The Wind Commands

The Wind Commands

Sailors and Sailing Ships in the Pacific

Harry A. Morton

Drawings by Don Hermansen and Paul Dwillies
from original drawings and research by Peggy Morton

Wesleyan University Press, Middletown, Connecticut
and
The University of British Columbia Press, Vancouver

THE WIND COMMANDS
SAILORS AND SAILING SHIPS IN THE PACIFIC

Publication of this book has been assisted by a grant toward the illustrations from The Leon and Thea Koerner Foundation

First published in Canada 1975 by The University of British Columbia Press

United States of America edition published 1975 by Wesleyan University Press, Middletown, Connecticut

For sale in the United States of America only

LIBRARY OF CONGRESS NUMBER 75-21906

INTERNATIONAL STANDARD BOOK NUMBER 0-8195-4089-7

PRINTED IN CANADA

To sailors everywhere and in every age

CONTENTS

PLATES

FIGURES

PHOTOGRAPHIC ACKNOWLEDGEMENTS

Plates 1 and 2 are from the Museo Maritimo, Barcelona. Plates 3, 15, 16, 17, 29, 32, 36, 49, 50, 52, 53, 56, 59, 60, 62, and 63 are reproduced by permission of the National Maritime Museum, London. Plates 4, 14, 33, 39, 40, and 43 are reproduced courtesy of the Special Collections Division of the Library of the University of British Columbia, Vancouver. Plates 5, 7, 8, 9, 10, 11, and 41 are courtesy of the Provincial Archives of British Columbia, Victoria.

Plates 6 and 54 are from the Musée de la Marine, Paris; Plate 12 is reproduced courtesy of the Hocken Library, Dunedin, New Zealand, and Plate 13 (Additional MS. 15743, f.2) is reproduced by permission of the British Library Board.

Plates 18 and 19 are British Crown Copyright, Science Museum, London, and Plates 20, 21, and 24 are Photos, Science Museum, London.

Plates 22, 25, 30, 42, 44, 58, 61, and 64 are from the Alexander Turnbull Library, Wellington, New Zealand—Plate 22 from the Kinnear Collection, Plate 25 from the Dickie Collection, and Plate 61 from the Making New Zealand Collection.

Plate 23 is reproduced courtesy of the Savings Bank of New London, Mystic Seaport Photo, Mystic, Connecticut, and Plate 48 is from the Mystic Seaport Collection, Mystic, Connecticut.

Plate 26 is courtesy of the Peabody Museum of Salem, Massachusetts, Plate 27, courtesy of the Mariners Museum, Newport News, Virginia, and Plate 28, courtesy of the Vancouver Maritime Museum, Vancouver.

Plate 31 is reproduced courtesy of the Rare Book Division, New York Public Library, Astor, Lenox and Tilden Foundations; Plate 34 is from the *Times* (London), and Plate 35 is by courtesy of the U.S. Naval Oceanographic Office.

Plate 37 is reproduced courtesy of Shaw, Savill and Albion Co. Ltd., New Zealand, and Plates 38 and 51 are from the Mitchell Library, Sydney, New South Wales.

Plates 45, 46, and 47 are reproduced courtesy of the Woodward Biomedical Library, University of British Columbia, Vancouver, Plate 55, through the courtesy of the Earl of Birkenhead, and Plate 57, by permission of the estate of the late Hon. Mrs. Clive Pearson, Parham, Sussex.

AUTHOR'S NOTE

The major problem in writing this book has been organizing into coherency a mass of material, but a difficulty secondary only by comparison was that of gathering widely scattered material together at the University of Otago.

The journals have been my mainstay; therefore, I thank those who helped me directly to assemble them. The staff of many libraries, but especially of the Library of the University of Otago and of the Hocken Library, have been always courteous, helpful and, if long suffering, smilingly so. The National Library of Scotland in Edinburgh and the Gloucestershire Records Office were most helpful, while the Interloan Service of the New Zealand Library Service has been invaluable in bringing me books from many places.

In order to preserve the flavour of the quotations from the sources I have not intruded "sic" after each example of odd spelling or misused word.

My wife and I would like to thank the personnel of the following museums for their courtesy and kindness during our visits: the War Museum at Vienna; the Science Museum at Munich; the Marine Museums at Bordeaux and at Nantes; The National Marine Museum at Paris; the National Maritime Museum at Greenwich; the Peabody Museum at Salem; the Kendall Whaling Museum at Sharon; the Mystic Seaport at Mystic; the Whaling Museum at New Bedford; the War Memorial Museum at Auckland; and, most particularly, the Otago Museum at Dunedin.

I thank Ruth Harper and Nola Hight for their assistance in preparing the manuscript and their forbearance when facing my hand-writing, my erasures, and my obscure directions. Mrs. Hight's suggestions have been invariably useful. My wife made preliminary drawings for all the figures in the book and suggested many of the other illustrations, but this was just part of the immense help and encouragement she gave me. Comments and suggestions from my colleagues and friends were most helpful—in particular those of Associate Professor G. S. Parsonson. I owe much also to Carol Morton Johnston who acted as research assistant for parts of the book and to Dr. Jane Fredeman and Andrew Pottinger of the University of British Columbia for their editing, always firm enough to be helpful, always sensitive enough to be tactful.

Any mistakes are my responsibility alone.

PACIFIC VOYAGES

Journeys referred to in the text

SHIP	NATIONALITY	CHIEF CHARACTER	DATE	PURPOSE IN THE PACIFIC
Adventure	BRITISH	Furneaux	1772	Exploration, as consort of Cook's *Resolution*
Africaansche Galey	DUTCH	Roggeveen	1722	Exploration, for trade
Albatros	AMERICAN	Gann	n.d.	Mid-twentieth-century yachting and cruising
Alert	AMERICAN	Dana	1836	Commerce, freighting from California to the eastern coast of the United States
Antelope	BRITISH	Wilson	1783	Commerce, from Australia to China
Archangel Michael	RUSSIAN	Spangberg	1738	Exploration, from Okhotsk to Japan
Argonaut	BRITISH	Colnett	1791	Commerce, Trading for sea otter fur in British Columbia
Astrocyte	CANADIAN	The Goulds	1966	Yachting and cruising
Astrolabe	FRENCH	La Pérouse	1786	Exploration, scientific as well as geographic
Astrolabe	FRENCH	d'Urville	1826	Exploration
Batchelor's Delight	ENGLISH	Dampier, Wafer	1687	Buccaneering
Beagle	BRITISH	Darwin	1835	Surveying and charting, the Straits of Magellan area

SHIP	NATIONALITY	CHIEF CHARACTER	DATE/PURPOSE IN THE PACIFIC	
Beeswing	BRITISH	Morton	1910	Commerce, freighting from the eastern Pacific to Britain
Boudeuse	FRENCH	Bougainville	1768	Exploration
Bounty	BRITISH	Bligh	1788	Transporting bread-fruit plants from Polynesia to the West Indies
Cap Pilar	BRITISH	Seligman, Burgess	1937	Cruising by adventur-ous young people
Centurion	BRITISH	Anson, Walter	1741	Raiding the Spanish Pacific empire, suffered greatly from scurvy, but captured a Manila Galleon
Challenger	BRITISH	Spry, Campbell	1874	Oceanic surveying
Charlotte	BRITISH, AUS-TRALIAN	White	1788	Transporting convicts to Australia, the first voyage
Charlotte Jane	BRITISH, NEW ZEALAND	Ward	1850	Carrying the first emigrants from England to the Canterbury Settlement in New Zealand
Chatham	BRITISH	Broughton	1792	Exploration and survey, as consort to Captain Vancouver's *Discovery*
Cinque Ports	ENGLISH	Dampier, Selkirk (Robinson Crusoe)	1705	Privateering against Spanish commerce in the Pacific, consort of the *St George*
Columbia	AMERICAN	Gray	1792	Trading, for sea otter and other fur in north-west America

SHIP	NATIONALITY	CHIEF CHARACTER	DATE/PURPOSE IN THE PACIFIC
Content	ENGLISH	Cavendish	1586 Privateering against Spanish commerce in the Pacific, consort of the *Desire*
Cutty Sark	BRITISH	Willis	1872 Freighting between the Pacific and Britain
Cygnet	ENGLISH	Swan, Dampier	1687 Buccaneering in the Pacific
Daintie	ENGLISH	Hawkins	1594 Privateering, against Spanish Pacific settlements and commerce
De Castries	FRENCH	Marion	1772 Exploration, with an eye to future trade, consort of the *Mascarin*
Desire	ENGLISH	Cavendish	1586 Privateering in the Pacific, the third circumnavigation, consort of the *Content*
Discovery	BRITISH	Cook	1778 Exploration and coastal survey, as a consort of Cook's *Resolution*
Discovery	BRITISH	Vancouver	1792 Exploration, diplomacy, and surveying in northwest America under George Vancouver
Dolphin	BRITISH	Byron, Wallis, Robertson	1765, 1767 Exploration, two separate voyages in the Pacific under Byron and Wallis
Duchess	BRITISH	Rogers	1708 Privateering, against Spanish commerce in the Pacific, consort of the *Duke*

SHIP	NATIONALITY	CHIEF CHARACTER	DATE/PURPOSE IN THE PACIFIC	
Duff	BRITISH	Wilson	1797	Carrying missionaries from Britain to Polynesia
Duke	BRITISH	Rogers, Dampier	1708	Privateering, against Spanish commerce, consort of the *Duchess*, captured a Manila Galleon. This expedition carried two competent authors, Dampier and Rogers
Elizabeth	ENGLISH	Drake, Winter	1577	Privateering, raiding Spanish commerce with Drake's *Golden Hind*, but failed to get properly into the Pacific
Endeavour	BRITISH	Cook	1769	Exploration, a scientific expedition which became a model for all successors
Essex	AMERICAN	Chase	1820	Whaling, sunk by a whale in the Pacific
Felice	BRITISH	Meares	1788	Trading for furs in British Columbia
Firecrest	FRENCH	Gerbault	1925	Yachting and cruising
Gallinule	NEW ZEALAND	Cole	1966	Carrying a family from Kenya to a new home in New Zealand, a trimaran
Garthwray	BRITISH	Eva Frampton	1921	Freighting from the Pacific to Britain
Géographe	FRENCH	Baudin	1802	Exploration, a scientific expedition along the coast of Australia

SHIP	NATIONALITY	CHIEF CHARACTER	DATE/PURPOSE IN THE PACIFIC	
Gipsy Moth IV	BRITISH	Chichester	1966	Circumnavigating alone
Golden Hind	ENGLISH	Drake	1577	Privateering, as a Queen's ship or privateer (it is not known). She raided Spanish commerce in the Pacific and became the first ship to circumnavigate the world under its original captain, Francis Drake
Golden Lotus	NEW ZEALAND	Clifford	1962	Cruising, a junk built in Hong Kong for a young New Zealander, who then sailed it to New Zealand
Heemskerck	DUTCH	Tasman	1642	Exploration, in a voyage which discovered Tasmania and New Zealand
Herzogin Cecilie	FINNISH	Karlsson	1928	Commerce, freighting between the Pacific and Europe
Hope	RUSSIAN	Walton	1738	Exploration, along the northeastern coast of Asia
Idle Hour	BRITISH	Long	1935	Yachting and cruising
Investigator	BRITISH, AUSTRALIAN	Flinders	1802	Exploration, surveying the coast of Australia
James Pattison	BRITISH	Ensign Best	1837	Bringing convicts to Australia
Janet Nicoll	BRITISH	R. L. Stevenson	1890	Pacific Island trading and passenger traffic

SHIP	NATIONALITY	CHIEF CHARACTER	DATE/PURPOSE IN THE PACIFIC	
Joseph Conrad	BRITISH, AUS- TRALIAN	Villiers	1935	Cruising, a world cruise with a largely apprentice crew, captained by a man as competent in writing as in seafaring
Kon-Tiki	NOR- WEGIAN	Heyerdahl	1947	Challenging established views, an experimental and didactic raft voyage westward from South America to Polynesia
Lady Nelson	BRITISH, AUS- TRALIAN	Grant	1800	Surveying the Austra- lian coastline, and testing removable centreboard keels for the Royal Navy
Lightning	AMERICAN, BRITISH	"Bully" Forbes	1854	Commerce, from the Pacific to Europe. A clipper famous for speed
Los Reyes	SPANISH	Mendaña	1567	Exploration, in the southwest Pacific
Marco Polo	CANADIAN, BRITISH	"Bully" Forbes	1851	Commerce, an emi- grant and passenger clipper to Australia, famed for speed and comfort
Margaret Oakley	AMERICAN	Jacobs	1835	Exploring and trading in the southwest Pacific islands
Mascarin	FRENCH	Marion, Crozet	1772	Exploration, consort of the *De Castries*
Nadeshda	RUSSIAN	Krusenstern, Hoppner	1805	Exploration, and a naval training cruise

SHIP	NATIONALITY	CHIEF CHARACTER	DATE/PURPOSE IN THE PACIFIC	
Novara	AUSTRIAN	Scherzer	1858	Exploration, a scientific expedition sent by the Austrian emperor
Pandora	BRITISH	Edwards	1791	Law enforcement; an expedition sent to find and bring to trial the *Bounty* mutineers
Providence	BRITISH	Broughton	1796	Exploration
Rattler	BRITISH	Colnett	1793	Exploration, to discover the best sperm whaling areas in the Pacific
Rattlesnake	BRITISH, AUSTRALIAN	Huxley, Macgillivray	1848	Exploring and surveying the northeast coast of Australia
Red Dragon	ENGLISH	Lancaster	1600	Commerce, the first expedition sent out by the East India Company to the East Indies
Rehu Moana	BRITISH, NEW ZEALAND	Lewis	1965	Catamaran cruising, sailed from Britain to New Zealand, crewed by a doctor, his wife and another woman, and which, on the way, tested Polynesian navigational methods
Research	BRITISH	Dillon	1827	Rescue, an expedition to find the fate, and survivors, of the La Pérouse expedition
Resolution	BRITISH	Cook	1772	Exploration, which reached ice at both the south and north ends of

SHIP	NATIONALITY	CHIEF CHARACTER	DATE/ PURPOSE IN THE PACIFIC
			the Pacific in two different expeditions
Rodolph	AMERICAN	Osbun	1849 Trading, in the Pacific islands
Roebuck	ENGLISH	Dampier	1699 Exploration, a King's ship under a buccaneer captain, Dampier
Royalshire	BRITISH	Lubbock	1899 Commerce, freighting between the eastern Pacific and Britain
San Pedrico	SPANISH	Prado y Tovar	1606 Exploration, consort of *San Pedro y Pablo*
San Pedro y Pablo	SPANISH	Quirós	1606 Exploration, the southwest Pacific
Scarborough	BRITISH	Easty	1788 Transporting convicts to Australia, the first voyage
Sheila	NEW ZEALAND	Hayter	1956 Cruising, a lone voyage home to New Zealand by an ex-officer of a regiment of the British Indian Army
Snark	AMERICAN	London	1905 Yachting and cruising
Solide	FRENCH	Marchand	1791 Exploration, a scientific expedition with attention to trading possibilities
Speedwell	BRITISH	Shelvocke	1719 Privateering, against Spanish commerce in the Pacific
Spray	AMERICAN	Slocum	1896 Cruising, the first lone voyage round the world
St. George	ENGLISH	Dampier	1704 Privateering, against Spanish commerce in the Pacific

SHIP	NATIONALITY	CHIEF CHARACTER	DATE/PURPOSE IN THE PACIFIC	
St. Jean Baptiste	FRENCH	de Surville	1769	Exploration, with hopes of trading
St. Peter	RUSSIAN	Bering, Steller, Waxell	1741	Exploration, from northeast Asia to Alaska
Suhaili	BRITISH	Knox-Johnston	1968	Cruising, the first lone nonstop circumnavigation
Swallow	BRITISH	Carteret	1767	Exploration, as consort of *Dolphin*, after involuntary separation she made a creditable voyage of exploration in spite of great shortcomings of the ship and equipment
Tartar Galley	BRITISH, INDONESIAN	Forrest	1775	Commercial exploration, an Indonesian ship and crew under an English captain in the East Indies
Te Hawai	POLYNESIAN	Whatonga	1150	Voyage of search (for grandfather) and settlement from Hawaiki, the ancestral home in the Central Pacific, probably in the Society Islands, to Raratonga and on to New Zealand
Te Pua-ariki	POLYNESIAN	Ru	950	Voyage of settlement (twenty specially selected women were taken) from Hawaiki to Aitutaki, Cook Islands.

SHIP	NATIONALITY	CHIEF CHARACTER	DATE/PURPOSE IN THE PACIFIC	
Tilikum	CANADIAN	Voss	1901	Cruising, a voyage to demonstrate the sea qualities of the British Columbian Indian dugout canoe, across the diagonal breadth of the Pacific to Sydney
Torrens	BRITISH	Conrad, Galsworthy	1893	Commerce, freighting from Australia to Britain with Joseph Conrad as chief mate
Trinidad	SPANISH	Magellan	1519	Exploration, as part of Magellan's fleet with the hope—justified in later Spanish sovereignty of the Phillipines —of finding rich trading territory east of Portuguese East Indian territories
Tzu Hang	BRITISH	Smeeton	1957	Yachting and cruising
Uranie	FRENCH	de Freycinet, Arago	1819	Exploration
Victoria	SPANISH	Magellan, Albo	1591	Exploration, in the justified hope of finding new territory for Spain east of the line of Portuguese-Spanish territorial demarcation as agreed in the Treaty of Tordesillas of 1494, resulted in the first circumnavigation of the world

SHIP	NATIONALITY	CHIEF CHARACTER	DATE/PURPOSE IN THE PACIFIC	
Vostok	RUSSIAN	Bellings-hausen	1820	Oceanic exploration, training cruise
Wager	BRITISH	Byron, Bulkeley	1741	Raiding, a consort of *Centurion*
Washington	AMERICAN	Gray	1788	Fur trading, in northwest America
Wentworth	ENGLISH	Barlow	1700	Commercial trading and freighting from China to Britain

INTRODUCTION

Sailors, Writers and Time

*But I have been as careful as I could: and tho' there are
some Matters of Fact that will seem strange, yet I have been
more especially careful in these, to say nothing but what,
according to the best of my Knowledge, is the very Truth.*

LIONEL WAFER
A NEW VOYAGE AND DESCRIPTION OF THE ISTHMUS OF AMERICA
1699

*And though, as I have said, I cannot affect a polished style, as
compensation I promise to tell nothing but the truth, and
that in my view is better than elegant writing. As my models
I shall take the famous seaman, the great Captain William
Dampier, and his mate Funnel. . . . These two men have also
given the world a description of their voyage, and though the
style of it is neither elegant nor learned, their books contain
only what is true and such news as the world craved.*

SVEN WAXELL
OF THE *ST. PETER*

There were special problems facing those who sailed the Pacific Ocean prior
to this century—or rather, the problems common to men and ships on any
sea became essentially different because on this ocean they were intensified in
degree or enlarged in scale. It is the vastness of the Pacific that made this so.
Hunger is hunger anywhere, but hunger for six weeks is a different problem
from hunger for six days; physical weakness and diseases of malnutrition see
to that. These effects, in turn, make the handling and maintenance of ships
difficult at the very moment when the rigging or sails or hull might be in need
of extra effort and attention. This wear and tear is also caused by the
sheer distance and time. While rigging wears and frays in the Mediterranean
and China seas just as much as it does in the Pacific, by comparison a ship
in those waters is never far from home and maintenance. Being near to home
means that supplies of clothing or ships' stores need not be so painstakingly
planned and selected, nor supplies of food so carefully preserved.

In the same way, the preservation of skilled men became not, as in short voyages, a matter of concern for the individual but a matter of survival for the group. A surgeon or a cooper or a carpenter could not be replaced five thousand miles from any European settlement in the way that a seaman could—by recruitment, voluntary or otherwise, of an inhabitant of the Pacific.

Important as such problems were, and still are, they were less so than navigation problems were. With distances so great and, over enormous expanses of the ocean, the lands so small as to mock the name, an error in direction—insignificant when sailing from Bristol to Brest—was multiplied by mile after lonely mile when sailing from Tahiti to Taiwan. European voyagers could no longer depend on the ancient pilotage techniques which had been maintained down the Atlantic along the length of Africa. They had to develop navigation; they had to leave behind, mentally as well as literally, landmarks of headland and cape and peak, and accept the guidance of the stars as the Polynesians had to do. It is true that Atlantic exploration provided many answers, but it is no coincidence that spherical navigation, although not developed for the Pacific, barely pre-dated the European exploration of its immensity, which was on a scale which itself expanded every problem and changed its nature.

There were problems of psychology too. Darwin saw the cause of these clearly: "It is necessary to sail over this great ocean to comprehend its immensity . . . for weeks together . . . nothing but the same blue, profoundly deep ocean." Problems of leading and following, action and reaction, plagued officers and mariners. Men of all races who sailed the Pacific were affected; many were broken and more were killed. Others could not bear to leave, and settled and multiplied into cultures of as many kinds as the vastness and variety ensured. The Pacific is not only the Pacific of legend, of smiling maids and whispering surf, for it is bounded by ice north and south, and by dangerous coasts east and west. Typhoons are as typical as trade winds, and giant waves can toss ships that only shortly before were becalmed.

The variety of hazards is matched by a variety of responses. Kamchatka's culture, Chile's or Canada's too, is part of the Pacific quite as much as are those of Samoa or Easter Island or New Zealand. So this book refers to many places and many peoples, to many different ships and many different men. All are related to one another by the problems that the greatness of the greatest of oceans poses. I discuss the problems and the answers to them because I have tried to make this a technical and a human book, not a comprehensive history. Modern yachtsmen should not hesitate to use the glossary; sea terms change from century to century, and much of the material comes from centuries ago. I hope that understanding will be aided by the diagrammatic sketches of ships and sails; appreciation of the hazards—and the beauty—will come, I trust, from the photographs and paintings.

Men and ships alike, whether bred or built on its shores or far away, had to measure up to the scale of the Pacific or disappear. Many who measured up decided to write about their experiences and so far as has been possible I have used the words of the men and women who faced the problems in person. Their journals, diaries, and narratives present a living world, a world seen and described by people who lacked modern advantages in mechanics and electronics, but seemed to be compensated by a patience and a clear-sightedness that has atrophied. Above all, their comments are expressed with an admirable directness and, in Elizabethan days, with a poetic simplicity that is most moving. John Davis prayed: "May it please His Divine Majestie . . . that we may rather proceed than otherwise; or if it be His Will that our mortall being shal now take an ende, I rather desire that it may be in proceeding than in returning." This great navigator, reared on the *Book of Common Prayer*, used its beautiful language to show he knew that much voyaging is beyond the will and skill of men. Drake knew it too. He closed a letter with the words: "The wind commands me away."

Not all the journals are Elizabethan. Many date from the eighteenth and nineteenth centuries. There are also first-hand accounts written within the last few years, for men are still sailing the Pacific, although now perhaps to find themselves—rather than to explore an ocean or to found a nation.

I selected only a limited number of voyages because I could not write about them all, and I have not included all the material available about the voyages I do discuss. Many of the voyages which are discussed have been described in the journals or in the captain's log or in books written after the ships returned. Some of these writings are contained in the notes, and more are in the bibliography. As a major purpose of this book is to arouse interest in the original publications, I hope that the bibliography will be consulted freely, and some of its suggestions followed.

Other authors perhaps would have chosen different ships, different voyages, and different men and women, but I have chosen each with a purpose in mind: to discuss a type of ship, to show that the French or the Russians were in the Pacific too, to talk about a ship because it was typical—or because it was not. Sometimes, I chose a ship because of the able men it carried, as with the *Beagle* (Plate 40) or the *Rattlesnake* (Plate 61); sometimes, because of the remarkable vessel that it was—as with the *Lightning*. Some men were chosen as much because they could write as because they had sailed the Pacific. In fact, one writer, Smollett, did not sail in the area, but his knowledge of the medical problems of men in ships seemed to justify his being placed with Melville, London, and Conrad. Each choice has a point to make. Ships sailed, ships sank, men died, men survived; finally, however, there are only *two* issues—the ship is a tool of man, and the Pacific is greater than man and his craftsmanship together.

In seeking to use the pungent descriptions written by the explorers, travellers, merchants, and settlers themselves, I consulted a wide variety of sources. These range from the journals and diaries of captains to reports by prisoners being examined for the Inquisition. Correspondingly, there is a variety of authors from fifteenth-century Italian merchants to twentieth-century Canadian yachtsmen. These authors wrote differently, not simply because they were different, but also because they were writing for different audiences. Some were writing for King Philip II of Spain, others for the equally majestic Admiralty in London; some were writing, as far as can be seen, to amuse themselves or their friends; others to excite a vast audience in the widely literate public of today. They were trying to achieve different things (including, sometimes, self-justification or self-glorification). Nevertheless, although many things will be explained, the main purpose of the book is to lead the reader to the writings of the men and women who were there themselves.

In the less literate earlier centuries, I have had to depend on the officers, often the leaders themselves. But where I could find another point of view—that of a sailor, or of a Spanish prisoner of the English, or of a convict, or of a woman, or of a non-European—then I have presented it. However desirable it might have seemed to use reports from the Polynesians and the Aleuts about, for example, their reaction to the appearance of strange vessels and strange men, it is almost impossible to do so. Where it was possible, I noted it; where it was not, I tried to change the perspective by insight, and to look, as it were, from the beach out to sea. So I begin with a description of the indigenous Pacific craft, granting them by right the place of honour, though of necessity these descriptions are by Europeans, laden with their assumptions and their values. The canoe was always longer or shorter than their ship; practically never was it expressed the other way around.

Most of the sources are connected directly with a particular voyage and a specific ship. For convenient reference a list of ships, in alphabetical order, with the writer of the book, journal, or diary in which they are mentioned, and the date they sailed the Pacific, immediately precedes this introduction (see pp. xvii-xxvii). But readers should not expect this book to be a history of Pacific watercraft; it is a technical and descriptive discussion of the problems of sailing and surviving in the Pacific. Nevertheless, readers must have some framework of time, although the dates have been kept to a minimum.

As far as possible, the seacraft are presented as they were seen by the men and women who were actually there; therefore, the discussion begins at the early sixteenth century and ends in 1974. There are plenty of footnotes to lead readers directly to the original material.

Nearly all the written material dealing with matters with which the book is concerned comes from this period; there is Chinese and Japanese literature from earlier centuries and, where it is pertinent, I have used it, but the discussion of the "Pacific proper" must depend mainly on reports from European travellers and explorers. The Chinese and Japanese did not sail there. The Pacific, by my definition, is bounded by the two Americas, by Asia, the Indonesian Islands, Australia, and Antarctica, and includes the various seas on its fringes. The "Pacific proper," then would be the huge ocean itself, spreading its immensity between Asia and Australasia on the west and the two Americas on the east.

The Portuguese reached the Pacific area, as defined, in the very first years of the sixteenth century, approaching it from the west, around Africa and across the Indian Ocean. Some of their reports to their king and petitions for support are available for study even though the Portuguese practised a most effective secrecy, seeking to gain and preserve a monopoly of the deep-sea carrying trade in Eastern spices and other exotic goods—the major reason for the voyages. Spaniards under Magellan (Plate 2), a Portuguese who had already sailed to the Indies around Africa, reached the Pacific by sea only a few years later by rounding South America. In the straits he discovered and which bear his name, he encountered all the dangers and difficulties of variable winds and currents which became mythologized for generations of later sailors. Then he sailed northwestward across the great ocean's vastness to confront the Portuguese on its western limits. His story is told in the journal of Antonio Pigafetta, an Italian gentleman who was one of the few survivors of this first circumnavigation. Magellan himself did not survive; he lost his life in a foolish intervention in a local war in the Philippines.

The Spaniards had first seen the Pacific proper in 1513, when Balboa stared excitedly from the Isthmus of Panama at "the Great South Sea." Across the Isthmus they soon established land communication with the Spanish territories in the Caribbean and built Pacific ships to help conquer and control another section of empire on the western side of North and South America. This empire was well described in the 1590's by Carletti, an Italian who had many of the experiences, although avoiding most of the risks, of Pigafetta.

Across the Pacific there was Spanish territory also—the Philippines— claimed by Spain because of Magellan's voyage. Communication between those islands and Mexico by means of the fabled Manila Galleon (a collective name for a series of ships spanning several centuries) was begun across the North Pacific to speed delivery of goods to Europe by a route which took advantage of both the vastness of the Pacific and of the Spanish convoys from Mexico organized to protect the riches of the Eastern trade from Spain's enemies. This usually, but not always—as will be seen—succeeded. Reports of those early voyages are found in Spanish archives; many have been sought out and published by American and English scholars.

The remainder of the Pacific, however, was not ignored by the Spanish. Between 1567 and 1607, a number of expeditions, interlinked by personnel and connected by their desire to expand both the empire of Spain and the sway of Catholic Christianity, sailed from Peru to the southwest Pacific. The names of the commanders, such as Mendaña, Quirós, and Torres, have survived in both history and geography. Their sailing orders, their reports, the accusations and counter-accusations poured into Spanish archives in attempts to explain and excuse the failures and the losses, as did their petitions to their kings, viceroys, and governors. These, together with those of men of lesser importance who accompanied them, help the southwest Pacific to be seen as the Europeans first saw it. Some of this material also helped contemporaries. Quirós's *Eighth Memorial*, widely read in several languages within a decade of its publication in 1610, was admired for both its spirit and its eloquence. By the time of the last of these South Pacific voyages, however, Spain had realized that an over-extended empire could crash of its own weight. Her attention henceforth would be devoted mainly to holding what she already had.

This Spanish Empire attracted the English to the Pacific. To increase their own fortunes, and as part of the long struggle between Spain and England (and between Catholicism and Reform), Drake (Plate 3) and Oxenham, reached the Pacific overland in the early 1570's in a dramatic raid on Panama. Oxenham came back overland again to build a pinnace, to capture and to lose his love, and to die by hanging. Spanish documents tell us his fate and so does gossip picked up by Sir Richard Hawkins while he himself was a prisoner of the Spanish in Lima.

Within a few years, Drake, Cavendish, and Richard Hawkins, in different expeditions, sailed into the ocean by Magellan's route, the straits between the southern tip of South America and the island of Tierra del Fuego. Each sailed his own ship; we remember one for his skill, one for his courage, and one for his wisdom. Such men had these qualities, and they also had England's national welfare close to their hearts, but personal factors, greed for wealth, desire for glory, religious bigotry, self-interest, pride, and pettiness, also affected their actions. They were able, but they made mistakes; much of the endurance that is admired in the sailors of the Pacific voyages was made necessary by mistakes in navigation or seamanship on the part of their leaders. Drake and Cavendish, after highly successful raiding on the Spanish American Empire on the Pacific coast, sailed home to England across the Pacific, but Hawkins was defeated and captured in a hard-fought sea battle off the coast of Peru and spent many years in a Spanish prison.

Drake's circumnavigation was chronicled by his chaplain, Fletcher, and that of Cavendish by a gentleman-at-arms, Pretty. It is a pity that the commanders' own reports, particularly Drake's to Queen Elizabeth, are not available. Hawkins wrote a book about his voyage, and about many other things concerning sixteenth-century ships and sailors too, which is as delightful to read as it is rewarding to study. His book was written after Queen Elizabeth's death. The language of the Elizabethan era lived on, but the spirit and enterprise did not. King James, whose upbringing in turbulent sixteenth-century Scotland perhaps engendered the desire for peace seen by many English contemporaries as often damaging to the English national interest, was more susceptible to Spanish sensibilities.

Spain claimed the Pacific for her own; indeed, she and Portugal between them claimed all the new territories in and around the Pacific. Sturdy Dutch seamen, of great technical skill in seamanship and of even greater skill and drive in commerce, were no more likely to accept any such claim than were the English critics of the peaceful King James. Spain was Holland's deadly enemy who, from 1580 to 1640, also controlled Portugal and her empire—in effect, most of the New World. Moreover, Holland recognized no claim that set limits to where her ships could trade unless that claim could be made good with force. One early Dutch expedition followed Magellan's route and reached the Philippines; after that, in the very last years of the sixteenth century, Dutch ships came to the Pacific as the Portuguese had—around Africa and then eastward. Within a generation they were firmly established in the East Indies, and most favourably situated for further exploration in the Pacific.

To become firmly based in that area the Dutch had to drive out the established Portuguese and drive off the importunate English who, under men such as Lancaster and Middleton of the East India Company, made persistent efforts to gain permanent footholds. John Davis, the great and inventive navigator, after surviving the icy hazards of Davis Strait in the north and Magellan Straits in the south, was killed during a voyage to the Far East. Many English died, most of them from disease, but many from equally ruthless Dutch action, and the English, although they continued to sail at times into the Pacific itself, were forced back from the Indies to make what they could of their chances in India itself. First-hand accounts of most of these voyages, as well as reports to the East India Companies of both Holland and England, are available.

Not all Dutch ships came in from the west. In 1615, about twenty years after the first Dutch voyage around South America, a ship and a yacht (the latter word being used in the seventeenth-century sense of a small, shallow-draught ship), captained by two brothers named Schouten, sailed in an expedition under the general command of Le Maire, on a voyage made memorable by the naming of the Straits of Le Maire after the commander and of Cape Horn after the expedition's hometown of Hoorn. Their small ship (the yacht was burned accidentally) was the first to sail around Cape Horn. The most famous, or infamous, of the corners of the Pacific, and of the four great capes of the world, had entered history. To preserve that history, Purchas printed translations of the first-hand stories of the Dutch voyages.

Less than a generation later, in 1642, another of these corners—and another of these notorious capes, Cape Leeuwin at the southwest tip of Australia —was passed by a Dutch ship. Abel Tasman, commissioned by the Governor of the Dutch East Indies, sailed eastward south of Australia to New Zealand with two ships, one a war-yacht, the other a flute (Plate 22), touching on the way at Tasmania—which he called Van Diemen's Land—and then crossing the Tasman Sea. He sailed northeastward from New Zealand to Tonga, northwestward to Fiji and then northward of west back to the East Indies. Both Tasman's journal and a narrative by one of his men are available in translation. Tasman had done much; the more driving and curious Cook would have done more; and Dampier would have seen and reported and speculated in a way that might well have made Europe think and act a century earlier than it did.

Dampier (Plate 56) was a buccaneer, a man in one of several groups of buccaneers who raided the Spanish Pacific Empire in the late seventeenth century. Some of the buccaneers, like Dampier, circumnavigated the world; others rounded Cape Horn in both directions; still others used the old Spanish method—and Oxenham's too—of linking the Pacific and Caribbean by land and then building or capturing ships in the Pacific. Dampier, because of his writing, has become the most famous of the buccaneers, proving perhaps that the pen is mightier than the cutlass. There were others who wrote too. Wafer was a buccaneer surgeon who presumably alternated his pen with a scalpel; his incisive and accurate observation of the Indians of Darien is a forerunner of modern anthropology. When we read the thoughts and the self-justifications of the literate and, to some degree, philosophical buccaneers, such as Dampier and Wafer, we should remember that the vast majority of them can be described best as piratical thugs, avaricious and cruel far beyond the standards of that day—standards which certainly seem lax enough to the modern mind.

Pirates are simply robbers at sea. Privateers are private citizens licensed by a nation's government during war to prey on its enemies. Buccaneers, nearly always English or French, looked on Spain as a permanent enemy in the Caribbean, whatever the policy of their governments might have been. When they operated during times of peace, the Spaniards treated them as pirates, with justification, but as most of them did not rob their own countrymen, they denied the charge. Even in wartime they did not always have the official "letter of marque" from their government which would make them privateers. Most honest observers considered them at least "semi"-pirates; some were unqualifiedly so.

Not all journals have made their owners famous or infamous in their own time, and not all seamen who wrote journals were buccaneers. Barlow, an English seaman and officer of the late seventeenth century, kept a detailed journal of his life at sea which was not published until 1934. Fortunately, on occasion he had sailed the western fringes of the Pacific, which opened up his insights, his prejudices, and his observations for us. Indeed, the first part of his journal was written while he was a prisoner of the Dutch at Batavia in the Indies.

The wars of the late seventeenth and early eighteenth centuries ensured that privateers would replace buccaneers as raiders of the Spaniards. What happened, of course, was that most of the buccaneers, properly or improperly, began calling themselves privateers. After all, they were an adaptable lot in an adjustable profession in an accommodating age. One buccaneer, Sir Henry Morgan, appears in history as buccaneer, pirate, privateer, and royal governor; another, Lancelot Blackburn, appears as buccaneer, privateer, and Archbishop of York! Dampier, at different times, was a buccaneer, a privateer, the captain of a King's ship, and a famous author. One of his seamen, William Funnell, saw enough to become a successful author too, and Captain Woodes Rogers, commander of a privateering ship in which Dampier was the chief pilot, wrote frankly and humorously of his famous raid into and across the Pacific in 1709.

The directness of Rogers contrasts with the prevarication of Shelvocke. This privateer, some ten years after Rogers, began his voyage in company with Clipperton, who is most famous for crossing the Pacific in an eighteenth-century forty-ton sloop. Shelvocke's story of his own voyage was widely distrusted because of his general reputation, but apparently it interested Coleridge enough to note his remarks about albatrosses. Privateers and buccaneers with the energy to raid seemed also to have a compulsion to write. It paid to do so; many people in Europe could read now and the linkage of publicity, publication, and profit was becoming obvious.

One captain whose blunt phrases seem to have been designed for circulation no wider than a board of directors was the Dutchman Jacob Roggeveen. A Dutch company was organized to seek profit in the Pacific proper east of the territories of the Dutch East India Company, and sent Roggeveen's little fleet of two ships and a galley to explore the possibilities of trade. It crossed the Pacific in 1722, discovering Easter Island and touching the Tuamotus, the Society Islands, and the Samoan group on the way to the East Indies. As was the case with Schouten and Le Maire, Roggeveen's ships were seized by the Dutch East India Company and charged with infringing their monopoly, but he and those members of his crew whom scurvy had spared reached Holland to win restitution in the Courts.

In 1741, Commodore Anson (Plate 52) of the Royal Navy, on a raid against the Spanish Pacific Empire in the War of Jenkins's Ear, led a squadron into the Pacific around Cape Horn, but found that his battle there against the forces of wind and wave was more hard fought than any battle that he later won. At Juan Fernández Island he made rendezvous with what was left of his ships, went north as far as Mexico and then west to China, stopping in desperation because of scurvy at Tinian in the Marianas. His share of the prize money gained from the capture of the Manila Galleon *Covadonga* (Plate 4) near the Philippines, after he had refitted in China, meant that he returned to England a wealthy man, having led as profitable a circumnavigation as had Drake and Cavendish. Anson's chaplain, Richard Walter, wrote a fine narrative of the voyage, although reputedly "aided" by a leading pamphleteer of the time.

While Anson was preparing his expedition, the Russians, or at least the Scandinavians in Russian service, had been active in the far north of the Pacific; indeed, they had begun some years before—and their efforts had been as hampered by scurvy in the sub-Arctic as Anson's had been in the sub-tropics. Bering's Herculean labours to solve some of the mysteries of the geographical relationship of Asia and America, his final success in 1740, and his pitiful and anti-climactic death, are well told by some of the able men who suffered with him. Spangberg and Waxell tell of difficulties overcome and hardships endured, while Steller, a brilliant but misanthropic scientist, has become immortalized, paradoxically, by a now extinct sea mammal which he described in detail in his journal of the voyage. Many voyagers brought back descriptions and sketches of Pacific peoples and artifacts, especially Dampier, Wafer, and Barlow, but Steller was the precursor of Humboldt and Scherzer in applying professional Teutonic thoroughness to the study of Pacific natural life.

One of Anson's original midshipmen, Captain John Byron (Plate 53), led an expedition of a ship and a sloop through the Straits of Magellan in 1765, when the end of the Seven Years' War freed Europe to think of other things. He sailed west-northwestward to the Tuamotus where he found (on Takaroa) some remains of Roggeveen's galley, which was wrecked there in 1722. He then sailed west, swung north through the Gilbert Islands, and then west around the Marshalls to Tinian in the Marianas where Commodore Anson had recruited his crew's health. Byron then sailed north of the Philippines out of the Pacific. Though less poetic than the work of his famous grandson, a thorough journal of this voyage was kept by Byron himself, who had already written one book about his experiences of surviving shipwreck, mutiny, and Spanish prisons on an earlier Pacific voyage.

Byron's ship, the *Dolphin*, was sent around the world almost immediately under Captain Wallis, this time accompanied by a consort ship under Captain Carteret. After a long and unpleasant struggle with the vagaries of wind and weather in the Straits of Magellan, the ships became separated. Wallis discovered Tahiti, bringing an apparent paradise to the world's attention and thus ensuring that paradise would be lost. The journal kept by the master of the ship, Robertson, is a fascinating account of a world where, of men's problems, only work and war occurred, and each of these seemed to be seldom fierce and never prolonged.

Carteret's claims to fame are his discovery of Pitcairn Island and his successful voyage in the old, slow and badly-equipped *Swallow*, whose poor sailing qualities and clumsiness belied her name. His journey through Polynesia and the Indies, Carteret says, was plagued both by disease and the difficulties of sailing a ship so leaky and worm-eaten that the Dutch at Batavia did not believe he could reach England in her.

Byron, Wallis, and Carteret had all encountered the French soldier, naval commander, and explorer, Bougainville, somewhere on their voyages. From this time on, the French would play a major role in the Pacific, although some of their ships had been there earlier. Commanders, such as de Surville, Marion, La Pérouse, Marchand and d'Entrecasteaux, played a prominent part until the Revolutionary Wars distracted the attention of that great people. Their contributions were not merely useful for the work they did, but invaluable in displaying the interaction of the ideas of the archetypal European civilization with the presuppositions of the various cultures being brought to world attention at this time. Nor are ideas—or emotions—as effective without felicitous expression and in this the French, as always, were foremost. Persuasive French writing about the "Noble Savage" helped immortalize if not originate the idea of primal innocence. Probably the eloquence of the French discussions owed much to the conditions in the late eighteenth century of France herself—it was France herself that made the desired point, and as is usual in ideological debates the objective truth came off second best. The savage, in truth, did not have to be noble at all to be lauded as such by people writing in the shadow of the Bastille. Knowledge of a life apparently free from most imperfections, as exemplified in Tahiti and reported by Bougainville, played some small part in creating the total climate of emotion and opinion from which sprang the great Revolution itself.

While the French were active in exploration and trade in the last part of the eighteenth century, the British and the newly independent Americans were doubly so. This period began with Cook (Plate 43) and ended with his protégé, Vancouver. It also contained many lesser figures, such as Furneaux, Broughton, Meares, Gray, and Bishop, some of whom were navy men, some traders, especially in sea otter furs in the North Pacific, and some, alternately, one or the other. Colnett, one of the narrators of this period, had a fascinating life as one of Cook's junior officers, as a trader in the North Pacific, as a naval officer in the wars, as an explorer in a whaling ship, and at the last as a surveyor of the coast of England in a galley. And no discussion of interesting lives at sea in the late eighteenth century can leave out the name of Bligh, or ignore the mutiny which blackened his name in the popular mind, or the four-thousand-mile voyage of survival in a longboat which burnished that same name bright again for small boat sailors everywhere for all time.

During this period, the convict ships were going out to Australia, and, as a result of this settlement, direct Australia to China voyages began. Captains Gilbert and Marshall left their names along this route. From ships' captains, or people who sailed with them, including some women, narratives survive which provide an insight into the changing and improving conditions at sea, and allow us to observe at only second hand the founding of struggling, straggling settlements which were to grow into a flourishing Australia. The exploration of Australia's coastline, tentatively begun by Dampier at one corner, and by Cook kitty-corner at another, provides stories and characters from the early nineteenth century: Flinders, Grant, Bass, Baudin, and de Freycinet and, somewhat later, Owen Stanley, Huxley, and Macgillivray.

Once well into the nineteenth century the journals and narratives became too many to mention in detail. Improvements in general education meant that there was much more writing done by ordinary seamen; Bechervaise and Bruce, who wrote under the names of "Quarter Master" and "Able Seaman," respectively, are two examples. Just as the literature was broadened by more writing from men in lower ranks, the presence of the Russians and Austrians in the South Pacific brought further competence and new points of view. The growth of the whaling industry all over the Pacific, together with some official exploration, left much valuable American information, while emigra-

Plate 1. Ferdinand Magellan's *Victoria*. This ship was the only one of Magellan's fleet of five to survive his 1517 expedition, and it became the first vessel to circumnavigate the world.

Plate 3. Sir Francis Drake (c. 1540-96). Drake won lasting popular fame for his raids on the Spanish colonial empire and for his part in defeating the Spanish Armada. He might as justly be remembered as a superb navigator and exceptionally astute commander of both ships and men. Like a great successor, Captain Cook, he displayed a sincere sympathy for indigenous Pacific peoples.

Plate 2. Ferdinand Magellan (1480-1521). A Portuguese by birth, Magellan quarrelled with his own king and led a Spanish expedition into the Pacific through the Straits which bear his name. His expedition was the first to circumnavigate the world, but Magellan himself was killed when rashly intervening in a local war in the Philippines.

Plate 4. The battle between H.M.S. *Centurion* (right) and the Manila Galleon *Covadonga* was the climax of Commodore Anson's 1741 expedition to raid the Pacific possessions of Spain. When captured, the *Covadonga* was found to be laden with enough treasure to make Anson a wealthy man and to set up his crewmen as publicans all over England.

Plate 5. John C. Voss (1858-1922). A retired Canadian sea captain, Voss (seated) was persuaded to try to rival Joshua Slocum, who had completed the world's first single-handed circumnavigation in the tiny *Spray*. Voss sailed the *Tilikum*, a British Columbian Indian canoe, around the world, much of the way single-handed.

Plate 6. Alain Gerbault (1902-41). Shown here on the bridge of his *Firecrest*, this French yachtsman cruised the Pacific in the 1920's. The books he wrote describing his solo sailing experiences and his encounters with the people of the Pacific are both acute and sensitive.

tion to Australia and New Zealand, and the need to control and protect the sea lanes to them, provided accounts of both emigrant and naval ships. Once European traffic became heavy enough to justify permanent naval bases, the pirates of the eastern seas had a harder time of it, and the narratives by navy men engaged in this policing provide a counterpoint to the tales of whaling and trading.

In this period too, the clipper ships were developed in the United States, almost as if in preparation for the mid-century repeal of the British Navigation Acts, which threw the sea lanes of a huge empire open to competition. Clipper ships took opium to China from India, tea to England from China, wool to England from Australia, people to Australia from England, miners to New Zealand from California; ships now crisscrossed what had been a lonely ocean. It is lonely again. Passengers now fly above it; the wool, the wheat, the tea, the meat, that once filled hundreds of sailing ships are concentrated in increasingly larger units.

The mid-nineteenth century also saw the beginning of "blackbirding," the recruitment of labour in Melanesia for the plantations of Queensland, a trade which employed the South Pacific brigantines and schooners left from the declining sandalwood trade with China. This handy type of ship, variously rigged, remained until the mid-twentieth century as part of the South Pacific culture; indeed, there are many sailing still. Today, the diesel is doing to them what steam did to the clippers.

Softwood American clippers gave way to wood and iron "composite" clippers and to iron ships built in Britain, and these in turn to great steel ships and barques from Britain, France, and Germany. These ships were jointly the climax of the days of sail, competing with steam and not really doomed until strategically placed canals made shorter routes which cut across the wind patterns in such a way that only engined ships could use them effectively. If the wind *does* command ships that sail, its mandates send them the long way round.

By the late years of the nineteenth century, a new phenomenon appeared—the cruising yachts. Their crews could now seek adventure without enduring hardships unnecessarily, although the risks of the great ocean have only diminished—they have not completely disappeared yet. Captain Slocum sailed alone around the world and wrote an entrancing book about it, but others without his compulsion for solitude have sailed in yachts—in the case of Captain Voss (Plate 5) in a British Columbian Indian canoe—and written about their voyages, although none quite with Slocum's ingenuousness.

Gerbault (Plate 6), cruising the Pacific sixty years after Captain Slocum, met men who had encountered the circumnavigator. So did Long; he also met a man who had been aboard the British Columbia canoe *Tilikum* when

Voss called at Sydney in 1903. In spite of the immensity of the Pacific, many of the people who wrote the narratives on which this book is based knew each other. Barlow himself sailed with the man who had inspired Stevenson's Long John Silver, while Dampier mentioned meeting Barlow; these three writers play important parts in this book. It is interesting to speculate on what influence, if any, the two keepers of journals might have had upon one another, or on Stevenson. It has been said that John Galsworthy, when in the *Torrens*, one of the ships discussed in another connection in this book, persuaded the chief mate to pursue his study of English. Joseph Conrad took Galsworthy's advice.

The writings of Conrad, Dana, London, Lubbock, and Melville, professional authors and knowledgeable sailors, have been used freely, as have those of Smollett for the eighteenth century. Some of these men sailed to earn a living and some to learn to live; all left a legacy of knowledge, whatever their motives were. Although associated with the nineteenth century, some of these men sailed, and most of them wrote, in the twentieth century too.

The great sailing ships of the twentieth century have also been described by able writers who were sailors as well. Karlsson, Villiers, Newby, Morton, and Course have written books entirely different from those by the yachtsmen, for few yachtsmen—retired Captains Slocum and Voss being exceptions— were professional seamen. These men were real sailors in commercial ships, and became writers as a result of this life and what they felt needed to be said about it. They have said it well.

A difference can be detected between the professional and the amateur, who is a sailor only temporarily and who consciously or subconsciously knows it. An amateur's references to the rest of his crew betray him; the "them" and "me" can be read between the lines. This in itself does not make his observations less valuable. Indeed, perhaps it is quite the other way around—how much is missed by those who see the day as one in an indefinite chain of days on into the future? How much more, on the contrary, can be marked of any place to which one might not return, or of any experience one might not repeat? This sense of enthusiasm makes invaluable the writing of yachtsmen who go to places in order to see, who try things in order to understand, who dare things in order to see and understand themselves. And exactly this self-analysis in the face of the problems of the Pacific makes Chichester, Smeeton, Knox-Johnson, Rose, and Hayter necessary reading. Perhaps this is even more true of Lewis and Heyerdahl, who deliberately set out to chip away some of the mystery which time laid over the solutions the ancient voyagers had found to problems we find difficult still.

One thing is certain, the Pacific itself is eternal; the answers have changed only because we have seen the folly in asking the same questions forever. We think we have solved the difficulties of this ocean, but we have only refused to face them. We fly high enough to outsoar typhoons and fast enough to conquer time, we dive deep enough for long enough that the surface waves climb and break without effect. But on that surface, where the wind still commands, even the greatest of craft ever built still hesitates before the Horn, and still demands of its captain, if not the daring of Magellan or of Drake, at least the assurance of Anson and the skill of Cook. Today, the largest of supertankers, in bulk and power greater than that of all the hundreds of nineteenth-century American whaling ships added together, still cannot ignore the Pacific when she speaks up. Magellan's ship, then, must have carried courage in direct proportion to her frailty.

Indigenous Pacific Watercraft

Floats must have preceded rafts, and rafts must have preceded boats, by the very sense of the matter. It probably was not too difficult to think of either; after all, one sees animals on floats during every flood and it would not have been too difficult to build one raft out of several floats. So this is where the book begins—with Chapter 1 discussing rafts and floats. Chapter 2 deals with skin craft of the North Pacific—boats of some complexity and the results of a great deal of ingenuity and of centuries of trial and error where the stakes were life and death. If floats come first as an example of the simple use of what are often simple materials, kayaks and umiaks should come next as examples of the effective use of meagre local resources.

The following chapters discuss the use of available material to meet varying local conditions south from Alaska along the Pacific coast of both Americas and across the Pacific to Australia. On and within both sides of the Pacific, bark and wood canoes were developed, quite independently. The wood canoes sailed on the Pacific; at least one crossed its greatest breadth, and although the bark canoes, with the exception of those in the area of the Straits of Magellan, were essentially riverain craft, they were used along the coast in sheltered waters and were often encountered and described by the men who wrote the journals. From Australia eastward to New Zealand and Polynesia, northwestward to Melanesia, Micronesia, and Indonesia, and north to China and Japan—all around this rim of the giant of oceans the exploring Europeans encountered watercraft which they described, in most cases admiringly, in some cases with genuine amazement. The craft were as different as the cultures of which they were a part, but they all performed, and many had the beauty which is created when form fits function perfectly.

CHAPTER 1

Rafts and Floats all around the Pacific

*The natives when they swim off, tie up a Bundle of Coopers
Rushes in the same form I have seen them in England, which
they place under them with the peaked end out of the water.
This bears them up so that they have only the toil of making
way through the water, which they Seem to do with great
ease. These Bundles I believe are only intended to support
them along side the Ship, where they Stay sometimes four
hours for I observed they often threw them away when going
for the Shore.*

CHARLES BISHOP
OF THE *RUBY*

Within the Pacific region itself variations of watercraft were much more
plentiful when the Europeans arrived than they are now. The interchange
of ideas has speeded up so immensely that better techniques and modifications
are adopted quickly, and those which are superseded soon die away. Certain
features seldom completely disappear, because they are answers to problems
posed by the ocean itself; for example, the problem of a low shore and a high
surf. They are specific answers to local problems. What have disappeared are
the ingenious craft designed to overcome a lack of better material. Knowledge
of craft such as reed floats must be gleaned from early journals, diaries, and
official reports, or through museum visits. Sewn animal skin, reeds, kelp, or
bamboo were used not only to give buoyancy to light cargo rafts in South
America, Hawaii, New Zealand, the Chathams, and China, but also to support swimmers, and in sealing and whaling to keep the harpoons and the prey
from sinking. There was also an emergency use for floats. Marco Polo admired the foresight of the Chinese, for in the event of a shipwreck they "carry
with them a number of air-tight skin bags ... then they lash them all together to form a raft."[1]

Surfboards are forms of floats, now used for sport, but in the old days for
fishing and short journeys as well. At Tahiti, Banks saw surfing with an old
canoe which "hurried in with incredible swiftness."[2] The crew of the *Discovery*

saw real surfboards in use at Hawaii, "a thin piece of Board about 2 feet broad & 6 or 8 long."[3] Natives on floats greeted the first ships to arrive at Easter Island in the eighteenth century laughing up from the mats of rushes or from the single planks on which they had braved the heavy surf. Carletti noticed the Indians of Peru fishing from reed floats, sometimes fifteen miles out to sea. He described these floats as being "like sheaves of straw that are thick at one end and thin at the other, six or seven arms long."[4] Apparently, the Indians sometimes sat astride, sometimes fully aboard with crossed legs, paddling many miles out to sea to fish, and on their return taking the float apart each time to dry out the reeds.

Easter Islanders sometimes abandoned their rush floats when they decided to swim back to shore. In the same way, floats were often mere temporary conveniences for river crossings, and were discarded as lightly as they had been built quickly. The Maoris made one-man floats, called "mohiki," from "raupo" (bullrush) stems. These could be shaped into cylindrical bundles tapered at both ends which could carry a man sitting astride and paddling with his hands, if nothing better were available. As noted earlier, floats, by a process of accretion, could have formed the basis of rafts; one log or reed bundle is a float, but several floats are a raft—once someone has thought of binding them together. The larger Maori craft were sometimes built up of their one-man floats, their final shape resembling closely that of the reed watercraft, seagoing and semi-permanent, of both the Peruvian coast and inland Lake Titicaca in South America. These Indian craft were, and indeed still are, too plentiful and too useful to be ignored. Although in shape they resemble a boat, the name is an honorary one, for the definitive feature of a boat is an outer surface through which water does not penetrate. This the reed craft do not have; so, whatever their shape, they belong in this chapter with the rafts and floats.

Tasmania has rush or bark-bundle "boats" rather like the New Zealand ones, and, across the Pacific in North America, Indian tribes—the Thompson of British Columbia, the Klamath of Oregon, and the Seri of California—all built and used similar craft. Vancouver, in his journal, described a straw "canoe" in California, but Colnett, the captain whose troubles with the Spaniards were a partial cause of Vancouver's voyage, was more precise. He said that while he was visiting the Indians near San Francisco, he saw "no Canoes, but floats that will only carry two people, made of Bull Rushes . . . three Bundles making the Bottom, and one each side, Bow and Stern."[5]

The vessels the Californian Seri tribe built were double ended, with tapering upward curves, which made excellent seacraft for coastal fishing. Although reed boats could carry heavy loads, they appear flimsy and impermanent to the modern eye. To some degree, however, this seeming impermanence was an advantage, for even though the material changed, the "boat" went on and on. As various parts decayed, they were replaced cheaply with new reeds—like a lumberjack's favourite axe which is given six new handles and three new heads. Such constant maintenance presupposed voyages which would not remove the vessel either too long or too far from the reed supply.

Drake's men mentioned meeting an Indian in Chile and taking him with "his owne canow (which was made of reed straw) to land him where he would."[6] This "canow" was made of several bundles of reeds lashed together, shaped like the craft Colnett had seen in California. Similar craft still used on Lake Titicaca in South America are very like the ancient reed watercraft of Egypt, as Heyerdahl's recent Atlantic crossing in the Egyptian craft *Ra* was meant to emphasize.

Wherever built and of whatever material—reeds or logs or brush or inflated skins—the construction of a raft that will float and carry a load is not really difficult, but moving the rafts through the water, especially against a current, and steering them, especially across a wind, are different matters entirely. Yet these problems were solved centuries ago, although the answers remained localized in area and then were obscured by time. The answer that the ancients found, movable steering planks, once conceived, was as simple in execution as sails, rudders, outriggers, or sea anchors. By setting planks in different positions and at different depths between the main logs, the raft could be steered and its drift lessened. The development of these movable "centreboards" was apparently arrived at independently in Formosa and Ecuador.

In Formosa, seagoing sailing rafts using this principle were highly developed (figure 1). These rafts were made of large bamboo poles with the thin ends forward and the fore end truncated and slightly upturned. They were up to forty feet long and about ten feet across. Usually, they were used as fishing rafts, but sometimes as cargo carriers, or as a ferry for goods and passengers, in which case the passengers sat in a tub amidships—sometimes an unsecured one. This protected them from wet feet, but put them in danger of being washed overboard, tub and all. A vertical mast stepped in a wooden block hoisted a square lug sail, and oars could be used to aid propulsion and steering. Three or more removable thin centreboard steering planks were let down through the bamboos to lessen drift and to aid steering.

On the Atlantic side of South America, the Brazilian fishing balsas were famed for speed and were often described and used for comparative purposes by sailors visiting the Pacific. Although they were small, they were nevertheless remarkably seaworthy and in this feature resembled their Pacific counterpart,

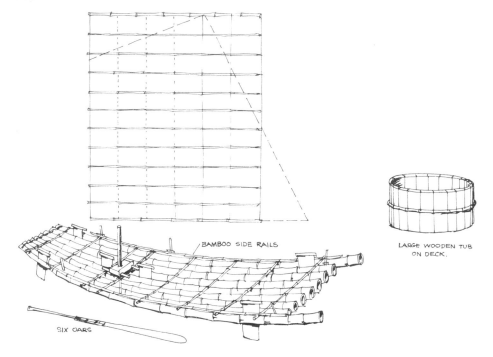

BAMBOO SIDE RAILS

LARGE WOODEN TUB ON DECK.

SIX OARS

Fig. 1. Formosan Raft

the small log rafts used for fishing in the Formosa Strait, which would appear to be smaller versions of the larger and extinct Formosan seagoing raft with centreboards. In 1797, Broughton of the *Providence* described fishing rafts near Formosa: "They were simply composed of bamboos lashed together, about 20 feet by 6 feet; the mast fixed in a wooden step in the centre, and they appeared to sail fast. Each float carried three men."[7] As with the small balsas of South America, their very shallow draught made them exceedingly fast in a breeze.

Even smaller bamboo rafts, about eleven by six feet, propelled by oars, were used for fishing in the Formosa Channel. Small junks acted as mother-ships and, instead of sampans, bamboo rafts operated from a parent-ship junk, just as Newfoundland dories do from schooners. The rafts were made of "ten or more giant bamboos . . . lashed together with cross-pieces of smaller bamboos to keep them in position."[8]

Far south and east of Formosa, off Peru and Ecuador, sailed other great seagoing rafts—the balsas of the South American Indians (figure 2). They were made from balsa trees, a very light wood today used in making model aircraft—either the tree was named after the raft, or the raft named after the tree. Similar in design to the Formosan bamboo raft, balsas were long rafts up to seventy-five feet long, the fore end slightly upcurved and tapered, not truncated, the centre log projecting at the truncated stern so that the steersman could use an oar, although his steering was aided by centreboard fittings like those of the Formosan raft. The Indian rafts carried a large square sail, but could also be paddled.

Log rafts of various kinds were used all around the Pacific. Some still are—the cargo balsas of inland Lake Titicaca, on the border between Peru and Bolivia, are still in use. The great seagoing balsas finally died out from Peru's seacoast some time ago, but they had lasted for centuries after the Spaniards conquered the country.

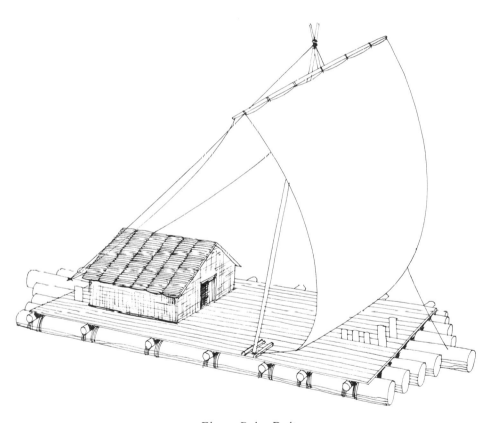

Fig. 2. Balsa Raft

Small balsas fished at sea as far north as California. The *Duke*'s crew saw "wild *Indians* who padled to them on Bark-Logs."[9] These craft were better built than the big Californian fishing balsas seen by Ulloa in 1539, which were made of "certaine thicke trunkes of Cedars, some of them of the thicknesse of two men, and three fadome long . . . laid along and fastened together."[10]

Dampier saw larger cargo balsas at Payta in Peru:

Others are made to carry Goods: the bottom of these is made of 20 or 30 great Trees of about 20, 30, or 40 foot long . . . on the top of these they place another shorter row of Trees across them, pinn'd fast to each other, and then pinn'd to the undermost row . . . they make long Voyages . . . 5 or 600 leagues. . . . They always go before the Wind, being unable to Ply against it . . . they are so made that they cannot sink at Sea. These Rafts carry 60 or 70 Tuns of Goods and up-wards.[11]

These cargo balsas were big craft, similar to the *Kon-Tiki*, which the anthro-pologist Heyerdahl sailed to Polynesia in 1947 to bolster his theory that at least some of the ancestors of the Polynesians had reached their islands from South America. He has some support in Polynesian legend for this theory. The *Kon-Tiki* attracted the attention of the world to herself, to Heyerdahl, and to his theories as she was meant to do. She was not a raft, but a reincarnation of an ancient culture and a vigorous, daring spirit. She was neither a restora-tion nor a replica, for they are merely a repetition of substance; *Kon-Tiki* was a making alive of legend.

Heyerdahl was right in arguing that the ancient balsas were fully sea-worthy. Many early European ships encountered them far from shore; Caven-dish captured one at sea in 1587. It was similar to those he had captured in a harbour, described as "foure or five great balsas, which were laden with plantans, bags of meale. . . . Our Generall marvelled what they were."[12]

Some critics of Heyerdahl and his theories have proposed that he in-validated his argument at the beginning by having the *Kon-Tiki* towed out to sea. He would not have been so foolish. The towing was merely a conve-nience; he and others knew that balsas can get out to sea. According to the Spaniards, the Indians of Peru used to go fishing on these rafts fifty or sixty miles out to sea, well into the Humboldt Current which sweeps north along South America and then west to the islands of Polynesia. It may well be, as Heyerdahl theorizes, that his *Kon-Tiki* was not the first South Ameri-can raft to reach Polynesia. But it must be emphasized that almost all expert anthropologists do not accept Heyerdahl's theories about an important ethnic connection between the Americas and Polynesia. What he did show was that survivors of a balsa raft expedition setting out from Peru or Ecuador could reach the Polynesian islands.

The *Kon-Tiki*'s crew was Norwegian, or Norsemen, with the exception of one Swede; what more fitting crew could there be for a long ocean adventure even in 1947? Yet their vessel—seaworthy, sturdy, strong, song-lifted as it proved to be—had none of the grace of a Viking longship. Nine huge logs of balsa were lashed side by side "with separate lengths of inch-and-a-quarter hemp rope."[13] The species of log is important, as a raft depends not on the shape of the craft, but on the buoyancy of the wood or other material used in its construction. Wafer described a wood like balsa wood in his account of buccaneering: "Tis so very light in Water that three or four Logs of it, about as thick as ones Thigh and about four Foot long, shall make a Rafter on which two or three Men may go out to Sea."[14]

With the longest log (forty-five feet) in the centre, the *Kon-Tiki* acquired the shape of a balsa, described by a Spaniard in 1524 as "like that of a hand stretched out, with the length of the fingers diminishing from the centre."[15] Cross logs were lashed on, a deck of split bamboos fastened on over them, a cabin of bamboo canes built on the deck, and two poles of mangrove wood lashed into a triangle across the width of the raft to serve as a mast for the large square sail. "Not a single spike, nail, or wire rope was used in the whole construction."[16] The nine big logs were each pointed to cut the water neatly, and fir planks were pushed down and lashed between the logs at irregular intervals to act as centreboards. "They were scattered about without system and went down 5 feet into the water, being 1 inch thick and 2 feet wide."[17] Spanish observers had written of these planks and said they were used for steering, but no one had explained how they worked. The *Kon-Tiki*'s crew eventually found how to operate the planks effectively, and it saved much effort at the steering oar. Effortless or not, the *Kon-Tiki* was steered, or steered herself, to Polynesia, where, according to Heyerdahl, she was greeted by the Polynesians as a successor to the great rafts of their own ancestors.

Raft navigation seems to have been of great antiquity in Polynesia, reaching a high degree of development in the early days. Linguistic and traditional evidence makes this plain. Tradition tells of rafts carrying defeated tribes into exile and of other rafts employed in inter-island traffic to transport heavy stones to be used for statues or in fortification. There is also a description of a raft at Mangareva forty to fifty feet long, made of large logs securely lashed and carrying an interesting isosceles-shaped sail.[18]

Different forms of log raft were found in most of the ancient Pacific. Australian aborigines used them, giving them a rough streamlining by placing all the thick ends of the logs at the same end of the raft (figure 3). Sometimes they used two rafts at one time by placing the front of one on the rear of another, tandem fashion. Many other forms

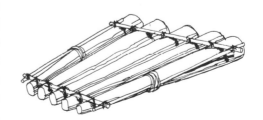

Fig. 3. Australian Log Raft

were used in the islands further north, an interesting variation being the log catamaran of the Solomon Islands, in which the logs were pinned and not lashed.

Not all Pacific rafts were large. Small outrigger rafts were used on the east coast of New Zealand well into the nineteenth century. Designed for two people to fish from, they were interesting double rafts, basically two pointed log floats held three to five feet apart by cross logs. Two paddlers, one on each float, propelled these craft out to sea and along the coast seeking the crayfish for which the area is famous. The catch could be piled on a platform built on the cross logs. It is tempting to see in the form of this raft a remaining New Zealand survival of the great double canoe and outrigger system of island Polynesia, a remnant of a progressive series of simplifications of construction to meet changing circumstances. A simple use gradually creates a simple replica of an old form, as tradition-based craftsmanship degenerates with the declining requirements.

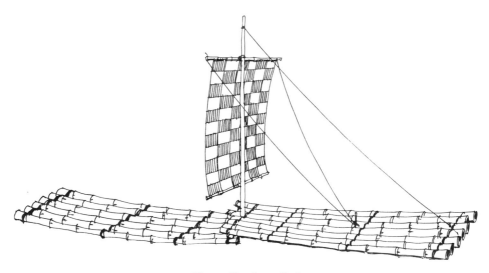

Fig. 4. Yachow Raft

Banana stems were used for rafts in the Marquesas, and bamboo was commonly used where available. Quite large craft have been made from bamboo; however, as their construction is simple, rafts setting out from one island to another with as many as thirty or forty people on board took care to wait for settled weather before starting out. "The lightest-draught general cargo carrier of the Yangtze, and quite possibly of the world"—the Yachow raft in China (figure 4)—is also made of bamboo; its "loaded draught is often as little as 3 inches and never exceeds 6 inches."[19] With their turned up bows and shallow draught, these rafts can slide over the rocks which almost break the surface of the water. Junk development is hidden in antiquity and, as Chinese rafts are common, authorities consider the raft the progenitor of the junk, much in the same way that the dugout canoes were the progenitors of the European ships. Some authorities claim that there were no dugouts in China.

As rafts are used in all the rivers of China, in all probability it is from a raft that the Chinese sampan is derived. The name means simply "three planks." Indeed, a sampan (figure 5) looks something like a raft; it is an open skiff, shallow, keelless, and bluntly wedge shaped. Each gunwale rail is extended beyond the stern as an upwardly curving projection, like great horns —in a way, evocative of the great ancient seagoing rafts of Formosa. Sampans are either rowed with two long oars by a rower standing and facing forward, or sculled over the stern. It is easily seen that from raft to sampan is one step, and from sampan to junk possibly another. The great rear horns on a large craft would produce the overhanging stern of the junk. On the junk's sampan-type blunt stern the sampan steering oar could become the hanging rudder.

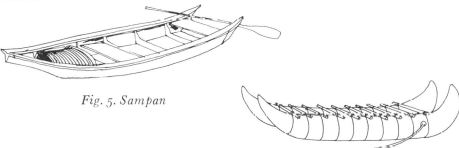

Fig. 5. Sampan

Fig. 6. South American Skin Balsa

A craft as interesting as a junk or sampan was encountered by Cavendish's *Desire* far across in South America in 1587. In southern Chile, the Englishmen reported seeing boats "marvellous artificially made of two skinnes like unto bladders, and are blowen full at one ende with quilles: they have two of these bladders blowen full, which are sowen together."[20] Drake had seen a sealskin raft off Chile even earlier, and his men said that it "rowed very swiftly, carrying in it no small burthen."[21] A privateer captain described a sealskin raft in 1720 and has left an excellent picture. In Chile, a special feature was that the skins were formed into shapes somewhat resembling boats by using a frame of poles, whereas in Peru similar craft were shaped by filling them with hot sand to dry the hides into the desired form (figure 6). Some of these craft are still in use.

Fig. 7. Skin Float

Skin floats (figure 7) were also used in rafts in China. After use, the skin floats could be deflated, the raft taken apart, and the flattened skins easily transported back to the original departure point to await re-inflation for another trip. In the same way, the Chilean skin balsas were sometimes taken apart and put under cover out of the sun. When kept greased they did not leak much air—naturally they took in no water where air was escaping—and were easily kept inflated by the boatman who kept a tube on hand for this purpose. The balsas were an excellent adaptation of local materials, for they suited the conditions of heavy surf in South America and could not be swamped, and, in any case, were unsinkable. As Drake's men had pointed out, their shallow draught made them both swift and able to bear heavy loads.[22]

In the absence of skins suitable for floats or trees suitable for logs, all kinds of materials were used ingeniously. Local adaptation reached its height in the Chatham Islands near New Zealand where the early Polynesians, often called Moriois, used flax, tree-fern, and, in a special way, the broad-leafed kelp, a large seaweed. Their rafts had many features of framed ships or canoes—perhaps a survival of an earlier New Zealand culture—but they were not boats. They were rafts, the lower sections being completely submerged beneath the water and, because of this, they were unsinkable as long as the cords of phormium, or New Zealand flax, which lashed them together held firm. The large ones gained buoyancy from inflated kelp used as flotation chambers, and were big enough to take sixty or seventy people as well as strong enough to carry large baskets of earth on which cooking fires could be built. These rafts were slow, ungainly, and ponderous. Although there is not much evidence, there is good reason to believe that they were not paddled, but rowed—something rare in the South Pacific and perhaps a very early cultural adaptation of an observed European technique. The rafts had the strength required to support pins for the oars to work against, but, more important, their crews had the strength of will to brave the dangerous seas which separate the various islands.[23]

When reading about the variety of watercraft of the Pacific and looking at illustrations, there is often reason to marvel at the unique solutions to unusual problems. There is also reason to ask about the unusually similar solutions found for corresponding problems half a world away. Perhaps the umiak (Plate 8) or the Pitcairn surf boat did not influence the Northumberland lifeboat, yet does not each show a common response to the problem of beaching a laden craft through rough seas on an open coast? Why did the Formosans and Peruvians find identical solutions to the problem of sailing unwieldly rafts in directions other than directly before the wind? Did the Vikings ever build ships near Vladivostok as some authorities have suggested on the evidence of striking similarities of boat construction in Scandinavia and parts of East Asia or did Viking influence creep east or west around the roof of the world, or were there people in the ancient East who independently reached the same answers as were reached in the ancient West? Did the great pines of New Zealand and British Columbia offer only the same facility or is there a closer connection between the war canoes of Keri-Keri and of Kitimat? Did the Isles of Lateen sails adopt their graceful triangular form of sail from the Portuguese in the sixteenth century or did the Pacific send the idea west previously, or had both areas received it from another central source? Where does influence begin and independent invention end?

CHAPTER 2

Skin Boats of the North Pacific

The baidars, or boats, of Oonalashka, are infinitely superior to those of any other island. If perfect symmetry, smoothness, and proportion constitute beauty, they are beautiful; to me they appeared so beyond anything that I ever beheld. I have seen some of them as transparent as oiled paper, through which you could trace every formation of the inside, and the manner of the native's sitting in it; whose light dress, painted and plumed bonnet, together with his perfect ease and activity, added infinitely to its elegance. Their first appearance struck me with amazement beyond expression.

A MEMBER OF THE BILLINGS' EXPLORING EXPEDITION, 1790

. . . the hole is skirted with loose skin, which, when the man is seated, he draws close round him, like the mouth of a purse, and with a coat and cap of the same skin, which covers his whole body, makes the man and his boat appear like one piece; and thus clad, and thus seated and surrounded, he fears neither the roughest sea, nor the severest weather.

JOHN RICKMAN
OF THE *DISCOVERY*

Miracles of courage and endurance by our standards are commonplace to the Arctic people on both sides of Bering Strait. They exhibit not only these passive virtues, but active inventiveness and creativity which have made other miracles happen in adapting so little to so much. There are no better examples of such adaptation than the Eskimo watercraft of the North Pacific and Arctic Oceans.

Very few primitive watercraft have become models for modern boats, but two of the common boats of early North America have earned this distinction —the kayak (Plate 7) and the bark canoe (figure 14). Each is still recognizable in form, although built of different materials. By "kayak" is normally meant the single-seater skin craft in which an Eskimo in fact becomes part of the boat, or perhaps one should say the boat becomes part of the Eskimo, making him a sea animal in the sense that gliders turn men into birds. And the Eskimo can start off by himself and is dependent only on himself for propulsion.

Kayaks vary in detail of construction from place to place in the Arctic and North Pacific, yet basically they are the same boat from Greenland to Alaska (and in a small area of northeastern Siberia, too). They are seagoing hunting craft, a wonderful example of the use of limited local materials, and a tangible expression of a culture. Of the singular beauty that form suited perfectly to function always creates, kayaks are really long, fully-decked, skin canoes with certain variations to suit the local conditions—for example, the V bottom, flat bottom, and multi-chine bottom forms, the last being the normal Pacific type (figure 8).[1] Decoration is added in the form of tribal totems or figure-

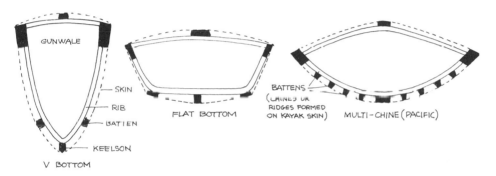

Fig. 8. Local Variations in Kayak Cross-Section

heads carved on the stems, often a representation of a seal's head carved with the moulded simplicity which graces Eskimo art. A hole right through the bow represents the eyes and also frequently serves as a lifting handle.

Kayaks must be fast and easy to paddle, able to face a strong tide or wind, yet also portable on land and ice. Such conditions dictate a small low boat with decking to keep out the water of the rough and icy local seas. Generally, it is meant for one person only, but Kodiak kayaks often have man-holes with room for two to sit back to back.[2] There are also kayaks for three—possibly the result of Russian influence. The *Resolution* saw a kayak —called a "baidarka" by the Russians—which contained a Russian trader and two Aleut paddlers. Large three-hole kayaks, up to thirty feet long were used by Russian officials, and two-man kayaks are used in the Aleutian Islands for hunting whales and sea otters.

Sometimes, one or more "passengers" crawls in and lies lengthwise within the single kayak, travelling along almost under water in a semi-transparent and extremely confining craft. Ledyard, a corporal in Cook's expedition, who certainly led a most interesting life, once travelled in this way, and "the Skin of the Canoe being transparent he could see the Water plain enough, in which he was in a manner buryed & only defended from it by thin Leather."[3] The *Vega*, the Swedish ship which first accomplished the northeast passage from Sweden to Japan by the Arctic, also saw "boats from which, when the two rowers had stepped out, a third person crept who had lain almost hermetically sealed in the interior of the *kayak*."[4] The Siberian kayak is shorter and wider than the American kayak, and rather weakly built, but very fast and handy provided the water is not too rough.

   In all kayak construction, the main strength comes from the gunwales. Some designs have stiff keels, but most merely have a frame of light longitudinal battens which, together with light ribs, serve merely as a framework for the skin cover which is not fastened to the frame in any way except at the manhole (figure 9). The skin cover is held out by the longitudinal battens; the ribs, placed inside the battens, do not touch the skin so that there will be no cross ridges to cause drag. Some kayaks have no stemposts or sternposts, coming to a point in all dimensions, but many have intricate stempieces carved from blocks of wood, and plank sternposts as well (figure 10). The stems of some models are "bifid," or split, as Cook reported. Decking is very light—only the thwarts at the manhole having much strength—as apparently strength seems of much less importance than lightness. Steller, the scientist with Bering's *St. Peter*, saw an "American" carrying a kayak in his right hand, his paddle in his left; he "carries it thus because of its lightness on to the land anywhere he wants to and back from the land into the water."[5] Perhaps we should remember too that the great strength of Eskimos was noted with envy by a number of observers.

   The timber used in kayaks is usually driftwood, for there is little other

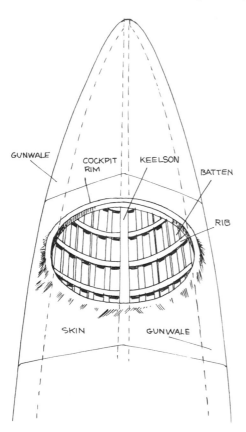

Fig. 9. Kayak Construction

GUNWALE
COCKPIT RIM
KEELSON
BATTEN
RIB
SKIN
GUNWALE

timber available where they are built. Fir, pine, spruce, or willow is used for
the long frames; the bent ribs are usually willow. Sinew is used for both lashing
and sewing, and all lashings are set in flush to prevent chafing. When a kayak
is being built, the gunwales are set up first, then the heavy thwarts for the
manhole, then a few bent rib frames to control the shape, then the long

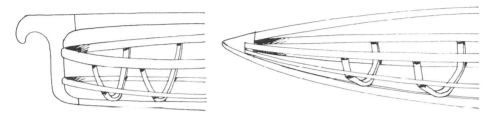

Fig. 10. Kayak   with and without stem post

battens and, finally, the rest of the ribs are lashed in to complete the frame.
The manhole rim is fitted and the cover stretched on. This process may be
reversed depending on whether the rim is to be under or over the cover, a
distinguishing feature of local areas (figure 11). Most Alaskan kayaks—the
Pacific ones of interest here—have the rim under the cover. All the sewn seams
meet along the top when the cover is properly fitted. It is stretched and
stitched on, but rarely secured directly to the frame anywhere except at the

Fig. 11. Kayak—alternative methods of fixing skin at cockpit

manhole. It is a cover, not a part of the structure. Probably because of a
shortage of material other than skins and also because the icy seas make dangerous any wetting at all, the Eskimos designed a craft which would go through,
as much as on, the water and yet keep its occupants dry. It entails quite a
different principle from building a craft with high sides which floats high on
the water.

Bearded sealskin usually is used for the covers for Alaskan kayaks and sea
lion skin for Aleutian ones. One of Cook's sailors said the skin was "dyed of
a kind of a purple colour," but most others described the colour as brown.[6]

Walrus skin is stronger than sealskin but loses its oiled waterproofing much faster. Any water that gets into the kayak is sucked out through a tube near the paddler, a reverse process from that of blowing air into the skin craft through a tube as in Chile. Cook, however, reported that sponges were used for this purpose.[7]

The hunter enters the kayak by putting in one carefully wiped foot—any dirt or stones would injure the skin cover—and steadies himself on the shore with the double paddle while wiping the other foot before bringing it in. He then slides down into the hole, working his legs under the deck until he is seated, with his hips jammed into the hole rim and sitting on a temporary and loosely fitted seat of heavy furred skin. His waterproof jacket, often made of whale intestines, has long sleeves and a hood with drawstrings to close them snugly; at the waist it is fitted tightly over the manhole rim to make the kayak and paddler a waterproof unit, a kind of hybrid, hunting, sea animal which can do anything except dive—and skilled kayakers can do almost that. By deft use of the paddle, the kayaker can roll the canoe, perhaps to avoid an angry or wounded animal, or perhaps just for fun. All kayakers are not skilled and the roll is not always completed; stuck upside down in the water, they have to be rescued by friends. Hunters in kayaks use darts and harpoons, the harpoon line being attached to skin buoys.

Occasionally kayaks are lashed into pairs to master very rough water or to ferry large loads across streams. In some parts of Alaska they are even formed into a rough catamaran with a sail. Whether this idea came from the Indians to the south, or from further afield with the Pacific ships, or was an independent invention, is not known.

Some authorities have theorized about the development of the kayak from the bark canoe, especially from the unique ram-ended canoe of the Kootenay and Salish Indians. This is a type of canoe which differs from all other North American canoes, although a somewhat similar version can be found in Asia. Birchbark canoes and kayaks are built by principles of construction as different as the two principles followed in European clinker- and carvel-boatbuilding (figure 43).

Kayak frames are built first and then fitted with a cover, whereas canoe frames are forced into an already assembled bark cover (figure 14) and held in only by a rigid gunwale structure. In this particular feature, canoes might be described as clinker-built and kayaks as carvel-built—the two types of European boat construction which will be described more fully later. Of course, neither canoes nor kayaks have planking. The strength of the gunwale of kayaks and canoes is their only common feature. When a kayak cover is removed for the periodic waterproofing with oil, the frame remains intact ready for recovering, but if the bark were to be removed from a canoe, the whole frame, except for the gunwales, would collapse—even in the ram-ended canoes of the Northwest. Interestingly, when Indians built skin craft on the prairies (where there were few birch trees), they used the canoe principle of attaching the covers to the gunwales and then forcing in the ribs.

The umiak (Plate 8) of the extreme northern seas is one of the seagoing types of primitive skin boats—primitive only in the sense of being ancient and limited by materials—rather like the Irish curragh. Compared to a dugout canoe, the hide boat is so much lighter and roomier in proportion to its length

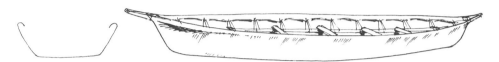

Fig. 12. Umiak—length, 30 feet. Midship skin shape is flat-bottomed and the skin is lashed over two framing poles running the whole length of the craft.

that it could carry much heavier loads while still keeping its gunwale high enough above the waves to avoid swamping, whereas a heavily laden dugout would sink very readily. The walrus hide cover on the umiak is immensely strong, and since the boat has a minimum of framing—partly by design and partly because of the scarcity of wood—its flexibility enables it to withstand both grounding on beaches and bumping into ice. A umiak resists the ramming of floating ice by allowing not only a distortion and sliding of its skin cover, but a distortion and recovery of its elastic frame with its lashing joints.

Main framing pieces run full length inside the umiak (figure 12), the most important being the keelson along the bottom and not, as in the kayak, the gunwales along the side. Construction begins (for these craft are still built this way) by building the frame—quite the opposite to a bark canoe—by lashing cross members to a keelson (a keel inside the outer covering of a boat), side frames and floor timbers to the cross members, and round poles to the frames for gunwales. The cross frames are in three pieces, one on each side and one across the bottom, forming a type of U-shaped rib. All are lashed together with sinew which gives slightly under stress without damage to the frame. Then the outside battens are lashed along each side and the frame is complete. All lashings are through holes or countersunk. Timbers are of fir, spruce, or willow driftwood, and the keelson is formed by two of these tree trunks scarfed together, with a root knee at each end serving as stem and stern.

The skin cover for this frame is prepared by removing the hair and fat by scraping or "by spreading fermented fish-spawn over it, and allowing it to remain till the hair rots off."[8] Blind seams, in which the needle does not penetrate through the skin, are sewn. Green pliable skins are used if possible, but in all cases the cover is soaked in seawater before being stretched over the frame and pulled taut with lacing. If the cover does not fit perfectly, gores are cut out and the skin re-sewn. Once shrunk smooth and tight it is soaked with animal oil to waterproof it; it requires drying and re-oiling every few days. Whymper, an Englishman travelling with Alaskan natives in the 1860's, asserted that the covers "were taken off their frames, re-patched in rotten places, soaked in water & c., and then again put on, well oiled, and fat rubbed into the seams." He had travelled extensively in umiaks and claimed that "a skin boat has its advantages; the tough flexible skin will *give* for several inches without necessarily tearing." He thought them much safer and stronger than either "cedar canoes of British Columbia" (dugouts) or "birch-bark" canoes.[9]

As well as being strong in relation to the load they can carry, umiaks are very light, a most important property in a boat which frequently has to be portaged over pack ice. "It is so light that four men can take it upon their shoulders, and yet so roomy that thirty men can be conveyed in it."[10] One explorer claimed umiaks would hold forty people. "Quarter Master" saw one carrying twenty-two people yet drawing only one foot of water, and a traveller in Alaska rode in one with over two tons of provisions on board.[11] With the hull so light, the bottom flat, and the sides flared, a heavy load causes little extra draught. Being so light and flat-bottomed they can be paddled easily, sailed, or towed by kayaks; more recently, outboard engines have been used. In earlier times, umiaks needed to be fast as food sources were far apart. The shallow draught and flat bottom that makes them easy to move through the water also makes both beaching and loading easier.

Alaskan umiaks vary in size, from cargo carriers forty feet long down to small, very fast eighteen-footers which are used for hunting walrus. Whaling umiaks are wide, light, and more strongly built than are cargo carriers and have covers of sealskin, split walrus hide, or even bearskin. Because of these hide or skin covers, umiaks on shore have to be stored up on a platform away from the ever hungry dogs. Probably due to European influence, umiaks are often rowed with oars using thong loops as tholes. Occasionally, ancient models show very different bow types; in one case, a bow looks very like that of a Malayan proa. Umiaks seem to resemble closely the European whaleboat, but the similarities probably are due more to function than to imitation.

Compared to boats of a similar size anywhere in the world, the umiak rates high for strength, lightness, and efficiency, just as the kayak is perhaps the most efficient hunting boat anywhere. Given the paucity of resources, the

Plate 7. This model illustrates very clearly the skin shape and interior construction of the kayak.
Note that in this example the skin is fixed over, not under, the cockpit rims. Three-hole kayaks were
developed under Russian influence when the Russians owned Alaska, and exploring ships often
encountered Russian fur-trading officials, seated in the central hole, being paddled by two Aleuts or
Alaskans.

Plate 8. Umiak. This type of Eskimo skin boat was called a women's boat because it transported the whole family and effects from island to island or along the coast. Umiaks were very efficient freight carriers, often carrying several tons of supplies and a number of people in one trip.

ferocity of the animals hunted, and the almost unremitting harshness of the climate, the designs of these two Eskimo boats in all probability are the supreme examples of a cultural response to challenge. Even the justly famed flying proa of the Carolines, beautiful craft of a lovely and predictable climate (in spite of hurricanes), is not an equal triumph of design. The umiak's strength lies in its flexibility, the kayak's in its lightness; this is a paradox, but also a fact. Most people who have studied the matter agree that the differences in the two North Pacific skin boats are not related to the relative timing of development, but strictly to function.

Umiaks were found on the Siberian coast of the Pacific and a short distance westward in Arctic Siberia. There they were called "baidars," and the kayaks were called "baidarkas" (little baidars). Somewhat further south, the Ainu of northern Japan used "leather canoes" very like the baidars or umiaks. Some journals mention that they used dugout canoes as well, so apparently they had adapted, or adopted, techniques which could use the materials available in their location in the border area between middle and north in the northern hemisphere. Both baidars and Alaskan umiaks are sharper at stem and stern than are the Greenland umiaks to which the European sailors constantly compared them. In Greenland, umiaks were used only by women for transporting goods, but in the Pacific men used them for whaling and hunting. As a result, more variations in detail and type are found. In spite of their adaptation to hunting, however, Meares, the captain of the *Felice*, pointed out that the Alaskans never made war in their large "womens' boats."[12]

It is claimed that baidars used sails even before the Russians moved into the Pacific. They certainly did latterly. One traveller in the 1860's saw not only umiaks "hoisting several masts and sails," but also what "might be called 'full-rigged' canoes, carrying main, gaff, and sprit-sails, but these were probably recent and foreign innovations."[13] A very graceful Asian type, the lightly-framed Koryak baidar, was sometimes sailed with a rectangular deer-hide sail lashed to a tripod mast. The larger Chukchi baidars had sails and rigging which appeared to owe much to European influence, and, in a feature more reminiscent of South America, some baidars carried inflated sealskins lashed to the gunwales to "serve as floats when the canoe heels over."[14]

People as inventive as Eskimos (and the trait displays itself in many ways other than boatbuilding) are bound to see the advantages inherent in certain European techniques. They are not too conservative to adopt them readily. Whatever is adopted, however, will only improve and not fundamentally change the designs of watercraft which have already proved themselves. Considering the challenges they have had to face, the very fact that there *are* Eskimos is proof enough of the superb suitability of their sea tools.

CHAPTER 3

Wood and Bark Canoes
of America and Australia

*Their canoes were of an uncommon length, many of them from
30 to 40 yards long, made of the main body of one of their
enormous trees, of which we have already spoken; their
breadth from four to five feet over in the middle, and gradually narrowing, like all others to both ends, but the stem much
higher than the stern. . . . Some of those canoes were roughly
carved and painted with the figures of the sun, moon, and
stars, probably the objects of their worship; but what was remarkable, they had no outriggers to prevent their oversetting,
like those in southern isles.*

JOHN RICKMAN
OF THE *DISCOVERY*

*At Broken Bay, in August, 1847, a singular couple of aborigi-
nes whom I met upon a fishing excursion had a small canoe
formed of a single sheet of bark tied up at each end; on the
floor of this they were squatted, with the gunwale not more
than six inches above the water's edge. Yet this frail bark contained a fire, numbers of spears, fishing lines and other gear.*

JOHN MACGILLIVRAY
OF THE *RATTLESNAKE*

The possibility of some cultural connection between the wood canoes of America and of Polynesia (and there certainly are striking similarities) has often
been discussed, but there is no real basis for argument that the birchbark
canoes of North America or the beechbark canoes of Tierra del Fuego are
connected with the bark canoes of Australia. The similarities that exist are
almost certainly inherent in the material itself. The differences probably are a
reflection of cultural development, which, in turn, is a reflection of the importance of watercraft in each individual area.

A fishing culture was almost predetermined on the northwest coast of
America, where the sea is kept temperate by the North Pacific Drift from the
Philippines sweeping over past Japan to America. The huge and delicious

salmon, which are still an important food item in many British Columbian homes, were so plentiful that they became part of the staple diet.

Northwest American Indian craft (Plates 9, 10), although they displayed tribal differences, were single canoes very similar to those of the Maoris at the diagonally opposite corner of the Pacific, and Northwest American canoes of size, durability, and beauty could be hewn from the giant trees of the great pine and cedar forests which even today cover hundreds of thousands of square miles. Cedar wood in particular is straight grained, easy to split, and very water resistant. Wood easy to split is also easy to work, but it is subject to cracking and leaking when a canoe is pounded by the waves.

With huge trees readily available, the Indians made the largest dugouts in the world; the crew of Cook's *Discovery* saw some they described as being "from 30 to 40 yards long,"[1] far longer than the ones mentioned in any other reports. Cook himself described one seven feet across and forty feet long, while others claimed to have seen hulls of seventy feet by six and a half feet by four and a half feet, holding one hundred people. In the method of canoe construction as well as in basic design, the Indian way of making canoes closely resembles the Maori pattern. A ceremony was performed in which the builders apologized to the chosen tree and explained the urgency of their need. Once felled with stone adzes and controlled fire, the tree was dubbed into hull shape on the spot. Sometimes wedges pounded in with a stone sledge hammer split the tree into halves, from which the better or bigger half was selected. The builders hollowed the hull with adzes and fire before dragging it with bark ropes down to the sea.

Both Cook and King described the canoes at Nootka as being similar to Norway yawls, probably because they were pointed at each end. Samwell called them "altogether much like a Thames wherry," a sharp, light, and shallow boat with both ends alike. An officer of the American ship *Columbia* said: "Their models was not unlike our Nantucket whale boats."[2] As the available trees were so large, extra planks along the sides were not needed on most canoes, but when required they were made by dubbing or splitting as in Polynesia. Stern and bow pieces varied from tribe to tribe and were a distinguishing feature by which a canoe's tribal origin could be recognized. Often these pieces were decorated with carving, paint, or seashells just as they were in much of Polynesia. Some early visitors claimed to have seen human teeth used instead of shells; others said that the shells looked like teeth until closely examined. Some traders reported that sea otter teeth were used for decorating coffins, and it is possible they were used on canoes too.

Totem heads of a guardian bird graced each side of the front of some canoes, while other prows curved up like a swan's neck only to end in a monster's head. A major difference between this canoe carving and that of the Maori is that the typical spiral (figure 17) of the latter is not found in American carving. Painted designs varied locally. Larger canoes were painted with a brush of hair tied to a stick, with black and red being the conventional war canoe colours. These colours were also found in China, in Polynesia, and in Melanesia; probably they were the simplest to produce, while still vivid or emotive enough to have impact.

The cross section of the canoes varied tribally (figure 13); those in Nootka

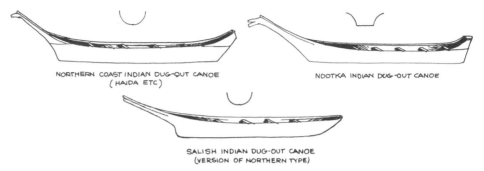

NORTHERN COAST INDIAN DUG-OUT CANOE
(HAIDA ETC)

NOOTKA INDIAN DUG-OUT CANOE

SALISH INDIAN DUG-OUT CANOE
(VERSION OF NORTHERN TYPE)

Fig. 13. Different Forms of Northwest Coast Indian Dug-Out Canoe (midship hull shapes shown above each canoe)

were angular with an almost flat bottom, while those further north were much more rounded. None had either keel or rudder, and propulsion was by paddling not rowing: "one sets in the stern and steers with a paddle the others set by pears and paddle over the gunwall next them, they all kneel in the bottom of the canoe and set on their feet."[3] King, with the *Resolution*, said: "There is not the smallest appearance of their ever using Sails, nor cou'd we perceive they had any idea of their use."[4] King was wrong; like the Maoris, the Indians did use temporary sails for running before the wind (Plate 9). Bishop's ship was approached in the 1790's by a "Cannoe under Sail full of People," not far from the present day Alaska Panhandle.[5]

Observers in the French ship *Solide* saw sails used on Queen Charlotte Island canoes in the 1790's, and one example still exists of an Indian sail made of strips of wood sewn together with spruce roots. Sails were used on the double canoes which were made for temporary purposes by lashing canoes together with a plank platform. A traveller on Vancouver Island in 1862 tells us he had "many times seen the Indians of that coast, when migrating from one village to another, employ *two canoes*, set a little apart, but parallel to each other, and covered with planks."[6] He added, "a small sail is often hoisted on the top of the planks."

One Indian canoe sailed so well that it became world famous. The *Tilikum*

(Plate 11), "an enduring eccentricity among little ships,"[7] sailed over 12,000 miles at the very beginning of the twentieth century, even though she was smaller than an ordinary ship's lifeboat. When she started her great voyage it was already forty years since the giant red cedar from which she was formed had been cut, and almost as long since she had first taken the water as a British Columbian canoe. So it was a well-seasoned hull which her owner, Captain Voss, decked over in 1900. The *Tilikum* handled well, with all her three masts rigged with the fore-and-aft sails which most people would argue were a European addition. There seems to have been a great many for her thirty-eight-foot length (slightly longer than Captain Slocum's *Spray* [Plate 42], another small craft which astonished the world by its circumnavigation under a retired sea captain born and reared on a Canadian coast). But Hoskins, an owner's representative in the American trading ship *Columbia* met an Indian chief on the British Columbia coast in 1791 who "had just come from Clioquot in a large canoe with four masts."[8] Perhaps Captain Voss was following Indian practice in using several masts on such a small craft. In any case, the *Tilikum* proved to be seaworthy; "I then put the helm down and she ran up into the wind most beautifully."[9]

Vancouver did not commend the canoes as seacraft, but on the expedition of 1804-06 Lewis said that the canoes near the mouth of the Columbia River were "remarkably neat light and well addapted for riding high waves."[10] He saw them at sea, seemingly unconcerned by the waves in which "I should have thought it impossible for any vessel of the same size to [have] lived a minute." His partner Clark admired their occupants as "the best Canoe navigaters I ever Saw."[11] The Indians took excellent care of their craft, taking them on shore whenever they landed, or if heavily laden, at least when they camped overnight. Lewis and Clark knew a great deal about the qualities of these craft, for they had built some out of large pines. Like the Indians, they used fire to help hollow out the hulls, because their axes were neither big nor good enough.

Vancouver's crew watched a great fleet of war canoes manoeuvering in a disciplined manner, and on some canoes saw shields through which loopholes were cut for discharging arrows. In another case, the Indians shot arrows from behind the canoes in the same way that prairie Indians shot arrows while hanging on the far side of their horses. The *Margaret Oakley* saw similar tactics used by Papuan natives diagonally across the Pacific.[12]

Further south, the Indians built somewhat similar canoes. In California, near the present location of Santa Barbara, Vancouver saw some good wooden canoes decorated with shells, and just south of Monterey he saw a wooden canoe with the Indians using double paddles. Colnett reported seeing Indians near San Francisco who used paddles "pointed at each end, held by the middle and used alternately."[13] This is most intriguing, for double paddles are seldom reported elsewhere except in connection with kayaks, or canoes near the kayak area. Three small Spanish ships sailing north along the Pacific coast from Mexico in 1539 first found Indians using rafts of canes, and then "canoes of cane" and then "Canoas made of wood, as we might discerne, and not raftes or Balsas, for so they call those floats which are made all flat with canes."[14] These wooden canoes would be of the same type that Vancouver saw later.

Further south in Central America, the French and English buccaneers built many canoes of the large soft cotton trees. Occasionally, they used cedars instead. One canoe was described as being thirty-six feet long and nearly six feet wide. They used axes to "hew and chizzel them," as did the Spanish, although the Indians who usually helped them preferred to use fire.[15] Cotton trees served to make piraguas as well as canoes, differing, Wafer said, "as Lighters and small Barges do from Wherries," which would mean that they were larger, not double-ended, and probably less graceful and handy.[16]

Planks were a further development, usually considered the result of a shortage of large enough tree trunks and not as a sign of higher cultural development. However, it often meant that much larger craft, free from the limitations of the shape of a tree trunk, could be built. The piraguas of Chiloe Island, just off the southwestern coast of Chile, were constructed of planks laced "together with a fine lashing that they lay up from certain tough canes called *colegues*, thus making a veritable seam."[17] (The Russians used boats in Siberia that were sewn together "with twigs," presumably in much the same way.) Shelvocke, on his privateering cruise near Chiloe, confirmed "that they, for want of nails & other utensils, sew their boats together very artificially [artfully] with oziers." He also said that the Indians rowed "in the same manner that we do,"[18] which may have been an adaptation from Spanish methods. While these South American piraguas were as neat and trim "as an ordinary boat or small vessel. . . . They are precarious craft . . . apt to capsize."[19] They resembled the Solomon Island mons (figure 22), but were much heavier and more clumsy. A unique feature of them was a type of sail made of strips of cloth pinned together with split cane which could be taken apart in port and used by the crew "as shawls or coverings for their bodies."[20]

Other American watercraft were sewn with tree products, for the bark of certain trees was a waterproof material for boat covering which was more available in some areas than the skins of animals, and almost as easy to work with. Although not as tough as hide, the barks nevertheless have their own virtues. The most beautiful craft seen anywhere in the world is the birchbark

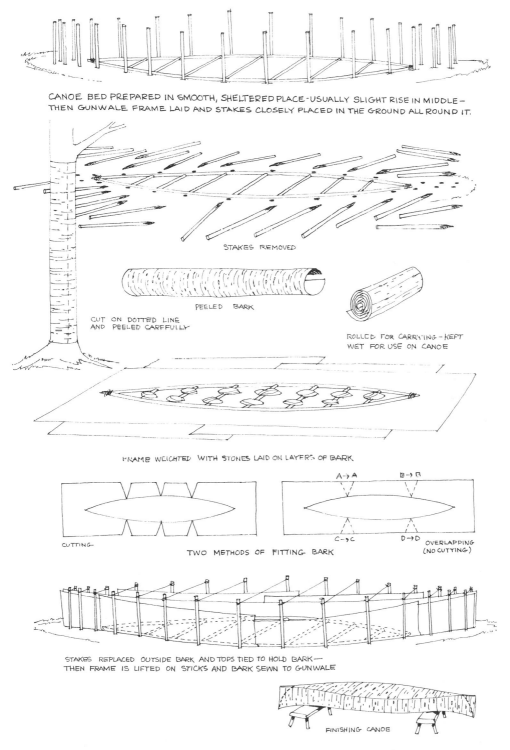

CANOE BED PREPARED IN SMOOTH, SHELTERED PLACE-USUALLY SLIGHT RISE IN MIDDLE—
THEN GUNWALE FRAME LAID AND STAKES CLOSELY PLACED IN THE GROUND ALL ROUND IT.

STAKES REMOVED

PEELED BARK

CUT ON DOTTED LINE
AND PEELED CAREFULLY

ROLLED FOR CARRYING – KEPT
WET FOR USE ON CANOE

FRAME WEIGHTED WITH STONES LAID ON LAYERS OF BARK

A→A   B→B

C→C   D→D   OVERLAPPING
                  (NO CUTTING)

CUTTING   TWO METHODS OF FITTING BARK

STAKES REPLACED OUTSIDE BARK AND TOPS TIED TO HOLD BARK—
THEN FRAME IS LIFTED ON STICKS AND BARK SEWN TO GUNWALE

FINISHING CANOE

Fig. 14. Basic Stages of Birchbark Canoe Construction

canoe, formerly used throughout northern North America, including the Yukon and other Pacific coastal rivers. Consisting only of a light frame of willow or birch with a covering of birchbark (figure 14), these canoes were as graceful as they were fragile. When the seams had been sewn with fir roots and caulked with spruce gum they were perfectly watertight. If the canoes were damaged, the materials for repair could be found on the river banks without the problem of hunting a suitable animal; bark also was simpler and cheaper than the thin lead plates carried for emergency boat repairs by Vancouver's small boats in the same area. Birchbark canoes usually were propelled with single paddles, although on the North Pacific coast sometimes double paddles were seen, perhaps copied from those used in kayaks.

At the other extreme of America, the *Golden Hind* had encountered a bark "cannowe or boate" in Magellan Straits of "most dainty mould, bearing in it most comely proportion, and excellent workmanship." The bark almost certainly would be that of the Antarctic beech. It seemed to Drake literally fit for a prince, "yea of some Prince," and was so well sewn with sealskin thongs that it was watertight without caulking.[21] In 1766, the *Dolphin* saw good bark canoes there also, but these were caulked with rushes and the "out side seemd to be paid with some sort of Sticky Stuf, which I supose preserves the Bark from being water Soked."[22] Earlier, Hawkins had seen "a cannoa . . . artificially [artfully] made with the rindes of trees, and sowed together with the finnes of whales."[23] A yacht sailing in that area 300 years later described canoes of plank and bark sewn with whalebone. The usual report in the 1760's was that canoes were "of bark badly contrived," but during her first voyage under Byron some of the *Dolphin*'s crew saw a canoe of a quite different kind "from any they had seen in the Straits before, she being of plank sew'd together, those we had seen before were of the bark of large Trees."[24]

Practically everyone who wrote of the Fuegian canoes reported that they carried fire in them, presumably, as Cook said, "that it may be allways ready to remove a shore wherever they land."[25] This was done in Australia too, and in British Columbia, an Englishman noted that "several canoes again accompanied us, each with a wooden bowl or birch-bark basket of embers on board, the smoke from which kept off the musquitoes, and enabled the travellers to raise a fire ashore at camp time, or when their craft required repairs."[26] An American noted that the fire in Fuegian canoes was built on a bed of clay laid on the bottom of the canoe. In their simple canoes the Aborigines of Australia, thousands of miles to the west, carried fire bedded in seaweed instead of clay, but otherwise in much the same manner and no doubt for the same reasons.

Bark was used for boatbuilding in Australia although never so skilfully as in the Americas. No one has ever suggested that the Australian bark craft (figure 15) were fit "for some Prince." However, the aborigines of Australia are not thought of as related to the sea in the way that Polynesians or the Eskimos are; with a vast hinterland there was no necessity for them to be. They had a variety of boats, however, from the bark bundle canoes of Tasmania to the outriggered canoes of the north. The most common type of canoe in Australia was made of bark (one observer referred to it as "cork," but presumably meant a kind of thick bark).[27] Construction was extremely simple; the *Rattlesnake* saw one at Cape York "made of bark, with small saplings tied along the side."[28] In another place, Macgillivray, who was the *Rattlesnake*'s naturalist, tells that the bark was from the gum tree and that a small square piece held in the hand was used as a paddle. While Cook saw this kind of canoe and thought it to be "the

Fig. 15. Australian Bark Canoe

worst I think I ever saw," his ship passed other canoes on the beach on the east coast of Australia "which to us appear'd not much unlike the small ones of New Zeland."[29] His statement would suggest that they were small dugouts, but as the ship had to stay outside the surf it is more likely that they were bark canoes not clearly identifiable as such at a distance. Explorers encountered the Australian bark canoe on salt water. The *Rattlesnake* met one in Whitsunday Passage; "a small bark canoe . . . came off to within a quarter of a mile of the ship." Hornell described a bark canoe from northern Australia as "built for use both in the sea and on rivers." One similar had been paddled "across 20 miles of open sea."[30] However, it seems that they usually stayed in sheltered waters.

Most of the Australian bark canoes were merely tied together at each end, but one seen in 1801 near the site of present day Melbourne was framed with timber, the ends "left open, the space being afterwards filled with grass worked up with strong clay."[31] Thomas Huxley, a young man on the *Rattlesnake* expedition, was destined for greater fame than his diary of the voyage would earn him, although he did acquire on the journey a good working technique and a wife, both of which proved lifelong. He said that the canoes at Melbourne were paddled by squares of bark in each hand, that there was "copious leakage," and that bailing consisted of "scratching the water out as it were with the paddle. The action is excessively ludicrous."[32] On the other hand, Lieutenant Grant of the *Lady Nelson* said that Aboriginal bailing was done "dexterously," and that the canoes went "very swiftly."[33]

The Australian bark canoes seemed so frail that Europeans avoided using them. A seasoned traveller commented that Australian canoes "fell very short of those which I have seen among the American or Musquito-shore Indians [British Honduras] who, in improvements of every kind, the Indians of this country are many centuries behind."[34] A scientist with the *Novara*, the Austrian ship which made a Pacific exploration in the 1850's, went further and said most inaccurately that "the black populations of Australia seem to be the sole savage race inhabiting the coast of an ocean, who possess no means of transport by water, and are unable to swim!"[35] This was simply not true. In the *Rattlesnake*, Macgillivray noted that the Australian canoes (only fifteen to thirty feet long) were much smaller than those on the islands further north. But even so, a thirty-foot canoe with a double outrigger is a perfectly efficient means of transportation. He also saw some canoes under sail at Cape York, although his description of a leaky and leewardly craft does not allow favourable comparison with those of Tonga or the Carolines. It is possible that the Austrian scientist meant that any reasonably good watercraft in Australia were the result of island influence from the north and had not been developed on the mainland.

One European observer suggested that the extreme hardness of Australian woods and the scarcity of tools explained the use of rushes and bark for canoes in the south. He said the European tools suffered for "most of those we had being either worn out by the hardness of the timber or lost." In addition to the problem of tools, he said that the wood was so heavy it would not "float on the water. . . . It is a great misfortune to us that we cannot find proper wood in this place wherewith to build a boat."[36] Sir Joseph Banks also noticed the lack of tools. Commenting that the north of Australia had much more advanced boats than the south, he was puzzled by a northern dugout: "How they had hollowed her out or cut the ends I cannot guess, but upon the whole the work was not ill done."[37]

The better built boats in northern Australia were attributed to influence from the islands of Melanesia. Banks and Cook spoke of canoes with double outriggers on the northeast coast, which would indicate Melanesian influence. Macgillivray said that canoes on the northeast coast of Australia were "altogether a poor imitation of that used by the islanders of Torres Strait." Of those on the north coast he said: "Formerly bark canoes were in general use, but they are now completely superseded by others, hollowed out of the trunk of a tree, which they procure ready-made from the Malays, in exchange for tortoise-shell."[38] So he saw, or thought he did, two different but direct outside influences operating in the development of Australian canoes.

No one in the north of Australia suggested what Furneaux of the *Adventure* said of Tasmania; we "never saw the least signs of either Canoe or boat, and it is generally thought they have none."[39] This, like the suggestion of the Austrian scientist about Australia, was quite inaccurate. The Tasmanians, like the Australians, did have watercraft, but their use of them was not as important a part of their culture as it was of the Polynesian, Melanesian, or northwest American. Men went to sea only when necessary. As Hawkins mused long ago, "the sea is naturall for fishes, and the land for men."[40]

Even though the sea allegedly is meant for fish, men everywhere have found a need to solve the problems it poses. The canoes of northern Australia generally are considered to prove that men will always be willing to adopt the solutions found by others as well as search for their own. Outside influence in the design of watercraft operated extremely slowly in the days when there was great risk, before modern aids and modern attitudes lessened the physical dangers and increased intellectual receptivity. This influence seldom was strong, unless craft of superior design appeared carrying men who remained long enough to justify and convert others to their confidence in the new methods. Many questions come to mind here. How quickly is a new idea accepted in ages and in cultures not dedicated to the idea that new is necessarily good? Does not the coracle of modern Wales show the length of time an ancient, simple, and effective idea can survive? Are sailors and farmers conservative men because both life and livelihood depend on correct solutions to their problems? If so, what has been tried and tested and proved acceptable would obviously seem preferable to what is merely extolled.

By and large, men are convinced that their way is best—or, if not best, that it at least has the virtue of familiarity. Few outriggers are seen at Hong Kong or Acapulco or Victoria; the rafts of Yachow did not replace the canoes of Quebec, although both craft were solutions to the problem of shooting rapids. Where striking similarities in watercraft are encountered, probably the problems posed should be studied first, then the possibility of long-term cultural interchange, and only lastly the possibility of a fleeting, contingent influence. By all odds, an independent solution of a similar problem would seem the most likely explanation to most of the intriguing similarities. The elements force men to find answers that work, and there is not an unlimited supply of such answers.

CHAPTER 4

Polynesian Watercraft

It wasn't real. It was a dream. That canoe slid over the water
like a streak of silver, I climbed out on the outrigger and
supplied the weight to hold her down, while Tehei (pro-
nounced Tayhayee) supplied the nerve.

JACK LONDON
OF THE *SNARK*

. . . the common fishing Canoes had nothing but the face of
a Man with a monstrous tongue . . . but the larger sort which
seemed to be intended for War were really magnificently
adorned, their heads were formed by a Plank projecting about
3 feet before the Canoe & on their sterns stood up another
proportioned to the size of the Canoe from 10 to 18 feet high;
both these were richly carved with open Work, & covered
with loose fringes of Black feathers that had a most graceful
effect.

SIR JOSEPH BANKS
OF THE *ENDEAVOUR*

There were, and still are, many Polynesian watercraft, for Polynesians are a
people of the sea living on small islands, the only large ones being those of
New Zealand, in a huge triangle of the Pacific cornered by Easter Island, New
Zealand, and Hawaii.

The Polynesians have a strong claim to be considered the greatest navigators
of all time. That they lived on the sea and from its bounty is not the basis
for this statement, for the produce of the sea was not as important to them as
it was to the Eskimos. Nor did they produce watercraft better adapted to local
needs and local resources than those of the Eskimos, the American Indians,
or the Chinese. But the distances the Polynesians conquered from east to west
and from north to south across the world's greatest ocean are adequate foundation for such a claim. There is much scholarly debate about all this. Interested
readers should follow it up in the bibliography and form their own opinions.
It is apparent that Polynesian navigation was highly developed and that their

great voyages were comparatively recent, extending well into the fourteenth century. They are one people still—if of mixed descent—of one language and one culture, with only very minor local modifications. A common genealogy of five centuries ago unites them, in the same way that New Zealanders may claim descent from the same ancestors as Americans or Australians, Englishmen or Canadians.

There is debate, too, whether there were planned migrations with retained contact, or one-way voyages only, accidental ones caused by storms, or deliberate ones caused by defeats in battle. There are accidental voyages even today; a clipping from a New Zealand newspaper of 1971 describes such a voyage. Plenty of the early European explorers found evidence of drift (*i.e.*, accidental) voyages and even met survivors of them. In the 1820's, Dillon of the *Research* met some who had been drifting at sea for five months.[1] He said that the Polynesians were quite conscious of the likelihood of drift voyages and took their women and animals in canoes as insurance. Some boats found drifting at sea had women on board: "His companions in the drift outrigger canoe were seven natives—a woman of the Tuamotus . . . and two men and four women from Rakahanga."[2] An early English explorer in British Columbia found that Japanese boats and crews sometimes drifted to British Columbia and drew the conclusion that "such facts as these . . . should, I think, make us very cautious in our ideas on the limitation of native migrations."[3] But myth-history of the earliest Polynesian days claims that storms were not the only motivation, and winds not the only impelling force.

In a seaman's journal in the National Library of Scotland, Edinburgh, I read the following interesting account of motivation—and of hardships and risk—in such voyages.

A family quarrel frequently happens which ends sometimes in a truly lamentable manner, their prophets pretend to tell them of fine Islands uninhabited with all Kinds of food in great plenty, that they have nothing to do but make a canoe and go and take possession, great numbers have gone led by these uncertain tales, now suppose some canoes may have reached some yet unknown Isle or two another canoe comes in the same track and comes to land those that have first got possession will not suffer a second to land on any account whatever the [sic] must pass by in search of another Isle, a canoe cannot live but a few days at sea even in very fine weather I have seen several canoes that set off on these unhappy discoveries, some of them perhaps may have 30 or 40 souls on board cramped up no room to stir for several days their limbs get benumd the canoe, very leaky they are wearied of bailing the water out the canoe gets swamp't and I make no doubt their poor hearts overwelm'd with grief no land in sight down they sink thus terminates their truly pitiable and untimely fate—I have frequently been ask'd to go with several families offering me their daughters in marriage to conduct them to their promised land, I have told them with tears what they might expect, nothing could change them it has often griev'd me to the heart to see a handsome young lady weeping with her neighbours a few days before her departure, It happens sometimes when a family thus leaving their country is belovd by their neighbours the canoe gets broke to atoms and they led back to their houses, sometimes this step has the desired effect and sometimes not, for they will hire a small canoe and go over to another Isle and build a canoe for their purpose and come over unexpected in the night time and take on board all that is concearnd, sometime some repents and swim on shore again.[4]

This kind of defeat in war or feud sent many Polynesians wandering. Custom allowed them to go in the same manner in which European customs of war allowed a defeated garrison to march away disarmed. Overpopulation on small islands, the search for traditional homelands, and adventure, are all motives; no one who has read of Odysseus or Beowulf could fail to understand. It should not be hard for a Quebecer to look back to the France of the 1660's or an Australian to look back to the England of the 1790's to see why some Polynesians left their homes to build a new life somewhere else.

There were other motives too. For example, the great Polynesian leader, Whatonga, was searching for someone, not mutineers, like those of the *Bounty* that Captain Edwards of the *Pandora* had sought, but the survivors of an earlier voyage—just as Captain Dillon was looking for survivors of the La Pérouse expedition.[5] The three-piece hull of his great voyaging canoe *Te Hawai* had been painted red with shark oil and ochre. She was a big vessel with twenty-six thwarts, two bailing wells and two anchors, capable of carrying sixty-six men and, as on many later Pacific ships, some women too, in order that the land they settled could be held permanently. The myth is specific enough to raise questions which cannot lightly be dismissed.

Myths and legends abound to describe the earliest days of Polynesia, just as they exist for the Saxons, the Franks and, above all, the Vikings. Saga has its Polynesian counterpart; the important point is that in all cases most of the stories interlock to reinforce one another. For example, in the Pacific, similar heroes and traditions feed the imagination in Hawaii as in New Zealand; the same tradition of a Friendly Alliance convening to the sound of the great drum *Tangi-moana* (Sound-at-Sea) stirs the racial memory in Raratonga as it does in Rai'atea.[6]

Authorities still argue about the location of the original Polynesian homeland; even more uncertain is the route by which they came to their islands. As it is accepted that different groups of somewhat different colours and cultures arrived at different times, it seems quite possible that the routes varied also. As part of their oral traditions, Polynesians have many beautiful legends which purport to explain and describe these things. Many capable writers—particularly Sir Peter Buck—have dealt with the subject.

To win a reputation as navigators, a people must have accumulated knowledge, highly developed techniques, and, above all, seaworthy craft to take them where their skill guides. Such craft were available to Polynesians. In this chapter, many of them are mentioned, but the building of only the Maori war canoe is discussed in detail. Although details of the craft in which the Maoris landed in New Zealand are not known, some at least would have been canoes with two hulls—double canoes—and in one myth there is reference to an outrigger. Both double canoes and outriggers in New Zealand are examined in this chapter, but by the time of the written descriptions their use was already declining. The great Maori war canoe (Plate 12) is the culmination of the canoe builders' art in beauty as in performance; it stands literally on its own among Polynesian watercraft. They are still being built, although now to preserve, rather than create, a proud culture.

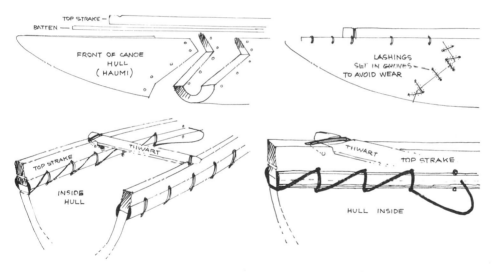

Fig. 16. Maori Composite Canoe Construction

The major Maori watercraft was the single canoe, of various sizes, but always based on a dugout hull (figure 16). The beautiful kauri and totara trees were big enough and plentiful enough for Maoris to be able to hollow one out for a single hull without worrying about waste. Plank canoes in other parts of Polynesia were not a display of higher cultural achievement, but evidence of a paucity of suitable logs.[7] Maoris gave the large canoes additional depth by adding one plank strake to each of the top edges of the hull, and some of the very largest had extra lengths of dugout hull, called "haumis," spliced on. These composite hulls, which might be the result of repairs rather than of an effort to gain size, were never made of two pieces joined at the centre, but always of pieces joined near the ends so that the centre portion remained strong. This precaution was taken also with the planks used to heighten the sides.

Tongue and groove fitting, lashing with fibre, caulking with dried raupo leaves or fibre, countersinking of lashings on the exterior to prevent wear at beaching are all evidence of Polynesian skill in designing large canoes, and of careful craftsmanship in their building. Care was needed, for the war canoes sometimes exceeded seventy feet in length and could carry one hundred men.[8] As with all strange craft with a pointed stern and stem, the Maori canoe was sometimes said by Europeans to be "something like our whale boats."[9] One can easily see why this would be said in New Zealand. Brenda Guthrie, a child of early settlers, described whaleboats used in Canterbury: "they were about thirty feet long, sharp at both ends (which were gaily painted and stood high out of the water), were steered by an oar, very fast under sail, and wonderfully safe in a gale or rough surf."[10] She might have been describing a Maori canoe. It was largely the length and slenderness of the canoe that led to this comparison, but it was true also that in spite of this tremendous length in proportion to breadth, these beautiful vessels could stand very heavy seas. Nevertheless, they usually were considered too precious to be used for ordinary tasks, such as fishing; if they were so used, the carved stempieces and sternpieces were removed temporarily.

It took over two years to build a first-class war canoe (figure 17), which was partly due to the extensive and elaborate carving which adorned them.[11] Building one was a serious and important matter, equally as vital to a tribal economy as is the design and construction of a new liner to an industrial nation, and it was hedged around by conventions meant to emphasize the importance of the task and to call forth the highest degree of response from all concerned. Each great canoe became, as was the *Queen Mary*, or a new battleship, a truly "national" concern.

When a great kauri or totara tree was selected for a canoe, the Maoris reserved it by clearing the surrounding bush. If distance so decreed, they built a temporary workmen's village at the site and planted crops for food. Before the tree was felled, the builders performed various rituals; perhaps the most fascinating of these was the explanation to the tree of the tribe's need. The tree, like the Maori, was the offspring of Tane, the fertilizer; the tree was the Maori's brother. Custom dictated certain precautions to be taken about clothing, cooking, and the presence of women near the canoe. Like the prayers at the launching of a European ship, or Viking and Indian customs, these *tapu* were meant to protect the canoe and all who rode in her from gusts and gales and the wrath of the gods.

Plate 9. A British Columbian Indian canoe running before a "fair" breeze; the second canoe is running "wing and wing." The Indians tended to use several small masts and sails, probably because the masts were often taken down and because strain had to be distributed evenly over a frail, long, and narrow hull.

Plate 10. A fairly small Nootka-type dug-out canoe in British Columbia. The grain of the beautiful red cedar wood is as plainly visible as the animal figurehead so like that of Captain Voss's canoe, *Tilikum*.

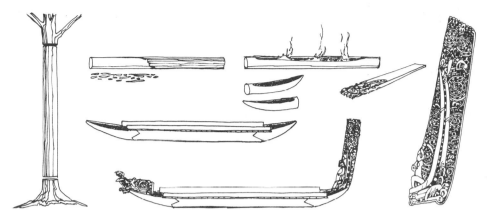

Fig. 17. Basic Stages in Maori War Canoe Construction

The felling took days, for the stone adzes, even when assisted by fire, made slow progress against the forest giant. When the tree had been felled and the top removed, more ritual preceded the dubbing down (removing of excess wood from the outside of the trunk), and the hollowing out of the hull. Adzes—the most commonly used being made of basalt, although greenstone adzes were prized for finer work—did the rough dubbing down, but fire was of great assistance in the hollowing out.[12] This was true also in the construction of American dugout canoes. Fire, carefully controlled, charred the wood for easier chipping; this charring and chipping process was repeated patiently until the hull was hollow. Stone adzes were all that were available before the Europeans came. They were seldom strong enough to be used for splitting hard wood to get planks, and using them to dub or cut required an immense expenditure of labour; however, Banks and Wallis describe seeing Tahitians use wedges and fire to split planks from green trunks. The creation of the great canoes of Polynesia was certainly a fine technical achievement; it was even more than that when it is remembered what tools were available. Dubbing a single plank from a tree with tools of stone is not a job that many people would face happily; however, some Europeans said that when they saw stone adzes in use they were utterly amazed at how well they cut.[13] Their chief defect was the need for constant sharpening.

No original blueprint or sketch was needed, and no cutting pattern was marked on the tree; design decisions followed discussions, and skilled eyes —artists' and craftsmen's eyes—saw what was needed. This was common practice in building indigenous craft, even with the large Chinese junks. However, this complete dependence on the shipwrights' skill was not unknown in building wooden craft in European and American shipyards—even well into this century. Co-operation was important, for the various groups worked at different tasks. Organization and planning were doubly important, because planking to heighten the sides was being prepared from other trees while the hollowing of the hull was proceeding, and even at this early stage, the decorative carving was often started.

Once the bulk of excess wood was removed, the rough hull was hauled to its launching site. Skids, guide ropes, hauling ropes, all came into play as this major project got under way. People who know both the forests and the topography of New Zealand can appreciate the effort required, and so the hauling was encouraged by singing special hauling songs, in both purpose and rhythm, similar to the hauling sea shanties. Canoes were tracked upriver at portages in expeditions in America and New Zealand to exactly the same type of song.

Dubbing down was completed in an open shed built for the purpose at the launching site, leaving the exterior of the hull either smooth or patterned, as some Maoris had a theory about water suction on a smooth hull which foreshadowed modern aerodynamics.[14] They thought that extruding patterns left on the hull exterior broke up the water flow in a way that increased the speed of the canoe. On a somewhat similar principle, the Chinese made holes in the rudders of their junks.

When the basic canoe hull was finished, the topstrakes, thwarts, figurehead, sternpiece, and flooring would be added, in that order, while the carving continued all the time (figure 16). The planks to be added to raise the sides— called topstrakes because the side planks of boats are called strakes—were dubbed out of trees which had been cut at the same time as the trunk had been felled for the main hull. If necessary, planks were lengthened by joining a smaller one to the end. After the planks were bowed inwards to the shape of the canoe by a form of tourniquet, the builders lashed them to the top of the hull. The workmen used bow drills or stone chisels to drill the necessary holes; to tighten the lashing they used a forked stick as a lever; and to caulk the hole through which the lashing passed they used wooden plugs and wet plant material. They had already placed raupo leaves and fibre as caulking between the planks and the hull. Battens were then placed along the exterior seam, covering the joints not only between topstrake and hull, but between the stem and sternpieces and the hull.

Canoes with topstrakes need thwarts for support. These were either laid on top of the strakes, or scarfed (so shaped that a shoulder rested against the inner edge at each end) and then lashed into place. Thwarts were never rested on the inner battens, for this would have strained the joins; this mistake is often made in museums when recreating modern thwarts for canoes. In large canoes, the paddlers sat on the thwarts, but in smaller ones they sat or knelt on the floor in the fashion of North American Indian paddlers. When the topstrakes were securely lashed into position, and especially when scarfed thwarts were used, the vessel was again as solid as if hewn from a single log. If—and this is a matter of opinion—these canoes were not as graceful as Viking ships or birchbark canoes—which were not limited in design possibility by the proportion of a tree trunk—they were good seagoing craft; the birch canoes were not. It might be difficult to choose which was the stronger—the Viking longship or the Maori canoe—for they acquired their strength in different ways; the longship was flexible and the canoe was rigid. In the voyaging achievements of each vessel, there is honour enough to share.

Canoe floors were usually rather rude gratings, supported on cross pieces fastened in a variety of ways to the hull, depending on the technique of the particular tribe. During voyages the grating was covered with rush mats. In large canoes, two gaps were left in the flooring to allow bailing, and some fishing canoes had a special hold for the catch. A drain hole was drilled near the bow so that when the plug was removed any water would run out while the canoe was being hauled stern first onto the beach.

Canoes were painted with ochre and oil, so most of them were red with black relief;[15] red represented the chiefs, black the common people. In the north, the figureheads and sternpieces were stained black with the same swamp mud which was used to dye the fibres for the Maori skirts, but elsewhere the sternpieces usually were red—fair enough too, for the stern in all ships is officers' territory, the seat (or standing room) of authority. Some canoes had designs painted on them, the finer designs being done with feather brushes, the coarser ones with fibre. Maori canoes were beautifully carved, especially the head and sternpieces (figure 17), some of which were several feet in height. One special feature of these beautiful works of art—the Maori spiral patterns—are not found anywhere else.

When finished, a canoe would be launched with a ritual, which placed it under the care of the gods and lifted the *tapu* so that ordinary people could use it. Long ago, it is said, a slave was sacrificed at each important launching as a propitiation of the gods. In some tribes, an elderly man would volunteer his spirit for the canoe—a sacrifice for its general well-being, as noble in intention as an old Eskimo's walking out into the storm—the great war canoe was heart-centre of the tribe.[16] Feasting followed its trial trip. Most of these ceremonies were paralleled wherever Polynesians built canoes, and if the ceremonies were not the same, they all had the same intention—to emphasize the central importance of canoes in Polynesian life. There is an excellent description of the Tahitian ceremony which was used at the launching of the schooner built by the *Bounty* mutineers on that island.

Maori women were as at home with the paddle as were the men, even though in most of Polynesia the chief role of women was that of bailer. One early European wrote appreciatively—albeit about a select group of girls—of their "peculiar grace and easiness of attitude, while the pliancy of the action displayed their fine forms to the greatest advantage."[17] The same grace was often remarked in the men: they paddled "as if the movers were animated by one Soul."[18] When the Maoris, men or women, used their large oval paddles, they timed the strokes with boat songs, as was done in the birchbark canoes on the Canadian rivers of the fur trade routes. In both cases, folk music of haunting beauty resulted, with the rhythm and beat being dictated by the task. Maori fuglemen, who kept time by example and exhortation, were so effective in inciting exertion from the paddlers that they often had to stop for fear of wearing them out. Sometimes, as Ensign Best saw, they kept time "to the waving of a battle axe dressed with feathers."[19]

When possible, the paddlers—and fuglemen—were spared such exertion by sails made of raupo stems or flax. They were triangular sails on one or sometimes two masts, or occasionally a rectangular sail between poles set one on each side of the canoe.[20] The rounded bulge of the sides of the canoe in part replaced the keel in imparting steadiness. Nevertheless, the absence of a keel allowed drift, and so these craft could not sail nearly as close to the wind as the Tongan double canoe, which, it is claimed, could sail within three points of the wind's direction. Except in heavy seas, where the risk of nosing under was too great, the canoes could run before the wind at great speed. Maori canoes were not miracles of stability; they were good craft with normal limitations. When Dillon of the *Research* was at the Bay of Islands, a chief was visiting his ship "in one of his war canoes, when it swamped alongside, the sea running very high."[21] Ensign Best wrote in his diary of "a report that a Canoe with one of the principal Chiefs and 30 natives from Queen Charlottes Sound was swamped yesterday in a tide rip & all perished."[22]

Smaller versions of the war canoe were used for travelling and fishing. These vessels were still efficient seacraft, for their construction was similar, except for the less elaborate ornamentation. While some war canoes were over eighty feet long—and at least one canoe was said to have carried four hundred people—the fishing canoes usually were about forty to fifty feet long.[23] Even smaller dugouts, with simple hulls lacking strakes, thwarts, and adornment, served as jacks-of-all-craft round the coasts and rivers. Working craft, sturdy craft, for earning a living or carrying travellers across the bays or rivers, these were the boats of everyday, no ceremonies or ornamentation for them. Frequently, they were poled, rather than paddled, especially in the face of the swift currents and rapids as in the Wanganui River. As in all descriptions of Maori men or women paddling, in an 1840's description of poling, the emphasis is on gracefulness, the rhythm, and the skill. This was the Maoris' life, not just their living.[24]

Maoris had centuries of sea life behind them before they came to know New Zealand's rivers and lakes. Part of their extensive tradition is the outrigger, although conditions in New Zealand were such that its use gradually declined. The Maoris used the huge trees to make hulls large enough for a single top plank to be all that was needed to give sufficient free-board for safety even at sea. Maori single dugout canoes were exceeded in size only by those of the Indians of British Columbia in the North Pacific, where even larger trees were available. That the British Columbian and New Zealand canoes resemble each other so closely in many more ways than in size alone has led to much speculation about the direction from which the Maoris reached New Zealand. After all, an Indian canoe from British Columbia (the *Tilikum*) fully demonstrated its capacity to sail anywhere in the Pacific when it carried Captain Voss from British Columbia to Sydney and on to London. This speculation, however, is much more interesting than it is convincing. But experts have pointed out, with much weight, that the name "canoe," given to various Pacific craft by Europeans, has caused an underestimation of both their seaworthiness and their size. This, in turn, has led to an underestimation of their ability to undertake extensive voyages.[25]

The Maoris must have arrived in New Zealand in Polynesian craft—by definition, indeed—and their legends of the famous fleet of six canoes, as well as those relating earlier voyages, mention both outriggers and double canoes. The outrigger apparently fell into disuse well before the double canoe did, but both types were still in use in Cook's time for "they sometimes joined 2 small Canoes together, & now & then made use of an Outrigger."[26] Even in the mid-nineteenth century some knowledge of outriggers either had survived or been reintroduced. Two generations after Cook, Ensign Best had some Maoris build him a canoe: "My little canoe was finished today & I went out in it with a Mauri when some distance from the land the outrigger broke."[27]

A single canoe from Polynesia would have needed an outrigger in order to survive the rough sea passage to New Zealand; therefore, if some Polynesians had arrived in New Zealand as a result of being swept away to sea during inter-island voyaging, probably in a few cases at least they would have been in this commonly used single outrigger canoe. Bligh's description of a canoe on Sunday Island is interesting in this regard, for if a canoe like that could get to Sunday Island, then others, accidentally or otherwise, could have reached New Zealand.[28]

In 1642, Tasman apparently did not see any outriggers in New Zealand, for he describes the canoes as "two long narrow prows fastened together, over which were placed some boards or other seats."[29] As a few weeks later he noted the "wings" (outriggers) on canoes further north, surely he would have mentioned outriggers had he seen any in New Zealand. Banks mentions seeing double canoes in 1769, but they seem to have been abandoned fairly soon afterwards, except for those joined together temporarily for specific purposes. In the Bay of Plenty in 1873, for example, one was made in order to pay out a large seine from the platform.[30] Cook saw many double canoes in the South Island and yet mentions having seen only one in the North Island; there is a great deal of further evidence that the use of the double canoe survived longer in the South Island. This may have been because of rougher seas and shallower rivers; on the other hand, the reputed conservatism of South Island New Zealanders may have begun with the Maoris.

Double canoes and outriggers were not really needed in a country where trees were big enough to form dugout hulls which were stable without any balancing device. Moreover, New Zealand was large enough and agriculturally productive enough for there to be no real pressure to travel on the open sea, except to cross Cook Strait to trade for greenstone or to find refuge after a defeat in battle. In addition, New Zealand rivers and creeks were generally unsuitable for the large double canoes because of narrowness and rapids.

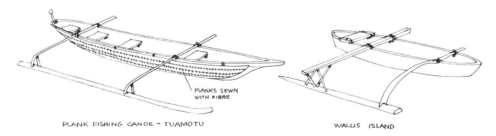

PLANKS SEWN WITH FIBRE

PLANK FISHING CANOE - TUAMOTU   WALLIS ISLAND

Fig. 18. Local Variations of Outrigger Canoe

In other parts of Polynesia, where travelling on the open sea is often necessary, the outrigger remained important. The outrigger canoe is the major example of a design variation for practical purposes. The dugout hull, limited by its material, was too narrow and unstable for the open sea or under sail without balancing devices being fitted to one or both sides. Probably the idea originated either in Indonesia or on the inland waters of Asia, but it is agreed that the outrigger canoe developed into a seagoing vessel in Indonesia, and from there spread across the Pacific. Outriggers are found in the areas east and west of Indonesia in the equatorial belt of the Indo-Pacific area and nowhere else. The outrigger is a feature of craft found only in the Indian and Pacific Oceans and naturally has caused much comment by Europeans.[31]

Dampier described a canoe in Nicobar which had two outriggers and a sail. One canoe at Java was said by an early Dutch observer to have "on both sides of the Boat two big Reeds, at the distance of a Fathom from her."[32] In the Pacific, double outriggers were not used much, although some say there is evidence of their former use in Polynesia.[33] Most authorities agree that the double outrigger is confined to Indonesia, the western part of New Guinea, and the coast of East Africa. Men of the Dutch ship *Heemskerck*, however, saw double outriggers near New Ireland which is *east* of New Guinea: "the canoes were with 2 wings." Tasman says of some other canoes in the same area that they had "a wing of bamboos on both sides."[34]

In double outrigger canoes, logs of light wood are held out at an equal distance from the sides of the dugout by poles lashed across the gunwales in such a way that the log floats rest lightly on the surface when the canoe is on an even keel (figure 23). Sometimes, the poles holding the floats curve down naturally and gracefully to the water; sometimes, they are straight and connected to the floats with multiple stanchions of various types pegged and lashed in place. But there were eccentricities in this also, and the Tahitians, for example, had one curved and one straight boom on their single outrigger canoes.

Lashings to hold on the booms were varied and meant to be permanent, in spite of the description in one Polynesian song of outriggers being carried to be lashed on only when a storm seemed close. One indication of intended permanence is the lashing called "the skirt of Luukia," a figure-eight form of lashing designed originally as a chastity belt, with its natural connotation of inviolability.[35] One would need a touching faith to sail with that one, and lashing sometimes did come loose.

In the open sea, clear of the island sheltered waters of Indonesia, the double outrigger is a handicap. In a squall, the lee float (the one on the opposite side to the wind) is plunged under water as the craft heels over. This creates a dangerous drag which causes difficulty in steering, and when the drag is sudden and strong enough it may even break up the canoe. Dampier was thoroughly frightened once when "the Poles of the Outlagers going from the sides of their Vessel, bent as if they would break, and should they have broken, our overturning and perishing had been inevitable."[36] Gradually, one outrigger was abandoned (usually the port or left one), because the single outrigger was found to be safer for long voyages or for fishing far out at sea. There is no certain evidence that the double outrigger ever reached Polynesia.

Single outriggers are characteristic of Polynesia, Micronesia, and all Mela-

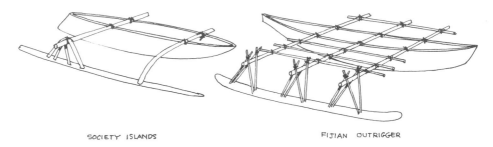

SOCIETY ISLANDS   FIJIAN OUTRIGGER

Fig. 19. Local Variations of Outrigger Canoe

nesia, except the Solomon Islands and the western part of New Guinea. Local variations of detail are almost infinite (figures 18, 19)—usually there are two booms for the outrigger, but there may be three or, in the Indies, sometimes only one.[37] Even the single outrigger can drag dangerously if it is on the lee side away from the wind; canoes in Melanesia and Micronesia were built pointed at both ends to be able to sail either end forward and thus keep the outrigger to windward. At Guam, in Micronesia, an early French explorer noted: "As the islands are situated in a row running north and south, and as the wind blows from the east almost all the year round, it is an advantage that their boats should have no stern. Their boats are therefore built with bows at each end, so that they never require to be turned round."[38] An English captain thought this certainly helped in tacking, as "the headmost proa . . . tacked in a very expeditious manner, by shifting its latteen sail (by which means the head became the stern), and went off at a great rate."[39]

Another answer to the problem of balancing narrow hulls in rough seas, which some authorities claim to be the origin of outriggers, is a platform on which a crew member could sit to counterbalance the effect of the wind, the same principle being used by the crews of modern racing yachts. The crew then literally rides the seas, balancing the changes in stress as do skilled horsemen or motorcyclists. Outriggers can be balanced this way too. Using this principle, Jack London sailed on a canoe: "I climbed out on the outrigger and supplied the weight to hold her down."[40] The *Idle Hour*'s captain, Long, saw canoes "manned by half a dozen Tahitians who shift themselves about on the platform as human ballast."[41]

Timbers big enough to build large and stable craft were needed in order to do away with balancing devices. In many places, good local materials simply were not available, and much ingenuity was needed to find substitutes for large timber. In the Chatham Islands, canes were used—as they were in California and Chile—and, in Easter Island and New Zealand, rush floats were used as temporary craft. In New Zealand, giant canoes could be formed from one huge tree, but in Easter Island craft had to be sewn together from bits and pieces of driftwood. Old techniques sometimes could be used with new materials, but in many cases techniques had to be altered to suit the available resources. For example, Maoris used flax for lashings and rope or to tie together anything that broke, whereas on the volcanic islands further north the Polynesians used the bark of the wild hibiscus. Perhaps this bark was also used for canoe rigging. Ellis, the missionary, who wrote so much about early nineteenth-century Polynesia, said it was, and certainly hibiscus bark was used for this purpose in South America.[42] Quite noticeable cultural differences grew up between the homelands of Polynesians because of the differences in the resources.

Because of their narrow hulls, almost all the canoes of the South Pacific required either outriggers or double hulls to be stable enough for the open sea. This need is emphasized by a native prophet of Rai'atea who predicted that a wonderful canoe without an outrigger would come to Polynesia. His prophecy was a source of wonder precisely because the outrigger was accepted as the natural thing.[43] The twinning of canoe hulls could also act to balance watercraft. Double canoes were effective craft, and some great voyages have been reported to their credit. One example will suffice. In his ability to dream, the great navigator Hotu-Matua was like Slocum, the first lone circumnavigator, who claimed he had the pilot of Columbus's *Pinta* to help him steer.[44] Hotu-Matua's dream showed him Easter Island, and so he sailed his great double canoe 1500 miles to see it in reality.[45] Heyerdahl thinks Hotu-Matua came from Peru on a great raft like the *Kon-Tiki*; Buck said he came from the Marquesas in a double canoe. The double canoe, whether used by Hotu-Matua or not, was one Polynesian answer to the problems of the open sea.

Ideally, if it were possible to find a tree trunk large enough, a boat "dug out" of it would have enough width to give stability. There were no trees of this size, unfortunately, except in New Zealand and America, and even these barely gave the size of craft needed for lengthy or rough sea voyages. In an attempt to achieve both size and stability, therefore, a craft with a double hull was introduced, and its characteristics are finding new favour today.

The *Rehu Moana* (Sea Spray) is a modern catamaran, her twin hulls reminiscent of the great double canoes of Tonga and Tahiti. She is important, because in many ways *Rehu Moana* is like a Polynesian double canoe, and so something was learned about that craft from her operation by David Lewis who is so interested in Polynesian vessels and navigation.

She is said to have been the first double-hulled craft to reach Easter Island after the one sailed by Hotu-Matua.[46] Her overall length is forty feet, her beam is seventeen. In spite of this beam, similar to the one-to-two, or the one-to-two-and-one-half ratio of the old northern European "round ship," she is very light, her displacement being only seven to eight tons. She is very stable, and fast too, her captain claiming fifteen knots on two occasions; her ease of movement is shown by her crew's satisfaction with one four-horsepower outboard motor used mainly for shifting in harbour. These particular qualities of double craft have been known for centuries. An experienced English captain in the East Indies in the 1770's was so impressed by the speed of double craft using Pacific sails that he urged their adoption. "Lash two London wherries together, and give this double vessel the tripod mast and [Indonesian 'pointed sail'], it will beat the fast sailing boats, at least three to two."[47]

The *Rehu Moana* was rigged as a cutter when she crossed the Pacific. (A cutter rig has a triangular mainsail, a staysail, and a jib.) Each hull had a drop-keel which could increase the draught from three to eight feet. After some difficulties, these were replaced by permanent skegs (small false keels) bolted beneath the rear of each hull.

On her modern voyages, the *Rehu Moana* has demonstrated the great advantages that the stability given by breadth can bring to the comfort of the crew. In long-distance voyaging, crew comfort is important for survival. Seasickness, wetness, and fatigue are all lessened by a stable ship, and it is interesting that today it is found that both stability and speed are lauded as advantages of the multi-hull craft. This, the Polynesians had already found, although their reasons for this solution were different; they were seeking size in order to attain distance. It is true that they could have increased further the height of the sides of a canoe by adding planks, sewn edge to edge carvel-fashion, upwards from the upper edge of the dugout sides. But the need to paddle placed a limit on height, and when the hull could not be raised it had to be broadened. The answer was the double hull, formed of two canoes linked by a platform. This gave buoyancy, room for cargo and passengers, and the stability to carry a large sail, which are exactly the advantages claimed for the modern catamaran. Development of the double canoe vastly extended the possibility of travel and of transport; there are records of voyages lasting one month.[48]

Some double canoes do not have twin hulls but unequal ones. When one hull is appreciably smaller than the other, it is considered by some authorities that doubling to enlarge and stabilize the canoe is an offshoot of the outrigger system.[49] This type of double canoe was often seen in the Cook Islands. Even when unequal in size, both hulls were used for passengers and cargo, and in most types of double canoe the booms connecting the hulls carried a platform as well. On some canoes this platform was walled against the flying spray; on others it held a deckhouse for both shelter and cooking. On special canoes it held a stage for the chief.[50] The large Tongan double canoes had a hut, decked hulls, and an extensive platform, and could carry 200 men to war or transport cargoes of great stones for royal tombs. Double canoes provided advantages other than extra cargo space. Broughton of the *Providence* thought Hawaiian double canoes (figure 20) were "safer conveyances" in surf than were ships' boats; "the surf seldom permitted our own boats to land."[51]

Because of local conditions, traditions, and materials, variations of design and construction were almost as numerous as the islands of the South Pacific. Double canoes of the Tuamotu Archipelago had tortoise shells covering the seams (where the Maoris had used wood battens), and they also used lashed-in ribs as a support for the side planks. Easter Island canoes were made of various pieces of driftwood "put together with manifold small planks and light inner timbers, which they cleverly stitch together with very fine twisted threads."[52]

In Tahiti, planks split from trees by the use of fire and wedges were used to build canoes. The planks were lashed together, but "this [the lashing], however, soon rots in the salt water; it must be renewed once a year at least; in doing so the canoe is entirely taken to pieces and every plank examined."[53] Besides being carefully maintained, Tahitian canoes were kept in boathouses when not in use; this was also quite usual in Polynesia and Melanesia. Sketches of these canoes show the tremendous upturn of the stern and prow, especially of the war canoes. Banks, with the *Endeavour*, reported that "the head and stern of these are considerably raised above the body in a semicircular form, 17 or 18 feet in height when the centre is scarcely 3 feet."[54] Such sterns were functional in heavy surf, because "their high round sterns recives the force of the Sea in Such a manner that none ever enters the Vessel."[55] Some were flat bottomed; others had sharp keels. The hull was not usually decorated. Instead, the decoration was lavished on the high sterns and on the pillars which held up the platforms from which the warriors fought, very much like the way the French and English used platforms for soldiers fighting in the sea battles of the Hundred Years War.

Cook saw two canoes being built in Tahiti, each 108 feet in length, slightly longer than his own *Endeavour*. Banks said that he was told that they undertook voyages of up to twenty days.[56] When possible, voyages were carried out by island hopping (Banks's informants named over a hundred known islands), because they could not carry enough provisions for much longer than twenty days. Sails of matting were very effective; so that ". . . their canoes go at a very good rate, and lie very near the wind, probably on account of their sail being bordered with wood, which makes them stand better than any bowlines could possibly do."[57] These wood-bordered sails were unique, although wood is used in other ways to strengthen and extend sails, as with the battens in junk sails or even the sprit of a spritsail. In British Columbia, one type of sail for canoes was made entirely of strips of wood.

Robertson said Tahitian canoes could sail "about one forth faster nor our ship." This was said of the *Dolphin*, a copper-sheathed frigate;[58] on the other hand, her rowing boats were able to pass the canoes easily when the canoes were paddled and not under sail. Not all Tahitian canoes were double, for "all those that go single both great and small have what is call'd outriggers which are peices of wood fasten'd to the gunel and project out on one side about 6, 8 or 10 feet."[59]

In the nineteenth century, "Quarter Master" described the same very narrow Tahitian canoes with one outrigger and a lateen sail, about which the Spaniards in 1775 had commented "these craft are extremely fleet."[60] Jack London described them too: "I had noticed a tiny outrigger canoe, with an impossible spritsail, skimming the surface of the lagoon."[61] The *Idle Hour* saw some carry up to two tons of copra on a platform on the outriggers and still sail well, for "they skim the surface of the water like a flying-fish and they are about the fastest sailing craft afloat—making better than twenty knots under favourable conditions."[62]

Craft of other islands had their own characteristics, just as each island had its own traditions. The Cook Island canoes had the tradition of the *Te Pua-ariki*, the voyaging canoe of Ru, a great chiefly ancestor, to vindicate; the voyagers themselves could boast of their ancestor Tangiia, who is said to have sailed from Tahiti to Indonesia and Easter Island before settling in Raratonga.[63] The earliest Spanish visitors to the Cook Islands reported both small and large doubles, with decks "capable of carrying fifty people."[64] This was not many; Wilson on the *Duff* reported canoes in Tahiti which could carry 300.[65]

The Russians left a sketch of an old-time Tongarevan (Penrhyn Island) canoe from the Cook Islands. In the twentieth century, new materials have been adopted: "The old type of canoe has completely disappeared and a modern form is made from imported sawn timber. Though shaped like a flat-bottomed boat with sharp bow and stern, the outrigger is retained."[66] This description shows that although the material has changed the principles of design have not. These boats are built to cope with the dangerous reefs which surround some of the atolls. Squalls and storms are dangerous too, and many a Polynesian canoe has been lost in bad weather.

In Samoa, the canoes for home waters were small, but "very neat and fast, for when we set off, we sailed with a topsail's breeze before the wind and they could keep up with us handily with three paddles."[67] In the early days, they had had larger double ones lashed with sennit in the Tongan style, with flanges on the inner sides of the planks. As elsewhere, dugout size is set by the size of the available trees. Thus, because the breadfruit trees had been destroyed in a hurricane ten years previously, the new sennit-lashed canoes Long described in the 1930's were small.

Samoans adopted the outriggerless European hull very early. An American, Jennings, is one of the many examples of Europeans who, attracted by the way of life in Polynesia, stayed to alter that culture by the introduction of techniques and attitudes. At the request of the Samoans, he built a copy of H.M.S. *Calypso*'s longboat, which was then re-copied, using home-made planks with sennit lashings. Jennings's craftsmanship ensured him a long life in the islands, where he founded a family. Mrs. Robert Louis Stevenson met a descendant of Jennings at Olesanga when she and her husband visited there in the *Janet Nicoll*.[68]

Polynesian canoes also were found north of the equator in Hawaii. The greatest pride of its Polynesian inhabitants is the navigation they used to guide canoes from Tahiti to Hawaii and back again, and not the canoes themselves. According to the many legends, the stars were used successfully as guides on voyages which were found to be extremely difficult by European sailing craft even in the twentieth century.

In Hawaii, Captain Cook found both major types of Polynesian canoe— the double canoe (figure 20) and the single outrigger type. One of the huge doubles was "a most superb vessel, in which were four idols, two at each end, representing men of a monstrous size."[69] Vancouver saw in Hawaii a monstrous canoe, over sixty feet long, ". . . made out of an exceedingly fine pine-tree . . . drifted by the ocean . . . probably the growth of some of the northern parts of America . . . which, by the lightness of its timber, and the large outrigger it is capable of supporting, is rendered very lively in the sea."[70] Usually the outrigger canoes were small; the huge one Vancouver saw probably was made after the Hawaiians had given up hope of building a double canoe, if and when a matching-in-size tree arrived as a gift of the sea. The bigger the original log for the canoe, the less extra planking was needed on the hulls and, therefore, the huge Oregon pines which sometimes drifted to Hawaii were greatly prized. The difficulty of obtaining two trees of the same size in this fortuitous fashion is obvious; therefore, Hawaiian chiefs preserved logs for years, waiting for a twin to arrive to provide the second hull.[71] The Lewis and Clark expedition saw "monsterous trees maney of them nearly 200 feet long and from 4 to 7 feet through" floating out to sea from the mouth of the Columbia River.[72] This is one definite link between North America and Polynesia, and there is no lack of speculation about others.

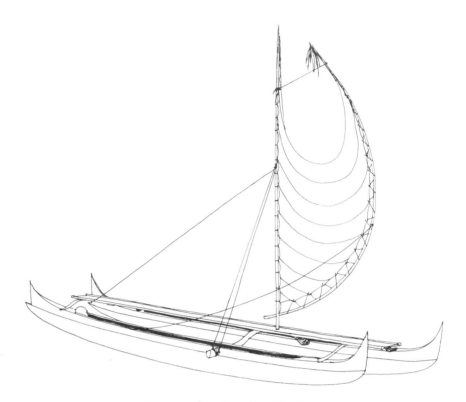

Fig. 20. Hawaiian Double Canoe

At another extremity of the region live the Tongans, the greatest canoe builders of Polynesia, although they did not have the kauri pines of New Zealand or the Oregon pines which drifted to Hawaii to work with. One European captain thought they had learned much of their shipwrights' skill from Fiji, although he granted the Tongans a "superior enterprizing spirit in affairs of navigation."[73] They had the means to match their enterprise, for Cook thought the large Tongan canoes (Plate 13) well suited to distant voyages. Most authorities tell of Tongans building canoes for the Fijians, and since it is agreed that the timber in Fiji is much better, it is probable that there was this trading of skill for material. Tongan workmanship was superb. According to Clerke, who became Cook's successor in command, the canoes were "put together with as much nicety, and their Seams are as fine, as any Cabinet work."[74] Another of Cook's officers said that "no Canoes that we have seen in these seas can bear the least Comparison with these in point of neatness & workmanship."[75] In spite of this commendation, one European captain reported that sometimes outriggers were not well adjusted and that this slowed the canoe. One Tongan canoe seen by an American ship had a mast fifty feet high with a "triangular sail made of matting. . . . These canoes tack and wear in all weathers, are good sea-boats, and sail from eight to ten miles per hour."[76] The sail was almost a true lateen with its point down to the bow, quite different from the sails in the other parts of Polynesia.

Design varied widely in the South Pacific, often for practical reasons. One such variation was overhanging platforms on sterns to use when spearfishing or when landing on steep beaches. Sometimes the designs seemed to be merely local vagaries; yet, whether practical or aesthetic, they marked the canoe as being of one culture or another, or even as coming from one island within a particular cultural grouping. Yet, when the Europeans arrived, there was a similarity in watercraft as there was in other cultural features, which to the pragmatic scientist confirms better than legend the oneness of Polynesia. With their skill, their stone tools, and their varied but limited materials, the Polynesians made the sea their hunting ground and highway.

CHAPTER 5

Watercraft of the Western Fringes

*The proas from Magindanao and Sooloo issue forth in such
swarms, that it becomes dangerous for a weak ship to sail those
seas. These proas are manned with an hundred, and sometimes an hundred and fifty men, well armed, and generally
mounting pieces of cannon of six or twelve pounders. As soon
as a ship is captured by them, a carnage ensues,—and the
unhappy few who survive it are carried into irredeemable
slavery.*

JOHN MEARES
OF THE *FELICE*

*Piling aboard, the crew got their stone anchor up and we
fairly sped through the water. . . . These fleet craft . . . share
the honour with the very similar canoes we had seen at Tahaa,
of being the fastest sailing-vessels in the world. As we skimmed
over the surface of the sparkling waters, we received the impression of flying in mid-air.*

DWIGHT LONG
OF THE *IDLE HOUR*

Melanesians inhabit the islands in the area of sea cornered roughly by Fiji,
New Caledonia, New Guinea and the Solomons. They are a different people
from the Polynesians, although there has been some mixing. Tonga and Fiji,
even though several hundred miles apart, had much contact with each other;
influence in many areas of culture, including their watercraft, no doubt ran
both ways. One example is the Fijian method of lashing their seacraft
(figure 21), which was adopted in western Polynesia and which differed from
the Maori and eastern Polynesian method. All the lashing was done through
special rims left projecting for this purpose on both hull and plank, a technique
which resembles Viking shipbuilding.

Like the Polynesians, the Fijians had large double canoes, often with decking
and houses, the planks and decks being lashed together. The Fijian single
outrigger canoes, however, were pointed at both ends. When tacking, the sail

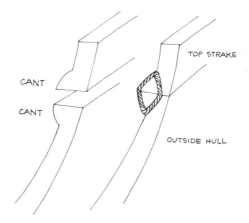

Fig. 21. Fijian Canoe Lashing

could be shifted without the canoe having to turn round in order to keep the outrigger on the windward side.[1] These double-ended canoes are characteristic of Micronesia, Melanesia, and of Polynesian Tonga, but not of the rest of Polynesia. The sail was a very large lateen type with a yard as long as the canoe. The similarity to Tongan work was strong enough that when Bligh passed Fiji in his launch and saw some canoes, he noted that "if I may judge from the sail of the vessels, they are the same as at the Friendly Islands."[2] It is possible, of course, that he saw some Tongan canoes on the way to or from Fiji.

These similarities were strong, but the differences increased further west from Polynesia. Cook thought New Caledonian double canoes "very clumsey & heavy," and noted the major dissimilarity was that "they do not Paddle, as all the other Nations in these seas do, but work them with large Oars."[3] In fact, they did not row, they sculled. Compared to paddling, rowing has the major advantage of leverage, for one pulls with both arms and the whole weight of the body against a fixed fulcrum. In paddling, the pivot point is one of the paddler's hands, in effect cutting down his applied strength. In sculling, which is commonly used in China, the sculler faces forward and works the oar in a rotary movement. It is not as effective as rowing, but has some advantages; for example, it takes less room in a crowded waterway. New Caledonians also used "one or two Latteen sails, extended to a small latteen yard, the end of which fixes in a notch or hole in the deck."[4]

An officer in the *Resolution* did not particularly admire New Hebridean canoes when he compared them with those of the Polynesians; he said "the Workmanship is very rude when compared with those of that truly ingenious People."[5] Cook agreed: "The Canoes which were by no means a master piece of workman Ship, were fitted with outriggers."[6] But in the "marvellous jumble of black and brown, of custom and manners in eastern Melanesia," there were some skilled boatbuilders too.[7]

Solomon Islands mons (figure 22) were particularly handsome craft, of beautiful shape and often so well finished that their separate planks could not be seen as such. The Austrian frigate *Novara* saw a resemblance to the deep-waisted, high-ended boats of Madeira which, of course, had a Mediterranean inspiration.[8] Mons are shapely craft, and were compared to whaleboats by an early American observer; others saw a resemblance to Viking ships. This double comparison was natural enough, for whaleboats are very like small Viking longships. The construction, and indeed the final shape of the mons, remind even expert observers of ancient Scandinavian ships, although the planks are not overlapped in clinker-fashion. In spite of their not having

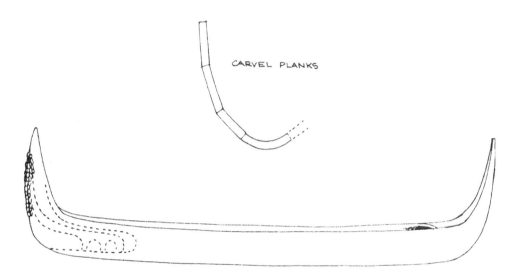

CARVEL PLANKS

Fig. 22. Solomon Island Mon. The slightly curved bottom of the canoe is a dug-out small tree. The sides are built by adding planks carvel fashion and lashing them to curved framing members.

available the giant trees of New Zealand, the Solomon Islanders were able to create a hull large enough for stability by following the same principle of construction as did the Maoris; however, instead of one plank above a large dugout hull, they used several planks above a small dugout hull. Edge to edge, carvel-fashion, curved to form the graceful shape of the sides, the planks were bevelled, lashed, and gummed along the seams in a technique of construction showing a high degree of ingenuity in the use of local materials.[9] Mons, already beautiful in form, were made colourful as well with decorations of paint and pearl shell. "Frigate birds and dolphins are favourite motifs for the paintings."[10] Mons are stable enough not to need outriggers, although these were not unknown in the Solomons. The *Novara* saw very fast narrow canoes with one outrigger near the Solomons, but probably they were fishing canoes.

New Guinea canoes were not famous for beauty—in spite of carving that "shews an ingenious Fancy."[11] Several early observers compared their shape to coffins. They were dugouts, sometimes with added planks, and in some areas were truncated for "the bow was sharp, but the stern square, as if effected by cutting a very large canoe in halves, and filling up the open end."[12] Knees, the curved supports which brace the sides of boats and ships and support the beams, were also used, being an advanced design feature. Sails were often but by no means always rectangular, sometimes described as oval, and were hoisted diagonally as is a lateen sail. Asian influence in sail shape was beginning to counteract the Pacific influence, for triangular sails of various kinds were overwhelmingly in the majority throughout the Pacific proper.

Huxley, visiting New Guinea in the *Rattlesnake* in 1848, said of a canoe sighted southeast of New Guinea, "We saw no mast or sails."[13] Many, probably most, New Guinea canoes did not use sails. "All the heavy canoes are pulled with oars, working in cane gromets, the others are propelled with paddles."[14] There was a form of double canoe which consisted of two, sometimes three, canoes lashed together. In the *Firecrest* a century later, Alain Gerbault was passed by "a strange craft" off New Guinea. "Three long dugouts were lashed alongside one another . . . propelled by two curious triangular sails."[15] Such craft were used mainly for transport—the war canoes used outriggers.

In addition to canoes, Huxley saw catamarans in constant use. He surmised that ". . . they are permanent constructions and of common use . . . from the elaborate carving bestowed upon the pointed ends of the middle logs—the outer logs are shorter than the middle one and though not carved are smooth and pointed at each end."[16] Whether thirty or nine feet long, these rafts nearly always consisted of three logs—Macgillivray of the *Rattlesnake* said "three thick planks" and Huxley wrote elsewhere "of three spars lashed together"—joined with rattan.[17]

Different islands and different areas were marked by their canoe design. Even when "there was no marked physical distinction between these inhabitants . . . the canoes . . . are as different as the language."[18] This is a remark which could well have been made by the New Guineans about the Dutch and English ships. Nations in Europe as close ethnically and closer geographically than were New Guinea and the Louisiade Archipelago (just southeast of New Guinea) about which Macgillivray was writing nevertheless had very distinctive features in their ships. In spite of stressing the difference in the canoes of these two areas, he repeated a New Guinea analogy about Louisiadean canoes, "a narrow coffin-like box, resting upon a hollowed out log."[19] Perhaps the cramped conditions of shipboard life were making him gloomy. Louisiadean canoes, beautifully carved and decorated, had a single outrigger and sometimes an oblong sail. They did not sail well into the wind, but the canoes from the eastern ends of the Archipelago, perhaps more greatly influenced by the requirements of the ocean itself, could work to windward handily.[20]

Most people seek beauty as well as performance in watercraft. Sometimes, the beauty is stated boldly in decoration; sometimes, it is implicit in the form. Melanesian canoes were often brightly coloured. The *Margaret Oakley*, an American brig, saw canoes which "were perfect gems; the bow and stern represented the neck and beak of a bird, and were painted red." One was painted "handsomely, with colours that would not rub off!"[21] Solomon Island canoes were "often painted with designs in black, white and red,"[22] but the American brig also saw plainer ones and "remarked that their canoes were whitewashed, and that they were very particular in keeping them clean."[23] Tasman saw a canoe near New Ireland which was "lime-white," carved with "elegant figures" and with a "wing" on the side.[24]

Likening an outrigger to a wing—Tasman once said "gull wing," giving an idea of the curve of that specific boom—is particularly apt when the canoe is seen sailing across the wind with the outrigger raised well above the water, acting not simply as a float, but as a balance against the pressure of the wind on the sail. Apt too because modern flying boats use outrigger-type floats on the wings, as Long noted when he saw a great American flying boat at Daru, anchored near outrigger canoes.[25] If outriggers and flying are related even today, then it should be appreciated all the more what the word "flying" meant to Magellan, or to Anson two hundred years later, when applied to anything man-made. It meant speed—especially speed—but also it meant the lightness and grace associated with birds. Tasman's "gull wing" defines something curved and beautiful; it is an attempt to define something almost magical in the days before man had built himself wings.

Bird-like lightness, grace, and magic: such words suit the impression made on Europeans by the canoes—the flying proas (Plate 14)—of the Caroline islands of Micronesia, the islands north of Melanesia and west of the northern Polynesian islands. While in the *Cygnet*, Dampier praised their speed as "the best of any boats in the world. . . . I believe she would run twenty-four miles in an hour."[26] Anson saw them from the *Centurion*—he was a fine and experienced sailor—and he thought they would do twenty knots, a speed not reached again until the late nineteenth-century clippers, and then only rarely. A French officer who estimated a speed of ten knots said he had been told they occasionally could reach fifteen. The chaplain of Anson's ship stated they could run before the wind "with a velocity nearly as great, and perhaps sometimes greater, than what the wind blows with."[27]

More interesting than their speed was their ability to sail close to the wind. An Englishman in the *Desire* in 1588 obviously spoke before understatement became an English trait: "they saile as well right against the winde, as before the winde."[28] This windward ability, Anson thought, was due to their peculiar construction:

...for as it is customary to make the head of the vessel different from the stern, but the two sides alike, the proa, on the contrary, has her head and stern exactly alike, but her two sides very different; the side intended to be always the lee-side being flat, whilst the windward side is built rounding, in the manner of other vessels.[29]

His description of the operation of these craft, it should be noted, is in one respect quite the opposite to the descriptions of Dampier, and of Crozet, captain of the French ship *Mascarin*. Dampier said: "They keep the flat side of the great boat against the wind, and the belly side, consequently, with its little boat, is upon the lee."[30] Crozet said of the ones he saw at Guam that they were "built flat on that, the windward, side and rounding on the lee side, which, being more under water, requires a more suitable surface for cutting through the water."[31] As Dampier did, he also states clearly that the outrigger was on the rounded or leeward side of the boat.

Anson's statement makes more sense than Crozet's, for it leaves the outrigger to windward where it could act as a balance, and where it would not be pressed down into the water, with all the concomitant drag and strain. However, as Dampier and Crozet depict the canoe itself exactly as Admiral Anson did, it is probable that they saw the proa being sailed in a different fashion from that normally used. In light winds, the proa certainly could be sailed with the outrigger to leeward. Crozet claims actually to have sailed in one at a high speed and, as an experienced seaman, he should have been able to see how it was done. However, one is inclined to agree with Macgillivray of the *Rattlesnake* when he says of some other outrigger canoes that "while under sail either the bow or stern of the canoe may be foremost, this being regulated by the necessity of having the outrigger on the weather side, unless in a very light wind."[32]

Lateen type sails extended almost the length of the flying proas, and tacking was done simply by reversing the sail around the yard, taking the steering paddle to the other end, and proceeding with the opposite end foremost. A modern touch was that "at the foot of the sail is another small yard to keep the sail out square, or to roll the sail upon when it blows hard."[33] Modern yachts often reef their mainsails in a heavy wind by rolling them onto the boom. Proas were good craft, but their owners knew that they had limitations.

Captain Wilson of the *Antelope* was told by a Micronesian at Palau Island that the canoes were not taken out when there was "too much wind and sea," and sailors of the *Antelope* actually were in one when it was upset by a squall.[34]

Crozet said of Micronesian boatbuilding, "in this respect they had nothing new to learn," but another Frenchman had some doubts.[35] When the *Uranie* visited the area, her scientist saw that a "proa, not having time to brail up the sail, was upset . . . a hint to those who bestow exaggerated commendations on the goodness of these boats." However, in spite of "such frail boats," he did admire "these daring men, [who] unassisted by the compass, and guided only by the stars and their own experience, would venture to undertake voyages of more than six hundred leagues."[36] Dampier mentioned hearing of voyages of nearly 500 leagues in 4 days, which would give them daily runs equalling the best that the clipper ships made, the very best being 430 miles made by the clipper *Lightning*.

If true, this feat of the proas is most remarkable, because crew fatigue is a factor in long-distance small craft sailing, particularly in solo yachts. Dampier complained that he "had been rudely tossed about in the proas, which, though lighter than our boats, and keeping the wind much better, are far more fatiguing."[37] Aside from the discomfort which accompanies speed in a small craft, the Micronesian craft were famous for many other qualities. Those of Palau Island were handsome craft. Some Europeans thought that "those of PELEW surpassed in neatness and beauty any they had ever met with elsewhere."[38] Colour and decoration added to the comeliness of the shape itself. Usually, they were painted red both inside and out, and inlaid with pearl shell, all very carefully done; the king "had taken down with him a design of his own for ornamenting some canoes then building, and this design was marked on a board with great accuracy, in different colours, to work after."[39] This is an interesting contrast to the Chinese or Maoris working by "rule of thumb." Palauans used wood resembling English ash for their canoes, a "lucky" wood. Some woods were considered "unlucky" for boats; in all probability this was a folk recognition that some woods lacked the strength, flexibility, or endurance required of boat timbers.

Canoes were as precious and important "a national asset" to Palauans as they were to the Maoris: "The obtaining [by capture] a canoe, however trifling it may appear to a reader, is equal to the capture of the largest ship of war in EUROPE." These assets were well guarded, the observer added, and carefully protected from the weather in well-made boathouses, "not unlike those that are made in England."[40]

Indonesia has a great variety of watercraft. Here the double outrigger

Fig. 23. Corocoro—note the twin outriggers

(figure 23) could be used in the waters sheltered by the myriad islands. The *Golden Hind* saw there "... canowes ... of one tree ... prowe and sterne they had of one fashion, yeelding inward in manner of a semicircle.... On each side of their canows, lay out two peeces of timber about a yard and halfe long.... At the ends whereof was fastned crossewise a great cane."[41]

Two hundred years later they were much the same, as the record of the voyage of the *Tartar Galley*, an Indonesian craft, shows. During the journey, Captain Forrest saw many beautiful and interesting boats: "A corocoro is a vessel generally fitted with out-riggers, having a high arched stem and stern, like the points of a half-moon" (Drake's semicircle). Corocoros could be paddled by men sitting at the gunwales and also on "fore and aft planks" placed on the outrigger booms. Forrest noted that "in smooth water they can be paddled very fast, as many hands may be employed in different ranks or rows," and mentioned an interesting feature in that, when sailing light with the gunwales well above the water, "they use oars; but, on the out-riggers, they always use paddles."[42]

Both Forrest and Dampier noted that the Dutch adapted corocoros for their own use, with the addition of a rudder and European rigging. The Indonesian boats sailed well. Near Java, the earliest Dutchmen had encountered

". . . a sort of Boats which run so fast, that it is almost incredible . . . they put on both sides of the Boat two big Reeds . . . tying them to two sticks . . . by that means the Boat carries so great a Sail, that one admires to see it run."[43]

However, not all the Indonesian boats sailed well. At Nicobar a century or so later, Dampier exchanged an axe for an "extremely crank" narrow canoe with "good Outlagers lash'd very fast and firm . . . [so] the Vessel could not overset, which she would easily have done without them."[44] The price of them was still reasonable 150 years later. A rajah ordered a new prahu (proa) "fifty feet long, fitted for service, with oars, mast, attops &c. . . . which completed was to cost thirty reals or sixty Java rupees, or 6L [pounds sterling], English."[45] As in the European galleys, the oars would be used under the same conditions and for the same reasons—in calms or in harbour manoeuvring.

Galleys (or ships very similar to them) were common enough in the western Pacific. John Davis, the famous navigator and captain, tells of a galley at Achin carrying 400 men. The king there had 100 galleys.[46] Saris, captain of a Dutch ship which visited Japan in 1612, saw Japanese galleys with thirty oars.[47] Indigenous galleys were common in the Indonesian Archipelago, and sweeps were used in the Euro-Asian hybrid craft—lorchas and others—as late as the 1890's.

In the nineteenth century, Borneo pirates used large proas pulling up to fifty oars and mounting European cannon. In spite of the cannon, their main tactic was boarding. They were strongly built ships, rather slow but very similar to a European galley in posing a potent danger when sailing ships were becalmed. Admiral Keppel described their "strong bulwarks or barricades, grape-shot proof, across the fore part of the boat."[48] A similar idea was ascribed by de Surville, the French explorer, to the canoe builders of the Solomon Islands. He said their canoes had a high prow and stern "apparently for the purpose of defending the warriors in them from arrows, by presenting either end to the enemy."[49]

Oared galleys native to Chinese and Japanese waters served as merchant or pirate vessels—sometimes both—the galley's purpose depending on the estimated strength of the potential customer or victim. Some were "biremes," that is, they had two banks of oars, one above the other, like the galleys of ancient Phoenicia, Greece, and Rome.[50]

Pirates operating from the Philippines used galleys which, from Dampier's description, somewhat resembled the Javanese proa, being "more round, like the Half-Moon almost . . . Outlagers on each side . . . 1, 3 or 4 Foot above the Water, and serve for the Barge Men to sit and Row and paddle on."[51] They

Plate 11. *Tilikum*. It was in this craft, converted from a British Columbian Indian canoe, that Captain Voss sailed round the world. The *Tilikum* is shown here in Samoa.

Plate 12. "The Last Maori War Canoe." The Maori carvers' characteristic spiral pattern adorns the intricate prow of this beautiful canoe.

Plate 13. A sailing double canoe of Tonga, as seen by the artist with Captain Cook in 1774. Note the decked canoe hulls of somewhat different size and shape, the two large steering oars, the heavy rope lines, and the hut on the deck or platform. Some of these craft were said to be big enough to carry 200 people.

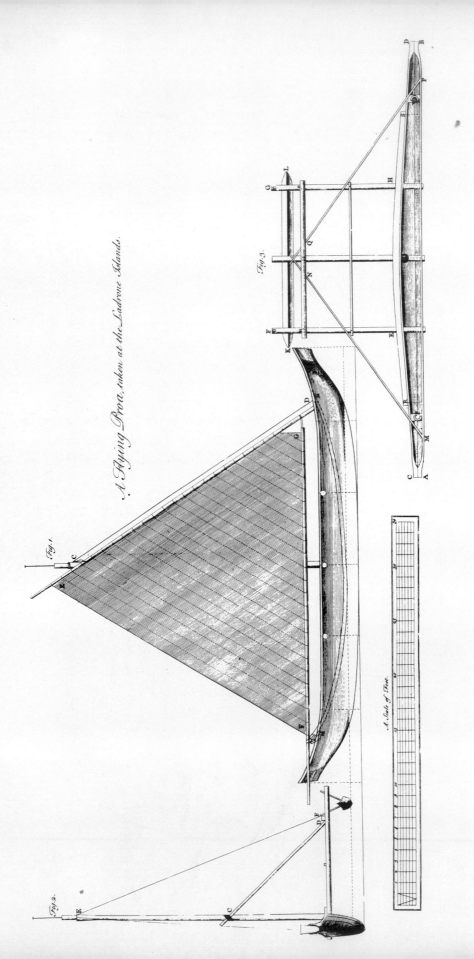

A Flying Proa, taken at the Ladrone Islands.

Fig. 1.

Fig. 2.

Fig. 3.

A Scale of Feet.

Plate 14. Flying Proa. This plan of a flying proa, done in 1742 by Brett, an officer on Anson's expedition, shows the distinct difference between the two sides of the craft. Sailed with the outrigger and the rounded side to windward, the great drift-resistance of the flat leeward side enabled the craft to sail at a very small angle to the wind. The craft's name is indicative of its speed and grace.

were much the same as the one Cavendish had seen a century earlier when he noticed a "canoa of a great bignes ... which was builded up with great canes, and below hard by the water made to row with oares."[52] Forrest described one of these craft with sixteen oars a side, "making a great angle with the horizon," and another with forty oars a side, the rowers sitting on projecting galleries.[53]

In the latter half of the nineteenth century, the Austrians of the frigate *Novara* described four quite different kinds of boats in the Philippines: a dugout canoe called a "banca"; a big and clumsy rowboat called a "lorcha"; a kind of rectangular barge or raft called a "casca"; and a form of Malay proa, the "paraho"; only the latter had any resemblance to the galleys the pirates had used. Probably they simply missed noticing them, for pirate galleys and junks were endemic in the area of the South China Sea during the nineteenth century.

This area was a meeting place of trade routes, of peoples, and of cultures, and naturally boats of many kinds were to be seen. In the Philippines, lorcha was the name given to a rowed boat, but the name was also used for the boat with a European hull and Chinese junk rigging which the Portuguese developed to use on their eastern trading voyages. Names of ship types were, as they are still, somewhat interchangeable.

The name, "flying proa," associated with Micronesia, was also used for Achin boats, "which are built long, deep, narrow, and sharp, with both Sides alike, and Outlagers on each Side, the Head and Stern like other Boats."[54] Many of the interesting solutions to the problem of balancing a narrow hull at high speed apparently had found their way over great distances.

The watercraft of the western fringes of the Pacific Ocean still exist in tremendous variety. The early plenitude of types suited the former dominant European powers in the area—Portugal and the Netherlands—for it matched the variety of small craft used in the homelands. European influence altered the hulls and rigging of those craft seen as being of most use to the Europeans, but in the more remote islands historic types have survived to the present day as a treasure trove of men's ideas about movement and the sea.

CHAPTER 6

Junks of China and Japan

The ships which sail in the South Seas are like big houses. . . .
A single ship carries several hundred men. It has stored on
board provisions for one year. They feed pigs and ferment
liquors. They put aside all thoughts of life and death, for once
they enter the dark blue distant sea, it is no more a human
world.

CHOU CH'Ü FEI
TWELFTH CENTURY

Junks are seaworthy craft which reached the peak of their development hundreds of years ago and, until recently, had changed very little. Those of North China are among the oldest known types of vessel, for the craft on their northern routes did not encounter foreign influence and therefore their basic design remained almost unmodified. The situation was somewhat different in South China, but in both very different from the steady development in ship design and building methods in Europe, especially from 1400 onwards. Static conditions in the Chinese shipbuilding industry were reflected in the attitude of its shipwrights. Clifford, a young New Zealander, who sailed his own junk from China to New Zealand, found it very difficult to get Chinese shipwrights to accept modifications of traditional design when they were building his *Golden Lotus* in 1962.[1]

Junks (Plate 15) are very interesting vessels in spite of their unattractive name—a name which has caused as much underestimation of these craft as the name "canoes" has of the ships of Tonga or Tahiti. Although the junks of China and Japan did not sail into the main Pacific, these ancient watercraft played a major part in later European trade and exploration along its western edges. With none of the features of the clinker- or carvel-built European sailing ships, presumably they must have had a different development and, possibly, parentage. In spite of this, seagoing junks had exactly the same function as their Western counterparts; they were marine cargo and passenger carriers, with wind as their propellant force.

European craft (figure 24) consist of a keel along the bottom, with a stem-post and sternpost curving upward at each end, bent internal ribs for strengthening curving upwards from the keel, and side planks curved to meet the end posts. Clinker-built differed from carvel-built craft only in that they had their planks overlapped and not edge-on-edge (figure 43). Also the ribs were put in after, and not before, the plank sides were erected. The most typical junks, however, before European influence modified some features, had no keel, no stempost and, usually, no sternpost. Planking was placed across the stem and stern to form the foremost and rearmost of a number of bulkheads (walls) which divided the ship into watertight compartments. This design feature was attributed to the Chinese adaptation of the bamboo structure with its watertight divisions, but in spite of its soundness, the feature was not adopted in the rest of the world until within the last century and a half. This was not because Europeans did not know of it; Marco Polo pointed out that in the case of a leak the junk would not sink, because the "cargo is shifted from the damaged compartment ... [and] the bulkheads are so stoutly built that the compartments are watertight."[2] A damaged junk would be repaired from within if possible, but, if not, "devil divers" would work from the outside.

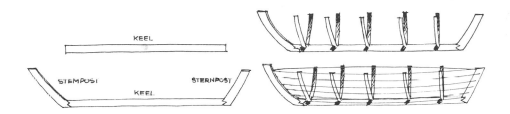

Fig. 24. Basic Principles of European Craft Construction

Building a junk was a very different process from building a European ship (figure 25). Planks were laid lengthwise on the ground and pinned together, bulkheads of dovetailed boards were built across them and then side planks were nailed along. A process of bending, charring, and adzing produced any curves necessary in the planks. Deck beams were laid along the tops of the bulkheads and let into the top side plank: "The Bulk of the Ship was joyned together after the same manner as a Cooper joyns the head of a Cask."[3] Only at this stage were prepared frames inserted into the hull. In this, there is some similarity to the inserted ribs of the clinker-built boats of the Vikings or Solomon Islanders, or to the bark canoes of North America. Stem and stern were built simply as bulkheads at each end, and then the deck was nailed on. It was a process of boatbuilding quite different from boatbuilding

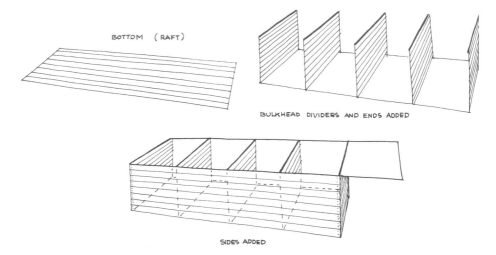

Fig. 25. Basic Principles of Junk Construction

anywhere except in East Asia. It was, and indeed is, all done by rule of thumb: "Wung Kee never referred to the plans from the time the timbers were selected to the time the junk was launched."[4]

Early observers said that the work of the shipwrights was most roughly done; great cracks and holes had to be filled with putty or bamboo shavings, and other planks were often put inside the seams to hold the caulking. In Polo's day, the caulking was "lime and hemp chopped up very fine and [pounded] together with the oil of a tree . . . it sticks like glue."[5] It set hard and white and watertight. Marco Polo saw that "the entire hull is of double thickness: that is to say, one plank is fastened over the top of another, and this double planking extends all the way round."[6] Repairs were simple, for all they did was "nail on another layer of planks all round, over the top of the original two. . . . Then they caulk her afresh . . . till there are as many as six layers."[7]

As with the junk hulls, the Chinese favoured propulsion which emphasized effectiveness; they paid little attention to appearance. Chinese sails are as efficient as the hulls are buoyant. The junk balance-lug sail is characteristic, resembling in appearance a lateen with the fore point removed, but stiffened with battens of bamboo so that its surface lies flat to the wind to form a most powerful propelling surface (figure 26). Each batten has a bowline which helps enormously in keeping the sail flat to the wind. Battened lug sails look clumsy to the eyes of European sailors, but they are very effective close to the wind. The sail folds up like an accordian and therefore is easily reefed, *i.e.*, the surface area reduced in strong winds; it also comes down very quickly when sail needs to be removed. Carletti, on his way to Japan in 1597, sailed "on a vessel of the sort that the Japanese call 'somme' ... when they want to furl the sails, these fold up like a fan."[8] All that is necessary to bring down the sail is to slacken the halliard (the line which hauls the yard up) and the weight of the sail and battens will bring it down as freely in a squall as it will in a calm. It is almost jam free; but the system also has its disadvantages. "A junk rig may be the easiest to handle, but junks have huge masts and even then are constantly breaking them."[9] Clifford, after sailing one, felt the major disadvantage of junks was that they were slow to windward, but he admired the advantages of the high poop and the simple rigging.

The battens so strengthen the sail that weaker cloth may be used, but in any case holes are not a matter of great concern. Junk sailors found (as snow fences in Canada demonstrate every winter) that a slotted surface breaks the wind more efficiently than does a plane one. Junk builders sometimes used

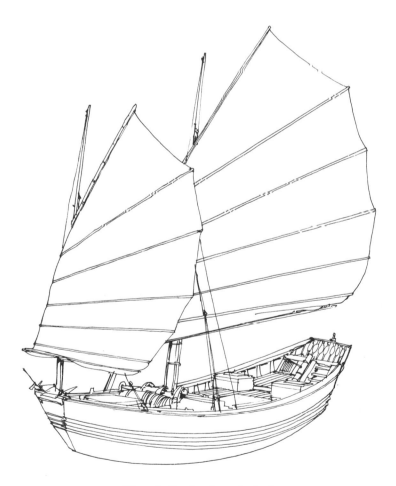

Fig. 26. Junk—length, 80 feet

this same principle on their rudders too, by perforating them with diamond shapes. The idea of holed sails, in a strongly modified form, was used on some good ships in the 1890's, although an Italian was given credit for the idea at that time. Many experienced captains used and liked them. Several advantages were claimed, including easier furling in an emergency, but what seems a paradox was the claim that holed sails were of great advantage in light winds.[10]

The junk sail is hoisted with about one third of its area in front of the mast. Various positions, heights, and rakes (forward or backward leanings) of the masts are used, and masts are sometimes staggered in port and starboard positions. Broughton, sailing the China coast in 1797, said that nearly every junk he had seen had had three masts, but he spoke of one with four, the additional one being outside the hull at the bow.[11] Different shapes of sprit-sails, trysails, headsails and spinnakers are used to supplement the mainsail; only occasionally are topsails used. Junkmen often add a small foresail on a foremast to improve the airflow past the mainsail, which it does by performing a slotting function similar to that of the modern yachting jibsail or staysail.

The balanced rudder, which can be raised and lowered at the stern, is the most typical junk rudder. Junks have square sterns—perhaps this made the stern rudder a fairly obvious device. At any rate, they were in use in China a thousand years before they were used in Europe, for, as in Polynesia or America, boats in Europe were steered with steering oars until (in historical terms) comparatively recently; the changeover took place during the late thirteenth and early fourteenth centuries.

Chinese junk rudders cannot be hung on hinges on a sternpost because usually there is no sternpost. Instead, they are hung in a well left open in the projecting portion of the after (rearward) upper works of the hull and then held steady by rope tackle. The rudder is lowered several feet below the bottom of the hull, so that it can act as a drop-keel as well as a rudder. In a similar way, Lewis in the *Rehu Moana* found that his twin rudders acted as keels to some extent. Once the junk is in shallow water, the rudder is hoisted up.

Carletti said that as the rudder was fragile and often damaged, ". . . to protect it from the waves and keep it from being damaged, they usually carry two large thick beams in the style of the oars from one side to the other . . . they lower these deep into the water, thus breaking up the waves of the sea."[12] Actually, this sounds more like a description of leeboards. Without doubt, it was this length and movability which caused Marco Polo to call the rudder a "steering-oar";[13] in all else his description is that of a typical large junk.[14] As mentioned earlier, the surfaces of some rectangular hardwood rudders are perforated with diamond-shaped holes, because the Chinese think, quite correctly, that water creates more resistance eddying through a holed surface than it does when glancing off a plane surface.

These rudders are very efficient. The *Golden Lotus* had one and Clifford wrote, after a harrowing experience in her, that "then more than any other time I was thankful that she would turn almost in her own length."[15] All these features make junks perfectly seaworthy craft. Many centuries ago, they were capable of sailing great distances; Fa-hsien sailed from India to Canton via Java in A.D. 413 in a merchant ship carrying 200 men. A Bureau of Trading Junks was established in the eighth century to register junks and collect duty on them. Measurements for customs duties affected their design, as indeed they influenced Dutch ship design also. Breadth and depth were measured at the "tallest mast," so the Chinese placed a very tall foremast forward where breadth and depth were small. There are some interesting accounts of American skippers attempting to swindle the Chinese customs authorities by putting up temporary masts; the Chinese, characteristically, were not fooled.[16] No doubt skippers, other than American, tried the same kind of trick.

These early merchant junks which plied only the western edges of the Pacific, not the broad reaches of the ocean itself, were large ships—of several hundred tons burden—with broad hulls, huge lug sails, both longitudinal and transverse bulkheads, and separate staterooms for passengers. They reached a higher standard of safety and comfort than did the Portuguese carracks 1,000 years later.

In some manuscripts, ancient merchant junks were described as being ". . . square like a bushel . . . one makes use not only of a stern wind but also of wind off or toward the shore. It is only a head-wind which drives the boat back. . . . On board a large . . . ocean-going junk, there are several hundred persons."[17] Even allowing for poetic licence, they must have been quite large.

Actual dimensions given for one junk in 1763 were 100 feet long and 20 feet wide; it was not much later that Captain Forrest of the *Tartar Galley* measured one at 120 feet long and 30 feet wide at the deck "but more below."[18] Marco Polo estimated the cargo capacity of similar junks to be from 200 to 600 tons.[19] Either the huge size of the early junks was not overstated, or the "several hundred persons" must have been crowded in conditions even worse than those in the contemporary European vessels. There is a record of a Shantung five-masted junk 150 feet long and 32 feet wide, which is considerably larger than the others mentioned.[20] For short journeys hundreds of people certainly could have travelled on it.

Huge war junks were patrolling the West Asian seas before Europeans knew that the area existed, and a fleet of junks under Cheng Ho sailed to

Africa in the fifteenth century. Not much is known about the early ones, although their potential or actual opponents gave some good descriptions of war junks in the nineteenth century. Large junks carried two or four guns, while the smaller war junks usually had only two swivel guns. By European standards they were so under-armed that they stood little chance in a gun battle with a frigate or ship-of-the-line. Royal Navy observers reported that they were large, unwieldy-looking masses of timber of about 250 to 300 tons (some up to 800 tons) and of shallow draught.[21] Silting up of river-mouth harbours required the gradual reduction of the draught of seagoing junks; there is evidence that earlier junks had been much larger. Some authorities claim that some of the fifteenth-century junks had nine masts and were over four hundred feet long, but this seems an incredible length for a wooden ship.

Some very early war junks were said to be so large that ladders scores of feet long were needed to board them. Ancient woodcuts show huge ships with dragons' heads at their prows, dragons so large that men are on lookout from the monsters' mouths. Junks were richly decorated with flags, paint, and carving; the motifs often were the colourfully fierce dragons or tigers. Two very noticeable features were the flatness of the straight stems or bows and the considerable sheer of the hulls. The junks were usually painted black and red —common colours in the Pacific—and they were personified by a huge eye painted on each side of the bow. In fishing junks, the eyeball was set low in the white of the eye watching for the fish; in trading junks, the eye looked straight ahead to perceive and avoid distant perils invisible to mortals.

Smaller war junks were "less shapeless" than the large nineteenth-century ones; they had neater lines, were a great deal faster, and they could be propelled by ten to twenty oars in a calm sea.[22] Some junks were driven by paddle-wheels, an ancient Chinese invention. General Li-Kao (A.D. 733-92) built "fighting ships with two paddle-wheels on each side so that they ran as fast as swift horses."[23] One very old woodcut shows a paddle-wheel war junk carrying archers. Presumably these wheels were turned by a treadmill or capstan operated by the crew; in the late nineteenth century, riverboats in eastern China were still using paddle-wheels operated by human labour. They were not the only human-powered paddle-wheels in the Pacific. In the South Pacific in the mid-nineteenth century, Jennings, the American who had copied the whaleboat for the Samoans and thereby altered Samoan watercraft, built a paddle-wheel to be run by handcranks.[24]

The great northern junks from Shantung were built of pine with hardwood bulkheads, strengthened because of their great length with a central longitudinal plank of heavy hardwood. This necessary strengthening raises a question about the junks which were claimed to be 400 feet long. Junks had to be designed for extremes of climate and for both deep ocean and shallow coastal waters. To meet these conditions of differing depths, the Chinese developed removable keels, using both leeboards and drop-keels or centreboards, similar to that of the *Lady Nelson* (1800) and of many later Pacific schooners. Perhaps the Chinese borrowed the idea of centreboards from the great rafts of Formosa. Some authorities claim that the Dutch, who still use them extensively, got the idea of leeboards from the Chinese. Broughton was not impressed by leeboards on at least one junk: "They had lee-boards; but notwithstanding, she went bodily to leeward, and she sailed very heavily."[25]

Very seaworthy small junks at Amoy co-operate with rafts, using bamboo rafts for fishing boats instead of sampans (the same mother-ship idea used by fishermen on the Newfoundland Banks, by whaleboats, and by modern Japanese fishing ships). All the fishing junks are built with watertight bulkheads, and some have free flooding front compartments, perhaps a throw-back to raft origins. The *Centurion* encountered many fishing junks near China, "their number incredible, since I cannot believe . . . there were so few as six thousand."[26]

Women were not allowed on fishing junks, it is claimed, just as women were not allowed in Polynesian fishing canoes. In contrast to both these cultures, Pigafetta noted at the Ladrones that the Micronesians' "amusement, men and women, is to plough the seas with those small boats of theirs."[27]

European influence affected junks, and this may be best seen at Hong Kong where there are all kinds of interesting hybrids. One example of European influence in another part of China is the Kwantung trawler; its standing rigging and its underwater lines are strongly foreign. Some of these changes were due to the importation of woods, such as teak, which required different handling. Clifford's modern junk was built of "rich smooth teak from the keel to the waterline and honey-coloured hardwood above that."[28] His reference to a keel might also indicate that some European features had been adopted by his shipwrights, in spite of the conservatism he mentions.

Lorchas built and used in Macao were a hybrid of Portuguese and Chinese design; they retained the Chinese bulkheads, but in a more slender European hull. Chinese balance-lug sails on the three masts retained the advantages of that rig (apart from the fact that the rigging was cheap and easy to obtain), while the change in hull gave much greater speed. Another hybrid was the coasting ketch developed for the southeast Asian timber trade in the nineteenth century. In appearance reminiscent of seventeenth-century craft, it looked very similar to Van der Velde's Dutch yachts, but it had the brown cotton sails and the diamond-holed rudder of a Chinese junk.

Not everyone is an admirer of the junk. If Clifford admired the design, he also modified it in the *Golden Lotus*. Gann of the *Albatros*, the American author who writes so well of modern yachting and flying, certainly does not like junks. Speaking of a "typical small cargo junk of the Hong Kong-Canton area," he reported that:

Any craft of such dimensions, [6o feet long with only 3½ foot draught], including a large wooden tub, is bound to sail fast—downwind. . . . The *Li Po* would not sail anywhere near the wind, showing even less style than a square-rigger, and when on a reach she made appalling leeway. . . . What was not apparent was the shocking inefficiency of her gear, which was the fault of stubborn adherence to ancient design rather than economics.[29]

Some Russian observers thought the junk sailors handled rigging poorly and that the junks were slovenly craft.[30] Holman, knowledgeable and observant, after travelling around the world, thought that the Chinese were remarkable for their skilled handling of small boats, but he quoted Gutzlaff, a European missionary who had lived in China for many years, in order to criticise them as crew members: "There is no subordination, no cleanliness, no mutual regard or interest."[31] Krusenstern, the great Russian explorer of the Pacific in the early nineteenth century who demonstrated convincingly that Russia's global interests and intentions coincided with her advancing naval techniques, agreed with this view, saying of the seamanship of one Chinese fleet: "and we were witnesses to the unskilfulness and difficulty with which they hoisted their sails."[32]

It is fortunate that in China sailing junks of essentially the ancient design can still be seen as working craft. At least until recently there were exotic variations also: the houseboat, sometimes with 100 occupants; the floating brothels, now probably a casualty of the new Chinese puritanism, but at one time a static Asian equivalent of the Caribbean cruise ship; the duck boats, which are mobile duck farms; and the fishing boats which use trained otters or flamingos to dive down to catch and retrieve the fish.

The Chinese also had rowed craft which showed the same creativity of design and independence of thought seen in their sailing vessels. Looking ahead to the principle of the screw propeller, one vessel was actually propelled by the rotary or screw motion of a gigantic oar projecting over the stern. This rotary motion was made by an ingenious arrangement of a rope and pivot with the energy coming from men's muscles. Propulsion was absolutely continuous, not intermittent as with standard oars, and a vessel of several hundred tons propelled by two or three of these oars would move at up to four knots. The Chinese had early learned the lesson that it pays to increase the size of the oar and the number of men working it, rather than to increase the number of oars; some of these *yulohs*, or sculling oars, had ten men working them. At Macao, an observer saw huge sculls using twenty men.[33] They used standard galleys (in the Western sense) as well, and a European sailor in the South China Sea saw a galley with fifty oars. So much of the colour and vitality of the amazing Chinese culture, with its conservatism barely containing its exuberance, found expression in its myriad watercraft.

Across the East China Sea in Japan, the watercraft, like so much in Japanese culture, were both like and unlike those of China. As with most techniques, the Japanese showed their amazing ability to adopt and adapt in shipping and navigation. As pragmatists, they thought the merit of an idea of technique much more important than its source. In Japan, therefore, early sixteenth-century visitors saw adaptations of the Chinese junk (figure 27), and early twentieth-century visitors saw adaptations of American schooners. Neither type had remained exactly the same as the original. It is debatable whether or not the changes were improvements, but each craft had the durability built in by the superb Japanese craftsmanship.

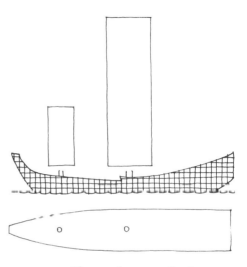

Fig. 27. *Japanese Junk* (*profile and plan*)

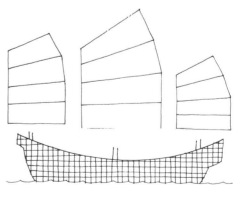

Fig. 28. *Chinese Junk* (*profile*)

Japanese junks were unsuitable for long sea voyages. Captain Colnett described them this way: "Their Large sailing Vessels have only one mast, which they use in Common with a Lug sail of Cotton, which are Bonnetted together in Cloths Vertically; each Cloth having a Bridle, which is made fast to one Sheet, that the sail appears like a Purse at the Foot."[34] Much like the fifteenth-century carracks, these junks were high pooped and, having only one lofty narrow mainsail, they could not work well to windward. La Pérouse noted that the Japanese "ships, of about one hundred tons burden, had a single, very high mast and carried an immense sail," but he did not comment on their sailing qualities.[35] The Russians commented in a rather non-committal way: "They sail well, but as a rule like to wait for a fair wind," and they thought they were not too seaworthy.[36] However, they were large. In 1613, Captain Saris saw "a Juncke of eight hundred or a thousand Tunnes of burthen, sheathed all with yron."[37] (The sheathing was protection against shipworms.) Their breadth meant that they could carry a great deal of cargo, but it also slowed them. Even if, as has been claimed, the Japanese junks were the most durable of all wooden vessels, because of their heavy construction and the very good craftsmanship, nonetheless the resulting weight and deep draught made them very slow.

The Japanese quickly adopted European models, even though these did not displace their own craft. The Shogun Ieyasu asked the Spaniards to send ships' carpenters from the Philippines to show the Japanese how to build ships after Spanish models; he also asked for pilots and navigators to assist and train his own. At one time, by Japanese law, a Portuguese pilot was required on each Japanese long-voyage ship. Will Adams, an English pilot of a Dutch ship, was kept in Japan in the early seventeenth century in order to build ships, although his only knowledge of shipbuilding, so far as is known, was acquired in the "setting up of a Pinnace of fifteene or sixteene tunnes in bignesse," at the Straits of Magellan on his way to the Pacific. As Adams himself said, "I was no Carpenter, and had no knowledge thereof."[38] Nevertheless, in 1610, one of his ships, the *San Buenaventura* of 120 tons, sailed to Acapulco, and there was purchased by the Spaniards with "goods and money: which shippe the Spaniards have now in the Philippinas."[39] In spite of this successful voyage, domestic policies in Japan prevented any large or long-term development in cross-Pacific commerce.

Early Russian explorers of the North Pacific described the Japanese fishing boats as being something like a European ship's longboat in shape and dimension, but "they always ply their oars standing and they row very fast."[40] By the twentieth century, many Japanese sailing ships were schooners modelled on those of Canadian and American seal hunters. There were distinctive modifications, however. In most cases, the two masts and their sails were similar in size, and a very long jib-boom carried two or three jibs besides the fore staysail. The Japanese schooners had no topmasts, and the square topsail was seldom seen.

One can assume that the Japanese did not sail the main Pacific, partly because they had no need to and partly because they deliberately isolated themselves from the world from the early seventeenth to the middle of the nineteenth century. But in addition, the North Pacific east of Japan is an area of particularly bad weather. It was the lack of adequate incentive to overcome the weather which held back the capable Asian seamen; it was not because they could not have adapted both equipment and techniques. Their world was a sufficient one.

European Ships

During the period covered by this book, Japan deliberately isolated herself inside her own sufficient world for over two centuries, ignoring where possible, and where not, rebuffing, all from the world outside. In contrast, Europe's interest in the world expanded with explosive speed and force, and at almost the same time the New World of the Americas and the Old World of East Asia were being reached by ship. During the following three and a half centuries, from 1500 to 1850, the New Worlds in the North and South Pacific were to be probed and then possessed by a variety of European peoples. All this had far-reaching cultural, economic, and political effects everywhere, on the civilizations of Asia, on the more simple cultures of America and the South Pacific, and, equally as important, on Europe herself.

During its explosive expansion, Europe brought two things of vital importance to the several new worlds that together made up the Pacific. The first was her mathematical navigation, still nascent and still incomplete, but, by 1500, tested enough that men were assured that navigation was the future, and that pilotage, although not quite the past, now was certainly the periphery of seamanship. The second and vital thing the Europeans brought was the ship-borne broadside cannon. It is not a complete coincidence that European expansion began dramatically around 1500, and that the first ship's sides were pierced for cannon in 1501. Mathematics now could guide Europeans where they willed, and cannon—broadside cannon—ensured that they could stay. It was not greed, or aggressiveness, or commercial skill that the Europeans brought—these were already there. But the safe and strong ships, capacious and defensible ships which they brought enabled them to explore, to exploit and, in some cases and places, to stay.

This section contains a discussion of the types of warships and working ships that came to explore, how and why they were chosen, and how they developed up until the nineteenth century. Once the routes had been explored and the possibilities of commerce realized, a number of factors coincided to make the nineteenth and early twentieth centuries the climax of Pacific sailing: America was independent; the great European wars of the early nineteenth century were over; and Europe was free to turn her attention away from Napoleon and outward to the world. The Industrial Revolution needed the products of whaling and of Australasian wheatfields and pastures—and men had to sail to the Pacific in order to harvest these products. Whale ships, convict ships, emigrant ships, wool ships, wheat ships, gold clippers, tea clippers, opium clippers—a galaxy of every size and quality crisscrossed the great ocean in an immense crescendo of bartering and empire building.

These new, or at least vastly increased, demands resulted in major developments in the vessels themselves. First, fast wooden clippers replaced Indiamen and wallowing cargo craft; second, iron hulls modified the clippers; and third, steel hull plates and steel rigging made possible construction of the long, mighty windjammers. Steam, aided by inter-ocean canals, in the end drove the big sailing ships from the seas, but in the beginning it helped them by towing the unwieldy craft in and out of harbours, and by powering winches to hoist their huge sails.

The period was a true climax in that it saw both splendid achievement and complete decline—all within a century. It was this growth and this decay which made it a fertile period for great sea writing.

Plate 15. Chinese Junk. These very seaworthy watercraft of ancient design were built on entirely different principles from European ships. Watertight bulkheads, as in the square bow of this example, were used instead of ribs to form the vessel's frame. In the fifteenth century Chinese junks made voyages as far as Africa.

Plate 16. Caravel. Caravels were beautiful, small, and handy craft of the Iberian Peninsula, used particularly by the Portuguese to explore southward along the west coast of Africa searching for water routes to the far east. The original caravels, as in this model, carried lateen sails on all masts.

Plate 17. *Caravela Redonda*. This particular caravel has three masts with lateen sails but also a foremast with square sails to help in long-distance voyaging before the wind. Columbus, for example, rerigged the caravel in his fleet with a square sail on the foremast to help her run ahead of the Trade Winds to America.

Plate 18. This cutaway section of a 60-gun ship shows clearly the complicated interior structure of even the old wooden warships. Open stern galleries for the officers, plainly visible here, were a revival in the late seventeenth century of an Elizabethan structural feature. This type of warship's prominent beakhead had its origin, as did that of the galleon, in the ram of the galley; the beakhead survived partly as decoration, but mainly as a convenient place from which to work along the bowsprit and as privies—the "heads"—for the crewmen.

CHAPTER 7

Warships and Working Ships

Sailing a ship made one realize that man, when creating the
wind-ship, had been inspired by a power greater than himself.

ELIS KARLSSON
OF THE *HERZOGIN CECILIE*

Without the sail real ships would not have been evolved;
without real ships the continents and their people would have
remained separate entities.

ELIS KARLSSON
VETERAN OF TWENTIETH-CENTURY SAIL

Without the sailing ship, the "expansion of Europe" could not have taken place; the ship was the sword of policy or the tool of commerce, whichever the kings and councils decided. To be these things in the Pacific, however, required qualities other than mere mobility. The sword of policy becomes blunt and worn when it is too far from the facilities of its power base. The vehicle of commerce or of exploration faces requirements of sturdiness, capacity, and self-defense which the more confined waters of the Mediterranean and Atlantic already knew, but only mildly in comparison. For centuries, when Pacific bound, European ships, whether Kings' ships carrying out national policies, or trading flutes carrying calico to clothe Eve, were sailing into vast leagues of the unknown. It was realized soon that this required a definite type of sailor, one willing to endure beyond the normal—presuming, of course, that he had any choice in the matter. The officers always had a choice; their ambitions, and the endurance of the seamen will be discussed later. Gradually, it also became clear that the Pacific voyages required ships that had been modified or adapted for conditions which are, it is worth repeating, the conditions of other seas writ large. The problems were not unique but simply larger than life—there was no vastness like the central Pacific, no waves like those at the Horn, no winds like those of the Roaring Forties east of New Zealand. Only some of the ship types designed for lesser waters were found suitable for Pacific conditions. Strength and endurance, for example, proved to be of greater importance than speed, and, paradoxically, ships, such as Cook's *Endeavour* (Plate 44), designed for commerce among the sandbanks of the small and foggy North Sea, proved superb craft, by the standards of their day, among the coral reefs of the huge and sunny South Pacific.

All the details of hull and rigging have their own importance in enabling or hindering Pacific exploration and exploitation, and in the effects these factors of design had on the crews and commanders. These effects were some-times far reaching. The size of the *Bounty*, if it be accepted that confinement exacerbates tension, had an enduring effect on British naval discipline and even on the English language; "Bligh" is a byword for severity—if unfairly so. The strength of the *Golden Hind*, which saved her more than once, was the foundation of a reputation which saved England. Men will flock to follow a reputation—even against an armada.

It was not only the hull shape or the strength of rigging that mattered, for each voyage had a purpose which would affect the choice of craft. Drake selected a craft which could capture treasure by fleetness and force, yet have the capacity to carry home what was a nation's ransom, much less a king's. Anson chose great warships for a great operation of war; Bligh sailed a plodding trader on an odd King's errand which required a floating greenhouse; Quirós selected small ships to explore a myriad of islands; the Dutch developed great Indiamen which could carry tons of wealth and the guns with which to defend them.

Sometimes, it is true, the commanders took whatever they could pry loose from a grudging king or admiralty—as with Anson's crew or Carteret's sloop *Swallow*. In these cases, there are fewer lessons to be learned about judgment than there are about duty, ambition, and perseverance. When some people argue that the Russians could have built exactly what they wanted in the North Pacific, then it must be appreciated that building ships there in the 1730's was in itself a feat. European ships required great trees for the great timbers, the beams, the massive knees, and the masts, but the coast of the Sea of Okhotsk does not have a good climate for trees. The iron for the bolts, the pintles, and the spikes to hold the craft together had to come overland for thousands of miles.

There was no easy answer to the challenges of the Pacific. Should the explorer speed across her vastness in a frigate and risk oversetting if the ship ran aground on one of the uncharted reefs or shoals? Should he plod across in a flat-bottomed cat, safe from oversetting, yet compounding the risks of scurvy by the increment of time? In the beginning, there were poor and tentative decisions by governments in Europe which did not yet know enough about the Pacific. But they soon learned about it as their seamen sailed on her—Portuguese, Spaniards, English, Dutch, French, Russians and Americans. They developed in Europe and modified for use in the Pacific important craft of great variety: caravel, carrack, cat, Indiaman, pink, war-yacht, flute, frigate and galleon. The names themselves are like a song; the ships were in reality prosaic. While it is true that men shape their tools to suit their purpose, it is equally true that the tools they have to hand will alter and shape their actions—as will be seen. Once the risks had been run and the charts drawn, then the clippers and the corvettes could go safely and swiftly where their business took them. But that came later.

European ships which reached the Pacific, from both West and East, from the sixteenth to the early nineteenth centuries, were of various nationalities, and are dealt with in the order of each nation's appearance in the Pacific, except that Portuguese and Spanish ships are grouped together. During the discussion, sometimes ships of different centuries are mentioned; if so, this is clearly stated. Where it seems pertinent, I mention features of certain ships which seem to relate them to ships of another nation—sometimes a nation of Europe, sometimes one of Asia, as in the comparison of the virtues of European lateens and Chinese lug sails, or in the discussion of Dutch and Chinese leeboards, and the English centreboard. Later on, at various places in the book, other ships exemplify certain problems or give weight to important points. None of these vessels, however, is of a different type from the ones to be discussed in this chapter, except the modern ships from the 1840's to the present day. Even these may be considered the same in type; such changes as are apparent are not fundamental, but simply the effects of new and strange materials.

The Portuguese came first as a result of complex economic and historical forces, mainly that of location. Portugal faces west and south onto the seas. In the mid-fifteenth century this meant that her people faced the future, and as a sea people they had developed ships which proved equal to its challenge. Perhaps the most famous of the early Portuguese ships was the caravel (Plate 16). This hauntingly beautiful name now belongs to a famous French airliner, but caravels were originally small coastal craft which gradually developed finer lines than did most contemporary West European ships, influenced in both hull and rigging by Arabian and other Mediterranean craft. Usually of only about sixty to seventy tons, and sixty-five to one hundred feet long, the caravel's beam of twenty to twenty-five feet made it at least comparatively fine lined.

Some early caravels had one complete deck; others had only half-decks. Whatever their decking, they did not have raised forecastles and carried only modestly raised poops above their transom sterns. At first, they had only two lateen-rigged masts, but later three or four (all with lateens) were common (Plate 16). Lateens were large triangular sails slung to a long pole-type yard whose higher end stretched far above and behind the masthead while the lower end swung barely clear of the gunwales. They were like the Chinese junk lug sail in one thing: "The virtue of the lateen, which at first sight seems so ill-suited a sail to such squally coasts as those of the Mediterranean, is that it can always be let go with a run in a heavy blow."[1] Some of the triangular sails already in the Pacific—although there is some argument about this—were of the lateen type, and were called lateen sails in the early journals. Probably Mediterranean lateens, which include Arabian and Egyptian developments, had reached the Pacific from the East, across Darien, almost as soon as they had reached it from the West, but in any event, triangular sails had been in the Pacific for centuries. Much later, twentieth-century Italians "fished out of San Francisco under lateen sail."[2]

Lateen sails act not only as sails taking the pressure of the wind as a direct push, but also as a form of airfoil—a type of "wing," in fact as in poetic descriptions. They are excellent sails in light and cross winds and so caravels were ideally handy ships for the increasingly longer coasting voyages, as Portuguese exploration during the fifteenth century stretched itself southward past Africa. But the huge yards were heavy to handle and the lateen was not as suitable as the square sail for lengthy voyages before the wind; therefore, a type of caravel—the *caravela redonda* (Plate 17)—was developed, with square sails on the foremast and lateens on the mainmast (at the centre) and the mizzen mast (at the rear). This was something like the rerigging that Columbus gave one of his caravels at Madeira before he crossed the Atlantic ahead of the trade winds. This rigging was a forerunner of that used on the modern barquentines, brigantines, and schooners, all of which played a great part in Pacific commerce. Already the pressures of distance were altering form to cope with an altered function. Some caravels had two masts with square sails and only one mast with a lateen. Square sails helped in running before the wind, the retained lateen or lateens helped in manoeuvring. By the time the Portuguese had reached the western portions of the Pacific, these *caravelas redondas* had become *caravelas de armada*—that is, full members of the fleet, capable of sailing anywhere.

The *San Miguel* was a Portuguese *caravela de armada* of only 100 tons burden, built in 1505 for the Orient trade, around Africa to the Spice Islands (Indonesia) on the western fringes of the Pacific. She was designed with a shallow draught for operating in the coastal waters of India and the East Indies. The hull was beamy, or wide, built clinker-style, with overlapping oaken planks—unusual, by definition, in caravels (carvels)—and reinforced by vertical planking in strips up the sides, with rubbing strakes (figure 29) outside of those strips for protection when near docks or other ships.

The tall mainmast carried a mainsail of hand-woven canvas which could be enlarged in good weather by lacing on an addition—called a bonnet—at its foot. A square sail only was carried on the foremast, and a lateen only on the mizzen, but the ship, in addition, had a short mast rising from the outer end of the bowsprit for a small square sail to help in manoeuvring. A rudimentary tiller below the square deck was operated by a man directed by an officer on deck who conned the ship by watching the compass and the sails.[3]

At the top of each single mast (there were no removable upper masts, the hallmark of the later full-rigged ship) was a walled platform to hold archers or musketeers during battle and lookouts during sailing. These platforms, called "tops,"

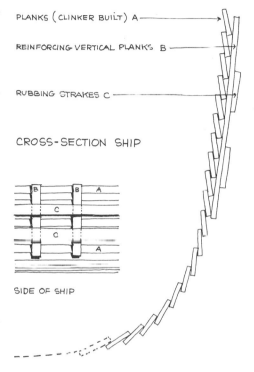

PLANKS (CLINKER BUILT) A

REINFORCING VERTICAL PLANKS B

RUBBING STRAKES C

CROSS-SECTION SHIP

SIDE OF SHIP

Fig. 29. Rubbing Strakes

were quite large on later and larger ships. Melville's character, White Jacket, was a topman in a nineteenth-century American frigate, which meant he was stationed in the tops ready to climb higher to furl or unfurl sails; the platform on which the topmen were stationed was big enough to hold thirty men.[4]

The *San Miguel*'s crew lived forward, almost unprotected from the spray, while the officers lived in tiny cabins in the aftercastle. It was an uncomfortable life for most people, even on shore, in 1501. Accommodation in caravels was always cramped and uncomfortable for longer voyages. For this reason, bigger ships were preferred, and later on, caravels tended to be included in fleets only as auxiliary vessels for inshore work and for carrying despatches. In fact, they were used exactly as Sir Richard Hawkins described English pinnaces being used during the following century, although caravels were somewhat more imposing vessels than pinnaces and were not meant to be rowed.

Even at this early stage, the Pacific was drawing attention to a problem which needed to be solved. Was an entire fleet required in order to have cargo capacity, defensive strength, crew comfort, and yet the ability to probe and explore and chart? Or would it be possible to build a ship which included all these prerequisites?

All the major vessels in the early Portuguese East Indian fleets had to be built to stand the rough seas of the Cape of Good Hope. The new type of caravels were always fully decked and greatly strengthened, and given much more free-board (the distance between the top of the gunwale and the sea), higher bulwarks, and a forecastle as large as their existing aftercastle. The use of the word "castle" to describe the structures at the upper front and rear of ships comes quite simply from the time when they *were* castles, built on board to give soldiers both protection and the advantage of height. With their crenellated shape, they could not properly be called anything else. Later they served as living quarters; the crew lived forward, the officers aft.

Occasionally, a Portuguese ship would sail east into the Pacific proper; one sailed to Mexico in 1589, quite illegally, for although Philip II was King of Portugal and King of Spain the two empires were kept separate and distinct. But it was from the other side, and two generations before the King of Spain had become the King of Portugal as well, that the first crossings of the Pacific had begun. The first European ships on the eastern Pacific were those of Magellan, a Portuguese commander of a Spanish fleet, forced to sail for the Spaniards after a quarrel with his own king. Magellan argued that the eastern islands of the East Indies were far enough east to be in that half of the world the Pope had assigned to Spain in the Bull of 1494. This great diplomatic encounter was by no means so simple, but this is the clearest way of expressing it. Magellan argued that in fact his voyage, as it was undertaken for Spain, was none of Portugal's business. The King of Portugal did not accept that view and tried hard to stop Magellan from sailing.

By this time, Portugal was feeling the draining effects of a century of effort: "Heaven curse the man who first launched timber on to the sea or first unfurled a sail!" their greatest poet wrote. Portugal was straining her energies in exploiting and in protecting what she had already claimed.[5]

Historians do not know many details of Magellan's ships which entered the Pacific from the east around South America in 1517, twelve years after the *San Miguel* was built, but in most ways they would be like her. They averaged about the 100-tons burden of the *San Miguel*; his smallest ship was 75, the largest was 120. The flagship, the *Trinidad*, was 110 tons, about the size of Drake's famous ship of two generations later, and about one third the tonnage of Cook's *Resolution* (Plate 51). She would not have been very different from her fleetmate, the *Victoria* (Plate 1), of which there is a likeness, the only ship of Magellan's fleet to reach Portugal again. The hulls were of seaworthy design, with good underwater lines, but they carried high poops and bows. These upper structures, combined with the limitation of early sixteenth-century rigging, meant that the ships would not sail well to windward.

The ships themselves, although old, had been examined and tested by Magellan's Portuguese lieutenants who had seen the power of the great waves that rolled south of the "Lion of the Seas." By this time, the fierceness of the storms off the coast of Africa was appreciated. (The Portuguese called the Cape of Good Hope the "Lion of the Seas," because of this fierceness.) A Portuguese consul said Magellan's were old and patched ships with "ribs as soft as butter" in which he would not sail as far as the Canaries, but like many consuls he wrote what his master wished to hear.[6] The patching he decried was actually rebuilding and strengthening carried out in Seville under the eyes of men who knew the risks and wished to minimize them. This "patching" succeeded—after all, the *Victoria* did sail home around the world, and not one of the others foundered because of debility. Moreover, forges and grindstones were carried in order to keep the ships in repair. A long voyage, in effect, was almost a community in motion and except when settlement was the object it lacked only women and children to make it complete.

As the Portuguese trade with the East thrived, larger ships did most of the carrying, but because of the growth of the caravels, distinctions between them and cargo *naos* became blurred. "Naos," a rather general term, like "ships," were of about 100 to 300 tons, had adequate upper structures fore and aft, and were ship-rigged, that is, they used square sails except for the lateen mizzen.[7] Columbus had one, and da Gama's and Magellan's fleets also contained both naos and caravels.

Once trade was established, larger vessels, the *naos da carreira da India*, usually called "carracks" (figure 30), were used. The name comes from the Arabic word *qaraqir*, meaning merchant vessel.[8] These were simply the medieval North European cogs, or merchant vessels—so wide they were called "round ships"—as they had been redesigned in southern Europe. A carrack bow—triangular and projecting—was built on above the forecastle. The aftercastle was square, lower than the forecastle, and really rather ugly. Carracks were not handsome ships, but they were capacious, and when built well they were seaworthy too. Carrack rigging had developed from the cog's square sail to the rigging of a full-rigged three-masted ship with the lateen mizzen, particularly suitable for long voyages before the wind, but still reasonably handy in adverse conditions.

By 1500, some Mediterranean carracks were as large as 1,800 tons, equal to the tonnage of a large sailing ship even 400 years later. Portuguese carracks in the East seldom exceeded 1,000 tons, and the more common size was about 500. Even so, they were thought to be too large, for "... whereas five galleons sailing in company amount to a powerful fleet, three *naus* are but three helpless carracks ... when three *naus* leave Goa they cannot all arrive safely without a miracle."[9] This anonymous critic, in 1651, quoted the case of the *Reliquias*, which "foundered on setting sail before actually leaving the port."[10] Using similar reasoning, the Spaniards tended to use galleons which were smaller, faster, and more manoeuvrable—except for the sometimes huge Manila Galleon which sailed annually from the Philippines to Mexico and back. These ships became bigger and bigger until one, the *Rosario*, was over 1,700 tons. Often, Manila Galleons were 1,000 tons, but even so they were usually so grossly overloaded as to be in danger.[11]

It was one of the giant Portuguese carracks, the *Madre de Dios*, rated by Hakluyt at 1,600 tons, that the English captured on her way home in 1592. The *Daintie*, an English ship mentioned later, played a most active part in the battle. The cargo of the *Madre de Dios* made some Englishmen wealthy. Spices, silks, damasks, brocades, satins, pearls, sandalwood, coral, ivory, and various drugs—rhubarb was first imported to Europe as a medicine—were part of her fabulous freighting. Even Drake's voyage through the Pacific had done little more to fire the imagination of the English; the merchants and the statesmen realized that trade with the East was a road to wealth, and both English and Dutch decided to follow it.

For decades the Portuguese had had the East almost to themselves, and on the network of trade routes they used both Western and Eastern watercraft, including a great many junks. They used carracks for sailing to Macao in China and for going to Japan, but there were *galeaos* (galleons) too, primarily war vessels. At first, it was hard to draw a clear line between galleons and carracks, but as the carracks increased in size—in spite of laws prohibiting this—the distinction became clear; galleons (figure 30) were not only handier but also smaller. However, some Portuguese galleons of over 1,000 tons were built. The major difference was the different ratio of length to breadth, the galleon being much longer and narrower than the carrack; the most obvious difference in appearance was that the galleon had a beak head while the carrack had its distinctive forecastle.

Most of the great Portuguese carracks—"mountains of wood" as Admiral Corte-Real called them when attempting to reform the Portuguese Navy[12]— were built in the East, because of the excellent teak timber that was available. Teakwood is beautiful, durable, and resistant to worms and splintering. Gradually, as local pilots led them around the ancient Eastern trade routes to the ancient Eastern ports, the carracks and galleons passed China and reached Japan. Here they were known as *Kora Fune* or "black ships"—a name revived by the Japanese 300 years later for the ships of the American Commodore Perry which led Japan into the modern world. Carracks were used in the Japanese trade until the attacks of the English and Dutch in the early seventeenth century gradually forced dispersal of the annual cargo into several faster and smaller vessels.

Spanish vessels were very much like the Portuguese, and certainly sailors of each nation often sailed in ships of the other. Although galleons are the ships usually associated with Spain, she used carracks and caravels as well. During the seventeenth and eighteenth centuries, vessels from both countries of the Iberian peninsula developed in similar ways to the vessels from Holland, England and France. There were always national differences, but the similarities in European ship development—for example, in the various Indiamen—far outweighed the distinctive details brought about by national taste or economy as the problems of sailing in the Pacific forced similar solutions.

One interesting misconception which shows the similarity of development is the confusion about galleons. They are usually thought of, romantically, as Spanish ships, whereas in many ways the English led both in their design and in their use. To think of Spanish galleons is to think of Sir Francis Drake, by almost unconscious association, yet it was in an English galleon (Plate 19) that he sailed into and across the Pacific to circumnavigate the world.

Drake's ship, the *Golden Hind* (Plate 62), was of exceptionally sturdy build. Perhaps her intended preservation at Deptford implies that she also was built there as a Queen's ship expressly for the great voyage of 1577. She was of about 100 tons burden and carried 18 guns; the number of guns is confirmed by the testimony of prisoners, after Spanish defeats in the Pacific.[13]

To modern eyes, the *Golden Hind* would seem a tiny ship. Exact information is not available for her as it is for later ships, such as those of Byron or of Cook, but apparently her keel was about forty-seven feet long, her beam (or width inside the planking) about eighteen feet, and the depth of her hold about nine and a half.[14] Only twenty-three good paces would encompass her overall length of slightly over sixty feet, less than twice that of the tiny *Spray*, which was so small that Slocum could sail her round the world alone 300 years later. Yet Drake had to stow aboard guns and a crew, and the supplies for both. Once gold and silver had been captured and taken aboard, it is no wonder that the ship sat disconcertingly deep in the water. Every prisoner noted, with much personal feeling in most cases, that the ship was well ballasted "with silver, chests of gold, and reals of eight."[15] Whatever her other deficiencies, her ballast was sufficient to see her home, and to ensure that her captain became an immensely wealthy and famous knight.

Some weight had to be jettisoned to save her when she grounded on the way home, but essentially she was saved by her smallness and strength. All Spanish reports agree that the *Golden Hind* was "in a great measure stout and strong"; she was said to be of French pattern—an early compliment to French skill in shipbuilding.[16] In writings about the sea, this laudatory reference to French ships is often found: "French-built, isn't she?" "Yes, my lord. They are great ship-builders."[17] It should be noted that actually it was the French design that was superior. English shipbuilders built very competently, but their creativity was hampered by conservatism.

Most reports by the Spaniards who had fought the *Golden Hind* greatly exaggerated her tonnage, armament, and crew. In one statement, she was estimated to be of 400 tons; in another, the "Corsair's vessel" was said to carry 150 men, only 14 short of the total of the crews of Drake's original fleet of 5.[18]

In spite of her strength, she needed repairs and overhaul, having battled and survived the worst seas in the world at Cape Horn before these particular Spaniards saw her. No wonder she needed repair—a small sixteenth-century vessel had lived where many large ships of the culmination of sailing ship design were to die. One Spaniard spoke of the *Golden Hind*'s need to be careened, another of her leaking when the sea was high, "whether sailing before the wind or with the bowlines hauled out."[19] "The bowlines hauled out" meant that she was sailing across the wind with the bowlines hauled tight to hold the windward edge of the sail into the wind. It was for the purpose of attaching these bowlines well forward that the bowsprit, a spar extending forward from the bow, was first designed. Sailing across the wind, battling the sea, would make the ship "work," or flex, which might well make her leak. The Spaniard, however, also observed that she carried workmen and a forge and was obviously prepared to make repairs. A Flemish prisoner of Drake's, when released, told the Spaniards he thought Drake intended to strengthen her "with a solid wale so as to enable her to carry more sail and be fit for the long voyage she would have to make in order to reach the Moluccas."[20]

Few people in England underestimated the wealth that could be won, albeit won hard, in the Spanish American Empire, but there were many who looked to trade and to the Portuguese Indies as being easier and even more rewarding. The capture of the *Madre de Dios* by an English fleet had shown what wealth was there; spices were almost as valuable as gold and could be gained without fighting either the Spanish or the gales of the Straits of Magellan.

English ships began to challenge the Portuguese domination of the Far East at about the same time as the Dutch did, at the end of the sixteenth century. In the very first years of the seventeenth century, Sir James Lancaster's *Red Dragon* approached the Pacific, as had the Dutch and Portuguese ships, from the opposite route to Magellan's *Victoria* and Drake's *Golden Hind*; he had come from the West and they from the East. Sir James was more a merchant than a warrior and aimed to trade with the Orientals and not to raid the Spaniards. Perhaps this is the reason why, when he bought the *Malice Scourge* from the Earl of Cumberland, he renamed her the *Red Dragon*, as evocative then as now of the distant East. The promoters of the voyage knew that Lancaster had been and still was essentially a merchant. They organized themselves into the famous East India Company while the ships were being readied, and the decision was made not to appoint a high-born commander. The promoters thought it better "to sort their business with men of their own quality."[21] Although a merchant, Lancaster also had been a good soldier and his proven capacity for command, hard won in the West Indies and Brazil, earned him the appointment of General of the Fleet of the (English) East India Company.

The *Red Dragon* was a vessel of 600 tons and, of necessity, was as much prepared for war as she was for trade. Violence was, and remained so until at least the mid-nineteenth century, a problem of Pacific waters. When a ship traded for sea otters in British Columbia, it had to be prepared for defense; when a ship sailed the South China seas, it had to be armed against pirates. Danger was so much a day-to-day event that the sailors thought it almost normal, but there was the special hazard of a ship out of contact with the world for months at a time, hailing another European ship without knowing if she was friend or enemy, without knowing who was fighting whom at home.

Lancaster's ship could not have been very different from the *Daintie* of Sir Richard Hawkins. It is likely that she was a large, three-masted galleon-type ship of the kind that developed later into the East Indiamen of both Holland and England, although a large ship of that time might well have had a fourth mast. A contemporary sketch shows one with four masts.

Even if they were well adapted to the needs of the seventeenth and eighteenth centuries, one could argue that the pattern of Indiamen (figure 30) proved too successful, for their excellent adaptation to eighteenth-century conditions inhibited their changing to meet those of the nineteenth. They were not changed, except very slowly and in minor detail, and those of the English did not improve enough to face strong competition until the American clippers forced a drastic reappraisal of British ship design after the removal of commercial protection in the mid-nineteenth century. It had to be forced before it was faced. Shipbuilders, like sailors, are conservative, for the very good reason that they know men's lives depend on their efforts.

As Indiamen were a combination of cargo ships and fighting ships, they developed in the same way, and came to look very much like the frigates— fast fighting ships equivalent to a modern cruiser. They were deliberately painted to look even more like frigates in order to discourage pirates. Eighteenth- and nineteenth-century Indiamen were as smart as Royal Navy ships in appearance and discipline. The most famous Indiamen were those of the English East India Company, and they occasionally sailed as far as China; however, the English sailed real warships and real cargo ships in the Pacific also. Both types had their advantages. The cargo ships, at any rate the small handy type used, were safer in unknown and possibly reef-studded waters, because they were both manoeuvrable and comparatively flat bottomed. But they could not be well enough armed to deal with hostile warships or well-armed pirates, and they were also slow on the long ocean voyages outward and homeward.

A famous British fleet which combined several sizes of warships with cargo ships is that of Commodore Anson, which was sent out in 1741 during the War of Jenkins's Ear to damage the ports and shipping of Spain's Pacific Empire. His chief ship, the *Centurion* (see Plate 4), circumnavigated the globe and brought home a treasure comparable to Drake's.

The *Centurion*, a ship-of-the-line, and flagship of Anson's fleet, reached the Straits of Magellan in early 1742. She was a warship sent to make war— the other hazards of sailing in the Pacific were beside the point. Yet she became the classic example of several of these hazards. A ship-of-the-line was a ship built strongly enough to play her part in the line of battle, hence the name "ship-of-the-line-of-battle," and today, by simplification, "battleship."

The name "ship-of-the-line" evolved from the description of a battle tactic. In 1653, the English Navy (because Parliament said there was no king, it was not called the Royal Navy at that time) issued instructions which required the fleet to sail into action in line astern (one behind the other) in order that their broadsides would be more effective, as most of the great guns fired only to the side.[22] This tactic had been foreshadowed in the battle against Spain's Armada. All ships had to be sufficiently strong to cope with any potential opponent in the enemy line; therefore, the ships of war were divided into rates describing their strength. A first-rate ship had over ninety guns, a second-rate over eighty (Plate 20), a third-rate over sixty (Plate 18), a fourth-rate over thirty-eight, a fifth over eighteen, and a sixth over six. Only the first three rates were considered heavy enough to be in the line of battle.

"Heavy" was meant literally, for the ship had to be built to be strong enough not only to carry over sixty heavy guns, but also to stand their recoil; big enough to carry not only the powder and the shot to feed the guns, but also the men to handle them. Such a ship would also need to be strong

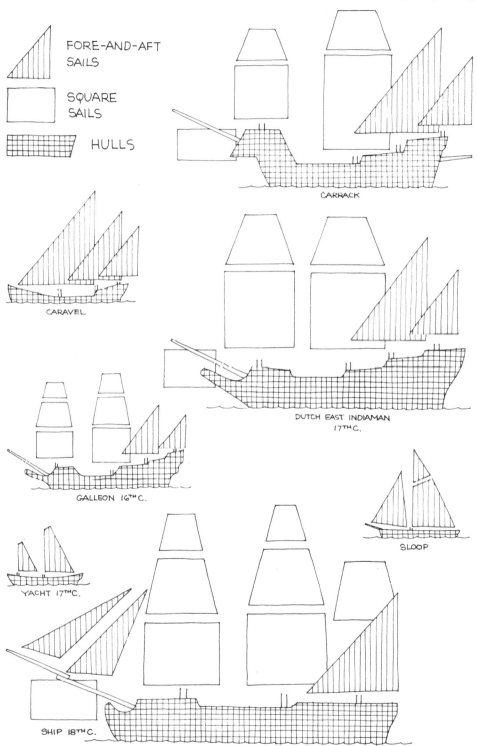

FORE-AND-AFT SAILS

SQUARE SAILS

HULLS

CARRACK

CARAVEL

DUTCH EAST INDIAMAN 17TH C.

GALLEON 16TH C.

SLOOP

YACHT 17TH C.

SHIP 18TH C.

Fig. 30. Profiles and Sail Plans of Representative European Exploration Vessels

enough to stand up to enemy fire. By the nineteenth century, some ships-of-the-line had hulls of solid oak more than a foot thick at the waterline.[23]

Keeping station in line of battle required both the ability to take punishment, and skill in sailing tactics and in handling sails. The line itself could not have been formed or maintained if the developments in rigging had not kept pace with those in gunnery and tactics. Eighteenth-century ships-of-the-line were full-rigged ships with three masts (figure 30). By the mid-eighteenth century, many of the lateens at the mizzen had been replaced by gaff sails which were simply lateens shorn of the canvas in front of the mast. During that century, the jib replaced the spritsail topsail at the bow, but a small sail under the jib-boom was retained on many ships.

The *Centurion* was the first ship-of-the-line in the Pacific. The Pacific also saw the last of the purely sail-driven ships-of-the-line, H.M.S. *Ganges*.[24] In the Pacific too, the last of the old-time broadsides were fired near South America when the wooden corvette H.M.S. *Amethyst* and the iron-built but unarmoured H.M.S. *Shah* fought the Peruvian ship *Huascar*.[25] There were many small actions under sail, but the great battles between Pacific fleets did not occur until the twentieth century when steam and armour had changed many things. The tactical principle remained valid, however; Japanese, Russian, British, German, Dutch, Australian, and American ships all fought at different times in line of battle. In spite of this, the story of Pacific sailing is not really a warlike one; there were raids, but no great battles in that ocean during the days of sail. At that time the Pacific was peripheral; the enduring fame of Anson and Drake is centred on the English Channel and the coast of Spain.

In addition to his ship-of-the-line and other warships, Anson's fleet contained two "pinks," the *Anna* and the *Industry*. Developed from the Dutch flute, pinks were carriers which could be operated cheaply, because they provided a great deal of cargo space in relation to crew size, and therefore were an excellent choice for supply ships. It is likely that pinks were built in England in large numbers in the early eighteenth century as replacements for the Dutch ships which had been captured in the wars of the seventeenth century.

Up until late in the eighteenth century, a ship usually took its name from its hull rather than from its rigging; from then onwards, it was the rigging that determined the name, although many of the names were still vague and indefinite. Sterns were a distinguishing feature of hull types. A pink was a pink-sterned ship, the word "pink" having nothing to do with colour, but meaning that the stern is narrow at the top and wider below, something like the flute stern (figure 31), as would be expected. It is commonly seen today on small boats. Sterns could also be the mark of the nationality of ships. The *Centurion* had a round stern. In the seventeenth century, this would have marked her as an English ship, but the extra strength achieved was such that by the mid-eighteenth century many ships of other European sea powers were also being built this way.

All the merchant vessels—flutes, pinks, and galiots (figure 48)—would seem to have been quite suited for exploration as store ships or for special tasks, such as the *Bounty*'s transporting breadfruit plants. They were comparatively easy to handle and not too big for the narrow shallow channels and lurking reefs they would encounter; yet they carried plenty of cargo to ensure a provision margin on long voyages away from bases.

This was the reasoning that led to the choice of a specific type of merchant ship for Cook's voyages. The *Endeavour* is famous as the first ship Cook sailed on the Pacific; her association is with the greatness of her captain, yet she had her other qualities too—and she was with Cook because of them. The qualities were of a type rather than of an individual, for she was a cat, built at Whitby, a typical collier for the east coast coal trade from the North to London. The name "cat"

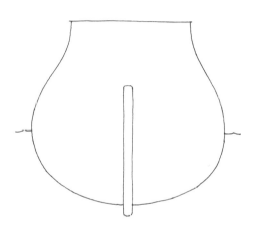

Fig. 31. Flute Hull, End-On

probably is of Norse origin, and to say a ship is "cat-built" is a way of describing her wide bow, without the beak head of a pink or a frigate, and her flat roomy hull.[26]

One hundred and six feet in length, the *Endeavour* was more than one and a half times the length of the *Golden Hind*, but she was not large for her day. She was nearly 30 feet wide and of 368 tons burden, but it was her shape that was important. As she was built to carry a great deal of cargo, she could carry a good many men and provisions. She was almost flat bottomed, and so Cook knew she would not overset if she took the ground (ran onto a submerged rock or reef or sandbank) in the strange seas he intended to sail. In spite of the Royal Navy's successful experiment in coppering a frigate, her flat bottom was not coppered to prevent damage from shipworms, but instead was sheathed with a thin extra outer plank and "filled" by having flat-headed nails driven in so closely together that they covered the sheathing. The rust which formed sealed the sheathing completely.

A ship of the *Endeavour*'s size would normally be either ship- or barque-rigged, and her fitters had the choice when remasting her. If completely ship-rigged, she would have had a lower, top and top-gallant mast at each of the fore, main and mizzen positions. In fact, her mizzen mast had no top-gallant mast. If barque-rigged, she would have set only fore-and-aft sails on her mizzen mast, whereas in fact she set a square mizzen topsail. She was strictly neither barque nor ship; she was "a sort of ship-rigged cat." It is possible her riggers thought that a square mizzen topsail would give her better before-the-wind qualities than a barque would have in Pacific long-distance cruising, and yet wished to avoid, for reasons of simplicity of maintenance, the mizzen top-gallant mast and sail of a ship.

Some of her interior deck space was divided into cabins for the scientists and artists that she carried. In addition to these extra people and the extra equipment for them, the stowage of two years' provisions also justified the choice of a cargo ship instead of a frigate. Seaworthy if slow, she sailed at her best pace at about only eight knots. The *Endeavour*'s only fault, according to her famous captain, was a tendency to drift to leeward, which could be expected of her flat-bottomed build.

Both the *Resolution* and *Adventure* (Plate 38) of Cook's second voyage were built at Whitby by the same builder who had built the *Endeavour*, which was now far away acting as a store ship in the Falklands. Their purchase was a great tribute to the *Endeavour*'s qualities. The first new ship was almost 100 tons larger than the *Endeavour*, the second was 30 tons smaller. The *Resolution*, the bigger ship, was nearly 111 feet long and of 35½ feet maximum width or beam, with the round-cheeked bow and roomy hull of her type; the smaller ship's dimensions were 97 feet by 28 feet. The *Resolution* was classed as a sloop-of-war—the smallest warship if the smaller cutters, which usually were either coastal or ship's auxiliary craft, are not counted. Sloops-of-war were rigged either as ships or snows, two-masted vessels differing from brigs only in having the fore-and-aft sail on a spar just behind the mainmast instead of on the mainmast itself.

The *Resolution* had three masts, and she was rigged as a ship, having a mizzen top-gallant mast which the *Endeavour* had lacked. Both she and her consort were altered in order to accommodate more men, more stores, and guns. Sheathed and filled against shipworms, just as Cook's first Pacific ship had been, the ships were not given any special protection against ice, even though it was intended that they would be sailing in high latitudes. Care and efficiency were to be their safeguards. Cook was already famous, and the *Adventure*'s captain, Tobias Furneaux, was a competent seaman, who, even

Plate 19. An English galleon of the type Sir John Hawkins did so much to develop. During the reign of Elizabeth I, Sir John's nephew, Francis Drake, and his son, Richard Hawkins, sailed the Pacific in ships looking very much like this model. The two rear masts of this galleon's four would carry lateen rather than square sails.

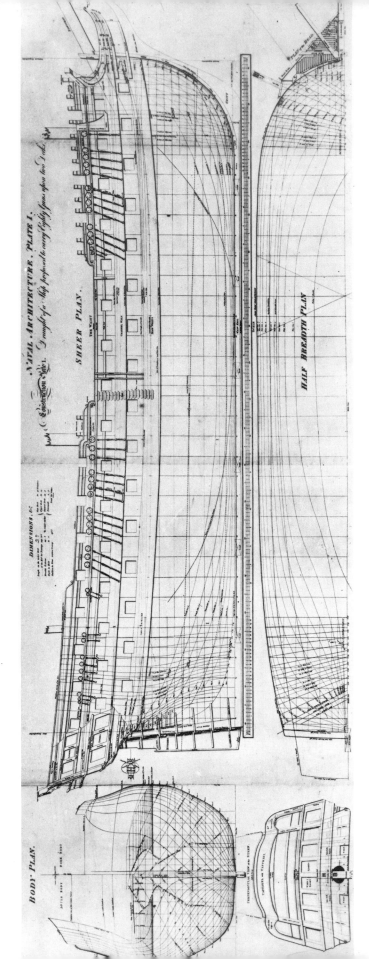

Plate 20. 80-gun ship. These lines, or plans, of a ship were used as an aid in designing a new vessel. Roughly the equivalent of contour lines on a map, the lines on this plan represent in two dimensions the three dimensions of a ship's hull. These lines could be "taken off" a particularly successful ship and used as an aid in copying her.

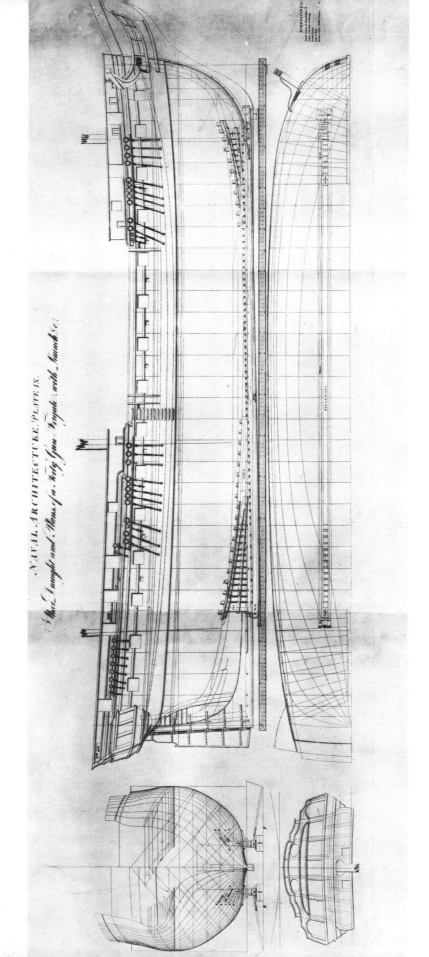

Plate 21. The lines of a 40-gun frigate, slightly larger than the *Dolphin* or *Boudeuse*. The frigate differs from the 80-gun ship-of-the-line (Plate 20) in having only one complete gun deck. Occasionally two-decker ships-of-the-line were converted to frigates by removing one gun deck. The frigate was in some ways the equivalent of the modern cruiser—relatively well-armed yet extremely fast and graceful.

Plate 22. The *Heemskerck* and the *Zeehaen*. In 1642 the Dutch explorer Abel Tasman led an expedition in these two ships from the Dutch East Indies south of Australia to New Zealand, Tonga, and Fiji. His *Zeehaen* (left) was a flute, with the extremely narrow stern and strong tumble-home of her type; the

if he lacked Cook's enterprise, nevertheless was the first man to have sailed twice around the world—once from east to west, and then from west to east.

All Cook's ships were small, but their lack of size was certainly no indication of potential fame. The most famous ship of the Pacific, the *Bounty*, was not imposing in appearance nor exciting in performance; she won her fame, not because of beauty or achievement, but partly by the manner of her going and partly by being the stage for an epic human drama. That drama made the name of Captain Bligh at first famous, and later infamous. His name is as linked with the name of his ship as the names of Drake and Slocum are linked with theirs.

The *Bounty* (Plate 58) was a small ship, 215 tons, 8 guns, and only 46 men, although, given the personalities, these proved at least 2 too many for a peaceful voyage. It was the confinement in small ships which proved to be their greatest disadvantage under the conditions of the Pacific. What is bearable in the Atlantic Ocean for six weeks is not necessarily bearable in the Pacific for six months. The *Bounty* had been the merchant vessel *Bethia* and, like several others of the ships being discussed, her name had been changed. She was bought by the Admiralty because she had room enough in her to carry something special—not the plants most scientists were collecting about this time to add to the world's knowledge, but breadfruit trees to transplant to the West Indies. She was only ninety-one feet long and twenty-three feet wide, a tiny ship to loom so large and so long in the imagination of men. But, although small, she was nevertheless a fully-rigged ship, nearly new and newly coppered. The *Bounty*'s figurehead was a woman, who, for some reason known only to her creator, was in riding habit.

If there were cats like the *Endeavour* and pinks like the *Anna* or the *Industry* among the merchants ships used for exploration, there were also warships other than ships-of-the-line. Frigates were good ships, fast and handy; indeed, the famous clippers of the nineteenth century are directly descended, through American privateers, from French frigates. They were used by Spanish, British, French, Russian, and Austrian explorers of the Pacific. Frigates (Plate 21) were medium-sized warships with one gun-deck, developed from a Mediterranean vessel which originally could be rowed. The prototype French frigate was probably built in Dunkirk as a fast ship to be used as a privateer, and the English and American frigates, at least many of the best ones, were copied from those of the French. (The famous eighteenth-century warships are meant here; the sixteenth-century Spanish frigates were actually merchant ships.[27] One name has been used for two quite different types of ship. As with both rigging and hulls, there was much that was indefinite in nomenclature.)

Perhaps they were too fast, perhaps so beautiful and strong as to evoke un-warranted confidence, but when the days of exploration were over the frigates did not have the record of success and survival that Cook's less beautiful, less swift, and less prestigious vessels had; nearly all the humble ships got home, with very few losses in men. Cook, the master mariner and explorer, should have known, and he kept using Whitby cats.

The *Dolphin* (Plate 63), a frigate, was 130 feet long, 34 feet wide, and 511 tons burden, much bigger than any of Cook's ships. She was a fifth-rate, with thirty-two guns, normally rigged with fore, main, and mizzen masts, and no royal. Her main distinguishing feature was an unusually long quarter-deck which reached almost half-way forward. She was the third ship of the Royal Navy to be copper sheathed, and as the procedure was still experimental, dockyard officers made complete inspections after her second circumnavigation under Captain Wallis. Their reports of the absence of shipworm damage and of weeds and barnacles vindicated coppering. Copper rudder braces and pintles (a form of hinge arrangement) had also been used, because it was already known that copper injured iron fittings, although it was not known that the damage was the result of electrolytic action. The *Dolphin*'s voyages under Byron and Wallis immediately preceded those of Captain Cook. Probably his knowledge of these frigate voyages had something to do with the type of ship he chose for his own exploration.

Dutch exploration began later than the English, if Drake and Cavendish are to be classed as explorers as well as raiders. The first Dutch ships reached the borders of the Pacific from the same direction as the Portuguese, and from the opposite direction to the first English or Spanish ships. These Dutch ships had unique features arising from the need to build ships fit for long voyages in stormy waters, but still able to navigate the particularly shallow and confined waters of the Netherlands itself. To get to the East Indies—the main area of Dutch imperial interest—a ship had to round the Cape of Good Hope; called at first the Cape of Storms, it came to be called *the* Cape—the singular form implying *the* cape of capes. Yet the same deep-water ships had to be able to bring heavy loads into the docks at home. The Dutch achieved this compromise in design as they achieved so many other things—by in-genuity and application. Sir Walter Raleigh thought Dutch enterprise amaz-ing—they had no trees, yet were famous for good wooden ships; they had shallow home waters, yet were famous deep-sea navigators. Dutch ships seemed ubiquitous. By 1610, it was reckoned that there were 16,000 of them trading wherever there happened to be ports: "And, blowe which way the winde would, they [*i.e.*, the Dutch] had shipping to come thither, eyther from the East or from the West."[28]

Because of this emphasis on shallow draught, Dutch ships were more lightly built and less heavily ornamented (there is a relationship between draught and ornamentation, of course) than either the English or French ships. The Dutch also used clinker-construction on upper works, such as the quarter galleries and the planking of the poop, with the idea of combining lightness and strength. Because of these construction features, their ships differed slightly in appearance from those of other European sea powers. Again because of their shallow home waters, ships of the Dutch line-of-battle usually had only two gundecks, compared to the three gundecks of many big English, French, and Spanish ships. Moreover there was a Dutch move to simplify rigging, the success of which was emphasized when Raleigh complained that an English ship of 100 tons required a crew of 30, while the Dutch could handle a ship of that size with only 10 men.

The Dutch developed well-armed Indiamen for their Eastern trade, as did the English and French. Indiamen were sturdy and comfortable ships, capable of carrying a large cargo and of defending it, for trade in the East bore some resemblance to war. These were not the qualities needed for exploration, for the main quality required of a successful exploring ship was manoeuvrability in confined waters. But the Dutch tried some exploration with Indiamen, and their sturdiness and comfort proved useful.

In 1641, a standard Dutch East Indiaman, the *Oostcappel*, proved barely sturdy enough for the storms off Japan. Her commander, Tasman, learned enough about weather in that area to add to the already formidable reputation those waters had.[30] Japanese waters have maintained that reputation. Captain West, a whaler in the nineteenth century, described sailing east of Japan as cruising in "snow, fog, hail, wind and rain mostly."[31] A Russian with Krusenstern, during the first years of the same century, found that the bad weather off Japan "exceeded all my expectations."[32] This kind of weather, plus the North Pacific's reputation, delayed its exploration for another century, although the Dutch tried once more under a Captain Vries. Then their eyes turned southwards, and to explore there they chose a different type of ship.

The Dutch East India Company in 1642 gave the tough and experienced Tasman the *Heemskerck* and a consort, the *Zeehaen* (Plate 22), in order to search for the "still unreached South and Easternland" and other lands too, "for the improvement, and increase of the Compy's general welfare."[33] The *Heemskerck* had sixty men aboard and the *Zeehaen* fifty. They were able to sail successfully in company, seemingly without the difficulties of keeping together that other pairs of exploration ships had encountered, except for a constant bickering about signals and the acknowledgment of them. The *Heemskerck* was a small three-masted war-yacht of 120 tons, and the *Zeehaen* was a flute, also with three masts. Tasman's war-yacht, in contrast to the flute, had a square stern, a sharper bottom, and greater width.

Dutch waters were, and still are, full of a variety of small craft and the lone voyage yachts encountered in the twentieth century have derived many features besides their name from the seventeenth-century Dutch yacht (figure 30). "Yacht" is a Dutch name now adopted internationally. In the 1640's in Holland, a yacht—as opposed to a war-yacht—was a small vessel designed originally for personal travel on the canals and local waters. Usually yachts were rigged with one mast carrying a fore-and-aft sail, with a three-cornered foresail on the stay from topmast to bow, or with two fore-and-aft-rigged masts and a jib-boom with jib hoisted to the fore masthead. The two-masted rig was definitely a schooner, although the name "schooner" is American and of uncertain derivation. Schooners (figure 48) are now a common rig in the South Pacific; the Dutch had brought in variants of that rig years before any American schooner had sailed that ocean.

Tasman's flute, the *Zeehaen*, was different in hull shape from his war-yacht. Essentially, the difference was that the flute was round sterned, flat bottomed, and narrow, with a pronounced tumble-home, or slope inwards of the sides from just above the waterline (figure 31). Hawkins, the English sea commander, discussing at length the loss of his beloved *Daintie* to a Spanish fleet, mentioned the disadvantages of the tumble-home, this "overmuch homing." He claimed it cut down room, made the ship "tender sided, and unable to carry sayle in any fresh gaile of winde."[34] He was right; expert opinion today argues that tumble-home made a ship top-heavy. Opinions varied, but most seventeenth- and eighteenth-century ships had some tumble-home of the sides, because the builders believed it helped keep the decks dry in a crossing sea.

Flutes will be discussed at greater length later, because they entered the Pacific as the standard cargo carriers of several European countries, the Netherlands among them, in the seventeenth and eighteenth centuries. Even this one type of craft varied according to the nationality of its builders, but it was not only the details of hull construction that made the ships of the various countries recognizable. Rigging had national characteristics, so did the way the ship was handled. National differences in both food and regard for hygiene affected the odour of the vessels; a ship in a fog or dark could often be recognized from leeward (or downwind) as Portuguese, Dutch, English, or French, if a particularly odorous freight (for example, slaves, *guano* or copra) did not outscent the infused odour of the ship as a living organism. For all these reasons, the first Dutch ships to visit the East would be recognized by the Portuguese as intruders, almost as readily as the Maoris would recognize Tasman as one.

Tasman's flagship, the *Limsnen*, on a second southern voyage, carried fifty-six men, and his second main ship, the *Zeemeeuw*, carried forty-one. They were fairly large vessels, possibly with three masts, and probably were war-yachts similar to the *Heemskerck* of his first southern voyage. The galiot *Brac* (Beagle) carried fourteen men. Besides early yachts in the Pacific there was also an early *Beagle*, if the waters between the islands of Indonesia are to be counted as part of the Pacific, as they are in this book. Normally, a galiot was a small trading vessel with a main and a mizzen mast gaff-rigged, with a square topsail on the main and a triangular fore staysail, a jib, and a flying jib. But, as the Swedish expert Landström points out about Europe's boats, "the small coastal vessels showed a multifarious collection of sails," and a particular rig cannot be guaranteed.[35]

Dutch shipping in the Pacific retained its own character mainly because of conditions at home, and not because of the conditions of the Pacific. Its hallmarks were simplicity, utility, and adaptability, as befits a nation of meagre resources, but great ingenuity. The Dutch adjustments to Pacific conditions, however, did not differ greatly from those of the other European nations, that is, they used large Indiamen for safe commodious transport and smaller, handier craft for exploration. The Dutch, English, and French, like the Portuguese and Spanish, had arrived in their own ways at roughly the same conclusions.

Although French nationals had been in the Pacific as buccaneers and traders much earlier, the great days of exploration by France in that ocean were from the 1760's onwards. She too used a variety of ships. In the eighteenth century especially, France had a well deserved reputation as a builder of good ships. The *Boudeuse*, like the British *Dolphin*, was a famous eighteenth-century frigate of Pacific exploration. The *Boudeuse* was a comparatively small frigate of twenty-six guns. She was not well preserved, but as became her French design and building, she was both beautiful and fast. In the time of the *Boudeuse* the frigate as the type of ship known by Nelson and Villeneuve, the "eyes of the fleet," had only recently reached its definite form. By the 1760's, it was a fast square-rigged ship with one gundeck carrying usually twenty-eight to thirty-two guns; the *Boudeuse* with twenty-six was small. So was her storeship, the *Etoile*, but she was so sturdy compared to the frigate that the commander of the expedition thought they could always sail home in her if necessary. In many cases, it was the sturdy workships that became famous.

The *St. Jean Baptiste* was not quite one breed or the other. Her 650 tons and 36 guns made her frigate-size and frigate-armed, but she was built as a merchant ship, to be commodious. She was decorated in the beautiful fashion of French, English, and Iberian ships—the practical Dutch spent their money on hold space and efficient rigging—with sixteen windows set in her graceful stern. In effect, she was a French Indiaman.

De Surville, her commander, had a fine naval record as a "man attentive to details, who has commanded the King's ships with distinction."[36] His second-in-command, Labé, like Jacques Cartier (the discoverer of Quebec and of spruce beer) came from St. Malo in Normandy, a nursery of the fine seamen of the Newfoundland fisheries and the French merchant marine. By definition, Normans have ancestral links with both France and England, and oddly enough Labé had just given up the command of a ship called the *Concorde*. His story of the *St. Jean Baptiste*'s voyage exists, although Commander de Surville did not survive.

A number of French explorers had reached the same conclusion as Cook and used merchant vessels. The *Mascarin* was a flute, but her consort, the *De Castries*, at sixteen guns, would have been rated as a sloop-of-war in England. These ships reached the Pacific in 1772 by sailing eastwards from the Indian Ocean along 46° S, a little north of the *Resolution*'s first track. On the way, they stopped at the Marion Islands, named after the captain of the *Mascarin*, Marc Joseph Marion, Sieur du Fresne. An excellent sailor, Marion had been commander of the *Prince de Conty* which had taken Bonnie Prince Charlie, the Young Pretender, back to France after the Battle of Culloden.

The exploration vessel, *Astrolabe*, was a flute of approximately 500 tons altered and called a frigate for navy listing, but used by La Pérouse on his voyage of exploration in 1786 for the same reasons that Cook had used a collier cat—because of the hull capacity which the flute's cargo carrying purpose ensured. Her bottom was protected from worms by being "filled" with nails, and she was also given extra keel protection to fit her for Pacific exploration. She rounded Cape Horn as easily and fortunately as had the *Endeavour*, so her commander, La Pérouse, was convinced that "the difficulties that one expects to meet are the result of an old preconception that should disappear."[37] He did not live long enough to learn differently.

European ships were also being built in the newly acquired Russian East Asian territory to the north of Japan. For the leadership of the expedition which expanded the already huge Russian Empire across the North Pacific into America, Emperor Peter the Great chose Vitus Bering, a highly competent Danish sailor. Bering's two ships, the *St. Peter* and *St. Paul*, the names reminiscent of Quirós's one ship, the *San Pedro y Pablo*, were launched there in 1740. Each was eighty feet long, twenty feet wide, and nine feet in depth, with two masts which were brig-rigged.

Bering's ships—Waxell calls them packet boats—carried fourteen small guns each; no one knew what they might encounter. Guns, anchors, and all other iron fittings had to be brought laboriously overland from Russia, although some of the fittings were made at the iron mines in Siberia.

While Bering's ships were being built in the 1740's, another Russian expedition sailed for Japan in vessels which had been constructed at Kamchatka by Captain Spangberg, one of Bering's officers. The *Archangel Michael* was a hooker and the other, the *Hope,* was a double sloop. A hooker (figure 48) was a Dutch-type vessel. The Dutch had much influence over Baltic and Russian shipbuilding; Peter the Great himself had once worked in a Dutch shipyard. Hookers were also used extensively in the Baltic, and, as Spangberg was a Dane, perhaps this was the source of the influence. They were small vessels with a large square-rigged mainmast and a very small gaff-rigged mizzen, and instead of a foremast they used a large jib and a flying jib on a jib-boom, a retractable extension of the bowsprit.[38]

The term "double sloop," when applied to the *Hope* is less simple to explain. A sloop-of-war in the eighteenth century was a warship smaller than a frigate and usually rigged in the same manner, although some authorities specify cutter rigging. Spangberg was not building a warship, as such, although during the entire eighteenth century it was possible to mistake for warships the many other ships which sailed long distances through pirate-infested seas. As the latter carried guns for defense, the layout of decks and ports actually was influenced. It was not necessarily always defense; the merchant ships were built with the possibility of privateering always present in the designer's mind.

A sloop (figure 30)—as distinct from a sloop-of-war—usually was defined as a single masted vessel with fore-and-aft rig; presumably a double sloop would have two fore-and-aft rigged masts, like a fore-and-aft schooner. Under the difficult conditions of Okhotsk, the *Hope* probably differed from a fore-and-aft schooner by doing without the gaff topsails. Muller, a scientist with the expedition who wrote an interesting account of it, calls the *Hope* a double shallop, and the shallop was definitely a successor to the early pinnace. The double sloop or shallop would closely resemble some developments of the small Dutch yacht, but to classify it more closely as a schooner or ketch type, it would be necessary to know the relative height of the two masts.

French or British, Dutch or Spanish or Russian, the height of the masts or the shapes and sizes of the ships varied, and so did their names. Some are familiar names to fire the imagination, such as caravel or galleon, frigate or Indiaman; some are not familiar, such as nao or flute, pink or cat. As one would expect, the latter are the working ships—the plain, overlooked ones.

However, the Pacific, like all challenges, was overcome by skill, not glamour; by effort, not elegance; by perseverance, not speed. The plain ones had their day.

CHAPTER 8

Galleys and Other Rowed Craft

... about the middle of May, at breake of day, wee had sight
of each other, thwart of Cañete, wee being to windwards of
the Spanish armado some two leagues, and all with little or no
winde. Our pinnace or prise being furnished with oares came
unto us, out of which we thought to have taken our men,
and so to leave her ...

RICHARD HAWKINS,
OF THE *DAINTIE*

Europeans used small craft in the Pacific. Some they brought, some they
built; in some cases they both brought and built them, several ships bringing
pre-cut smaller craft to be assembled as soon as the Horn was behind them.
Most of them could be rowed. As craft they were interesting, evoking memories
of Roman galleys and Viking longships, and their uses were interesting too.

Craft small enough to be rowed yet large enough to keep up with a fleet
under normal sail were found useful by all the European powers in Pacific
conditions. In the earliest days in each successively explored area of the Pacific,
they were used to precede and protect the larger ships from the hazards of
reefs and shallows, to survey anchorages and coastlines, and to carry despatches.
King Philip II of Spain spelled out their uses clearly in his instructions to
commanders. In time of war, the rowed craft were used to reconnoitre and
to capture prizes in the supposed safety of shallow waters, and at all times
the small craft were maids-of-all-work and rescuers in distress. Their functions
may be summed up as surveying, scouting, and succour, and these functions
will be dealt with in that order.

In the Indies, on the western fringes of the Pacific where the waters are
enclosed, the Portuguese used several types of small oared vessels as well
as their smallest galleons. *Pataxos* were similar to the English pinnaces;
navetas were swift despatch vessels; *galiotas* were similar to the English gal-
leasses—a kind of galleon which could be rowed in windless conditions. They
also used junks of all sizes as well as proas of various kinds, and interesting

hybrids developed. These various craft were used in both trade and exploration, their major advantages being their ability to travel through shallows and to move when the wind did not.

The Spanish were fully aware of the advantages to be gained by the use of small handy vessels in exploration. Mendaña (the pious and persistent Spanish leader who discovered the Solomon Islands) of the *Los Reyes*, built a small vessel at the Solomons; Gallego, who was there at the time, called it a brigantine, and Vaz, who was not present, called it a "pinesse." Translation may explain the different names, but in any case there was little difference, except in the rigging. Brigantine or pinnace, it was a wieldy sailing vessel which could also be rowed when deemed desirable. It was most suitable for detailed island exploration.[1] Quirós said that he deliberately chose two small ships for his voyage to Melanesia, which was following up those of Mendaña, although he could have had two large ones.[2] Estimation of tonnage seemed a difficult matter at best, and, in reading reports, it should be remembered that the size of their ship was a measure of their prestige to some commanders. They tended to exaggerate when discussing them; in the same way, their detractors tended to understate.

In addition to Quirós's two chief ships which, as he said, were small ones, the Viceroy of Peru, who bore the responsibility for the expedition, assigned a "zabra" to the fleet. At that time, a zabra was a large launch which could be rowed or sailed, and it has been defined as a "Spanish pinnace." According to Prado, the officer who succeeded to command after Quirós's own ship became separated from the others, the zabra was to be sent back to Peru to report if and when the discovery of La Austrialia del Espíritu Santo had been made. The zabra must have been of reasonable size to face that voyage alone; apart from that, she was also under orders to explore in detail any new lands which were discovered.

Philip II himself had prescribed in his "Ordinances on New Discoveries" that smaller vessels should be included in fleets of discovery to explore coasts and rivers, and to find suitable anchorages for the larger ships.[3] This was a sensible order and describes exactly the techniques used later by Captain Cook. Cook's *Resolution* carried framed vessels packed in cases "for exploring or surveying or any emergency," although he did not use them on either of that ship's voyages.[4] Captain George Vancouver, who learned his trade from Cook, used small craft in his work on the indented British Columbia shore line, which is so like the southwestern New Zealand coast both men also explored. Vancouver had been to southwestern New Zealand as a midshipman with Cook, and, later, following as in most things his great mentor's example, used that area himself as a refitting and resting place on his own famous expedition.

Vancouver complained in his journal that his small boats had been out twenty-three days along the British Columbia coast, travelled seven hundred miles, and yet had surveyed only sixty miles of the coastline.[5]

This method was used by all nationalities. Large ships cannot adequately explore new coastlines without the aid of auxiliary craft. When there was not one available, one was built, just as Mendaña had done at the Solomon Islands. Spangberg, one of Bering's captains in Kamchatka, built a shallop (a later name for a type of pinnace) which used sails when possible and oars when not. He did so "to make use of it the better to discover the islands."[6] Spangberg built himself the little craft of birchwood and called her the *Bolsheretsk*. It was fast and handy, sailing well close-hauled, and it proved very useful during his Japanese voyage.[7] She is described by Muller as a decked shallop, with twenty-four oars, a repetition of the idea that any voyage of exploration needs a craft big enough for safety at sea, but small enough to be rowed inshore for detailed examination.

George Bass, for whom the straits between Tasmania and the Australian mainland are named, undertook his most famous exploratory voyage through the straits in a whaleboat less than twenty-nine feet long. As Flinders said of his friend: "A voyage *expressly* undertaken for discovery in an open boat, and in which six hundred miles of coast, mostly in a boisterous climate, was explored, has not, perhaps, its equal in the annals of maritime history."[8] The *Rattlesnake*'s exploration and survey along the north coast of Australia and the south coast of New Guinea were aided by the flotilla of small boats that she and her tender, the schooner *Bramble*, carried. They had "two splendid Gallies, 32 feet long a very fine Pinnace and two first-rate cutters."[9] Even in charting and surveying the coastal waters in Europe large rowed vessels were used. Captain Colnett, whose journal of his Pacific exploration is so useful and fascinating because of the individuality and self-confidence of the man himself, used a galley to conduct a survey of the English coast in 1795-96, after his return from his voyage in the *Rattler*.

The Dutch had built a sloop in 1599 in the Straits of Magellan from prepared parts they had carried with them. Sloops could also be rowed, but were essentially sailing craft, very like a pinnace in size and purpose, and basically a development of them. Before proper charts had been made, the search for decent anchorages in the Straits of Magellan was vitally important, because the weather was dramatically uncertain and the winds vicious and unpredictable. In straits, by definition, there is no sea room, that is, room to manoeuvre the ship or to flee before the wind. Naturally, the smaller rowing boats which were carried on the ship or towed behind it were used for the same purposes as sloops or pinnaces. These boats, with interesting names, such as cock-boat, or dinghy, or light-horseman, now called a gig, a fast rowing boat, were too small to travel far or to stay long at sea because of the lack of space for provisions.

The use of small craft for warlike reconnaissance began early in the Pacific with the *Golden Hind*. In his ships, Drake had four pinnaces "brought from home in peices with us."[10] English pinnaces had developed, through row-barges, from Mediterranean galleys, although the Saxons' and Vikings' oared ships would be part of their cultural ancestry too. They could be used, like galleys, to attack sailing ships during calms, or to perform warlike reconnaissance. Drake set up one of his pinnaces as early as his call at Mogodore in West Africa, and therefore it must have been large enough to sail with the fleet. (It is true that some early very small ships had made amazing voyages —Clipperton, a privateer captain, sailed a captured Spanish vessel of only forty tons seven thousand miles across the Pacific from Mexico to the Philippines in the early eighteenth century.) Pinnaces (figure 48) were small ships rather than large boats, although the distinction cannot be one only of size. Gradually they became smaller, and their role changed somewhat; Cook's pinnace was carried aboard his ship to be used as a ship's boat. Earlier, many pinnaces had accompanied fleets as separate ships, as Drake's had been. In effect, pinnaces were meant to be sailed, but could be rowed.[11] Rowed pinnaces developed into shallops and then into sloops. On the other hand, ships' boats were designed to be rowed, but could be sailed; that is, the masts were removable and normally carried lying in the boat itself. Until the nineteenth century, small ships preferred to keep open to them some alternative to sail or to towing; sloops, and even frigates, could be rowed through oarports—openings in the ship's side—usually located between the gunports but sometimes a deck lower.[12]

Early pinnaces had permanent masts and could be quite large. Oxenham, the first English captain to sail on the Pacific, had built a pinnace with a reputed keel length of forty-five feet, only two feet shorter than the keel of the *Golden Hind*. This description came from a Portuguese named Vaz, whose report to his government was captured at sea by the English.[13] It may be exaggerated. Oxenham's pinnace was really a very small ship, and its building an accomplishment in itself. Unfortunately for Oxenham, he captured, together with much gold, a Spanish lady "of singular beautie, married, and a mother of children." Smitten with love at first sight, the English captain released the other prisoners at the lady's request. The prisoners, naturally, although ungraciously, sought and received help from Panama, which enabled them to find and capture Oxenham. Richard Hawkins, who was a prisoner in Lima only a few years after Oxenham had been hanged there as a pirate, said Oxenham had carried "by peecemeale, and in many journeys, a small pinnace," to a river running into the Pacific and then "hee fitted it by time in a warlike manner."[14] Oxenham had been schooled correctly in both daring and achievement; he had been one of the men with Drake when he crossed the Isthmus both to raid and to gaze on the Pacific. In crossing the Isthmus and building on the south side, he merely was adopting the normal Spanish way of putting ships into the Pacific, whereas Drake adopted the method and route of Magellan. Hawkins suggests, when telling Oxenham's history, that his fate should be a warning "to shunne such notorious sinnes, which cannot escape punishment in this life, or in the life to come."[15]

Oxenham's swift end was no fault of his ship, but he did tempt fate, according to Hawkins's views, by the role he expected the pinnace to play: "Any pynaces to meddle with ships, is to buy repentance at too deare a rate. For their office is, to wayte upon their fleete, in calmes (with their oares) to follow a chase, and in occasions to anchor neere the shore, when the greater ships cannot, without perill; above all, to be readie and obedient at every call."[16] This is probably a fair statement of the opinion of both Drake and Philip II of the role a pinnace should play.

A century after Sir Richard Hawkins wrote his famous book about the sea and sea warfare, English explorers brought a somewhat different type of rowed craft to the Pacific for the same purposes as their predecessors had brought their pinnaces. Like the earlier pinnaces, galleys could be sailed, but were designed and fully equipped to be rowed when and if necessary. Because this requirement influenced design, they had a distinctive hull shape and construction. One distinguishing feature of the galley hull, when compared to that of a frigate, was the decking. Galleys were flush-decked, that is, with all decks on one level, sometimes called galley-decked, whereas to be frigate-decked meant the decks were discontinuous throughout the length of the ship. As oared vessels they were low and long and narrow, very manoeuvrable, and swift under the right conditions, that is, smooth seas. Although, in reality Mediterranean craft, the galleys that the North European powers built retained recognizable galley features even when they had been modified for rougher seas. Certainly the *Drake Galley* of seventeenth-century England, of which there is a full account, was long and narrow even though she saw little of smooth seas.[17] But the northern galleys of this time were essentially sailing ships which relied on oars more than was normally the case.

Dampier entered the Pacific in 1705 in the twenty-six gun ship *St. George*, with the *Cinque Ports*, a ninety-ton galley of fifteen guns, as consort.[18] The *Cinque Ports* was definitely not a pure galley in the sense that contemporary French and Spanish galleys of the Mediterranean fleets were. It is clear from the journal of Barlow of the ship *Wentworth*, the sailor whose writing gives a clear look at life in the lower ranks of the seventeenth-century Royal Navy and merchant service, that not too long before this English galleys were small frigates which fairly frequently used oars as well as, or instead of, sails. He served in one, and writes with first-hand knowledge of several, including that of the notorious Captain Kidd, whose craft Barlow describes as the *Adventure Galley*—frigate-built.[19] On several occasions, he calls them frigates. Probably they were not very different, except perhaps somewhat larger, from the pinnaces of Drake's day.

Galleys, pinnaces, and sloops were sailed far more than they were rowed, but Barlow points out the obvious advantage of the general type when he tells of the *Martaine Galley* "leaving the rest behind us till such time as they had wind to bring them out."[20] To some extent, the oars were the equivalent of the modern yacht's auxiliary engine, which is not used for cruising, but for getting in and out of port or for drive in calms.

Oared ships were obviously most useful on the Pacific coast of America, where calms often coincide with currents in such a way in the Doldrums that sailing ships drift helplessly miles beyond their goal and face a long beat back when the wind rises from the wrong direction. For example, sailing ships making for the ports of Iqique or of Callao from the south have to be very careful not to get to the northward or they would almost certainly have had great difficulty in beating back against the wind and current.[21]

Wafer, a buccaneer surgeon who left an excellent account of his adventures (which contains particularly interesting insights into the cultural attitudes of the Darien Indians), described the ordinary condition of the sea on the Peruvian coast as having a great swell, "though smooth as the Surface of a River, here being little or no Wind to curl the Waves."[22] Light winds of constant direction, calms, and smooth seas would make men consider alternatives to sails. The *Cinque Ports* was rowed on occasion; she "put out her Oars, and rowed towards the Island" at Juan Fernández.[23] Off Australia, the *Lady Nelson* used her sweeps in cases of calm; "at 4 calm, out sweeps to pull ahead."[24] The American sloop *Lady Washington* often used her sweeps on the mountainous and indented British Columbia coast where winds are so variable, and where anchorages in her time were uncharted. Emergencies could bring out oars or sweeps. The American brig *Margaret Oakley* was equipped with ten sweeps which could move her at two or three knots in a calm; she needed them near the island of Floris to escape a waterspout.[25] In one crisis, Cook's *Endeavour* used sweeps hastily made from planks and studding sail booms to assist the boats towing her. However, once the mass of the ship was moving boats could accomplish much. Two small rowboats once towed a "2,000-ton steel barque for two miles out of a land-locked harbour via a narrow channel in the face of trade-wind driven rollers"[26]—which sounds rather incredible.

There were countless uses besides towing for smaller craft: fishing, visiting other ships, loading supplies, seeking anchorages, and hunting seals or penguins. Pirates or men-of-war used small craft to extend their line of vision when searching for victims or enemies, or watching for friends. Anson carried an eighteen-oared barge with him to use for all the various tasks an easily managed vessel could do. He often used it to land troops on shore in amphibious operations, as well as for an extra rowing pinnace for the usual ship's errands. Some of these ships' barges were fine craft. "Quarter Master," a century after Anson, described a ship's rowing barge as "clinker built of mahogany, coppered, and copper fastened . . . rigged very neatly as a schooner."[27] In spite of the special attention and exemption beauty so often attracts, this barge proved both functional and useful.

Small boats on or with ships are naturally associated not with their functions as auxiliary tools, but with their additional use as means of escape from dangers of various kinds; visitors to ships tend to call every boat they see on board "a lifeboat." Escapes in small boats from wrecks or maroonings were plentiful in the Pacific. Convicts in Australia sometimes took their chance in small craft; one group, which included a woman with two children, successfully sailed a small boat to Batavia from Port Jackson.[28] Others were less conventional, but just as successful. A convict known to Mortlock, one of the convicts whose journal has been useful, escaped in Tasmania by crossing an arm of the sea in a washtub.[29]

In the most famous escape of all, that of Bligh in the *Bounty*'s launch (figure 32), eighteen men were packed into the twenty-three-foot craft, not only crowding each other unpleasantly, but sinking the boat low in the water; they had been given no chance to enlarge or alter her. Presumably the leaders of the mutineers thought they had seen the last of Bligh and had

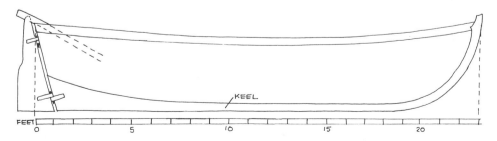

Fig. 32. H.M.S. Bounty's *Launch—length, 23 feet; breadth, 6 feet 9 inches*

merely salved their consciences by giving him a fighting chance. The very low free-board (or distance between the waterline and the top of the boat's side) of only nine inches meant that the sea kept washing in, and the men were debilitated by being continually wet through by the spray and breaking waves, and having to bail constantly to keep the boat afloat. Bligh found navigation very difficult, because his papers kept getting soaked, but his greatest navigational problem lay in making good observations from the pitching craft. He succeeded, and he and his crew survived.

In another remarkable survival, one of Bering's ships became famous not only for the difficulties of her building, but because she was built twice, in different sizes but with the same name. During his second voyage of exploration to Alaska in 1740, scurvy decimated the crew, and partly because the surviving men were too weak to handle the ship properly, the *St. Peter* was wrecked. From the wreckage, a new *St. Peter* was built. This resurrection was accomplished mainly by a Cossack who only knew of shipbuilding "just what he had seen of it in Okhotsk, when he was employed there as a labourer during the time our packet-boats were being built."[30] Later his captain was able to have this talented Cossack made a Siberian nobleman.

Whatever might have been expected of a Cossack cavalryman acting as shipbuilder, the new ship was well built from the salvaged materials; her forty-foot keel was made from her namesake's mainmast and her sternpost from the former capstan. Some masts and yards were re-used in their original capacity and the remainder were sawn into planks for the hull. She was properly beamed and kneed with salvaged beams and knee-timber. Ships' knees (figure 33) are the more or less right-angled pieces which join the beams to the timbers (frames) and on them depends much of the strength of the ship. Wood which was naturally of the correct angle—roots or branches— was very valuable because of scarcity, and ships' knees from the immense forests of northwest America became an item of trade with China. These salvaged knees must have added the required strength to the reconstruction, for the Cossack's ship lasted as a transport vessel for years after carrying her builders home.

Rigged as a one-masted hooker, the second *St. Peter* was also given four sweeps on each side for rowing. She both sailed and steered so well that a flying foresail and jib were enough sails off the mainmast, and there was no need for a spanker (the gaff sail used both for balance in steering and for help in turning to tack). Tar for the rigging and caulking was laboriously and ingeniously melted out of the cable.

Mere survival justified such labours, but excessive physical effort was not the only horror of this episode. Semi-starvation and scurvy made the building

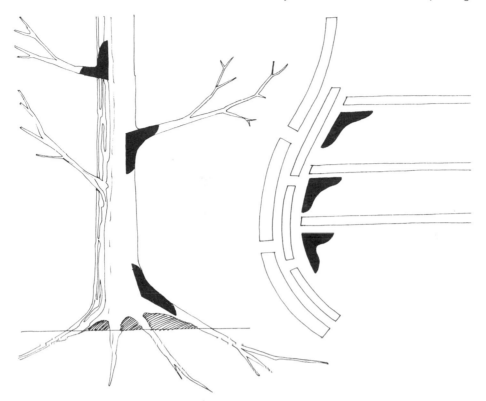

Fig. 33. The tree's natural branching points provide the great strength needed for a ship's "knees."

of any ship—much less this stout ship—almost a miracle of endurance and perseverance. Lieutenant Waxell, Bering's successor in command, also built a type of small craft, called a jolly-boat, a name which thoroughly belies the effort and the motivation behind its building: "In the wreck we found two reserve anchor-stocks of birchwood. Half of one stock went to make hafts for our axes, but the other three halves were sawn up into planks ¾ and ½ an inch thick, and from these we built a jolly-boat capable of holding eight to ten men."[31] Building the second *St. Peter* had already strained that crew's resources of material, and morale and energy as well. Building a boat to accompany the ship they had built to save their lives must have seemed a matter of urgency or the Russians would not have done it; ships simply could not operate effectively in unknown waters without supporting craft. In spite of this auxiliary role, seamen, in fact, did travel immense distances in these tiny craft, but these voyages practically never were matters of choice—except insofar as escaping from an even worse fate could be considered a matter of choice. Oddly enough, a third ship, or at least a large boat, was built by another shipwrecked crew from what little was left of Bering's ship. This small ship, consisting mostly of driftwood, was called the *Capiton*, and, like the second *St. Peter*, it carried its builders to safety.

Shelvocke, wrecked on Juan Fernández, built a boat with a thirty-foot keel and sixteen-foot beam while he was on the island; old Spanish swords provided the iron, while the bowsprit from the wreck of his ship became the keel. Shelvocke did not have a creator's love for his new *Recovery*: "I dare say the like was never seen, and I may safely affirm that such a bottom never swam on the surface of the sea before."[32] His statement was not meant to be laudatory. Shelvocke's crew sailed this crazy craft successfully, if unpleasantly, for the forty men were packed in on top of two thousand smoked eels—their only provisions. There was only one frying pan and the sizzling noise of eels frying was continuous and apparently nervewracking. Fortunately, they met and captured a Spanish ship, attacking it with the desperate valour of people who, even when almost unarmed, feel they have nothing to lose.

Besides building from scratch, ships' boats could be lengthened or strengthened to make them truly seaworthy; the *Wager*'s longboat became the twenty-three-ton schooner *Speedwell*, when the wrecked crew lengthened her and changed the rigging. After her voyage from southern Chile to Montevideo, all who saw her remarked on her smallness for such a performance in those dangerous waters: "they were surpriz'd that thirty Souls, the Number of People now living, could be stow'd in so small a Vessel."[33]

The mutineers of the *Bounty*—the less convinced ones at any rate, those who felt least implicated in guilt—built a schooner at Tahiti which, after capture, became a Royal Navy ship, a token repayment at least, even though not intended as such. Perhaps she did not have the necessary naval qualities, because there is some evidence that she finally ended up sailing between Asia and northwest America as the Portuguese ship *Florinda* of Macao. An American sailor who saw her near the Queen Charlotte Islands thought her "the most miserable thing that ever was formed in imitation of the Ark."[34] Many of the escape craft would have fitted this description; certainly Shelvocke did not admire his.

But many of the galleys and pinnaces had been handsome as well as useful craft, graceful when under sail and rhythmically lifelike when being rowed. It was this very ability to live and move when the wind had abdicated its command that made them useful in exploration and dangerous in war. These craft, in some form or other, survived until the auxiliary engine gave even the smallest schooner the equivalent power of a Roman trireme's banks of oars.

CHAPTER 9

Pacific-built European Ships

. . . carved into many Devices, viz. *some Fowl, Fish, or a Man's*
Head, painted or carv'd: And though it's but rudely done,
yet the Resemblance appears plainly, and shews an ingenious
Fancy.

WILLIAM DAMPIER
OF THE *ROEBUCK*, 1699

. . . the Spaniards cheeke by jole with us, ever getting to the
wind-wards upon us; for that the shipping of the South soa is
ever moulded sharpe under water, and long; all their voyages
depending upon turning to windwardes; and the brese
blowing ever southerly.

RICHARD HAWKINS
OF THE *DAINTIE*, 1594

Europeans began to build their own types of ships immediately after they
arrived in the Pacific. Naturally, they modified the design to suit local
conditions, such as the southerly winds off Peru, or the stormy Tasman Sea.
But rigging could be both lighter and more carelessly maintained in a ship
which remained in the Pacific than in one which must fight her way in or
out and past the great capes. In many parts of the area, hulls could be
lighter too, and to save cost or time or both, Europeans often bought hulls
of indigenous design and construction. These they always rerigged to improve
handling—from a European point of view—and at least to give the security
of familiarity. Regardless of the nationality of the builder of the hull, the
craft became European, and gradually the indigenous people adopted many
of the features for their own use. It was not all rational and practical;
artistry found its place too. In this, European and Pacific dweller agreed;
both loved painted and carved decoration and figureheads.

Pacific-built or rerigged ships avoided certain major problems. Ships from
Europe coming to the Pacific had to be rigged to pass either the Cape or the
Horn, but they also had to sail through the Doldrums on the way. Too little

sail area meant a slow trip through the light variable winds of the Doldrums in an age when the danger of scurvy and the hardships caused by poor food preservation made the loss of time on voyages hazardous. On the other hand, too much mast height and the extra rigging supporting it added to the dangers of gale-force winds and the immense seas off the Cape or the Horn. A compromise made both passages possible, but it left some things not quite right both in the Doldrums and off the capes.

Most captains re-stowed the ships (that is, re-positioned the different factors of the ship's load, for example, by dismounting the guns on deck and putting them in the hold) after passing the Doldrums and before reaching the rough seas further south. Unless the ships were very poorly supplied, new sails were put on before the rough passages of the capes were reached. This also was done before entering the bad weather area east of Japan. Felicitous always, Dana said, "for a ship, unlike people on shore, puts on her best suit in bad weather."[1] (A complete set of sails is called "a suit.")

Other rigging, when possible, was overhauled as well. Dana said that "our rigging was all overhauled and mended, or changed for new, where it was necessary . . . and other preparations made in good season, that the ropes might have time to stretch and become limber before we got into cold weather."[2] These chores were not necessary for the Pacific-built Spanish ships, because these were preparations for hazards they would not encounter. Shelvocke pointed out that a non-Pacific ship could be told at a distance by its good rigging; well-maintained rigging was rare in the Pacific. The neglect of an important routine such as rigging maintenance must mean that it was thought to be unimportant. A Peruvian ship could be recognized by its white cotton sails which contrasted vividly with the brown and often patched and battered European canvas. Similarly, years later, American ships could be recognized by the "snow-white cloths," the white cotton sails of the clippers.[3] Peruvian cotton sails caught fire easily and burned fiercely, and this, together with the light build of the ships and the naturally half-hearted service of semi-enslaved and naturally apathetic Indian crewmen, could be a partial explanation of the many easy victories by European ships. In the simple sailing conditions of the area, the ships also tended to carry very small crews.

Some particular European designs with new techniques, such as coppering, sound materials, and conventional construction were well suited for work in Pacific conditions. But it was soon found that in certain areas of the huge ocean, conditions were so unusual that specialized ships were needed. Some accounts by early voyagers tell of these specific types. One such account is that of an Italian merchant, Francesco Carletti, who travelled around the world from 1594 to 1602, mainly on Spanish ships, trading astutely, observing acutely, and reporting clearly to his ruler, Grand Duke Fernando Medici of Tuscany. He described a particular type of Pacific ship developed solely for the special conditions of the route between Panama and Callao, the port of Lima, Peru.

Carletti claimed that the wind came from the southern quarters all year, an observation confirmed by many others. This meant that the ship had to travel south in a series of tacks. The captain chose to tack for twelve hours at a time, heading in toward land all day and out from land all night, in order not to run ashore in the dark. Usually, it took two and a half months to travel the 1,200 miles even though the hulls had been specially designed to have little surface to resist the wind. This special design did not allow for the usual superstructures to protect the passengers, and Carletti complained bitterly.[4] The ships had hulls wider toward the prow and narrow toward the poop, a rather interesting streamlining feature of design, which almost describes the *Spray* of Captain Slocum, or the famous French luggers of the American War of Independence, from which many fast American ships are very indirectly descended.

Spain quite sensibly avoided the Cape Horn route and built up, in effect, a Caribbean fleet and a Pacific fleet (by "fleet" is meant a number of vessels, and not a group setting out with a particular purpose) connected in terms of policy and freight by land communication across the Isthmus of Panama. Because the Spanish Pacific ships, except the Manila Galleon, were built for local trade only (although local trade in the Pacific could still mean long, hard voyages, as Carletti had discovered), and because this meant sailing in between the tropics along a coast available for refuge, these ships were lightly built, fine weather vessels. It is possible that this was due to factors other than regional climate. In a very human fashion, the Spaniards built lightly where there was a chance of getting away with it. Meares said, for example, of their voyaging from the Philippines: "After October the passage to and from Manila to China is always certain [for] even the worst of the Spanish ships, and they are the most miserably equipped of any vessels in the world."[5] There were some advantages to the lighter built ships. Hawkins speaks of "the advantage which all the South-sea shippes have of all those built in our North-sea"[6] in a context implying that the strength necessary for "North-sea" ships made them slow in comparison with the more lightly-built Pacific ships. Cameron, writing in *Lodestone and Evening Star*, suggests that it was considered characteristic of Peruvian ships to be difficult to handle under little sail.[7] They were designed to carry a great deal of canvas. Sailing when and where they were built to sail, they would not have needed either strength or storm worthiness. Shelvocke, the privateer, found his Peruvian-built ship worked her seams loose in a heavy sea very quickly; on the other hand, flexible ships were fast, as Hawkins had seen. Some ships were actually designed to enable the crews to remove stiffening beams when extra speed was required.[8]

European shipbuilding had begun early in the Pacific. Pizarro sailed to conquer Peru in a ship he built in Panama, and by the time Drake's *Golden Hind* and Cavendish's *Desire* raided the eastern Pacific there were many ships at sea which had been built in Peru by Europeans for Europeans. In addition, of course, there were the indigenous giant balsas and other Indian craft. Although Oxenham's pinnace of the late 1570's is considered to have been the first English-built ship in the Pacific, she did not precede by very many years the ships that Will Adams, formerly an English pilot on a Dutch ship, built in Japan, for Ieyasu, the great Shogun. It is interesting to speculate what effect Adams's ships would have had on the Pacific, if at that time the Japanese had not shut themselves almost completely away from the rest of the world, following a policy deliberately designed to guard against the danger of foreign control.

Less advanced indigenous peoples were usually as interested in European shipbuilding techniques and the vessels which resulted as were the Japanese. European influence on indigenous shipbuilding spread. The schooner built on Palau Island in the Carolines by the crew of the wrecked *Antelope* for their successful escape bid was European in design, Pacific only in her materials. She was much admired by the Carolinians. Some European-built Pacific craft were more prosaic in conception and plebeian in design. A flat-barge, twenty-two feet by six feet, was built at Tahiti by men from the *Duff*, a very uninspiring vessel when seen alongside the beauty of the local canoes. Whatever her looks, she was easy to build, carried forty-three people, and worked well for short inter-island freight and passage.

Europeans built ships in the Pacific for non-Europeans, and their designs soon were favoured nearly everywhere in the Pacific because of their sturdiness. When an Englishman built a vessel named *Britannia* in Hawaii for "King Tamaahmaah [Kamehameha]," it was a standard framed hull with a thirty-six-foot keel.[9] Some interesting mixtures of Pacific and Atlantic craft developed elsewhere: "the Dutch, as I have before observed, do often buy Proe-bottoms for a small Matter, of the Malayans, especially of the People of Jihore, and convert them into Sloops, either for their own use, or to sell."[10] These sloop-rigged proas were a comparable hybrid to one the *Nootka* saw at Hawaii, a "double canoe, schooner rigged," which at a distance everyone thought to be a European ship.[11]

The *Tartar Galley*, in which Forrest sailed from Balambangan in the East Indies to New Guinea, in the western fringes area, was a ten-ton "Sooloo prow," with twenty rowers, lateen sails, and two steering oars. It was an Eastern ship in every way, with an interesting wind-up boom to reef the sails, by description very like that used by many modern yachts. Finally, Forrest rigged her as a schooner and impressed his crew with the ease of tacking with this European rig compared to their own, in which the whole yard of the lateen had to be shifted to the opposite side of the mast in order to tack. European alterations did not always take the form of Western rigging fitted to Eastern hulls. In the lorchas of East Asia one found Western-type hulls with Chinese-type rigging, the Chinese lug sail being particularly easy to reef and hence valuable in an area subject to heavy and sudden squalls.

Rerigging is done for practical reasons, and beauty is incidental. The shape of the hull is also intended to be strictly functional; however, because the designer is usually seeking speed, and this means streamlining, hull shapes, like aircraft shapes, are very often beautiful. For example, the bow of the *Albatros* was commented on for its boldness. A ship's bow is as important to her beauty as a woman's face is to hers. But there is more than beauty to the bows of ships. Ruskin wrote of them:

One object there is still, which I never pass without the renewed wonder of childhood, and that is the bow of a Boat. . . . The sum of navigation is in that. You may magnify it or decorate as you will; you do not add to the wonder of it. . . . I know nothing else that man does, which is perfect, but that. . . . Without it, what prison wall would be so strong as that "white and wailing fringe" of sea.[12]

John Smith, that practical soldier and colonizer, also waxed lyrical about ships' bows. In the *Sea Grammar*, he says that "a well bowed Ship so swiftly presseth the water as that it foameth, and in the darke night sparkleth like fire."[13]

Beauty was so much a part of sailing that the most hardened sailors were aware of it (although they had so many hardships that their softer or aesthetic feelings apparent in so many journals are cause for wonder). One of the most beautiful of brigantines, the *Ryno* (named from Ossian's "The Defeat of Swaran") was "built on the east coast of Auckland by an old Nova Scotian Highland shipwright" and became famed in island song because of her beauty:

> Oh, the *Ryno*'s the ship of Niué-é!
> Haul away, O haul away![14]

Most of the early island ships, such as the *Ryno*, had European officers and Polynesian crews, but soon many Polynesians became proficient schooner captains, as one would expect of their centuries-old tradition of voyaging. Tradition and legends told them of dangers and of the facing and solving of problems;

neither dangers nor problems had altered and, if the choice of solutions had been broadened, so much the better.

Europeans in the southwest Pacific became famous for shipbuilding, and seamanship too. In Tasmania the "blue-gum clippers" became as famous in the nineteenth century as the Tasmanians themselves did as competent sailors and skippers. Perhaps it was because they lived on islands that the British settlers in Tasmania and New Zealand retained their sea skills and sea life as vigorously as they had done at home. It was not only the settlers—Maoris and the Tasmanian aborigines took up the life on whalers and trading brigs and schooners with notable success. The excellent Pacific clippers, and the crewmen they supplied for large British and American ships, made Tasmania and New Zealand important in the sailing ship world until the present century.

The remarkable success of New Zealand and Australia in world yachting competitions during the present century had its beginning in the early days of the Australasian colonies. References are often made to the interest in shipping, to the abilities of the men as sailors, to the excellent ships that were built in both early New Zealand and the Australian colonies. Joseph Conrad says: "These towns of the Antipodes . . . took an interest in the shipping, the running links with 'home.' . . . They made it part and parcel of their daily interests."[15]

Sydney in particular has a yachting tradition that goes back to its earliest days, and a reputation for yachtsmen that "carry sail." Today, the Sydney-Hobart and the Hobart-Auckland races are yachting classics of the modern world—they are based on the traditions of "Sydney sailors," of "blue-gum clippers," and of "Waipu skippers."

North across the Pacific in what is now British Columbia, the first ship built in northwest America was launched in 1788.[16] Within four years, the *Discovery* reported that both English and American traders were building shallops. The builders of these particular boats had available in British Columbia the best supply of huge trees in the world (some early traders had found Indian dwellings carved into living trees). In European fashion, they sawed these into planks rather than hollowed them out directly into hulls. They also had some very challenging and remarkably beautiful sailing waters to test their shipwrights' skill and the design of their ships. Nevertheless, these were European boats, which in inspiration owed more to the fiords of Norway than to the local conditions of British Columbia.

Pacific shipbuilding was not entirely a matter of economics or convenience, concerned only with rigging or sails or hulls. There was room also for the irrational and the artistic. Figureheads were an interesting feature of early ships in the Pacific—indigenous canoes as well as European barques. The

Plate 23. "Nantucket Sleigh-Ride." The natural reaction of a harpooned whale is to flee or to dive. If he fled on the surface, the careering of the whaleboat towed behind him was called, by American whalemen, the "Nantucket sleigh-ride" and, by the French, *promenade dans un wagonnet*. Sometimes the boats were towed 30 or 40 miles before they could be pulled hand over hand up to the whale to allow the officer to kill him with a lance thrust to the heart or lungs.

Plate 24. Whaleship *Alice Mandell*. This model of a typical whaleship, her whaleboats hung ready to take the water, is equipped with fittings characteristic of the later nineteenth century—the boats, for example, have tillers and rudders rather than the great white ash steering oars of earlier days.

European ships built in the North Pacific could have blended in an Eskimo artistic influence from kayak figureheads, in which case they would have been simpler figureheads, less realistic, but more symbolic of the truths of the sea.

The *Tilikum* had a fierce dragon of a figurehead, almost certainly done by an Indian carver, because she was a genuine Indian canoe, already forty years old when Voss bought her. The *Adventure*, a sloop built in British Columbia in 1791, had "a handsome figure head and false badges, and other ways touch'd off in high stile"[17] but there is no report that any totem carvers were involved in carving these ornaments.

In the South Pacific, where the great canoes were central to the tribal life, every war canoe, like the Viking ships to which they are so often compared, had a figurehead. Carving one often took years, and resulted in singularly fine examples of woodcraft. So valuable and valued were they that a figure-head often was re-used by attaching it to a new hull. Marquesan carving was almost as good as that of the Maoris, some of whose figureheads were stylized representations of the human face. Sometimes the figurehead wore a wig of *kaka* (New Zealand parrot) feathers. Forster described the figurehead of a Maori double canoe as a "mishapen thing, which with some difficulty we perceived was meant to represent a human head, with a pair of eyes of mother of pearl, and a long tongue lolling out of its mouth."[18] Forster obviously had no appreciation of surrealism.

Maori sternpieces also were elaborately carved, and both stem and stern pieces often had extra feather decoration to make a fine show in the wind, tossing in greeting to the guardian sea gods. The carving was continued long after the European influence had become important. Ensign Best saw an old man "carving a head piece for a war canoe with a couple of old chisels . . . instead of the old mauri instruments of green stone."[19] However, non-metallic instruments could produce good work. Cook saw on a Tahitian canoe "the image of a Man carved in wood, very little inferior [to] work of the like kind done by common ship carvers in England."[20]

European ships also carved and mounted their tribute to the irrational. The iron-hulled *Joseph Conrad* has a "magnificent head of Conrad" at her prow to dare the waters her great original had sailed.[21] Figureheads usually were directly connected with the name: "That gun-brig the *Elk* enjoyed a curious sort of fame in Auckland and Sydney, 1859-60" because her figure-head (mounted only while in port, for it was too precious to be exposed to the spray of the sea) was "the stuffed head and neck of an American elk."[22] The *Penang*, a three-masted barque of the 1920's, to the resentment of her mate, had a "worthy moustachioed gentleman" as a figurehead.[23] In his opinion: "The image of a beautiful woman was the proper ending to a sailing-ship's bow; for a wind-ship was an amazon, a *sköldmö* (shield-maiden) or a *valkyria*, with strength and skill to do battle, but she also possessed most of the main characteristics of woman, foremost of these a grace and beauty definitely feminine."[24] It was always a "beautiful woman"; the crew of the *Boadicea* hated the ugly representation of the fierce queen who led them. Ugly or beautiful, femininity was emphasized. A great navigator once reminded all sailors that a ship was a "wayward 'she,' " and needed handling accordingly.[25]

A plaided Highlander—surely no one will think his kilt a compromise with this last expressed view—faced the sea on the *Highlander*, his tartan carefully repainted at each overhaul, exemplifying the care lavished on figureheads. They were important to the sailors, partly as charms of fortune, partly as something irrational in the hard, grim realism of all else about them. Like the eyes painted on Chinese junks, figureheads represented the personality of the ship, the living, wayward part of her that made her different from all others. A condor, as on the *Esmeralda* of the Chilean Navy, represents the freedom of spirit, the grace of wing and winged movement, the beauty of the "carved instants" of soaring; all are as much a part of "white-winged ships" as they are of the kings of Andean air.

The "sea-horse" head of the *Resolution* could claim for the immense body behind her a sea life of her own as wide ranging, as single minded, and as successful as that of any sea animal that lived by the chase and the capture. Not all figureheads capture the spirit of the ship so well, nor are they always what is expected. There is a picture of the *Rattlesnake*'s head, looking more like a devotee of yoga than the fearsome serpent the ship's name would suggest. Figureheads of certain kinds could be a dangerous luxury in certain places. Golnett suggested that when a ship going to Japan has a figurehead it should be one of the animals; "the Japanese have all heads to their Vessels which is a Bell fix'd horizontally. I would have no figure representing the human Species on any part of the Vessel, that they might not take them for Catholic saints."[26] In Colnett's day, the Japanese were thoroughly and dangerously anti-Christian.

Conrad said of the figureheads at the quays, saints or sinners:

It was a noble gathering of the fairest and swiftest, each bearing at the bow the carved emblem of her name as in a gallery of plaster-casts, figures of women with mural crowns, women with flowing robes, with gold fillets on their hair or blue scarves round their waists, stretching out rounded arms as if to point the way; heads of men helmeted or bare; full lengths of warriors, of kings, of statesmen, of lords and princesses, all white from top to toe; with here and there a dusky turbaned figure, bedizened in many colours of some Eastern sultan or hero.[27]

Whether in ships with a figurehead or of a more functional design, the arrival of the Europeans and their assumption of dominion over great areas altered Pacific life as it altered Pacific watercraft. During the nineteenth century, the economic exploitation of Pacific resources was to force even greater changes; at its end, the whales had gone, and wheat and wool were the new staples of Pacific commerce. The old ways had gone too.

CHAPTER 10

Whaling

*. . . some of the authors of narratives relating to the pursuit
and capture of the whale are easily entitled to wear cham-
pion belts as masters of pure fiction. Whaling is one of the
least hazardous, the most commonplace, and, taken altogether
about the laziest occupation that human beings have ever been
engaged in upon the sea.*

A CLIPPER SHIP OFFICER

"My God, Mr. Chase, what is the matter?"
I answered, "We have been stove by a whale."

OWEN CHASE
FIRST MATE OF THE WHALER *ESSEX*

*A school of whales passed by. They wallowed southward,
blowing wispy feathers of steam that turned to rainbows as
they fell.*

ADRIAN SELIGMAN
OF THE *CAP PILAR*

Explorers had seen enough whales to suggest that the Pacific could become
an incomparable hunting ground, but it took some time for the best local
areas to be found and reported. Historically, however, exploitation has tended
to follow exploration very closely; the first British whalers entered the Pacific
by Cape Horn in the same year (1788) that the first convict ships reached
Australia, and these two events signalled the beginning of changes that were
to shake and shape Pacific life speedily and brutally, as Cook had foreseen
with sadness. The settlement and commercial exploitation of Australia and
New Zealand, and the discovery and commercial exploitation of the various
Pacific whaling grounds meant that the long night of dreams was over. The
morning was short and metamorphic. In one century—by 1888—all had
changed. It is not necessary to accept the whole concept of the Noble Savage
to see him as such in contrast to many of the whalers, convicts, and even
settlers.

Sperm oil—a good whale yields sixty-five to eighty barrels—was used for lamps and stoves; hence the discovery and development of petroleum was a blow to whaling. The cooper, or barrel maker, was important in all early sailing ships, but he was especially so in whalers, where from pre-packed rings and staves he made the barrels to hold the cargo of oil. Whalers also filled their emptied provision barrels with oil. Animal oils of many kinds were needed for lubricants, for the sizing of cloth, and for cooking. The oil from the Australian whaling grounds was particularly good, fetching £10 a ton more than oil from elsewhere. Spermacetti, a very light wax, found in the sperm whales' heads, where it acts as a mechanism somewhat like the buoyancy tanks in submarines, is used to make candles and ointments, and for lubricating delicate instruments. Ambergris, a fatty substance found in the intestines, is highly valued as a fixative in costly perfumes.

Baleen, or whalebone, from the horny plates in the mouths of the toothless species of whales is very valuable too, sometimes fetching thousands of dollars a ton. Plumed knights got their plumage not from birds but from whales, baleen being shredded and artificially coloured. The tiny waists that marked the hour-glass shaped female figures of the late nineteenth century were made slender by baleen stays. The essential quality of flexibility so valuable in corsetry meant baleen was also used in chair seats and as brush bristles and whip handles. These uses made whale products important in the culture of the day; however, the discovery of petroleum and plastic meant the end of the whaling boom, as these products were just as good—and cheaper into the bargain.

The Pacific opened rich new hunting grounds for European whalers, although the Pacific people themselves were whalers too and used centuries-old techniques. Cape Horn had long been known as a haunt of whales, but its heyday as a whaling ground had to wait on the demands of the Industrial Revolution for lubricants for its machines and for sizing for the cloth to clothe the rapidly increasing population which operated the machines. The *Speedwell* reported so many whales so close that the stench was offensive. From the *Dolphin* "Great Numbers of Whales and Grampuses" were seen as they approached the Horn, to the delight of "Some of our men that was formerly in the Greenland Trade."[1] Whalers from the North Atlantic appreciated well enough the possibilities opening up in the Pacific once the routes had been discovered and described. The whales did not yet fear the whalers and "they swam pompously within pistol range" of the *Astrolabe*.[2] Forty years later, the *Nadeshka* and *Neva* saw so many whales disporting themselves near Tierra del Fuego that the watchkeepers reported their splashing as breakers. A shoal of porpoises (a small species of whale) leaping like "a pack of hounds in full cry"—Banks was a country gentleman—created the same effect near the *Endeavour*: "any Man would have taken them for Breakers."[3]

"Breakers ahead"—the waves literally breaking on rocks or shoals—is the ocean's most feared warning, a peril that can be both seen and heard, and a ship could strike a whale just as easily as it could a rock or shoal. The *Dolphin* nearly did so when, in a huge herd, "another blew the water in upon the Quarter Deck & they are of the largest kind we ever have seen."[4] The *Argonaut* did not strike, but was struck by one. Perhaps it was as the mate of the *Cap Pilar* said: "Whale, sometimes dey rub dere backs on de bottom of de ship to scrape off de fleas."[5] Hitting or being hit by a whale can be a serious matter. In May of 1972, an English yacht sank in the eastern Pacific after striking or being struck by a whale, and another yacht was sunk by a whale in 1973. Whether deliberate or accidental, these sinkings, from which there are survivors to provide an explanation, may be clues to the fate of various small craft which, before modern lifesaving and communication equipment, simply disappeared.[6]

Bulk and power enable the whales to outmatch ships if they so choose; fortunately, they rarely attack, diving being their usual evasive action. Sperm whales "dive straight down and remain below for from fifteen to forty minutes, though individuals have been known to remain below for an hour and a half."[7] Contrast this with human diving times—although Meares, captain of the *Felice*, claimed to have clocked one Hawaiian diver as being underwater for seven and a half minutes.[8]

Gray whales and sperm whales, others only occasionally, will fight to protect their young. In 1604, Middleton fought a mother whale who "bestowed one bange on the Generals pinnesse that split all the timbers and boards."[9] Finback whales were avoided for decades because they were so dangerous, although eyed with speculation; one Scot invented a rocket harpoon in the early nineteenth century which he claimed—incorrectly—would add finbacks to the harvest.

Whales were not the only ocean inhabitants to be feared. Purchas tells of a swordfish ramming a Dutch ship, apparently deliberately. The rudder of the *Idle Hour* was hit by "a gigantic fish of some sort,"[10] Long told Zane Grey, who replied that the ketch could have been capsized, "for natives of Polynesia have often described such a fish as destroying canoes with one powerful flap."[11] Captain Colnett of the *Rattler* saw the manoeuvres of sharks which apparently were attempts to overturn outrigger canoes. Haida Indians feared the large sharks in the sea off the Queen Charlotte Islands and claimed that "they frequently break their canoes and eat the unfortunate occupants."[12] The whale shark which followed the raft *Kon-Tiki* sounded frightful enough, but surely not so bad as the one the *Cap Pilar* saw: "His mouth was fringed with loose and bestial-looking lips; in and out of it there swam and slithered obscenely white sucker-fish, like snakes on the Gorgon's head. He was the incarnation of blind brutality; the spirit of all earthly frightfulness."[13]

Whales, however, have much more mass and power than sharks. A steamer of 400 tons is said to have been sunk by a sperm bull, but the most famous sinking, the one on which the book *Moby Dick* was based, was that of the whaler *Essex*. Deliberately ramming the ship twice, the huge bull whale smashed in the side completely; the men out in the boats chasing whales returned to find their base sunk by their quarry. Fortunately, the men remaining in the ship were able to launch a boat and save two quadrants, two compasses, two "practical navigators" and six hundred pounds of bread. In their choice can be seen the vital importance of navigational instruments in seamen's eyes. The way in which the men in the boats survived is told elsewhere in this book, but by an almost unbelievable coincidence another whale, of another species, attacked one of the surviving boats.[14]

The *California* had a boat smashed by a sperm whale; this was not an uncommon occurrence because of the need to approach closely enough to the whale to kill it with a lance held in the hand. Any violent flurry at this close range could smash a whaleboat, and this often happened. The size of a whale, however, made even its accidental approach cause for fear. "Whales I was frightened of" said Knox-Johnston, a young circumnavigator. "A large blue whale would not have to exert itself to turn over a boat of *Suhaili*'s size."[15] Dumas, another lone yachtsman, was worried when a fifty-foot sperm whale made "a couple of passes" at his yacht.[16] Marco Polo was told by Chinese seamen that they were afraid that whales would smash their ships.[17]

It is easy to understand why the Chinese would be afraid; whales are monstrous. Sanderson, a writer and an authority on whales, as a boy wriggled "through the main artery of a seventy-foot whale into the heart of the animal."[18] They are big enough for Jonahs:

In a German book published in 1895, a whaleman named James Bradley was said to have been swallowed by a whale which was caught and killed the next day. It was immediately opened and the luckless Bradley taken out of its stomach, still alive but entirely comatose. It is said that he lay in a swoon for hours and was found hard to revive, though this is not difficult to imagine, and was out of his mind for three months afterwards. According to the account, he then revived completely and was entirely normal.[19]

Pacific inhabitants have their Jonah stories also. In one, a British Columbian Indian, swallowed canoe and all by a whale, saved himself by cutting up and setting alight his canoe.[20] The resulting heartburn had the desired effect. Such stories are presumably an accurate psychological indication of men's reactions to the size and menace of whales.

The record blue whale was 113 feet long—2 feet longer than the *Resolution,* almost twice as long as the *Golden Hind*—and she weighed 170 tons. The female blues are often bigger than the males. Nor is a whale's power any less impressive than its size. A finback whale once ran ahead of a steam yacht doing twenty knots "for hour after hour, day after day, and it could still dash off at twice that speed, at least, to grab a fish or something, apparently without even changing gear."[21] They are efficient gears, in truth, for a finback's tail, using the whale's (typical) semi-rotary sculling motion, has been estimated by British naval engineers "to exert a drive over twenty times more efficient than that of 'any screw of similar dimensions we have so far devised."[22] No wonder a large female blue whale was able to tow a ninety-foot steam whaler, with its engines full astern, for seven hours at eight knots.

The immensity of such power makes most men fear whales. "Leviathan" has a sinister ring to it, no matter how reassuring are the tales of friendly dolphins. But whales have had centuries of being afraid of men; whaling began in prehistoric times, as the carvings and drawings of Neolithic man show. Adzes for cutting blubber, which are hundreds of years old, and harpoons which were made 16,000 years before Christ are displayed in museums. Phoenicians hunted the "blower," or sperm whale: "in ships of Arvad he rode; a blower in the great sea he slew."[23] No one knows how they killed whales, but it is conjectured that they were hunted by small boats launched from large ships, in which case harpoons would have been used. It can only be guessed how the Phoenicians kept the dead whales afloat.

A prehistoric ethnic group in Japan, prior to the Ainu and long before the Japanese, harpooned whales and kept them afloat by using floats made from sewn skins or from the stomachs of seals, almost identical to those used in the Neolithic Hebrides or those being used by the Eskimos of Alaska when the exploration ships arrived. Further south on the American Pacific coast, Indians at Cape Flattery used copper harpoons with elk-horn barbs, the harpoons fastened with whale sinew to sealskin floats. This is exactly the technique reported in British Columbia by Haswell; ". . . the harpoon is made of a stout mussle shell barbed with boan . . . their worps and lines are of Whale sinue and they have a number of Seel skins turned inside out and blown up with wind these they have to Keep the Whale from diving deep."[24] He described a whale "with sixteen Bladders fastened to him with harpoons," and commented of the Indians that "we must allow them expurt Whalemen."[25] Other expert whalemen—Japanese shore whalers—used floats so profusely that in some pictures the whole sea looks a mass of lines and buoys. Floats were necessary because most whales sink when dead. Some claim that "right whales" have this name because they are the "right" ones to hunt—they float.

At Nootka Sound on Vancouver Island, the *Discovery* bought 100 gallons of good whale oil for its lamps, and the Indians told the crew how the whales were harpooned from canoes. Each harpoon was attached to a large bladder which hampered the whale enough so that the canoes could keep up with him; finally, the Indians killed him "with large Whalebone Spears."[26] This was not essentially different to the way in which whales were killed by Europeans in the boom days of the 1840's. The only real difference was that the European whalers used the whaleboats themselves as the floats.

In the South Pacific, "according to the legends, the Polynesians continued for many centuries to hunt [whales] both for their flesh and for their teeth." A survivor of the *Port au Prince*, a European ship captured by the Tongans, has written about the value placed in Tonga on sperm whales' teeth used for personal decoration.[27] (Queen Elizabeth was given a sperm whale's tooth as an official present by the Fijians in 1953.) Maoris made extensive use of whalebone and whale teeth, but little is known of their method of capture.

It would be safe to presume that even the bravest of the brave descendants of Toi, an early leader of Maori settlement in New Zealand, would not use the method Hawkins, apparently in all seriousness, attributed to the Indians of Florida. On seeing a whale near shore, the Indian took two "round billets of wood," sharp at one end, swam out to the whale and mounted his neck, Hawkins said, and even when the whale dives

... the Indian forsaketh not his holde, but riseth with him, and thrusteth in a logg into one of his spowters, and with the other knocketh it in so fast, that by no meanes the whale can get it out. That fastned, at another opportunitie, he thrusteth in the second logg into the other spowter, and with all the force he can, keepeth it in. The whale not being able to breath, swimmeth presently ashore, and the Indian a cock-horse upon him.[28]

Whatever the methods used, whaling was not new to the Pacific, but the large-scale commercial exploitation of the resource was. It was a ruthless exploitation so speedily accomplished that some wooden ships lasted throughout the entire period; the *Maria* whaled from her launching in Massachusetts in 1782 until being scrapped exactly ninety years later in San Francisco.[29] One of the reasons given for this longevity is that the whale oil, which over time seemed to reach everywhere throughout the entire ship, was an excellent preservative. The last of the real old-time whalers in action was wrecked with a hold full of oil in 1924 at Cape Hatteras.[30] At Mystic, Connecticut, the *Charles W. Morgan*, which whaled from 1841 to 1920, is being restored to perfect repair as a nineteenth-century whale ship. This is a genuine restoration for this is a genuine whaler, with many logs of her voyages still available for study. An inspection leaves two dominant impressions: one, that, even to a modern eye, she appears to be a functionally efficient commercial craft, and, two, that the men who worked and sailed her were cramped and crowded beyond belief. Parenthetically, one might point out that wooden ships are much more durable, through rebuilding and remodelling, than those built of iron or steel. Good ships, well built of oak, could remain in use for 100 years without difficulty.

A good example of a sturdy whaler, and an example which had the advantage of a mission—to explore—and a literate captain—to describe—was the *Rattler* of Britain. It is not known whether the *Rattler* had the deadly figurehead that *Rattlesnake* had not, but perhaps even if she had, that fearless and fearsome reptile might have hesitated to attack a sperm whale. The *Rattler* was a converted Navy sloop of 374 tons fitted out by Sam Enderby and Company of London in 1792 in order to examine thoroughly the prospects for sperm whaling in the Pacific. Her main task was to explore, but she did hunt, killing six sperm whales on May Day, 1793. She had a crew of 22 to work a ship that the Royal Navy had crewed with 130 men, yet the only change in rigging was a slight reduction in sail area; there was no need, it is true, for large gun crews. Navy ships were often bought for use as whalers because of their sturdy construction.

Exploitation of the whales was large scale. The American whaling fleet at its peak in 1846 consisted of 680 ships and barques, 34 brigs, and 22 schooners, most of which cruised in the Pacific.[31] The American whalers drove the once great British whaling industry off the seas in spite of government support and subsidy. In the main, the Americans did it by hard work and superior skill, but the hard work, which actually amounted to brutality to the crews, was the more important factor. (Incidentally, there are several oil tankers now afloat, each of which has a greater tonnage than the total of those 736 American craft.) In addition to the Americans, there were substantial British, French, and Dutch whaling fleets in the Pacific in the early nineteenth century.

Men spoke out against the slaughter; de Freycinet of the *Uranie* calculated, and regretted, that 17,000 sperm whales a year were captured.[32] An historian of whaling tells of "whale after whale killed and abandoned untouched, except for the extraction of its baleen.... This was one of the stupidest and most wasteful actions in history."[33] But then, at the same time, tens of thousands of bison on the plains of America were being shot only for their tongues.

Men used both shore and ship for bases from which to catch Pacific whales. "Bay whaling" in Australia and New Zealand began in Tasmania, where whales were at first so plentiful "that what was described as their 'snoring' once kept the governor awake in his residence."[34] The first whale caught off Australia was worth £1,000 in bounty. In bay whaling, whales were spotted from lookout points on shore and then pursued by open boats, clinker-built of cedar. In each boat there was a harpooner, a steersman with a long steering sweep, and usually four oarsmen, one of whom was responsible for the correct functioning of the long harpoon line, kept coiled in a tub until performing its function of holding the wounded whale "fast." These boats were practically identical to the whaling ships' "double-ended craft with cedar planking and oak timbers and keel, designed for buoyancy and speed,"[35] which also had a crew of six (figure 34).

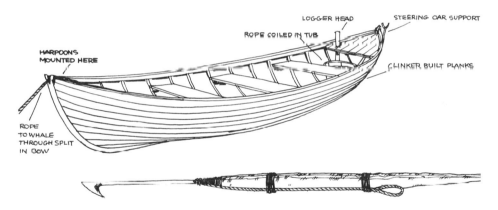

Fig. 34. Whale Boat and Harpoon

A whaling ship's officer, survivor of the *Essex*, spoke with feeling of the frailty of the lightly-built whaleboat; designed for speed, its main advantage was buoyancy to ride the sea. Once fast to a whale the boats acted as gigantic floats dragging on him, and, then, according to an historian of whaling, ". . . the oft-told procedure of burning lines rushing between the cleats, entangled human limbs, desperate backing and pulling on the oars, lancing, shouting, cursing, bloody foam, flailing tails, and miraculous escapes took place."[36] Most whales, when firmly held, were finally brought to the ship, or the ship to them. The whales were cut up and the oil extracted—the process so well described by Melville in *Moby Dick*.

Because of the value of whale products, an enormous industry was built up in the Pacific. The hundreds of American and scores of British and French ships operating from Alaska to Antarctica searched remorselessly for the great mammals. This very scrutiny gave a distinctive appearance to the whaler: "the vessel under short sail, with lookouts at the mast-head, eagerly scanning the wide expanse around them, has a totally different air from those engaged in a regular voyage."[37] Occasionally they heard, rather than saw, the whales. Captain West tells of hearing a male bowhead, the sound coming through the bottom of the ship. It is possible; modern recording devices have picked up and preserved for all to hear a whole variety of whale calls and songs, some audible for miles under water. Old-time whalemen used to say that a male bowhead could hear a female calling from the equator; an exaggeration, without doubt, but perhaps less so than we formerly imagined. One modern underwater listening device at Bermuda heard and recorded the sound of an underwater explosion near Australia.

A rather fanatical scrutiny of the ocean was not the only difference to be seen between whale ships and other types of craft "A 'spouter' we knew her to be, as soon as we saw her, by her cranes and boats, and by her stump top-gallant masts, and a certain slovenly look to the sails, rigging, spars, and hull; and when we got on board we found everything to correspond—spouter fashion."[38] Nevertheless, Dana thought "there are no better seamen" nor "so venturous and skilful navigators" than those on whalers.[39] And this was so, although good men from men-of-war and from merchant ships would try to avoid shipping in them. Opinions varied. An officer of a lordly clipper said that his men thought whales harmless and whaling easy; they referred to whale ships as "butcher shops adrift."[40] In return, not all seamen admired clippers or their captains. One writer probably gave a commonly held view: the *James Pattison*, his ship, he said, was "no brand-new clipper, sharp-built and overmanned, throwing aloft sails with fancy names."[41]

American whaling ships (Plate 24)—and the British and French were not much different—were shaped rather like the old "round-ship," with very blunt bows and square transom sterns. Some navy ships and Atlantic packets, bought second-hand for use as whale ships, naturally had the hull lines to be expected for their original purpose, but were converted by the addition of try-works (the furnace and boiler for extracting the oil) and cranes. Three-masted whalers were usually rigged as barques, square-rigged on fore and main, and fore-and-aft-rigged on the mizzen mast. The whaling ships were specially strengthened so that the huge heads and chunks of blubber could be hoisted by the cranes.

When the first of this type of whaler—English in 1788 and American in 1791—came round the Horn into the Pacific, they found that the Spaniards in Chile had already built up a whaling tradition to complement the ancient whaling traditions of the Basque caravels. (It was on one of these early caravels that the rendering down of the blubber into oil aboard the ship was first begun, the fires, then as later, using the "crackling" as fuel once the process of "trying" was under way.) Some historians claim that the trade brought by whalers to the Pacific coast of South America—a trade increased against the will of Spain—was a major factor in the drive for independence of the Spanish colonies there.

One captain who studied the matter concluded "after reading hundreds of log books and sea journals, that the old whaling vessels had more than their arithmetical proportion of madmen."[42] This extreme statement may have been true. If the nineteenth-century American sailor, J. R. Browne, is to be believed, "we have a whaling marine in which cruelty and despotism are fostered with special care."[43] Granting Melville's knowledge of the subject, it would be depressing to believe that Ahab of the *Pequod* was more real than allegorical. One old whaling man, on taking the wheel of Villiers's latter day frigate, the *Joseph Conrad*, burst into "Shenandoah"—haunting, nostalgic, deeply moving.[44] His life on whaling ships cannot have been all bad—perhaps he had been a harpooner.

If harpooners were the aristocrats aboard whaleships, their prestige was threatened as early as 1731 when someone "invented a new sort of gun for shooting with gunpowder the harpoons into the bodies of whales."[45] This idea, in spite of some initial success, did not take hold until a better model was invented in Norway during the middle years of the nineteenth century.

Many people had tried to invent something along this line. In the Public Records Office in London, there is correspondence about the development of a rocket harpoon in the 1820's, which would have enabled the swift and dangerous finbacks to be captured. Apparently, it came to nothing. By 1859 some American captains were using a "Bomb lance gun" to kill the whales. It too must not have been widely

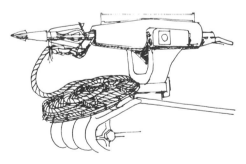

Fig. 35. Harpoon Gun

adopted.[46] These ideas were foreshadowed in the Pacific by "the little short arrowes" which muskets on the *Daintie* fired in battle with "singular effect and execution" in 1593,[47] although these were meant to kill more dangerous, if smaller, animals than whales.

The Pacific had several advantages for whalers. First, there was a good supply of whales, once the habits and migration patterns of the different species had been learned. From the coast of New Zealand in the early 1840's "it was estimated that American whalers alone took away £140,000 worth of bay-whale oil in one year."[48] Profits could be immense: "the *Lagoda* in twelve years earned $652,000 and in one year paid a dividend of 363½ per cent. She cost less than $5,000 to build!"[49] Second, there were good bases in New Zealand, the islands of Polynesia, Hawaii, and northwest America. Third, the mid-Pacific was a pleasant place to cruise, and whalers were often sent out on "between season" cruises to overhaul the ship and make her boats ready for the Arctic whaling in summer. Cheaper than holding the ship, for instance, in San Francisco, thereby risking the loss of a good crew, it had the additional advantage that "a school of sperm whales in the vicinity of the Pacific islands"[50] might be found.

Captain West, who kept a journal, once had $10,550 for his share at the end of one voyage. He enjoyed recording this as a record of his competence as a whaler and not simply because of the money.[51] Whaling wages had their origin in the whaling co-operative in America, which was "a joint enterprise, initiated by co-operative labour, and entirely without subscribed capital."[52] Ownership of ships became private, but wages were still shares or "lays," divided according "to his or her investment in money or labour."[53] It was important that the system be understood. Dillon tells of a Maori crewman greatly disgruntled when he received no pay when there had been no catch.

As a matter of interest, the sandalwood trade operated on the same system: the master received one twelfth of the market value of the wood, while the shares of the others varied from the mate's one twenty-eighth to the seaman's one seventy-second. There was a somewhat similar system used in both buccaneering and privateering, and also in national navies. It was called "prize money," and the money accruing from the sale of captured ships and cargoes was divided among the crew members present at the capture. (The definition of "present" often caused trouble, but in the Royal Navy and in the Courts it was usually defined as "within sight of".)

Shares in sandalwooding, prize money, and whaling would seem to favour the captain disproportionately, at least to modern eyes. However, whaling captains had to be tough men, for they had both rough crews and a hazardous trade to master. Rose de Freycinet was not favourably impressed with those she met. She wrote of "the usual harshness of the whalers of the New World." Unfair perhaps, but then she had already said, unfairly, as have others before and since, that "Americans in general think only of commerce and have rough ways into the bargain."[54]

Whaling—and not only American whaling—was a rough and crudely exploitative industry. What remains of it is still so. Courage and endurance are necessary qualities in whaling men, but they do little to justify a slaughter just as repugnant as that of the prairie bison. Although some far-sighted people, such as de Freycinet, did protest, nonetheless the early nineteenth-century men were operating by the standards of the day. The slaughter still goes on, in spite of strenuous efforts to control it; possibly, it will not stop until the whales become as extinct as the Nantucket wooden whaleships which Melville knew.

CHAPTER 11

Clippers and Windjammers

. . . the graceful, yacht-like clipper, perhaps the most beauti-
ful and life-like thing ever fashioned by the hand of man.

A CLIPPER SHIP OFFICER

[The steel ship] . . . at its least attractive, a wall-sided, blunt-
ended, but powerful-looking vessel, with most of the delicate
grace of the old clipper hull gone; at its best, it was a hull
which combined power and grace harmoniously blended, and
aesthetically a masterpiece.

ELIS KARLSSON
OF THE *HERZOGIN CECILIE*

Tall ships were the creation of the nineteenth century. Sails were hung higher and higher on immense masts in order to catch and use the driving power the hulls were designed to endure. The hulls could both endure it and use it, and speeds were attained under sail in the 1850's that would not disgrace a modern steamer.

This chapter is about the ships towards the end of the days of commercial sail, and about speed and the freights which demanded it and were willing to pay for it. Importers demanded speed. The first tea from China each year fetched a premium on the London market. Gold in California, in Victoria, Australia, in British Columbia, and in Otago made men willing to pay for speedy passage; the goods and the food the passengers needed boosted the ship's earnings. Emigrants to New Zealand and Australia who could afford to pay demanded both the luxury of speed and other extras as well. It was all interrelated, as was so much else at sea. A speedy passage meant less skimping with water and food; people were willing to pay for both speed and good living; more money to shipowners meant more money to spend on improving conditions to attract more passengers. In a buoyant period, conditions can improve very quickly indeed.

Plate 25. The *Cutty Sark*. This tall ship lies now at Greenwich, England, preserved as a relic of the great days of the tea clippers and the annual race home with the new season's tea. One of the most beautiful ships ever built and named for the robes of Tam O'Shanter's witch, she contained a spirit that bewitched men of the sea—there are *Cutty Sark* clubs all over the world.

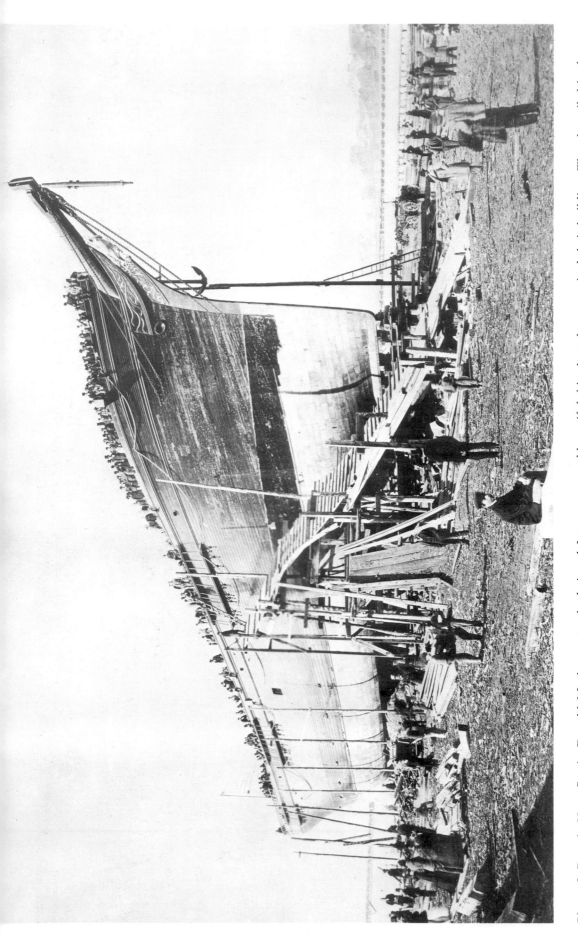

Plate 26. Born in Nova Scotia, Donald Mackay not only designed fast, strong, and beautiful ships but also supervised their building. Then he sailed in them to gain the practical experience needed to build others even better. He is shown here (in top hat) at the launching of the hull of the clipper *Glory of the Seas*

Plate 27. The *Marco Polo*. This clipper was a favourite vessel with passengers and freighting firms alike. She was built at St. John, New Brunswick, in the nineteenth century, when New Brunswick and Nova Scotian ships and seamen were famous throughout the sailing world. Her speed and comfort, even luxury, won for Canadian shipyards many orders for ships to work the Australia run.

Plate 28. The *Herzogin Cecilie*. Named for the Duchess of Mecklenberg, the *Herzogin Cecilie* was a twentieth-century steel ship. Of only slightly greater tonnage than the biggest wooden clippers, she was much longer and much stronger than any of them. Her steel-won strength, below and aloft, allowed her to carry sail in heavy winds (in light winds she spread over one acre of canvas), while her length enabled her to achieve great speed. In one famous hour's

Later in the century, competition with the plodding dirty steamships, which ignored the winds except when they raged, forced the sailing ships to cut costs and to carry more passengers and freight. Simplified rigging cut crew costs, with only a minor sacrifice in speed, and redesigned hulls still carried bulk cargoes efficiently. But as steam engines improved and canals were dug, the end came clearly into sight. Sailing ships lasted until the 1930's, although fewer sailed each year from the early years of the century. However, even today, there are many people still living who knew them and crewed them, and who still will argue the merits of this ship or that in terms of beauty, of comfort, or of speed.

Some sailors argue that the *Thermopylae*, a British clipper designed for the tea trade to China, was the fastest sailing ship, over a passage, ever built. On her first voyage, she broke the record for every passage, that is, from one port of call to the next. She was 212 feet long and 36 feet wide as compared to the American-built *Lightning*'s 244 feet by 44 feet, a ratio of 5.88 length to breadth compared to 5.54, respectively. The *Thermopylae* made fast passages, but not very fast individual runs, probably because she was too narrow to be driven hard in heavy weather, in which the beamier American ships had their greatest advantage. She was famous for speed when winds were light; "she has been known to have gone along 7 knots an hour [sic] when a man could have walked round the decks with a lighted candle."[1]

The clipper ship *Cutty Sark* (Plate 25) is very famous, perhaps because she can still be seen in dry dock near the National Maritime Museum at Greenwich, England—although over 100 years old. Very narrow (212 feet long by 36 feet, a ratio of 5.88, the same as that of the *Thermopylae*), she was stretched quite a bit from the length-to-breadth ratio of about 3.6 of the *Golden Hind*, which was a fast handy ship of her day. Because of her length, this clipper was very fast and purposely so. She was built at Dumbarton in 1869 specifically to "lower *Thermopylae*'s colours," her designer using the lines of a famous speedster the *Tweed*, which had been developed from the lines of a very fast French frigate. Not only beautiful ships were fast; there were other fast ships which were similar to "the marvellous *Tweed*, a ship, I have heard, heavy to look at but of phenomenal speed. . . . She had a great sheer, high bows, and a clumsy stern . . . nothing much to look at."[2] Nor were the great windjammers of the twentieth century particularly beautiful ships, yet their strength was such that they were fast, for strength meant the ability to carry sail when the winds were strong.

The *Cutty Sark* had great days in the Australian wool trade as well as in the tea trade from China; she did better in the Australian voyages, while her rival, the *Thermopylae*, a fine light-wind sailer, proved superior in the voyages to China. The *Cutty Sark* was known as a wet ship. The "long, snaky hulls" of the British clippers had the disadvantage of making them wet ships; in a high wind and sea, the water would sweep many of them from end to end.[3] This point was emphasized when Gann, in describing the *Albatros*, said she was narrow, "being only 20 feet, 6 inches at the waist. I presumed this would make her a wet ship and I was right."[4] The *Cutty Sark* carried a sky sail on her mainmast, and spread a tremendous area of sail. Her masts were placed like those of the *Tweed*, with her foremast particularly far aft, and all masts handsomely raked. She is a beautiful ship, her figurehead a beautiful witch "with her long hair and cutty sark flowing in the wind."[5]

Many claim that the most beautiful tea clipper of all was the *Sir Lancelot*, and that she may be regarded, in most ways, as the ultimate in sailing ship design. The tea clippers, however, had the weakness of any design which is meant for one purpose only; when the purpose changed, the design died. Yet miniature clippers, built to copy the lines of the *Thermopylae, Cutty Sark, Sir Lancelot*, and other immortals were still being built in Ceylon as late as the 1930's. Solidly built of teak and schooner-rigged, they made durable and handy island trading vessels, preserving a traditional beauty in a functional world.[6]

An American sailing ship man of great experience considered that the British tea clippers had "probably combined the good qualities of a merchant ship in a higher degree than any other vessels that have ever been built."[7] It is important to remember that clipper design varied to fit the requirements of the trade for which the ship was being built, *e.g.*, tea or immigrants. Speed, strength, carrying capacity, and economy were blended successfully into beauty. Low running cost was perhaps the most important feature ships could have, for without it they could not survive. Although not as famous for beauty as were the various clippers, the great German steel ships of the twentieth century were probably the best of all, which is why they survived to be the last of the large sailing ships.

Old sailors everywhere argue about the comparative fleetness of various sailing ships. Often the arguments are confusing. It is important to understand the distinction between a maximum speed attained in running before high winds, and the speed of a ship averaged over a whole voyage. Some big ships could sail very fast in heavy winds, yet were slow in light winds, or had to sail at such great angles to head winds (thus lengthening the total miles sailed), that their high maximum speed did not get them home any sooner than a ship with a slower maximum speed which could handle unfavourable conditions better. An analogy might be that of a race between a Land Rover and a racing car, in which two thirds of the course covered rough and stony hill paddocks.

When discussing the speeds of ships, what is actually meant must be carefully specified: total passage time between distant ports, maximum sailing speed per hour, or the distance run per day or per week. This is particularly true of fast small yachts, for, in a one-man operation, comfort is important. Endurance is necessary over long passages: "It was comfort that lay behind the *Spray's* great runs. This comprised many things—stiffness, easy motion, dryness, and roominess."[8] The *Spray*, in other words, would sail well in rough conditions, yet remain comfortable enough for Slocum to endure many consecutive days and nights of hard, fast sailing.

A ship's maximum speed depends theoretically on her length at the waterline—the longer the faster. By formula, her speed in knots should be equal to the square root of the waterline length in feet multiplied by one and one third. Chichester, in a very thorough discussion of this in *Along The Clipper Way*, explains that when a ship moves it creates a bow wave in the water.[9] As the speed increases, the distance from the crest of one bow wave to the crest of the next lengthens. When this distance becomes too great, the stern of the ship is not held high enough and the ship has to climb her own bow wave, requiring much more driving force from her sails. Because a long ship can go much faster before being forced to climb her bow wave, her potential speed, given good sails and rigging, is greater. But this is a theoretical maximum speed which needs favourable conditions before it can be reached.

A better way of judging the speed of ships is the day's run—or better still a week's run—the longer period giving the chance of more varied conditions. An underestimate of longitude one day and an overestimate the next would give a cumulative error—and observational errors of a few miles are easy to make in conditions of swell and add much false distance to a single day's run. Chichester was sceptical about accepting less than a six-day run as an indication of sailing ability.

Some big sailing ships in the early twentieth century could average fourteen knots for a seven-day run. The *Cutty Sark* averaged fifteen knots for six days on two separate occasions. The point about *two* occasions is important; exceptional conditions can make an exceptional run for what is really only a good ship not a great one; only a great ship can do well consistently. The *Thermopylae*, British-built like her greatest rival, practically always made fast passages and once went from London to Melbourne in sixty-one days. Because of the immense distances and the variety of conditions encountered—the sailing ship voyages from Europe to Australia had to pass through the Roaring Forties and the Doldrums each way—the passages are measured in days. The

Lightning, an American-built clipper, went from Melbourne to Liverpool in sixty-four days, although, according to Lubbock, this passage was at the cost of some spars and much risk.

Speed was important for several reasons. For example, early clippers entered the opium trade to China, and became known as "opium clippers." They were lavishly equipped, as befits a trade of vice, and they had to be fast because of pirates. Both the exceptional currents and tides of the China coast and the monsoon winds of the China Sea made a strong ship essential, and clippers had this quality or they could not have carried the sails necessary to get their speed.

Clippers were originally American—although Donald Mackay (Plate 26), the designer of the biggest, fastest, and most famous clippers, including the *Lightning*, was Canadian born and reared, and later naturalized in the United States. Like Captain Slocum of the *Spray*, he came from an area of Canada where until recently beautiful wooden ships were built almost by eye and hand, and where the famous "bluenose" schooners—the supreme fishing boat design—were developed and built.

America's sailing ships were beautiful ships from the earliest days. The schooner was developed there and very good, fast frigates, but, above all, so were the clippers. Although Britain and the United States were the only countries which built and sailed clippers, much of the inspiration for the development of fast and beautiful ships had come from French design of the second half of the eighteenth century. French frigates and luggers were studied thoroughly when they were operating from ports in the United States during the War of Independence. (A "lugger" is a fast small ship named for its lug sails.) The beautiful lines of both these French types affected the design of the privateers and frigates built in the United States. From these, the clipper ship developed through a process that changed them quite drastically, giving them finer underwater lines.

By 1824, an Englishman in Liverpool had written about the "long, sharp built, beautifully painted and rigged" American ships, contrasting them with "the English vessels, short, round and dirty, resembling great black tubs."[10] One device which helped Americans design and build beautiful ships was the invention in 1794 of a type of lift model made of thin sections joined by screws. Taken apart, its lines could be transferred easily to full-size working plans. Thus, when the designer was satisfied with the model's appearance and potential, it was taken apart to get the cross-section shapes, which were enlarged for working drawings. Only then was the ship built full scale.

American designers were not hampered by the obsolete laws which taxed

Fig. 36. Clipper Hull Profile above the Waterline

ships according to their tonnage. These regulations required the measurement of tonnage by a formula that made it seem more profitable to build ships which were too narrow to be the most effective sail carriers, even though the rigging had been improved to give the strength necessary for the huge sail areas which the modern demand for speed in commerce had made essential.[11] Commercial monopolies, such as that of the East India Company, held back improvements in the design of British ships for years, because, as only East India Company ships could trade, there was practically no incentive to improve the East Indiaman ship design for anything other than greater comfort on leisurely voyages. Competitive speed did not matter. When this stultification was removed, British designers and builders did their job well enough; the *Cutty Sark* shows it. But by this time the Americans had vastly improved the square-rigged ship. As early as the 1830's they had developed ships which had the ability ". . . to carry sail, to beat to windward, and to 'tack in a pint o' water' . . . a ship of 450 tons, which, handled by 18 officers and men, could carry half as much freight as a 1,500-ton British East Indiaman with a crew of 125, and could sail half again as fast."[12]

British clippers were narrow compared to the American, partly to defeat the tonnage measurement regulations—the same inhibiting influence on ship design of treasury bureaucracy as was seen with Chinese and Dutch ships. More wisely, the Americans built ships to be good, fast ships, regardless of tonnage regulations, believing that they made more profit from the extra speed their width gave them than they lost in tonnage tax in foreign ports. For a time, American ships could cross the Atlantic five times to four for British ships; it is the same major advantage that fast jet airliners today have over the slower propeller-driven aircraft. The greater number of passages can increase the number of passengers carried as much as bigger capacity can. The "Concorde" hopes to prove this point again.

American design improvements culminated in the clippers—the word comes from clip, to run fast, that is, to go at a good "clip." Known at first as "Baltimore clippers" from their city of origin, they were at that time small vessels; they were "brigs, brigantines, fore-and-aft or topsail schooners, and rarely exceeded two hundred tons register."[13] Like their French prototypes, the Baltimore clippers tended to have their greatest width well forward and to have a graceful tumble-home, while a long clean after-body gave the "time-honored cod's head and mackerel's tail."[14]

As these lines were made for speed, they were originally used for small craft; big ships were built full bodied in order to have a roomy cargo stowage or to be stable gun platforms. What made the later big clippers so different was that they were built as big ships on speedy small ship lines. An early example was the *Ann McKim*. According to some nineteenth-century ship historians, she was the first large clipper, but a more recent authority states that "she was a 'Baltimore Clipper,' no more and no less."[15] For some reason (probably too small cargo capacity), she was not directly copied, but she was both interesting and successful enough to encourage American designers to try to improve the lines and the sailing qualities of large ships. Encouraged in their turn—perhaps even stung—designers and builders in Canada and Britain, and particularly Scotland, built some of the best big clippers.

One of the first "extreme clippers" was the *Rainbow*, with her long fine bow and with her greatest width placed much further back; this latter was a major change in design. Chinese junks, in one of their many contrasts to European design, tend to have their greatest underwater width very far back, a quite recent feature in Western ships. The *Rainbow* proved to be very fast and seaworthy, demonstrating that the clipper design was an excellent one. The lines were good. A reporter said of the clipper *Lightning* on her first voyage: "We have seen many vessels pass through the water, but never saw one which disturbed it less. Not a ripple curled below her cut-water, nor did the water break at a single place along her sides."[16]

American clippers, compared with contemporary British ships, were broad, and lightly built of soft timber that did not last. They were fast ships of short life, which is said to be true of all that is beautiful. Lightness of a ship increases her speed, but often decreases her ability to manoeuvre—exactly the point Gann made about the shallow-draught Chinese junks. In the *Wager*, the ship from Anson's squadron which was wrecked in southern Chile, Bulkeley's crewmates once had to lighten ship by throwing cargo overboard in order to escape pursuit. It worked—the lightened ship sailed faster and escaped—as Bulkeley tells in his journal of his famous escape in the *Wager*'s reconstructed longboat.

Racing clippers used a variety of tricks to increase their speed and each captain quickly learned his ship's best sailing trim. One, in use as a troop ship, went noticeably faster when the troops were in bed below deck, presumably because the weight was lower. In order to help win a race, the troops, nothing loth, spent most of their voyage in their hammocks instead of drilling on deck.[17]

Some sailors argued that American clippers made exceptionally good speeds only when new and light, because the softwood of which they were built gradually soaked up water and waterlogged them. Softwood ships also leaked badly compared to oak or teak ships, and many sailors refused to ship in them in order to avoid long hours at the pumps. The breadth, or beam, that was an essential feature of the design gave the American clippers speed, because it gave them the buoyancy needed to carry full sail in strong winds. Long narrow ships could not do this. In the days of steel rigging, four-masted German barques from Hamburg achieved eighteen knots, as the *Lightning* did, but "to set more sail, when that speed was reached, only buried their barque's [sic] bows in the sea, and reduced their speed."[18] This was an important limiting factor, especially for ships with narrow hulls.

British shipbuilders fought back against American superiority of design; excellent composite clippers were designed and built specifically for the tea run from China to Britain. "Composite" describes ships built by applying wood planking over iron framing. There were good reasons for this technique. Wooden hulls did not present the condensation problem of iron hulls and they could also be sheathed with copper as long as care was taken to keep the ironwork separate from the copper in order to prevent the electrolytical decay of the sheathing. Copper sheathing was considered so important that British naval vessels of this composite type were built as late as 1874. With the *Sapphire*, built that year, wooden shipbuilding came to an end in a navy that in one form or another had been in existence since Saxon days.

Copper sheathing gave very smooth bottoms which reduced friction with the water; this, combined with the narrow British hulls, made composite tea clippers very fast ships in ordinary weather. The *Thermopylae* and *Cutty Sark* are the most famous composite clippers—beautiful, swift ships. Perhaps the perfection of the American clipper-type was the *Stag-Hound*, with "graceful sheer, finely formed midship section, and beautifully moulded ends."[19] Like another very beautiful ship, the first *Royal Sovereign*, the *Stag-Hound* was completely destroyed by accidental fire.

Despite their beauty, clippers were not handy ships; twenty big square sails meant a lot of manhandling and trimming each time the ship had to tack. Clippers were ships for long distances and strong, consistent winds. Within those limits, they were of the beauty that the successful relationship of form to function always grants wherever men seek speed.

Not all the speed of the clippers was due to their design. Clipper captains had a reputation for keeping sail on: "Bearing down on us, with the wind on her quarter, was a ship, a huge square-sailed vessel bearing full topsails and, like a gesture of defiance, above them a close-reefed topgallant on the main. . . . By her snow white cloths and her glistening black hull—for she lifted with the speed of an express—we knew her an American."[20] As a result of this personal factor, ships which changed captains often changed reputations at the same time. Some ships that had seemed slow began to move faster; some with a reputation for speed never made another fast passage. The *Marco Polo* (Plate 27), a very famous Canadian-built ship, lost her reputation for speed after a change of captains. As with the *Lightning*, her record at least is in part due to Captain "Bully" Forbes.

Perhaps the best example of the relationship of captain to speed is Captain de Cloux's success in different ships in the great grain races from Australia to England in the late 1920's and early 1930's. Of the 1932 race, Villiers says: "It was the same old de Cloux, though *Parma* was no *Herzogin Cecilie*. I believe if de Cloux had had the sluggard *Mozart*, he would still have won the grain race twice in three starts."[21] Captains who sailed ships which had a reputation for speed were often criticized for recklessness, just as captains with well-disciplined ships were often called brutal. The latter charges are nearly always anachronistic (when made today), or were made by people who had no conception of either the responsibility of command nor "had experience in handling degenerates at sea."[22] According to a person who had known both the responsibility and the experience, American merchant captains "enforced their authority by sheer power of character and will against overwhelming odds of brute force, often among cut-throats and desperadoes."[23] These seem strong statements, yet they are corroborated in the main by evidence from other journals and autobiographies.

Sailed by such captains and driven unrelentingly at speed, the clippers set standards of speedy and reliable service far beyond anything yet seen. It was on the Britain to Australia run that the *James Baines*—a Donald Mackay ship—sailed at twenty-one knots, the fastest recorded speed of a ship under sail.

Clippers were passenger liners as well as cargo ships. The *Marco Polo*, already mentioned as a fast ship, was designed and built in New Brunswick (in that part of Canada most distant from the long Canadian coastline of the Pacific), and set the standards for speed and comfort for passengers on the long run from England to Australia. The *Marco Polo* was damaged at her launching and some sailors said she was "hogged," that is, drooping at bow and stern. It did not slow her; in fact, it may have speeded her up. Certainly, she was not beautiful; she was said to be "as square as a brick fore and aft, with a bow like a savage bulldog."[24] But others have described her quite differently, "in fact, with a bottom like a yacht, she has above water all the appearance of a frigate."[25] Her success led to many orders for

New Brunswick ships for the Australia run. She sometimes logged over sixteen knots, in spite of the fact that passenger ships, out of consideration for passenger comfort, were not driven as hard as were cargo clippers. A favourite vessel with passengers and one of the greatest of wooden ships, the *Marco Polo* was most luxuriously fitted out internally with upholstery "in embossed crimson velvet," and public rooms richly ornamented with all the glories of Victorian interior decoration.[26]

Life at sea was changing. Clippers could afford to wine and dine the passengers tastefully (Plate 50). Some of them were as famous for good food as many ships of a century earlier had been notorious for bad food; however, some passenger ships which predated the clippers had done well enough in this regard. The ship *Hope* in 1838 would seem to have been comfortable for passengers, for they could "... breakfast at half-past eight and such *capital breakfasts*. Hot rolls, new bread and about a dozen different dishes such as mutton chops, liver and bacon, cold fowl, ham, fine hambro beef, anchovies, herrings, etc., etc. Tea, coffee, chocolate."[27]

Passengers could be fed well on clippers because speed meant short passages and high profits. The four-masted barque *Great Republic*, designed and built by Mackay as the largest wooden merchant ship ever launched, once rounded Cape Horn east to west from 50°S round to 50°S again in a little over nine days. Sailing on that particular trip in 1857, while freights were still high, she grossed a quarter of a million dollars in her ninety-two-day voyage from New York to San Francisco.[28] Profits poured into the American clippers as a reward for their swiftness: "Many of them more than cleared their original cost in less than one year, during a voyage round the globe, after deducting all expenses."[29]

Clippers had disappeared by the 1880's, not because they were not good sailing ships, but because sails were becoming obsolete as the source of power in commercial shipping. Although the complete changeover from sail to steam on the open sea took place roughly between 1840 and 1940, sails were doomed because they depended too much on men and too completely on the wind. Steam power promised certain scheduling, a means of getting from port to port with little worry—never, of course, with no worry at all—about winds or tides or being embayed. When the Suez Canal was finished, the tea clippers to and from China were finished too, even though they lingered for a while. When the completion of the Canadian Pacific Railway gave another fast all-British route for valuable cargoes from East Asia to Britain, the first tea crop of the year could go *via* ship to Vancouver, train to Montreal, and then by ship to Liverpool.

Yet sailing ships of a size and strength to make good use of the "Brave

West Winds" of 40°S remained competitive cargo carriers for bulky products, such as wheat and wool from Australia, for another half a century. At the beginning of the twentieth century, sailing ships were still an important part of national merchant marines. The British Empire was using 1,956 wooden sailing ships with a total tonnage of 564,797 tons, and iron- or steel-hulled sailing ships of a total tonnage of 1,914,150 tons. The United States had 2,287 wooden sailing ships, of 1,123,307 tons, and 83 metal-hulled sailing ships of 149,608 tons.[30] Germany and France had great steel sailing ships in service, and other powers, such as Sweden, Holland and Portugal, had large sailing fleets. It can be seen, therefore, that even in the twentieth century sails have powered commerce as well as provided cruising pleasure. But even these ships were doomed when the Panama Canal shortened the distance to Europe and made roaring past the Horn an unjustified risk.

There was no hurry for wheat and wool to reach market, but the load had to be big enough to be economic; bulk carriers needed hulls of capacity and great strength: "A modified clipper hull, built of iron, with a larger cargo capacity than the yacht-like tea clippers, appeared . . . excellent vessels in every way: handy, fast, and durable."[31] The *Melbourne*, one of these ships, once averaged over twelve knots for seventeen days, a remarkable run.

The development of iron hulls put industrial Britain in a position to regain the merchant ship supremacy which she had lost to forested America. Britain had the resources and the skill to produce fine iron products, and she had built one iron-hulled ship as early as 1800. Iron ships meant a fresh start in which Britain's skills and capital could be used to advantage; iron hulls ended the supremacy of wooden ships built in the eastern United States and Canada. They also made dry ships, because they had no seams to work. "Bluenoses" and "Down-easters," both ships and men, gradually faded into legend. The last wooden, square-rigged ship built in the United States was the *Aryan*, launched in Maine in 1893. Fortunately, a handsome, iron-hulled four-masted ship, the *Falls of Clyde*, built in Scotland, is being restored for exhibition at the Bishop Museum in Hawaii. Iron hulls have great endurance. The *Joseph Conrad* (Plate 29) "was built of Swedish iron, the most indestructible of ship materials."[32]

These fine iron ships were replaced gradually by large steel ships, far longer, wall-sided, blunt, powerful-looking, but not as beautiful as the wood or iron clippers. The large steel ships were called windjammers, an American name said to come from sailing with the yards jammed into the wind. They could carry almost twice as much cargo as clippers of the same dimensions, because of the different underwater shape of the two hulls (figure 37). Although these big ships were nearly as fast as the clippers had been, they got their fleetness

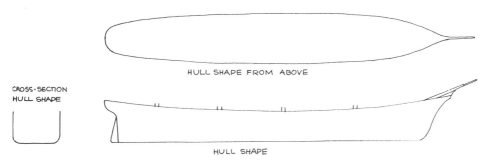

HULL SHAPE FROM ABOVE

CROSS-SECTION
HULL SHAPE

HULL SHAPE

Fig. 37. Late Nineteenth-Century Windjammer—note wall sides of cross-section

not from a fine shape, but from their length and from their strength.

Steam power helped in this development of sailing ships. Steam tugs to tow these big cargo carriers in and out of harbour meant that the ships could be designed for long, hard ocean passages without worrying too much about handiness near land. Sails and yards were raised or braced, and anchors were raised by steam-powered winches. Light, but immensely strong, steel standing rigging and masts added strength aloft while also subtracting weight; in the *Seaforth*, an iron ship built in 1863, twenty-one tons weight aloft was saved by using steel spars and rigging. Another advantage was that this greater strength was provided with much less wind resistance. Rigging and sail plans were simplified, so that fewer men were needed; some big German four-masted barques had all three square rigged masts the same, with interchangeable yards and masts.[33]

Increasing worry about a shortage of fossil fuels and the dangers inherent in producing nuclear power has made engineers begin to discuss a renaissance for large cargo-carrying sailing ships. They propose that these should have their sails raised and lowered mechanically, and also trimmed for direction and effective area at any given time by the same computer that is navigating the ship. Engines would be retained as an auxiliary feature, as in modern yachts or the earliest long distance steamships, to be used only when entering or leaving harbour, in calms, or in emergencies. These ships, still only a gleam in some designers' eyes, are different from the last of the great windjammers only in increased mechanization and in the use of computers. At least one modern commercial sailing ship is beyond the "gleam-in-the-eye" stage: "A Sydney naval architect has been commissioned to design a 2,000-ton sailing ship for the Pacific trade. . . . The ship will have a low-speed engine for inshore work and when it is becalmed. . . . It is intended to carry bulk cargoes that need no lifting gear, such as blue metal and timber."[34]

The great windjammers still depended on strong men and capable officers. A fine example, coincidentally a ship in which Conrad once sailed, is the

Herzogin Cecilie (Plate 28), a German-built ship (originally a four-masted barque of 3,000 tons registered), long, very strong, and very fast—the length was no problem when building with steel. "But with a gale blowing, *Herzogin Cecilie* was in her element, and it is doubtful if any ship that ever sailed could have sailed her under the horizon [leave her behind out of sight] in a force nine gale."[35] The *Herzogin Cecilie* claimed twenty and three quarter knots, only slightly less than the record speed of the clipper *James Baines*. These steel ships had the length to allow them a high maximum speed and the stability of hull and strength of rigging to allow them to carry sail when lesser ships were furling theirs. Morton once compared them to the *Beeswing*: "when we met the heavy westerlies ... and had to reduce canvas, the big boys would keep going."[36]

Not all the big boys could keep going, not even the strong ones of the twentieth century. The French three-master of almost sixteen hundred tons, the *Bretagne*, was so battered by the storms in July and August of 1900 that she was abandoned and her crew taken off by an English ship. In 1913, the English three-master *Dalgonar* was stricken by a gale and an "enormous wave," and her crew was rescued by a French ship. But it was not the dangers or hardships of sailing that brought the end of the big, beautiful ships; it was the attrition of economy. Beauty at sea, at least for working ships, was as doomed by accountancy as was craftsmanship on shore.

Maintenance and Movement

This section discusses the repairs and maintenance of the ships' hulls, the significance of and maintenance of the ships' rigging, steering, anchoring, and the ways of rolling with the punches of wind and wave (all of prime importance for small wooden craft) and navigation, routes, and dangers which were important to all craft. Each of these problems—or challenges—was greater in the Pacific because the Pacific itself is greater. As men found their way around it, they built up a body of knowledge about its dangers and the best ways to avoid or cope with them. Gradually ships' hulls and rigging were improved, and the techniques of navigation and operation were both simplified and made more certain.

At the same time, just as gradually, a network of favoured routes was woven—where the winds commanded the ships onward—as the captains learned to shun the regions which the winds forbade.

CHAPTER 12

Navigation

The first & most principall thing for any seafaring man or traveller, is to know toward what part of the Earth he meaneth to go & then being upon the sea, there he seeth no path nor mark to travell by, but only the use of the Nedle or compasse.

WILLIAM BOURNE
A REGIMENT FOR THE SEA, 1574

When we enquired of our pilot by what means they guided their vessels during their long voyages, he cut some pieces of bamboo and made a compass with them, indicated the winds which blew most generally in his country, pointed out the places of the stars and constellations, and gave them names; adding, that when these guides failed them, they regulated themselves by the currents, the course of which was known to them by many years' experience.

JACQUES ARAGO
OF THE *URANIE*

Accurate navigation was important to deep-sea sailors on all oceans. But on the huge Pacific it was vital, for against its vastness even the width of the Atlantic seemed insignificant. In 1517 when Magellan found a way into the Pacific from the east, perhaps it was as well that longitude was still difficult to know with any certainty. If he had known this ocean's true width—and its incredible emptiness—it is possible that even his spirit would have been daunted. As it was, he pressed on, and his circumnavigation was the major achievement of deep-sea navigation, comparable to the first manned orbit in space travel.

Magellan had to face extraordinary problems of navigation. Ordinarily, a navigator knows where he wishes to go, in what direction, and how far; Magellan knew only the first. A navigator, to know the direction of his destination at any time, must know where he is himself and he must also have some way of telling accurately in what direction he is going. These things are difficult enough on land, but, on the open sea when the sky is overcast, they are impossible—without instruments. The story of Western navigation, therefore, is largely one of the development of instruments to supplement the senses: the instruments of direction, such as various forms of compass, and the instruments of measurement, such as those which measure the angle of the sun from the horizontal, or which measure speed, measure time, or measure distance—all of which are related. A navigator cannot measure the distance travelled unless he knows both where he started and where he is (and the angle of the sun gives only half the answer to that), nor can he find his speed unless he knows both the distance travelled and the length of time the journey took.

There may be problems that these measurements enable him to offset. For example, if he finds, when sailing north before a southeast wind, that he is further to the east than he estimated, then something, a current perhaps, is moving his ship east; in future, therefore, he must head a little more to the west rather than straight towards his destination. Anyone who has rowed across a flowing river knows this. On the other hand, perhaps his ship had been pushed by the wind further west than he had thought would be likely. From then on, he will allow for this. But he cannot do these things without knowing where he is, and knowing where he is today means that tomorrow he will know where he was yesterday; this allows him to calculate things such as average speed. Without all these answers and the resulting calculated allowances, he will not know the direction in which to point his ship, nor will he have any idea of when he will arrive. This last estimate affects planning— for food and water, for example.

In the Pacific especially it is necessary to plan well. An accurate estimate of time was, and still is, important in planning for provisions or equipment for the voyage. It was important in estimating a potential profit in a commercial venture; would it pay to make the voyage at all? It was important in wartime, when speed and timing meant surprise and hence success. It was important to the health and the morale of the crew, especially when scurvy was still a scourge, without any known prevention other than a speedy voyage. Yet no one had answers to direction or to the probable length of a voyage without instruments of measurement carefully used, and the readings accurately computed. So this chapter deals—necessarily briefly, but in order —with the mathematics of computation, with the compass and the problem of variation, with the finding of latitude by measuring the angle of the sun, with the measurement of time at sea before the invention of accurate clocks which could withstand the ships' motion, with log-lines and estimation of speed, with the long search for a reliable and simple way of finding longitude, and with the importance of theory and training in navigation. Above

ate 29. The *Joseph Conrad*. This small, but extremely sturdy, iron-hulled ship—"the last surviving
igate"—sailed round the world under the Australian sea writer Alan Villiers. She now lies berthed
Mystic, Connecticut.

Plate 30. The *Snark*. Jack London's difficulties in provisioning this beautiful yacht and the mishaps he suffered while voyaging in her inspired him to add many touches of bitter and sarcastic humour to the literature of Pacific sailing.

all else, there is need for accuracy and care in the use of these methods. All of them involve measurement and calculation; calculations are of no use when observations are wrong.

In any discussion of the Pacific, it is interesting to note that the Polynesians navigated—and well too—without, so far as is known, any theoretical base of the mathematics on which all of the European navigation depended. The mysteries of navigation, as opposed to the practicalities of pilotage, are mathematical mysteries. In pilotage, persons go from point to point as reckoned by the observation of nearby land itself; it is highly skilled, but depends entirely on memorized or published knowledge of the local area. Navigation depends on the navigators' observation of heavenly bodies to find their ships' positions, just as pilots use their lighthouses, their capes, or their islands. Navigation is pilotage on a global scale, made essentially different by the distances involved and by the fact that the earth is a sphere and not a plane. Pilots can act as if the earth were flat, navigators cannot. It was mathematicians who solved, by calculations based on spheres, the problems for Europeans who wished to navigate the great oceans.

Some of these mathematicians were also seamen, for example, Edward Wright of Cambridge (see Plate 31), who had sailed after Spanish treasure ships in 1589. It was he who solved the problem of "the representation of the earth's curved surface upon a plane surface in such a manner that courses and distances could be accurately plotted by the navigator."[1] His solution is known as the Mercator's Chart. On this chart, all points are on their correct latitude and longitude, for the purpose of "charting a course" from one point to another, but at the price of a distortion of the shape of land masses increasing with distance from the equator.

At about the same time, another genius, Napier, in Scotland, developed logarithms to make navigational calculations easy.[2] Laborious multiplication and division were simplified into operations involving only addition and subtraction, using tables which took decades to calculate. When Gunter "exposed these numbers upon a straight line" (that is, invented the ancestor to the modern slide rule), immense amounts of calculation could be avoided— together with their manifold possibilities of error.[3] Navigation was not the only place in the world of ships in which better calculations were required. These new methods speedily found their place in shipbuilding as well as in ship steering, for instance, in the calculations for price and ordering of all the materials needed for a ship of a certain projected size.

Navigation could be defined, as Dr. John Dee did in 1570, as finding out "how by the shortest good way, by the aptest direction, and in the shortest time, a sufficient ship . . . be conducted."[4] Yet, finding "the shortest good way," is not a simple matter. While cruising in the *Snark* (Plate 30), London decided that young men who learned navigation "at once betray secretiveness, reserve, and self-importance" because "the average navigator impresses the layman as a priest of some holy rite."[5] London learned to navigate in a few hours—by his own story at any rate—but remembered with appreciation the "mathematicians and astronomers" who had made it possible by providing the simplified methods and the ready-made calculations.[6] Competent observation is still up to the individuals. According to the navigators' care and skill the ships can proceed, each along their own version of "the aptest direction." Nothing, not even a computer, is likely to relieve navigators of their ultimate personal responsibility.

In the early days of Pacific exploration there were problems that appalled and events that amazed, in spite of the assumption of this personal responsibility and of the most careful procedure. The surviving crew members of Magellan's *Victoria*, the first men to sail around the world and lose a day of time, were startled because ". . . they told us that it was Thursday with the Portuguese. We were greatly surprised for it was Wednesday with us, and we could not see how we had made a mistake; for as I had always kept well, I had set down every day without any interruption."[7]

One who was "greatly surprised" by the loss of a day was an educated Italian gentleman, Antonio Pigafetta, who fortunately survived the voyage and wrote of it so well that more is known of Magellan, "so noble a captain," of his naming of the Pacific, and of his death in a rash and foolish military action, than any ship's journal could have told. The loss of a day in circumnavigation had interesting effects later in the Pacific; when explorers coming from the east met those coming west, their days did not coincide. In Alaska, the Russians' Sunday fell on the Americans' Saturday—with some business inconvenience each weekend. The inhabitants of the Wallis Islands solved the problem neatly—they had two Sundays.[8]

The major news brought back to Europe by the *Victoria*, therefore, was of the size of the great ocean. This had not been known; even when it was known its significance was not always understood. Even today the scale is not always fully appreciated. Darwin thought that "it is necessary to sail over this great ocean to comprehend its immensity . . . for weeks together . . . nothing but the same blue, profoundly deep ocean."[9] It was this immensity which made time a major factor. Without measurement, whether month or minute, there is, in effect, no time in any comprehensible sense, and so time and its measurement became both enemy and friend. It was the passing of time which decayed the rigging and rotted men with scurvy, but it was the measurement of time, when accurate enough, which solved the problem of longitude. When location became certain, there was less time wasted and, therefore, fewer lives lost from scurvy. Magellan's voyage was primarily a feat of navigation and a confirmation of navigational theory. All the problems of oceanic navigation which were gradually solved during the next three centuries were either encountered or were the subjects of experiment during this voyage—from checking the accuracy of sun-shots to the finding of the compass variation in each locality in the hope of finding some pattern which would help solve the problem of longitude.

Out of sight of land, navigators can look only to the sky. When the weather is clear, they have the sun by day and other stars and the moon by night. But, when the weather is bad, there are neither landmarks nor skymarks. Europeans, by the very nature of their cultural tradition, would fall back upon a machine or an instrument of some kind. The basic one in navigation, over land or sea, is the compass. In its simplest form, the compass itself is a very small magnetised bar of iron floating, or pivoted, in a container so that it is free to remain pointing north no matter how or which way the container moves. The compass card is a card marked with the directions. In a hand compass, it is so fastened to the container that when "North" on the card and the direction of the needle coincide, users can then read off the other directions; that is, place N on the card at the N indicated by the needle, and west is 90° to the left. It was a natural development to fix the compass container to the ship, and the compass card to the needle, so that as a ship altered direction, with the needle and card remaining pointing north, the direction in which the ship was pointing could be read directly from the card. To steer west, the ship was turned until the "West" on the compass card was in line with the centre line of the ship and pointing forward. But this implies that a person cannot steer true west unless the compass is actually showing true north. In local pilotage, true north, as such, did not really matter, because pilots steered from sighted point to sighted point by compass bearings, or simple direction; however, when ships became involved in deep-sea navigation, out of sight of land for days and weeks, then their positions had to be found by relation to the sun and stars. There were no other marks relative to the ships.

True north, towards the Polar Star—which by dispensation or good fortune sits almost immediately above the axis of the rotation of the earth—was a fixed guideline. However, in daytime or in cloudy conditions, when the Pole Star was invisible, a compass which showed true north was necessary; any difference between true north and compass or magnetic north (what the compass showed as "North") became important. Various causes for this differ-ence were discussed, including error by the navigators, but it was centuries before it was understood.

By the end of the fifteenth century, it was realized that the compass did not point to the true north and, even more important, that the difference between the needle's direction and true north was not the same everywhere. This puzzled early navigators. This difference between true north—directly towards the North Pole, as marked in practice by the North Star almost directly above it—and the direction the compass actually points, was caused, it was found, by the focus of the radiation of the lines of magnetic force, the Magnetic Pole, being at some distance—and a changing one at that—from the geographic pole or the focus of the radiating and regular lines of longi-tude. When persons sail only in a restricted local area, this small difference can be allowed for by off-setting the compass card the correct number of degrees, but this will not work over great distances because the difference alters.

The distance between the North Pole and the North Magnetic Pole does not matter too much near the equator, as it is thousands of miles away, but it is a matter of great importance closer to the poles, in the same way that two trees six feet apart seem close together from a mile away, but far apart at a distance of a few feet. In the first case, to point to both trees, for all practical purposes, an arm would point in the same direction; in the second case, that arm would need to swing a certain number of degrees. This is what the compass must do when approaching the two poles.

As a result, variation—as the difference in compass direction came to be called—was more important in high latitudes, that is, in the areas closer to the poles than to the equator, or within the "high" numbers of the parallels of latitude. These are numbered from 0 at the equator to 90 at each pole, and high latitudes are those over 60. London is roughly 50°N latitude, there-fore, English ships sailing to northern Norway would encounter this greater variation. (The importance of this was made clear in the sixteenth century as the English, among others, searched for a Northeast Passage to China and Japan around Europe and Asia.) It was important in Pacific exploration during the search for a Northwest Passage back to Europe through the Bering Straits and the Arctic, and in the high-latitude Antarctic exploration as well, dating from Cook's voyages onwards.

There were two important matters involved for the European navigators. The first was that the compass is not a completely accurate indicator of direction unless the local variation is known and allowance made. The second was the not unreasonable idea, held for many years, that variation would be consistent, that is, would change at a fixed rate as a ship went north and south, or east and west. If it had changed at a fixed rate, the problem of finding longitude would have been solved. It was this search that led navigators to hope that the solution would be found in an instrument of observation and not in an instrument of the measurement of time. It was known that accurately measured time would give longitude, because the earth revolves 15° in an hour, but it was thought that the required accuracy was impossible to obtain; therefore, navigators continued to try observation and plotting of variation, hoping to observe a consistency which would be useful. Various forms of instruments were developed to find variation. A variation compass was invented as early as 1460 and was used by the Portuguese in the sixteenth century. Some of these instruments were quite useful and, in spite of failures and difficulties, navigators and inventors kept on trying to improve them. Robertson, in the *Dolphin*, reported one experiment:

The Ship being very steedy and the Water smooth I tryd the Variation with Docter Knight's new Invented Compass, and found the Variation to be 24°: 30′ E'erly. At same time it was tryed by the Docter's old Compasses and they all agreed within a few Minutes. The New Compass is a very fine Instrument for observing the Variation when the Ships in smooth water. It is likeways very good for Observing the Variation ashoar, but will not answer at Sea in bad weather when the Ship has a quick motion. It then runs round and neaver Stands Steedy.[10]

If one of the variation compasses had worked easily under all conditions, and if variation had been consistent, all would have been well. The "ifs" had it.

Variation was not consistent and, therefore, finding it did not solve the problem of longitude. Observing it and noting it at each locality proved to be the only way to deal with it; charts had then to be prepared marked with the allowance to be made for local variation. But, in order to chart consistency or, as it turned out, lack of it, the variation had to be found accurately. An obvious way, when a fixed true north-and-south line can be laid out on the ground or by bearings on fixed marks (as in modern "compass swinging" of ships and aircraft), is to align the compass correctly and then read off the variation the needle shows. This was seldom possible at sea, because of "the shipps Motion and the Needles quickness," even when the ship's masts were kept reasonably in line with the North Star.[11]

Various new methods and instruments were finally devised which were no more difficult to use at sea than the standard navigation instruments were. One observational technique was to compare the bearing of the sun at noon— the time of maximum elevation of the sun at any given place and thus the regulator of local time—with two other bearings, either at sunrise and sunset, or at other times provided they were equidistant in time from noon. The bearings would give true north, which could then be compared to the noon compass direction. The difference would be the local variation. An alternative was to use a shadow cast by the sun at set times to give the true bearing, which could then be compared with the compass reading.

When it became possible to calculate the variation easily and accurately, the observed inconsistency of variation was accepted by the best navigational theorists as early as the middle of the sixteenth century. As the local variations were plotted, it became apparent that longitude could not be found by using them, for no definite pattern was emerging. Also, it was found that variation changed in local areas over a period of time—"the secular change of variation," which is caused by a shift in the position of the Magnetic Pole. Hope died hard—Dampier in the *Roebuck* in 1699 observed and studied variation in the hope of finding longitude, and Cook discussed the matter, although negatively, in his journal of his third great voyage three quarters of a century later.[12]

Latitude is distance north and south of the equator; longitude is distance east and west of an agreed point of reference. Latitude can be found comparatively easily north of the equator by measuring the angle between a line from the eye to the horizon and a line from the eye to the North Star. The smaller the angle, the further south—the angles running theoretically from 90 at the pole when the star would be overhead, to 0 at the equator when the star would be at the horizon. However, this worked only at night and only in the northern hemisphere, so another method had to be found. The solution became more urgent as the Portuguese pushed south along the coast of Africa, and the North Star sank lower and lower behind them.

In 1484, the Portuguese worked out a way of finding latitude by measuring the altitude of the sun at noon, *i.e.*, when the sun was at its highest, applying for each specific day the difference made necessary because of the sun's apparent movement north and south between the tropics as the seasons change, and subtracting this from 90. The changes to be applied because of the sun's apparent movement were prepared in published tables. The system was checked in 1485, found to be successful, and became the foundation of solar navigation, which guided ships through the Pacific until after World War II when radio and radar largely displaced it.

Different instruments were used to measure the sun's altitude. But "all instruments used in the Navigation, of what shape of forme soever they be, are described or demonstrated upon a Circle, or some portion of a Circle, and therefore are of the nature of a Circle," said John Davis succinctly.[13] One of them, the quadrant, was a metal instrument forming a quarter-circle (hence the name), with two sights along a straight edge, and a plumb line hanging from the apex. The sights were aligned on the sun or a star (usually the North Star), and the reading was taken where the line crossed the graduated scale.

Astrolabes were much more complicated. A graduated full-circle with a sighting bar, it was read where the bar crossed the graduations. Each of these instruments had to be held perpendicular, and naturally this was very difficult to do in a moving ship. To make observation easier, cross-staffs (Plate 32) were developed, long rods held pointing from the eye to the horizon, and worked by sliding a cross piece until its top was in the centre of the sun and then reading off the angle marked. A back-staff was invented by John Davis to use the shadow cast by the sun and thus spare the eyes. Both were large and awkward instruments, but their simplicity and accuracy when properly used made them popular.

Later, the sextant with a scale on one sixth of a circle was the instrument used to find latitude, its advantages being its convenient size and an artificial horizon. Variations and developments of the sextant are still in use. Pilots and navigators had many more instruments than these: ring dials, nocturnals, and azimuth compasses, and many other implements for particular needs. They had, as well, journals and pilot books (called "rutters" from route), charts, almanacs, and traverse boards. Ships still got lost occasionally, but not because the equipment could not find the latitude, that is, if it were being used correctly.

The older instruments were not completely accurate. Quirós had trouble finding his way back to Santa Cruz along a latitude, because an error south on his first voyage added to an error north on his second put him thirty minutes, or half a degree, north of where he had actually been. And none of the latitude finders will work when the sky is consistently overcast. The ancient cross-staff and back-staff were very difficult to use when the horizon was obscured, in the one case toward, and in the other away from, the sun. Long, in the *Idle Hour*, still had problems with obscured horizons in the 1930's.

Observation could also give local time. Keeping time at sea was a problem for many years. Noon could be found accurately each sunny day by beginning latitude readings well before and continuing well after noon. The high reading would naturally be noon local time. One interesting result of this difficulty in keeping time was that sailors kept their reckoning at sea from "myddaye or noone, and ended it the next noone folowynge,"[14] as indeed they still do. For example, the dating in early ships' journals commenced the twelfth day of the month at what on land would have been noon of the eleventh day.

Shorter intervals of time were measured on European ships by hour, half-hour, minute, and half-minute glasses, very much like the three-minute egg-timers still seen. Chinese junks used incense sticks which burned at a standard rate. For activities requiring precise timing, such as the firing of salutes or the reading of an early type of log-line to measure the speed of the ship, ships' officers in Western ships learned to keep time by reciting verses or formulas under their breath. Practice in front of a minute glass could make this method of finding "a knowne part of an houre by some number of wordes," quite accurate.[15]

The interval from the moment the glass was turned until all the sand flowed into the bottom was a set time. Turning it was not always easy, for, although a half-minute glass might be only two inches in diameter by six inches high, hour glasses were quite large. A four-hour glass to regulate the calling of the watch might measure a foot in diameter and stand two feet high. (The name "watch" is derived from its early sense of "to guard" and, in shipboard context, means group, all seamen being in one of two or three watches, which change duty every four hours. Accuracy was important in order to be fair.) All glasses had to be checked, for many were carelessly made; both Barlow and Fleurieu complained of faulty sand glasses. A captain who was particular might use more than one at the same time and take an average. As a result of all these problems, people tried for years to find an instrument like the sundial which could use the sun directly for telling time at sea. On land, the sundials are accurately aligned, built for the latitude, and held firm, but these conditions could not be duplicated at sea.

Time in conjunction with speed was important for reckoning the distance covered, but both time and speed were rough estimates by modern time-keeping and speed measurement standards. Speed was measured by an English invention called the log, a small weighted piece of wood fastened to a long line in such a way that it held its width across the water, meeting resistance and thus hauling out the line over the stern of the ship. When the line was stopped from running out at the end of a prescribed time, the resulting jerk tripped a cross-line at the log and allowed it to be hauled in easily, end on.

The amount of line which ran out in a set amount of time, usually one half-minute, was translated, by proportion, to nautical miles per hour, that is, 30 fathoms of line in half a minute would be 30 times 120—3,600 fathoms in one hour. This, divided by the number of fathoms in a nautical mile, gave the speed. Usually, these arithmetical calculations had all been done before-hand. A refinement described by Champlain, the French explorer and founder of Quebec, which he saw when he was a prisoner in an English ship, had a knot every forty-two feet of line, so that when one length of forty-two feet (one knot) ran out in one half-minute the speed was one mile per hour, later called one knot. In Champlain's time, the English mile was 5,000 feet. The major advantage of this method was that it required no calculation at all on the part of the seamen operating the log.

An alternative was the Dutchman's log; this was a mark on the line which was timed passing a set distance along the deck when it was being hauled out in the same way as the English log-line was. This operation could not be done with a time glass, for the obvious reason that they were, and still are, made for set intervals of time. Although a special one was developed, it was not sturdy enough. Navigators had to learn to count rhythmically at a set rate, a method similar in principle to the rhyming verses mentioned earlier. It is apparent that there were too many variables for the Dutchman's log to prove as useful as the standard log.

Many captains used neither method, but relied instead on their skill in estimating speed and course. Quirós's pilots in the *San Pedro y Pablo* did not use logs, only judgment. This required great experience, much knowledge of the individual ship, and, as Villiers says, "considerable optimism."[16] Norwood, both a practical sailor and a mathematician, after observation, did not believe "that the way which the ship maketh may be knoun to an old Sea-man by experience (as they say)."[17] He devoted himself to finding better ways of navigating.

That there is much more to seamanship than instruments few great seamen denied, certainly not Slocum:

I think I have already stated that I kept my longitude, at least, mostly by intuition. A rotator log always towed astern, but so much has to be allowed for currents and for drift, which the log never shows, that it is only an approximation, after all, to be corrected by one's own judgment from data of a thousand voyages; and even then the master of the ship, if he be wise, cries out for the lead and the lookout.[18]

Magellan's pilot was wise. He used lead and lookout carefully, and his methods in general sound very much like those of Slocum; each would have been at home with the other's methods, in spite of nearly four centuries of development in navigational methods.

But lead and lookout, intuition and experience would not solve the problem of longitude. The solution to that was an instrument—and a very complicated and expensive one. Sailors had cried out for it for long enough. "I can say that only half the navigation is known [i.e. latitude] and by many the other half is ill understood," Quirós rather petulantly complained.[19] For although variation, the observation of latitude, and the accuracy of estimated positions were all problems, the vastness of the Pacific meant that the major problem on that ocean in the first 250 years of European ships was knowing how far they were east or west of any given point. "European" ships has been used advisedly, but in all probability no earlier navigators of the Pacific had solved the problem of longitude either, in the sense of knowing accurately their position east or west of a distant point at a given time. If they did solve it, the solution was not handed down.

Unlike latitude, longitude could not be observed comparatively easily. Longitude is the distance east or west of a known position, now measured—by convention—from Greenwich, England. It is as essential to know the ship's position east and west as it is to know the more easily found distance north and south. A ship's navigator might know he was at the same distance south of the equator as Dunedin, New Zealand, but he also needed to know whether he was near Chile or Tasmania. It would make a difference to the course he would steer if the ship's master wished to go to Wellington.

Such differences in estimated longitude, although rarely as extreme as this example, were great enough and dangerous enough in many cases; a British fleet had been wrecked on the Scillies, near Britain, due to an error in longitude, and Tasman thought New Zealand was 170 miles west of its true location.[20] Longitude could be as much as 30° in error, which, on the equator, would be 1,800 sea miles or about 2,000 land miles.[21] With such an error a ship could think she was near Hawaii when, in fact, she was near Mexico. A more usual error would be that made by Bougainville, which was of approximately forty miles or two thirds of a degree (about forty-six land miles at the equator), checked against an astronomic observation.[22] According to Captain Edwards of the *Pandora*, who tried to find the mutineers of the *Bounty*, Carteret had been thirty minutes out in longitude, marking Pitcairn Island as being far to the westward of its real position.[23] This was about thirty land miles in the latitude given, and would almost certainly mean missing a small island.

This might be more than important: it could be vital. The *Centurion* suffered severely from scurvy because of the uncertainty of longitude (Plate 33). Because of such errors, islands were marked on charts as being in many different longitudes and therefore could only be found by latitude sailing; that is, going to the right distance north or south of the equator and then sailing along the latitude, east or west, to the island. But a ship might not know whether to turn east or west. Anson's *Centurion* thought herself to be westward of Juan Fernández when she was to the eastward; they sailed even further without realizing the mistake until Chile was in sight. It was a miscalculation that scurvy made fatal to some; by losing nine days, the *Centurion* "lost between seventy and eighty of our men whom we should doubtless have saved, had we made the island that day."[24] The *Centurion*'s experience also indicates that scurvy and unknown longitudes were intimately linked by the factor of time. Accurate navigation saved time, and time saved meant lives saved. Oddly enough, the problems of scurvy and of the calculation of longitude were solved at about the same time, and Captain Cook had much to do with the testing of both solutions. Even so, both present difficulties even today.

The compass needle's variation from true north did not give the solution to finding longitude, mainly because variation changes with the passage of time. Magellan in his *Victoria* had hoped to find his longitude by using a system of finding variation, but found it did not work. Neither did Sebastian Cabot's divine revelation of the correct method of determining longitude prove to be either divine or particularly revealing—even to the man to whom he told it. "But I thinke," his friend said, "that the good olde man, in that extreme age, somewhat doted."[25]

Until the development in the eighteenth century of measurements of the relationship of the moon and certain stars, all that seamen could do, in practice, was to keep a close reckoning of the courses steered, the time elapsed, and the speed of the ship. Yet, by modern standards, not one of these factors was absolutely known. Compasses, time pieces, hour glasses, and the log, were all instruments which some experienced navigators, even in the 1890's, either ignored or interpreted as they thought their experience warranted—as Slocum did in the *Spray*.

In theory, if a ship were steered accurately southwest, with a favourable north wind, for ten hours at five knots, she should be about thirty-five nautical miles south, and about thirty-five nautical miles west of the departure point. Tables had been developed which showed the change in longitude to be expected in a given change of latitude on a set course. The distance south could be checked by the cross-staff, or later by the sextant, but the distance east or west could not be checked by instrument. If a current (which is invisible) had been moving the ship west, then she would be further west than the distance reckoned. Or perhaps the ship had been making greater leeway, that is, drifting sideways in the water because of the sideways pressure of the wind, to the east than had been allowed for; then, she would be further east than estimated. If the ship were singularly fortunate, the westerly current would have countered the easterly leeway and she would be where she should have been. But how would her captain and his crew know? Hawkins found that ". . . the error which we fell into in our accompts, was such as all men fall into where are currants that set east or west, and are not knowne; for that there is no certaine rule yet practised for triall of the longitude, as there is of the latitude."[26]

In the seventeenth century, captains of East Indiamen tried to measure currents: "I hoysed out my Schiffe, and sent her to ride neere us, to prove the set of the Current: she found by the Log-line, the Current to set South-east by East two miles a watch." The skiff rowed to windward at the wind's speed to try to stand still in relation to forces other than the current. The result was at very best an approximation. Robertson, when in the *Dolphin*, tells of a boat's compass newly invented "to tray [try] the currents." Log-lines could be used to measure currents with some accuracy, where the ship could be anchored, or where a boat could be held in one place by a heavy kettle lowered a hundred fathoms or so below the surface currents to act as a sea-anchor, as Bellingshausen did.[27]

In shore voyages, particularly if the destination were a point on a large land mass, these things did not matter; one could hardly miss Africa sailing south from Toulon, or America sailing west from Europe. Eventually, a body of knowledge about currents would be built up and carried in a book, and masters in time would learn their own ships' tendencies to make leeway. This leeway could be estimated approximately by throwing out astern a line affixed to a lead-weighted piece of wood carrying a pole to serve as a mark for compass bearings taken from the stern of the ship. But, in the Pacific, distances were vast, islands were small, the currents unknown, and the problems extreme. "Outside a particular course it is almost fatally easy to miss," Beaglehole aptly summed it up.[28]

A better way to find longitude than by reckoning the course and the speed of the ship had to be found. Lunar observations were developed in the 1490's. Columbus had tried to find his longitude by using eclipses of the moon, but precise timing of observations in a long process such as an eclipse proved impossible. Centuries later in the *Vostok*, the Russians decided that "the determination of longitude by lunar eclipses has not the required accuracy," confirming Columbus's findings.[29]

By the middle of the sixteenth century, longitude on land could be found by measuring the change of angle of bearing between the moon and different planets. As the moon was changing its apparent position relative to the earth more quickly than was the chosen planet, the different bearings, or angles of sight, could be used to find distance east or west of another point on earth for which the angles at given times were known to the observer. In 1600, Dutch navigators had worked out longitude by using the conjunction of the moon and Jupiter, and comparing their figures to tables prepared in Venice. This was difficult both to observe and to calculate—too difficult for ordinary navigators at sea; but by the late eighteenth century the observed distance of the moon from fixed stars had been tabulated and could be used to find longitude in an improved method, perfected mainly by Halley, better known for his comet.

Much earlier, the basic Halley system had been used with some success by navigators, such as Baffin, who had even obtained his longitude by this method while at sea in 1615. But this system was too difficult for lesser navigators; the observations were hard to make on a ship's pitching deck. In Baffin's time, many masters still mocked men who navigated by instrument as "star-shooters and sunne shooters," and preferred to lie-to at night when near land, and by day to check their position by sight, by soundings, and even by the smell of land. They were still basically pilots, not navigators.

Halley's lunar observation methods were of great value to true navigators. The *Endeavour*'s officers used them to Cook's satisfaction, although he feared that many officers would be put off by the calculation required, and pointed out that "they would not find them so very difficult as they at first imagine."[30] Cook's astronomer in the *Resolution* was instructed ". . . to teach such of the Officers onboard the Sloop as may desire it the use of the Astronomical Instruments, and the Method of finding the Longitude at Sea from the Lunar Observations."[31]

In the *Dolphin* in 1766, Wallis took lunar observations which in general turned out to be more accurate than his estimated ones. Bellingshausen's Russian navigators checked their longitude constantly by observing lunar distances, taking the mean of "a large number of lunar distances"; that is, between the moon and a fixed star.[32] Unfortunately, most modern navigators cannot amuse themselves as Gerbault did in his *Firecrest* "by calculating the longitude by the distances from the moon to stars."[33] Some nineteenth-century captains had also amused themselves this way; Lubbock said of some Blackwall frigate captains that "lunars with them were a recreation."[34]

Most modern captains do not bother. Chronometers had made finding longitude comparatively simple. Chronometers are—simply—very well-made clocks. It is the adjective "well-made" that points out the difficulty. It was perfectly understood that the earth revolves 15° in one hour (after all, it revolves once, or 360°, in one day of twenty-four hours). When the time at a fixed point on earth was known—for example, London—and if it were 2 p.m. there and noon at the present position, then the ship had to be two hours, or 30°, west of it. To operate the system, the chronometer was set at London time and read when the noon observations for latitude were taken; thus, longitude calculations could be made as well. This method had been explained clearly as early as 1558: "Before commencing the journey, the watch should be set at the time of departure and care taken that it does not stop on the way. On reaching a certain place, the time should be calculated by use of the astrolabe (i.e. by observation of the sun), compared with that shown upon the watch, whereupon the difference will be the longitude."[35] The difficulty lay in making a clock that would keep accurate enough time over a long period—and on a rough sea. This was the difficulty—it was simple and yet seemed insuperable.

In 1714, the Board of Longitude in London offered £20,000 to anyone who could establish longitude at sea to an accuracy within 30 miles. In spite of all the good work by the astronomers, the solution, probably contrary to their expectations, was an accurate chronometer and not any refinement of the lunar system. This exceedingly accurate chronometer was built by John Harrison in Yorkshire; it had compensating arrangements for climatic changes and it found longitude within eighteen miles. Its complete vindication came with Cook's voyage in the *Resolution*, when, at the urging of the Astronomer Royal, a thorough check was made of the chronometer against competent and complete astronomical observation. Precautions with this experiment were of stringent quality. Among other things ". . . the Commander, First Lieutenant and Astronomer on board each of the Sloops [i.e., *Resolution* and *Adventure*] had each of them Keys of the Boxes which contained the Watches and were allways to be present at the winding them up and comparing the one with the other."[36]

Precautions were always necessary with chronometers—most ships carried two in case one broke. When ships "spoke" each other in the late eighteenth century, they compared the time on their chronometers, and the instruments, as has been seen, were checked constantly against lunar observations in cases where navigators were competent to make them. These observations were used both to check the chronometers and to train navigators. On his Russian Pacific voyage, Krusenstern had concluded that if chronometers and lunar observations were within one quarter of a degree, then the navigators would take the chronometer's result; if, however, several good lunar observations were in agreement and differed from the chronometer's indication, then, perhaps the latter was wrong. Vancouver used lunar observations to check his chronometers; so did La Pérouse.

The check was simple in principle. If a satisfactory lunar observation showed the ship to be further west than the chronometer indicated, then the chronometer was running slow; if further east, then it was running fast. Before setting out on a long voyage, ships' masters had their chronometers checked—often at Greenwich itself—where an elaborate organization and a form of ritual had been developed to maintain accurate time for longitude finding.

Nowadays, ships are able to check their chronometers by the noon radio signal. Before radio, or lacking one, if navigators could not do lunar observations and calculations, ships would check them (when possible) by lying near a point of land of known longitude, and also by comparing them with those of other ships whenever they had a chance to "speak" one. Suspecting an error in her chronometer, the *Cap Pilar* tested it by passing over a shoal of known position called the Victoria Bank and finding the bank by sounding (measuring the depth of water).[37]

In spite of all these precautions, chronometers still gave some trouble. One of Cook's got wet when water leaked into the bread room "where the clock & other instruments were put as the driest & best place."[38] Vancouver found that the temperature changes from Mexico to northern Alaska were extreme enough to affect his chronometers. Half a century later, in the *Rattlesnake*, "the firing of shotted guns . . . strangely altered" the time shown on her seventeen chronometers, and so she stopped firing them.[39] In a somewhat similar way, the *Vostok* found that active sports played on deck affected the compasses, but Bellingshausen considered the health and morale of his crew to be the more important factors in his sailing.

Chronometers are still vitally important instruments; however, other methods of finding longitude are now known. After reading Dana's description of the problems of navigation encountered by the captain of the *Alert*, Chichester of *Gipsy Moth IV* worked out a new way of finding longitude. His method uses an observation of the moon computed as sun-moon fixes for two different guessed-at Greenwich times, plus an ordinary noon latitude sighting. A line is drawn joining these two sun-moon computations, and where it crosses the observed latitude line is the longitude. From this, inversely, Greenwich Meridian Time can be calculated. This method requires only a sextant to make the actual observations.[40]

Naturally, no instrument or method will work unless good care is taken in its working and its calculation. Magellan often had his pilots disembark to correct errors in their observations, as they had only primitive instruments and needed a steady platform. Centuries later, Knox-Johnston described the care he took in making his observations. Bellingshausen was adjured by the Russian Admiralty to make plenty of careful observations and, in exactly the same tone, Quirós outlined what he expected of his pilots. The Board of Longitude in England gave detailed instructions to the astronomers in Cook's *Resolution* and *Adventure*. In the *Endeavour*, observations were taken so regularly and so carefully that they were continued even when the ship appeared to be drifting helplessly onto a reef. This particular zeal may have been overdone, but it is only by such careful observation that accurate navigation can be guaranteed.

Correct and exact observation is also derived from thorough training, and the training of young officers was a major part of all the great exploring voyages; "for training in navigation and seamanship in time of peace there could be no better sphere than the arduous and often perilous one of the polar regions."[41] Sailing ships in some ways were better than steamships for training—and are considered so even today. There is room in the hull for the men (because there are no huge engines), and the men who are being trained can earn their way by acting as sailors and sail-handlers, at least saving the fuel costs. The beautiful four-masted barquentine *Esmeralda* is used by the Chilean Navy as a training ship and still cruises the Pacific.

Portuguese and Spanish supremacy in early exploration was as much a result of their pilots' training schools as it was a cause of them. The navigational systems of both countries were admired and copied by the English, French, and Dutch. Nearly all the early books on navigation were published in Spain, a country which produced naval officers of the highest quality— contrary to much popular belief in the Anglo-Saxon countries. Spain's training schools were successful and, by the seventeenth century, their navigators were thoroughly versed in the several sciences of mathematics. Much of the entire maritime system of Spain was copied, albeit in modified form, by sixteenth-century England and, by the end of that century, the English had caught up. It was from Spanish sources that *The Arte of Navigation* was translated and compiled by Richard Eden and published in 1561. A leading authority on navigation calls it "one of the most decisive books ever printed in the English language. It held the key to the mastery of the sea."[42]

Some historians have argued that Drake's circumnavigation depended on captured Spanish and Portuguese pilots. That Drake grasped information where he found it is undeniable—and it was undeniably sensible of him. Yet surely not even his justified self-confidence and unbounded optimism would have led him to set out on an important voyage vaguely hoping to capture, on the way, co-operative pilots possessing exactly the right knowledge. Drake had the latest information with him, captured more, and used his instruments carefully; he dared much, and he won his way home. That Sir Francis used Spanish knowledge no doubt he would have been willing to admit, delighted that he could use Spanish methods to hurt Spain.

The Spaniards who encountered Drake on the voyage (an expedition on which no Spaniard was killed) were in no doubt about his abilities as a navigator: "this Corsair ... is so well versed in all modes of navigation."

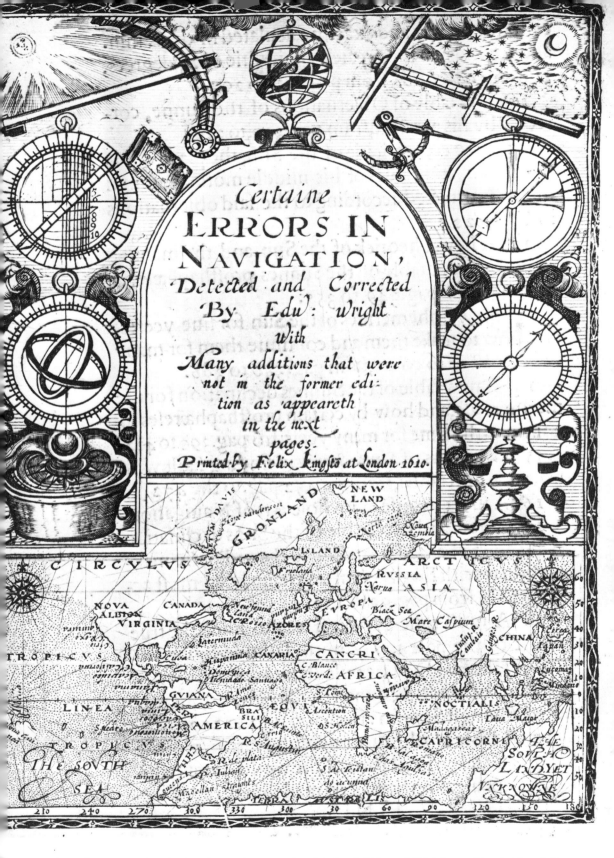

Certaine ERRORS IN NAVIGATION, *Detected and Corrected By Edw: Wright* with *Many additions that were not in the former edition as appeareth in the next pages.* Printed by Felix kingsto at London 1610.

Plate 31. *Certaine Errors in Navigation,* title page. In this book Edward Wright, a Cambridge fellow with sea experience, set out to correct, as the title implies, the navigational errors inherent in the methods of the late sixteenth century. Wright considered contemporary charts "an inextricable labyrinth of error," and one of the many navigational improvements he suggested in this book, his Mercator chart projection, is still used.

Plate 32. Seventeenth-century instruments of navigation. Upper left is a globe, and lower left, a marine astrolabe. Lying on the map of the world (which has much still unknown and unmarked) are a measuring compass, or divider, and a cross-staff. Upper right is a Davis Quadrant, or Backstaff while mid-right is a sand-glass, probably for one hour. Below the map is a Gunter's Sector, an instrument in some ways like a slide rule, which enabled navigators to find a ship's position without laborious calculation.

They thought his care in learning from captured pilots equally as impressive as his ability to chart with paintings the route he followed: "each thing is so naturally depicted that no one who guides himself according to these paintings can possibly go astray."[43]

Navigators can always go astray. As scientific navigation with its ready-made tables developed, there were complaints in England that young men would not serve their proper apprenticeship in navigation—a cry echoed in many trades throughout the centuries. There was also concern that practical navigators might have things made so simple for them that they would ignore and forget the mathematical and astronomical basis of their art, and that by using tables they would forget calculations and thereby fail to appreciate the necessity of understanding the foundations of compilation. This fear also has a modern echo; computers are lauded and arithmetic decried. Course, when discussing conditions of half a century ago, tells of students who "struggled with *Nicholl's Guide*," a book widely used at the time by aspiring ships' officers. These officers, now veterans, envy modern lads their "excellent nautical schools ashore which give pre-sea training, mid-apprenticeship coaching and preparation for the examinations."[44]

In Polynesia there were some counterparts of European schools of navigation, for pilots learned to navigate by using the stars as rough guides to a location, and then using local signs, such as alterations in ocean swells or colour, the habits of birds, sighting of land-created clouds or lagoon reflection, and even smell, to find the last landfall. Winds and currents had to be learned for each local area; they were learned—and thoroughly. People still argue about how well the Polynesians could navigate. In order to assess their ability, their failures as well as their successes would need to be known, and this information has not been recorded.

Though there has been, and still is, much scholarly debate about the original sources on which much of this book is based, it seems undeniable that the Polynesians were competent navigators; they spread across the Pacific over a great period of time and, even in the days of early European exploration, were still making voyages of significant distance.[45] Lewis, who tried their methods in the *Rehu Moana*, was satisfied that they work reasonably well; so was Gatty, who wrote *Nature Is Your Guide*.[46] These are only two of many writers on the subject, and both of them have tried what they debate.

The Polynesians' knowledge of stars and winds impressed early European navigators. Bellingshausen said that "they have some notion of the course of the stars, a conception of which is a necessity for them."[47] Banks and Cook noted with respect their practical astronomy, but a French scientist was somewhat less impressed by a lecture on navigation in the Carolines of Micronesia. "What imperfect guides!" he said, yet from his description of the kenning of winds and stars and of the dead reckoning, it could be assumed that their seamanship—except for instruments—was very much indeed like the European.[48]

More modern European seamen have not ignored the stars. They were essential guides to Captain Voss in his British Columbian canoe *Tilikum*. "Having lost the binnacle I had nothing but the stars to steer by at night, and I would have managed right enough but for the gales."[49] This qualification is a vital one; to navigate by the stars requires at least an approximate knowledge of where the ship is at a given time. Voss came to depend on something else less fixed in their course, but with the advantage of being palpable as well as visible: "the guides I had to steer by were the sun, moon, stars, and the ocean swell, but I soon discovered that the ocean swell was by far the best to keep the boat making a good course." Cross swells and cloudy weather caused problems, but Voss would "heave to until the weather cleared up" and, when necessary, he would "put the drag out and let her drift."[50] As if to show that ancient methods go with ancient craft design, Clifford in his Chinese junk, like Voss in his canoe, sometimes steered by the stars.[51] Slocum's *Spray* never doubted her position, even without using the compass at all at night, for the Southern Cross was there at night and the sun by day: "I wished for no other compass to guide me, for these were true."[52]

These statements ignore the problem of poor visibility, but this, of course, existed for instruments users too. Bligh of the *Bounty*, who performed the most famous of all long-distance feats of small-boat seamanship and navigation, complained when there was "not a star to be seen to steer by."[53] Skilled modern commanders such as Villiers comment that near Tierra del Fuego the "difficulty was data for astronomical observations, for sun and stars down there were so often obscured."[54]

All navigators used the stars, for the sun is a star too. One of the riddles of Polynesian navigation is how they could use them so effectively without the instruments needed to measure accurately the changes in relationship. If they found a solution to the problem of finding longitude while at sea it is no longer known. One does not need to share "European ethnocentricity" to ask simply, "How did they do it?" The answers given up to the present have indicated only a masterly knowledge of practical astronomy and local pilotage and a form of navigation similar to the European practice of running along the latitude. All of these were mastered in Europe too, centuries before the problem of longitude was solved.

There is an important point which has to be considered when discussing the navigation of canoes. It is very much more difficult to sight low islands from the hull of a boat or canoe than it is from the masthead of a ship. Lewis of the *Rehu Moana*, who tested Polynesian navigational methods, was fully aware of this problem. He gives a formula for "... finding the approximate distance at which an object whose height is known in feet becomes visible over the horizon. The square root of the height of the object added to the square root of the height of the observer's eye gives the distance in miles."[55]

Gann mentioned this problem when explaining why he preferred to keep old-fashioned shrouds and ratlines on his *Albatros*. "There is nothing quite so reassuring as a quick trip up the ratlines to spy an island or reef [which from] the deck would be visible over the horizon, or to pick up a distant buoy, or navigate a difficult channel. The area visible to a sailor whose viewpoint is 10 feet above the water is a mere 3½ miles!"[56] A low island could easily be missed by a boat in the vastness of the Pacific, and probably many small boats and canoes sailed past such havens just out of eyeshot and went on to disappear into the open sea.

Failure to find the destination is a failure in navigation, but it was an excusable one in the days without radar or radio. Today, in spite of sophisticated equipment, ships and aircraft still get lost. European or Polynesian, modern or ancient, all navigators are trying to follow John Dee's advice to find "the shortest good way"; this was and is the purpose of navigation. Yet the "shortest good way" is always relative. Weather, season, fortune, might all conspire to waft the sailors gently or to smash them back. A wise choice of routes could lessen these risks. In an ocean like the Pacific, with ice at each extremity, and gales and calms and always distance, the methods by which the navigators found the way were often less important than the way they chose to go.

CHAPTER 13

Routes, Winds, Other Dangers of the Elements, and Superstitions

*Windes, Raine, Hailes, Snowes, Sicknesse and Contention . . .
accompanied with losses of Anchors, Cables and (that which
is most irrecoverable) time.*

OLIVIER DE NOORT
OF THE *MAURICE*

*The inanimate works of nature—rock, ice, snow, wind, and
water—all warring with each other, yet combined against
man—here reigned in absolute sovereignty.*

CHARLES DARWIN
OF THE *BEAGLE*

*Behold Tainui, Te Arawa, Mataatua,
Kurahaupo, and Tokomaru . . .
These are the canoes of Uenuku
Whose names resound unto the heavens.*

ANCIENT MAORI SONG

There is no easy way into the Pacific by sea. Ships must pass Cape Horn, or Good Hope and then Leeuwin, and risk the storms and waves. Which route was chosen depended on their destination—when Australia or China, the way was past Good Hope, but when British Columbia, Hawaii, or Peru, the ship beat past the Horn. Of all the Pacific routes that were sailed, the one westward past Cape Horn is the most notorious. It has become a byword, and to have sailed past the Horn in a sailing ship—either way, but especially westward—sets a sailor apart as a "Cape Horn man." This cape is feared both for its winds and for the waves that they push around the world without hindrance. In the remainder of the Pacific, winds, or even lack of them, could make sailing difficult, especially if, in innocence, it was hoped the ship could sail directly from port to port. Embayment, leeshores, and calms were all dangers. The strong winds were so capricious that one can easily see why sailors thought them uncanny and took philosophical refuge in superstition.

Some experienced captains claimed that individual gales at Cape Horn were not as bad as those in the West Atlantic and that it was the prodigious waves that made the area so dangerous. Many seamen with experience in both oceans argue that the North Atlantic is the most dangerous of oceans; having a greater share of all perils, it is by cumulative effect the most dangerous. This may be true, yet winds of over forty-five miles per hour blow on twenty-two days out of thirty at the Horn, and for most of these days from the westward. One recording at the entrance to Magellan Straits measured a wind velocity of 120 miles per hour. They are so fierce that trees on the outer islets of the area grow along the ground instead of upward. A combination of such winds and seas meant death to many ships and men, even if sometimes only indirectly—such as through delay causing scurvy.

The route around South America was discovered by Magellan; the name of his straits commemorates this. The sea route further south was found by Drake; it is called Drake Passage. Both men were already famous for skill and determination before the voyages which needed so much of both characteristics took place. These waterways have been notorious in all centuries since, and to use them as commercial routes—even for the great steel ships of the twentieth century—required the same degree of determination the two great navigators had demonstrated. Few men went westward past the south extreme of South America without definite orders, such as Anson, Byron, Cook or Colnett had. It was feared right from the beginning. There were some men—comparatively few—who were lured by the hope of great wealth gained by force or by speculation, the kind of hope which brought the privateers and then the clippers. Not many seamen regretted the completion of the Panama Canal, unless it were in a nostalgic dream of the challenges youth had outfaced. Today, the route which knew Drake, and Anson, and the captains of the clippers is seen as the ultimate challenge to sailors and their seamanship.

Above all, it is the great waves of an unhindered global sweep which make this challenge good. Drake and the *Golden Hind* knew these waves first, waves that "rowled up from the depths, even from the roots of the rockes . . . and being aloft were carried . . . to water the exceeding tops of high and loftie mountaines."[1] The first Dutch ships reported that the "Surges of the Sea rose higher than the Masts, and tossed the Ship with such strength that it was a Miracle she was not overturn'd, and split in pieces."[2]

In spite of such warnings, Anson's fleet sailed into the Pacific by Cape Horn on his way to raid the Spanish Empire. After an easy passage through

Le Maire Straits it was blown back (see Plate 33); this kind of setback was a frustration suffered by many in this famous sea corner. It took three months to get into the Pacific, fighting the seas and storms, the notoriety of which Anson's chaplain said he had believed a fairy tale before personal experience showed him better. Even a proud and heavy ship-of-the-line like its flagship the *Centurion* was vulnerable to such weather; forty years after Anson's voyage another ship-of-the-line foundered in a storm.[3]

Heavy seas smash hard at a ship which is fighting into them, as a ship must do to round the Horn east to west. Anson's fleet laboured against them, sturdily fronted them, yet they tossed even the *Centurion*'s great hulk around so violently that one man was thrown overboard and many others suffered broken bones. Her upper seams worked loose and all within her suffered from the "deluge of water that came in upon them."[4] But the direct suffering of the crew and the damage to the ship were not the most serious consequences of this three months' battle; worse was the lost time. In the days before antiscorbutics were properly used, the lengthening of the time at sea favoured the most dangerous, yet most insidious enemy of all—scurvy—which could take a far greater toll than could the sea itself.

Horn seas have been described often enough since the *Golden Hind* rode them. In a great windjammer 150 years later, a sailor said that ". . . on the top of one of the great Cape Horners, looking forward was like looking from the top of a mountain. . . . I am very certain that it was a good deal nearer two miles than one mile from crest to crest of these enormous seas."[5]

The greatest Cape Horners are the especially large waves, which, according to mathematical odds, can occur in any set of waves. At Cape Horn, where all waves are large, such special waves are gigantic. Not all "rogue waves" in the Southern Ocean occur near Cape Horn. The author nearly lost a son-in-law in May, 1974, when the small, eighty-seven ton, research supply ship he was in, the *Acheron*, was badly damaged by such a wave two hundred miles south of New Zealand. Chichester mentioned two reports of giant waves; one was said to be 112 feet high, the other 120 feet high. According to the expert he quoted, when the waves are of an average height of 30 feet then one wave of every 300,000 can be expected to be 120 feet high.[6] The *Herzogin Cecilie*, a vessel 337 feet long, was once lifted high at the stern with her bow in the trough between two seas, which gives some idea of the size and power of waves travelling faster than a ship going at 17 knots.

Some ships simply disappeared in such seas, others reported damage to hull, to upper works, and even to rigging. Sometimes, waves swept the decks completely clear. Cooks in American ships, whose galleys were usually built on deck, were in particular danger, since they could not see what was coming.

Small yachts have vanished without word or trace. Perhaps, like Smeeton's *Tzu Hang*, they were flipped stern over bow, but could not recover as she did. Losses have been high; fifty-three windjammers foundered rounding the Horn in the short period between 1900 and 1914, in most cases with all hands lost.[7]

In the days before accurate finding of longitude was possible, the heavy east-running current at Cape Horn was a major problem. Anson's navigator found they were ten degrees of longitude further to the east than they had estimated, and all this windward distance had to be regained. (Whether caused by currents or not, ending up to leeward of the objective is still a worry for sailing-ship navigators, as Long found in his ketch: ". . . or was it Tapuacmanu, sixty miles to leeward? . . . I thought dismally of the days and weeks it would take us to regain all those miles to windward if I had guessed wrongly."[8])

South of the Horn itself, Drake Passage is wide, but prevailing wind, seas, and currents, are all against the ship. Course, who had sailed round the Horn, thought that the longest time taken was ninety-two days by the French three-masted barque *Cambronne*, and that the shortest was six days taken by the German four-masted barque *Priwall*.[9] Some captains fought through the weeks of time which were so often required; others, including Bligh, gave up and ran the other way round the world, ahead of the winds. Going from west to east is so much simpler. One early clipper was able to speed around the world by staying with a single storm.

As early as 1600, Spanish pilots were advising that ships for the Straits of Magellan should leave Europe by early August and Rio de Janeiro by mid-November; later, one whaler suggested that ships should be even earlier, reaching Chile before November if possible. On the other hand, Colnett, who had rounded the Horn, suggested early winter, when there was likely to be both moonlight and east winds. Broughton obviously did not reason as Colnett did, "as I intended, in consequence of the lateness of the season, to proceed to the South Seas by Van Diemen's land [Tasmania]."[10] Most captains thought as Broughton did. Anson and his officers blamed delays in the preparation of the fleet for forcing them "to make our passage round Cape Horn in the most tempestuous season of the year." Byron, in his journal, complained similarly of the season being "*far advanced*"; he recommended that ships be "*at the East Entrance sometime in the Month of Decem^r*,"[11] that is, in late spring.

Sailing ships could not go where and when they pleased, even given a sufficient depth of water. Not only the direction but the timing of arrival or departure was set by tide and wind. Captains simply had to wait for a reasonable wind, and, when it arrived, they sailed—and quickly. Drake, in his direct Elizabethan English, expressed it clearly: "The wind commands me away."[12]

Even when the South American route had been chosen, there was still some choice. Ships could pass either through the Straits of Magellan, or else round the Horn through the Straits of Le Maire or through Drake Passage further south. The dangers in Magellan Straits were the confinement, the tide rips, the sudden gusts of hurricane-force wind hurtling down the mountain sides, the rocks, and the whirlwinds. Slocum took the *Spray* through the "Milky Way of the sea, which is northwest of Cape Horn," the mere sight of which, Darwin said, would give landsmen nightmares.[13] (No wonder the original accounts of Magellan's and Drake's voyages both mention that natives in this general area worshipped "Setebos, that is to say, the great devil."[14] Shakespeare, so alive to all concerning England and the sea, did not miss this; Caliban cried his invocation to Setebos.) For strong, well-equipped sailing ships of the late nineteenth or early twentieth century, these hazards were worse than the gales and huge seas of any open passage. Such a passage would seem to them claustrophobic—strong ships fear the land, not the sea.

In the early days, with smaller ships and weaker rigging, things seemed different to many commanders. Byron, who had been shipwrecked as a midshipman in the *Wager* shortly after passing the Horn with Anson's fleet, knew as well as anyone the hardships and dangers of the area. He chose the Straits passage: "*I would prefer it twenty times over to the going round Cape Horn.*"[15]

Any route around South America in either direction was hard and dangerous for sailing ships. When the *Princess Royal*, of only fifty tons and fifteen men, went round from east to west in late 1786 and early 1787, it was commented on up and down the west coasts of the Americas. So was the passage of a fifty-two-ton ship fifty years later. Villiers states—and he knows the Horn—that this alternative route into the Pacific need not have made the Dutch East India Company fear growing competition, for it "was more deterrent than aid."[16]

Yet the Horn route was not invariably bad, and Whymper, the English artist who tells so much about umiaks and canoes in Alaska and British Columbia, wrote that the "weather was superb, the sea almost a lake and the regulation terrors of the passage were nowhere!"[17] However, such a statement is so rare that the notoriety of the Horn must be accepted as completely justified. Even the passage from west to east was feared—the route of the great grain and wool and gold clippers, and of the grain, nitrate, and *guano* windjammers that sped through the last great days of sail. It was only the westerly gales common in the Great Australian Bight that prevented a much greater use of the windy but fine weather route from Australia to Europe by Good Hope, using the southeast trades to the northward of the west of Australia and avoiding even the eastward run past the Horn.[18]

Sailing tactics for rounding South America were as varied as were the captains. This may explain why the *Dolphin* and the *Swallow* separated. Apparently Wallis preferred to get through Magellan Straits quickly at the risk of losing rigging, while Carteret preferred—the *Swallow* was not a good strong ship like the *Dolphin*—to preserve his equipment at the risk of not making headway. One of Lubbock's captains suggested that most captains were too cautious at the Horn; he thought the way was to "cram on sail and force your way against the Westerlies."[19] This would take the best of ships and the most self-confident of captains, whereas many of them, such as Bishop, captain of the ship *Ruby*, were bound to be cautious. He had read about Anson's voyage—not reassuring literature. Other captains, even one as justly famed for seamanship and resolution as Cook, disagreed with the route itself. He recommended entering the South Sea by the Cape of Good Hope and then sailing south and east to New Zealand. The French captains de Surville and Du Fresne agreed, although their decisions were probably guided by their eastern starting points. On his second voyage, Cook came into the Pacific from the west, past Good Hope and Australia to New Zealand. In doing this, he was using the westerly winds of the "Roaring Forties" (and the Fifties, too) instead of fighting them. Coming in from the east by the Horn he had found what Byron and Wallis had found—the likelihood of getting set too far to the north. The *Dolphin* had edged north "as we had no chance of getting westing in this latitude."[20]

Cook's route took him past two of what Chichester claims are the three worst capes in the world: Good Hope in South Africa and Cape Leeuwin— "the dreaded region of the Leeuwin, the south-western tip of the vast Aus-tralian continent," as another experienced captain called it;[21] the third is Cape Horn. Villiers, of the *Joseph Conrad*, adds to this list a fourth—Cape Flattery (which Cook named) in the northwest United States. Cook saw all the great corner hazards in his lifetime.

Cook's *Resolution* stayed hundreds of miles south of Cape Leeuwin, in the latitudes of the fifties and sixties, checking the existence of a southern continent. Here she encountered ice (Plate 38), but no southern continent, and was glad enough to swing north to New Zealand. In the same way, Tasman's *Heemskerck* and *Zeehaen*, after sailing as far south as 50°, had been happy to turn north and then to drive east to New Zealand along the 44th parallel. Half a century later, the *Vostok* sailed in the same area, the

Russian officers reading and thinking of Cook's voyage; their journals described the hardships almost in the English captain's words. One of the difficulties of ships dependent on the wind is well exemplified in this area. North winds from warmer latitudes move the ships south, but as the warm winds blow over the cold sea they also bring bad visibility with all its risks; south winds off Antarctica bring clear weather, but the ships have to fight against the wind to get south and have to worry about loose ice blown off shore.

The Cape of Good Hope route became favoured by whale ships coming into the Pacific in the following century, because it saved the battle at the Horn. However, the route chosen depended somewhat on the month the ships left Europe or the United States, and the subsequent time of arrival in the South Atlantic.

Sailing-ship navigators had always to think of the winds quite as much as compass routes, and they had to be aware of wind patterns. Villiers said of the *Joseph Conrad*'s routes that, as she was a square-rigged ship, "usable winds matter to her far more than mere distance."[22] Meares thought of sailing to British Columbia from India by going around Australia; Seligman set out from Auckland on a course south of east, to get the Westerlies, although his ship's objective was the Gambier Islands east-*north*-east of Auckland. One of the earliest examples of the dependence of sailing-ship routes on the winds —where the longest way round often does prove to be the shortest way home —is the path used by the Manila Galleon for centuries. She went from the Philippines north to the belt of Westerlies, across to America and south to Mexico. To come back, she sailed westwards more or less ahead of the north-east trades.

A vital contribution to navigation using wind routes was Maury's Wind Chart, worked out during the nineteenth century by Captain Maury of the United States Navy (Plate 35). Dampier had been a pioneer in this science. The latest parallel advance, announced in 1972, is the use of "information radioed from 'wave gauges' often situated on the tops of under water mountains." The information enables ships to "pick their way through rough seas along the smooth channels which usually exist even in the worst weather."[23] Even when this forces ships to travel greater distances, they need not reduce speed, and the total time of the passage is less. Even today this is important in the Pacific.

Ships might have to sail a greater distance to avoid a prevailing wind pushing them onto a leeshore (*i.e.*, the shore on the lee of the ship and therefore the shore onto which the wind is blowing), a great hazard to ships which do not operate well in beating against the wind. The *Beeswing*, on the way to

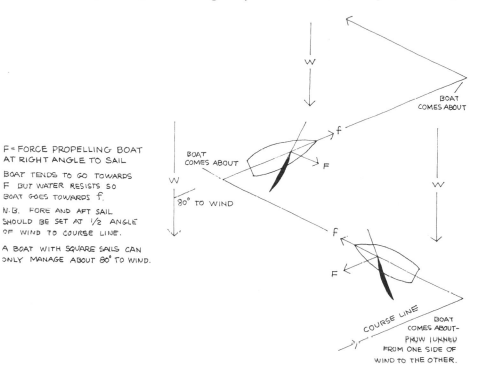

F = FORCE PROPELLING BOAT
AT RIGHT ANGLE TO SAIL

BOAT TENDS TO GO TOWARDS
F BUT WATER RESISTS SO
BOAT GOES TOWARDS f.

N.B. FORE AND AFT SAIL
SHOULD BE SET AT 1/2 ANGLE
OF WIND TO COURSE LINE.

A BOAT WITH SQUARE SAILS CAN
ONLY MANAGE ABOUT 80° TO WIND.

Fig. 38. Principles of Tacking—in order to sail against the wind

Europe from western North America, had to go far to the west of Chile so that she could clear the Horn "on the port tack with the prevailing Westerly winds."[24] When windjammers did not clear the Horn, but instead got close to the Chilean coast further north, they had a terrible time beating out to the westward; therefore, skippers tended to play for safety and get far to the west before turning southeast for the Horn. The dangers were recognized as early as Drake's time. One of the pilots he had captured said that "all the stormes of the North sea come from the land, but in the South sea all the windes and stormes come off the sea, and force the ships to run upon the leeshore."[25] Navigators fear land, and a leeshore most of all: "Isn't 60 miles away enough for you?" Lewis asked his very competent female navigator in the *Rehu Moana*, the modern catamaran discussed in the section on Polynesian double canoes. "The farther away the better," she answered.[26]

An extreme example of these limitations of sailing ships is that of Pizarro, conqueror of Peru, who tried without success for seventy days to get his ship out of the Bay of Panama. He was embayed (that is, his ship was in a bay with the wind blowing directly in), and he lacked room to manoeuvre by a series of tacks. Certain bays, because of their shape and the prevailing wind direction, are particularly dangerous. The Bay of Panama is a bad one. A

French barque in the twentieth century failed to get out of this bay after ninety-two days—time enough for scurvy to decimate her crew and for worms to destroy her hull. One wonders why the men did not go ashore sooner.[27]

A difficulty which arose because of all the variables in navigation was keeping company in a fleet of vessels, even with only two ships. If they became separated, they would, in all likelihood, not see one another again until the rendezvous which every foresighted commander appointed. Hawkins found that "commonly one ship, though but a bad sayler, maketh more haste then a whole fleete," and so ships left behind by accident sometimes reached the rendezvous first.[28] His father, the great Sir John Hawkins (Plate 36), left five commandments of the sea:

> Serve God daily, . . .
> Love one another;
> preserve your victuals;
> beward of fire;
> and keep good company.[29]

This list covers most of the problems. Hawkins starts with what, to him, was the most important; the last precept is not "Polonius-type" advice about friendship, but means that ships of a fleet should stay together.

Carteret found that his exploration sloop, the *Swallow*, in spite of the promise of her name, could not keep company with the *Dolphin* (Plate 63), a fast frigate. According to her captain, the *Swallow* was not only old but "one of the worst, if not the very worst of her kind."[30] To Robertson, master of the *Dolphin*, she was "our poor, dull Consort."[31] Bougainville, sailing on after speaking her at sea, left her "as it were at anchor."[32] As a result of her poor sailing qualities, "she mist tacking more than once" and sometimes even had to use boats to tow her around to tack.[33] Her steering was so bad that its balance was not even altered by furling all sails forward of the mainmast and setting all sails from the mainmast aft to the stern, a circumstance, Carteret said, which "appeared strange enough to us, and I believe will be thought so by others."[34] Even broadening the rudder by adding a piece of wood made no difference.

So even if the *Swallow* had been "an extraordinary good sea boat, (which was the only good quality she had)," it would have been difficult for her to keep company with her frigate consort and most certainly frustrating.[35] Although thinly sheathed against worms, she was not protected by "filling" with nails. As a result of this deficiency, on her way home she had to be repaired in the Dutch base at Batavia, simply by adding sheathing to her bottom over the old planks—for fear that any further examination would see her con-demned.

A great many of the fleets found difficulty in keeping together because of mis-mating, such as the *Swallow* with the *Dolphin*. Spanish pilots emphasized the importance of matching ships well: "such a pair when sailing that in all the rains and fogs we met with, they were never separated" was considered a description of the ideal.[36] Usually, however, separation was caused by storms, in the same way that the *Elizabeth* became separated from the *Golden Hind*. The *Wager* was blown away from the *Centurion*; in fact, all of Anson's fleet was scattered, and not all reached the rendezvous at Juan Fernández.

Wind was not the only hazard which could separate ships, but, like a woman, it could be either cruel or kind, depending—it seemed—on whim, and worth placating. Most other dangers simply appeared, or did not. The *Vostok*, not far from Macquarie Island, but nevertheless out in the open sea, "suddenly felt two violent shocks, as if the vessel had run on a shoal."[37] Her consort, subject to the same distress, sounded with the leadline and found no bottom at over 350 feet. Canvassing the possibilities, from shoals to sleeping whales, it was finally decided it had been an earthquake. (It was once thought the *Dolphin* had run into a whale; one had hit the *Argonaut*, so by no means was it an absurd suggestion.)

Near South America, the *Golden Hind* and her pinnace, "riding very neere an English mile from the shoare, were shaken and did quiver as if it had beene layd on drie land."[38] And it was near South America that "on board the *Beagle* it was as though the ship for a moment had slipped her anchors and was bumping on the bottom."[39] Quirós's ship once felt "a great trembling of the sea and of the ship—a notable thing and new to me."[40] Near Juan Fernández, the *Batchelor's Delight* was so shaken by an earth-quake that several men were thrown out of their hammocks and the captain right out of his cabin; the sea—and perhaps the buccaneers—"seemed then of a Whitish Colour.[41]

Ships reported these shocks from various parts of the Pacific, in every case describing the shock as similar to that of running aground. Course discusses a ship that "shook as if she was bumping over a shingle bottom" and the *Black Swan*, an immigrant ship on the way to New Zealand, "was shaken violently, and a peculiar sound was heard, as if she was grating over the bottom."[42] Only in one instance was actual damage to the ship reported—the crew considered that the earthquake had opened a cock at the bottom of the ship. The shock of an earthquake would be a frightening experience, but still harmless enough in the open sea. The real danger lay in being in harbour at the time of the shocks, for earthquakes are known to cause tidal waves which could sweep anchored ships far inland. The Pacific is rimmed with lands subject to earthquake and volcano, therefore it is to be expected that some convulsions would occur beneath that sea, and that all shocks, by sea or land, would send out waves. The crew of the barque *Archos* was actually on the lookout for Anjer Point on Krakatoa Island when in 1883 a great volcanic eruption removed two thirds of that island from the face of the earth.[43] The *Archos* and her crew survived, although tens of thousands of people perished. Tidal waves sped throughout the Pacific flinging ships ashore, smashing ports, and roaring over coral atolls.

Icebergs were also a menace, but, if sighted, they could be avoided. They are not like the lightning and storms which seem to seek out ships; an iceberg has to be run into. Ice can be a menace in the southern oceans from roughly the 40th parallel south; the danger varies from year to year. The great commercial sailing ships taking wheat, meat, or wool from Australia and New Zealand eastward past the Horn and northward to England had to sail in this danger zone to make a short passage, because a "great circle" route, or as close as can be to it, from Sydney to Cape Horn would mean going as far south as 60°S, 800 miles within the iceberg zone. The bergs were huge, many times the size of a ship: "Four bells, passed a big 'berg, judged to be about 180 feet high and 600 to 700 feet long."[44] That particular one was on the latitude of Christchurch, New Zealand, although thousands of miles east past the Horn. In an amusing but not entirely convincing calculation, Captain Bellingshausen estimated that the fresh water that could be obtained by melting down one particular iceberg he saw to the southeast of New Zealand in December, 1820, would supply one pail of water a day for "22 years and 86 days" for each of the 845 million people he thought to be alive in the world.

Captains claimed there was a warning of the presence of ice by a sudden cooling of the air. Chichester was told by a veteran of Cape Horn that "you could smell ice ahead in the southern ocean well in advance"; Chichester reasoned that the ice, moving downwind in the same direction as the ship, would leave "a trail of cold water behind it," a confirmation of the cooling theory.[45] "Able Seaman," writing of the North Atlantic, says the custom there was to take the water temperature every two hours as a means of detecting the proximity of icebergs. In the twentieth century, foghorns are sounded, "and breaths were held on deck, listening for an echo to come through the noises of sea and wind."[46] Radar uses the same principle, sending out radio waves that echo back from solid objects to show a reaction on a screen.

Even the sharpest lookout might not be sharp enough in poor visibility. Conrad, in "a Clyde-built barque of 1,000 tons" in the extreme South Pacific, nearly hit a piece of ice which had been swept much further north than was usual. He saved his ship only by the good fortune of being aloft repairing the rigging during daylight; any later and "no eye could have made out in the dusk that pale piece of ice swept over by the white-crested waves."[47] A question could be raised by what could be seen, not only by what it was feared might be concealed. On one iceberg, a fully clothed man, lying as if asleep, was seen plainly by the whole crew of the *Marco Polo* in 1861.[48] Unable to reach him and certain he was dead, the men left him to ride the berg mysteriously until it, and he, went back to become part of the sea.

Waterspouts are easy enough to see, and they are an awe-inspiring sight. One came near the *Dragon*, "which we feared much ... if they should light in any ship she were in danger to be presently sunck downe into the sea."[49] Dampier saw waterspouts and, as with so many things he saw, he left an excellent description.

A Spout is a small Ragged piece or part of a Cloud hanging down about a Yard, seemingly from the blackest part thereof. Commonly it hangs down sloping from thence, or sometimes appearing with a small bending, or elbow in the middle. I never saw any hang perpendicularly down. It is small at the lower end, seeming no bigger than ones Arm, but 'tis fuller towards the Cloud, from whence it proceeds.

When the surface of the Sea begins to work, you shall see the Water, for about 100 paces in circumference, foam and move gently round till the whirling motion increases: and then it flies upward in a Pillar, about 100 Paces in compass at the bottom, but lessening gradually upwards to the smallness of the Spout it self, there where it reacheth the lower end of the Spout, through which the rising Seawater seems to be conveyed into the Clouds. This visibly appears by the Clouds increasing in bulk and blackness.[50]

One passed one of Cook's ships "within fifty yards," and another came close enough to Bligh's ship to frighten its crew and captain.[51]

It is during a calm, at the very time when sailing ships have no ability to manoeuvre, that waterspouts occur—for the same reasons that prairie whirlwinds and tornadoes build up in hot, still afternoons. They are not necessarily fatal to ships. One day, when a "light wind from the north barely filled the sails," the *Penang* hit a small waterspout: "a low hum came from aloft ... the ship seemed to be halted and held still by a giant's hand for a moment; then the fore-rigging filled again, and the ship sailed on as before."[52] Apparently, Dampier's belief about them was well-founded, "but though I have seen, and been beset by them often, yet the Fright was always the greatest of the Harm."[53]

The conditions that create waterspouts also create thunderstorms, and the lightning is a menace to ships. A Dutch Indiaman lost all her masts to lightning while anchored close to the *Endeavour*, whereas Cook's ship was saved by its lightning conductor which "carr[i]ed the Lightning or Electrical matter over the side Clear of the Ship."[54] A convict ship lost a top-gallant mast to lightning and was sunk by it, and the *Rattler* had men wounded by electrical phenomena while at sea.[55]

Fire was the greatest of all dangers to wooden ships, with their highly inflammable sails, hulls, and rigging. At sea, a wooden ship was extremely vulnerable to lightning or to human error. At war, the shore batteries defending harbours—although lacking the mobility of ships—had the advantage of being able to heat red-hot cannonballs to fire at the ships' wooden hulls. Spontaneous combustion was a great danger on ships with bulky cargoes, such as coal or wool, and the *Lightning* and many other good ships caught fire this way, nearly always burning to the waterline in spite of water all around. In one of Vancouver's ships, fire was started by the spontaneous combustion of some mattresses. Oddly enough, ice was "the most inflammable cargo . . . ice sets up gases below, the sawdust in which it is packed catches fire as easily as cotton or jute, and there is an end of the ice ship."[56] Another coincidence of cold and fire occurred on the "fast and handsome sailing ship, *Dunedin*" (Plate 37) which took the first shipment of frozen mutton from New Zealand to England in 1882. She struck some extraordinarily hot weather on the voyage and her steam-fired boilers, used to run her refrigerating plant, kept setting her sails on fire.[57]

But carelessness was a more potent menace than shore batteries, steam boilers, or spontaneous combustion. The fire in the *St. Jean Baptiste*, caused by a candle setting fire to some brandy while its level in the cask was being checked, was successfully quelled by the item which had caused Vancouver's trouble—a mattress. This foolish use of candles was criticized in early Australian emigrant ships, in which naked lights might be carried to illuminate the activities of an officer charged with the drawing of ardent spirits from a darkly stowed cask.[58] The *India* caught fire because of this type of carelessness.

The *Daintie* caught fire while pitch was being heated by someone "who had a better name than experience," and Hawkins put it out by using "rugge 'gownes'" (heavy sea coats) soaked in the sea. Hawkins went on to tell of various ships burned by the careless use of candles and matches, and of one, the *Roebucke*, which burned "with drinking of tobacco."[59] Barlow, just home from China in 1696, saw the huge *Royal Sovereign* "new launched and rebuilt at Woolwich, being made the finest ship in the world."[60] She had been

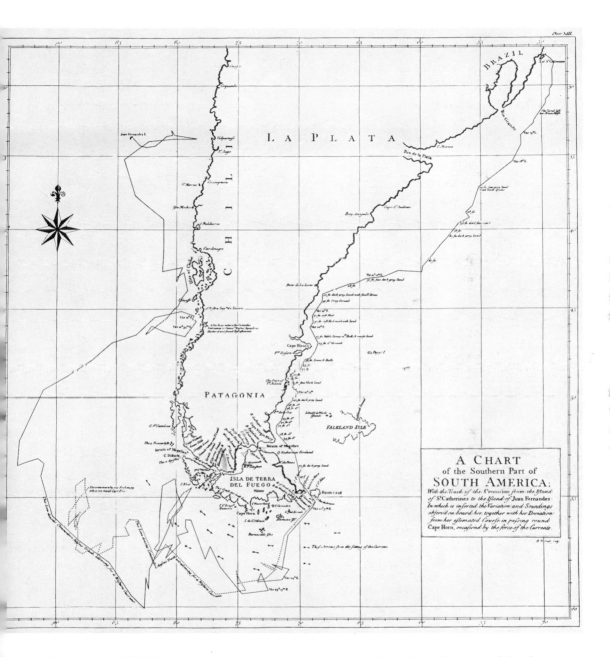

Plate 33. The track of H.M.S. *Centurion* from east to west around Cape Horn. Because of the danger from on-shore winds along the coast of South America, Anson naturally wished to sail as far west as was practical before turning north. But without chronometers to help determine his precise east/west position, he had to estimate the *Centurion*'s track from day to day by dead reckoning. The broken line shows the track Anson estimated he was following until, as shown by the unbroken line of his actual route, he found himself at Cape Noir—at the same *latitude* as his estimated position but hundreds of miles east of it, still nowhere near far enough west for safety. The extra time used to sail west again, against the Westerly wind, this time allowing for the western current (arrows), caused Anson to lose so many men to scurvy that he had to abandon and sink a consort ship for lack of men to work her.

Plate 34. *Gipsy Moth IV*, sailed by Sir Francis Chichester, rounds Cape Horn. Of the four great continental capes, the Horn was the most feared by sailing ships because it was there that they encountered the huge seas pushed by the strong Westerly winds sweeping completely round the world. To have sailed around Cape Horn in any ship set one apart as a Cape Horn Man, and few have done it alone, as Chichester did, in a small craft.

Plate 35. Matthew Maury (1806-73). After he had served briefly as an officer in the U.S. Navy, Maury's interest in improving naval administration led him to an appointment as superintendent of both the Depot of Maps and Charts and the Naval Observatory, which were soon merged. His most solid work was done as an oceanographer, preparing charts and books on winds and currents for American seamen, and he was instrumental in having a uniform system of recording oceanographic data adopted by the shipping industries of the world.

Plate 36. Sir John Hawkins (1532-95). Sir John did not himself sail the Pacific, but many of the devices he invented or introduced into the marine industry of Britain (movable top masts, boarding-nettings, chain-pumps, anti-shipworm sheathing) assisted such men as Sir Francis Drake and Sir Richard Hawkins on their Pacific expeditions.

Plate 37. The *Dunedin*. A refrigerator ship, the *Dunedin* took the historic first load of frozen mutton from New Zealand to Britain. The steam boilers operating the refrigeration plant constantly set fire to her sails, but the voyage was successful nonetheless.

Plate 38. H.M.S. *Resolution* and H.M.S. *Adventure*, 4 January, 1773, taking in ice for water. Getting fresh water was a problem for eighteenth-century ships on long voyages. One solution was to obtain and melt ice from icebergs, although occasionally sailors complained about ill effects from such water.

Plate 39. Crossing the line. A measure of license was allowed a crew in such ceremonies as that which celebrated crossing the equator, or "crossing the line." The ritual could become coarse, even brutal, at times, depending on the state of the crew's feelings, but it practically never got out of hand. It was a valuable release of tension for men crowded together, performing strenuous but monotonous work in what were often, in early sailing days, dangerous and unknown circumstances.

built originally at tremendous expense in 1637 as the *Sovereign of the Seas,* with the ship money collected by Charles I—her size and beauty indirectly costing the king his head. Famed as the most richly decorated ship ever built, she was a good one too, and never lost a battle in spite of seeing action in all the seventeenth-century English wars. Although the Dutch and French had tried in vain to beat her in war, shortly after Barlow saw her she was completely burned because of an overturned candle.

These other dangers were real, but very unusual. It was the wind that counted most near land or in the open sea. The wind was necessary for movement, and sailors would put up with a rough sea as long as progress was made, because "among seamen, a 'good wind makes a good sea.' "[61] Although winds set limits to the direction sailed, calms left the ships motionless, except for the little that ships' sweeps or the oars of ships' boats could do. It is true that some optimists looked on a calm as being "half a fair wind"; after all, there could have been a wind blowing the ships off course. Even a calm did some good. Calms brought sailing ships together—in exactly the same way that a damaged bridge or road brings automobiles together—for, when progress stops, there is a pile up. One six-week-long calm off the Azores in the late nineteenth century brought 300 ships together: "this is a bit hard to believe, but it has been verified."[62] Such meetings gave a chance for ship-to-ship visiting and gamming (or the exchange of information and news). Boatloads of ladies and gentlemen of the *Randolph*, one of the "First Four Ships" of Canterbury, New Zealand, exchanged visits and dinner with passengers of the French ship *Active* in September, 1850, during a calm. The French captain at first did not wish to dine aboard the *Randolph* "but in the end yielded to the solicitations of the ladies, who were very anxious to stay."[63]

Without wind, the sails flap and the ship rolls in the swell or, even worse, psychologically speaking, she lies unnaturally still. Seas rise quickly with the wind and fall as quickly with a calm; "up wind up sea, down wind down sea" is a sailors' saying in the tropics. When down wind, down sea for too long, tension built up among the crew; at such times the famed superstition of sailors and the sea held sway, as Coleridge vividly portrays in "The Ancient Mariner." Superstition affected morale, and morale was of overwhelming importance in long voyages. Almost any Pacific voyage was a long one. Discontent broke down both discipline and, to a lesser degree, health; the men either would not or could not do the work properly.

There is a vast treasure house of stories about the superstition of seamen which, like prayer, is one of men's reactions to elemental forces they cannot control. This treasure house contains much that is important rather than merely interesting, for the irrationality of men is itself an elemental force to be reckoned with. Unlucky captains or unlucky ships tend to be prophecies which fulfil themselves, simply because the seamen's beliefs lead to a lack of confidence which affects action. The *Peppercorn* was an unlucky ship. Not only did fourteen treenail-holes prove empty of treenails, but the cook set her on fire and her admiral's ship ran into her. There have always been some ships known as unlucky ships; today, there is the *Melbourne* of the Royal Australian Navy, whose collisions have caused some sailors to remember ancient superstitions. There were also lucky ships. The *Torrens*, associated with Conrad, with some reason was felt to be a lucky one. Not only were her recorded passages outstandingly successful, but odd anecdotes survive. Once, having run out of oil for her lamps, she picked up a barrel floating out at sea—it was full of lamp oil.

Winds, or the lack of them, were not always thought to be matters of luck. During one calm, Morton saw that in his ship everybody "is looking for a 'scapegoat' on the ship to see who brought these horrible conditions on to them."[64] When present, the usual scapegoat was "that most terrible of men amongst sailors, a Russian Finn."[65] Finns were believed to control the winds and so could be blamed for either plenitude or dearth—as circumstances warranted. Some sailors went even further: "the sail-maker was a Fin, and could do anything he was of a mind to."[66] It was reported, perhaps not too reliably, that one captain shut a Finn down in the fore-peak until he made the wind change. This superstition was still firmly held into the twentieth century: "We can't fight '*trolldom*,' " said Sam, the Swedish mate of the "regular old clipper" *Beatrice*, when speaking of the captain of the Finnish four-masted barque *Herzogin Cecilie* in 1927.[67] None of this stopped Seligman signing on a Finn for the *Cap Pilar*. Nowadays, middle-class sailors who are really sailing for the fun of it are probably less concerned with the supernatural.

Finns were not the only men whose presence supposedly created trouble with the elements. Byron, midshipman in the *Wager* and commander of the *Dolphin*, as an admiral was famous as "Foulweather Jack." Seamen firmly believed his presence meant gales for the ship or the fleet, and with good reason—as may be concluded from reading of the gales he survived. In the *Rattler*, not only the superstitious among the sailors were distressed by a woman screaming in agony for hours from the sea near the ship. Whatever it was—a seal perhaps, Captain Colnett thought—one can imagine how upsetting it was to even the most cynical. Sailors fear a hen crowing on board, but surely a hen crowing is unusual enough anywhere to cause comment. Sailmakers, often the tough old survivors of a long life at sea, were usually the undertakers too. One of their customs was to put a stitch through the corpse's nose when they sewed it into sail cloth for burial—to keep it sewn in so that it could not return to haunt the ship.[68]

The scientists of the eighteenth-century enlightenment were not cynical in the face of the forces of nature and of men's puny equipment to resist them. "We were drifting under the might of God," said Steller of a gale which tossed the *St. Peter*. "There was much praying, to be sure, but the curses piled up during ten years in Siberia prevented any response."[69] Two centuries earlier, Spanish sailors thought Drake's raid "a great plague of God justly inflicted upon us for our sinnes."[70]

Curses and sins were intangibles, and ordinary sailors everywhere piled them as high in Siberia as they did in Peru, no doubt. But they also feared actual things which were as far beyond harming them as a curse could possibly be. A boy in the *Conrad* found his looted souvenir skull blamed for the storm which battered the ship. Allowed to keep it only if the wind changed, he asked the skull to change the wind. The wind changed. This was more dramatic, but no more successful, than when the Polynesian priest in the *Endeavour* prayed for wind—although, as Banks observed, "he never began till he perceived a breeze so near the ship that it generally reached her before his prayer was finished."[71] Wafer, the buccaneer surgeon, was not allowed to keep the Peruvian mummy he had found, a relic of a Spanish massacre. He saw it tossed unceremoniously into the sea, and his scientific spirit reacted with "great Vexation."[72] Probably Wafer had little choice other than to let his mummy go in the face of a determined and superstitious crew, if even the strict Cook saw the wisdom of humouring a crew's whim by sailing on the 12th of July—a lucky day. "The superstition of a seaman's mind is not easily subdued,"[73] one of Cook's officers, Colnett, gradually learned.

Sailors and seamen of all ranks had their ways of placating fate ahead of time. A ship's name, for instance, would seem to be of much less consequence than her maintenance or navigation. Yet, to sailors, ships' names were and are important. Like figureheads, intrinsically unimportant, names nevertheless have a psychological and emotional significance that wise leaders know how to use to advantage to maintain morale. Men's reactions to the elemental dangers they had to face in Pacific sailing were often irrational; yet, since morale is more important than material, such reactions and any overt actions which illustrate them, are significant. Two early examples of this belief are interesting, because, although each name was changed to one more euphonic and more positive, the fates of the ships were very different. One name is still world renowned; the other lost its fame when it lost its battle.

Drake of the *Pelican/Golden Hind*, like Cook of the *Endeavour*, knew his men and their fancies; no doubt he had his own as they had theirs. When the *Pelican* set out, none could have foreseen her triumphant coming home as the *Golden Hind*—golden in fact as in fame. At the beginning, her commander had deliberately made her magnificent; his quarters contained "all sorts of curious workmanship," and at his table he ate from silver while expert musicians played. Perhaps he intended to display the "magnificence of his native country" to all the world. Queen Elizabeth contributed "dainties and perfumed waters" to the commander and, by doing so, presumably gave her blessing as well. The *Pelican*'s setting out with splendour and the *Golden Hind*'s returning with wealth—two names, but one ship, one spirit, one commander—were to flaunt the greatness of the rising maritime nation and that of her captain too.

Drake was no stranger to the deepest feelings of true seamen, for he had not been born to a quarterdeck, nor to own a famous ship either. He had made his way upward as painfully as Cook was to do. As an omen of success, and as a tribute to his friend and sponsor, Sir Christopher Hatton, and perhaps even with history in mind, off South America, Drake changed the name of his ship to *Golden Hind*, after the majestic deer which was the Hatton family crest. With the new name, there was meant to be a renewing of purpose and unity, and a steeling of resolution for the hardships and dangers ahead. It worked; Drake's ship did not turn back.

Although she was the second ship to sail around the world, Drake was the first captain to command his own ship from the beginning to the end of the voyage. The man who had learned his trade on the bleak North Sea—one of the worst of seas—had now mastered the South Atlantic, the Pacific, and the Indian Ocean in an English ship. This feat linked the names of captain and ship inseparably. An Englishman with Magellan had sailed the Pacific; John Oxenham had built a pinnace and had been the first English captain to command a ship on that ocean. Together Drake and the *Golden Hind* had done both, and more besides.

A cousin of Drake's wished to emulate this, and he had a ship he thought could dare the Pacific. Sir Richard Hawkins was very proud of the *Daintie*: "doubtlesse, the *Daintie* was a very good sea ship, and excellent by the winde; which . . . made fezible that which almost was not to be beleeved."[74]

From drawings, attributed with some reason to Elizabethan master shipwright Matthew Baker, it is known what the ship would have been like. Sailing ships, at this time, were not built to a blueprint; variations were myriad. Naturally, some attempts were made to copy vessels known to be good sailers, and the Hawkins family had plenty of experience with ships and shipbuilding to draw upon by the time Sir Richard built the *Daintie*. He was of the third of three generations of famous and successful seamen. There is little reason to think that he would depart very far from the most successful design, largely his father's creation, which had been vindicated just before the *Daintie*'s building by the great victory over the Armada. She would have had a mainmast, a foremast ahead of her forecastle, and possibly two masts instead of one aft of her mainmast to balance the foremast.[75] The picture which exists of her shows her with four masts, but it is not certain that the artist ever saw her. If she had had two aftermasts, both would have carried lateen sails, the sail on the more forward of the two masts to add to her performance when sailing on a wind, and that on the mast farthest aft to aid the handling of the ship.

Hawkins's loss of the *Daintie* to the Spaniards, after the most heroic defence, was a bitter blow. This ship had damaged King Philip II's purse severely even before her protracted battle with the Spaniards off Peru. She had been a major partner in the capture of Philip's great Portuguese carrack, the *Madre de Dios*, in 1592, "the vast body of this carak . . . being in burden by the estimation of the wise and experienced no lesse than 1600 tunnes."[76]

The *Daintie* was of only from 300 to 400 tons, but Hawkins described her as "pleasing to the eye, profitable for stowage, good of sayle, and well-conditioned."[77] Apparently, she was a handsome ship, for Queen Elizabeth renamed her the *Daintie*, disliking as much as Hawkins did the gloomy name of the *Repentance* that his stepmother had given her.

Hawkins and Elizabeth were right. The names of ships are important, even setting aside the element of superstition which is involved. Names should be pleasing to the ear, be memorable, be evocative of glory, or of beauty, or of intention. The *Golden Hind* commemorated both the beauty of an animal and the pride of a great family. Clifford named his Chinese junk of the 1960's *Golden Lotus*, recalling the beauty of an early Chinese "wicked lady."

England, on the whole, has named her ships well, and so has France. Contrast, for example, *Solide*, *Boudeuse*, *Uranie*, or *Royal Sovereign*, *Halcyon*, *Endeavour*, with the dreary procession from the saints' calendars of Spain and Portugal—or the unimaginative state and city names that Americans so often use. Sometimes, Americans do even worse and choose individual names—initials as well. How could names, such as *R. B. Forbes*, *Charles W. Morgan*, or *Thomas W. Lawson*, ring as mellowly through history as do *Cutty Sark* or *Etoile*? Names as euphonic as *Tamar*, for example, have had a representative in every age, and several of the ships have been as beautiful as their name. To be fair, however, the *Flying Cloud* and the *Lightning*—both American ships—should be remembered. The Maori names for their great canoes were simple and euphonic; the beauty of *Takitimu* or *Tainui* matched the grace of the vessels themselves, and is as haunting as those of *Ariel* or *Boudeuse* or *Sir Lancelot*. Beautiful Maori names still grace New Zealand ports: the *Aranui* plies Cook Strait, the *Waiata* lies in Otago harbour.

Sometimes, names could imply a relationship, as with Rogers's pair of ships, the *Duke* and *Duchess*. One Dutch fleet setting out to the Pacific consisted of the ships *Faith*, *Hope*, *Charity*, and *Fidelity*. Perhaps, in case these names might prove merited, a fifth ship was called the *Good News*. A name could be most inapt; there was a warship called H.M.S. *Quaker*. Certainly, some names can go too far. A schooner built for the government of Tonga was called "*Koe Bamu oe Utukalogalu*"—her skipper called her *Bamu*! There is no record of what the Spanish skipper usually called his *Nuestra Señora de La Encarnación Desengaño*. Probably, she would be referred to as the "Capitana" (the vessel of a fleet commander) or the "Almiranta" (the vessel of the second-in-command of the fleet).

A name conveys an aura, a reputation; it is the "mana" (a word of Melanesian and Polynesian origin, meaning the power of the elemental forces of nature embodied in an object or person) that goes with a ship, compounded over the years out of marine talk, of personal gossip, of the stories that glorify her achievements and gloss over her failures. "All that talk makes up her 'name,'" Conrad said, rightly enough.[78] It is an important matter, the choice of a ship's name, the one to be painted on and pointed out, the one to which all rumour or compliment or complaint is directed. Queen Elizabeth was right, and Hawkins, and Conrad. And so, perhaps, Villiers, as a writer, was the most right of all—he renamed his handsome ship the *Joseph Conrad*.

As well as honouring someone who was admired, or evoking the magic of the gods of the sea and the moving air for oneself, there could be diplomatic and tactful reasons for a change of name. For Cook's second great Pacific voyage, two ships had been commissioned—the *Drake* and *Raleigh*—names as fitting for both success and high purpose as one could wish. Political caution intervened, however, and to avoid offending Spain, the ships sailed as the *Resolution* and *Adventure*, felicitous choices for a voyage that constantly required the former and richly attained the latter.

There is an amusing story of a Cunard line spokesman's attempt to tell King George V that the great new liner of the 1930's was to be named the *Queen Victoria*. He began diplomatically be saying that the ship was to be called after a great queen who was also a noble woman. The king's reply, "My wife will be so pleased," was touching, simple, and inspired. Who, of an earlier generation, would have had the *Queen Mary* called otherwise? Too much can be easily made of all this; it is the qualities of the ship as a ship, and the qualities of her crew and commander as well that, in the long run, as Conrad implies, make her "name."

One superstition that has lasted until today is the ceremony of "crossing the line" (Plate 39). It is an ancient one, used mainly as relaxation for the crew, but formerly also used as a form of blackmail to get free drinks. Nor was the opportunity lost to pay off some old scores within the crew, or between the crew and passengers. In one case, however, £100 damages were won in court by an irate passenger.[79] It was not all one-sided. By custom, a ducking at the line entitled the receiver to a treat in the pub at home, so some new sailors on Rogers's *Duke* insisted on being ducked several times. Informed opinions about it have differed. Anderson, one of Cook's surgeons, thought the ceremony should be suppressed because of the bullying, yet de Freycinet firmly believed in its value as a morale builder. Customs varied, and ". . . instead of the usual amusing horse play that takes place in British ships, the proceedings on board the *Passat* [a Finnish barque] appeared . . . blasphemous. This, however, might well have been due to the fact that there were no women passengers on board."[80]

Innocent fun or vindictive mischief, the horseplay was a relief for the tensions that built up in the crowded conditions aboard ship. With the limitations of the vessels, the impersonal power of the ocean, and the seeming capriciousness of the all-important winds, it is little wonder that superstition flourished among the crew members. The officers, busy with plans and choices, could take some refuge from their tensions and frustrations in mental effort.

CHAPTER 14

Materials, Measurement, Shipworms, Grounding, and Repairs

The fourth prevention [for shipworms], which now is most accompted of, is to burne the utter planke till it come to be in every place like a cole, and after to pitch it; this is not bad.

RICHARD HAWKINS
OF THE *DAINTIE*

The much-esteemed stempiece was from the butt of the smartest kind of a pasture oak. It afterward split a coral patch in two at the Keeling Islands, and did not receive a blemish. Better timber for a ship than pasture white oak never grew.

JOSHUA SLOCUM
OF THE *SPRAY*

There are certain aspects of shipbuilding, common to all ships, which should be known in order to understand the problems involved in repairing damage or wear. Shipwrights built ships of certain materials and in particular ways for reasons that seemed good to them. The size and shape of ships that resulted were important in Pacific conditions; so was the way they were described. It is interesting to note, for example, that the size of European ships is described in terms of tonnage, and the size of European small craft in terms of length or of the number of oarsmen—for example, a 300-ton ship or a 12-oared captain's barge. This custom ensured that Chinese junks would be described by tonnage, and kayaks or canoes by either length or the number of paddlers; knowledge of them, therefore, is shaped by the viewers' preconceptions. National characteristics played a part in shipbuilding too, as with the use by the Dutch and Chinese of sheer and leeboard in their ship design, or with the selection of materials by the British and Americans. It was not simply the availability of material that was decisive; cultural attitudes counted as well. After all, Baltic pine was easily available in Britain, and there was plenty of oak in America. The oak ships of the Royal Navy were as steadfast and solid as was the tradition that shaped its men, and both discipline and ships seemed often to have a corresponding heaviness and inflexibility. In contrast, the beautiful and speedy softwood clippers of the Americans were an early example of built-in obsolescence; their years of speed were few, though supreme. For all their beauty and importance, it is worth noting that American ships were not the only softwood ships in the Pacific.

Oak was the most famous wood used in shipbuilding, but many northern countries—Sweden, Russia, Canada—used pine, or fir, or sometimes even spruce. So did one southern country, New Zealand, and so did the United States. Her ships were immortalized by the contemptuous phrase used by an Englishman about American "fir-built frigates." However, the Englishman spoke too soon—those powerful ships proved to be a match for any frigates of oak that the British had in 1812.

Different woods had their own virtues in shipbuilding; however, in nearly every case, ships were built to a price, and the choice of wood was governed by availability rather than by intrinsic quality. Oak was tough and very durable, but chemically hard on iron bolts, whereas teak preserved iron rather than rusted it. Because teak was used so much in Eastern shipbuilding, it became known as "Indian oak." Teak did not splinter easily either, and was much superior in nearly every other way to elm, which was also known for this quality. Naturally, in warships, some attempt was made to avoid wood which splintered badly, more wounds being caused by splinters than by shot; therefore, elm was used for shielding devices at times, "for that it shivers not with a shot, as oake and other timber will doe."[1] Elm was also used for outside sheathing against shipworms, because of the same special qualities that caused its use in some clippers with their beautiful curves: "it ryveth not [does not split], it indureth better under water, and yeeldeth better to the shippes side."[2] Ships of durable teak from India still sail in Pacific waters and so, if accident has not intervened, must the ships built of wood with an even greater claim to endurance—the "everlasting wood" of Paraguay.

Russian pinewood, especially the unseasoned wood used in the exploration vessel *Vostok*, made no such pretense to immortality, and her captain, Bellingshausen, more than once must have wished it had. His Russian-built sloop suffered from many ills. She was about 130 feet long and 33 feet wide, of the same build and dimensions as the Russian sloop *Kamchatka*, which had successfully sailed around the world. The *Vostok* was to have a most successful voyage under Bellingshausen, a skilled navigator and a splendid leader of men. Built of unseasoned pinewood, somewhat reinforced underwater, and then sheathed with copper, the *Vostok*'s construction is interesting because it was roughly about this time (in some cases, a little earlier) that a great number of

American ships built of various softwoods began to appear in the Pacific. The *Vostok* was built of Baltic pine, but Russian Pacific exploration in softwood ships had begun even earlier with the ships Bering had built at Okhotsk.

Whether built of softwood or hardwood, a wooden hull requires a great deal of protection and maintenance. The distances in the Pacific and the time it took to traverse them wore out ships and gave their enemies, such as shipworms (figure 39) and decay, sufficient chance to cause severe damage. In the earliest days, the lack of fully equipped shore bases meant that repairs had to be left undone or done hastily and inadequately. Ships required maintenance and repair, particularly against the ravages of shipworms, but also against the breakage or straining caused by running onto shoals, shores, or rocks. The removal from the wooden hulls of the marine growths which both hindered and injured the ships was as essential for the survival of the ship as was the replacement of broken planking. Good ships' officers knew as much about these things as they did about seamanship; carpenters, for centuries officers, were important men on any wooden ship. Their maintenance efforts were lessened or increased in proportion both to the skill of their own ships' officers in navigating well enough to avoid dangerous losses of time, and to the conscientiousness of shipyard officials (which was often nearly nonexistent) in preparing the ships for the hazards of long voyages.

The success and survival of many early wooden ships, as Magellan's *Victoria* shows, were very often because of foresighted preparation before sailing. That Sir Francis Drake's *Golden Hind* completed her circumnavigation was largely due to her extra sheathing against the ravages of shipworms. This protection was recommended by Drake's uncle,

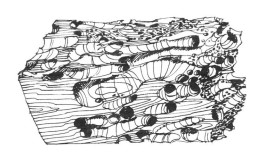

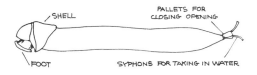

SHELL

PALLETS FOR CLOSING OPENING

FOOT

SYPHONS FOR TAKING IN WATER

Fig. 39. Wood Bored by Shipworm and (below) *a Shipworm* (teredo navalis) *out of Burrow*

Sir John Hawkins, who introduced many sensible regulations and useful inventions into the Royal Navy. His interest in naval medicine is important. Much more important, giving him immortality through English history, was his major role in the creation of the *"Revenge"* type of warship which played such a part in defeating the Armada. It is worth repeating that, although it was these ships which were the true "galleons," that name has become linked with ships of their opponents, the Spaniards.

Hawkins is credited with inventing chain pumps and anti-boarding nettings, but by far the most important of his technical innovations was his method of protecting ships against shipworms (*teredo navalis*) which were quite capable of ruining the planking of a ship's wooden bottom in a few weeks. "Worm" is a misnomer, for it is a form of bivalve mollusc related to the cockle and mussel. Nor are they worm-like in size; some tropical species grow to be six feet long and to the thickness of a man's arm.[4] Not only do they ruin the wood, but the heads of these marine creatures are so hard that they ruin saws which attempt to cut through the foraminous planks in any efforts to repair the ships.[5]

In the double sheathing method devised by John Hawkins, sheathing of thin elm boards, smeared thickly on the inner side with tar and plasterers' hair, was nailed over the bottom planking (figure 40). Hawkins's son, Richard, knew a great deal about the ravages of shipworms, having seen ships in such

a condition "that the most of their plankes under water have beene like honey combes."[6] In spite of this forewarning, he lost much of his fresh water on his *Daintie* voyage, when the worms, picked up while getting water at a river mouth, ate through the water casks. He also lost his "shalop," a small boat they were towing, to worms which had "wrought into the planke as with a gowdge."[7] Neither casks nor boats could be protected by his father's technique.

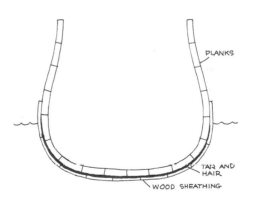

Fig. 40. *Early Anti-Shipworm Sheathing*

Hawkins was not the only famous Pacific voyager to suffer their ravages. Pizarro, the conqueror of Peru, had earlier lost his ship, not to a storm or to the Incas, but to the *teredo*.[8] Two hundred years later, Funnell, Dampier's mate on a privateering voyage, described their ship as being so honeycombed by worms that a thumb could easily be thrust through the bottom. In 1710, Rogers had to sell one of his privateers because her bottom was a perfect honeycomb—a metaphor so many journals use and which seems apt enough.

By the late sixteenth century, concurrent with English double sheathing, some Spanish and Portuguese ships were sheathed on the bottom with very thin lead, but this added greatly to the weight and was not durable. Another protection was to char the planks and then put pitch on them, as Cavendish, an English circumnavigator, did to his *Desire* at the Isle of Puna. In some ships, the nails joining the elm boards to the bottom planking were placed so closely together that the nailheads and the resulting rust formed an extra sheathing, but the main protection was the hair and tar held to the planking by the outer boards. When the worms ate through the outer sheathing, they were stopped by the mixture, which they apparently found unappetizing.[9]

A most dramatic demonstration of the effectiveness of the method was the examination in Mindanao in the Philippines in 1686 of the buccaneer ship *Cygnet* and an accompanying tender. Although they had sailed through the same seas for the same length of time, the unsheathed tender was no longer fit for sea, because she was eaten through by worms; however, the ship was sound, because the worms had not penetrated past the hair and tar between the sheathing and the planking.[10]

It was not only the bottom planks that suffered. Rogers, a privateer, lost the rudder of the *Duke* to worms on his very profitable cruise in the Pacific in 1709. The damage was not confined only to European ships; however, most of the native canoes were sufficiently protected by being hauled up on shore when not in use. The drying of the surface of the canoes destroyed the pests. Polynesians at least were conscious enough of the problem to note and state that wood from the breadfruit tree was resistant to worms.[11] The Australian wood, *jarrah*, was also thought to be worm resistant.[12]

Copper sheathing (figure 41) for wooden ships was to prove the best solution against worms. The beautiful wooden clipper ships of the nineteenth century were sheathed with "red copper" up to the waterline. This gave an additional advantage in speed over iron hulls which lost their smoothness much more quickly than did copper or the later improvement, "yellow metal." In the Royal Navy, the first ship to be coppered was a frigate in 1761; Byron's *Dolphin* was the third, when she was sheathed in preparation for her Pacific voyage.[13] Not only were worms repelled, but, as the inspectors reported, the ships stayed "always clean and fitt for Immediate Service."[14] Sailing was speedier with clean bottoms, and handling qualities improved, but there was one reported disadvantage no one had foreseen. Some journals claimed that fish refused to follow a ship with a copper bottom.[15]

Coppered ships could cruise much longer without visiting either a base or some tidal flat to careen. This was of particular advantage to ships in the Pacific, since it removed one of the problems associated with the time spent covering the great Pacific distances. The length of a cruise would now be limited only by provisioning and psychology, for sailing ships were not tied to bases by a need for coal or oil as steamships still are. (Atomic power may free ships again from this dependence.)

There were other disadvantages to copper sheathing apart from its un-attractiveness to fish. Copper was so soft that it could be easily scraped off. The *Lady Nelson*, a small ship which helped chart parts of the Australian coast, had some copper sheathing rubbed off the bottom and jammed into the case of one of her centreboards, or sliding keels, preventing the keel from being lowered. Colnett's *Argonaut* suffered a speed loss when her copper plates became partly unfastened and caused considerable drag. Weight was a disadvantage too; it took thirty-five tons of copper to cover the under-side of a seventy-four-gun ship-of-the-line. Coppered bottoms also made repairs difficult and many captains preferred *mailletage* (covering timber with nails). One experienced seaman thought it would be a good idea to have wood sheathing under the copper—a case of wood to buffer the copper which protected the wood.

Copper sheathing was held on by copper nails, and a shortage of these caused difficulty at times. Fastening with copper instead of iron was

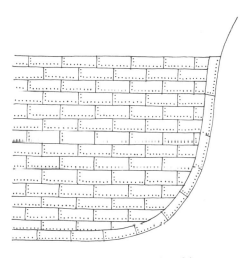

Fig. 41. Copper Sheathing

important, because reaction between copper and iron in salt water corroded the iron by an electrolytic process. Such corrosion could also destroy the iron bolts in the ships' frames and the iron work holding and hinging the rudders. During repair work on the *Providence* at Nootka, Broughton found that "another bolt below the forechains, was decayed through the planking; and that part which remained indicated that it had been corroded by the copper."[16] The *Margaret Oakley*, the American brig which used its oars to escape a water-spout, had copper nails, spikes, and bolts; the importance given the technique is clear from nineteenth-century advertisements announcing that ships were "*coppered and copper-fastened.*"[17] Corrosion was not the only problem caused by chemical reaction. In the *Rattler*, bad quality tar destroyed both copper and iron, and, in one French corvette, the copper—supposedly too pure—was found fretted with holes like lacework.

In addition to these hazards, the copper wore away easily, as might well be expected of a soft metal. In the case of the *Dolphin*, it was reported in July, 1768 that "upwards of 600 out of 900 of the 1st plates put on in May 1764 are worn off"; this was reasonably explained as "occasioned by friction from the great Velocity of the Ship in passing through so Great a Distance through the sea in Two Voyages round the World."[18] It might be noted that, although these experiments and reports were made in the 1760's, nearly 200 years earlier a Spanish report about Drake's *Golden Hind* had said, "she is not new, nor is she coppered nor ballasted." As this seemed anachronistic and did not agree with Wagner's translation in the 1920's, I had this checked at the Mexican National Archives where the original documents are stored. According to them, the translation would more properly be "leaded" than "coppered." This would seem reasonable on other grounds as well, for the Spaniards were using lead as a protection against shipworms by the late sixteenth century, as noted earlier.[19] Interestingly, many South American ships in the Spanish cultural areas are still coppered, demonstrating a conservative faith in metal sheathing.[20]

There were other satisfactory solutions to the shipworm problem. As early as 1769, Captain Cook expressed his satisfaction with white lead as a coating for ships' boats, for it had completely protected his pinnace. However, from Banks's journal, it is learned that the longboat, protected only with pine varnish, fared badly and that "every part of her bottom is like a honeycomb, some of the holes being an eighth of an inch in diameter, such progress has this destructive insect made in six weeks."[21] Across the Pacific, Chinese junks were protected by a special varnish which repelled the worms, while the Japanese used "a certain bitumen made of lime and oil with beaten oakum which, when it is all mixed together, they call *seiucui*, and which is known throughout the Indies as *galagala*."[22]

In view of the success of these mixtures, it is interesting to find that the modern glue used in marine plywood repels the *teredo*. A small schooner, the *Sea Wyfe*, rebuilt in 1964 after being driven onto a reef at Huahine, was "sheathed in plywood as a protection against worm."[23] In another early Pacific recipe, Indonesians at Banda Island used coconuts beaten "very well with a Mallet into Tow, in order to caulk the Vessel," and "a Composition made with Lime and other Matters, which preserve the Ships as well as our Pitch and Tar."[24] Lime, alone and in combination, apparently repels shipworms. Captain Forrest's *Tartar Galley*, like other East Indies ships, was protected from the *teredo* by a bag of lime suspended in the water at the bow, presumably releasing a solution washing back over the hull.

Metals other than copper were used later. Seligman's interesting ship, the *Cap Pilar* of the 1930's, used zinc sheathing successfully. Woods and metals are not the only sheathing—the trimaran *Gallinule* in 1963 sailed the Pacific clad daintily in nylon.

Even when shipworms were repelled, there were other reasons for repair. A ship of euphonic name, the *Desire*, the chief ship of Cavendish's small fleet left England in 1586, 400 years before the *Gallinule* sailed the Pacific. At 120 tons, she was slightly larger than the *Golden Hind*, and, as far as is known, of much the same design. The *Desire* proved sturdy enough to get through the Straits of Magellan, across the Pacific, home to England around the world, and even once more out to Magellan Straits and home again under the great John Davis. No wooden ship of the sixteenth century could have done this without repairs of many kinds, and one of the fascinating aspects of these early voyages is the way the ships were maintained without properly equipped bases. Foreign bases could not be counted on as being friendly, and it was the mid-nineteenth century before reasonably good base facilities were available in the North Pacific for British ships. Australian bases were available fifty years earlier. Fortunately, wooden hulls meant that material for repairs was widely available; many ships that set out built of seasoned English oak came home partly built of raw Chilean pine, or Tahitian breadfruit, or New Zealand beech. Captain Cook's *Endeavour* came back to England with bottom planking from the Dutch East Indies, after repairs done, much to Cook's satisfaction, in a good Dutch base. Two centuries had seen a major change since Cavendish's day, when there were no friendly bases away from home.

Often the repairs, like those of Cavendish, were simple maintenance, such as scrubbing the ships' bottoms to clean them of the weeds or barnacles which slowed them down. The metal sheathings, first lead and then copper, used later to protect the planking against worm damage, were not so liable to weed growth as was wood; iron, later still, could become quite overgrown. Even sucking fish sometimes attached themselves to ships. While buccaneering and privateering in the Pacific, Dampier saw how much these peculiar fish cut down the ease and speed of sailing. Cumulative marine growth creates dangers even today, as Hayter found when his *Sheila* became overgrown with goose barnacles, a small shellfish growing on a stalk about an inch long: "I could deal with the continual pumping out, the short rations of food and water, for a reasonable length of time; but a dirty ship would tend to prolong that length of time beyond my endurance (and very nearly did)."[25] A slow ship, made so by being "dirty," can be dangerous, and the effect, even with later iron ships, could be almost unbelievable. "The ship, in mid-Pacific, refused to go any further; she had been more than three years out of dry-dock, and her bottom plates were a mass of great barnacles, trailing sixteen feet of weed and rank sea-growth." That particular ship, the *Hellas*, was

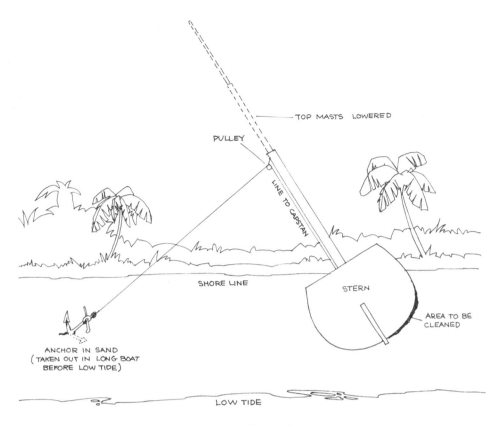

Fig. 42. Careening

abandoned, for no other reason than that these conditions slowed the ship so much that the crew was running out of food.[26]

Cavendish was not short of food, but he needed speed to capture Spaniards. In his case, to help increase his speed, he cleaned, singed, and re-tarred the *Desire*'s bottom planking by hauling the ship aground on the Isle of Puna, and working at low tide. It was probably managed by careening—heaving the ship over by a line from mast to anchor in order to expose one side at a time (figure 42). This had to be done carefully. Cleaning his ship at Bahia Salada in Chile, Drake nearly capsized the *Golden Hind* in careening her and only saved her by the quick use of another anchor on the opposite side. Once the ship was heaved over, burning or singeing the bottom had its risks too. Schouten's Dutch ship *Horne*, from the town after which Cape Horn was named by her commander, was completely burned near the Straits of Magellan while burning off the bottom growth with dry grass.[27] More exotic fuels were sometimes used. Rogers saved a number of bales of "Pope's bulls" which he had captured in order to use them to "burn the Pitch of our Ships Bottoms when we careen'd 'em."[28]

Plate 40. The *Beagle*. The *Beagle* is most famous for having carried Charles Darwin on the voyage which led to his theory concerning the origin of the species. She is shown here careened at the mouth of the River Santa Cruz. The upper masts are down but, even so, her hull is sufficiently rounded to need propping up.

Plate 41. H.M.S. *Discovery* leaving Falmouth in 1791. It was in the *Discovery* that Captain George
Vancouver made a single great exploration voyage linking what are today the four English-speaking
powers of the Pacific. His experiences in Australia, New Zealand, British Columbia, and California ar
recounted in a series of masterly volumes on the voyage.

Drake applied tar to the *Golden Hind*'s planking, adding grease and sulphur as well, both to impede weed and barnacle growth and to preserve the wood. Eighteenth-century ships' journals often mention that underwater portions had been scrubbed during a calm; probably the ships were tilted as far as reasonable in each direction to make this easier. For her scrubbing on shore, Cavendish's *Desire* had the good fortune to find an especially good place with a large and luxurious house nearby in which to quarter and stand guard.[29] Although he and his crew were attacked there by the Spaniards, the advantages of this site were so great that his second ship, the *Content*, was also "haled on ground, to grave at the same place in despight of the Spaniards."[30] A good site for graving, or cleaning, should have a firm bottom of a suitable slope and also have enough tide to help to position and later to refloat the ship. The shape of the ship itself was important—the bottom needed to be flat enough to take the ground without oversetting.

Protection from shipworms by double sheathing saved ships from other dangers, because of the extra strength it gave. The *Daintie, Golden Hind*, and *Endeavour*, and the *Aquila* of the Spaniards all hit reefs, ledges, or rocks. All of them thanked the extra sheathing for saving them from even worse damage than they had suffered. Some authorities argue that it is probable that sheathing added as much extra tonnage as extra strength, but there can be little doubt that extra sheathing would protect the hull during the grounding better than would copper or lead.[31] Whatever the material of construction, strength of the hull counts, as Villiers knew. When his iron-hulled *Joseph Conrad* was grounded on Wari Reef, he was "devoutly thankful . . . that she belonged to a day when ships were built with pride of construction and of workmanship, when craftsmanship still counted."[32]

"Grounding" simply means running onto ground. Sailors guarded against it by careful lookout and by sounding (measuring the depth of water in which they sailed in order to be warned by any decrease in depth). Sounding would not work if the menace were a reef jutting upwards as abruptly as a cliff falls away, for a ship could be in deep water one minute and on a reef the next. When the *Endeavour* struck ground east of Australia, the leadsman had just called 17 fathoms (102 feet) and yet "before the Man at the lead could heave another cast the Ship Struck and stuck fast."[33] She floated off again, largely because her flat bottom kept her standing upright at low water, whereas when the frigate *Pandora* grounded she fell over on the reef when the tide receded.

Survival often depended on the state of the tide at grounding. If the ship went aground when the tide was relatively low, one could count on help from the high tide in refloating the ship. The basic procedure was to lighten ship and pull her off the reef or sand or rock at high tide by using the capstan to wind in an anchor which had been carried out some distance by a boat and dropped, usually in a position astern of the ship. In theory, this moved the ship off the rock or shoal by pulling the ship to the anchor. It worked when the sea had been calm and the ship had not been pounded further and further up onto the ground or had not had her bottom badly damaged by the waves working her on the rocks.

The survival of Cook's vessel was also partly due to luck, for the coral which had pierced her bottom broke away from the rear and remained in the hole in the hull, as if to apologize for its damage. The main factor, however, was neither the flat-bottomed design nor the *Endeavour*'s luck; it was the good seamanship of the officers and crew. So many things had to be done quickly, but in order: down sails so she will not press forward; anchors out to a distance to be ready to haul against; yards and uppermasts down to lessen leverage as the swell moved her; guns and other dispensable weight tossed overboard to "lighten her by every method we could think off."[34] Some of those guns have been recovered. The ship survived. (So did the grounded *Golden Hind* in a similar crisis by throwing over some guns and three tons of cloves—but none of the silver or gold.)

The *Endeavour*'s leak was somewhat lessened by pulling a stretched sail filled with oakum over the hole as a temporary repair, a process called "fothering"; variations of this process are manifold. Hawkins described a similar process which he learned from the Spaniards as using "a round wicker basket . . . with peeces of a junke or rope . . . as oacombe . . . under water, care is to be had to keepe the baskets mouth towardes the shippes side."[35] An East India Company ship, in similar circumstances, had used "a dooble line to wch occum was fastined."[36] In all these methods, the oakum was sucked into the hole by the pressure of the water. The same principle was used for a slightly different purpose in the East Indies—to find leaks in ships. Divers let "their hair loose, thinking that their hair . . . would indicate to them the leak."[37]

Many of the ships discussed here ran onto ground. The *Ruby* struck a rock in a British Columbia channel, at least partly because of the failure to take proper soundings. She got off without damage, sparing the crew from being "cast away on this Wretched, Savage coast."[38] Vancouver's two ships both survived going aground on the British Columbia coast. Not all ships survived; the *Pandora* was completely wrecked on a coral reef and the *Uranie* was pierced fatally by a "submerged rock."[39]

Risks such as grounding were to be expected in uncharted seas; hence, it was important to choose the right type of ship and to use extreme care in handling her. Even mariners such as Cook and Drake ran aground in unknown seas for the simple reason that no one knew where the shoals and reefs were. There were some most peculiar and coincidental wreckings. The *Derby Park*, on its way to Sydney from Vancouver with Canadian timber for the Melbourne Exposition, was wrecked on a reef at Penrhyn. After a time, the schooner *Flying Venus* was sent with more Canadian timber to repeat the unfilled order; she also hit a reef and was wrecked only eight miles from Penrhyn.[40] The *General Grant* not only grounded, she went underground. In a calm, this ship was actually drifted by a current into a cave; "the ship was trapped in a huge vault of wet, slimy rock."[41] There she sank after the swell had lifted her against the roof of the cave, forcing the heel of the mainmast out through the bottom of the ship.

After the Pacific was charted, groundings were often the result of the ships being "run ashore" because of navigational error rather than "driven ashore." There is tragedy in this. Conrad put it well: "A ship may be 'driven ashore' by stress of weather. It is a catastrophe, a defeat. To be 'run ashore' has the littleness, poignancy, and bitterness of human error."[42] Human error can lose a ship quickly and in the most familiar of waters—a ship can kill, as Villiers said, and a ship can die, also. However, killing or dying depends largely on the skill and strength of men. Naval cadets in France smashed the *Firecrest* "the very first time it was used . . . Gerbault had sailed it all the way round the world!"[43] In spite of all the dangers and disadvantages, men love their ships. Only men like Conrad and London could say so in words to match the strength of their emotions, but after wreckings the anguish can be read in the curt language of less literate logs and journals.

Sometimes groundings and other tragedies were caused by the errors of the shipbuilders and outfitters rather than by the errors of officers or sailors. Ships ran aground because rigging failed at a crucial moment, or because poorly forged rudder pintles broke, or because anchor cables were not strong enough. Naturally, not all poorly prepared ships were wrecked. During Cook's third voyage he suffered great worry and strain from trying to cope with the poor fitting out of the *Resolution*, as well as with poor quality rigging and sails. Even more dangerous and annoying than weak canvas, however, was the poor workmanship used during the naval refit. During an early part of her voyage, because of improper shipyard caulking, seams in the *Resolution*'s sides were gaping "so very open that every trifling shower of rain runs through them."[44] Before she reached the equator in her run south through the Atlantic, not only were the officers and crew suffering, but the stored sails had been badly damaged by rain getting into the sail room. Anderson, the surgeon, saw the sea coming into the crew's quarters through "the negligence of those who caulk'd her," and thought it sufficient grounds for an enquiry.[45] It was natural enough that he should be upset, for of all the leaky cabins, the two worst, said Williamson, the third lieutenant, were "mine & ye Surgeon's."[46] Anderson's complaints had been cried aloud before his time, just as they have been echoed since. "Truely there is little care used now adaies amongst our countrimen in this profession," Hawkins said of the English caulker, and suggested he be liable for "losse occasioned through his negligence."[47]

Negligence often involved much more than faulty caulking. The *Peppercorn* constantly leaked, and the carpenter found "two trennel [treenail] holes, left open by the carpenters who built the vessel, and completed the number of fourteen holes similarly discovered."[48] A treenail hole was simply the hole for the wooden pins, treenails, which fastened together the planks and timbers of the early ships. Several of the ships described here suffered from similar carelessness: the *Providence* had an empty "auger hole," the *Duff* an empty "bolt hole," and the *Columbia* an unfilled "spike hole." Plain vessels were not the only ones to suffer; even the fabulously expensive, beautiful, and mighty *Royal Sovereign* suffered from treenail neglect.

Captains and crews alike expressed the hope that in this world—and, as that was probably too much to hope for, then at least in the next—some of the designers, builders, shipwrights, and provisioners, would have to use their own product. The even-tempered and gentlemanly Bellingshausen, deploring the water coming down through the decks, declared that "these and similar mistakes are due to shipbuilders never going to sea in their own ships," and spoke of "strong expressions of opinion by naval officers about shipbuilders delivering unreliable fittings to vessels."[49] Labé, the second-in-command of the *St. Jean Baptiste*, complained bitterly about the persons in charge of her fitting out, "what is certain is that they are an ignorant lot."[50]

"Ignorant," as a word applied to shipbuilders, is hardly a fair description. The shipbuilding industry was, and still is, slow to change, but in the days before the plenitude of choices of material available today, the shipwrights who worked in wood were bound strictly by the limitations of their material. Although their work was the culmination of centuries of development, there are only so many things that can be done with a wooden plank. It is not iron—much less steel; it is not ferro-concrete—much less fibreglass.

Two terms should be understood when discussing wooden shipbuilding: clinker-building and carvel-building (figure 43). These illustrate the limitations of method in wooden shipbuilding, inherent in the material before the days of plywood, and they have to be used descriptively in every culture which built wooden watercraft. They are interesting terms historically as well as technically. Clinker-building, the distinguishing feature of all early north

European ships, means simply that the planks are laid edge over edge and nailed together through the edges with the nails clinched (hence "clinker") over washers. To say a ship was completely "clinker-built," originally implied that only *after* the hull had been constructed, by curving full length planks from the sternpost at the rear to the stempost at the bow, were ribs inserted to add extra strength. It was replaced for most ship and boat building by the carvel method in which the planks are placed edge to edge and the resulting seams are caulked with a soft material. In this type of construction, which is very strong, the frame of the ship is built first, and the planks are then fastened to the ribs. In one journal, Captain Wilson of the *Antelope* tells of the amazement of the natives of Palau, an island southeast of the Philippines, as they watched European sailors build a craft carvel-fashion. When the frame was first erected, the "rajah" said he could

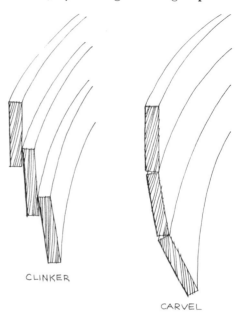

CLINKER

CARVEL

Fig. 43. Clinker and Carvel Hull Construction

not understand how such a craft could float; he did not foresee the covering of the ribs by planks. He was accustomed to craft being built by adding planks above the sides of a canoe carved out of a whole tree trunk, and never—at any stage—unable to float.[51]

Historically, the most famous clinker-built vessels are those of the Vikings, combining strength, flexibility, and lightness with the legendary grace which flowed from the completely natural curves of the planking. Most European whaleboats were clinker-built for the same reason that the Viking ships were —they had to be strong, speedy, and light. In the South Pacific, the Solomon Island mons, and, in the North Pacific, the plank-built boats of the Ainu have enough clinker features to have caused speculation about a Scandinavian influence.[52]

There are other characteristics of the early European ships, apart from the use of wood as a material, which apply to those of every nationality. For example, flutes—sometimes called flyboats in England—were essentially merchant vessels needing room for cargo, and so one might wonder why there was such constriction of width at the top of the hull (see figure 31). The answer is simply that the duty levied at many ports was based on tonnage calculated partly by the width of the top of the ship amidships.

A ship's tonnage is a way of expressing her capacity and size. In the early days, these were described by saying how much the ship could carry—just as is done today with trucks—a "three-ton truck." It was standardized on the number of "tuns" of wine (each casked in two barrels of half-a-ton weight) a ship could carry, each "tun" thus weighing about 2,240 pounds—a long ton. A sixty-ton caravel was of a size large enough to carry sixty "tuns" of wine. Present tonnages of cargo ships are based on measurement—110 cubic feet to the ton—and the formulas for measurements are formidable because of the curves of the ships' hulls. Naval ships use displacement; the actual weight of water they displace is their tonnage; this is done, of course, in order to make allowance for their armour. Measurement of tonnage has been a problem ever since the measurers stopped counting barrels. One letter to the Board of Trade which I found in the Public Records Office in London proposed a novel solution: by using closable openings in the hulls of new wooden ships sink them to the normal loaded waterline by letting in seawater, then close the inlets, pump out the water, weigh it, and register the tonnage permanently. This technique was *not* adopted.

During the three centuries under discussion, the tonnage of most types of ships greatly increased. However, there was a very definite limit to the length of a wooden ship; a very long wooden ship could not be prevented from "hogging," or sagging at each end. A ship's tonnage could be increased greatly without increasing her dimensions very much. To understand this, a rectangle could be used as a model ship. The rectangle should be three inches long by one inch wide, made three-dimensional with a depth of one inch. It contains three cubic inches. To double its capacity to six cubic inches, only one third to its length and one half to its breadth need be added, making it four inches long by one and one half inches wide by one inch deep. If its dimensions were doubled (making it six inches long by two inches wide by two inches deep), its capacity would be multiplied by eight, that is, to twenty-four cubic inches.

It is this principle, together with modern materials, that today makes possible the building of steel supertankers of huge tonnage. In the seventeenth and eighteenth centuries, however, the trade and exploration of the Pacific was carried on by very small wooden ships and, necessarily, in the busy areas such as the East Indies, there were thousands of them. It was in this area that the Dutch and Chinese met, with some interesting results in the design of Pacific—and even European—ships and boats. Some of the design alterations are still in use, and many of them enabled safer and easier exploration of unknown waters hiding uncharted reefs and shallows. One Chinese invention which the Dutch adopted and adapted (there is some argument about independent invention), the movable leeboard, gives the important quality of handiness in shallow water, so important to both Chinese and Dutch craft. Small Dutch vessels have used leeboards for centuries and the Chinese for centuries before that. Leeboards are wide boards pivoted on the sides of the boats or yachts, to be lowered in deep water to serve the same purpose as a keel, and raised in shallow water or when sailing before the wind.

The centreboard was an improvement on the leeboard principle. It certainly helped the sixty-ton *Lady Nelson*, for she was so small that many considered distant exploration beyond her powers. Yet she was the first ship to sail parallel to the entire south coast of Australia, and the first ship to sail through Bass Straits between Tasmania and the mainland of Australia, waters close to Tasman's route.[53] She was designed to try the newly invented centreboard keel, which, in simplest terms, was a keel which could be raised or lowered at need (figure 44). In its lowered position, it helps a ship to sail to windward without making too much leeway; in its raised position, it allowed the *Lady Nelson* to sail in very shallow waters. With "her three sliding centre-boards" up, her draught was only six feet. It is a device still used in many modern yachts and smaller boats, and it was used in nineteenth-century Pacific schooners, even in quite large ones, as well as New Zealand trading scows and American whaleboats.[54]

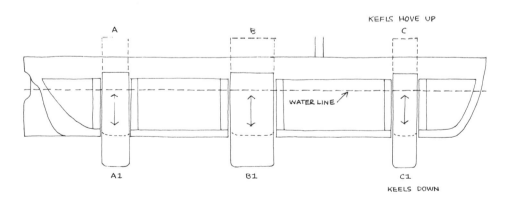

Fig. 44. Sliding Keels in a Late Eighteenth-Century Cutter

Centreboards enabled smaller ships to beat out from leeshores when necessary and, by retracting them, to go close to shore when they wished. They could avoid some of the hazards to hulls; however, as has been seen, centreboards themselves could be a source of trouble. Wooden ships' hulls, all parts of them, require constant maintenance just as their rigging does, and when the maintenance is good, wooden hulls protected against shipworms will sail for over a century. But this was not the main point to sailors of sailing days. Good maintenance meant speedy voyages; speedy voyages meant safety. So did a well-equipped and well-prepared ship fresh from the shipyards and, when there was faulty preparation, there was anger among officers and seamen.

It is no wonder they felt this way. Shipbuilders certainly profited, but the sailors might perish. Bitterness was compounded by the knowledge that delay for any reason could be fatal. Avoidable delay was even more enraging. For example, Anson was delayed—though as much by Admiralty dithering as by shipyard dereliction. His fleet reached the Horn too late, and the time taken there fighting the weather of the worst season of the year enabled scurvy to decimate his crews. Before lemon juice and proper food preservation, time was a hazard in the Pacific more deadly than distance. Fair winds and sound ships could overcome distance; when ships were in disrepair, or when there was bad weather, time went by whether or not the ships made progress. Yet, if delays were a dangerous result of negligence, the ancient shipyards were no worse than some more recent ones. The *Snark*, London says, was plagued by delays in 1906: "not one union man and not one firm of all the union men and all the firms ever delivered anything at the time agreed upon."[55]

CHAPTER 15

Rigging and Stability

*The sea has ever been more conservative than the land, for
the simple reason that at sea every attempt to step forward has
to be paid for in human life rather than coin of the realm.*

BASIL LUBBOCK
OF THE *ROYALSHIRE*

*The great difficulty was to get a large ship, say from 1600 to
2,000 tons, that would sail fast in moderate winds. If she had
canvas enough to drive her along in a light breeze, the chances
were that in a gale something was bound to carry away aloft.*

ARTHUR CLARK
OF THE *VENUS*

Most of the ships which explored the Pacific were square-rigged ships. These
are ships with two or three masts (and later, even more) carrying "square"
sails, with the sails spread across the ship (see figure 45). Even the earliest
ones would have had at least one "fore-and-aft" sail, spread more or less
along the centre line of the ship, but far forward or far aft, because they
were mainly to aid steering. Square-rigged ships developed in the fifteenth
century and, by the end of it, this type of ship had six sails: mainsail and
main topsail, foresail and foretopsail (which were basically driving sails), and
a lateen on the mizzen mast and a small sail under the bowsprit (which were
really steering sails). These were the basic sails, and remained so until the
end of commercial sailing.

Refinements altered the shape of the sails and even the location of them.
The need for power added sail after sail upwards, while the drive for economy
of manpower forced improvements in the lines and equipment which moved
them. These were developments which affected all types of vessels, but there
were different kinds of changes which might have altered the types of sails
used on individual vessels. Often owners rerigged vessels because they wished
to change their usage or wished to sail them in a part of the seas where

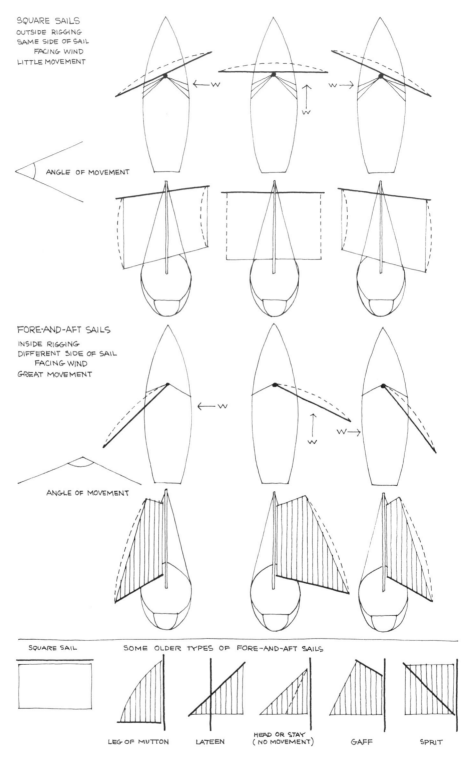

SQUARE SAILS
OUTSIDE RIGGING
SAME SIDE OF SAIL
FACING WIND
LITTLE MOVEMENT

ANGLE OF MOVEMENT

FORE-AND-AFT SAILS
INSIDE RIGGING
DIFFERENT SIDE OF SAIL
FACING WIND
GREAT MOVEMENT

ANGLE OF MOVEMENT

SQUARE SAIL   SOME OLDER TYPES OF FORE-AND-AFT SAILS

LEG OF MUTTON   LATEEN   HEAD OR STAY   GAFF   SPRIT
                            (NO MOVEMENT)

Fig. 45. Relative Movement Allowed by Fore-and-Aft and Square Sails

conditions were different. Rerigging could involve changing masts as well as the sails, and changing either meant altering the maze of lines and ropes that web a ship.

Whatever the type and number of sails gracing a ship, working them meant that the masts had to be strongly supported, the yards had to be hauled up and down to spread the sails and be trimmed at different angles to let the sails catch the wind, and the sails themselves set, or reefed, or taken in, to suit the weather of the moment. "Standing rigging" supports the masts and stands fast for strength; "running rigging" (figure 46) moves the yards into position and spreads and furls the sails. As the second quotation at the beginning of the chapter indicates, there is an element of compromise involved in rigging a ship; nowhere was a mean so golden found as in the famous clippers (figure 47). These could coast along in light airs and yet gallop safely in gales. Clippers were American ships originally, and were rigged for speed and built to be strong enough to take the battering that speed implied.

Rigging suffered when the ship was battered in a gale, and suffered almost as much when the ship rolled in a calm or a cross sea. Stability, obviously vital to safety and comfort—plenty of ships have turned over—is also important in lessening the strains on the rigging. It takes only a little imagination to shudder at the thought of the stresses on the shrouds (or supports from each side) of a 160-foot mainmast at the extreme point of a roll, when the topmost shrouds have to begin to pull that mast upright again. Sailing-ship design, as with maintenance, is a matter of the interrelationship of strengths and strains, and stresses and supports. This means constant adjustments as well as sound design.

The most common rigs, in descending order of size, were ships, barques, brigs (with variations, such as snows), brigantines, schooners, galiots, hookers, ketches, cutters, and yawls (see figure 48). Hulls could be rigged in different ways for different conditions; for example, privateers rerigged captured Peruvian ships to suit other areas, just as Columbus rerigged a caravel before he headed west with the trade winds. Rerigging could be described in different ways; the sloop *Lady Washington* was rerigged in 1791 in China and was reported afterwards by three different observers as being a brig, a brigantine, and a snow.[1] Whatever she was, the hull was unchanged, and the descriptions referred only to the rigging.

Rigging was used to classify ships, and still is used for classifying yachts. Dwight Long's *Idle Hour* was ketch-rigged whereas Gerbault's beautiful yacht the *Firecrest* was cutter-rigged. Slocum's *Spray*, the vessel which began solo voyaging, was yawl-rigged.

The same hull can be rigged in different ways, according to purpose or preference. A cat hull could be barque-rigged, for example, or it could be rigged as a square-rigged (or full-rigged) ship. In the eighteenth century, a barque would have had three masts, the foremast and mainmast square-rigged (that is, with square sails spread by yards running across the ship), while the mizzen mast, the mast at the rear, would be fore-and-aft-rigged (that is, with sails spread "fore-and-aft" along the centre line of the ship by spars known as gaffs and booms). Combining the two types of rig, in various degrees, was always done to gain the advantages of both and thus obtain both power and handiness. Conrad says that fore-and-aft rig "requires less effort in handling; the trimming of the sail-planes to the wind can be done with speed and accuracy; the unbroken spread of the sail-area is of infinite advantage; and the greatest possible amount of canvas can be displayed upon the least possible quantity of spars. Lightness and concentrated power are the great qualities of fore-and-aft rig."[2] Conrad makes it plain that fore-and-aft rig, by its ease of handling, allows great economies in crew strength. However, square rig had its advantages too, especially on long voyages with steady and favourable winds. A ship, as contrasted with a barque, would have had square top and top-gallant sails on removable masts above a fore-and-aft sail on the mizzen mast.

Barquentines were developed from the barque by having fore-and-aft sails on mizzen and mainmast, and square sails only on the foremast, in a way a return to the *caravela redonda* of the early Portuguese. These square sails on the foremast gave much better "on the wind" performance. Underhill discussed a fore-and-aft schooner converted to a barquentine which was much improved by the change: "it transformed her over night ... from a very mediocre performer into one of the crack ships of her day."[3] A variation called

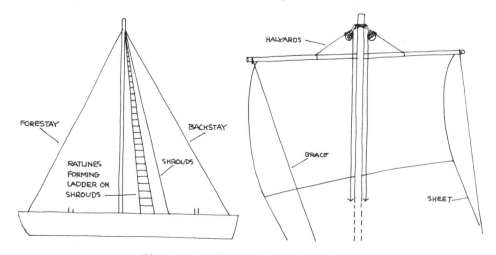

Fig. 46. Standing and Running Rigging

a "jackass barque" had square sails on the main topmast and the main top-gallant mast, with a fore-and-aft sail on the lower mainmast, retaining square sails on the foremast.

The particular form the rigging took—called "the rig"—depended partly on the size of the hull and partly on the conditions under which the craft would normally be sailed, a point emphasized in discussing the rerigging of one of Columbus's ships to add square sails to improve performance in what he foresaw would be different conditions.

The combination of square and fore-and-aft sails gives many advantages in sailing. Many owners rerigged ships to get these advantages, but some did so for quite different reasons, such as defense, as in the case of the *Nautilus* in northwest America: "Her Main boom of 42 feet, having been twice carried away, is now laid aside, and in the room of making a new one, we have turned her into a Barque by stepping a Mizzen Mast, and by this means enabling us to keep the boarding nettings up always under Sail or at Anchor, a circumstance now become highly necessary."[4] Even today the rig of ships is changed to fit a changing purpose, or to suit their destinations. The schooner *Albatros*, important as the yacht of a fine modern writer who cruised in the Pacific, was rerigged in America as a hermaphrodite brig. This rig differs from a barquentine in having only two and not three or more masts, that is, each type is square-rigged on the foremast. The barquentine has more than one aftermast. The usual purpose of this kind of rerigging, whether with two or more masts, is to improve performance on long runs with the wind; this is very important in the Pacific with its long trade-wind sweeps.

Two-masted ships—brigs, brigantines, ketches and schooners—were commonly used in Pacific island trading. During the nineteenth century, brigs gradually gave way to brigantines or schooners. In the eighteenth century, to be brig-rigged meant to be square-rigged on both masts, but, in addition, to have a large gaff fore-and-aft sail on the mainmast. Casson explains the creation of the nineteenth-century brig very clearly and briefly: "Brigs and brigantines go back to what, about the beginning of the eighteenth century, was a two-master completely square-rigged on both masts. The brigantine was created by *doing away* with the square mainsail in favor of a fore-and-aft mainsail. . . . The brig . . . was created by *adding* a fore-and-aft sail. . . ."[5] Basically, this system combined the mizzen and the mainmast by adding the gaff to the mainmast (see figure 48) or to what is essentially the same thing—the small trymast just behind the mainmast. A gaff is a spar which is mounted at an angle to the mast, butting against it, in order to spread the top of a fore-and-aft sail. In a sense, it is the rear portion of the lateen yard which remained after the front portion had been removed as unnecessary, when seamen realized that the balancing and steering advantage of the mizzen mast lateen could be gained just as well without the entire triangle. (For years, larger ships kept the entire mizzen yard without the before-the-mast portion of sail in order to have a long spare yard or a temporary replacement mast if needed. Such repair or replacement of a mast was often called "jury rig," and the temporary mast a "jury mast.")

Brigs were really very efficient small ships in terms of sailing ability, but expensive to crew compared, for example, to schooners. Schooners developed from the early two-masted types, such as Dutch yachts, and had fore-and-aft mainsails and a variety of rigging on the foremast. When square-rigged on the foremast, the ship was called a schooner, "or a *hermaphrodite brig*, and later—somewhat improperly—a *brigantine*."[6] "The true brigantine," Underhill says, "was a two-masted craft, fully square-rigged on the foremast and fore-and-aft on the main but with the addition of square topsails on the main topmast."[7] A distinguishing feature was the boom extending the foot of its main gaff sail—the "brigantine sail." Today, the brigantine is rigged as a hermaphrodite brig, or schooner, except that the "brigantine's foremast is proportioned in ship fashion and has a shorter lower mast and a longer topmast than a schooner's."[8] A schooner with a square topsail on the foremast is a "topsail schooner" and these give better "before the wind" performance. Most English schooners were topsail schooners, because they crossed wide oceans, whereas American coastal schooners and Pacific island schooners, sailing in tricky seas with tricky winds, tended to be fore-and-aft schooners (completely fore-and-aft-rigged on the foremast as well as the main) for handiness in tight conditions.

This is a particularly graceful rig, famous in Nova Scotia and in the Pacific, and especially in New Zealand where so many former Nova Scotians lived to build and skipper ships. One day in early Auckland there were nine vessels anchored, all commanded by famous Nova Scotian skippers from Waipu, New Zealand. There are some schooners with this beautiful nineteenth-century rig still at sea. The author saw a gaff-sailed fore-and-after in Agamemnon Channel while cruising as a guest on the Vancouver yacht *Halcyon II* on the British Columbia coast in 1973. She did not have gaff topsails set, and our modern rig left her behind, but we cast lingering looks back at the sailors who had chosen aesthetic perfection before performance.

Some fore-and-aft schooners reached immense size; the *Thomas W. Lawson* was of over 5,000 tons, had 7 masts, and yet was manned by only 16 men. Simplification of rigging in order to reduce manpower could hardly go further than this. But, while prosperity was still possible for sailing-shipowners, and speed was the key to achieving it, they were less anxious to skimp on crews and more anxious to pile on sail. Great spreads of sail meant many sailors to handle them and strong rigging to support them.

Speed, sails, and strength are exemplified in the clippers. The *Lightning* was typical of the American beamy softwood clippers, 244 feet long, 44 feet wide, of 1,468 registered tons.[9] Built by the famous clipper shipbuilder, the Nova Scotian American, Donald Mackay, she was only one of his many superb

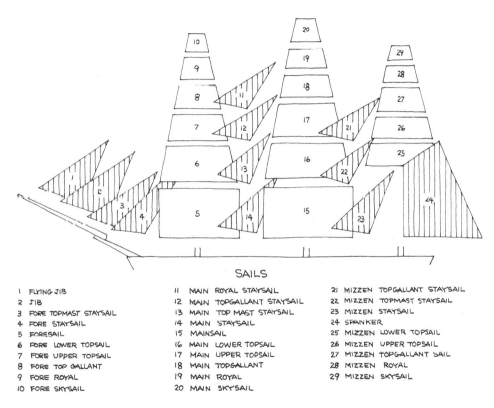

SAILS

1 FLYING JIB	11 MAIN ROYAL STAYSAIL	21 MIZZEN TOPGALLANT STAYSAIL
2 JIB	12 MAIN TOPGALLANT STAYSAIL	22 MIZZEN TOPMAST STAYSAIL
3 FORE TOPMAST STAYSAIL	13 MAIN TOP MAST STAYSAIL	23 MIZZEN STAYSAIL
4 FORE STAYSAIL	14 MAIN STAYSAIL	24 SPANKER
5 FORESAIL	15 MAINSAIL	25 MIZZEN LOWER TOPSAIL
6 FORE LOWER TOPSAIL	16 MAIN LOWER TOPSAIL	26 MIZZEN UPPER TOPSAIL
7 FORE UPPER TOPSAIL	17 MAIN UPPER TOPSAIL	27 MIZZEN TOPGALLANT SAIL
8 FORE TOP GALLANT	18 MAIN TOPGALLANT	28 MIZZEN ROYAL
9 FORE ROYAL	19 MAIN ROYAL	29 MIZZEN SKYSAIL
10 FORE SKYSAIL	20 MAIN SKYSAIL	

Fig. 47. Clipper Sail Plan

ships—beautiful, fast, well-built. She could set one and one quarter acres of sail, which was supported by miles of rigging, and in her best day's run she claimed a speed of over eighteen knots. The *Lightning* was one of the sharpest ships to be built, with long concave waterlines and a handsomely raking stern. Her figurehead was a life-sized and graceful young woman holding a thunderbolt in an outstretched hand. She was a comfortable as well as a fast and beautiful ship, with a most unusual eight feet of headroom in her 'tween decks, which meant excellent passenger accommodation. Her really novel feature was her iron water tanks capable of holding 36,000 gallons. On her speedy passages, no passenger needed to be thirsty or dirty.[10]

The *Lightning*'s first captain was "Bully" Forbes, notorious for keeping on sail; that is, because of his desire for speed, refusing to reduce sail area when winds were strong, in spite of the greater likelihood of smashing rigging. The immense pressures on large sails driving big ships at high speed made strength of rigging a problem, even without captains like "Bully" Forbes. Before steel rigging was developed the weight and wind resistance of the heavy hemp stays were a major disadvantage: the *Lightning*'s shrouds, supporting her masts, had to be almost four inches in diameter to give the strength to support a main-mast 164 feet high. After all, she had the distinction of being one of the very few ships that regularly used a moonsail—a sail above the skysails, usually the uppermost sails even on ships considered heavily canvassed.[11]

Today, so much strength is possible for so little wind resistance. Modern yacht rigging would make Magellan or Donald Mackay green with envy: "her rigging was all of stainless steel, and it was new, and her sheets and halliards all of terylene."[12]

Rigging had steadily developed in complexity, but also in performance, from the fourteenth to the mid-nineteenth century, as the number of sails increased from the basic six to twenty or more. Materials and techniques improved apace, but wood and hemp still imposed lower limits on the ships' size, weight, and strength than those which became possible once the Industrial Age poured out iron and then steel for hulls and for rigging. With the advent of wire rope in the nineteenth century, rigging became strong enough not only to match the great iron and steel hulls, but also to answer the demand for speed. The Industrial Age gave its materials to bring sailing ships to the peak of their performance, exemplified by the great windjammers running grain and wool to England from Australia past Cape Horn, or running the easting down (running straight east from far south of the Cape of Good Hope along the latitude of Tasmania) to return to Australia.

In one case, the Industrial Age wed the Age of Exploration: Villiers's little ship *Joseph Conrad* (Plate 29) was full-rigged or square-rigged, looking just like the frigates of the Napoleonic wars. She was "the last surviving frigate in the world," when Long saw her from the *Idle Hour*, "a picture of grace and beauty."[13] She was a square-rigged ship, not a barque or bar-quentine, and at about 200 tons much the size of the *Bounty*. A product of the Industrial Age, built by builders who thought strength was essential to safety, the *Joseph Conrad*'s masts and hull were of iron, her rigging of iron wire, her watertight bulkheads of steel. From her teak deck to her hand-sewn sails, she was strong and she was handsome, with "the strength of a sperm whale in the ocean, and the grace of a swan."[14] Her figurehead was a ruggedly carved head of her namesake.

Possibly a bit too short to be fast—ten, perhaps twelve, knots was her limit—her shortness was an advantage in Pacific voyaging where the seas are long. It meant that the *Joseph Conrad* was never strained by two seas at one time. Except for her iron-given strength, it was very much the kind of ship that Byron, Bligh, Bougainville, Carteret, and Cook had used—as Villiers pointed out—and so he too sailed to the Pacific. Half his crew were young men from fifteen to twenty-four years of age who had paid fees for their adventure, for learning to hand, reef, and steer, and for braving the height of mast and threading the maze of rigging.[15] By a singular piece of good fortune, the author is able to visualize what this meant. When he saw the *Joseph Conrad* in 1973, berthed at Mystic in Connecticut, some young employees of the Whaling Museum—including a girl—demonstrated the furling of her foresail and jib.

At the same time, the Industrial Age gave its techniques to the steamships, and they ended the days of sail, not quickly or dramatically, but remorselessly and inevitably. Competition with steam ground away profits, forcing owners to try every simplification of rigging to save manpower and, thereby, wages and keep. In this process, many combinations of large hulls and simplified rigs were produced. Sails were made interchangeable between yards and masts of the same length, and yards and masts were made interchangeable too. This simplification blurred the distinctions between rigs, but they are not, were not, and never have been absolute. As Underhill sees it, "most of the names and definitions carried entirely different meanings at different periods, to say nothing of those which had several alternative meanings at one and the same time, as for example the common cases of ship, sloop, and cutter."[16] In general, ships were classed by hull until late in the eighteenth century, and from then on by rigging; but the names of either hull or rig are not really of very careful definition. Common hull shapes were frigate, hagboat, pink, cat, and barque (and barque is a rig as well). Although some modern authorities do not agree with the practice, seventeenth-century writers such as Barlow often called ships by their name and classification combined, for example, *Drake Galley, Bantam Pink, Chamber Frigate.*[17] The practice of combining name and classification was officially accepted; the Admiralty Secretary used the term "*Discovery Sloop*" in writing to Cook.

Simplification of sails to save labour was a matter of altered rigging, not hulls, and could mean discarding as well as changing them. The process began well before the age of heavy industry. Upper sails, with romantic names like royals (after the *Royal Sovereign*, supposedly the first craft to use them), skysails, and moonsails, were done away with—they took too much manpower to spread or to furl. Sometimes it consisted of discarding an earlier

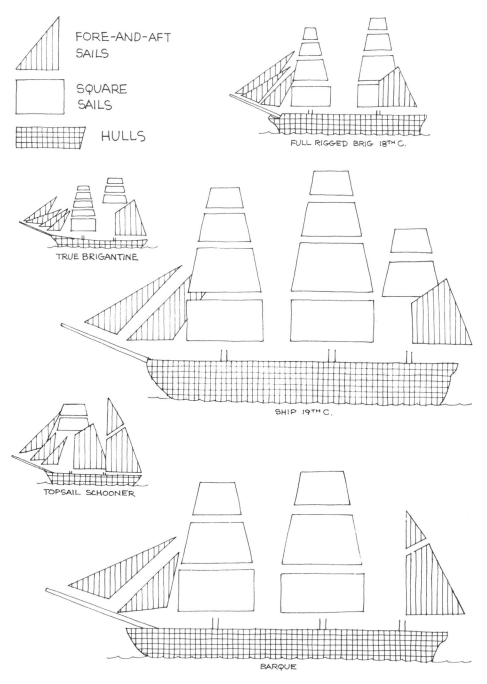

FORE-AND-AFT SAILS

SQUARE SAILS

HULLS

FULL RIGGED BRIG 18TH C.

TRUE BRIGANTINE

SHIP 19TH C.

TOPSAIL SCHOONER

BARQUE

Fig. 48. Eighteenth-, Nineteenth-, and Twentieth-Century European Rigs

FORE-AND-AFT SCHOONER

GALIOT

PINNACE

HERMAPHRODITE BRIG

HOOKER

CUTTER

KETCH

BARQUENTINE

SEVEN MASTED
FORE-AND-AFT SCHOONER

complication possibly brought about more by fashion than function. Bowsprits were originally designed to provide both a place to stay, or brace, the foremast and a place to fasten bowlines well forward. Bowlines, a Norse invention, were lines which held the leading edge of sails so they would catch the wind properly, and improve the "across the wind" performance of square sails. Some bowsprits were given a small mast at the tip (originally a flagstaff) and, during the seventeenth century, a little sail on this mast, the spritsail topsail, was used (like the spritsail under the bowsprit) to help balance the steering. This particular sail, although absurd in appearance, was used throughout the seventeenth century. It was abandoned in the early eighteenth century in all but the biggest ships and, by the 1770's, it had been replaced by the jib, or else was set under the jib-boom (an extension of the bowsprit). This is where Cook's *Endeavour* set her spritsail topsail.

It has been suggested authoritatively that the fact that Cook's spritsail topsail wore into rags indicated that the *Endeavour* tended to swing into the wind when the setting of all forward sails depressed her bow, allowing her stern to swing as a wind vane would. In any ship, too much sail forward pushed down the bow. A spritsail topsail, being so far forward, yet too small to add much to the depression effect, would help to counteract this tendency to swing. Villiers condemns the original spritsail topsail as "the most optimistic, and useless, piece of canvas ever spread from a square-rigged ship," and its successor of Cook's day, set under the jib-boom ahead of the spritsail on the bowsprit, as "little if any better."[18] However, Cook must have used it often to have worn it out.

Most certainly these early sails look both cumbersome and inconvenient out on the bowsprit, and no doubt their pressure on the bowsprit would add to the tendency of "the tightest ship" to "leak more or less round the heel of the bowsprit and the bitts." Dana bitterly complained of this on the *Alert*. The *Endeavour*'s bitts also loosened (bitts are the wedges which secure the foot of the bowsprit). By the nineteenth century, the spritsail as well as the spritsail topsail was replaced by the jib, a triangular sail, and later a flying jib was added in front on the jib-boom.

The *Endeavour* must have managed well enough, without the unreplaced spritsail topsail, however, because her captain did not discuss the matter in his report on her sailing qualities. Her tendency to turn into the wind—if indeed she did—was matched by a similar problem in a modern catamaran 200 years later, and with much the same cause. The *Endeavour*'s bow was thought to have gone deep with a press of sail; in the *Rehu Moana* "the trouble was caused by the hulls being too shallow aft."[19]

Sails themselves were improved to make them stronger, and gradually they were designed and sewn to lie flatter. New types of fore-and-aft sails (called staysails because they were spread along the stays, the braces securing the tops of the various masts) were developed, mainly by the Dutch, to help the square-rigged ship beat into the wind. These are used on modern fore-and-aft-rigged yachts too and are important sails, for "the staysail definitely pulls the boat more than its proportion of the sail area would lead one to think. . . . I think it must fill the gap between the jib and main-sail creating a slot on each side of itself, which doesn't exist otherwise as the sails are too far apart."[20]

Without good rigging and strong sails a ship could be in danger—if, for example, it could not carry enough canvas in a gale to keep the ship answering the helm. For a rudder to work, a ship must be moving through the water and have what is called "steerage way," that is, enough movement through the water to allow the rudder to bite and swing the ship. Sails also steadied the ship, and a sailing ship, with a wind blowing, "rolled but little because of the 'holding' power of the wind in the sails . . . the pitching and tossing was generally of a slower and more gentle character in the old-time sailer than in the steamer of anything like equal tonnage."[21] Storm sails steadied the ship in a gale and were made with extra care. For a different reason, sails and rigging need to be particularly strong for modern catamarans, such as the *Rehu Moana*, and presumably this was also true of the Polynesian double canoes. A ship with an ordinary hull will heel over (lean) with the wind, spilling some wind from its sails, but the beamy catamaran will remain upright, holding the wind in its sails, and thus maintaining the pressure loading on them.[22] There are recent reports of a German development in multi-hull craft in which the flexibility given by heeling over in a single-hulled vessel is paralleled in the multi-hull by a flexible mast bending from its pivoted foot in order to spill the wind and ease pressure.

All equipment needs to be well made for good service at sea and, as already emphasized, in every century of Pacific sailing there were complaints about shipyard inefficiency or corruption. Distance and time were tests of material as well as of men. In the *Resolution*, it was found that the rigging from her collier days, already well worn, still stood up better in hard conditions than did the new rigging from the naval yard. Bolt-ropes broke and lost the ship a whole suit of sails. (Bolt-ropes are the ropes around the outer edge of sails to which the canvas is stitched—a kind of flexible frame for the sail.) When the bolt-ropes were strong enough and the canvas blew out, this frame would remain to be incorporated into a new sail. This was the custom in the best merchant ships, but their contractors were more likely to be held directly responsible for faulty supplies than were the graft-ridden Admiralty yards of Cook's century. Cook found "that the bolt-ropes to our sails have not been of sufficient strength, or substance, to even half wear out the Canvas."[23]

As better masts became available (and finding these was always a problem), and as the rope for rigging improved, sails crept higher and higher until by the mid-nineteenth century some American clippers had moonsails positioned six sails above the deck, and up to thirty-five sails in all. The statistics are impressive. One clipper had a mainmast 164 feet high, braced by ropes of approximately 4 inches diameter; a later steel barque had masts almost 200 feet high, when measured from the keel.[24] Sails themselves were of impressive size and weight, some mainsails weighing one ton when dry, much more when wet; one big ship, the *Herzogin Cecilie*, had 18¾ miles of running rigging to set 59,000 square feet of sail.

One sailor spoke of the "magnificent lookout one gets from the royal yard of a ship," but also of the effort and the danger when "the sail . . . hitting you in the face, tries to knock you over backwards; then if you have not got firm hold of the jackstay you are bound to go—to land on the deck 150 feet below, an unrecognizable mass, smashed like a rotten apple."[25] Burgess, on the *Cap Pilar*, agreed about the magnificent lookout, but added that even small ships could be dangerous. It was true. In his ketch, Long had a companion who "said he would rather take in royals on a swinging yard one hundred and sixty feet above the deck than try to climb half the thirty-five feet of my mainmast, with the *Idle Hour*'s jerky, uneven motion."[26]

Huge masts, with immense spreads of sail—all developed from the original square sail of the Viking ships, or some ships like them—required networks of braces or stays (called standing rigging, because it was still), and great numbers of lines to haul up the sails, to control them, and to help furl them (called running rigging, because these lines were moved). To learn to use the various lines, each with an appointed place and a specific name and purpose, was a problem in itself. Maori sailors were famous for being quick to "learn the ropes." Everyone had to learn them, for "only with experience can a sailor do the right things quickly without thinking."[27] "Able Seaman" said that the profession of seamen "consists mainly in a multiplicity of detail," and journals tell of occasional mistakes and of the punishment or disaster that followed.[28] An officer in the Peninsular and Oriental Line, who had been a midshipman in a clipper, said, "the easy toleration extended to first voyagers who made mistakes in the identity of ropes lasted for only one calendar month after joining the ship. The mates made no mistake over the expiry of that period of grace."[29]

All lines and ropes were not of wire or hemp. Pacific rigging was often made from coconut coir, and it was considered better than hemp. Cook and Forster mentioned seals, "the skins we use for our rigging," and Dana spoke of "topgallant sheets and wheelropes, made of green hide, laid up in the form of rope."[30] (A sheet is not what it sounds to be, but is a line attached to a corner of a sail by which the sail is kept tight.) Hide rigging had an additional advantage—more than once it was eaten by desperate sailors on long voyages, with whatever flavour and softness soaking in seawater could give. Although possibly less versatile than the leather rigging seemed to be, an excellent long-lasting rigging was made from the bark of the *maho* tree (*Hibiscus tiliaceus*) by the Indians of Darien.

Maintaining all rigging, of whatever it was made, provided endless employment: changing new lines for old, checking for wear, and winding on yarn and canvas to prevent deterioration. Keeping the rigging tarred, something done about once every six months, was considered to be the worst toil on a sailing ship, with only occasional exceptions—such as the time the sailors on the *Duff* received sprightly assistance from unclad Polynesian girls whose skirts had been eaten by the goats aboard ship.[31]

Constant maintenance was not for rigging alone. "On board *Herzogin Cecilie*, for instance, we used up approximately 3 tons of paint and oils, 2 tons of first-class manilla, some of it waterproofed, and about a ton of flexible steel wire rope, annually."[32] Good officers kept a crew at work in fine weather passages when the sails themselves needed little attention: "No merchant vessel looks better than an Indiaman, or a Cape Horner, after a long voyage, and captains and mates stake their reputation for seamanship upon the appearance of their ships when they haul into the dock."[33] Rigging was taut and true, as well as tarred, by then. The work on rigging is always made more difficult by the interrelationship of the whole webbing: "You cannot stay a mast aft by the back stays without slackening up the head stays, etc., etc."[34] Sometimes, captains deliberately slackened one side of the shrouds (the permanent rigging bracing the masts to the side) in order to swing the yards around further to sail closer to the wind. But the shrouds and back stays could chafe the sails and rigging when the ship beat into the wind for too long.

All this interrelationship of multiple shrouds and stays gave strength, but seldom enough. For centuries men sought for stronger materials, only to find that when they had them there was a disadvantage to them too. The *Royalshire* once heeled over until the lower yardarms were in the water, and was nearly lost because "in a modern wind-jammer, with masts of iron and shrouds of the strongest twisted wire, this [using axes] is impossible, and you can no longer save your ship by cutting away the masts."[35] In earlier days, although weak materials had disadvantages, losing masts, or cutting them away, was a kind of safety clutch; "it is a very bad ship whose masts crackt not asunder . . . before she over-set," Hawkins said in 1605.[36]

Seamanship was an important factor in the endurance of masts and rigging, and, in spite of her being lightly sparred by modern standards, the *Endeavour*'s masts suffered surprisingly little during Cook's epic voyage. Once, when they did suffer, the captain placed the fault squarely on his being "over desirious of makeing the most" of a "fresh gale at north." On one occasion, though, the top-gallant mast broke in "light breezes and fine clear weather."[37] Masts sometimes gave way because of excessive rolling, particularly if the standing rigging had become slack. Sailing ships rolled excessively "in a rough sea or heavy swell *with only a light wind*" when the wind pressure on the sails was not enough to steady them.[38]

Banks suggested that the *Endeavour* was "at first but ill provided" with sails, and that the subsequent wear was a factor which altered the route that was taken home.[39] There was wear and there was damage, for after all it was a long, hard voyage, but Cook prevented even more damage by keeping a healthy crew and using it to send the yards and removable upper masts down when the winds roared too loudly. During the second half of the sixteenth century removable topmasts had been developed; John Hawkins adopted them for the Queen's ships. A further development was removable top-gallant masts, which, like the topmasts, would be brought down in bad weather to increase stability and to save them from harm.

A healthy crew was the clue to this success. All factors are closely interrelated on sailing ships—crew, health, rigging, design, and seamanship. A captain's greatest hazard in harbour, whether in Plymouth or Tahiti, was that of losing healthy men by desertion. A sailing ship could sail without fuel, but not without sailors. It was important in most latitudes—and vital in some—that sails could be furled as speedily as set, for otherwise a sudden squall or gale could smash the masts. Journal after journal tells of the inability of the crews to handle sails or masts, even in harbour, because so many of the men were ill. The *Daintie* was a very special case; her lack of men "to amaine our sayles" was due to her three-day battle against heavy odds.[40] Sailing ships simply could not operate without enough men, and this was always an incentive to further simplify rigging. Several squadrons sailing the Pacific had to sink some of their own ships in order to combine the crews for the remaining ships. Anson blew up the *Gloucester*, at least in part to release her men for the *Centurion*, and the grim necessity was emphasized when all lamented having to destroy such a beautiful ship, "justly esteem'd the Beauty of the English Navy."[41] Sailors and sails are as linked as the words imply.

Wear because of time and distance, or lack of care because of an ill or unseamanlike crew were not the only hazards for rigging. It was also subjected to immense stresses as the ships rolled. The inertial forces exerted on the supporting standing rigging as the top of a 200-foot steel mast swings back and forth through an arc of 30° or more are very great indeed. Anything in the design of the ship or in the seamanship of its officers which either increased or decreased the rolling of a ship directly added to or lessened the strains on the rigging. The way in which the cargo was stowed directly affected the weight distribution of the ship which was, in turn, the major factor affecting the extent of roll. Practically all the problems of a ship are closely interrelated.

This is exemplified by the problems faced by Captain Shelvocke, an English privateer who came to the Pacific in the ship *Speedwell* in company with Captain Clipperton in the *Success.* (Prosaic enough names for ships—although hopeful. These ships had originally been called the *Eugene* and the *Starhemberg* and were intended to be privateers of the Holy Roman Empire; as such, they would have been the first Imperial ships in the Pacific since the days of Charles V. The main fame of this voyage is that it was one of Shelvocke's crew who shot the albatross to which Coleridge gave immortality. The voyage might have had other fame, too; Shelvocke found gold in California. He reported it, but because of the dubious reputation he had acquired he was not believed.) Shelvocke's first problem with his ship began early in his voyage. Overloaded, particularly at the upper deck level, his ship was "tender," a problem common with the highly-built ships of the early sixteenth century, but usually much less so by Shelvocke's time. Possibly the fact that most of his overload on deck was his consort's brandy made the problem seem more tolerable to Shelvocke.

"Tender" in reference to a ship means the instability caused by the weight and, therefore, the point of balance being too high. A canoe can be made "tender," or unstable, by standing up in it. It is to overcome this problem that ballast is used, or heavy keels are put on small yachts; it was to overcome the problem that ships' guns were nearly always stowed down in the hold before the ships faced Cape Horn. (In Europe, the brand new Swedish warship, the *Vasa*, capsized in harbour in 1628, apparently because of "the great weight of her hull, the excessive weight above her water line."[42] The placement on her upper gundeck of heavier guns than were originally intended no doubt added to what became an instability fortunate for later ages—the *Vasa* has been recovered and restored, and so there exists a complete seventeenth-century warship to examine and admire; a ship that, paradoxically, is brand new.)

One answer to instability is to put extra weight low down, another is to remove weight from higher up; stowing away the guns did both, for it took weight from above and put it low down. Ballasting merely adds useless weight low down. Finding ever stronger and lighter material for masts, sails, and deckhouses removes weight from above and is a better solution. This was an aim of all shipbuilders, so they chose their materials carefully. New Zealand trees were often criticized as being far too heavy for masts because they would force the ship to carry too much weight too high.

A particular problem of weight distribution was one common to early Pacific voyagers leaving from Europe—the immense amount of provisions and supplies which had to be taken for a voyage of two or three years away from well-equipped and friendly ports. In this case, distance could mean overloaded ships, for the provisions required seem staggering. "The *Tamar* took on board: peas, 13 bar. and 3 gal.; beef, 1,320 pieces; brandy, 817 gal.; wheat, 16 bushels 7 gal.; oatmeal, 28 bushels 9 gal.; mustard, 166 lb.; pork, 2,556 pieces; bread, 6,272 lb.; oil, 145 gal.; vinegar, 60 gal."[43] These were large weights, but there was no way to avoid them.

The dietary scale in Tasman's time was something as follows:— To each man, one good cheese for the whole voyage; 3 lb. of biscuit, a quartern of vinegar, and ½ lb. of butter per week; on Sunday, ¾ lb. of meat; on Monday and Wednesday, 6 ozs. of salted cod; on Tuesday and Saturday, ¼ lb. of stockfish; on Thursday and Friday, ¾ lb. of bacon with grey peas; and at all times as much oatmeal as could be eaten.[44]

At the beginning of any long voyage a ship would be heavily laden, but for a Pacific voyage especially so.

Shelvocke's attitude to the weight of the deck-stowed extra provisions in the *Speedwell* was that the crew would "eat and drink her into a better trim."[45] The same philosophy comforted the captain of the sixty-ton *Lady Nelson*, sent to Australia in 1800 as a survey ship. Although she was very heavily laden, he "believed, however, that the consumption of coal and provisions would soon bring her to a proper degree of buoyancy."[46] Slack, of a modern yacht, claims that a ship's crew "eat her out of the water as they cross the Pacific," almost exactly the expression Robertson had used about the *Dolphin*.[47]

It was not always as simple as it sounds. Stowage—correct stowage—was an art as well as a science, and it was usually the responsibility of the first mate, or first lieutenant, or, in the early days, the master (in all cases the officer immediately below the captain). Stowing hides, as in Dana's *Pilgrim*, or wheat or wool as in the great Australian shipping trades, was both an art and hard, heavy work. Cargo was packed in tightly both to make a more profitable load and to prevent shifting during the ship's rolling. A loose cargo was a potentially fatal one, so the mate's responsibility was great.

Conrad, when a new first mate, had tried too hard to stow efficiently. It is true that he had read *Stevens on Stowage,* a book he called "a portly volume with the renown and weight (in its own world) of Coke on Little-ton."[48] Stevens said that no two ships could be treated alike, no matter the rules and principles, and this was true of other things besides stowing. All ships, for example, have a particularly good position for sailing—some quite odd—which their captains gradually find out.

In his efforts to gain stability by keeping the weight low, Conrad had over-done it on his ship and created a violent roll. The ship returned too quickly from being forced over by wind or wave, something like the action of a tumbling jack. Falconer, an eighteenth-century authority, said of a ship's centre of gravity that "by having it too low, she will be in danger of rolling away her masts."[49] Rolls could be violent. The astronomer of one ship re-ported that "the greatest Angle he observed her to Roll was 38°, this was on the 6th Inst. when the Sea was not unusually high, so that it cannot be reckoned the greatest Roll she had made."[50]

At least weight too low was safer than weight too high. Barlow, the English sailor whose journals give such an excellent picture of maritime life in the seventeenth century, tells about a

... good ship of near 400 tons, having delivered all her goods ashore, and had taken about thirty hogs of sugar and some log-wood, being hauled off from the quay and "rid" at her moorings, she, being a little top-heavy, would not bear herself very well; and all the men running over on one side to do some work, she was fallen over and overset and sunk down to Rights, and about ten or a dozen men "drownded" and all the sugar lost.[51]

The great nineteenth-century sailing ships built for carrying grain were some-times so top-heavy when unloaded that giant logs, which were reminiscent of Pacific outriggers, would be fastened to them temporarily to keep them from oversetting.

The stowage of a ship and the strength of her rigging were related. Anything that made a ship roll and recover sharply put a tremendous strain on the masts and their stays and shrouds. A top-heavy ship could overset; she could also strain her rigging by her over-leaning. It was a top-heavy condition which caused trouble with Cook's *Resolution* after much additional building had been done on her upper decks in order to accommodate Banks. Such extra structures on the upper decks, like the high forecastles and aftercastles of the early Portuguese carracks, made ships difficult to handle into the wind. This same problem recurs as a result of the recent trend for British Columbia power-boat owners to build high, upper-deck steering bridges on their craft. In most cases, although they give better visibility, these upper works spoil the contours of the hull aesthetically, increase the effect of roll, and make the craft difficult to handle at low speeds in a cross wind.

Cook said about the *Resolution*'s problem that "we had reson to think that she would prove Crank, and that she was over built," as well as "a good deal lumber'd a loft with heavy, and some useless articles."[52] She had to be restored to her original condition, as Cook's hopes of a cure "after we had consumed some of our Provisions" was thought to be not certain enough.[53] This particular example illustrates very well the interrelationship between food, stowage of cargo, accommodation for passengers, and the safety of the rigging and, therefore, of the ship. Dana defines "crank," the term which Cook used, as: "The condition of a vessel when she is inclined to lean over a great deal and cannot bear much sail. This may be owing to her construction or to her stowage."[54] It is another term for "tender." The strains on the rigging would be tremendous, and the mental strain on the sailors even greater. A ship and her crew make up a corporate body in which every weakness is multiplied by its relationships; the only answer is to provide and maintain strength in every element.

CHAPTER 16

Sea-Anchors, Anchors, and Steering

A small yacht, we said, will ride easily over and among great waves if she is hove to or allowed to drift broadside under bare poles; you have only to watch a seagull riding out a storm upon the water, we said. Perhaps we failed to notice that the seagull spreads its wings now and again to get out of trouble . . .

NEVIL SHUTE
ENGINEER, AUTHOR, AND YACHTSMAN

. . . one said "Starboard the wheel" to turn the ship to port, and vice versa . . . pig-headed conservatism from the days when ships were steered by a tiller, which is pushed in the opposite direction to the intended turn.

BRETT HILDER
NAVIGATOR IN THE SOUTH SEAS

When distances are great and the crew is small—sometimes of one man only —endurance means survival. The endurance of ships and men is fully tested in most Pacific voyages. When the ship is small she must be able to ride out a storm; she cannot win by fighting against it. She must be content to survive. In this "rolling with the punches," sea-anchors help by keeping the vessel in such a relationship to the direction of the waves that she is not overwhelmed or overturned. Easy steering, or even better self-steering, is also of major importance once the storm has been survived and the course is resumed. Getting the job done with the least effort, and comfort, are important aids to endurance, and hence to success. The voyage of Slocum, the first solo yachtsman to circumnavigate the world, made the point about each of the problems, and his *Spray* (Plate 42) is worthy of detailed examination. She has been widely copied; many replicas of her are still afloat.

The *Spray* is perhaps the most famous, as she was the most copied, small yacht in history. Because of this fame she and (for other reasons) Captain Voss's British Columbian canoe *Tilikum* (Plate 11) are the best examples to use in a discussion of sea-anchors. Nearly everyone has heard of the *Spray*. Already over eighty years old before she became well known, she was rebuilt in 1893 by Joshua Slocum, a Nova Scotian who had become an American merchant captain. Slocum had commanded the *Northern Light*, which he called "the finest American sailing-vessel afloat."[1] Such a statement, normally to be doubted, would be tempered with Nova Scotian caution—after all, he did qualify it by using the adjective American—and may be taken at face value. Having sailed a canoe home to New York from a shipwreck in Brazil, Slocum knew not only ship-handling but boat-handling. His long and varied experience gave him definite ideas about the qualities to be built into a ship and those to be drilled into a man to make both seaworthy.

Slocum rebuilt the *Spray* from an old sloop, a small, one-masted vessel, but, as was said of another ship, "it is a law in Lloyd's that the *Jane* repaired all out of the old until she is entirely new is still the *Jane*."[2] He built her solidly: oak for keel and ribs, stem, and sternposts, and also for the breast hooks (the specially shaped timbers that support and brace the stem-piece from within) which were doubled in case of meeting ice; Georgia pine for planking; white pine, white oak, and cedar for the stanchions; a single Hampshire spruce for the mast. Every piece was carefully shaped by the handwork of the man who was to sail her: "It was my purpose to make my vessel stout and strong."[3] In this case, the shipbuilder *was* sailing in his own craft— Captain Bellingshausen would have approved.

Slocum painted his sloop with a preparation of copper on the bottom, and white lead on the top just before launching, and she "sat on the water like a swan."[4] In 1895, Slocum set off to sail around the world, and he did so, taking three years, and writing a book about it all—a book which is a gem of literature quite apart from the intrinsic value of an accurate account of the first solo circumnavigation. It contains titbits such as an interview with President Kruger of the Transvaal in which Slocum, who had reached South Africa by circumnavigation, failed to persuade the old Boer statesman that the world was round. After being completely convinced of the *Spray*'s seaworthiness in her survival of a monster wave off South America, and of the safety inherent in her design, Slocum decided to devote his "best energies to building a larger ship on her lines." He thought her "such a ship as I should call seaworthy in all conditions of weather and on all seas."[5] Unfortunately, he never got the chance; he, and the *Spray*, disappeared together while on a voyage in 1909, probably to South America, an old haunt. But it was not the end, for "the *Spray* sails still—kept afloat in its continued reincarnation by yachtsmen; old copies and new, but worthy vessels all."[6]

The *Spray* was not quite thirty-seven feet long by fourteen feet wide, a beamy boat by the builder's design and choice. Although the lines of this famous sloop were said to have been "those of a North Sea fisherman," Slocum had widened her somewhat. Extra beam (or width) is an advantage in the swells of the open sea where the *Spray* was to sail, compared to sailing in the short waves of the North Sea.[7] The width dampens down the roll, and it provides the platform which will allow enough sail to be carried to steady the ship before a following wind and sea. Even in moderate gales Slocum could "hardly realize that any sea was running at all, so easy was the long, swinging motion of the sloop."[8] This quality was of paramount importance in the Pacific where the distances involved meant great cumulative fatigue in the crew, particularly when, as with Slocum, there could be no relief.

Beam would also give advantage when lying a-hull (drifting sideways, moving with the sea), a course chosen when, for some reason, the ship is unable to keep facing into the sea or wind, or does not have the room to run ahead of them. It was often done with small ships. Davis said the *Desire* was "inforced to hull" in 1591 during her second voyage to the Magellan Straits.[9]

Extra beam, if for either of these reasons a craft were lying a-hull, might also prevent her from being overturned by an especially heavy sea. A modern English yachtsman, Smeeton, said that if he were building a yacht to round the Horn again, "she would have broader beam than *Tzu Hang* and shallower draft, and then perhaps she would not be bowled over if ... I was forced to lie a-hull."[10] Lewis's catamaran could lie a-hull very successfully because of her great beam and because she was also very light and buoyant, floating more like a raft than a ballasted ship.[11] When yachts lie a-hull, they do so in the hope that Darwin was right: "It appears the very insignificance of small vessels is their protection."[12] One leading authority described Chinese junks bobbing "like corks," arguing that they were safe because they were so short as "to fit neatly in the trough of the sea between the two wave crests or else ride on the crest of one wave only."[13]

When conditions became too bad at sea for comfortable sailing, Slocum would normally heave to: "The *Spray* was all right, lying to like a duck."[14] To lie-to "is to stop the progress of a vessel at sea, either by counter-bracing the yards, or by reducing sail so that she will make little or no headway."[15] This was a course of action adopted with confidence when a captain knew his ship and when there was plenty of sea room. Sometimes it was used over-confidently. Wakefield, the early New Zealand settler mentioned earlier as describing Maoris poling canoes up river, amusingly describes the brig

Guide lying-to in a violent storm near New Zealand with every officer and man sound asleep. He decided that as he was only a passenger he might as well go back to sleep too.[16]

In very bad conditions, Slocum would sometimes lay out a sea-anchor, a canvas bag held open by a ring and fastened by a line to the ship (figure 49). It drags heavily in the sea to keep the boat's bow or stern facing into the sea, depending on the end of the craft to which the line is fastened. It can also be used as a device to slow up a ship entering a crowded harbour, or when a captain wishes his vessel to seem slower than it is in reality. The *Golden Hind* used a form of sea-anchor, dragging "cables and mattresses," or so Drake's nephew told the Spaniards.[17] In fact, she was dragging water-filled wine jars or casks in order to stay well behind the fabled treasure ship she later captured, to avoid being seen, or if seen, to appear slow in order to lull Spanish fears.

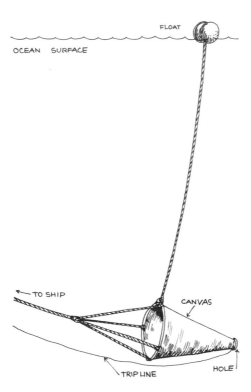

Fig. 49. Sea Anchor

Most sea-anchors are not used to deceive an enemy, but to save the craft. The Chinese used huge bamboo baskets which would float on the surface of the sea and keep the junk's head to the wind.[18] Captain Forrest, in command of an Indonesian galley, described how Filipino boatmen used similar devices in exactly the same way: "In bad weather they throw out a wooden anchor, and veer away a long ratan cable, which keeps their head to sea."[19] The Polynesians used sea-anchors, and the greatest modern proponent of their use was Captain Voss who crossed the Pacific in the British Columbian Indian canoe so like those of the Maoris. He designed a sea-anchor which he both used and publicized.[20] The *Astrocyte*, a modern Canadian yacht, from exactly the same part of the world as Voss's canoe, used her sea-anchor successfully in 1968: "In another 2 hours, the wind and seas were so high that we took in all sails and very shortly set out the big sea anchor, from the stern. . . . We lay fairly comfortably with this about 4 points off."[21]

Not everyone was as satisfied with sea-anchors as Voss had been. Two modern copies of Slocum's sloop used them, one with happy results and one not. Knox-Johnston, in his ketch *Suhaili*, preferred to trail warps and ropes to control the boat: "You could almost walk on the ropes astern!"[22] He found that streaming a warp as a bight (that is, letting a great loop of heavy rope stream behind the boat) was more satisfactory than using a sea-anchor, partly because it was simple and partly because the stretch in the rope cushioned the jerks caused by the heavy waves. Clifford, in the modern junk-yacht *Golden Lotus*, also used trailing warps successfully.

However, methods worked out by one sailor for his own ship may not be successful for a different craft. Nor can sailors ever be certain that they have seen the worst that sea and wind can offer. The *Tzu Hang* had plenty of trouble which dragging a warp did not prevent, even though 360 feet of 3-inch rope streamed in her wake. Smeeton concluded that either a very heavily constructed sea-anchor or the yacht's dinghy slung in a rope net would serve better. London found the *Snark*'s sea-anchor as unsatisfactory as nearly every other patent device he had so foresightedly bought for her. He had to buoy the anchor with a timber to keep it afloat at all, and the ketch—"the *Snark* that wouldn't heave to"—towed both timber and anchor as if she did not know what they were for.[23] However, she was fifty-five feet long and of fifteen foot beam, almost as big as the *Golden Hind*. There is an important dispute embedded here which divides small craft sailors. Some of them argue in favour of running before the wind, streaming warps to both slow the ship and keep her from broaching to, *i.e.*, turning sideways to the waves, in danger of turning over. This requires a minimum of sea room in which to run. Others argue that the ship should lie-to and ride out the storm, using a sea-anchor to keep the head safely into the wind and seas. Some have survived by using either way; those who did not survive have not told which, if either, method they were trying.

Even large ships have used sea-anchors, sometimes made from spars and sails. Course, a modern writer who sailed in twentieth-century sailing ships, spoke to one of the men who made such a sea-anchor, built quickly and used in an emergency by the *Garthwray*: "It appears to have been thoroughly successful."[24] The *Lady Nelson* used a "drag sail in order to steady her," probably very much like the drift sails used by fishermen in the North Sea. That craft was particularly suited to this tactic: "owing to her small draught and flat bottom, she rose like a piece of cork on the top of every wave."[25] Another use of the sea-anchor principle was the patent machine which so impressed Cook at Capetown (and which the Admiralty bought for him), designed to allow a ship to be dragged towards it by winching, in order to pull off a reef, for example, or to turn.

Sometimes, instead of changing the operation of the craft, sailors tried to alter the sea itself. Oil was spread to smooth a following breaking sea. Smeeton had little success with this, but Course said that when the *Garthsnaid* used it "the oil flattened out the tops of the seas and caused the barque to lay much quieter and without the danger of being overwhelmed."[26] The *Joseph Conrad* also used oil: "we had been hove-to twenty hours in the wild sea with the oil-bags out."[27] Others reported little success with this ancient method.

Sea-anchors are meant to prevent huge seas simply overwhelming a ship by keeping her lying correctly to the sea's force, but ordinary anchors, made to grip the ground and hold the ship in one place, had their problems. Rocks could wear through the cables and shipworms could eat away the shanks, or even entire anchors, for the Chinese used huge anchors made of hardwood. The Polynesians and Melanesians used anchors of stone, shaped to hold the lashings, and there could be trouble with the lashings. These stone anchors depended on weight and not on bite, whereas European anchors depended on both weight and bite. Some weighed as much as four tons; one rule of thumb was that for large ships the two bower anchors combined should weigh seven and one half pounds per ton of the ship's burden. Sometimes anchors held too well and if the ship had to leave quickly they were abandoned— hence, the phrase "cut your cable." As the crew of the *Providence* kedged in to Tahiti (that is, dragged themselves in by pulling the ship up to an anchor by winding in a cable from the anchor to the capstan), ahead of them they found a dropped anchor abandoned by the *Bounty* when the mutineers left in haste.[28] Ships could abandon anchors, but anchors did not abandon ships. Conrad claims that "an anchor is forged and fashioned for faithfulness; give it ground that it can bite, and it will hold till the cable parts."[29]

Sea-anchors are used to slow a ship up, anchors to hold a ship still, but the *Spray* was more famous for her movement and for her captain's skill in directing it. A good sail plan, combined with the steadiness given by her width, made Slocum's craft particularly easy to steer. In theory, a fore-and-aft-rigged craft sailing downwind would tend to turn into the wind because her sails extend to leeward of the hull, making forces unbalanced. It is seldom possible to wing and wing the sails accurately enough for complete balance. To "wing and wing" is to set one fore-and-aft sail to the starboard and another to port, so as to set the maximum sail area across the vessel to take advantage of a following wind. In fact, the *Spray*'s most famous quality was her ability to steer herself, even when running ahead of the wind. She once ran 2,700 miles, with Slocum at the helm for only 3 hours out of the entire 23 days, and this was without the self-steering devices seen in the pictures of modern yachts.[30] Easy steering was a vitally important feature in seacraft, one that made day and night the same when clear of land; the *Spray* had no need to lie-to while her crew slept. This quality of Slocum's yacht was so remarkable that many sailors are still not convinced. London's yacht also could run within two or three points of before the wind "without being steered," but London forecast that "they'll call me a liar when they read this; it's what they called Captain Slocum when he said the same of his *Spray*."[31] Smeeton's famous ketch also did well in this regard: "When she is under a balanced rig, she can be left alone for hours and hours, and sometimes for days."[32]

Balancing of sails was important in making steering easy, and some big ships were almost as famous for easy steering as the *Spray*, whereas others were notoriously difficult. The *Loch Torridon*, a four-masted barque of the Australian shipping trade, was lauded by her captain because of her easy steering: "being perfectly sparred, the ship is easy to steer, and even in the worst weather the smallest boy on board can keep her on her course."[33] Sails were an indirect influence; steering was done by the rudder, turned either directly by a tiller, or by whipstaff or wheel operating on the tiller. Rudders caused many troubles, being, while in operation, subject to great pressures, yet bound to be lightly supported because of the need to swing. Pintles wore through or suffered from the electrolytic effect of copper near iron—and always the seas battered. If the rudder broke while the seas and the winds were up the ship became endangered. Vancouver's launch, Bligh's launch, one of Cook's ships, Smeeton's yacht, Middleton's ship—all suffered from rudder trouble. Most of these were forced to rely, temporarily, on the ancient device of the steering oar. It is true that it was possible to alter direction by changing sail settings, particularly of the mizzen course, but that could hardly be called steering—it was slow at best and impossible in the very conditions when steering was vital.

Early steering oars had been either turned directly by hand or with the assistance of a small lever, which was a rudimentary tiller. The early European steering oar was on the right side, which came to be called the steer-board side, now starboard side. As a result of this impediment, ships put their left sides to the wharf to be loaded through the "ports" (doors cut in the hull); this left side finally came to be called the port side. The left side had been called the larboard side for centuries; no doubt the change to the name port was made to avoid confusion in commands.

A change of importance in the eighteenth century, which affected steering, was the change from tiller and whipstaff to tiller and wheel for moving the rudder. The tiller is the bar which is set directly into the head of the rudder

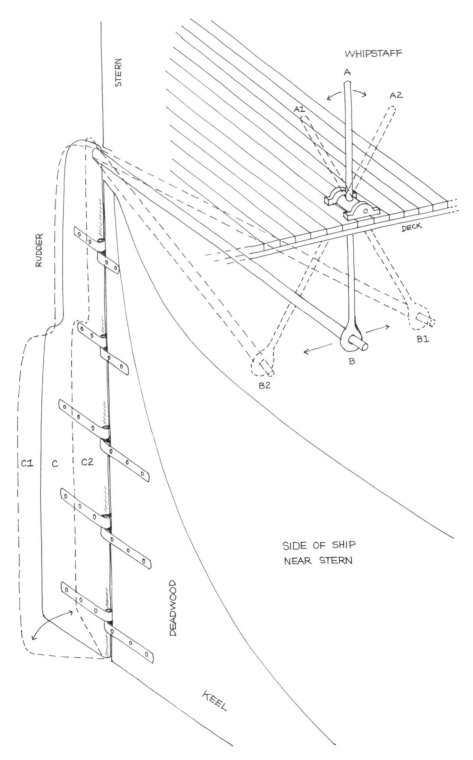

Fig. 50. Whipstaff Steering Gear

to gain the advantage of leverage, and turns it by direct movement as in small boats. A whipstaff (figure 50) is a pole attached vertically to the end of the tiller, going up through the half deck, able to move up and down as well as to lever in either direction through a fulcrum in the deck. When moved sideways, it moved the tiller to turn the rudder, but the pole had to slide down as well because the end of the tiller moving sideways would increase its distance from the fulcrum above it in the deck. As a result of double pivoting, the whipstaff was moved to the starboard (right) to turn the ship right, whereas with a direct tiller it is moved left to turn the ship to the right. This movement of the tiller in the opposite direction to the turning of the ship left its traces in English ships' orders up until the 1930's: "To alter course to port the order 'starboard' (your helm) . . . was given."[34] The advantage of the whipstaff was that it let the helmsman stand on deck to see the sails; watching the effect of the wind on the sails, showing shifts of direction or changes in velocity of the wind, is important in steering.

The wheel began to replace the whipstaff in the early eighteenth century; there is a model at Greenwich marked 1706 with both a wheel and a whipstaff pivot. In the new device, a rope was so fixed to the axle of the wheel that when the wheel was turned the rope was slackened in one direction and tightened in the other.[35] Led through pulleys, the tightened end would pull the tiller while the slackened end would allow it to move. In a further development, a screw device conveyed the movement of the wheel to the rudder. It is with the wheel that the helmsman of fiction and of metaphor appears. It is difficult to imagine a prime minister at the whipstaff of state.

Steering a ship is a skill that can be learned—on easy ships or difficult ones. But the skill can be used only when there is the will to go, and the courage to do so. Slocum was the first man to circle the world alone in a small sailing craft, and the attention he and his book attracted made it certain he would not be the last, for in lone voyages the sailor appreciates best the relationship of man, craft, and sea. When one sails alone the slightest slip can be disastrous, for there is no help with injury, no one else to tend the sails, to calculate the course, to steer, to decide. There are problems of psychology too—"the sea is so big, and I am so small"—no one to love, no one to hate, no relief from boredom. Slocum saw a ghost steering his craft, and claimed to be happy to have his company.

SECTION FOUR

Health and Diet

Before the great age of machinery began in the nineteenth century, sailing ships required large and vigorous crews if they were to move, and, even more critically, if they were to stop. Sailors handled the sails; it was a matter of pride to them that they be set quickly, but it could be a matter of survival that they be taken down quickly. It had to be done under any conditions of weather, and it was hard and wearing work. Keeping the crew healthy was as important to the voyage as keeping the hull in good repair. In this matter of health, the vastness of the Pacific made worse all the problems of sailing, in particular, the one problem so intimately linked with the length of the voyage—scurvy.

Vigour is not simply freedom from disease, malnutrition, and poisoning. A sound diet can do more than merely avoid illness, it can create energy and endurance. But in the Pacific it was hard to preserve food—and even water—properly as the basis of a good diet (much less an attractive one) until the modern methods of food preservation were invented in the nineteenth century. Before that, food was dry, and salt, and dull, particularly with the unimaginative preparation that seemed to be standard procedure. An interest in food, beyond the nagging void of hunger linked with the crushing workload, was aroused only when the native foods of the Pacific, vegetable and animal, were used to supplement the oatmeal and salt meat. This interest was not always a positive one—which was only to be expected if boiled lizard or roasted bat were served. Variety had its hazards as well as its delights.

CHAPTER 17

General Health

*Notice, Gentlemen, that much of this fish is jaundiced, namely
that which has black teeth, and it is pure poison, do not eat it
but throw it into the sea and only eat that which has white
teeth . . .*

A SPANISH SAILOR
IN THE *SAN PEDRICO*

*And I was always thinking that beggars had a far better life
of it and lived better than I did, for they seldom missed of their
bellies full of better victuals than we could get: and also at
night to lie quiet and out of danger in a good barn full of
straw, nobody disturbing them, and might lie as long as they
pleased.*

EDWARD BARLOW
OF THE *WENTWORTH*

*His real diseases spring from causes peculiar to a sea life;
laborious duty, change of climate, and inclement seasons, bring
on premature age, and few of them live to be very old.*

THOMAS TROTTER
A FAMOUS NAVAL SURGEON

Oars, and paddles, and sails, all had to be handled by men. The words,
"oarsman," "paddler," and "sailor," are indicative of this; even more indicative
is the famous cry, "All hands on deck!" The health of the crews was as
essential to voyages as the cleanliness of hulls or strength of sails and cables.
Without surefooted sailors on the foot ropes, the great canvas "wings" could
neither be spread nor folded; without strong men at the capstan, the anchor
could remain fast in the harbour bed. Even the handiest and fastest of ships
could not fight its way out from a leeshore if the men were too ill to handle
the sails and braces.

Illness was common, because the work was hard and dangerous; the food was
poor beyond modern belief; the discipline harsh; and the medical attention—

if present at all—was nearly always unskilled and not always well in-tentioned. The mortality was shocking; the wearing out of men even more so. Nearly all sailors seemed old, very old, beyond their years. Their health in retirement must have seemed as expendable as their lives had been in action; otherwise much more would have been done much earlier to ameliorate the conditions and lessen the risks. There were good surgeons and good com-manders in every century who recommended reforms, but given the importance of vigour and energy on a sailing ship, some of the shipowners—and too often the naval administrators—showed a singular lack of foresight in the way the ships were provisioned with food and medicines, and provided with medical skill. Too much depended on the captains, who, although grand officers when afloat, still could not browbeat owners or admirals when ashore.

Captains, then, had to look after their men as best they could; the crew's strength was just as vital to success as the captain's skill. The good captains tried, and the greatest of them, given the limitations of their time, were those who were as successful in dietetics, provisioning, even in surgery, as in naviga-tion and leadership. For although the preparation of food was the cook's responsibility, the rationing the purser's, and the medical treatment the surgeon's, the oversight the captain gave and the response his known attitudes elicited made all the difference.

The ship's handling and the ship's maintenance were affected by what happened to the men in the ships. It worked reciprocally; the conditions on board and the length of the voyage, often directly due to the state of the rigging or the hull, affected the health of the men. In slow sailing ships, before food could be properly preserved, and before the use of citrus juices to ward off scurvy was an accepted practice, the time spent on the open sea was a danger to the crew. Starvation as well as scurvy decimated Magellan's men:

... we remained three months and twenty days without taking in provisions or other refreshments, and we only ate old biscuit reduced to powder, and full of grubs, and stinking from the dirt which the rats had made on it when eating the good biscuit, and we drank water that was yellow and stinking. We also ate the ox hides which were under the main-yard, so that the yard should not break the rigging: they were very hard on account of the sun, rain, and wind, and we left them for four or five days in the sea, and then we put them a little on the embers, and so ate them; also the sawdust of wood, and rats which cost half-a-crown each, moreover enough of them were not to be got.[1]

Yet the scurvy was even worse. This scourge affected Pacific voyaging for centuries, and was not effectively countered until the end of the eighteenth century. Scurvy was not the only hazard. Under the hard shipboard conditions of the days of sail, the sailors' work and the officers' work predisposed them to certain ailments. Arthritis of various types plagued many. For a long time, it was ascribed mainly to the damp, but it is now thought that other factors, such as infections and chronic Vitamin C deficiency, may have been more important causes. Cook, Vancouver, Furneaux, and Carteret are four captains who suffered from some form of this crippling and painful affliction.

As might be expected, dampness was a major factor in a variety of ills. Knox-Johnston spoke of skin irritation; others spoke of boils and the refusal of cuts to heal. Most of the early surgeons thought dampness contributed to scurvy, while Broughton deplored "the prevalence of the easterly winds and foggy weather, which concurred materially to have affected the health of our people, who were universally afflicted with the dysentery."[2] Even when the deck seams were watertight (and too often they were not tight enough "to keep the water which pours in in bad weather from swamping our bunks out"), the constant influx of men in wet clothes coming off watch brought moisture into the forecastle (the quarters at the bow of the ship where the seamen lived).[3]

Men tried to have waterproof clothing available; Dana described oiling cotton twill with linseed oil to be ready for Cape Horn, while other sailors who had been to the North Pacific bought the weatherproof parkas made of whales' gut from natives of the region. (The word "parka" comes from the North Pacific, for it is the Russian word *parki* for shirt, used to describe the Aleut or Eskimo hooded coat.)[4] Cook's men were given "a Fearnought Jacket and trowsers" each, and he also gave out needles so that his men could mend clothes.[5] In Wallis's ship, cloth was distributed and when "the Jackets was cut out the Capt. Cabin was filld of Taylors, and every officer that hade the least room in his cabin took two or three men in to sew."[6] This, or something like it, seemed to be a general practice in English ships; in the *Duke*, for example, spare blankets were made into clothes for the Horn. In Roggeveen's Dutch ship, the men got "the woollen clothing of coats, breeches, hose, shoes, shirts, mittens and caps which were provided by the Lords Directors."[7]

Quite apart from outside moisture coming in, the quarters were so confined that even the breathing of the men produced enough dampness to encourage tuberculosis, pneumonia, and various rheumatic complaints. Asthmatic complaints were common at sea. Captains tried to keep the men's quarters dry by heating them intermittently, but it was a losing battle, even for the cabins of the officers. When wooden ships came into warm weather after having been long in cold latitudes, the iron bolts sweated until the entire hulls reached the warmer temperature of the air around them.[8]

Conditions became even worse with the advent of iron ships in the nineteenth century, for condensation gathered on the hulls and bulkheads in cold weather and sweated off again in warm. (Because of this "sweating," shippers of tea did not favour iron-hulled ships; therefore, wooden planking—albeit over iron framing—was used in the tea trade for years longer than it was used for ships carrying wool or wheat or passengers.) Whitewashing of the crew's quarters helped, and the introduction of sand instead of seawater for scrubbing decks did away with at least one source of dampness.

Attempts to ventilate were not completely successful, although they did some good. Various types of ventilators were constructed, either on a chimney principle to suck out the warm damp air from confined quarters, or on the opposing principle of trying to force some of the wind's draught down through the quarters. One captain declared that "this evil, unhealthy stench" arising from the hold when many men were ill was enough to make anyone else ill; using sails to deflect some breeze into the ship's hull was never sufficient to overcome this.[9] Trotter, a very famous naval doctor, described "these foul airs that are apt to be generated in ships" as an "atmosphere of its own surrounding it . . . it requires a more considerable force of wind to displace it than has been usually imagined."[10]

When ship's air was so bad that it was thought it caused disease, then, by corollary, it should be thought that land air was beneficial—so seamen attributed their cures to land air rather than to the respite, the change, and, most important of all, the diet which the land afforded. One of Cook's sailors asserted that the "dry soft air of the African mountains proved a restorative superior to all the physic in the world."[11] Noting correctly enough that the Dutch stopped there with many ill on board, both in going to the Pacific and in returning to Europe, he gave the credit for an improvement in their health not to the world-famous garden of the Dutch East India Company, but to "the efficacy of this salubrious air."[12] Roggeveen also believed this strongly: "little notice can be taken of the journals of others, testifying that by a bag of greens, or by the use of fruits, their people in a short time were improved . . . our experience bears out the opposite of this, for to cure a sea-scurvy . . . not only must fresh good food be used for nutriment, but in addition to this a fresh and agreeable land air."[13] Roggeveen tended to be dogmatic about many things.

The casualties from illness were enormous, even after scurvy was overcome. The mortality rate at sea was still double that on land as late as twenty years after lemon and lime juice were officially recognized for issue in 1795. But there was more to concern seamen than the risks of bad health. It was understood—by the sailors better than any others—that a sailor's life was hard and that he worked and endured beyond the lot of most men. "No man will be a sailor who has contrivance enough to get himself into a jail," said Dr. Johnson many times.[14] He was using his imagination. But Richard Hall wrote that "it is worse than a prison," and he was in a ship.[15] Melville, also experienced, thought that the "sons of adversity meet the children of calamity" in the Navy.[16] Old sailors knew what the risks were and what voyaging was like. The *Discovery*'s officer/author, Rickman, humorously commented, although it is almost certain he was not amused, that "those who had never been employed on discovery before, were more impatient to depart."[17]

"Few of them live to be very old," said Dr. Trotter of sailors, and listed the reasons.[18] In spite of these hazards afloat and ashore (and even "the pox" was not contracted only ashore, as one sailor of the *Duke* could testify, having caught his disease from a captive female in the ship), some sailors lived long, as "The Ancient Mariner" implies. Bulkeley described the death at sea of an eighty-two-year-old, but this leaves room for scepticism, as Cook spoke of a man as seventy or eighty when the records show him to have been only in his late forties. It is possible that Cook may have been right, and the man may have lied about his age in order to obtain his position, but, on the other hand, it may be the common case of a sailor looking old beyond his years. Cook mentions that this old man was the only one *not* ill in the ship's company in spite of (or, perhaps, because of) "his being generally more or less drunk every day."[19] This tough old sea-bird was a sailmaker, in some ways like Dana's sailmaker, "the oldest and best seaman on board."[20]

In the *San Pedro y Pablo*, an eighty-year-old friar died, nearly home and much mourned after a hard and hazardous voyage. It seems a most advanced age to set out on a long seventeenth-century voyage; yet perhaps he thought, as had Sir Humphrey Gilbert somewhat earlier, that "Heaven is as near by sea as by land." An even greater age, and a much happier sequence, was celebrated in the trimaran *Gallinule*, when the captain's mother observed her ninety-third birthday aboard. This was in the twentieth century, but the craft was a small one, its route unusual, and the lady's spirit matched that of her seventeenth-century peers. Course knew a seventy-year-old mate on a windjammer, a tough enough job even for a young man, and one of Bering's sailors was seventy when he died after the shipwreck of the *St. Peter*.

Buccaneering may seem an occupation for the young—at least it is today— yet the *Batchelor's Delight* lost an eighty-four-year-old veteran who had seen service under Cromwell; he "would not be dissuaded from going on the enterprise against Leon."[21] Surely no other Ironside could have been shot in action in 1685.

Accidents, just as often as scurvy or starvation or bullets, were the cause of the cutting short of sailors' lives. The *Centurion* tried to keep its station with the other ships in a storm by "manning the fore-shrouds"; that is, to help keep the ship on course a number of the crew was sent up into the rigging which braced the foremast to substitute for the sails which could not withstand the gale. In doing this, the ship lost one of her best seamen who was "canted overboard." Men fell overboard fairly often. Captain Voss lost his mate overboard from the *Tilikum*, and, in a way even worse, lost the compass with him. In sailing ships, it was more likely that a sailor would fall because of the work in the rigging, and less likely that he could be rescued, because the ship could not stop quickly or go astern as could steamers or paddled craft. One sailor was rescued by Vancouver's *Discovery*, but mainly because he was an excellent swimmer; the ship lost another.

Some escapes were miraculous; a sailor on one storm-battered ship was washed off by one wave and back on with the next.[22] James Bissett had this happen to him too. With such luck, and great abilities, he survived an apprenticeship in sailing ships to become captain of the *Queen Elizabeth*. Some deaths were quick; when a sailor fell from a top-gallant yard, the sea was almost as unyielding as the land. Some deaths were not so quick: "the sea birds ... would not allow him to go down in peace."[23] Captains and crew did their best. The *Resolution* had a life-saving device to try, a float which would support a man and would be both seen and heard, because it was brightly painted and carried a bell. One life was saved by its use, and in an account of the incident by one of Cook's midshipmen is found the first use of the word "lifebuoy."[24] Melville's "White Jacket" of fact/fiction was also saved by one of Cook's lifebuoys. But rescues were rare; even today the odds are against a man who falls overboard. Captains such as Gann maintain that: "We had smoke buoys, light buoys, and a thorough drilling on how to organize and keep track of a departed crew member in the water, and yet I had a minimum of confidence in finding anything without a powerful assist from luck."[25]

Men could be pulled from a ship as well as fall from her. One of the *Resolution*'s crew became entangled with a buoy rope and went to the bottom with the anchor. He survived. Falls were not always into the sea; many seamen died from falling on board rather than overboard. In the *Providence*, a crew member who fell to his death on the deck was the only non-volunteer in the crew. Risk as well as hardship was, and is, the lot of sailors; there were few ships which lost no men.

On one rough day, Lancaster's ship lost more than a man: "we saw a great sea breake over our Admirall, the *Penelope* ... and after that we never saw them any more."[26] Hazards of many kinds other than "great seas" could destroy a ship quickly and completely. There are many ships whose fate will never be known.

Accidents were always a possibility anywhere, but at sea one of the real hazards was the lack of skilled attention to the injured. Sometimes so arduous and unpleasant was the work that even an accident was welcomed—something like a "Blighty wound" in World War I. Lubbock admitted this, after very badly injuring his kneecap: "Although I was in great pain all night as I lay in my sleeping-bag, I could not help gloating over the fact that I had so many hours of warmth and rest whilst the sea and wind roared and battered on the deck outside."[27]

One of the unfortunate coincidences of sailing-ship life is that the hardships of storms and the efforts of reefing or adjusting sail go together. Even calm did not always mean rest; it often meant attempting to tow the ship with its own boats. A good trade-wind passage with sails and helm constant, and no anchorage ahead for hundreds of miles should mean rest. Not so; it would find the mate anxious to tidy ship and to repair rigging, supported by the captain who was almost invariably worried about mischief and idle hands. As one mate expressed both points: "Keep all hands through the day in good weather employ'd in the various departments of the ship; it is best to keep them moving."[28] It was true in all ships of all centuries and of all nationalities:

> Six days shalt thou labour
> and do all thou art able;
> And on the seventh, holystone the decks
> and scrape the cable.[29]

Dana quoted this verse in an American ship in the 1840's, and he was echoed by the crew of an English ship in the 1930's; however, there was nothing new about it even in Dana's time. Two hundred years earlier, Hawkins "devised to keepe my people occupied . . . to divert them . . . from play . . . and other bad thoughts and workes which idleness is cause of."[30] Spanish sailors "were kept occupied . . . that they might not be idle nor have time to indulge in evil thoughts."[31] In both instances, a touch of sixteenth-century religious morality was added to a realistic fear of a completely secular mutiny. In spite of the more enlightened interests and attitudes of an English gentleman of the nineteenth century, Spry, in the *Challenger*, affirmed that "scrubbing, washing, and holystoning of the decks . . . are all measures which tend to enforce the discipline so essential to good government."[32]

Although it is probably true that idle hands find devil's work, all this unremitting exertion, whatever its purpose or justification, took its toll. An average seaman of forty-five looked "to be fifty-five, or even on the borders of sixty."[33] Beaglehole, in his remarkable edition of Cook's *The Voyage of the "Endeavour,"* speaks of the physical strain imposed on the crew by hauling up the anchor with a capstan, a slogging job too much romanticized by the modern enjoyment of the ballads and shanties sung while the sailors strained to turn it. It was sheer hard work. Capstans (figures 51, 52) were simply verti-cal winches turned by men pushing against horizontal bars placed in slots in the upright cylinder at waist height. Great leverage was obtained in this way, but not enough leverage to make easy the breaking free of a heavy anchor held in the sand or mud of an anchorage. In his book on Captain Cook, Villiers gives an excellent ex-planation of this device, with clear diagrams.[34]

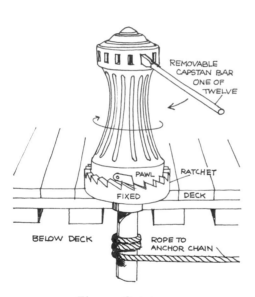

Although officers did not work at the capstan, their health broke down too. Most of Cook's officers died comparatively young, and Cook him-self was ill on his last two voyages. It was said of Conrad, novelist, sea-man, and captain of the *Otago*, that, after his retirement from the sea at the age of only thirty-six, "his life from then on [was] increasingly one of physical pain and break-

Fig. 51. Capstan

downs, the tortured years as an author for which he is remembered."[35] Vancouver, de Freycinet, Wallis, Carteret—the list of men of broken health is a long one.

Yet much of the seamen's life was not so much dangerous—indeed, some of the things already described are hazards only by the cumulative debilitating effect they had—as it was thoroughly unpleasant. Keeping clean was a problem on ships even with the water of the great ocean so near; having enough fresh water to drink was difficult enough without providing fresh water for bathing. There were some alternatives. The fictional Captain Hornblower had the crew pump seawater onto him and "he pranced grotesquely under the heavy jet."[36] This was exactly Ward's solution in the *Charlotte Jane*, one of the "First Four Ships" of the Canterbury settlement of New Zealand. He thought that "it is

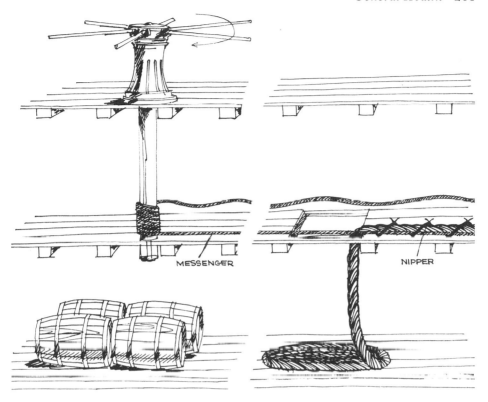

Fig. 52. Capstan Operation—note the short lengths of rope, "nippers," that secure the anchor cable to the continuous rope attached to the capstan shaft.

an improvement upon the shower bath" which had been "rigged on deck like an ordinary bath made of canvas; through a perforated roof the sailors throw buckets of water."[37]

Some crews swam in temporary swimming pools made by submerging sails, but these could be used only on days of complete calm; otherwise, they depended on rain for shower baths or simply did without. "Just before nightfall we had a torrential downpour and nearly everybody was skylarking on deck in a state of nature, having a really good bathe."[38] The difficulty in keeping clean was a distressing feature of sailing-ship life, but, as with discipline, food or confinement, it was not too dissimilar to contemporary standards ashore.

A French ship visited Kamchatka where Bering's *St. Peter* had been built. Here the crew, sitting naked on a tier of benches in a little hut, enjoyed a Russian steambath; the water, thrown onto a red hot stone oven, "immediately rises in the form of steam and causes the bathers to perspire most profusely."[39] Apparently, "the true 'Russian steam-bath' was always to be obtained at these posts."[40] The *Vostok* even set up a Russian steambath in a tent at Port Jackson, although surely a steambath near Sydney, even in March, would seem redundant. Such baths could be encountered elsewhere; a sailor in the *Tonquin* described an Indian sweatbath in California.

Ships carried with them the attitudes as well as the habits of the lands from which they came, but found humanity much the same wherever they landed. This discovery of common solutions was as true of attitudes as it was of personal habits. Ships both carried and discovered honour and treachery, honesty and dishonesty, love and hatred, and virtue and vice as well as filthiness and cleanliness. All these intangibles came in European ships; it was disappointing for the idealists to find they had long since arrived.

After saying that cleanliness is not merely a virtue, but a necessity on board, Karlsson admitted that in the *Herzogin Cecilie* they suffered from "this fiendish insect," the bedbug, in spite of keeping clean. In one whaler, the crew even introduced cockroaches to get rid of the bedbugs, believing them to be preferable—merely bad rather than horrible. Cockroaches were a plague in at least one ship of the Canterbury fleet of 1850, and the year before they had been so bad in the exploring schooner *Bramble* that she was deliberately sunk for a week to get rid of them: "perfectly destroyed them for the present though I have no doubt they will appear again."[42] In some ships, the crew made the best of a bad situation and used the cockroaches for racing. "Little black so-called copra bugs," something like ladybirds, were less unpleasant: "if one carried copra one had to put up with tens of thousands and millions . . . [but] they had no vices such as biting or stinging."[43]

Other vermin were worse. Sick sailors were "devoured with vermin hatched in the filth that surrounded them," Smollet discovered as a surgeon's mate on shipboard.[44] In the *Red Dragon* in 1604, many men "fell sicke of the scurvy, calenture, bloudy flix, and the wormes," and in Cavendish's ship in 1590 men were terribly afflicted with lice in clusters "as big as beanes."[45] Some of Anson's men were "almost devoured by Vermine insomuch that I have frequently seen by a modest Computation above a Peck of Lice on a Man even after he was dead."[46] Not all shipboard insects attacked only the crew. In one ship, white ants ate through a mast, making extensive and expensive repairs necessary.

When sailors landed, it could be even worse: ". . . the insect tribe are pretty numerous here [British Columbia] particularly gnats, moscheto, and sandflies whose stings are exceeding venomous some of our people who were on shore on duty were stung to such a degree that their limbs swelled so as to become totally useless."[47] In the water, as on land, lurked other unpleasant creatures. Buccaneers in the eastern Pacific had to beware of catfish with fins containing venomous bones, whereas right across the southern breadth of the

Pacific sailors could receive punctures from the dorsal spines of frogfish and be incapacitated for a fortnight.[48]

Strange foods to which sailors were driven by simple hunger or by a craving caused by the monotony of shipboard diet could also be dangerous. In addition to food poisoning, any sudden change of diet had its risks, and there is evidence that unfortunate effects often occurred. Some crewmen of the *Endeavour* suffered heavy vomiting from eating nuts of a kind which they were sure Australian aborigines had eaten. Men from a very early whaling ship vomited after eating some beans and prickly pears. Bligh, in the launch, recorded his fear of his men being poisoned by odd foods and plants and tried to judge their safety by seeing whether or not birds ate them. Crewmen of various ships died from eating machineal apples; one sailor died six months after eating them—"from which time he wasted away till he became a perfect skeleton."[49] A famous New Zealand physician says that "this is hard to believe." A surgeon from a French ship in 1790 cautioned his men about the dangers involved in promiscuous selection of wild vegetables, a point which had been stressed in Carteret's report to the Admiralty on his return with the *Swallow*.

Strange wild vegetables could be dangerous for unwary sailors avid for a change of diet, and so could certain fish. It was not that the literate among them, mainly the leaders, had not been warned. Often sailors recorded in their journals that they had eaten fish they did not recognize, because hunger for fresh food had overridden the caution induced by warnings about poisoning in earlier journals. At Tinian Island, Byron complained bitterly about Anson's chaplain's use of the word "surfeit" in describing the cause of the illness that the crewmen of the *Centurion* suffered after eating fish caught there. Byron justly asserted that "surfeit" means "too much," whereas the fish really were poisonous, and that he had nearly lost some men because of this lack of clarity.

A knowledgeable sailor in the *San Pedrico* had warned his officers not to eat a certain fish. Pigs and cats on which this fish had been tested died within two days; in the meantime, Quirós and his officers in the accompanying *San Pedro y Pablo* had refused to heed the sailor's advice, only to call within a few hours not only for the surgeon, but also for the confessor. Although some officers were ill for a fortnight, emetic oil given by the surgeon relieved the confessor of his duty by serving as an earthly purgatory. Sailors in Quirós's ship attributed this toxicity to the fish having eaten a herb called "manzanilla." At Tahiti in the 1930's, Long heard of fish that were poisoned by eating "coral when it is in 'bloom' "; he was told that natives of the area died from eating the fish.[50] "Red fish" caught by the *Resolution* in 1774 produced in the men who ate them "violant pains in the head and Limbs . . . with a kind of Scorching heat all over the Skin."[51] This had happened in spite of the cook having "Boiled a Spoon" with the fish and watched for discoloration, in an old test for poison.[52]

Retching and pain were major symptoms in most cases of fish poisoning. During one Spanish expedition the officers had very bad attacks of diarrhoea from eating what appeared to be "a large and excellent fish," and, by way of contrast, in the North Pacific, Waxell reported constipation caused by too much fish.[53] Other symptoms were mentioned in other accounts. Hayter suffered from food poisoning when he was on a diet of fish: "After about a week on nothing but fish my body revolted, and my stomach (which usually only worked once a week on such a diet) became racked with pains and demanded unpleasant attention; the glands in my throat became swollen and ached, and a splitting headache throbbed with the slightest movement."[54] The *Ruby*'s journal reported some crewmen "ill to day from Eating the Large Pearl Muscles which lines these shores" in northwest America; exactly the same thing happened to the men on Vancouver's ship.[55] The symptoms as described sound very much like those of a violent allergy to shellfish, not uncommon but most unpleasant.

Dysentery and diarrhoea caused by food were common afflictions, and spread misery from the sick men to all near them. Hawkins thought the "purging" in his ship, perhaps somewhat less serious than dysentery, was caused originally by the eating of a strange nut. "A violent purgeing" of some of the men in the *Dolphin* on her second voyage after "Eating the Scurvy Grass and purslin" was not of great consequence, and the good that these foods did for those suffering from scurvy seemed more important.[56] The cause was not always food, of course. "Violent heat & perpetual Rains" had been blamed by "our Doctor" for the "flux" in that same frigate two years earlier, just as Broughton blamed the weather for the dysentery in his ship. Dr. White cured "obstinate dysentery" in his convict ship with sap or gum from the red gum tree.[57] Any of these "purgings" could have been caused by a variety of things. Most were probably a form of mild food poisoning, although White blamed his epidemic of dysentery on the dreadful stench which arose from the bilge after a leak had made the ship take water.

A strange poisoning occurred in another convict ship on her way to Australia, producing symptoms like those of mumps in adults, a swelling of the glands under the jaws and of the testicles. It probably was mumps, but White thought not, and suspected at first that it had been caused by a verdigris on the copper cooker. As a good cleaning of the copper seemed to make little difference, the cause still remains a mystery. The patients were cured by an emetic and by "the motion of the ship," a cure which sounds even more mysterious than the cause.[58]

If these incidents were strange, they were also frightening. What would seem minor incidents on land may be major ones at sea. When Lubbock cut his thumb in the *Royalshire*, it was a serious business, "as a sailor's thumb is a very necessary part of him, and cuts won't heal off the Horn."[59] Again and again, mention is made of this refusal of wounds to heal in the cold and the salt of Horn conditions: "sea cuts, which eat down to the bone, are very common, and many of the men have got bad sea boils on their wrists and arms."[60] In the *Beeswing*, Morton had his share of "a great epidemic of sea boils."[61] If he had been in the *Rattler*, he might have been cured by the tea made from molie tree leaves and mint, which was Captain Colnett's prescription for the complaint.

Colnett was interested in medical matters and discussed scurvy, yellow fever, and less important diseases, such as boils and diarrhoea, both sensibly and at length. He was interested in indigenous medical practice in the Pacific and once treated crewmen wounded by St. Elmo's fire with Tahitian massage. (St. Elmo's fire is an electrical phenomenon during which balls of fire appear on high structures, such as masts of ships and steeples of churches.) As a captain in a ship without a surgeon he thought that "it became a duty in me, to make part of my study, such an important subject, as the health of my crew." His motives might not have been completely altruistic: "It frequently became a nice point to judge, whether a man neglected his duty from idleness or sickness."[62] Seasickness was seldom mentioned by anyone. Perhaps it was so common that it was ignored, although Dillon did say that "the water of a roasted half-ripe cocoa-nut" was a remedy; in the *Novara*, Scherzer was told that the Maoris found "roots (roi) of this fern, baked and ground" an excellent preventative for seasickness.[63]

Other illnesses were more closely related to the attitudes of the persons who were ill. Intemperance in drink was blamed for some deaths in ships. Venereal diseases were mentioned in the records often, but, as sailors were docked pay when they reported a venereal complaint, some of the milder cases probably did not get into the records. Early ships' surgeons and captains saw a relationship between "an ill-cured venereal complaint" and scurvy, "for the Scurvy seems to bear a great proportion in his disorder."[64] Dr. Lind, after considering another medical writer's clinical reports, saw scurvy as "seeming constantly to awake any sparks of the venereal poison lurking in the body";[65] from one of Rogers's consorts: "August 29. Capt. *Cooke* buried one *John Edwards*, a Youth who died of a Complication of Scurvey and the

Pox."[66] There may have been a confusion of symptoms, for Lind is found quoting Martini Lister that "they are nearly allied; having so many symptoms common to both," and not easily told apart, "but by an experienced physician."[67] This is exactly what was so often lacking, especially when competence as well as experience is demanded.

Illness at sea, when acute, becomes an emergency even today. Without radios or helicopters, lacking most modern medical knowledge, fortunate when they had a surgeon or a surgeon's mate at all—much less a skilled one, early sailors found almost any illness dangerous. "The want of a skilfull Chirurgian" was an important matter in the *Delight* in 1590 in the Straits of Magellan, because of disease and accident. In those days, in the Straits, ships had to operate completely within their own resources.[68]

The ships' surgeons were sometimes grossly unskilled, not only by the standards of today, but of their own time. This can be inferred from the constant complaints, for it may be assumed safely enough that at least the officers had reasonable standards of comparison ashore. These were the days when the physicians—unlike the surgeons—were university men, interested in a great many aspects of health, both in prevention and treatment, relying mainly on rules of living, including careful diet and wise choice of "airs," and, when these failed, on physic or medicine. They were, in their own and in others' eyes, gentlemen, and this, as much as their learning, set them apart from the surgeons. The surgeons' was the more direct of the two professions, relying on "bleeding" and amputation and bonesetting, and it was well on into the nineteenth century before they began to amass the prestige which graces the group today. In the early days in English ships, the surgeons were often the unwilling choices of the Company of Barber Surgeons, which had to provide ships' surgeons on request and, by the early seventeenth century, surgeons were quite openly "impressed," or conscripted, to go to sea. Drunkenness was commonly a cause for surgeons to ship, or be shipped, on a voyage. Bligh's surgeon in the *Bounty* was constantly drunk. A surgeon's standing at that time may be judged by noting that his stipend per seaman was twopence a month, whereas that of the chaplain was fourpence. Of course, this may be merely a realistic assessment of the proportion of cures to deaths. However, somewhat later, Smollett said that Random received "a warrant, appointing me surgeon's mate of the *Lizard* sloop of war, which put me on a footing with every first mate in the service." Nevertheless, in one ship the captain was "too much of a gentleman to know a surgeon's mate, even by sight"—one measure of the social gap between warrant and commissioned officers.[69]

The captain would usually act as the surgeon when the ship did not carry one, and in one ship there was an outspoken attack on her captain for having "consumed those sweete meates, which were layed up in the shippe onely for the reliefe of sicke persons."[70] Fortunately, other captains acted differently; de Surville in the *St. Jean Baptiste* ordered that the poultry be reserved for the sick, "and only for the sick."[71] Good commanders were careful of the health of their men and thoughtful of the sick, but by no means were all captains good commanders. Dana tells of a saying in the American merchant fleet in the 1830's that "a sick sailor belongs to nobody's mess."[72]

In one interesting experiment, the chaplain of the *Red Dragon* was to act as the doctor also. He gave no satisfaction; it was reported that "our phisition shipt for that purpose being as unwilling as ignorant in any thing that might helpe them."[73] Bulkeley, of the *Wager*, wrote that their surgeon would not treat a wounded officer because he had quarrelled with him. The care taken in English ships may seem most inadequate, but Hawkins said that "the Spaniards, in generall, are nothing so curious in accommodating themselves with good and carefull surgeans, nor to fit them with that which belongeth to their profession, as other nations are."[74] It is certain that the Spaniards seemed happy to capture a group of buccaneer surgeons and to spare their lives in return for service.

There were plenty of good surgeons, however, energetic and curious men who added to mankind's knowledge, not only about life in the ships, but also about the life of the different people they encountered. Wafer was a buccaneer, anthropologist and writer; Anderson of the *Resolution* was a naturalist and writer; and Patten of that ship's first voyage represented science on board in quite a different way than did the navigators and astronomers. The concern of these surgeons was with men's relationships to other men and to themselves, a subject just as absorbing and just as important as the relationship of a ship's position to the stars.

Sometimes this importance was officially recognized. In the convict and emigrant ships bound for Australia, the surgeons had great power in relation to the captains—too much perhaps. The anxiety of the surgeon to get his charges ashore forced the captain of the *Cataraqui*, an emigrant ship on her way to Australia, to press on in poor visibility, and this, combined with faulty navigation, led to a disastrous shipwreck. Interestingly, the estimated position was considerably wrong in both longitude and latitude—yet this was in 1845, not 1545.[75]

One great difference between the role of medical men in peaceful exploration and their duties in a man-of-war in wartime was that in the former they acted largely as physicians, and in the latter all too often as surgeons. Ships' surgeons had to amputate the limbs ripped by grapeshot or splinter, or shattered by ball or blast. There was a deadly and unfortunate rivalry between the scholarly physicians and the surgeons, who, in the physicians' eyes, were little above—in skill or class—the barbers and horse leeches from whose ranks they had been drawn. The surgeons for their part looked down on "doctors' work"—cutting, speedy cutting, was their job. This is graphically pictured in Melville's *White Jacket*. It is to be hoped that the character of Chief Surgeon Cuticle in Melville's U.S.S. *Neversink* was grossly overdrawn.[76]

This professional rivalry had unfortunate effects upon naval medicine. Trotter, who is remembered as one who did so much to help the victims of scurvy and who will be discussed later, was one of the few naval surgeons of the late eighteenth century who was also a physician. More might have been done earlier about scurvy, sanitation, and general diet if more physicians had gone to sea. Smollett expressed himself as less surprised "that people should die on board, than that any sick person should recover."[77] Under these circumstances, it is surprising to note that one early British hospital ship was named H.M.S. *Charon*; it seems unnecessarily productive of depressing thought.

Medical science ashore was not very advanced either, a point worth repeating about many things: medicine, diet, discipline, the class system, the attitude towards experiment and innovation, and the attitude to the real work of the world. If seamen were neglected, so were the agricultural labourers and miners. Few people ever examine the structural foundation of an economy or a society. They are conditioned to believe that power comes from the barrel of a gun, or the decrees of bureaucrats, or the eloquence of demagogues, whereas in reality it comes from the miners who mine the iron to make the guns, and from the farmers who feed the miners while they mine. As an extreme example (but only one example in one of many foolish countries), Britain remembered her seamen, her agricultural labourers, and her miners in 1914 and 1940, but proceeded to forget all about them as soon as it was again convenient to do so. After all, in the first half of this century, Britain has nearly starved twice, and, all too often, she has to repeat wartime blackouts in peacetime. It is little wonder that, in even less enlightened times, British naval medicine lagged so badly for so long, or that disease, especially scurvy, killed more sailors, many times more, than lost their lives in all the fabled battles of naval history put together.

Plate 42. The *Spray*. This beautifully built, beamy yacht was both comfortable and strong enough to enable its captain and builder, Joshua Slocum, to make the first lone voyage round the world. An ex-Nova Scotian living in Massachusetts. Slocum built and proved the *Spray* so successfully that faithful copies have been built in many parts of the world. Notice the yawl rig.

Plate 43. Captain James Cook (1728-79). The son of a farm labourer, Cook rose through effort and merit to recognition as the world's supreme navigator. Most famous for his three great Pacific voyages between 1768 and 1779, he was killed by Hawaiian natives during a brief, confusing confrontation, the details of which are still not entirely clear. His death was all the more tragic because of the concern Cook had always maintained for the welfare of the indigenous peoples encountered on his voyages.

Plate 44. H.M.S. *Endeavour*. Built to be a sturdy coal freighter on the North Sea, the *Endeavour* became, through her association with Cook, one of the most famous exploration vessels in history. This modern etching depicts her arrival in Botany Bay.

A
TREATISE
OF THE
SCURVY.

IN THREE PARTS.

CONTAINING

An inquiry into the Nature, Caufes, and Cure, of that Difeafe.

Together with

A Critical and Chronological View of what has been publifhed on the fubject.

By *JAMES LIND*, M. D.

Fellow of the Royal College of Phyficians in *Edinburgh*.

EDINBURGH:

Printed by SANDS, MURRAY, and COCHRAN.
For A. KINCAID & A. DONALDSON.
MDCCLIII.

Plate 45. *A Treatise of the Scurvy*, title page. This book by James Lind publicized the known facts about scurvy and recommended the final solution to the problem, the regular and frequent use of citrus fruit juices.

Extract of a Letter from Captain Cook *to Sir* John Pringle, *dated* Plymouth Sound, July 7, 1776.

I ENTIRELY agree with you, that the dearnefs of the Rob of lemons and of oranges will hinder them from being furnifhed in large quantities, but I do not think this fo neceffary; for though they may affift other things, I have no great opinion of them alone. Nor have I a higher opinion of vinegar: my people had it very fparingly during the late voyage; and towards the latter part, none at all; and yet we experienced no ill effects from the want of it. The cuftom of wafhing the infide of the fhip with vinegar I feldom obferved, thinking, that fire and fmoke anfwered the purpofe much better.

late 46. Captain Cook's very restrained recommendation about the use of citrus fruit juices aboard aval ships may well have held back for years the introduction of this scurvy preventative.

have them.   They all in general had putrid gums, the spots and lassitude, with weakness of their knees.   They lay together in one place, being a proper apartment for the sick in the fore-hold; and had one diet common to all, *viz.* water-gruel sweetened with sugar in the morning; fresh mutton-broth often times for dinner; at other times puddings, boiled biscuit with sugar, *&c.*; and for supper, barley and raisins, rice and currants, sago and wine, or the like.   Two of these were ordered each a quart of cyder a-day.   Two others took twenty-five gutts of *elixir vitriol* three times a-day, upon an empty stomach; using a gargle strongly acidulated with it for their mouths.   Two others took two spoonfuls of vinegar three times a-day, upon an empty stomach; having their gruels and their other food well acidulated with it, as also the gargle for their mouth.   Two of the worst patients, with the tendons in the ham rigid, (a symptom none of the rest had), were put under a course of sea-water.   Of this they drank half a pint every day, and sometimes more or less as it operated, by way of gentle physic.   Two others had each two oranges and one lemon given them every day.   These they eat with gree-

diness, at different times, upon an empty stomach.   They continued but six days under this course, having consumed the quantity that could be spared.   The two remaining patients, took the bigness of a nutmeg three times a-day, of an electuary recommended by an hospital-surgeon, made of garlic, mustard-seed, *rad. raphan.* balsam of *Peru*, and gum myrrh; using for common drink, barley-water well acidulated with tamarinds; by a decoction of which, with the addition of *cremor tartar*, they were gently purged three or four times during the course.

The consequence was, that the most sudden and visible good effects were perceived from the use of the oranges and lemons; one of those who had taken them, being at the end of six days fit for duty.   The spots were not indeed at that time quite off his body, nor his gums sound; but without any other medicine, than a gargarism of *elixir vitriol*, he became quite healthy before we came into *Plymouth*, which was on the 16th of *June*.   The other was the best recovered of any in his condition; and being now deemed pretty well, was appointed nurse to the rest of the sick.

B b   Next

Plate 47. *A Treatise of the Scurvy*, pp. 192-93. Here Lind describes experiments he conducted with some patients aboard a ship on which he was a naval surgeon. It was these experiments that led to his strong belief in the effectiveness of citrus fruits and juices. Beginning like Smollett, the eighteenth-century novelist, as a surgeon's mate, this "man of observation" was perhaps the first modern clinical investigator and made an enormous contribution to the health of the seaman at sea.

CHAPTER 18

Scurvy

*Who does not know that cheerfulness and contentment con-
tribute to good health, whereas weariness and dejection
create idleness and that want of cleanliness which helps to
produce scurvy?*

THADDEUS BELLINGSHAUSEN
OF THE *VOSTOK*

*Nothing was more hideous than the appearance of their face:
to the leaden complexion of the victims of scurvy was added
the prominence of the gums jutting out of the mouth. . . . The
sick gave out a fetid smell, which, when you breathed it,
seemed to attack the very root of life. I have often felt my
strength ebb away when I came near them. Their state of
weakness did not prevent them from retaining the use of all
their intellectual faculties, which made them feel all the more
cruelly the pangs of despair.*

A FRENCH NAVAL SURGEON

Scurvy had been a land disease of long winter months, a northern disease.
With the advent of long-distance sea voyages as Europe spread itself around
the world, it became a sea disease also. It was by no means confined to the
Pacific, but it was far worse there than elsewhere, because distance conspired
with disease to punish men for their desire to explore and their drive to
exploit. Apart from distance, some Pacific routes had another factor of time
involved—the caprice of the winds. At the Horn, they almost forbade entrance
from the east and nearly always exacted a heavy penalty in time. Since
scurvy was a deficiency disease, it was time multiplying the effects of poor
diet which induced it. In other areas of the Pacific, it was the calms that had
to be feared, for, in calms, ships lost almost as much time as when they were
driven back by contrary winds. These factors are discussed in the chapter on
sea routes. In this chapter, scurvy and the classic Pacific voyages which it
ravaged are the subjects. The most notable of these was Admiral Anson's,

when, in his flagship *Centurion*, he led a British fleet to the Pacific to harass the Spaniards during the War of Jenkins's Ear.

It was not until 1928 that Vitamin C was isolated and could be measured, although it had been conclusively demonstrated in 1917 that scurvy was a diet deficiency disease.[1] Scurvy had been little known in southern Europe where fresh produce was available the year round. In the north, it was different. Some early medical authorities stated it to be "endemic with the English," and Hawkins of the *Daintie* thought that "our nation is more subject unto it than any other."[2] If this were indeed true it was simply because England's northern location gave her such long winters. During the Pacific voyages, in which the vast distances had exactly the same effect as long winters, by creating long periods of time between fresh provisioning, sailors of every nationality suffered.

Dr. Lind's *Treatise on Scurvy* (Plate 45), published in the 1750's, was inspired by the dreadful losses from scurvy on Anson's voyage; and he may well have heard of Bering's fate as well. During Anson's expedition, 1,051 of 1,955 men died, practically all of them from scurvy, although it is true that the bungling of the preparations by the Admiralty (not by Anson) gave him many unhealthy men to begin with. At one point in the voyage, only 71 men of the 1,000 who had originally made up the crews of the three ships were capable of manning the guns of the *Centurion*, and in its battle with the Spanish galleon from Manila the British sailors had to fire and reload the guns by a form of shift work. Although these English losses were frightful, being of a different nationality certainly did not prevent da Gama's Portuguese, Magellan's Spanish, or de Castries's French crewmen from getting scurvy; the French ships of Baudin and de Surville suffered as badly in the Pacific as did those of the northern-reared Russian and English seamen.

With her crew already so riddled with scurvy that there were "few on board who were not in some degree afflicted with it"[3] after her lengthy and disastrous struggle round Cape Horn (Plate 33), the *Centurion* finally made her way north in late May, 1742 to the island of Juan Fernández, Robinson Crusoe's island. A high proportion of scorbutic patients died and the symptoms were not only revolting, but particularly terrible because they gave such definite and early warning of almost certain death. In April alone, "no less than forty-three died" in the *Centurion*; in May, "near double that number"; by the middle of June, although now at Juan Fernández, "above two hundred."[4] Symptoms of the disease were lassitude, depression, fevers, ulcers as well as spots all over the body, swollen and rotten gums, and a "luxuriancy of fungous flesh."[5] There were side effects too. A fall from the yards, in one case, was made much worse by scurvy, as the "parts soon mortified."[6]

Most of the early ships' crews suffered from scurvy to some degree and, although generally similar, the symptoms described in journals are not always identical. For example, the *Centurion*'s crew complained of fevers and body rashes, whereas the Russians of Bering's *St. Peter* did not. Waxell, in making this point, was specifically comparing their experiences, for he had read Anson's account by the time he wrote his own. The similarities were more important; both English and Russians suffered from loss of appetite, and what seemed most noteworthy to both Anson and Waxell was that seamen who ate well and seemed reasonably healthy could die on the slightest exertion, particularly on going on deck into the fresh air.[7]

In other Pacific ships, the reports show great similarities of symptoms: bad gums in the *Endeavour*; bad gums and legs swollen blue in Carteret's *Swallow*; "limbs black as ink" in the *Dolphin*'s first voyage; bad gums, stench, and "leaden complexion" in Taillefer's French ship; panic and paralyzed legs in the *Rattler*; swollen gums, bad legs, and stench in Dana's *Alert*; and bad gums in Dumas's *Legh II*, a modern cruising yacht.[8]

The symptoms were easily enough described and recognized; after all, they had been known since classical times. But though there were many theories, the causes were unknown. Many observers noted that those persons who had had scurvy once before and had recovered were the first to suffer it a second time; this may have been partly caused by a natural anxiety. Psychological causes were observed and considered important from the very first reports to the last. Dr. Lind, summarizing some conclusions of Cockburn, said that "it attacks commonly the weak, lazy, and inactive."[9] Muller, writing of the Russian ships in the North Pacific, speaks of fear and anxiety as both predispositions and symptoms. These emotions might very well have been a predisposing factor among the female convicts who developed scurvy in the *Prince of Wales*, one of the ships in the first convict fleet to Australia.[10] Men who had been drafted by force to crew naval ships were considered "extremely liable to its attack, by reason of their discontented state of mind" and, as a corollary, "those that are of a chearful and contented disposition, are less liable to it."[11]

Eminent doctors such as Blane and Lind had observed that excitement, action, and success lessened the incidence of scurvy, whereas failure increased it. Battle was the excitement they cited; Anson reported the same effect, although from an admiral's rather than a surgeon's point of view. In confirmation, Browne, in a lowly whaling ship, noticed that scurvy was "aggravated by the despondency arising from want of success."[12] Despondency was an effect even more than a cause. In the *St. Peter*, the only wish of the sick men was "a speedy death."[13] Byron's sick crewmen were "in a very desponding way," and there is some evidence of depression in every first-hand discussion of the disease.[14] This was natural enough in such an unpleasant and usually fatal disease—there was much to be despondent about.

Other observers noted that scurvy was a plague on dry land as well as at sea, telling of its ravaging Hudson's Bay Company employees, Roman Catholic monastic orders, and the Austrian army fighting the Turks in Hungary. Cook's successor in command found scurvy among the Russians at Kamchatka. His officers sent them some sauerkraut: "They were too lazy to gather the green stuff with which the country abounded."[15] The captain of the *Lady Nelson* found scurvy among the Australian colonists, perhaps for the same reason. It seems more probable that it was caused by ignorance of the value of fresh vegetable matter in both cases. Not even Pacific islanders were immune from scurvy on their beautiful islands, according to an Austrian scientist in the *Novara*, although this seems incredible to Europeans who have lived on island diets.[16]

As befits not only its importance, but its horror, theories about scurvy were almost as numerous as sea captains and surgeons. Experienced seamen such as Krusenstern and Bellingshausen of Russia, Colnett and Meares of Britain, and La Pérouse of France, were still emphasizing the dangers of wet clothes and damp quarters at the end of the eighteenth and in the early nineteenth century. Bellingshausen worried about many predisposing factors, and thought that: ". . . dress, salt provisions, not quite fresh water, and an atmosphere vitiated by many being crowded together, the smell of the bilge-water, the continual monotony and the consequent depression of spirits, little movement and exercise or too much rolling of the vessel, combine to produce scurvy and tend to spread it."[17]

Lind, the eighteenth-century English physician so famous for his emphasis on the importance of diet, thought wet conditions an important cause. As a result of this belief, most captains—prior to Cook's voyages and certainly after them—tried to keep the men's quarters clean and dry. In his ship, Vancouver lit fires between decks "to keep up a constant circulation of fresh air" and, in Bellingshausen's, the living quarters were dried out regularly by using stoves in the crew's space and by carrying red hot cannonballs into the tiny cabins of the officers.[18] Such efforts were not always appreciated. Meares complained that the sailors considered the smoke from his well-meant efforts to be a cause of scurvy, which still appeared, as he somewhat sourly commented, "in spite of our strict adherence to those admirable rules of regimen so happily conceived, and successfully practised by Captain Cook."[19] In a general way, no doubt, this suspicion of damp conditions was sensible, for it could be assumed that good health would postpone a deficiency disease such as scurvy and that stress would accelerate it. Today, stress is considered an important predisposing factor to many diseases.

Other authorities were doubtful of the efficacy of these measures in preventing scurvy, although they were not at all against cleanliness and comfort for the crew. Anson reported that all the "uncommon pains in sweetening and cleansing the ships" had little effect.[20] Sir Gilbert Blane observed with some interest that, after the Battle of the Saints in the West Indies in 1782, whereas the French ships were, by Royal Navy standards, defective "in every point of cleanliness and order," their crewmen were healthy.[21] It is true that he was mainly concerned with fever, but the "healthy" would naturally imply the absence of scurvy. La Pérouse of the *Astrolabe* thought the change from a cold to a hot climate was a cause of the disease, a theory early English mariners had also put forward. The most startling theory of causation, considering other descriptions of a sailor's life, was that of "the want of exercise."[22] Oddly enough, this theory was espoused during two Russian voyages, eighty years apart. One English captain argued that although scurvy caused an aversion to exercise, the exercise itself was a cure.

There was a widespread belief that small ships suffered less from scurvy than large ones. Frigates were said to be more healthful than ships-of-the-line, but considering their size and their role this probably was due to the fact that frigates put into port more often under conditions of blockade. Modern yachting voyages have shown that even the smallest boats with one-man crews can have scurvy aboard.[23]

Plentiful salt meat and too little fresh water were such common factors of crew life in Pacific ships that it was only to be expected that both surfeit of salt meat and shortage of fresh water would be blamed for the scourge. Late eighteenth-century British captains often mentioned a shortage of water as conducive to scurvy, agreeing with Barlow's view that supplying little water for men who had to eat dry biscuits and salt meat was a shortsighted economy. In his *Discovery*, after an outbreak of scurvy, Captain Vancouver seemed to find confirmation of this distrust of salt, when a cook confessed to having given skimmings from the boiled salt meat to the men. This was against explicit orders from Vancouver, who followed Cook's dietary principles faithfully; this incident seemed to confirm their wisdom.

Waxell, Hawkins, and Lind all attacked the diet of salt meat, the famous physician claiming that it is so difficult to digest that it "requires perfect health . . . to subdue it in the first passages."[24] It is easy to agree with Lind; on the other hand, it should be remembered that the ships were small and so extremely inflammable that the major cooking facilities needed to achieve real variety were forbidden. The food was monotonous and stodgy, mainly because very few foods could be kept at sea for any length of time. Also, there is, at best, only a limited number of ways of presenting oatmeal, or rye flour, or ship's biscuit, even though they were spiced up and varied with the mustard, olive oil, vinegar, or raisins usually carried.

Officers had somewhat more attractive food, because they were allowed to carry private provisions in addition to, or perhaps in amelioration of, the standard rations. However, officers in all navies developed scurvy—Bering died of it. While editing La Pérouse's report of part of the voyage of the *Astrolabe*, Valentin suggested that the "disease was not widespread among the seamen, but it attacked many of the officers and their servants who were unaccustomed to life at sea and were unable to tolerate the lack of fresh provisions."[25] This seems a version of inoculation or adaptation which is in interesting conflict with other statements about the relative health of officers and men. One of the many clues which led Lind to ascribe a dietary cause to this disease was a report in a book by Bachstrom that in the Austrian army in Hungary in the 1720's "many thousands of the common soldiers (but not one officer, as having different diet), were cut off by the scurvy."[26] It seems likely that scurvy, resulting from a poor diet, would act as a weakening factor rather than the mortal agent. Most important to history, however, is not the causes of Austrian deaths, but Lind's belief about those causes, for this helped to lead him to his conclusions about the relationship of scurvy and diet.

The astonishing thing about the ravages of scurvy in the mid-eighteenth century is that a successful preventative had been known for at least 150 years, that is, citrus juices. This seems astonishing only because scientific research and the practical application of its findings are now taken for granted. Today, people assume and accept a way of looking at things which not only demands new remedies for old ills, but even new ills for old remedies. Whole communities are based on a search for new products or new fashions or new knowledge. Indeed, a surprising number of people in modern educational systems are employed simply to seek questions for which others can then seek answers. It was not like this in Anson's day, nor had it been in Lancaster's time in the last years of the sixteenth and the early ones of the seventeenth century. For example, quite as astonishing as the general non-acceptance of the preventatives for scurvy which Lancaster knew about and used is the fact that a connection between mosquito bites and malaria was discussed as early as 1572 and yet nothing further was done about it.[27]

Discussing the incidence of scurvy in the *Red Dragon* during his voyage to the East Indies on the western edge of the Pacific in 1600, Lancaster says that he stopped at the Bay of Antongil "to refresh our men with oranges and limons, to cleere our selves of this disease."[28] He had brought in his ship "certaine bottles of the juice of limons" which he gave out by teaspoon as a medicine, and "cured many of his men, and preserved the rest."[29] Middleton, on the same ship's next voyage, also took lemon juice with him, but not nearly enough, and the crew suffered from lack of it. It is likely that Lancaster had learned this virtue of citrus fruit directly or indirectly from the Dutch, who freighted many oranges from Spain to Holland. He had noticed that crews in these ships stayed in good health; nevertheless, the Dutch were still losing crews from scurvy in Captain Cook's time.[30]

Sir Richard Hawkins wrote, "that which I have seene most fruitfull for this sicknesse, is sower oranges and lemmons," and spoke of his crew, which "with the sight of the oranges and lemmons, seemed to recover heart."[31] Obviously, not only Hawkins, but the crew of the *Daintie* knew something of their properties. Hawkins did not see them only as fresh fruit with no more virtue than that of plums or apples, for he wrote of "the power and wisedome of God, that hath hidden so great and unknowne vertue in this fruit, to be *a certaine remedie for this infirmitie*."[32] (Author's italics.) In another place, he spoke of oranges and lemons "as the remedie of our diseased company";[33] he definitely saw citrus fruits not only as a preventatlve, but also as a cure. It is odd that Dr. Lind, writing in the mid-eighteenth century, mentions Lancaster's experience, but does not refer to Hawkins's definite opinions, in spite of quoting his figures on the mortality caused by scurvy. As he mistakenly called him Sir Peter, and not Sir Richard, it seems likely that he had not read Hawkins's 1622 book which contained these definite statements.[34] Another book, *The Surgeon's Mate*, written by John Woodall, Surgeon-General of the East India Company, had commended lime juice in 1617.[35] *The Sea Grammar*, by the flamboyant John Smith, best known as the saviour of the new colony of Virginia and as a popular author and adventurer, put forward strong views about the diet of seamen and specifically recommended "the juyce of Limons for the scurvy."[36] Smith's book went through a number of editions, and was contemporaneous with Hawkins's. Purchas describes the making of lemon water by the barrel as early as 1607. However, all this Tudor and early Stuart knowledge seems to have been ignored.

A hundred years prior to Smith, Magellan had known that fresh fruit prevented scurvy. His problem was the same as that of every ship after him—to find fresh fruit at suitable intervals on a long voyage. Few fruits kept well and, when preserved, they lost many desirable qualities. Ships in the Pacific found the problem a particularly difficult one, for they sailed on an ocean one third the size of the entire globe, containing only a scattering of islands, miniscule in proportion and by no means evenly scattered. Obtaining fruit depended simply on finding land and, as Magellan's *Victoria* was the first, but not the last, to realize, it was possible to sail for weeks and months without even a sight of land. When islands were seen, the fruit seemed the most precious reward for discovery—even more important than gold or glory.

Calls during the first part of the way to the Pacific were well known—the Azores, the Canaries, St. Helena, Brazil, the southern tip of Africa—and all of them provided refreshing fruits and fresh provisions. When ships continued on to the Indonesian Archipelago—the Spice Islands of romance and fact— again there were fruits in abundance. The eastward route into the South Pacific from the Cape took ships past Australia, not today's continent of vineyards and orchards, but a land almost barren of easily gathered food— and on to New Zealand where provisions were plentiful, but fruit was scarce. The westward route went south and west to the barren regions around Cape Horn where little fruit grew.

Cape Horn is as far from the equator as is Churchill on Hudson Bay in desolate northern Canada, whereas the Cape of Good Hope is as close to the equator as the southern tip of Spain. Fruits at the one cape, therefore, would not be at all like fruits at the other. Although the currants, gooseberries, cranberries, and raspberries which are found in high latitudes (that is, far south or far north of the equator) seemed meagre fare compared to the fruits of South Africa, they were good anti-scorbutics; black currants, for example, have four and a half times the anti-scorbutic value of lemons.[37] The real problem in high latitudes is not that the fruits are not valuable, even if perhaps less appetizing, but that their season is so short. Only cranberries, rose hips, and hawthorns remain on the bushes for any length of time, and a seaman would pick long only to garner little.

In the Straits of Magellan, the *Endeavour* saw some berries which were used by the Indians. Cook called them cranberries, "because they are nearly of the same Colour, size and shape" and they were edible "raw or in tarts."[38] The Straits of Magellan area has much less fruit, even of the small and hardy high-latitude type, than is found in the equivalent North Pacific latitudes of Asia. Across the North Pacific, in America, many types of berries flourished. A sailor on shore on Vancouver Island reported that "we frequently meet with gooseberrys rausberrys currants blackberries strawberries and thimble berries."[39] It is thought that what Steller called the "scurvy berry" was the cranberry, which all North Pacific explorers used in various ways. The Swedish ship *Vega*, the first ship to sail the Northeast Passage around Asia, used cranberry juice very effectively to cure scurvy.[40]

In the South Pacific, however, once they reached northwestward from Cape Horn to the warm-latitude Pacific islands, the European ships encountered new fruits, as well as some tropical ones familiar to them from

East Indian, West Indian, or Brazilian experiences. Some fruits which they had neither encountered nor heard of, such as breadfruit, pineapples, coconuts, bananas, pawpaws, and mangoes, interested and amazed them. Many of the new fruits were effective anti-scorbutics; all of them looked appetizing to men long at sea. Because they were published for stay-at-home readers, many journals of voyages contain interesting descriptions of the new fruits, for the conditions of the day prevented the fruits from being brought home. For example, the chaplain of the *Golden Hind* described coconut meat as a "kinde of hard substance and very white, no lesse good and sweete then almonds" and the milk as "a certaine cleare liquor, which being drunke, you shall not onely finde it very delicate and sweete, but most comfortable and cordiall."[41]

Of all these fruits, coconuts seemed best for scurvy. Everyone who was ill of the disease longed for fresh fruit and vegetables; as Dr. Trotter said, "that longing desire for fresh vegetables . . . dictates the very method of cure."[42] Trotter, 130 years before Vitamin C was isolated, recognized "that recent vegetable matter imparts a *something* to the body, fortifies it against the disease."[43]

Lind often treated scurvy during the Seven Years War in the eighteenth century. In a later edition of *Treatise on Scurvy*, he said he had found that "the most quick and sensible relief was obtained from lemon juice; by which I have relieved many hundred patients."[44] One of the problems with citrus juice, however, was to find a way to keep it in sound condition. Lind gave careful instructions for preservation, claiming of some four-year-old juice that in water or punch "few are able to distinguish it from the fresh squeezed juice mixed up in like manner."[45] Banks, in the *Endeavour*, liked his "lemon juice No. 3" and his "Dr. Hulme's Essence of *Lemon Juice*," and thought it "little if at All Inferior in taste to fresh Lemon Juice," but then he took his in his punch.[46] The eminent naval surgeon and physician Thomas Trotter pointed out that many people had been cured "with the juice that had been near two years squeezed from the fruit," probably because "great attention was paid to its preservation." He suggested that ships calling at any place where they could get lemons or limes should buy them, squeeze out their juice, and keep it in a cask with two or three gallons of spirits: "Thus furnished, a ship may bid defiance to the scurvy."[47]

Attempts to cut down the bulk of the juice by thickening it into a "rob," or essence, lessened the Vitamin C content, which in part explains Cook's scepticism about its value (see Plate 46). His scepticism was very important. Coming from a man so successful in keeping scurvy from his ships by a combination of methods and foods, it was given such weight that it helped delay the full-scale introduction of lemon juice into the Royal Navy until 1795. Most of the hard-headed (and cost-conscious) owners of the merchant fleet did not adopt it for fifty years after that.

Lime juice was substituted for lemon juice as a scurvy preventative in the mid-nineteenth century because it could be obtained cheaply within the British Empire. This was an unfortunate, even if an explicable policy. It is now known that lime juice has only half the Vitamin C content of lemon juice and only one tenth the Vitamin C content of rose hip syrup (the wartime substitute for orange juice in World War II Britain, now commonly used for infants). The Vitamin C content of lime juice served in the same amounts as lemon juice—as commonly happened because its relative lack of efficacy was not known—was insufficient to prevent scurvy. This explains, in part at least, many of the recurrences of scurvy in the nineteenth century. Nevertheless, lime juice did reasonably well as an anti-scorbutic. After the British Parliament made it mandatory for British ships to carry and issue anti-scorbutics in 1854, they became known as "limejuicers." Their sailors therefore became "limeys," a name now often applied by Americans to any Englishman. Whatever the snide remarks from others, the sailors on "limejuicers" liked the protection and the drink: "I never heard anybody growl at having to take lime-juice, as, besides being a very good drink, each deep-water jack knows how good it is to keep off scurvy."[48] A modern sailor "enjoyed the tepid water, mixed with a teaspoonful of fortified lime-juice, my first encounter with this beverage."[49] These pleasant anti-scorbutics are still used. Gerbault took lime juice with him in the *Firecrest*, and Chichester took lemon juice in the *Gipsy Moth*.

Lind knew that there were many other valuable anti-scorbutics: the juices of scurvy grass and of many kinds of pot herbs and fruits, and the infusion of fir or pine tips. All were used in Pacific ships. In one way, spruce beer is even more important as an anti-scorbutic than lemon, lime, or orange juice; the resource materials for it are so much more widely distributed. Spruce beer first came to public attention with the return to France in 1536 of Jacques Cartier, who had survived a scurvy-plagued winter on the St. Lawrence River in what is now part of Canada. He gave credit for the survival of many of the French to an Indian recipe for a drink made from the bark and needles of the spruce. Lind was familiar with Cartier's account and, after study, concluded that the entire pine and fir family of trees "seem all to have analogous medicinal virtues, and great efficacy in this disease."[50] He suggested that if a ship did not carry spruce tops specifically for that purpose, then, even the fir tops used for fuel in the ships, if boiled and the liquid brewed, would be helpful. Lind noticed that spruce beer kept Newfoundlanders free of scurvy under conditions that he thought even worse than those in ships.

Ships brewed beer from New Zealand and British Columbian pines, New Zealand *manuka*, Siberian cedar, and no doubt other trees as well. All these beers seem to have been of some help. When possible, they were brewed in casks recently emptied of malt beer, and molasses and a formula of concentrated malt (called "inspissated juice of wort" by Furneaux, and "inspissated Juce of Beer" by Cook) were sometimes added.

La Pérouse allowed his crew to have wine at the same time as they had spruce beer—with excellent results. Exactly the same effect was observed in the *Lady Nelson* on her way to Australia, with "wine supplemented with spruce beer."[51] However, there were also failures of skill or knowledge. It seems odd that Bering, who used beer made from cedar and taught its use to the Kamchatkans with pleasing effect, did not receive more benefits from it for the crews of his ships on a voyage during which not only many men and officers but he himself died of scurvy. It also seems unnecessary that a man and a boy in the Spanish forces in northwest America in the 1790's should die of scurvy within sight of the greatest conifer forests in the world.

Many other drinks were considered anti-scorbutic, usually with little justification except the ease in getting sailors to take them. Beer itself was thought to prevent scurvy. Ships' surgeons reported a "rapid increase of Scurvy as soon as the beer was done," but, as some beers travel poorly, the crew often finished the beer fairly early in the voyage. Yet it is known that beer has no ascorbic acid (Vitamin C) whatsoever.[52] It may be suspected that the reported increase in scurvy, in all probability, was misleading, and that it seemed so only because by the time all the beer had gone scurvy had begun to appear. It is true that the French ship *Solide* had little scurvy while using fermented wort and sugar, but the explanation of health is to be found, it is believed, in her other precautions. Not all French commanders were so careful. Baudin's *Géographe* was riddled with scurvy during her exploration of the coast of Australia almost a generation after Cook had demonstrated that the disease need not be a scourge of seamen. This has been blamed on Baudin's incompetence, for "he caused his crew and the sick to suffer the most appalling privations."[53]

Wine has no ascorbic acid content, yet wine was recommended as a substitute for spirits in order to decrease scurvy, and the benefits the French received from its use were often quoted. One of the difficulties in knowing which remedy or preservative was the effective one is that several were often tried at one and the same time. From the *Dolphin*, Wallis reported of his scurvy patients that "wine was served to them; wort was also made for them of malt, and each man had a half pint of pickled cabbage every day."[54] It is now known, but it was not then, that sauerkraut has half as much Vitamin

C as lime juice, whereas wine and malt have none. When anyone's condition improved after having partaken of those particular remedies, there is little doubt that they would give the wine, and not the cabbage, the credit.

Cider was also commended at times. Both Furneaux and Lind speak well of it, the doctor prescribing "good sound beer, cyder or Rhenish wine."[55] Saloops (or saloups) were sent with Cook's ships for making a kind of sassafras drink, which had a rather unspecific reputation of being able to "do good."[56] Even more esoteric drinks were prescribed. Wormwood ale used by the Dutch gave the precedent for Lind to recommend wine and wormwood. In the *Golden Hind*, the sailors drank a tea made of an herb like the "herbe which wee commonly call Pennyleafe," and molie tree tea, prickly pear juice, elixir of vitriol, and especially coconut milk vinegar, were all highly praised by Colnett of the *Rattler*.[57] It is true that coconuts and coconut milk seemed to help those ill with scurvy, and were vigorously acclaimed: "The milk or rather water of these Nutts is an excellent and perhaps the best Antiscorbutick that is in the world."[58] Less enthusiastically—but with more chance of getting them—the crews of the Russian ships in the North Pacific favoured cranberry juice and tea as preventatives.

Food was as important as drink in the prevention of scurvy. From his trips to the East, Magellan knew about scurvy before he set off to find his Straits and, as has been pointed out, he realized that the cause was a lack of fresh fruits and vegetables. He planned to get them wherever and whenever he could.[59] Others were aware of such a relationship; Barker, with Lancaster in a voyage in 1591, attributed scurvy among the sailors to their "evill diet at home."[60] By Lind's time, a full realization of the effect of deficient diet was precluded by the eighteenth-century medical emphasis on climate and on good and bad airs. Yet, Lind recognized the relationship of diet and scurvy, speaking of greens, fresh vegetables and ripe fruits as "the most effectual preservatives against it."[61] He knew that they were also a cure, even though he did not know about ascorbic acid as such, but warned that dysentery could result from too sudden and too great an amount of such foods after a long period without them. His suggestion that all ships' captains should imitate some commanders with whom he had sailed by growing their own salads on board, particularly watercress, was excellent, but seldom adopted. Whenever it was, it worked. A midshipman in the famous wool clipper *Illawarra*, after the hesitancy normal for a boy, began to follow his father's advice and grow watercress on flannel: "Far from being regarded as a crank for producing this luxury after weeks at sea on salt horse, relays of it were in continual demand and the foresight and sagacity of my father went without question."[62] More recently, Knox-Johnston grew mustard and cress for vitamin supplements in the *Suhaili*. In fact, watercress has a higher Vitamin C content than has almost any other vegetable; it is as high as that of orange juice or scurvy grass.

Cook and Vancouver were right to emphasize the gathering of wild "sellery" and scurvy grass by their crews, although the vegetable the crews liked best was Indian kale. It was not that these particular plants were unknown before; Bulkeley who had been in the *Wager* with Byron, mentions wild celery as being good for scurvy. Byron and Wallis, while commanding the *Dolphin* on consecutive voyages, sent men out to gather "scurvy grass," and Wallis sent for "Cellery to boil amongst the White [wheat] and Pease."[63] At first, the crews did not like such dietary innovations and, when captains were successful in preventing scurvy, it was quite as much because they were strict disciplinarians as because they were willing to innovate. French cooking is reputed to be more innovative than English, although some authorities state that "food on board the 'Lime Juicers' was a little more varied than on French ships."[64] De Surville, in the *St. Jean Baptiste* put cress and wild celery into a "fish-based stew which the men had greatly enjoyed."[65]

The benefits from eating the vegetables appeared so quickly and definitely that usually the most hardened sceptics gave way. French sailors in the *St. Jean Baptiste* were speedily restored to health by island greens. Roggeveen had wild purslane and "garden cress" gathered for his sick men, although he had some definite reservations about greens—as he seems to have had about so many things. In the north, the Russians from the *St. Peter* could confidently eat a number of herbs, because they had the good fortune to have a botanist with them. One of their favourites was the sweet grass from which the natives made a wine, described as tasting "something like Russian *borshch*."[66] In this reminiscent taste, some "scurvy nostalgia" may be suspected, which Dr. Trotter discusses as one of the signs of scurvy—its main symptom being a longing for the home country.

Other exotic vegetables used as anti-scorbutics, but genuinely pleasant tasting, were various palm and coconut cabbages, the terminal buds of the trees. Dampier described one palm cabbage as being "as big as the small of a man's leg, and a foot long. It is white as milk, and sweet as a nut if eaten raw, and is very sweet and wholesome if boiled."[67] Boiled palm cabbage was so good—Banks said delicious—that the search for it often caused trouble with the natives. This was not at all surprising for the coconut trees had to be destroyed to get the cabbage. Two coconut trees would support a family, live up to one hundred years, and were correspondingly prized; yet the compensation paid by French sailors for a tree cut down in Papua was one pocket handkerchief.[68]

Most of these anti-scorbutic vegetables should have been eaten raw, but almost never were in the early days. Cooking destroys Vitamin C in most vegetables, especially when the water is thrown away. It is now known that Vitamin C is destroyed by cooking in copper utensils, and copper was the common material for ships' cooking boilers.[69] When vegetables were eaten raw, the point seems to have been proved. At least one French corvette captain in the Pacific, Lavard of the *Aube*, made his men eat a potato raw every day as they sailed to New Zealand in 1840. In one of Dana's ships, the *Alert*, a crew member with scurvy "brought himself to, by gnawing upon raw potatoes and onions," and Dana described fresh onions as "a glorious treat."[70] Lind thought onions to be essential vegetables and that when their fresh onions were all eaten then the "pickled small onions" would do. Chichester, nearly three centuries after Dampier, was told by a dietetic specialist that raw foods are the best preventative for scurvy and so on his yacht voyages Chichester followed this advice and ate many vegetables raw.

Raw food produced some dramatic results. Abandoned to his fate and put ashore as certain to die, a sailor racked with scurvy cured himself by grazing on grass while still too weak to walk upright. By good fortune, his pasture was the green known as scurvy grass. To give more hope and better choice, many captains, and particularly many surgeons, planted European vegetables on the islands they touched. The *Ruby* "clear'd a Small Island . . . and made a Garden, planting Indian corn and Sowing Reddishes, Mustard, cresses, salery, Cabbage and Turnip seeds."[71] The *Rattler*, *Discovery*, *Astrolabe*, *Mascarin*, *Tamar*, and *Lady Nelson* all planted gardens "for the future benefit of our fellow-men, be they countrymen, Europeans or savages."[72] Furneaux "in several places . . . planted seeds, limes, lemons and oranges for the benefit of the natives and refreshment of future voyagers."[73]

When tame or wild fresh vegetables were unobtainable, a second best was preserved vegetables. Sauerkraut or pickled cabbage as a preventative for scurvy was the subject of experimentation in the Royal Navy in the 1760's and 1770's. Lind had recommended "pickled cabbage" ten years earlier, based on Dutch experience, but the most effective patron of this form of vegetable was George III, who loved it.[74] On Byron's voyage, the *Dolphin* apparently had none, there being no mention of pickled cabbage when the captain's report lauded portable soup, a kind of concentrated beef extract, as well as "Wood Sorrel & Wild Sellary."[75] Some was sent on the ship's next voyage under Wallis, "but the Pickeld Cabage was only Served when the Surgeon thought it proper."[76] In Carteret's report from the *Swallow*, there was no reference to sauerkraut, and he asked later, in a way suggesting that he felt his ship had been slighted, how Wallis had obtained his pickled cabbage. It is probably safe to assume that his ship did not get it because of the unfortunate separation at the Straits of Magellan; the cabbage intended for the *Swallow*, a small and grossly overladen ship, had gone with the *Dolphin*.

Cook commended "sour krout" very highly, but reported some trouble in getting the sailors to eat it—which can be easily understood. However, his knowledge of the psychology of British seamen came to his aid; he gave it to the officers daily and within a week he "found it necessary to put every one on board to an Allowance."[77] Banks preferred salted cabbage to sauerkraut, but this was just a variant with somewhat less fermentation; the essential qualities were the same. In Bellingshausen's ship, the sauerkraut "had been a little over salted for its better preservation."[78] A much greater variant was described by sailors of a Swedish ship—a "sour-krout" of fermented willow leaves made by the Chukchi, a northeast Asian tribe with a culture much like that of the Alaskan Eskimos.

Sauerkraut kept well; Cook reported perfect condition in barrels packed for two years. It was used widely in the late eighteenth century, but never became very popular with English seamen. After lemon and lime juice solved the scurvy problem, little is heard of it. Nevertheless, "Quarter Master," who spent much time in Pacific ships in the nineteenth century, mentioned both sauerkraut and pickled cabbage as part of the food supplied by the Royal Navy, as well as portable soup, tinned meat, and preserved pippins.

All kinds of things were tried in order to prevent scurvy. Marmalade of carrots sounds at best only slightly appetizing, but it was tried in the *Endeavour* at the recommendation of a Baron Storsch of Berlin as a good anti-scorbutic. A German peasant food tasting rather like honey, it was not a success in spite of its aristocratic commendation. Honey blended with mustard seed was praised as an anti-scorbutic by a writer in 1608, who also spoke of the curative power of orange juice, only to be ignored in both recommendations as thoroughly as Lancaster, Hawkins, and Smith had been.[79] Mustard seed was a standard provision. It was regarded by some, particularly the Dutch, as anti-scorbutic, and by everyone as necessary to spice up the dull foods. "Spicing up" was important; there is even one report of gunpowder, after a wreck, being used to flavour food in the absence of anything else—surely an indication, even in emergency, of a revulsion against the insipidity of the food.[80] Quality could not be counted on in sea supplies, even in simple things such as condiments; on the *Resolution*'s return, Cook reported caustically on "the Mustard seed (if it was such)."[81] No one in his ship would eat it, so apparently it had not been needed as an anti-scorbutic on that successful scurvy-free voyage.

Other spices were often collected during the voyage. Hawkins's ship spent some time in Tierra del Fuego gathering a bark called "Winter's bark" after Captain Winter of the *Elizabeth* in Drake's fleet. In exactly the same way as Cartier had been directed to spruce bark, Captain Winter had been told of the bark by the Indians, who knew it as a cure for scurvy. Hawkins's crew gathered Winter's bark for its qualities as a spice, and they thought it "most comfortable to the stomache."[82] The *Dolphin*'s crew also used it "in pies, instead of spice," even though the original samples taken to England by Winter were said to have had "an intolerably pungent burning taste" which could be mitigated only by steeping it in honey.[83] The palatability of such a preparation may be measured by recalling that a common name for the tree from which the bark comes is the "pepper tree."

It is easy to see why spices were sought—appetizing foods were difficult to keep on long voyages. Portable soup, a beef essence similar to Oxo or Bovril (a piece that returned from a voyage with Cook can be seen in the National Maritime Museum in England), was invented in 1756 by a Mrs. Dubois, who prospered as a result. She contracted to supply it for the Royal Navy in partnership with—fittingly enough—a Mr. Cookworthy. The crews of the *Dolphin*, *Swallow*, *Resolution*, and *Adventure* all received a good deal of it and found it most successful. Its main success was that it helped to make wild vegetables more acceptable, and it was often boiled with peas, oatmeal, or wheat. As Carteret pointed out, portable soup "made the Seamen have a better liking to those kinds of Sea provisions which are accounted the most inoffensive";[84] that is, it weaned the sailors from meat towards wheat and peas. The soup was used on meatless days (Mondays, Wednesdays and Fridays), so that it would give at least the flavour of meat to relieve the dreariness of boiled peas or the oatmeal porridge called "burgoo." These meatless days were called Banyan Days after an Indian religious group which ate no meat. Days of the week on American warships tended to be named for the expected food—Banyan Day, Duff Day, Swampseed Day, etc., very much as Saturday is Fish and Chip day in certain British families.

Vancouver did not use portable soup on his major voyage until after the fresh meat was intentionally used up rather quickly before it spoiled. When there is enough of it and when it is not overcooked, fresh meat of any kind is anti-scorbutic. No fresh meat was as much favoured by sailors as beef. Most of the *Endeavour* sailors at Tahiti did not like oven-fresh dog, for example, and, in retaliation, the sailors proceeded to horrify the Tahitians, in turn, by eating fried rats: "most of the gentlemen in the bell-tent ate of them, and commended them much."[85] Some sailors suggested meat which seems even less appealing than dogs or rats. Pigafetta wrote that some of the sick men in the *Victoria* "begged us that if we killed man or woman, that we should bring them their entrails, as they would see themselves suddenly cured."[86] How, or if, they intended to cook the entrails was not made clear. A more detailed recipe of the East that Pigafetta mentions—and one that most certainly was anti-scorbutic—was that of raw enemy heart "with the juice of oranges or lemons."[87] On one occasion, when human flesh was eaten to prevent starvation—in a whaleboat of the *Essex*—the heart was the first part of a dead sailor to be eaten. Cannibalism also occurred in the other surviving boat of that ship, with murder necessary to accomplish it. Bligh says, however, that it was not a real issue on his long voyage, even when they were in the direst trouble.[88] At least one captain resisted the openly expressed idea. "No more of that," he said fiercely, "or I'll capsize the boat and drown the lot of us."[89] Although Dillon described the way in which the natives of one Pacific island dressed and cooked a human, on the whole there is less discussion of cannibalism, as an indigenous custom or as a last resort, than might have been expected.[90] It certainly was not discussed as a preventative measure against scurvy.

Indians in British Columbia told Meares that the scurvy from which the white members of the crew of the ship suffered was caused by their refusal to eat blubber oil. Nearly a century later, a traveller in the same area confirmed that men at one fur trading post who had eaten the Indian diet of walrus and seal blubber had no scurvy, whereas those at another post supplied with European food by the Russians had "suffered severely from the disease."[91]

An Indian girl on the coast of British Columbia told the men in Meares's ship that Indians sometimes got scurvy in the wintertime, but when they did, they went south and cured themselves with a diet of fish.[92] Tupaia, the Tahitian returning to his island with Cook, cured himself of scurvy with a fish diet and, thirty years later, Dr. Trotter strongly commended fresh fish as a preventative. Centuries before Tupaia or Trotter, crewmen from the *Daintie* had been set to fishing "either with netts, or hookes and lynes" for the sick who had been carried ashore, and it is quite clear that Hawkins realized the value of fresh food, including fresh fish. Among other things, he said that it "yeelded us some refreshing."[93] Captain Gilbert, however, claimed that in his experience fish was no cure for scurvy.

It is only to be expected that a great variety of cures for scurvy were tried. The ones of concern here are those that sailors tried and claimed to be of benefit. There is something psychologically interesting in the fact that so many sailors at sea who suffered from scurvy felt strongly that direct contact with land itself would be a cure. Colnett of the *Rattler* thought scurvy sores benefited from prickly pear poultices; he also thought laying the patients in fresh earth helped them. Some agreed with him: "We buried sevrall of our sick, up to the Hips in the earth, and let them remain for *hours* in that situation [and] found this method of great service."[94] Still others believed that scurvy could be cured by hot sandbaths or by placing the body in contact with the earth, but this certainly did not cure Bering, who died half buried. In the *Uranie*, hot sandbags were applied to scorbutic patients to no avail.

There is no externally applied cure for scurvy. The remedy is also the preventative—a good diet containing enough ascorbic acid. What were called "cures" were the recoveries evident when fresh vegetables and fruits, particularly citrus fruits, were freely available to men who were suffering badly from the disease. The swift return to health was so dramatic that "cure" is not too strong a word.

The Pacific saw cures, as at Tinian with the *Centurion*, but it was the Pacific voyages—Magellan's, Anson's, and Bering's—which became the classic casualties of the disease. It is fitting that prevention, through Cook, is also linked with the Pacific. The theories of Dr. Lind found successful application with this great explorer, more because he was a disciplinarian, a perfectionist, and an inspiring leader than because he had any new insight into the causes of the disease. It could be argued that the very success of Cook held back the adoption of the simplest preventative—citrus juice; however, it also must be accepted that his methods led not only to a less scurvy-ridden marine industry, but also to one in which healthful diet, cleanliness, and the cheering and supporting effect of strict and fair discipline were themselves appreciated.

CHAPTER 19

Food, Sea Cooks, and Cooking

*Few can live altogether on ship puddings, dumplings, or the
like, without being sensible of an oppression and uneasiness.*
JAMES LIND
NAVAL SURGEON

*Having discovered some valuable uses to which we can apply
the cocoa milk, we are now taking advantage of them.
Viz. it is an excellent substitute for cream in tea or coffee.
It answers all the purposes of eggs & milk in making custards
or pies. We have made some excellent pumpkin pies with it.
It answers us a good substitute for cream or milk & butter in
making light short cakes, some of which we have had baked
from verry indifferent flour, as good we all pronounced them
as we ever ate.*
ALBERT OSBUN
OF THE RUDOLPH

*At this time, to our great joy, the sea washed up a dead whale.
It was 8 fathoms long. Its blubber was slightly rank, it is true,
for it must have been drifting dead about the sea for some
considerable time; but we were highly satisfied with that piece
of good fortune and called the whale our provision store.*
SVEN WAXELL
OF THE ST. PETER

Sailors' diets were bound to be limited to what could be carried and kept. Before refrigeration and canning were developed, the very few ways of preservation limited the variety of tastes and ensured a certain monotony. Much more restricting was the small number of foods which could be preserved by salting or drying. This limitation meant that a well-balanced diet was hard to attain in the early Pacific ships. Animal protein could be carried as salted meat or fish, and there were always the hope and intention of catching fish during the voyage. Plant protein was supplied by peas and beans. Carbohydrates came in the form of wheat or flour, oats or oatmeal, potatoes, and the ubiquitous ship's biscuit, or hardtack. Fat could be carried as heavily salted butter or as whale or olive oil, although animal fats went rancid easily. The major deficiency was the fresh fruit and vegetable matter which contains the vitamins essential not only to avert scurvy but to maintain general health. There simply was no way to fill this gap completely until refrigeration allowed fresh meat, fruit, and vegetables to be carried. Lemon and lime juice helped, used sufficiently and properly, but there is more to malnutrition than scurvy.

Some sailors tried to overcome these difficulties by eating all kinds of strange fruits, vegetables, meats, and seafood; the list of what was tried is an exciting one and much longer than the list of what was enjoyed. Many sailors were too conservative and, unfortunately, in most ships, the cooks were both conservative and inept. They could neither outsmart blandness nor overcome salt, and most were horrified by the words "bake" or "roast." Cooking meant boiling; peas, coconuts, salt meat, fresh pork, bear, or tortoise were all one to the pot. Sometimes, there was hardly enough water to allow boiling, and sometimes it was already so thick that the peas seemed redundant. Sailors' diets, like their lives in general, were usually dull, generally debilitating, occasionally repellent, and sometimes downright dangerous.

There were several problems with food which were caused or intensified by distance and time. The first problem, and perhaps the least complicated, was preservation. In the sixteenth century, food could be dried or salted— this was simple. It had to be kept dry and kept salted—this was not. By the beginning of the nineteenth century, canning had improved matters, but only relatively. To think of bully beef as an improvement on anything is one measure of the earlier problems.

The age-old solutions to the problem of keeping food by drying and salting brought on another problem—the monotony of meals prepared from the food so preserved. Oatmeal, dried peas, and salt meat soon pall and, on the Pacific, there was usually a long way to go. It was no wonder that some odd foods were eaten, nor that all resources of fish and game were exploited—even at dire risk to palate or to health, or to both. After shipwreck, when starvation threatened, some very strange foods indeed were tried. When odd foods are used, and particularly dull foods, cooking—and hence cooks—are of great importance.

If food and its preparation were problems, then fresh water was doubly so—for water is as apt to spoil as food. It is true that it would remain wet against many odds, but it would discolour, and crawl, and stink, until it looked more like a devil's meal than a man's drink. A machine to make salt water fresh, or stinking water sweet, was as much sought after as was a recipe which could make salt meat palatable after four months at sea. Sometimes, food and water were not just unpalatable, they were spoiled completely. Even spoiling salt meat could be resalted if it were detected soon enough, but often it was not. One of Cook's men was not happy "with salt and maggots eating into the beef and pork, and the rats and weavils devouring the heart of the bread."[1]

It is surprising how few foods would keep unless the conditions were almost perfect. Before canning was developed, ships had to depend on the uncertainties of salting, smoking, drying, pickling, and fermenting, and on the use of casks as containers. There were some refinements by the time of Cook; the *Resolution* carried six half-barrels lined with tinfoil to see if this would help to preserve the flour, malt, oatmeal, "grotts" (groats), peas, and bread. It did. Butter was put in tight casks filled with "strong pickle," as this method had already been proven.

The *Africaansche Galey*'s good casks aroused the envy of the other Dutch ships of Roggeveen's fleet, whose peas, groats, and dried fish the admiral called "unsound, rotted, full of worms, mite, and a stale smell."[2] So much depended on good casks or barrels that the cooper or barrel maker was an important man on board. His duty was to make the casks airtight, otherwise the contemporary means of preservation would not work. In the *Providence*, "on opening the cask we found our mustard-seed entirely spoilt, the air having got into it."[3] Coopers were kept busy all the time; empty casks were usually taken apart and stored as staves and hoops in order to save precious space and to help the ship's stability. This was called "shaking" the casks. Normally, casks were hooped with iron to keep everything tight, but in the North Pacific the Russians once "had the casks reinforced with nooses or hoops of rope and these answered."[4]

Even iron hoops did not always "answer." Cook, in the *Resolution* in 1773, mentioned that on opening some casks he found a "good deal of the bread very much damaged" and "ordered the Oven to be set up to bake or dry such as was damp and not so bad but that it might be eat."[5] He blamed the green wood of which the casks were made—the very problem which caused such suffering in the Spanish Armada in 1588, because Drake had caused heavy destruction of seasoned barrel staves in his raid on Cadiz the year before. Even iron hoops could not prevent green wood warping as it dried, making cracks in the cask joins.

As a result, opening casks, even in the 1930's, could be interesting. In a salt meat cask, Seligman of the *Cap Pilar* "found enormous chunks of salt-encrusted brown substance, from which arose a curious odour, that transported the bystander rather abruptly to the slaughter-house."[6] Even though salt meat was notorious for its toughness, its salinity, its stench, and its age, few ships could have sailed the Pacific without it. Salt beef, which was the

English standby, just as dried or pickled fish was that of the Portuguese and Dutch (although the latter used much salt meat also), was provided at the rate of two pounds of beef per head (or one pound of salt pork) on alternate days. Occasionally, salt beef found unwonted uses; Dampier used a piece of salt beef to stop a leak in the *Roebuck*'s side. Quite naturally, the beef proved satisfactory, for its durability was notorious; Dana thought salt beef "like a rock at low tide—nothing could hurt *that*."[7] However, the *Roebuck* sank anyway—"foundered through perfect age."[8]

"Salt-horse" was the semi-facetious name salt beef bore—but only *semi*-facetious. Horses' hooves and horses' shoes had been found in it. Sailors in the *Alert* had a verse:

> "Old Horse! Old horse! what brought you here?"
> "From Sacarap to Portland Pier
> I've carted stone this many a year;
> Till, killed by blows and sore abuse,
> They salted me down for sailors' use.
> The sailors they do me despise,
> They turn me over and damn my eyes;
> Cut off my meat, and scrape my bones,
> And pitch me over to Davy Jones."[9]

No doubt this is why the cask of salt meat opened for distribution was called the "harness cask." Actually, horsemeat is palatable when treated properly, although French sailors in the *Uranie* thought it bearable only when fried or braised. They considered horse soup very bad indeed. Anson's sailors liked horsemeat well enough when they captured some in a Spanish prize.

An even more unlikely source of the origin of salt meat than that of the song was put forward in the *Herzogin Cecilie*: "some huge, prehistoric animal . . . evolved without muscular tissue, had been discovered in a Greenland glacier, and an enterprising ship-provisioner . . . sold it as salted beef for ships' provisions."[10] Horse or monster, or even, as seemed unlikely, plain English beef, English seamen ate it, "besotted in their beef and pork," in spite of unbelievably poor cooking on the one hand, or any efforts to tempt them to a better and more healthful diet on the other.[11] One sailor explained that there were good reasons why "sailors as a rule prefer the ships's salt meat to the fresh meat which they get in port, as this fresh meat is the cheapest that can be bought, in fact nothing but the refuse bits from the butchers."[12] French seamen were somewhat more discriminating than the English and, in Bougainville's ship, preferred rats and leather rigging to the available salt meat.

Some attempts were made to dress up "salt-junk"—another name for salt beef which probably refers to the size and not to the quality of the pieces.

Most of the recipes sound to be no better than the standard boiling—cooks in the eighteenth century, by regulation, were instructed "to boil the Provisions, and deliver them out to the Men."[13] Some men tried to get variety. Lubbock remembered the recipe for "crackerhash" as "save some of your salt junk from dinner, and mixing it up roughly with broken-up hard tack, have it baked by the cook."[14] The problem was made worse in some ships where "the red meat (the lean of the salt junk) used to go always to the cabin for the Captain and Mates."[15]

"Son of a sea cook" is a term which, to put it mildly, is meant to be highly critical. This seems hardly fair, considering the materials with which cooks had to work at sea and the conditions under which the work had to be done (see Plate 48). However, hungry men are not notably just, and with sailors being tough men of necessity their criticism might go well beyond swearing. As a result, many good men were reluctant to be cooks, and the position declined in status although not in importance. In *Song of the Sirens*, Gann contended that "even a leaking ship is better than one with a heedless cook." At one time full warrant officers, cooks finally became "Inferior Officers."

In spite of this decline in official status, however, cooks still had a position of power as "the patron of the crew," dispensing favours such as drying wet clothing or giving lights for pipes. A cook was called "Doctor," either because of what he did to the food, or because the crew suspected the source of his raw materials. "Doctors" stood no watch; as they worked all day, like the carpenters and sailmakers, they could sleep all night, but everyone in the crew had his exact station when the ship was tacking or wearing. The cook's position was at the foresheet, the line which held the leeward lower corner of the foresail.

The extreme length of Pacific voyages added to the importance of a cook; a good one meant better morale. Unfortunately, the strict discipline which was essential for the proper handling of sails and ship was used by many captains and owners to keep in check the justified resentment caused by uninteresting food poorly, even dirtily, prepared. In many ships, especially British ones, the attitude seemed to be that as the food was dull and badly preserved anyway, then unskilled or unclean cooks were good enough.

Naturally the quality of foods varied, even in salt meat, and this was hard on the cooks. And salt could not improve poor meat. According to the Russians, the Russian salt meat compared very favourably with the Irish and German products. There is no doubt that much of the trouble with salt meat was caused by carelessness, outdated regulations, or sheer profiteering by suppliers of every nationality. Profiteering was a problem everywhere in every century.

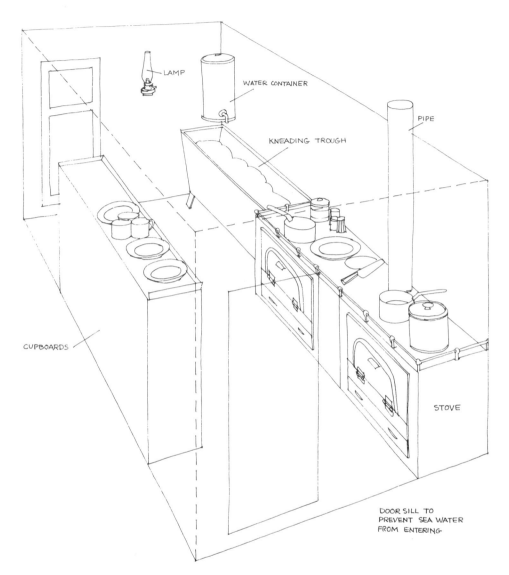

Fig. 53. Nineteenth-Century Galley

Hawkins complained bitterly of "certaine persons, who, before they goe to sea, either robbe part of the provisions, or in the buying, make penurious unholsome, and avaritious penny-worths."[16]

One Dutch ship was "short in each meat-barrel by forty, fifty, and sixty pounds of meat."[17] Culpable carelessness was sometimes charged: "the villian Cooper, had so ill prepared the Casks, that one third of our whole Stock was lost."[18] Barlow complained that his purser in the *Augustaine* "never buyeth that which His Majesty alloweth, but always buyeth the worst and putteth the rest of the money into his own pocket."[19]

This problem had not been solved by the twentieth century:

... we quickly discovered that our box of oranges had at some time been frozen; that our box of apples was mushy and spoiling; that the crate of cabbages, spoiled before it was ever delivered to us, had to go overboard instanter; that kerosene had been spilled on the carrots, and that the turnips were woody and the beets rotten, while the kindling was dead wood that wouldn't burn, and the coal, delivered in rotten potato-sacks, had spilled all over the deck and was washing through the scuppers.[20]

Nor was corruption confined to Europeans supplying Pacific ships—it could also be the other way around. In China, Anson complained bitterly about ducks fed with stones, and pigs heavily watered so that they would weigh more when sold.[21] At least one modern yacht avoided this problem of supply corruption in a very special way: "We had our own bottled and tinned meat from the farm in Canada, and bottled venison, as well as various other brands of tinned meat and tongue. We still had some salami sausage left, and all kinds of tinned vegetables. We had our own bottled plums, and our own tinned pears and apples."[22]

One early major difficulty was the Admiralty rule, comprehensible although shortsighted, that the oldest provisions must be supplied first. As a result, ships seldom got new curings of salt meat. Barlow thought himself hard done by one Christmas, "for we had nothing but a little bit of Irish beef for four men, which had lain in pickle two or three years and was as rusty as the Devil."[23] In spite of all this, Barlow thought Navy ships were better provided than merchant vessels. Cook said it was generally held among naval officers that "no stores are equal in goodness to those of the Crown and that no ships are found like those of the Navy,"[24] but he, himself, did not agree with this opinion. It seems a sad commentary on private enterprise, whether the discussion centres on food, like Barlow's, or on rigging, like Cook's.

Cook took a lively interest in food preservation as he did in everything affecting the health of his men. With this type of man, an interest led to both thought and action. He developed a method of salting pork which worked even in the tropics. Vancouver, Meares, and Bishop all followed his procedure with success, and acknowledged its merits gratefully.

Preserving food so that it would stay edible during long tropical voyages was a major problem not solved until forty years after Cook's voyage, near the end of the Napoleonic wars, when canned bully beef was first issued to the British channel fleet. Just as the meat was adopted and adapted from a French recipe for "bœuf bouilli," so was its name "bully beef" adapted and adopted. There was also the variant name, "Sweet Fanny Adams," allegedly from a prostitute murdered and chopped into fine pieces and said to have been provided as service rations. Whatever the promise of liveliness implied by that name, the arrival of "Sweet Fanny Adams" did not mean the end of monotony in food at sea.

Ships of other nations were usually more particular about their cooks than were the British—although complaints are not wanting in other literatures of the sea. By nature of the conditions and the food available, it was a difficult enough job, but to go further and reserve the position for "such cripples and maimed persons as are pensioners of the chest at Chatham," as the Royal Navy did in 1704, was surely carrying parsimony to the limit.[25] Even in the twentieth century in the *Cap Pilar*, Seligman found that cooking "in a small galley at sea, is an experience so heart-breaking that no one who has not actually tried it can possibly understand . . . holding a frying pan with one hand, trying to stir a pot with the other."[26] It is no wonder that drunkenness was a chronic problem with cooks, "a pattern which recurs with astonishing frequency."[27] One wonders whether they were good men frustrated, or just ne'er-do-wells posted to the least regarded position. In one ship, the drunken cook attacked the mate with a knife. Naturally, it was not always this way around—in the *Arend*, a drunken sailor tried to knife the cook—a much more natural consummation.

The cook in the *Endeavour* only had one hand. He did quite well in spite of his handicap, coping successfully with a succession of bizarre foods, and putting up with the constant supervision of a captain who was determined that his men would not lose their health because of any neglect by his officers or his specialists. The *Adventure*, the consort on Cook's second voyage, was not so fortunate. Her cook died of scurvy, "being so ver(y) indolent & dirtily inclined there was no possability of making him keep himself clean."[28]

There had not always been this unconcern for cleanliness and good cooking in British service kitchens. In 1612, cooks in ships on an English expedition to the East Indies were told firmly, in the commander's instructions, to ". . . be carefull yow have your vittualles well seasoned, both flesh and fishe, and that yt be provided in dewe tyme . . . that yow have a speciall care to keep your steeppstubs sweet and cleane, together with the furnace, kettles, pottes, and platters. . . . Faille not heereof, as yow will answeer yt, by sitting in the bilbowes 24 houres with bread and water."[29] This mandate and threat certainly seem to recognize the importance of cooking.

Anson also recognized it, but in another way, by taking a French cook with him only to lose him as a prisoner to the Indians in Mexico. One hopes they appreciated him, even though that appreciation might have crossed the national lines of conventional taste. Rose de Freycinet loved the puddings she was given at Sydney and aroused the indignation of the *Uranie*'s cook by suggesting that he learn how to make them. He refused indignantly, "saying that a French cook had nothing to learn from an English one."[30] Mme. de Freycinet was not convinced, but neither did she get her English puddings.

When dull monotony seems so much the rule at table on board that people wish for English puddings, a shipwreck could change attitudes dramatically. Shipwrecked scientists, like shipwrecked mariners, had to eat, and Steller, of the shipwrecked Russian ship *St. Peter*, made some comments on food which were as pungent as his comments on his companions. During the previous winter, the ship's company had lived on fish, reindeer meat, and a half ration of bread—luxurious fare in retrospect. But after the shipwreck in the following autumn, the "main means of sustenance" were sea otter flesh ("very tough and consists mostly of sinews") and sea otter entrails, which were, at least, tender.[31] Fermented rye flour fried in whale oil was all they had for bread. They loathed fur-seal flesh "because it has a very strong and very unpleasant smell, more or less like that of an old goat," and they gagged over the flesh of other types of seal, because it was "coal-black."[32]

There were some dishes more pleasant: spring herbs, ptarmigan, young sea lions of "peerless" taste, and, finally, the sea cow and her young. Steller remarked that the meat of the "sea-calf" was like veal, that of the cow "not to be distinguished from beef," and also that the meat would keep for two weeks in the open air, even in the summer. In addition to these remarkable virtues, the fat was a good substitute for butter, and the rendered oil of such "exceptionally good flavour and nourishment that we drank it by the cupful."[33] Steller discussed the animals at length; they are still called "Steller's sea cows," for he was the only scientist who saw and described them. Twenty-seven years later, they were extinct, as a result both of their tastiness and of men's stupidity.

The weak survivors of the shipwreck found sea cows hard to capture, not because of wildness but because of their tremendous strength and bulk. Attempts to capture them with iron hooks were replaced by harpooning from the repaired yawl, exactly as in whaling. Macgillivray, the scientist with the *Rattlesnake*—a very agreeable man as well as a capable scientist—described a similar technique for harpooning the dugong, a close relative of Steller's sea cow, from a canoe near Cape York in Australia. He said dugongs were a "favorite article of food," the blubber being "the most delicate part."[34] Over a century later, the crew of the *Golden Lotus* found that "it tasted like the most tender beef with a delicate oyster flavour."[35] Oddly enough, the meat of the dugong was considered excellent fare for people suffering from pulmonary disease. Dampier lauded the eating qualities of the manatee, another close relative of the dugong and the sea cow. After all this, it seems anticlimactic to record that the dugong and the manatee are said to be the original mermaids. Presumably, this legend grew because of the way in which they suckle their young, held to the breast while floating on the sea—not because they were a source of savoury food.

Sea cow flesh provided food for the return voyage of Steller and his fellow survivors. There was plenty of it; the flesh from one sea cow would feed fifty men for more than two weeks. Its keeping qualities meant that a great deal could be eaten while still fresh, and several barrels were salted down successfully for the return to Kamchatka. Salt "sea-beef," if such it may be called, was one of the more pleasant preserved foods the Russians encountered or developed during their voyages in the North Pacific. Their salted fish and dried fish were familiar to West Europeans, but the salt reindeer and salt geese were not. Bechervaise, veteran of British naval messes, enjoyed Russian beef flavoured from grazing on wild garlic. (Wild garlic was also salted down in barrels, and was considered to be anti-scorbutic as well as an excellent additional savoury spice. Krusenstern thought garlic water an appetizing beverage and picked up three barrels for his ship.)

Polar bears are excellent meat—as good as beef, especially garlic-flavoured beef. Vancouver's crew thought so, and even ate with appreciation the un-digested seahorse (a kind of seal) found in the stomach of one of them. Young black bear, too, is good to eat; the ship's company of the *Ruby* found "the Flesh of it Eating like venison" and, a little earlier, one of Cook's sailors had thought bear meat a "most delicate food."[36]

In the North Pacific, ships' crews got deer and reindeer meat as well as bear. Drake had noticed, and his chaplain had noted, that the further north his ship went from the equator, the hungrier his men became. Barlow also discussed this point. Provisioning for high-latitude voyages required differ-ent calculations of amounts and types of food. Real hunger had to be satisfied in the distant north or south. Palates were tempted by some northern food. Moose was a favourite: "its nose, properly stewed down, is a great luxury; better to my mind than the other extremity of the beaver, its tail, which is everywhere considered something specially delicious."[37]

In the Pacific, with such a range of climate and landform, sailors and sur-vivors ate many meats. To the officers of the *San Pedrico*, the Solomon Islands castor "was like venison" and, across the ocean, buccaneers often ate monkeys and thought them "sweet and wholesome food."[38] Cats on Juan Fernández were roasted as a change from the wild kid or from seals' "livers & hearts. . . . No other part is considered eatable."[39] To one traveller, any meat seemed gustful "when cooked by a bluejacket, whom I will back against many *chefs* to make strange eatables palatable."[40] Nonetheless, "strange eatables" seemed better when men had been at sea a long time. As Cook's successor once said, "we have not yet eat Salt Beef enough to give a Zest to these good things, which sometime hence we shall have a much better relish for."[41]

Food, such as bear, moose, or cat were comparatively conventional. The *Speedwell's* crew happily ate armadillo. One sailor in Funnel's ship claimed that iguanas made a person sick unless they were very well boiled, although Wafer and Dampier had praised "*guano*" meat, and other sailors had acclaimed it as being like a combination of good chicken and good fish. It is true that persons could get sick from eating lizards. In the North Pacific, a barrel of Smithsonian specimens was surreptitiously broached for its alcohol; once drunk, and "visibly affected thereby," the men, "feeling hungry, went on to eat the lizards, snakes and fish. . . . Science was avenged in the result."[42] However, freshly-caught sea snakes were supposedly very palatable and Dutch sailors of the *Zeeland* enjoyed eating an eleven-foot serpent. Starving or desperately thirsty men will try things that normally would cause revulsion; some seamen, after drinking turtles' blood when very thirsty, became violently sick. More desperate (or perhaps less sensitive) men from the *Centurion* had not suffered any penalty for doing the same thing.

There is disagreement about alligators and crocodiles as food; men in the *Rattler* and *Roebuck* ate them, but most writers say that the musk made them inedible. Crayfish were lauded, and the crew of the *Golden Hind* liked the land crabs "of exceeding bignesse, one whereof was sufficient for 4 hungry stomacks at a dinner, beeing also very good, and restoring meate."[43] Dampier also liked the crabs, but Seligman, stopping at Tahuata, described them as "huge, bloated and disgusting, looking like a lot of crawling skulls."[44] This was not simply an objection to crabs, for on another "evening we went out in the dory to catch the little brown crabs which were scuttling about the surface of the sea."[45]

Drake did not mention eating the bats he saw which were "as bigge as large hennes," but, in the same general area, the naturalist in the *Rattlesnake*—perhaps having read Hakluyt—said later that "the flesh of these large bats is reported excellent; it is a favourite food with the natives."[46] The *San Pedrico* found "some snails, each about two handfuls . . . excellent food."[47] Bats, crabs, snakes, snails, crocodiles: at best, they were delectable, at worst, they were interesting. Perhaps modern sailors should try them. Knox-Johnston came to the Pacific with his *Suhaili* too late for such titbits: "I relied far too much upon basics like bully beef and tinned vegetables . . . and for several months ate less than I ought to have done through sheer lack of interest."[48]

Russian recipes using local Pacific foods were adventurous, and often very toothsome. *Burda* was fermented rye-flour boiled as a soup, sometimes with whale oil.[49] *Saturnan* (flour fried in butter stirred with tea until creamy) was a Siberian drink, but was adapted in Kamchatka for Waxell's guests as rye-flour fried in whale oil and stirred with crakeberry tea. Apparently, it made everyone "quite gay and cheerful."[50] Cook was given an excellent salmon pie by the Russians, but Vancouver was not happy with cranberries in whale oil. Another sailor did not mind "berries in oil which they eat with spoons as in our country we do berries and milk."[51]

It is a pity that Sir Joseph Banks, who appreciated exotic fish dishes, did not sail the North Pacific where the Russian cooks offered ". . . some boil'd Halibut; round the bowl on the table was laid thick slices of boild whale, two bowls of the Juice of the large blue berry's. . . . The whale & halibut are eat together and with every two or three mouthfuls they take a spoonful of the berry juice."[52] Russian cooks had "the art to make indifferent things palatable . . . they made a kind of Pan-pudding of Salmon roe beat up fine and fryed that is no bad succedaneum for bread."[53] However, Ledyard complained that some Russian food gave "a composition of smells very offensive at nine or ten in the morning."[54]

Considering the sub-arctic area in which the Russians were living and the resulting difficulty in getting a variety of foods, their recipes sound little worse than some served in ships at sea. On occasion, Lubbock ate biscuit dust and molasses cooked as pudding. Karlsson and his shipmates in the *Herzogin Cecilie* "filled ourselves with pea soup until we could hold no more," because the rest of the time "there was porridge made from mouldy oats, rice and curry containing a few gristly sinews, stockfish that had seen better days, and diseased potatoes."[55]

Similar complaints about cooking and food enliven nearly every journal. Slocum's narrative of his single-handed voyage was an exception: "I found no fault with the cook, and it was the rule of the voyage that the cook found no fault with me."[56] On the other hand, he had to put up with the same cook for the whole voyage, whereas in Seligman's ship the cook was changed every week, so that "being sworn at by the forecastle" could be evenly distributed.[57] People on other ships simply became philosophical; in the *Tzu Hang*, "burnt toast is the hallmark of Beryl's wonderful breakfasts."[58] The ability to honestly link the words "burnt toast" and "wonderful breakfast" is surely the hallmark of philosophy.

Long's ketch had a Polynesian crew member who amazed the rest "at the way he prepared many shellfish and berries that they had never eaten."[59] Creating interesting dishes from the dull preserved foods on board was a challenge which most cooks failed to meet. Recipes, such as "biscuit pounded fine, salt beef cut into small pieces, and a few potatoes, boiled up together, and seasoned with pepper," tried to do so.[60] So did a more modern one: "Three-parts of ship's biscuits to one part of corned beef, very finely minced, judiciously seasoned and then frozen, makes a most excellent substitute for sausage."[61] In many ships, there was lapscouse: "mashed potatoes and turnip, with chunks of salt beef left over from the midday meal, onion and carrot, all mixed together."[62]

But if fresh food were available, the cooks could dare further. Whale brain fritters, young gannets "boiled with pickled porke," turtle soup made with wine, baked native pig stuffed with yams, penguin stewed together with salt beef and gruel and seasoned with vinegar, turtle guts stuffed with the yolks of turtle eggs and dried as sausage, braised horse flesh, green sea turtle curry with rice: all these exotic dishes made the most of what was available. But surely special mention is due to the *Rattler*'s sausages made from turtle meat and port wine.

The sailors and officers of the *Resolution* approved of porpoise meat: "the Harslet and lean flesh was to us a feast."[63] As both Bligh and Henry VIII liked it, the maligned captain and the great king are linked by more than Charles Laughton. Henry ate it with a kingly sauce of breadcrumbs, sugar, vinegar, and mint. Not every hungry sailor would agree with Bligh about porpoise, but they might agree with Henry if they tried his recipe. One early writer said that porpoise meat was "of a very hard digestion, noysome to the stomack, and of very grosse, excremental and naughty juyce."[64] If this be so, it is hard to imagine anyone eating it—much less liking it, but then Bligh and Henry seldom refused a challenge.

Wild poultry took exotic forms at times; "a Dish of Flamingo's Tongues being fit for a Prince's Table,"[65] proclaimed Dampier, while "ostriches thighs . . . in bignes equall to reasonable legs of mutton" found favour in the *Golden Hind*.[66] Not as well favoured in a modern ship was the *titi*, a mutton bird, "the taste of it likened to the smell of a blown-out oil lamp."[67]

As one would expect of cooks sailing on the world's greatest ocean, fish recipes are legion. Fish soup made with coconut water and eaten with fish and yams delighted Cook, who was certainly no gourmet. Banks savoured "a sauce made of the kernels of cocoanuts fermented until they dissolve into a buttery paste, and beaten up with salt water. . . . I should almost prefer it to our own sauces with fish."[68] Jelly made from boiled fish heads, sea eggs, sturgeon, sharks' tails, squid, dried salt ray, may be compared—in Banks's imagination—with "one of the best soups I ever ate," made from a dead cuttlefish much "pulled to pieces by the birds."[69] He also liked stingray tripe, "with a dish of the boiled leaves of *Tetragonia cornuta*," and approved heartily of kangaroo.[70] Sir Joseph either had catholic taste or else he was, most creditably, determined to accept things as they came.

The most intriguing of all the fish dishes is a very modern one. In the trimaran *Gallinule*, lime cordial, mistaken for cooking oil, was used to fry fish; "the result was quite delicious."[71] This was twentieth-century luxury; conditions were usually rougher in earlier days. The survivors in the *Essex's* whaleboats ate small clams from the boat's bottom before they began to think seriously of eating one another. Sometimes, there was not even that choice. Hayter, alone in his yacht in the early 1950's, enjoyed eating shellfish from the yacht's bottom: "Boiled with a dash of soya bean sauce they were delicious and also proved to be very sustaining."[72]

Fresh fish, in theory at least, was always a possibility at sea. In practice, it did not work out that way. Ships were encouraged to supplement their supplies of food by fishing, even if no one had scurvy, and hooks, lines, and nets were provided for that purpose. During the *Dolphin's* first voyage, Byron complained that no fish followed the ship *"which must be owing to our being sheathed with Copper,"* adding that they could see plenty a short distance away. This agrees with Slocum's dictum that "fishes will always follow a foul ship."[73]

The Dutch in the *Heemskerck* sent out her boats with nets, but most of the fish were caught by hook and line from the ship. There were voyages in which for some reason no fish were caught, and some of these fishless voyages took place long before there were copper bottoms on the ships. By contrast, tuna followed a French ship all the way from Easter Island to Hawaii, and "provided a complete ration for the crews almost every day for a month and a half."[74] In the North Pacific, exploration crews found salmon extremely easy to catch; La Pérouse's boats were filled when "sailors, using sticks, killed five thousand two hundred fish in an hour."[75] In any case, salmon was easy to buy on the northwest coast of America, either fresh or dried.

Naturally, fish was the most plentiful North Pacific food, and the most interesting way of preserving it was the making of "appan" by the Kamchatkans. Masses of live fish were thrown into deep pits in the ground, covered as a protection against the foxes, and then left to become "a gelatinous mass," a kind of fish sauerkraut or silage. Waxell could smell the pits from a quarter of a mile away and, needless to say, never ate the product, although he said that some Russians did.

Fat from certain fish was used as butter the whole year round, sometimes on the raw dried salmon which was used as a substitute for bread. Natives of Kamchatka ate the soft under-bark of the birch tree, spread with dried fish

Plate 48. The galley of the whaleship *Charles W. Morgan*. Considering the number of men needed to work a ship in the days of sail, ships' galleys were extremely small. On whaleships like the *Charles W. Morgan* this problem was particularly acute because of the extra men required to man the whaleboats.

Plate 49. "Dinner in an East Indiaman." This East Indiaman's passengers are not enjoying their "movable feast." The dining room is a large stern cabin, well windowed and comfortable although, even in 1818, the diners must eat beside guns. Apparently such disorder at dinner was not uncommon off

Plate 50. A splendid dinner table set attractively in the main saloon under the long poop of the *Macquarie*. The table is built around the mizzen mast. Note the free-swinging oil lamps and wine glasses—important for giving light and lightheartedness on the many repetitive days and nights of long colonial clipper voyages in the Pacific.

Plate 51. H.M.S. *Resolution*. Captain Cook's *Resolution* made two magnificent voyages round the world. It stitched the Pacific together, braving Antarctic and Arctic ice, anchoring in New Zealand, Hawaiian, and British Columbian bays, visiting Australia, Easter Island, Siberia, and China.

roe, as if it were biscuit and caviar. Fish in various guises, some almost unbelievable, was a food that was said to be anti-scorbutic and was known to be
nourishing. Dried and salted fish was staple fare, like meat, with the advantage that fish could follow a ship and animals could not.

New ways of eating fish were tried by the more adventurous. Banks learned
to eat raw fish with breadfruit; and found "it agreed as well as if dressed."[76]
Raw fish seems reasonable enough when it is remembered that oysters are
commonly eaten uncooked. Before they reached cannibalism in the boat of
the whale-smashed *Essex*, the sailors ate live flying fish.[77] Slocum and Heyerdahl did not eat flying fish raw, but they were able to catch them without the
effort of pursuit—the flying fish flew on board both their craft.[78] When a
large bonito jumped into Gerbault's yacht, he ate it, after giving thanks that
sharks did not jump in the same way.[79]

In the *Swallow*, three sharks were divided "between the officers & men all
alike."[80] In the *Discovery*, during Cook's last voyage, there was a subtle
difference in the division. A shark was caught just before she gave birth to
six young ones, so the babies were given to the officers and the mother to
the men. Soon after this, another shark was caught and the entrails went
to the officers and the body to the men, presumably with the assumption that
tougher men need tougher meat. (Baby sharks and entrails were not the
only thing of use found inside sharks; a prayer book was once returned to a
ship via a shark's stomach.) However, no one appeared to be very enthusiastic
about shark meat. One officer gave it very faint praise: "When fryed, it is
tolerable meat; but the fat is very loathsome."[81] Perhaps Ward in the
Charlotte Jane described it best; shark "smelt savoury but looked dangerous."[82]
Apparently, brown sharks are not edible—at least they were never eaten.
When one ship nearing New Zealand caught one, the sailors refused to touch
it; however, they did accept the advice of a Maori crew member to keep the
shark's meat as titbit presents for the Maori girls.[83]

Sunfish are much better eating, described as being "exactly like the Claws
of a Crab or lobster"; another "very sweet and luscious" fish dish is the
smoked eel of New Zealand.[84] Bonito brought mixed reports; one sailor called
it "coarse," but "very welcome on a hungry 'lime-juicer.' "[85] Stingrays were
often caught and eaten, apparently without much enjoyment by anyone. It
seemed "abominably coarse" to Banks, and his taste was far ranging.

An even more exotic seafood was the ugly sea squirt which Banks claimed
was "by no means to be despised by a hungry man."[86] Catfish, almost as
ugly, were found at the river mouths of Central America; they were thought
to be passable if caught young enough. Yellowtail, snooks, and jewfish were
perfectly edible, and there were other fish that early explorers did not recognize

—such as those "marked grey on white like grains of mustard," which Prado of the *San Pedro y Pablo* called *morena*, because it somewhat resembled a Spanish fish. Many varieties of fish were quite recognizable to Europeans; Cook's crew caught mullet, "macharel" and "cod and holybut."

Huge clams containing two pounds of meat apiece helped supply the *Endeavour* on the east coast of Australia and later the *Tartar Galley* near New Guinea. In New Zealand, Cook's ship got "lobsters which were allow'd by every body to be the best they ever had eat," and, across the Pacific to the east, the buccaneer *Trinidad* found both crayfish and lobsters "in abundance" at Juan Fernández.[87] Oysters were appreciated too. The same Captain Winter who had found the value of Winter's bark fed his crew of the *Elizabeth* with "very great muscles (some being 20 inches long)."[88] After him, all ships that came through the Magellan Straits feasted on the variety of shellfish to be found there. (Pearls were sometimes found in the oysters, but there are no reports of any of value, although perhaps this does not prove that none of value were found.) These shellfish saved many crews from starvation, and several types were very appetising. With them, even more than with meat or ordinary fish, the problem was preservation. Clams and oysters did not fit into the rather short list of foods that could be stored and carried.

Seafood, whether in emergency or as standard fare, must be supplemented by a carbohydrate or it very soon becomes boring. Breadfruit was the substitute for bread wherever sailors could get it in the Pacific. Yams had a definite value as an anti-scorbutic, keeping both Mendaña's and Quirós's Spanish voyages relatively free of scurvy. One particular species of yam root was sometimes "so large that one man alone could not manage it."[89] Other roots served the same purposes. In California, the Indians gave the sailors some roots which "taste exactly like the Roots of our English Burdock boil'd," and in New Zealand fern roots and sweet potatoes were basic foods.[90] The "root of a species of lilly" was used for bread in the north, and Nootka Sound Indians used "fibrous roots which they eat with oil [and] these appear to be the roots of clover and other grass and are by no means unpalatable."[91]

Bread of a sort, usually hardtack biscuit, was the main carbohydrate. There were oatmeal and peas for "burgoo" or porridge, but the sailors wanted bread, and prized it. On his first voyage, Cook had thought some damage to bread in casks was due to the "casks being wet when the Ship was a shore upon the rocks."[92] Whatever the reason for the damage, the coopers were kept busy opening and resealing casks as well as setting them up or taking them apart. Material in casks was occasionally examined and aired (gunpowder especially), and when there was damage the contents were salvaged, if possible. Lind suggested a method of sieving the vermin from oat-meal, peas, and flour, knowing and regretting that the contaminated food would still have to be eaten. There were some attempts to be philosophical (or facetious) about it. When Morton complained in the *Beeswing* that "the biscuits were full of maggots," the captain replied, "You are getting fresh meat with your biscuits."[93] It is said that some sailors refused to eat biscuit which had no vermin on the grounds that they would not eat biscuit which even the weevils refused.

Banks asserted that his ship's biscuit was infested with five different kinds of vermin, hundreds or thousands of them in a single biscuit, adding a flavour as strong as mustard. To fight them, rooms were cleaned, heated, and fumigated, but without much long-term success; they could be driven out by baking, but this was not possible to do for the entire ship's company. Not all the problems are solved even now. In the 1930's, Seligman had just as much trouble keeping macaroni sound as Cook had had with biscuit in the 1770's. In fact, he said that "the remedy was to serve 'George's mess' only in the evening, when the livestock passed unnoticed."[94]

The French baked bread on board their ships, but the British did not. Vancouver argued that bread could safely have been baked at sea if it had been attempted and, he might have added, if the Admiralty had cared enough. It was often done on a small scale for captains and, by the end of the late nineteenth century, British merchant ships sometimes baked "soft tack," or bread, when sea conditions allowed.[95] Many ships had an oven with them; Cook mentioned having one in both the *Resolution* and *Adventure*, "but this [baking] can only be done a shore."[96] Broughton had a copper oven in his ship too, but used it only on land. That seems to have been standard British practice.

Unground wheat kept better than flour, so the French overcame a major problem by carrying their grinding facilities with them in the ship and making fresh flour each day. In the *Astrolabe*, La Pérouse used little windmills (later turned by hand) to grind good flour for the bread baked on board. In one wheat ship, the crew ground grain from the hold in a coffee grinder for frying in rancid salt meat fat. In his ketch, Long carried wheat in an airtight tin with a carbide fume device to keep it fresh to be ground and boiled for porridge. Cook also used wheat directly, by boiling it into the old English dish "furmity," so well described in Hardy's *The Mayor of Caster-bridge*.

British crews, conservative in most ways and especially so about food, were happy with wheat and wheat flour and unhappy with the rye flour they got from the Russians in the North Pacific. Barlow said his crew was not pleased when they were forced to accept farina as a substitute for ship's biscuit, damning it as "stuff not much unlike sawdust of some white wood, having no taste but of a dry piece of stick."[97] French sailors, perhaps not so conservative—or else not so discriminating—were happy to accept bread-fruit sliced thin and baked dry into a biscuit which would keep "very much better than does our ships' biscuit."[98] Perhaps they were right. A Spanish sailor commended breadfruit: "It was roasted on board ship and it seemed very good. It tasted like baked chestnuts."[99] It would almost certainly have tasted better than the bread which was baked for the crew of the French corvette *Uranie*, after her shipwreck, from the flour used by her chaplain to powder his hair. Apart from such unusual emergencies, French sailors remained French, even in the Pacific, and the complaint that no one presented an acceptable sauce with the food was not uncommon.

The French were right, for there is no doubt that acceptable sauces would have made the over-preserved meats and the verminous or tasteless carbohydrates more palatable. That is what sauces are for. Rum and brandy performed a parallel service for the drinking water. It is often forgotten that the serving of "grog," a mixture of rum and water, was not designed merely to give a ration of alcohol, but was also meant to help make the water bearable. Bad water was a problem, but an even greater one was the shortage of any kind of water, good or bad. A heavy drain on the water supply of early ships was the livestock that many of them carried, usually as a source of fresh meat, although some stock was also carried to introduce useful animals to the Pacific islands. Because of their speedy passages, clippers usually could be generous with water for passengers and crew in a way that lesser ships could not. The relationship was between the water needs of the ship (men and livestock) and the length of the passage. Early ships were at a disadvantage in every way. They carried livestock because food preservation was an undeveloped science; they had large crews because rigging was not yet simplified; and they were slow.

Preserving fresh water was as difficult as preserving food and, as to be expected, many ideas were advanced, machines invented, and methods tried. Most of the methods, whether for salting pork or purifying water, had to be learned under the conditions of the voyages themselves, and many machines and techniques which had seemed so promising under English conditions did not meet the requirements set by the Pacific. Experiments went on. In 1765, Captain Byron was given command of the "true frigate" *Dolphin* for a voyage of exploration to the South Seas. Byron was an interesting man and as a midshipman had already survived to write about the wreck of the *Wager*, the subsequent dissension and hardships on shore, and his three years in a Spanish prison. His ship was given a consort, named *Tamar*, one of the most beautiful and famous of English ship names.

On board the two ships were experimental machines for making water fresh, or at least palatable, after it had been stored for long periods in casks. Air was circulated through the water to replace oxygen lost during storage. The machines operated on exactly the principle (re-oxygenation) that, in Canada, dictates pumping air to clarify water tainted and discoloured after ice has sealed the reservoirs for several months. Byron used the machine and he "*found it* [to] *answer very well.*" So did Wallis and Cook on later voyages.[100]

If some way could have been found to keep the water sweet in the casks, tanks, or other containers, it would have been an important discovery. Polynesians and Indonesians carried water in their canoes in bamboos, but I have found no discussion regarding how well it kept. The surgeon in the *St. George* advised the men to leave chickweed in the water when filling the casks, as this would preserve it. [101] At this particular watering place, the crew was able to use a canvas pipeline to fill their casks on board—an oddly modern touch. In 1770, Dr. Trotter, then surgeon of H.M.S. *Duke* (the Atlantic *Duke*, not the Pacific privateer *Duke*) found a way "to preserve water pure and sweet for any length of time" by charring the inside of the casks.[102] Like the pipeline mentioned above, this also has a modern ring to it for carbon is used today to absorb certain chemicals in many forms of gas and water purifiers.

In most ships, efforts were made to collect rainwater by using sails, as the Spaniards had done in the *San Pedro y Pablo*, funnelling the water into jars. This was a standard procedure in the Manila Galleon, and one so widely known that the awnings and other devices used for water collection gave her rigging such an odd appearance that she was recognizable at a distance. Carteret's British ship collected water with an awning he had constructed both for that purpose and for shelter. Cook caught rainwater in the *Resolution* and, as "we could get more by the rain in an hour than by the still in a Month, I laid it aside as a thing attended with more trouble than profit."[103] One of his sailors, however, objected to the colouring and taste of tar which was characteristic of rainwater collected in sailcloth on board a ship. Some modern yachts have such efficient collection systems that they need not take water from shore for a year or more.

Often the water available on shore for refilling the casks of the early ships was not good, and occasionally ships would encounter an uninhabited coral atoll which had no water supply at all. One crew could find no water, and the sailors had to chew green leaves; the crewmen of the *Rattler* watched a bird squeeze water from a berry into the mouth of its chick, and learned to quench their thirst in the same way. Others copied the land tortoises of Galapagos in eating the damp inner bark of trees. Although usually there would be water of a sort, there must have been many fevers and much dysentery as the result of drinking poor water. One ship could obtain nothing but water so stinking with alligator musk as to be practically undrinkable. Dampier once gained water for the *Roebuck* by digging a sand well in the beach, but found the water so unattractive that the ship used it only for porridge. An upsurge of scurvy cases made him regret that he had done even that.[104]

Like the *Roebuck*, every ship filled her casks at any place where it was at all possible to get fresh water. It was important for morale that the men be able to drink from the open cask of water—the Scuttle-Cask or Scuttle-butt—which stood on the quarterdeck. "Scuttlebutt" became the name for ships' gossip; this cask was the office water fountain, or coffee machine, of yesterday.

Entire crews have been known to die at sea from lack of water; for example, that of the barque *Craigmullen* which ran out of water between the Philippines and Taiwan.[105] In her case, only the first and second mates survived. A ship's crew, according to Dr. Lewis of the *Rehu Moana*, needs a great deal of water; an estimate for a modern yacht cruise in the Pacific is one gallon per person per day. (Knox-Johnston points out that alcohol is a dehydrant and should be used with care. In effect, it is not a substitute for water, but a drug which will cause a desire for more water. It is an interesting argument against the issue of grog not found in the early literature.)

Many ships, besides Cook's *Resolution*, carried stills to distill fresh water from the sea; not all rejected them in favour of collecting rainwater as Cook had done. Hawkins claimed such success in the *Daintie* that he "easily drew out of the water of the sea, sufficient quantitie of fresh water . . . wholesome and nourishing."[106] It must have been the same kind of device, using the ships' cooking coppers, that Cook carried later, but spoke about with less enthusiasm. Hawkins said that "with foure billets [of wood] I stilled a hogshead of water, and therewith dressed the meat for the sicke and whole."[107] If so, it is a pity that, just as with his comments about lemons and oranges, so little seems to have developed from these ideas of Hawkins.

The French in the *St. Jean Baptiste* had a machine for distilling water; Quirós had one in his ship too. Lind invented a still for use in ships, and explained it very clearly in the second edition of his *Essay on Preserving the Health of Seamen*. Another surgeon, Irving, had invented the type tried in the *Resolution* that seemingly had not been too successful. Today, there are excellent water-producing machines for ships of all sizes.

Sailors objected to the flat taste of distilled water. However, the Austrian frigate *Novara*, sailing the Pacific in the nineteenth century, discovered that if the distilled water were kept in iron tanks for a month it improved in flavour.[108] Some sailors claimed even more: "they say that rusty water is good for the system, being a nerve tonic."[109] Even without steeping in iron, the distilled water made as excellent tea and coffee as could be made from rainwater. Rain allowed Knox-Johnston to have tea as a treat in his ketch, the superb tea that can only be made with pure, soft water. Other soft water was sometimes regarded with suspicion. In the far south, the *Vostok* used melted ice only to make tea or in cooking, having read the scientist Forster's complaint from the *Resolution* that various illnesses had arisen from drinking melted ice directly.[110] Tea is so important to Russians that it is surprising that they would take the chance of spoiling it with poor water.

By the mid-eighteenth century, crewmen were allowed to supply their own beverages and to use water to make them. Tea was not introduced into the Royal Navy rations until 1790. Cocoa had been introduced ten years earlier. Sailors drank a great deal of tea, particularly in the Pacific, where it was the cargo of tea clippers in one corner of the ocean and the staple hot drink of Australia and New Zealand in another. There were few refinements with it on board ship; one can of condensed milk every three weeks was supposed to suffice a windjammer sailor for his tea, coffee, and burgoo as well. One sailor claimed to have "boiled weeds and molasses as a substitute for tea and sugar."[111] In the *Alert*, Dana was given tea made of half a pint of tea and one and a half pints of molasses, all in three gallons of water, stirred up so that each man got his share of molasses and tea leaves. One may question whether they all wanted it. A sailor in a New England whaler described, with American under-statement, molasses "so tarnation sour, we can sweeten it with vinegar" and "so thin, a little water will thicken it."[112] Unfortunately, the idea that water might thicken molasses may be a comment not on the thinness of the molasses, but on the thickness of the water.

By the middle of the nineteenth century, the fast ships with giant iron tanks (the *Lightning*'s would hold 36,000 gallons) had solved the problem of keeping water drinkable even over Pacific distances. Speed had lessened the problem of food preservation as well, and, at the same time, canning had almost solved it. Although not a modern luxury cruise, a voyage in one of the better ships after 1850 could have been taken without fear and—with only a little hardi-ness—for pleasure. But it would be conventional and not, in the culinary sense at least, adventurous pleasure. It was only very occasionally that the cooks adopted a native dish; the sailors were too conservative. In general, the cooks attempted to make the resources of the Pacific as much like the foods of home as possible—they were substitutes, not successors. Coconuts made into "pumpkin pie," the dogs like "English lamb," the gannets made into "goose pye," are all testimonials that food, like music, is a major vehicle of nostalgia.[113]

CHAPTER 20

Animals on Board

. . . our live stock, consisting of four bullocks, a dozen sheep,
a dozen or more pigs, and three or four dozens of poultry,
were all stowed away in their different quarters; the bullocks
in the long-boats, the sheep in a pen on the fore hatch, the pigs
in a sty under the bows of the long-boat, and the poultry in
their proper coop, and the jolly-boat was full of hay for the
sheep and bullocks.

RICHARD DANA
OF THE *ALERT*

Hunger is certainly most excellent sauce; but since we
have no fowls and ducks left, we find ourselves able to eat any
kind of bird (for indeed we throw away none) without even
that kind of seasoning. Fresh provision to a seaman must
always be most acceptable, if he can get over the small preju-
dices which once affected several in this ship, most or all of
whom are now by virtue of good example completely cured.

SIR JOSEPH BANKS
OF THE *ENDEAVOUR*

Pacific sailors needed fresh meat and vegetables. There seemed to be no
way of gardening on any major scale on board ship, although a few captains
and even some midshipmen grew some greens. Meat was a different matter,
because wherever men could go they could take their animals with them.

Given the difficulties of keeping food fit to eat, and the desirability of
some alternatives to the standard fare of biscuit and salt meat, the carrying
of animals on board ship was a natural development. The Polynesians and
Chinese had done so in the Pacific centuries before the Europeans came. Some
of the animals provided milk; some of the birds—and turtles—provided eggs.
All provided meat. This chapter contains an account of the various ways in
which voyagers tried to overcome the dullness of diet and the dangers of
malnutrition by taking animals and birds with them. None of the animals

could be consulted, or matters might have been different, for few of them liked shipboard life. But there were some exceptions even to this; some pigs and pigeons seemed happy enough, and many goats positively thrived. There were others—the pets and the parasites: dogs, cats, and rats sailed the Pacific too, and provided their quotas of exiles or deserters on the various islands. On the other hand, as with fruits and fish, some animals were picked up along the way, almost changing the ships from farmyards into zoos. Llamas, buffaloes, turtles, albatrosses, monkeys, rabbits, swans, penguins, tortoises, lizards—all joined the ships in their travelling and cheered men as much as they nourished them.

Cook's *Endeavour*, one of the Pacific's most famous ships, was a cat—because of her hull type and not her zoological classification. But, cat or ship, she carried an even more famous animal—a milk goat which circumnavigated the world twice without going dry. Feat though this be, there was even more; this nanny lived to retire to a green pasture and to have a Latin verse written about her. Another goat, in another ship, died and for the lack of a Latinist on board, had to make do with an eloquent eulogy in English:

Departed this life our dear freind *Nancy* the *Goat* having been the *Captains* companion on a former voyage round the Globe but her spirited disposition for adventure led her to undertake a 2nd voyage of Circumnavigation; but the various changes of Climate, and sudden transition from the Polar Colds to the tropical heats of the Torrid Zone, prov'd too much for a constitution naturally delicate, At 5 p.m. Committed her body to the deep. She was lamented by those who got a share of her *Milk*!!![1]

On her second voyage, the *Endeavour*'s nanny had to put up with the two greyhounds of Joseph Banks, whom she no doubt regarded with disdain as being both dry and inexperienced landlubbers. Dogs were carried in many ships and were not necessarily ornamental only. Even the aristocratic greyhounds showed their paces in catching specimen animals in Australia. Clifford's modern junk was saved from drifting into cliffs by her dog's growls, and a water spaniel of Dampier's *Roebuck* proved useful in retrieving birds which had been shot. Newfoundland dogs seem to have been favourites, which is natural enough given their gentle disposition, their swimming ability, and their loyalty. This loyalty was not directed solely to men; when Gambier Islanders tried to steal a small dog from an American brig, a Newfoundland successfully prevented them. Far more often, the dogs were companions, usually valued as such to the edge of men's starvation and even beyond—*Don Juan*, Canto II, notwithstanding. When Lord Campbell says that " 'Sam' is now on board—a charming great black curly-haired Newfoundland," it can be seen that it is the charm that he loved, although he valued the strength.[2]

The custom among many peoples of using dogs as food often horrified English sailors, most of whom possessed some of their countrymen's love for the species. But Cook and his men had learned to eat, and liked to eat, dog flesh: "few were there of us but what allowe'd that a South Sea Dog was next to an English Lamb."[3] Banks thought this flavour was due to the dogs' diet: "these in Otahite scarcely in their lives touch animal food."[4] A Spanish officer compared dog flesh to venison and may well have agreed with Banks about the reason for it. It is true that not every Englishman loved every dog. Huxley, with relish, related that in the *Rattlesnake* the captain's dog, weary "of leading a dog's life among the middies, committed suicide."[5] It may have been loneliness, for "the skipper and his dog had this in common, that they liked one another, and were disliked by every one else."[6] Dogs more fortunate (or less neurotic) were distributed by Cook to many islands in the hope that "they may prove the Adam and Eve of their species in this country."[7] Many of these were killed by men with less acquaintance or sympathy with Genesis.

The French historian, Count Fleurieu, opposed the introduction of strange animals to the Pacific islands on the reasonable grounds that the meat they supplied merely encouraged the visits of European ships which harmed the native populations. Most explorers did not agree with him, and so breeding livestock was often carried in Pacific ships from one place to another, as Cook had done with dogs. He also carried some horses to leave as gifts at various islands. Vancouver took cattle from California to Hawaii, because it was thought the Spanish black cattle would do well there. One attempt to take the same breed to New South Wales had failed because all but one cow died on the way. Despite this particular failure, Australia soon had cattle to give away and presented a milch cow and calf to the French corvette *Uranie*, probably as a gesture of gallantry to the captain's wife, Rose de Freycinet.

Cattle could be a nuisance on board ship, since they required bulky hay and much water and often became seasick, although, fortunately for the ships, cows cannot vomit. Seasickness, with its notoriously depressing effect, might explain why some very wild East Indian buffaloes suddenly became tame during their voyage. Buffaloes did not earn a reputation as good voyagers, often dying on board, whereas the usually more docile bullocks were more likely to survive. Cows had feminine unpredictability, and Ward, the diarist of the *Charlotte Jane*, became one of the few men to be tossed by a cow while aboard a ship.[8]

Turtles were the most docile and by far the most convenient of all sailing livestock; besides being excellent to eat, they would live for long periods on board without eating or drinking anything. Some whalers claimed it was possible to keep them alive for a year without eating or drinking, provided they were kept out of the cold; however, there is some disagreement about this. Barlow specifically stated that "they will live on board without victuals or drink four or five and twenty days."[9] Many turtles were caught on shore, but some were harpooned at sea where they were often spotted because of the birds perching on them as they slept on the surface. One smaller variety was fished for in an even more interesting way. A live sucking fish (*Echeneis Remora*), secured by a line passed round the tail, was thrown into the water in suitable places and swam about until it made fast by its sucker to a turtle; then, they were hauled in together.[10]

Some were too big for such handling. One turtle in Barlow's ship supplied enough meat to feed forty or fifty men. In addition, the females often contained two or three hundred eggs and, according to some sailors, these were as enjoyable as the meat: "they did eat very sweetly."[11] Because they did not eat, the turtles made no mess. Even if Barlow's belief in their comparatively brief life were balanced against a number of reports claiming much longer survival, his twenty-five days gave fresh meat for a fairly long voyage between ports. Turtle meat was tasty and healthful food. Sailors in the *Centurion* remained healthy as long as they had plenty of it, their chaplain reported. In many ships, besides using the meat, "the oil saved from them was kept in jars and used instead of butter to eat with dough-boys or dumplings."[12] Anson's chaplain said that the Spaniards would not eat turtle meat, although this seems odd considering the praise the French and English lavish on this food. It was probably their appearance. For example, there are reports that iguanas were so repulsive to look at that no sailor of any nation would eat them, though almost every journal praised their edibility.

Sailors were not often reduced to such creatures for fresh meat, for livestock could be fattened aboard. Shelvocke's ship carried llamas, and they smelled as rank on board as they had done on land. Most of the shipboard animal populations were kept for food. The *Alert* set out from California with enough varieties of livestock to make the ship virtually a modern ark. Some ships were more fastidious than Dana's captain or Noah. The *Uranie*, except for her Australian gifts, did not carry livestock because it needed so much water and feed, and "besides, what a source of uncleanliness and infection in the ship!"[13] Apart from these very practical points, the animals suffered greatly in storms and cold weather, many dying when the ships encountered rough conditions.

Sheep in the *Resolution* contracted what was thought to be scurvy. It certainly sounds as if it might have been—loose teeth, sore mouths, and other classic symptoms. In the *Vostok*, Bellingshausen thought his sheep had scurvy: "their hoofs and gums became blue and swollen." Modern medical scientists say that guinea pigs are the only animals other than men that have been demonstrated to get scurvy, claiming that "other animals apparently, are able to manufacture their own ascorbic acid."[14] Baudin, in the *Géographe* near Australia, would not have agreed. He had scurvy in his ship and "even the domestic animals succumbed to it and some of them, in particular two rabbits and a tufted monkey . . . died."[15] Moreover, the modern scientists were not on board the *Resolution* or the *Vostok* to see the sick sheep (or in the *Géographe* to see the dead monkey) which apparently not only had the same symptoms as men but, like the men, recovered quickly on a diet of fresh vegetation.

Some animals were guests or paying passengers; other were on board as stowaways. Rats were a persistent menace to the ships' food supplies; the fact that they provided fresh meat at times was insufficient compensation. French sailors ate rats in preference to salt meat on occasions and, in at least one English ship, "the gentlemen in the gunroom dined on a fricassee of rats, which they accounted a venison feast."[16] Bougainville, a French gentleman (although the discriminating taste to be inferred from that may have been blunted by his hard military campaigns), "ate some rats, and found them very good."[17] Rats sold for a ducat apiece in some Spanish ships when starvation threatened; this can be easily understood—most reports describe rats as being very good to eat.

Tasty or not, rats were a plague. So much has been heard of their intelligence about their leaving sinking ships and so on—that the ones who gnawed through the bottom planks in the *Resolution* either were suicidal or very dull-witted. The cleverness of rats is evident in their increase and survival under the most diverse of conditions. They survive even in association with men, who certainly do not co-operate in their survival. These vermin adjust to men's poisons, dodge men's blows, spring men's traps, and defy their canine and feline allies. Perhaps there is no other animal, except man himself, who is so adjustable in habit and temperament that it can become, in one and the same university, both a quarry for the exterminators and a playmate for the psychologists.

Cook tried hard to get rid of them, deliberately hauling the *Resolution* "within thirty yards of the Shore" at the island of Moorea near Tahiti. Then his sailors "Got a Hawser out of the Ballast Port with some Spars lash't upon it with a Design to get some of the Rats out of the Ship." Few of them, perhaps the clever ones, left and those who remained showed more confidence in the leaky *Resolution* than many of her men had. Cook did not say whether or not he thought the rats would be a livestock asset to Moorea, noting only that "we got clear of very few if any."[18]

Sailors fought rats constantly and unsuccessfully. In the *Daintie*, the pests began to eat the sails and the sailors' clothing as well as the food, "though we had diverse catts and used other preventions."[19] They were as omnipresent and omnivorous as they were clever. In one ship, they ate the hard skin from the soles of the feet of all the sailors during their sleep and, in only one case, drew blood.[20]

Cats did their best against the rats, and nearly every ship had at least one of these beautiful and useful animals. A midshipman in one of Cook's ships "had a favourite cat who never failed to catch and carry rats to her master: he divided the prey so that the cat had the fore part, and the back part was cleaned, roasted, and peppered for himself."[21] Such a thoughtful cat would be an asset to any ship, guaranteeing at least one sleek midshipman. From journals it is obvious that the companionship cats provide was essential to the sailors; the reminder of home and fireside, firm land, and trees to climb was even more important than pest control. Joseph, the ginger tom cat of the *Joseph Conrad*, had been reared in the ship and used the shrouds and masts as his landlubber ancestors used trees, climbing each morning to the maintop to look downward on the men and outward to the sea. When imperious and lovable Joseph fell overboard, the ship hove-to so that he could be rescued. He may have been merely careless, but it has been said that cats go mad in the tropics. The *Cap Pilar*'s cat would "run along the bulwarks at dizzy angles, shoot up into the rigging and lie in wait between decks."[22] Once she fell off the bowsprit to be saved only by the netting slung beneath, yet she kept on climbing the masts, presumably banking on eight lives more.

The *Cap Pilar* had another pet which kept away from the bowsprit, but from little else—a pig whose favourite sleeping place was the coiled starboard braces. The fat and growing pig had to be moved before the angle of the yards could be changed when the wind shifted. "Denis" had come aboard as a small pink porker with a ribbon on his neck. For some obscure reason, the pigs on board all ships were called "Dennis," and it is evident that the missing second "n" in this particular one's name made little difference. It was not until "he had grown too gross to command our affection" and too heavy to be easily moved off the starboard braces that anyone could face eating him.[23] Pigs often became pets. In the *Garthwray*, the pigs had the freedom of the deck in fine weather, and their Dennis "often went into the saloon aft to pay a visit to Mrs. Frampton and Eva," the captain's wife and daughter.[24]

Pigs were not meant to provide company, however, but fresh pork. To remain fresh they had to survive, and reports about their sea legs are varied. Reports from Cook's ships said that the Hawaiian pigs "die away at an incredible rate" once on board, and that island pigs "die like rotten Sheep as soon as you get to Sea and begin to dance a bit"; yet, in other journals, quite the opposite is recorded.[25] For example, Bligh thought that his hogs were better sailors than the sheep or the poultry. Pigs were fed largely on stale oatmeal, but naturally they shared the few scraps left by a hungry crew; no doubt because of careless feeding, they were subject to intestinal and urinary diseases. Farmers warn against giving brine from meat-curing to pigs, and brine—natural and otherwise—would be plentiful enough on shipboard.

Hunger was a risk for voyaging pigs, as it was for voyaging men, but in the case of the pigs it merely moved forward the date of their slaughter. Their deaths would help both to create food and to save food for the dominant animals in the ship. Far too often, the fresh pork was for the truly dominant of the men on board—the officers—unless a forced slaughter in hot weather made necessary a wider distribution. This made the sailors' protests about the filth and stench caused by the pigs and their sties easier to accept as being justified, because the men had the work and the stench, whereas the officers had the meat. There were hazards as well as delights in the fresh pork from shipboard slaughtering, but "the bouts of diarrhoea did not last long, and I am sure everybody considered that it had been worth it."[26]

Quite often, the longboat, or another large ship's boat, was used as a pig pen, being the handiest natural enclosure. Another enclosure for the pigs while in the Pacific, although just as handy, was definitely more strange. The export of live pigs from Tonga to Samoa was forbidden in order to preserve the market—the Polynesians, generously and genuinely hospitable, have never ignored the basics of commerce. One Samoan successfully smuggled live baby pigs to his home island by enclosing them in the body of a slaughtered pig, ostensibly being taken along as provisions.

At times there were exotic eggs available from shore: herons' eggs, ostriches' eggs, tabons' eggs, and gulls' eggs. Chickens were kept on board to provide more orthodox eggs for the officers' meals in some ships, and for broth for the sick in others. Other birds were kept on board too. One windjammer kept pigeons free to fly out to sea in the daytime, "always returning to their loft on board for the night."[27] Not all the pigeons were so faithful. One whaling captain's wife wrote of meeting the *Rodman*, a whaler, at sea: "they had Pigeons on board and four of them flew on board of us. They are very pretty and my Husband has had a nice house made for them."[28] Journals mention

Guinea hens, English geese, and Australian swans. In the *Bounty*, the ship's crew fattened the wild birds they had captured, to improve both the fleshing and the flavour. Some of the wild birds, however, were almost as convenient to kill as chickens; "stupid old boobies, perching on our yards and boats, were caught and ruthlessly skinned."[29] Hawks, eagles, terns, ducks, woodpeckers, dippers, shags, cranes: all were enjoyed in a catholicity of taste reminiscent of medieval days.

In many ships, albatrosses were caught with a hook or a special triangle on a line and kept aboard for food. Reactions to the flavour varied. No journal is so enthusiastic about them as to make readily credible recent reports from the Chatham Islands of New Zealand that they are being slaughtered by the truckload as delicacies for the islanders. However, the albatrosses were good for more than food: "Scar got the breast plumage, the cook the wing bones for pipe-stems, the nipper and Mac taking the feet for tobacco-pouches."[30] Their giant size—with wingspans up to twelve feet—and their superb airmanship ("They don't fly, they sail") intrigued the sailors, and these qualities are combined with a chaplinesque tragicomic way of doing things which is endearing. Their habit of keeping company with ships links the albatrosses to men at sea in a way shared only by dolphins. Albatrosses could also be kept on board as pets, although rather irritable and snappish ones. Penguins are mentioned in journals as often as albatrosses, for they too have an endearing quality. Sir John Narborough, who led an English fleet into the Pacific on a mission of trade and observation in 1669-71, said that they "stand upright like little Children in white Aprons,"[31] a simile which must have inhibited his appetite for them.

Gradually, with the improvement in preserved foods and greater regularity of calls at new Pacific ports, livestock and birds disappeared from the decks of sailing ships. The pigs seemed quite willing to help in this process, sometimes eating the poultry, sometimes eating their own young. Occasionally, the unfortunate animals on board met death at the same time and in the same way as their masters—in naval battles—just as cavalry horses always shared the risks of their riders. If the destiny of the animals were to become navy beef or pork, being killed in a real slaughterhouse on land rather than in its counterpart, a battle at sea, seems little to be preferred. But at least many cows, bullocks, and pigs were spared the pangs of seasickness.

Actions and Interactions

This section discusses the effects of the responsibilities, dangers, and temptations which burdened men—and women—in ships in the Pacific. Few voyagers in small ships survived long Pacific voyages without undergoing some change in their attitudes or health, or both. The hazards often were as psychological as they were physical, but in either case they were real and they were feared. Captains, mutineers, buccaneers, drunkards, emigrants, convicts, prostitutes, captains' and missionaries' wives, all faced them and, in most cases, outfaced them. When the voyages were over, the relationships of these changed people with the local inhabitants also changed, in turn. Sea life was life with the certainties removed—and uncertainty is a solvent of human behaviour.

CHAPTER 21

Command

*Good mariners grow not up like mushlooms [sic] without care
or culture. It is morally impossible, nay, it is naturally impossible, to have a brave, active, skilful, resolute body of sailors
without just and generous as well as understanding officers.*

BARNABY SLUSH
A SEA COOK TURNED PROJECTOR, 1709

*Captain Thompson gave his directions to the mate in private,
and, except in coming to anchor, getting under way, tacking,
reefing topsails, and other "all-hands-work," seldom appeared
in person. This is the proper state of things; and while this
lasts, and there is a good understanding aft, everything will go
on well.*

RICHARD DANA
OF THE *ALERT*

The ability to command skilfully is rare in most occupations; in an occupation
as complicated as handling large sailing vessels, it is doubly so. To command
acceptably is an ability even more rare, and marks a good captain; to command inspiringly marks a great one. The difference between skill and inspiration is the vital matter of human relationships, and nowhere was this more
evident than in crowded ships on long voyages. Under these conditions,
skilled control from the top was indispensable in physical matters; tactful
control from the top was essential in psychological ones. Nothing—not a
school, a hospital, an army, nor a society—works really effectively without
firm guidance from the men or women in control, in the position of responsibility where both the fame and the blame are centred.

Captains of ships are in this position, but it is made even worse by the
absence of peers, the constant pressures of risk while at sea, the demands of
business when in harbour, and the burden of discipline at all times. Captains
today are both sailors and leaders, but this was not always so; for years the
masters sailed the ships, while the captains led the fighting. Officers who

could do both had as much pride in their skill in seamanship as they had in their power and rank as captains. They paid dearly for this right to feel proud, paid in strain and in loneliness; many broke under the pressures, either in nerve or in health. In the meantime, the way they coped with the pressures and their own emotions affected the lives of all about them.

The skill derived from training and experience, the influence arising from charm and tact, the prestige attaching to a King's Commission, the certainties of an assured social position and rank, aided a commander to success; these are the components of command which must be examined. Leaders who lacked any of these acquirements or abilities had to fall back on the assertion either of ruthless personality or brute strength, or on the sustaining force of the state. Force could work, but never so well nor so permanently as inspirational leadership grounded in a happy combination of the positive virtues. A number of the famous Pacific sailors, by hard work, long study, and constant application built up this combination; this is the reason their names are still recognized.

If a few captains did not win their place fairly, as Barlow complained of the seventeenth-century navy and merchant marine, they all had to retain it in face of the job itself. Influence could win a position for a captain, and so could money, but these could not do the job for him. Training for command was important, although it was not institutionalized nearly so early as was the technical training for pilots. Training ships, specifically to train ships' officers, were not introduced into the Royal Navy until 1857. Such training as existed earlier had been done on board, not unlike a system of apprenticeship, by the serving officers. Theoretical knowledge was imparted in some of the larger ships officially after 1702 (and unofficially in a few earlier cases) by a "Schoolmaster" appointed to teach "the young gentlemen."[1] Aboard American ships the schoolmaster was known as "the professor."

The merchant ships of the more efficient shipping lines trained their own officers: "A boy in the *Hotspur* under Toynbee had little excuse for not turning out a scientific and clever navigator. Every morning at 10 some of his 'mids' had to attend in the cuddy (a cabin in the forepart of a ship) for navigation lessons."[2] It is true that theoretical knowledge was decried by many "practical seamen," but Melville tells of the fine book on naval tactics written by a man who had never been to sea.[3] Melville gives the answer of the intellectual: it is better to think when absent than to be present and not think.

There had to be definite rewards for effort and skill. Rules were gradually laid down, and even more gradually fully obeyed, which created classes of individuals from which higher appointments could be made. Qualifying to become a lieutenant while a midshipman did not make the officer a lieutenant—he had to be appointed to a ship in that capacity. Gradually, these classes of individuals capable of appointment became ranks; the rank of midshipman was held by persons capable of serving as midshipmen and therefore available to be appointed as lieutenants; the rank of lieutenant was held by persons capable of serving as lieutenants and, theoretically, capable of taking over as captains. In fact, the name "lieutenant" means literally "to hold instead of," or more accurately, "to take the place of," that is, to act as the captain in the captain's absence and to succeed him in the case of death, just as the words "captain" and "caput" mean "the head."

The duties of the captains (and their lieutenants) were to lead the fighting and to command, which are the reasons why the names of their ranks are military. From the beginning of sea fighting, soldiers—men of the ruling class on land—were given these posts, and it was not until the nineteenth century that the two tiers of officers were completely merged into the professional naval officer, trained from the beginning of his career to be both technician and fighter.

Masters, in spite of their heavy responsibilities, were ranked as warrant officers, that is, a grade lower than officers with commissions. The duties of masters were to see to the rigging and the anchoring of the ships and to help with the navigation. It was essentially the same office as the Portuguese and Spanish "pilot," although pilots were concerned much more specifically with navigation. Names and functions differed somewhat in different national marines; captain, master, and pilot were the three chief officers in Spanish ships.[4]

In Hawkins's time, the masters looked after the sailing, the mooring, and the rigging of the ships, "and the workes which belong thereunto, within bourd and without."[5] Masters were, and still are, responsible to the ships' owners for the safety of the ships as the chief officer in direct charge of their handling. Sometimes, as happened with Robertson, the master of Captain Wallis's *Dolphin* in 1766, a conscientious master would be accused of over-caution by a first lieutenant, a captain, or a scientist, who wished to take risks to further a particular aim.

Many masters of English warships had come into the Navy after experience in the merchant marine. Cook (Plate 43) is the most famous example; Robertson, like Cook, rose to independent command of Royal Navy ships. Masters were a relic of the days when ships' captains were fighting commanders—usually soldiers at least partially ignorant of the ways of ships who left the actual seamanship to the masters. Magellan was this kind of military commander, so was Mendaña, and later Bougainville; although they all knew something of ships, their main job was to command. The distinction existed because originally merchant ships were commandeered by the Crown for military purposes, and commanders who were soldiers were put aboard. Commanders gave the orders where to go and led the fighting forces when the ships arrived, but the masters remained responsible for the safety of the ships. Manifold possibilities of clashes were possible between these two types of officers, particularly as there usually stood between them a difference not only of function and responsibility, but of social class as well. Drake was both types combined. Like Cook, he had been reared in the merchant navy, but he was a soldier as well, and foreshadowed in many ways the later naval officers who handled the ships, used the navigation instruments, and controlled the fighting.

It is interesting to find the difficult relationships between the early captains and masters, or captains and pilots, recurring in the late nineteenth century, when it became the fashion for wealthy men to buy yachts in order to cruise and then hiring masters because they could not sail the ships themselves. In Dewar's yacht the *Nyanza,* in 1890, most of the problems of divided command on board a single ship that were seen in the *San Pedro y Pablo,* for example, were repeated.[6]

By the time of Wallis and Robertson in the *Dolphin,* the roles of captain and master were becoming defined. Eventually, masters disappeared from naval ships, their duties being divided between the first lieutenants and the navigating officers. In other ships, the meaning of the name "master" altered somewhat. By the late nineteenth century, a "master's ticket" meant a certificate entitling the bearer to command a merchant ship; the title of "captain" in the merchant service became an honorary one. A famous "P. and O." seaman of the present era took pride in his "ticket": "And so I put to sea as Captain; Commander; Master of my own ship: call me what you like. Personally I prefer Master. Anyone can be a Captain: few can be Master."[7] He is proclaiming his pride that "masters" are from the ranks of fully qualified seamen, whereas "captains" do not necessarily have to be.

Much was demanded of captains in sailing ships before the twentieth century. There were no radios on which to appeal for assistance and no helicopters to bring it; ships were on their own on the great oceans and, on the Pacific, they were most alone of all. The commander of the *Daintie* set himself a high standard: "being required in a commander at sea, a sharpe wit, a good understanding, experience in shipping, practise in management of sea business, knowledge in navigation, and in command. I hold it much better to deserve it, and not to have it, then to have it not deserving it."[8] Many captains would fall short of Hawkins's standards, and of those of

Quirós also: "worthy of esteem is the captain who, without resorting to force or other severities, governs and keeps what is entrusted to him."[9]

During the Tudor period in England, whole families of gentry or near-gentry, "by a tradition of naval service akin to apprenticeship, transmitted their naval lore to each successive generation."[10] They developed a tradition of skilled and just command at sea. Sir Richard Hawkins, of the third generation of such a family, wrote down much of this lore. In his writing shines the pride of his rank—not his rank of English gentleman nor even of dubbed knight, but of his rank or standing as a ship's captain who was also fully capable as a ship's master. In quite the opposite way, Roggeveen, who was not a knight or a knight's son, was reluctant to give the honourable and hard-won title of "captain" to the buccaneer Davis, declaring that fully qualified seaman and fighter to be a "so-called Captain."[11] Nonetheless, captains and especially Navy captains gained power and influence from their social rank.

In the early years of European Pacific exploration, in all navies, there had been a distinction between the captains and lieutenants who held commissions (and the midshipmen training for these positions) and the technical officers who held warrants, such as the masters, gunners, carpenters, boatswains, surgeons, cooks, and later schoolmasters. Each of these officers, made officers by warrant, had the specific duties that the names of their positions implied, but —and this had its importance—commissions came from monarchs and the warrants were made out by the admiralties.

Conrad describes the tension as seen from the point of view of a captain— and Conrad was a good one—possessed of a first mate not only willing, but anxious to assume responsibility. If captains could be hard on officers, officers, in turn, could be vindictive and petty towards captains. Warrant officers usually had better relationships with the captains, as they were less closely linked to them in their duties and were more secure in their specialities.

In later merchant ships, the custom was for the captains, who by this time were also masters, to give general directions and for the mates to give the specific orders: "The Old Man reappeared on deck . . . said something to the Mate, who put his whistle to his lips and blew three blasts, then bellowed: Call all hands! Break cro'jack buntlines! Man sheet and tack!"[12] Paradoxically, the direct interference of captains was resented, although they had the power as well as the responsibility. "Whatever the captain does is right, *ipso facto*," and yet there were ways of doing things which had "somewhat the force of prescriptive law" and which wise captains did not transgress.[13] When manoeuvres required all hands, "the master takes command and gives his orders in person, standing upon the quarter-deck," but, in the ordinary day's work, the masters gave general instructions to the chief mates, who saw that they were carried out.[14] In later years, when captains were always seamen, they took over in emergencies, but, even then, most of their orders were given through their officers.

At all times, the relationship between the captains and their officers depended on the force of the personality of the captains themselves, and specifically on their ability to delegate. Hawkins in the *Daintie* knew "that the more absolute authoritie any commander giveth to his under officers, being worthy of it, the sweeter is the command, and the more respected and beloved the commander."[15] It is a rare ship indeed which is remembered apart from her commander. To be successful leaders of men, sailors, like Carteret or Wallis, could depend largely on the habits and customs of a disciplined service, tempered by insight and humanity. Success would follow in most cases, unless a particular circumstance or a particular personality threw such habits and customs into confusion. Good captains—and the Pacific knew many—were those who knew the worth of habit, customs, and discipline. Cook also had that indefinable "something more" that makes a great leader of a good one. Service under such a man was considered both an honour and a benefit, and to have served with Cook to his satisfaction helped many officers to great distinction. As well as supreme competence, Cook had presence, movingly affirmed by the Maori boy who said of him that "a noble man cannot be lost in a crowd."

Drake had this presence, and, like Cook, prestige arising from success, although their sea vocations were somewhat different. Drake had charm, also, when he wished to use it, and, like all charming men he knew what people applauded and valued—in the less important aspects of life at least. He had noticed that Indian women in South America liked brightly coloured petticoats (Wafer later commented on this also), and so as a means of ingratiating his ship with the Indians he seized all the petticoats in Guatulco to "exchange them for victuals and articles of necessity and keep them contented."[16] It is trivial things such as this that accumulate in total to bring success.

Hawkins argued that a ship is "but a masse of dead wood, were it not managed and ordered by art and experience."[17] A tiny sixteenth-century ship had no room for idle passengers, or for dissension either. Here is where "art and experience" come in. Drake insisted that everyone on board his ship was to work: "For I must have the gentlemen to haul and draw with the mariner and the mariner with the gentlemen."[18] He did this both to gain effort from everyone and to assert firmly that there was only one commander.

In a rank-conscious world, in which Drake suffered at times from the barbed comments of superiors in birth and breeding, his view of the roles of

Plate 52. Admiral George Anson (1697-1762).
Anson was a competent seaman and an
inspiring leader. He is remembered mainly
for his raid against the Spanish Pacific colonies
in the early 1740's.

Plate 53. Admiral John Byron (1723-86).
Known as "Foulweather Jack," Byron wrote so
movingly of his adventures at sea and in
shipwreck that his grandson, Lord Byron,
adapted many of his descriptions for the epic
poem *Don Juan*. But, as a Pacific explorer,
Admiral Byron failed; few eighteenth-century
voyages of exploration discovered so little as
Byron's voyage in the *Dolphin* (1764-66).

Plate 54. Jacques Arago (1790-1855). Arago
was the draughtsman with de Freycinet's
Uranie expedition of 1817 to 1820 and wrote
engagingly, if sometimes spitefully, of the
people and events on that fascinating and
ill-fated voyage. The presence aboard of Rose
de Freycinet, the captain's beautiful young wife,
lends extra interest to every account of the
expedition, including Arago's.

Plate 55. Tobias Furneaux (1735-81). Furneaux was Wallis's second lieutenant in the *Dolphin* when their expedition discovered Tahiti, and he commanded the *Adventure*, the consort of the *Resolution*, on Cook's second Pacific voyage. In the *Adventure* he brought home Omai, the first Polynesian to visit Britain.

Plate 56. William Dampier (1652-1715). Dampier left his father's farm to become a buccaneer, privateer, captain in the navy, circumnavigator, and hydrographer. Without his ability to observe and describe, we might have known little of this highly coloured career. His writing is almost classical in simplicity, and his observation of natural phenomena and human activity would be creditable in a trained modern scientist.

Plate 57. Sir Joseph Banks (1743-1820). Lincolnshire gentleman, naturalist, President of the Royal Society, adviser to kings and cabinet ministers, Banks won his enduring fame in the *Endeavour*'s Pacific voyage under Captain Cook. Many believe that it was Banks's advice to the British government about Australia that led to the founding of New South Wales.

gentlemen and sailors, however sensible, might well have had little effect except for his exceptional powers of command. A Spaniard who had seen him in action called him "one of the greatest mariners that sails the seas, both as a navigator and as a commander." Approvingly, he referred to Drake's treating all of his men "with affection," and to their response: "they treat him with respect."[19] The spirit inculcated was such that his enemies, as well as his friends, knew that any ship he commanded would not hold back from daring what could rationally be dared.

Morale was as vital a key to the success of a ship as was technique or design. Captains who could maintain morale were more important than sound rigging or sturdy masts; their leadership qualities were central to the voyage. Only very exceptional ships, such as the *Royal Sovereign* or the *Cutty Sark*, are remembered when their captains are forgotten.

On the other hand, the *Golden Hind* is remembered because of Drake, and perhaps too for the golden ballast he won for her and for the euphonic name he gave her. It was fitting that it should be a bark of that name which was the first to sight and report the Armada. Considering her record, it seems strange that there is so little left of Drake's ship and, in some ways, so little knowledge. Queen Elizabeth gave orders to have her preserved on shore at Deptford, but, except for some brick walls built for the purpose of containing and protecting her, there is nothing left. The *Golden Hind* shared the decay of English naval power under James I, but a new *Golden Hind*, as exact a twin as possible, has been built recently. She is not the first duplicate. Research thorough enough to satisfy the Admiralty encouraged it to build a small-scale replica of the *Golden Hind* which cruised around the ports in southern England during the 1930's. While in Sydney, Dwight Long, who was cruising in the Pacific at this time, met the British naval officer who had played the role of Sir Francis Drake in this replica.

Anson (Plate 52) was as charming as Drake. He so impressed a Jesuit that the priest confessed to doubting that heretics were necessarily forbidden Heaven. Like Drake in this respect also, Anson was willing to work at whatever seemed important at the time; he sawed trees alongside his sailors on the island of Tinian, just as Cook later worked the pump with his men. It is worth noting that charming and eloquent commanders were often mentioned as being notably effective in their relations with the people of the different civilizations they encountered. Charm and courtesy are intercultural. Tasman, an able sailor, was deficient in these qualities, just as he was lacking in the curiosity which drove Cook to his successes. Diplomacy was as much a part of an explorer's task as was command—and not merely on the first ships. In the island schooners of the nineteenth century, the captain "was explorer, trader and diplomat" and, in the windjammers and clippers, as in the early Indiamen, he had great business responsibilities as well.[20]

Charm in commanders, when genuinely linked to thoughtfulness about the welfare of their crews, is successful only when it is not too transparently used for effect or accompanied by some other less desirable idiosyncrasies. Conrad, when known as Captain Korzeniowski, was noted for "the distinction of his manners," but as he "was always dressed like a dandy" it brought him more mockery than approval, especially from his fellow officers.[21] Charm, apparent in Hawkins, Nelson, Drake, and Anson, was in no case a symptom of weakness; each at times used his power directly and firmly. Of Bering, however, who was "of good manners, kind, quiet, and universally liked," Steller added that he was too lenient.[22]

Captains, unlike most other men aboard, could never alternate their tasks or shift their responsibilities completely. In every century, whatever the code of discipline to aid them, and whatever the assistance they got from their officers and warrant officers, every captain had to face alone the problems of command. Some altered under the pressure—the responsibility and loneliness overcoming them.

On his third Pacific voyage, when Cook's personality seemed to change, there were murmurings of discontent. This change in Cook is ascribed by Beaglehole to illness, and to a wearing down of physical stamina by the long sustained hardships and especially by the tensions of command. Bering also wore himself out in service, at the end wishing the responsibilities were neither so great nor his to carry. In his case, probably it was not command in his ship that wore him out, but the command of an expedition which, at an immense distance from home, had to create a base and build the ships before the exploration could even begin. He died as much from worry as from scurvy and hunger, worn out from labour and broken down under his load. His successor, Waxell, nearly broke too: "I speak from experience and can truthfully say that I did not get many hours' peaceful sleep during the five months I was away on that voyage, and never seeing known land."[23]

In spite of crowded ships, captains are always alone at the top. Conrad expressed it this way: "Call her a temple or a 'hell afloat' . . . the captain's state-room is surely the august place in every vessel."[24] Dana pitied his captain: "He has no companion but his own dignity, and few pleasures . . . beyond the consciousness of possessing supreme power, and, occasionally, the exercise of it."[25] In the Pacific, each captain is alone, and presumably lonely, for long periods of time.

The burden of command is always a heavy one, but it was particularly so for the commanders of voyages of exploration where they were, by definition, in unknown territory, facing hazards that could only be guarded against once the location was certain. Many of the great explorers did not survive; many who did were broken men. Sometimes their successors also broke, and expeditions returned under the third or even fourth commander. Their words reflect the burden.

Bering's successor, Waxell, for example, found the load heavy and felt himself to be in "a continual state of uneasiness, always in danger and uncertainty."[26] Cook made clear that, if "these anxieties cause the commander to abandon his purpose," he is not forgiven.[27] It is no wonder that some captains drank and others broke down. Yet, there were always men to take their places; no matter how lonely or arduous the post at the top there will always be men who seek it, or at least accept it, finding in it professional or personal satisfaction.

Some of them should not have been there—those who lacked the positive virtues and relied on fear. Roderick Random (admittedly a figure of literature) was "under the dominion of an arbitrary tyrant."[28] Apparently, there were plenty of tyrants; Lubbock named several, stating flatly that "downeasters" and "bluenoses" were notorious as "drivers" who maintained discipline "with belaying pins, knuckle-dusters, and six-shooters."[29] However, there is a chicken and egg situation here. If good captains attracted good crews, tough captains could get nothing but tough crews; when captains succeeded to or were appointed to the command of rough crews the methods necessary for control could condemn them throughout their careers. Lubbock pointed out that he knew better than to work in a ship so commanded. It was all rough, but it was not all one sided; it was not unknown for captains and mates to be murdered as well as for seamen to be beaten to death.[30]

Captains not only had to survive, but to see that their crews moved at their direction; some captains drove, some led. The best of them knew whether driving or leading was required, and had the hardness to drive when necessary, but the personality to lead when possible. A hot temper, like that of Cook or of Middleton of the *Red Dragon*, was easily forgiven when the causes of the outburst were apparent. Men in the care of other men do not respect softness with delinquency, even their own. The cardinal virtue in dispensers of justice, whether teachers, captains, or judges, is not kindness, but fairness. Kindness has its importance, but in quite different circumstances; effective captains were kind to the sick, but not to the men whose delinquency was putting their ships in danger. In the same way, it is quite a different thing to forgive a prank, as with the "Madeira swimmers" of the *Swallow*, than to shrug off men sleeping on lookout or losing their guns when on sentry duty.

The ways in which captains dealt with delinquency tell much about them and their times. Some captains had much more to contend with than did others. Bligh, of the mutinous *Bounty*, had no marines or commissioned officers to help him maintain discipline. Carteret had to cope with the *Swallow*, an ill-equipped and clumsy vessel; that he was able to keep his crew at work in such a ship is to his credit as a captain. Light may be thrown on his character and his methods by looking at the way he treated some of his "best men" who swam ashore at Madeira "to get a Skinfull."[31] By admonishing rather than flogging them (he seemed really rather proud of them, although it is almost certain he did not tell them so), he won their complete loyalty. Afterwards, on several occasions, "my bold & fearless Madeira Swimmers" gave special service. There were many captains who, on occasion, acted as human beings rather than as minor gods. The balance was always a fine one; in most large crews there would be men to take advantage of what they saw as weakness. The commanders who could relax successfully, that is, without a damaging and permanent diminution of effective control, were usually in the navy and had such auxiliaries of power as marines on hand. (Carteret had a corporal and ten marines on board when he left England.) Far more important than the direct power evident in the marines' discipline and armament were the awesome powers vested in and wielded by the Admiralty, as an expression of public determination to have dominance at sea. Deserters and mutineers lived in peril for the rest of their lives if they chose to live anywhere near salt water.

Even minor naval captains threw the shadow of giants. This being so, wise ones could sometimes overlook things which clipper captains, much more dependent on their own personality and resources and much less buttressed by maritime law, had to treat seriously. Not only did Carteret ignore the letter of the law and follow its spirit, but he realized that the kind of morale essential on an arduous and dangerous voyage could sometimes show itself in excess. Conrad, who knew the sea and seamen, described men such as Carteret's:

They had been strong, as those are strong who know neither doubts nor hopes. They had been patient and enduring, turbulent and devoted, unruly and faithful . . . they had been men who knew toil, privation, violence, debauchery—but knew not fear, and had no desire of spite in their hearts. Men hard to manage but easy to inspire; voiceless men . . .[32]

Karlsson put it somewhat differently, suggesting a response from seamen to the challenge of the power of wind and wave, for he argued that "these manifestations of primordial power have an exhilarating effect, stimulating them and enabling them to accomplish feats perhaps impossible under normal conditions."[33]

"Boys will be boys" is an effective attitude, as long as it is confined to misbehaviour of the prankish type—drinking and clowning. "The failings of brave men should be treated with kindness," said Carteret of his attitude, "there was neither malice nor want of honour in their conduct."[34] But such methods will not work when something really malevolent has been done; then, they are rightly seen as a sign not of understanding, but simply of weakness.

Captains used rewards as well as punishment; double grog was sometimes given after extra work. Drake gave a gold chain to the seaman who spied the treasure ship they were seeking, and he gave forty "ecus" to the man who first saw land. Cook named "Young Nicks head after the boy who first saw this land."[35] Little things such as these did more to prove the common humanity of captains and seamen than to change the effective working of the ships. There were larger rewards available for both officers and men, however, in prize money for ships successful in war and in the "lay" system of distributing whaling and sandalwood profits. Captains who were successful and therefore profitable to serve had little worry about discipline. It is well to emphasize the key position of the captains once more in order to reiterate the point that whereas force—direct or indirect—was an important auxiliary, the real key to effective discipline was the trust with which crews responded to skill. Drake, Anson, and Cook were effective captains primarily because they were superb seamen; they were great captains because they had so much more to add to that skill.

"Quarter Master" summed it up, from the sailor's point of view: "With such a ship, and under Captain R——, any man might be comfortable; he was a strict disciplinarian, a thorough bred seaman, and above all a good master; it is not to be wondered that this immense fabric, in all its evolutions should be like clock work, regularity itself."[36]

Discipline that protects peaceful men from bullies, skill in seamanship and navigation, and the ability to maintain the ships in a safe and comfortable condition were the criteria by which captains were assessed by men who had reason to judge and the means to know. Reward or punishment, leniency or tyranny, resulting in happy ships or hell-ships, it was the captains' words and whims that mattered. Ships, especially sailing ships centuries ago, are communities isolated from the world. This is why the traditions which fostered a code of behaviour, as well as training which guaranteed skill in action, were so important to the men in command who were both patrons and patriarchs and who had no peers closer than the nearest sails. They were of even more consequence to the men who sailed under them.

CHAPTER 22

Mutinies and Discipline

She was unseaworthy, had a decided list, and was manned by
the scum of the docks—desperate men, ready to take any
chance. To add to this unfortunate combination the craft had
a drunken captain, and in the latter part of the voyage the
food was scarce and unpleasant.

SIR HENRY BRETT
WHITE WINGS

They all knew him! He was the man that cannot steer, that
cannot splice, that dodges the work on dark nights; that, aloft,
holds on frantically with both arms and legs, and swears at
the wind, the sleet, the darkness; the man who curses the sea
while others work. The man who is the last out and the first in
when all hands are called. The man who can't do most things
and won't do the rest. The pet of philanthropists and self-
seeking landlubbers. The sympathetic and deserving creature
that knows all about his rights, but knows nothing of courage,
of endurance, and of unexpressed faith, of the unspoken
loyalty that knits together a ship's company.

JOSEPH CONRAD
THE NIGGER OF THE "NARCISSUS"

When the relationships between officers and seamen were unsound, mutiny festered below the surface. A proper relationship was one of mutual reliance on skill, although on one side the skills were more intellectual and, on the other, more physical. The relationship was qualified and shaped in every ship by the individual personalities involved, and, at base, was always one in which common humanity and common interest had to be recognized whatever the fears and passions which smouldered under pressure. When fear followed a breakdown in the seamen's faith in their commander's skill or the ship's seaworthiness, or when resentment of inhumane treatment could no longer be repressed, then mutiny could easily break out. The essential point is that good discipline is a matter of mutual faith, with the officers bearing by far the greater responsibility for its maintenance; however, as the quotations at the beginning of the chapter illustrate, this responsibility was not theirs entirely.

Effective discipline was much more than a matter of avoiding quarrels or mutiny. It was a day-to-day matter upon which both the health and happiness of the crews and the safe handling of the ships depended. Because of the danger to vessels, cargoes, and passengers, mutiny was regarded as one of the most heinous of crimes. Since discipline was so much a matter of trust, good discipline—not the kind enforced only by fist or lash or pistol—is being discussed. Since trust involves both respect and rapport, this "feeling" in a ship was much harder to maintain when the crew was a hodge-podge of nationalities with no common purpose except wages or plunder. Crews divided by language barriers and cultural attitudes had the same tensions and weaknesses as a society so divided.

The triggering causes of specific mutinies were not often as simple as might be expected. Judged by modern standards of expectation, the treatment, food, and care given to crews should have led to chronic mutiny; yet this was not so. Personal relationships seem to have been a great deal more important than physical conditions. The ways in which captains dealt with mutiny seem to have been as diverse as the personalities involved another illustration of the pivotal position of the commanders. Upon them the burden pressed; try as they might to call to their aid councils of officers or even committees of all ranks, the commanders still remained responsible. Sometimes, the councils were forced upon them—the commanders *still* remained responsible. It is the commanders' names which are associated with mutiny, and so history records that Bligh's crew mutinied against him (Plate 58), and that some officers mutinied against Magellan. Drake, Cavendish, Quirós, Dampier, Rogers, Anson, Roggeveen, Waxell, Meares, Shelvocke, Seligman, even the great Cook: all these and many other captains had crew trouble of some kind.

All the ostensible causes of discontent—food, scurvy regulations, pay after shipwreck—would be badly exacerbated by the vastness of the Pacific. Many Pacific voyages were of great duration, for there were surveying, trading, loading, diplomacy, warfare, and recruiting to be done, quite apart from traversing the distances of the immense ocean itself. Voyages of great length, as were so many whaling and trading voyages, were incubators of mutiny, because what could be endured for three months could not necessarily be endured for three years. Time was as hard on the equipment as it was on the men, and fear of the consequences of faulty material bred discontent. So did hunger, so too did the temptation of a better life ashore, which could be seen, or at least imagined, on almost any South Pacific island. But mutiny could also occur in good ships in the North Pacific. The relationship between commander and commanded—the basis of mutiny—is as complicated in a ship at Nootka as in a sloop at Tahiti.

Handling men is an art, made even more difficult during long voyages in small ships. Confinement, hardship, danger, boredom, heavy labour, all create tensions, even when some factors are cross-cancelling. In the Pacific, there was the peculiar additional strain placed on men who were of necessity celibate for months, who put up with dull food and damp cold quarters, yet who intermittently had access to willing women, fresh meat, and tropical fruit, all in the legendary climate of the South Sea Islands. In the face of such contrasts and alternatives, restlessness, desertion, and even occasionally a *Bounty*, are not to be wondered at as much as the maintenance of any discipline at all.

Mutiny was common: "I guess few men spend a life at sea without experiencing a mutiny of some kind," one veteran captain stated.[1] But the "of some kind" is an important qualification; many of the so-called mutinies would be considered now as only "go-slows" or "stop-work meetings." By modern standards, there was cause enough and to spare for these. Even Cook faced some obstruction, particularly in matters such as substituting spruce beer for grog when the men thought the weather was too cold for beer, or substituting fresh seal meat for all provisions except flour. In each case, the men's resistance was successful. Yet, by these orders, Cook was trying to save his men from scurvy and, moreover, was merely changing food, not stinting it.

Today's conditions show that three things have changed the situation markedly. The speed and mass of ships have so increased that decisions must be made quickly. Today, almost all seamanship near shore is at the level of urgency which was reached in earlier periods only when ships were actually drifting towards a reef. Crews are better educated, better informed, and come from social conditions on land where normal obedience and even simple courtesy, much less deference, are at a discount. These men need even more careful handling than those who were cooped up and crowded in an old-time forecastle. Today, the mystique of navigation has faded before the brightness of radar scopes, and its prestige has declined with the advent of radio advice from a distance. Entire relationships have changed and, paradoxically, there is less instinctive response to command at a time when speed and power and size would indicate there is more need. It is a trying time for leaders. While there are no more "bluenose" or "downeaster" captains (the notorious Nova Scotians and New Englanders), and no more "cats" (see Plate 60) or "knuckle-dusters," at the same time the roles and ranks of officers have been legally buttressed because of both tradition and the demands of modern technology. There is now both less discipline and less consultation than there used to be.

Stern discipline was the rule in sailing ships, partly because of the demands of the craft themselves and partly because of the type of men available. Crews in Pacific ships were a mixed lot, and this was true even of the crews of naval ships. However, in the nineteenth century, the French, by law, compelled their merchant marine owners to employ only French nationals.[2] In this way, they escaped much of the trouble that plagued British and American ships in the Pacific, where men of diverse attitudes and prejudices were crowded together for long periods of time. In European ships, this mixture of crews was true of even the very first of them; Magellan's *Victoria* had French, English, and Dutch sailors aboard as well as Portuguese and Spaniards. The *Golden Hind* carried "Frenchmen, Biscayans, Scotsmen and Flemings," as well as English. One of the reasons for the defeat of the *Daintie* was the incompetence, perhaps treachery, of her gunner, who for years had been a gunner in a Spanish ship; in the same battle, one of the Spaniards' gunners was English.[3] To prove his loyalty, each gunner boasted of what he would do to his former friends.

The Dutch often sailed with the English, and the English with the Dutch; Will Adams, an English shipbuilder in Japan, reached there as a pilot in a Dutch ship, and the master under Middleton in the *Red Dragon* was Dutch. The great John Davis piloted the second Dutch expedition to the East Indies, thereby acquiring the knowledge and skill which led to his appointment as pilot-major to Lancaster's fleet. Scandinavians were known as fine sailors in the fleets of every European nation. Carteret had a Quebecer in the *Swallow*, and many Americans (British Colonials at the time) sailed with Cook as seamen and officers, one of them, Gore, being the commander who brought the last expedition safely home.

Portuguese, mainly from the Azores, made up a large proportion of American whaling crews, "because they can be obtained at a lower rate of compensation than Americans."[4] The *Spray*, at Juan Fernández, met an Azorean Portuguese who "had sailed in New Bedford whale-ships and had steered a boat."[5] Now he was "king" of Juan Fernández.

Some captains and owners argued that mixed crews were less likely to unite in order to mutiny, but it is apparent from the journals that these nationality mixtures created problems at sea, whatever the seamanlike merits of the different groups might be.[6] It was the tensions caused by the mixtures which brought on the troubles, not the abilities or lack of them of the individual sailors of any nationality. The French showed great wisdom in preventing this particular source of friction; there were difficulties enough without including avoidable ones. The burden of command was made heavier, the danger of mutiny became greater, and the exertion of reasonable discipline was made more difficult; all the existing problems were exacerbated by the deficient maritime policies of Britain and America which allowed "catch-as-catch-can" crews. It seems incredible that such ridiculous deficiencies in man-made laws would be allowed to exist when all the challenges of nature had to be faced.

There were other ways in which the laws were deficient. For years, well into the present time, the welfare of the seamen seemed to be almost ignored. It is no wonder that, in long-term reaction, seamen's unions seem universally militant. Today, the hardships hardly seem believable: "a hard biscuit cake, or a piece of old salt beef or pork, and maybe both stinking and rotten," was all Barlow got when sick of dysentery in one ship.[7] This poor food, bad as it seems (and few ships in Barlow's time had any better), was all that was provided for the seamen. They had to get other essentials at their own expense. Even in windjammers two centuries later, "a common sailor before the mast has to provide all his own clothes, his soap, matches, eating utensils, blankets, and bedding."[8] In the *Royalshire*, this evil system was compounded by the provision of such poor oil that the binnacle lamps were constantly going out. The helmsman had to relight them with his own matches so that he could steer the owner's ship on the compass course set by the captain. Neither owner nor captain seemed to worry about it! This parsimony was perhaps one of the reasons for "Quarter Master's" preference for service in a warship rather than in a merchantman. But the benefits were only relative.

Somewhat earlier, Smollett described the space for the surgeon's mates (he had been one) in a ship-of-the-line as a "dismal gulph," and said that seeing it filled him with "astonishment and horror."[9] In his whaling ship, Browne complained bitterly of his lot: "It would seem like exaggeration to say, that I have seen in Kentucky pig-sties not half so filthy, and in every respect preferable to this miserable hole: such, however, is the fact."[10] Under these conditions, seamen were bound to become depressed and ill-natured, even allowing for similar social conditions ashore.

These were shortsighted policies. The safety of sailing vessels depended completely on the responsiveness of the crews, yet the men were often irritable and worn down by hard living. Many of the journals give the impression that the confinement in small ships was the most wearing of all the bad conditions. It is literally true to say that if today's society forced convicted murderers to live in rooms like the cabins of officers in the early ships, much less in the crew's forecastle, there would be howls of outrage from both prisoners and public. In the *Rattlesnake*, Huxley, five feet eleven inches tall, had a cabin with a height of four feet ten inches. Doubting that "Jonah was much worse accommodated," he was thankful for "a sort of skylight into the berth, so that I shall be able to sit with the body in it and my head out." Afterwards, his worst criticism of anything was that "it is *worse than a ship*"; yet he was travelling nearly three hundred years later than the *Golden Hind* and in a ship many times her size.[11]

In a small vessel, time seems to work inversely to space—the longer the time aboard, the smaller seems the space. The Pacific, therefore, made the space seem very small indeed, because of the distances involved. Bassett quotes a surgeon in a ship who spoke of the beneficial effect of pouring out a "bellyful of bile against some unfortunate messmate."[12] Indeed, it was hard to know how best to deal otherwise with this problem of irritability caused by confinement, for it was unavoidable; sails required crews to handle them, crews took up room in hulls already crammed—partly with their own provisions. Even missionaries noted how hard it was to keep their love of men intact in a ship, although usually they blamed the vices of the crew and not their own self-righteousness for the clashes. People were jammed elbow to elbow. It was impossible ever to be alone in a ship; sailors sought out the oddest perches or hidey-holes in search of solitude.

At sea, what was accepted stoically by some men moved others to desperation. Occasionally, men counted up their afflictions; forty-five distinct stenches were once listed in a ship's forecastle, the crew's quarters. Noises aboard ship were incessant and irritating; Huxley listed fifteen he had heard in one sleepless night, from the wind and sea (which was expected) to "goats bleating or rather moaning as Australian goats do"[13] (which was not). There are also two reports of another unexpected sound, which was made by "countless thousands of sea-snakes . . . of a rich bronze colour with diagonal stripes along the back . . . lapping the water with their tongues as they swam."[14] Some men loved the gentler sounds at sea: "And round the ship the sea rose and fell with its eternal mysterious murmuring, rumbling, whispering; licking the ship's side wetly, its well beloved child."[15] One sailor loved the stronger notes of shipboard harmony too; "it all blends together like a song, hummed together by close friends."[16] Conrad thrilled to "that wild song, deep like a chant, for a bass to the shrill pipe of the wind."[17] But, he admitted, "the weird effects of that invisible orchestra would get upon a man's nerves till he wished himself deaf."[18] Loved or hated, the sound had a use. Villiers said that good captains "slept only while the pattern of all these salient things maintained its familiar harmony"; today, captains and chief engineers will start from sleep at a change in the rhythmic beat of their ships' engines.[19]

Several journals state that the common shipboard custom of having different rations for officers and men caused resentment. Russian ships, even as early as the eighteenth century, seemed less prone to this fault than were the others.

In "lime-juice ships," even in this century, there was "wretched discrimination," although it should be remembered that most of the special food for the officers was supplied at their own expense.[20] Quirós instructed: "As for extras, he [the captain] must act as he thinks fit, always seeing that no grounds be given for just complaints." Bechervaise, a sailor for years, thought the share-and-share-alike distribution of food "one of the most sensible acts that could be done, as when a difference is made in favour of officers it invariably creates dissatisfaction and sometimes serious consequences result from it; but when a seaman sees his superiors bear with resignation the privations allotted to all, he can no longer murmur."[21]

Complaints were justified; there was corruption on board many ships. Food was often short, not because of supply, but to increase profits, especially "when the master is in part owner."[22] A common saying was that "pursers can make dead men chew tobacco," implying falsified crew lists from which the pursers and, sometimes, the captains benefited; in some ships, for example the *Bounty*, they were one and the same person. In order to line his own pocket, the steward of the *Pilgrim* tried to deprive Dana and his mates of molasses on Christmas Day, because they already had plums in their "duff"; but "we were not to be cheated out of our rights in that way.... Such are the trifles which produce quarrels on shipboard."[23]

The poor conditions on board were made to seem so much worse, as Bligh pointed out about the *Bounty*, by the prospect of easy and pleasurable living on shore. "The delights of Tahitian life and love had far more to do with their mutiny than the tactlessness of the able but somewhat overbearing Bligh," asserts Villiers about the *Bounty* mutineers, agreeing with Bligh.[24] (Yet a great contemporary, Vancouver, who knew Bligh well and had reservations about Tahitian women, was sceptical about their having been an important cause of the mutiny.)[25]

It was human relationships that really mattered; morale is to material, Napoleon said, as three to one. Melville wrote, with the feeling engendered of personal experience, of all the petty jealousies and cruelties of a ship. Two antipathies that were usually apparent, and sometimes even dangerously so, were those between sailors and marines in ordinary naval ships, and between sailors and soldiers in troop transports. The marines were seen as the force behind the discipline and were feared accordingly, but, as they were also an élite corps, proud, smart, and well disciplined, no doubt jealousy was in evidence too. Soldiers were merely held in contempt: "Mr. Wood is one of those curses of the service who has early imbibed an antipathy to the Red Coats and imagines that he can in no way show his *Naval spirit* to such advantage as by subjecting them to every inconvenience & rudeness possible."[26] "Sojer" (soldier) was a term of abuse for shirker; "marine" was merely a term for a man ignorant of seamen's work.

Most of the exploratory voyages had scientists with them, and their relationships with the officers and crew made a difference to general morale. Often it seemed clearly a case of the chronic clash between the intellectuals and the men of action, although the lines became blurred in times of crisis, such as shipwreck. A classic example of this blurring occurred after the wreck of Bering's *St. Peter*. Bering, because of illness, had effectively resigned what command remained to his lieutenant, Waxell. Maintaining the morale of his crew and preserving discipline in the dreadful conditions of the long northern nights were solved by the new commander acting "with the greatest possible mildness and calmness." As he said, "That was no place for exerting one's power and authority."[27] Social distinctions broke down. Steller, the scientist with the ship, along with others, "realized that rank, learning, and other distinctions would be of no advantage here in the future" and so "we began in the meantime to address everybody somewhat more politely by their patronymics and given name."[28] He frankly stated that this was "to win them over and be able to rely more on their fidelity in case of misfortune later on."[29] This somewhat cynical approach justified his fellow voyagers' opinion of him.

Although an able scientist, Steller was considered to be a singularly unattractive character, who "lacked tact, sympathy, and appreciation of the other man's point of view"; naturally, "his very insistence to be heard and his air of wisdom aroused opposition."[30] For all his ability and energy, Steller, like the elder Forster who, accompanied by his son, sailed with Cook as the naturalist on the second great voyage, was full of that unique venom which an academic training sometimes provides, and his youth gave it a double distillation. According to McCrae, "Steller was what would to-day be called an 'intellectual.' He was very intelligent, very young, very intolerant and bad tempered, and he held ordinary mortals, naval officers in particular, in supreme contempt. He gave his opinion, unasked, on every situation."[31] Again like Forster, he lacked a sense of humour, probably the most important ingredient other than kindness for successful living in confined spaces, a point Villiers underlines in his book about the *Joseph Conrad*.

Waxell and the Russian naval officers, on whom Steller "looked down as beneath his notice," had good cause to anticipate Cook's "Damn and blast all scientists!"[32] The scientists were a perennial problem. A later Russian expedition, a model one in every other way, had to sail without any, because the two who had been asked to go claimed they had not obtained the proper books. Bellingshausen felt aggrieved and disappointed: "I, as a naval officer, cannot help thinking, that all that a scientist need bring with him is his scientific knowledge."[33] Cook and Bering would probably have advised Bellingshausen to recognize when he was well off.

Steller as an individual is not important in a discussion of Pacific sailing, but the relationship of scientists to officers responsible for the ships and crews —if that relationship were producing tension—is important, for it was a factor in the operation of the ships. The relationship was so often of the destructive kind that it could be suspected that the tendency on the part of some intellectuals to regard all equals as competitors was partly to blame. Yet it would be wrong to suggest that all the blame was on one side. Men like Steller and Forster would be natural butts for the direct and earthy humour of men of action. Most officers did not take kindly to the "bedevilment" of their decks with "the damned stuff" the scientists collected.[34]

Naturalists were a nuisance in many ways. After all, the ships were very small and crowded. The *Uranie*, for example, was a corvette of only 250 tons. ("Corvette" was simply the French name for a sloop, the smallest ship-of-war.) No "professed naturalist" was taken with her, as de Freycinet, while with the French ships which explored the southern coasts of Australia from 1801 to 1803, had learned about the trouble they could cause a captain more interested in his own sciences of navigation and charting. On one occasion, de Freycinet said to Flinders: "Captain, if we had not been kept so long picking up shells and catching butterflies at Van Diemen's Land, you would not have discovered the South Coast before us."[35] It can be inferred from this rather unsympathetic remark that all the trouble did not come from the scientists. Along that coast during the same years, Flinders had trouble with his scientist, Brown, because the latter's desire to go ashore to collect specimens was so often frustrated: "Robert Brown made no effort to disguise his displeasure."[36] Sir Joseph Banks (Plate 57) had argued the same points with Cook a generation earlier; his displeasure with his captain's decision showed itself in snide remarks made intermittently for several years after the *Endeavour*'s voyage. The French found the way to short-circuit many of the charges and counter-charges by having as ships' captains naval officers with training in science, such as Dumont d'Urville. The combination meant at least one less body and one less personality in a small ship.

The ship which carried Charles Darwin, the most famous scientist of all, was a very small one. The *Beagle* (Plate 40) was a small barque of only 235 tons burden. She was a very handy craft of excellent sailing ability, which was demonstrated at the Horn, the testing ground for sailing ships. This very quality of handiness, partly dependent on smallness, meant crowded living conditions, and difficulties for naturalists. Some men could rise above irritations and hardships; Banks, Darwin, and Huxley, all scientists in Pacific ships, were gentlemen whose code of behaviour—and it was a real one—modified the direct expression of the irritation that various frustrations of their enthusiasm sometimes created. They all had quarrels with ships' officers, but bad outcomes of such quarrels were nearly always avoided by keeping quiet —they had all read of "soft answers." In this particular way, the amateurs, as in a sense all these young Englishmen were at the time of their voyages, made greater contributions than did the professionals. After all, much of their work depended on winning co-operation. Forster and Steller did not modify their speech or win co-operation, although perhaps the real problem was that neither belonged to the culture of the expedition's sponsoring nation. Fortunately, there were examples of complete professionals, such as Arago, the French draftsman in the *Uranie* expedition, who could temper zeal with tact and common sense, and who could, above all, avoid pettiness.

This problem occurred with even the smallest crews. Of later yachts, Long asked, "Have you ever wondered why so many sail alone?" and answered, "It is a rare exception to hear of two men ever getting very far in a small boat together."[37] John Fairfax, who rowed across the Pacific in 1971-72, made this very point. He solved the problem by taking a woman with him instead: "For me it would have been impossible with another man."[38] Only concerted efforts could overcome the problems of boredom and the resulting irritability, and such efforts require humour and goodwill.

In the *Joseph Conrad*, a good ship with a thoughtful commander, her captain perceptively lauded one of his crew for "his irrepressible humour . . . turning aside the little trials of the day always with a joke."[39] Humour was important and helpful, and readers can encounter plenty of it—some of it a little straightforward—in earlier journals. Endurance probably counted even more; de Freycinet expressed it well: "Continual vicissitudes—such is the life of a sailor! Dangers, forgotten as soon as over—such are men!" In other words, the attitude of the crews mattered as much as did the abilities of the officers. Commanders of long voyages of exploration were particularly keen to get responsive and responsible crewmen. They were quite aware of the dangers of having to use severe measures when the crew had been confined for overlong. Flinders said he deliberately transferred "two of my ship's company, whose dispositions required more severity in reducing to good order than I wished to exercise in a service of this nature."[40]

The longer the voyage, the more important this matter seemed. Trading voyages were very complicated in the late eighteenth and early nineteenth century, more so than they are today. Ships have been known to sail from England to northwest America for furs; to China to sell the furs; to Boston to sell Chinese goods and pick up trade goods; to northwest America for more furs and then to Hawaii for sandalwood and pearls; then back to China before returning to England. In the South Pacific, *trochus, trepang,* sandalwood, coconut oil, and pearls were all exotic trading products, while in the North Pacific in the mid-nineteenth century there was an even stranger trading oddity, a flourishing trade in Alaskan ice for California and Mexico, an American company having leased the trading rights from the Russians.[41]

The extended voyages arising from such diverse trade made it difficult to get and keep crews and to maintain the ships properly. Because fear is the mainspring of much irrational action, good equipment helps to prevent trouble from the crews. Confidence in the ships and their commanders is indispensable in maintaining the crews' morale, but there is much more to it than that. Seamen have to feel that the law is not stacked against them. Merchant crews in eighteenth-century English ships often were required to pay for all damage to goods, even when caused by leaky ships or faulty packing; a hundred years later, American whaling crews sometimes returned "to the United States, after their privations and hardships, *in debt for their outfits*!"[42] Yet by the nineteenth century officers did not have it all their own way. At San Francisco and Sydney in particular, lawyers in the ports waylaid seamen and persuaded them to lay charges of brutality and misbehaviour against officers, a practice policemen today might decry as bitterly and as justly as the ships' officers did then. Court cases cost a great deal of money, because they held up the ship. For this reason, no matter how clear a captain's conscience, he feared the courts and the men knew it; some used the threat of suit as blackmail. Moreover, because of ignorance, it was not necessarily justice that the courts dispensed. As one experienced sailor, who had served most of his life as a seaman, saw it: "I have often thought that a jury composed of landsmen cannot be regarded as competent to bring down a verdict in reference to offences committed at sea."[43]

One maritime custom, which worried the Dutch sailors who caused Roggeveen some difficulty, was stopping pay from the date of a shipwreck. This was done by almost all European maritime powers. Such a calamity in uncharted waters was not unlikely. If shipwrecked in Europe it was comparatively easy to sign on in another ship, but a wreck was of greater consequence in the Pacific where a disaster could easily occur far from any chance of re-employment or transport home in another ship. Until 1748, the authority of English officers became uncertain after shipwrecks; one can understand why if the men knew they were not going to be paid.

In shipwrecks, the officers tended to set a good example, although it might be inferred from Steller's words that they had little choice. Shipwrecks changed the circumstances so much that discipline was usually hard to maintain; cap-

Plate 58. The *Bounty*. A tiny ship with a choleric captain, the *Bounty* won an oversized reputation as a hell ship because of the exaggerations of the nineteenth-century Romantic poets and the anachronistic vision of twentieth-century film makers. This modern etching of the mutiny shows Bligh and the men who remained loyal to him leaving the ship in her launch.

To the Public.

WE, the Presidents and Delegates have taken it into consideration to convince the Evil-minded, that the Reports which have circulated through Plymouth-Dock and its vicinity, of the Cambridges' intention of turning our esteemed Captain BOGER on shore, is totally a fabulous story, and we wish to convince the Public of the high esteem we hold him in. We honour him as a brave Commander, and love him as a Father who has the incumbent charge of a large family. Also our worthy Lieutenants, who we can say have always singularized themselves as Sailors' Friends.

We have the honor to remain,

The Public's most devoted Servants,

&c.,   &c.

By order of the President and Delegates
of His Majesty's Ship Cambridge,

JOHN LLOYD, Secretary.

Dock, May 23, 1797.

CONGDON, PRINTER, DOCK.

Plate 59. Mutiny—"To the Public." Issued in the days when the French Revolution across the Channel must have been still in the minds of many, this handbill made it clear that the sailors of the *Cambridge* had no dispute with their officers, whom they saw as good men. If there was any dispute, it was with what they saw as an unjust system.

Plate 60. Flogging.—"The Point of Honor." Flogging at the gangway was one of the severest punishments used to keep discipline in days when order was as hard to maintain ashore as afloat. The deterrent intent is shown by the mustering of all hands to view the punishment. Few great captains flogged very many men,

tains of ships do not appear quite so majestic when they have lost their ships. Usually, they would try to augment their authority by calling a council of their surviving officers, an institution often used in early ships when important decisions had to be made. This procedure, used by most of the early explorers, went far beyond what today would be considered a normal consultation of subordinates. In practice, the working of the system, whether after shipwreck or not, depended very much on the personality of the nominal commanders. In the *Golden Hind*, a Spanish prisoner noted of Drake and of some of his gentlemen, that: "These form a part of his council which he calls together for even the most trivial matter, although he takes advice from no one. But he enjoys hearing what they say and afterwards issues his orders."[44] The reason may not be difficult to deduce. One early commander reported bitterly of his council that "their opinions were as divers as their names."[45]

In Tasman's little Dutch fleet, the council seems to have had a genuine influence, and the opinions of the members were sometimes solicited in writing, probably in order to share responsibility. Eighty years later, Roggeveen also asked for written reports; this seems to have been done in many of the Portuguese and Spanish councils. This lightening of responsibility by distribution may have been a reason for the lack of real drive or outstanding success in Tasman's voyage. The successful voyages, whether their aim was war or exploration, were those with strong individual leadership.

Apart from leadership, the motives for the voyages were factors in the discipline of crews, especially with buccaneers and privateers who sailed for profit. Mutinies in buccaneering ships were common, although the flux of official positions under those semi-anarchic conditions was so constant that a change of elected officers can hardly be called a mutiny. The ships' crews were in a constant turmoil of politicking, for every man sought to secure his own best interests by sailing with the men he considered to be lucky or capable commanders. Privateers too were particularly subject to disruption because of the difficulty of dividing spoils satisfactorily, as Cavendish found. Both of Rogers's ships had mutinies over the distribution of profits; however, pay was an issue in ships other than privateers. The crews of Roggeveen's *den Arend* and *Thienhoven* had to be assured about their pay in writing, although they were already in the Pacific. Attempts were often made to head off mutiny by devices, such as committees of management or councils of officers like those used during Rogers's voyage.

Sometimes, councils were set up for specific reasons and had limited roles; this happened even in the Royal Navy. One of Anson's captains in the mid-eighteenth century wrecked his ship, because (in the opinion of most of his officers) of his erratic judgment, and on shore the survivors decided he was fit for only a limited command. The men respected his knowledge, but distrusted his judgment; they placed him, by force, under a council of officers. Usually more formally constituted than this particular one, councils of officers had real power. In 1600, one Dutch council even marooned a high officer: "Here the Vice-Admirall for divers misdemeanours, was by a Councell of Warre adjudged to be set on land."[46]

During his major voyage for the Russians, Bering went so far as to have a meeting of his officers and crew "to discuss the question of going to the Harbor of St. Peter and St. Paul."[47] Michael, who translated from Danish the book by Bering's second-in-command, says that this was a standard practice in the Russian fleet and laid down as an official regulation. It is difficult to avoid concluding that, at least on this expedition, the system produced more silliness than sense. Though few captains of other nations (except the buccaneers) went quite so far in consulting their crews, there was ample and early precedent in England for consultation. The "Laws of Oleron," brought to England by Eleanor of Aquitaine, provided, for example, that if the weather were doubtful the members of the crews should be consulted before sailing. It was more usual for the captain to speak to the assembled crew at times of crisis and, with greater or lesser eloquence, urge them to support a course of action already decided. Anson mustered "all the Ship's Company on the Quarter-Deck, and there in a short Speech acquainted them with his Design."[48] Decisions, after all, were what leaders were for; nevertheless, successful captains knew what was happening, and what their men were feeling.

However, even today what works for one captain and crew will not necessarily work for another. Seligman of the *Cap Pilar*, in 1936, said that "a vote would always be taken by the whole ship's company upon every important decision," and that "the experiment was an unqualified success."[49] On the other hand, Villiers of the *Joseph Conrad* flatly stated "that ships and the sea are not to be fooled with lest they kill you. There was no debating committee."[50] During Villiers's cruise, he absolutely refused to have any kind of "silly co-operative venture," because, in his opinion and stated bluntly, "Co-operation and the sailing-ship do not mix and cannot be blended."[51] Some agreed fully; Newby, who sailed in the sailing ships from Australia to England in this century, said, "sailing ships do not stay afloat and make passages at the pleasure of committees of seamen."[52] Long ago, Captain John Smith best explained the position of those who command at sea: "there is no dallying nor excuses with stormes, gusts, overgroune Seas, and leeshores."[53]

Sir Richard Hawkins said of "murmurings and mutterings," that it is best "by prevention to provide remedie with expedition."[54] Anson felt the same way about "Murmuring and Discontents amongst the People," and in a speech completely satisfied his crew.[55] What other "remedies" were available—threats? Quirós "ordered a block to be placed at the yard-arm. Thereafter an uneasy peace existed in the *capitana* and Quirós lived in fear for his life."[56] The best way simply could not be known. Drake and Magellan succeeded with drastic action; Roggeveen, by giving in; the *Felice*'s commander found leniency bred more mutiny, while the *Wager*'s captain found his use of force did the same. Variables in the equation of personalities differed too much in ships for there to be any simple answer. Stronger leadership sometimes came to the mutineers from the lower deck than that provided by the captain on the quarterdeck, and then men could be moved to attempt to change things rather than to accept them.

All harshness did not originate with owners or officers. Seamen were as hard on each other as ever officers were. Mutinies within mutinies occurred, and in the tiny schooner *Speedwell*, built from the *Wager*'s longboat, the men wished to divide the rations according to their view of the worthiness of the recipients—less work, less food.[57] Rutter, who wrote about Bligh and the *Bounty* mutiny, explains this phenomenon; "men who have been kept in subjection are wont to be the hardest masters when they come to wield authority."[58] One man who did not abuse his authority after a kind of mutiny was the seaman who took over *de facto* command of the sailing ship *Victory* on her way to Otago, New Zealand, in 1848. In order to protect the crew from the sheer incompetence of the officers, he "took charge whenever the weather was rough, and from that point until New Zealand was reached the captain had very little to do with running things."[59] It was a successful voyage, but in spite of that the seaman was imprisoned for a short period.

Severity was not the complete answer. To seamen in ships in the Pacific, the powers of the Admiralty in London or its equivalent in Paris or The Hague were menaces less dangerous than the hundred perils in between. Even so, British captains criticized the deficient maritime laws of Britain, which fell far short of those of France or Holland.[60] This had not always been so, although practice had usually lagged well behind prescription. Sir Richard Hawkins complained of the English "that being the authors and reformers of the best discipline and lawes in sea causes, are become those which doe now worst execute them."[61]

Discipline was not maintained by distant authority, but by the commanders and the spirit they imparted to their officers. As Christopher Lloyd argued, there is a "variation between happy ships and hells afloat, invariably depending on the type of officer in command." De Freycinet ran no hell-ship; he punished a sailor for theft by capping his head with the ears of an ass. "Would you believe," said de Freycinet's wife, "that this children's penance from our infant schools has been more successful than blows in correcting this miserable man?" Hell-ships did exist. Villiers described the rage of an old Negro, who sailed in his frigate, when the ship *Panama* was mentioned. He remembered it as a "hell afloat."

One ship that nearly everyone has heard of as a "hell afloat"—although assuredly it was not—is a natural choice as an example of mutiny in the Pacific. All the questions are there: was discipline too arbitrary, too harsh, or both? Was the root cause the confinement of two clashing personalities for too long in too small a craft? Was it Tahiti, and the life of simplicity, ease, and sensuality that seemed to be at hand? These ideas of a Paradise to be gained are commonly held to be at the bottom of the most famous mutiny of all—that in the *Bounty*. Bligh, her captain, although an unpleasant and tactless man, has become unfairly infamous, made so by the anachronistic views of people who believe that the same actions could have been taken in the eighteenth century as would be taken in the twentieth. This is no more true when dealing with men than it would be of the techniques of operating the ships themselves. Sailors of that day were as different culturally from the sailors of today as is the small wooden barque from a modern destroyer.

Bligh did not operate a hell-ship by the standards of his day; neither was he operating a twentieth-century cruise ship. Undoubtedly unpleasant, he still made some firm friends and was recognized as highly competent by a mariner such as Cook. His total record as a navigator, explorer, master, and captain of a ship in battle speaks for itself. His naval career, at least, has been unfairly dealt with, not only by many popular writers, but by historians who should know better. His name is a byword, as Villiers found in the *Conrad*: "Because I always insisted upon immediate and proper obedience to all orders, I had heard in Samarai that I was another Captain Bligh."[63] At the time of the mutiny, there were few, and none in authority, who questioned Bligh's actions. His portrayal as a villain was largely the creation of the Romantic poets to whom he had the misfortune of being only slightly pre-contemporary; to be even slightly out of date will attract a charge of anachronism from the *avant garde*. In this circumstance, no one has the same advantage as the ancients have—that of being thoroughly and romantically dead.

It was nevertheless a mutiny against Bligh which has made the *Bounty* famous. There are still debates about the cause. It was not flogging, as such, or there would have been many more mutinies, for there was flogging in most of the naval ships of the day. Bligh, depending as he did on tongue lashings, was not a captain who used flogging much.[64] Months before the mutiny, Bligh wrote regretfully in his log about the first flogging that "I had hopes I could have performed the Voyage without punishment to any One."[65] It was Bligh's expressed view that the trouble was caused by the temptations of Tahiti, but these had operated in many other ships without such drastic results; however, there is support for him in Villiers's view of Tahiti and the mutiny. In Villiers's own young crew, in the present era, he felt there were some "who felt inclined to mutiny in Tahiti. Perhaps there is something in the air."[66]

It was not "something in the air"; it was, surely, the coincidence of Bligh *and* Christian in a small ship. Without Christian—and no other—there would probably have been no byword "Bligh." The spark flew from the clash of the personality and will of an overbearing Bligh with those "of a melancholy underling who has fallen in love at Tahiti," as Villiers rather cuttingly describes Christian.[67] But the effects of love, if any, were indirect. Other authorities claim that Christian was one of the mutineers who was *not* in love. Perhaps the most definite statement of this view is that of John Fryer, who was master in the *Bounty* at the time of the mutiny: "Christian was not particularly attached to any women at Otaheite."[68] Most of the talent in the *Bounty* left the ship and went with Bligh in the launch—there was not room for everyone—and some who stayed with the *Bounty* called out that they were compelled to do so, a plea later accepted by the courts. Did only the unskilled fall in love? Did not Tahiti at most seem a haven for those already disaffected?

It was during the voyage of the launch that the real quality of Bligh's seamanship and character showed, for he sailed a small boat nearly 4,000 miles under difficult conditions, and brought his men through to survival as a disciplined unit. The main hardship was the constant wet, although paradoxically this was of benefit as it saved them a good deal from the pangs of thirst. They had little food, but what they had was shared equally and most strictly supervised. If a bird were caught—fishing was not at all successful— it was shared by exactly the same children's game as was used by the crew of Melville's *Highlander* to share salvaged tobacco "chaws." A portion of bird meat was selected, held out of sight by Bligh, who called, "Whose is this?" to be answered by a selected crew member with a sailor's name, "John Smith," "Albert Robins," etc. No favouritism was possible as the crew member did not know what the portion was, and Bligh did not know who would be getting it.[69]

Whatever Bligh accomplished as a navigator, and however his actions may be justified as being within the limits of reasonable action in his time, in the eighteenth century, British naval discipline was harsh (though Royal Navy ships were preferred to French or Iberian ships because of cleanliness and diet). Although welfare was becoming a matter of concern in society at large, as yet no successful captain could depart too far from the necessity of being not just "the protector of the weak," but also a "terror to bad ones."[70] In the seventeenth century, "terror" usually meant flogging, although bizarre punishments, such as keel-hauling (pulling a man under the ship from one side to the other) were sometimes used. However, these punishments fell far short of ones used in the earlier days, when a man could "be hanged on the bowsprit end of the ship in a basket, with a can of beer, a loaf of bread and a sharp knife, and choose to hang there till he starve, or cut himself into the sea."[71]

This was in the early days indeed. In spite of myth, by the nineteenth century, British sailors in general were better treated than American sailors. Melville thought English officers and American officers from the South were much better liked by the seamen than were American officers from the North. Probably it was simply that class distinction led to an easy "habit of command" which did not need to over-insist. Many claim that English soldiers invariably preferred to be commanded by "gentlemen," who commanded as if it were the natural thing for them to do. Melville spoke of the "shipping of the quarter-deck face"; his implication was quite clearly that American officers, at any rate, too seldom allowed themselves to be human and natural, and too often forced themselves into a role.[72] "Able Seaman" confirmed Melville's view; in many American ships, he claimed, there was "a chronic state of hostility existing between officers and men."[73] He also thought that although American officers were better seamen, English officers were better navigators.

Some so-called mutinies, for example, those against Magellan and Drake on their circumnavigations, were not mutinies at all, but disputes about command or objectives among the higher officers themselves, differing from mutinies in the same way that a *coup d'état* differs from a revolution. Two of this type of dispute found their culmination on the same spot, after trials which were fully reported and which have certainly been fully discussed since. Drake's executioner did his grim duty in sight of the gibbet that Magellan's hangman had used. Because of this coincidence, Dutchmen in Drake's crew spoke of the stark and barren Port St. Julian, in Patagonia, as "fatal to Mutineers," not knowing the historical debates that would swirl around both block and gibbet later on.[74] Probably, on the spot and at the time, they made the soundest assessment. When discussing possible violent punishment, the critics of the dispensers of justice should beware of judging by standards different from those the culprits would themselves have accepted. Mutiny is not romantic, really, any more than piracy is; the motives are more often sordid than noble. Greed and ambition could govern action in the lower decks as well as in the officers' cabins, and so the only valid basis for judgment would be the clear results and not the clouded causes. King Stork was often worse than King Log.

CHAPTER 23

Buccaneers and a Bottle of Rum

*Gold was the bait that tempted a Pack of Merry Boys of us
near Three Hundred in Number . . . to list ourselves in the service of one of the Rich West Indian Monarchs, the Emperour
of Darien.*

BASIL RINGROSE
OF THE *TRINIDAD*

*The love of gain, strengthened by the love of the marvellous,
smooths the difficulties of a long voyage.*

JACQUES ARAGO
OF THE *URANIE*

*. . . you may be surprised to hear that the worst part of going
to sea is the deadly monotony.*

BRETT HILDER
NAVIGATOR IN THE SOUTH SEAS

Buccaneers are interesting. People love stories of violence; many of them can
rationalize their own irresponsibilities remarkably easily by making Robin
Hoods out of men who are simply thugs and thieves, as they often do with
hijackers. There ought to be scepticism regarding motives then and now, but
the reasons why individual men became buccaneers are not what is important
in this discussion.

What is important about buccaneers here is that there were so many acute
observers and capable writers among them. Their writings show that, although
this collection of semi-pirates and brutal thieves may have been romanticized,
the life they led was one of monotony and boredom—as a life that lacks
creative purpose is bound to be. Drink was one anodyne, sex another, violence
a third. Drink, in fact, was a relief to many sailors in many ships and in many
ports. No wonder men like Dampier (Plate 56) and Wafer never quite fitted
in; no wonder Rum and the Lash are forever linked in men's minds.

The name "buccaneer" comes directly from the hunters of cattle on the

Caribbean islands, who preserved their beef by drying it over a fire on a grate which the Indians called a "barbecu." "Barbecu" is an interesting word. Wafer, who lived with Indians in Darien, sometimes used the word "barbecue" as a verb, when speaking of the Indian cooking of fish and their choosing either to boil "or else *barbecue* or broil them," and sometimes as a noun: "a Barbecue or Grate of Sticks."[1] This conforms with modern usage. Dampier saw meat being dried in exactly the same way in the East Indies, so it was not exclusively a Caribbean technique. The product, something like the "jerky" of the American buffalo hunters, or the "biltong" of the African Boers, was called "boucan." It was a short step—if the water may be forgotten—from hunting cattle on the islands to hunting Spanish ships on the seas around them. Boucan became a stock provision of the buccaneering ships.

Dampier sailed the Pacific in buccaneering ships, privateering ships, and Royal Navy ships. Fortunately, he wrote about his voyages with an observant eye and in a straightforward style. Although the trade the buccaneers followed was a form of piracy, in the seventeenth century there were many shades and distinctions within it. Many contemporaries thought of them as pirates—whatever they called themselves—and were not put off by euphemisms. Part of one famous man's career is described as "when he was out a *Roving on the Account*, as the *Jamaica* Men call it, but it is downright Pirating, they making their own Commissions on the Capstane."[2] As the capstan is the lever and wheel device by which crews hoist the anchors—no doubt of a convenient height to use as a writing table—this was an accusation of forgery as well as of piracy. The accusation was possibly literally as well as metaphorically true. Melville says the capstan was often used as a desk, with the slots being convenient for filing papers. All the Maori land around Wellington Harbour in New Zealand was signed away on the capstan of the ship *Tory*.[3]

An excellent discussion of buccaneering and piracy may be found in Burney's book, *History of the Buccaneers of America*. There is an interesting link between Caribbean buccaneers and Chinese pirates, showing the community of human psychology. The West Indian buccaneer, Henry Morgan, was knighted and made a governor, and in China a great pirate was "ennobled under the title of the 'Sea-Quelling Duke' by which method he was at once pacified and extinguished."[4] Piracy was still rife in Chinese waters in the nineteenth century; becalmed clippers were sometimes boarded by rowed junks, so piracy was still being practised in Pacific waters until nearly the twentieth century.

French buccaneers, as well as English, pillaged the Spaniards, with an official letter of marque (a letter from the government making a private vessel, in effect, a ship-of-war), if and when they could get one, but without one if necessary. With the letter, they were privateers. "Pirats," said Richard

Hawkins, "are those who range the seas without licence from their prince." The English, with that flair for the "concealing word" that has been inherited by every English-speaking land, insisted on calling themselves privateers, whether or not they had the letter of marque. Probably the simplest way of looking at it is that if the buccaneer's own country were at war with Spain, he became a privateer; if his country were not at war with Spain, he became a pirate. However, some people argue that seamen are pirates only when they rob their own countrymen as well as other nationals—in peace or war.

Whether pirates, privateers, or buccaneers, 300 of them crossed the Isthmus of Panama into the Pacific in 1680 to raid the Pacific coast and to get away from increasing pressure in the Caribbean. Their first watercraft on that sea were Indian canoes, but in these they captured a small barque almost immediately. The canoes in that part of America were simple dugouts made from the trunks of either cedar or cotton trees and were much like the cedar or fir dugout canoes of northwest America. Even without the captured barque, which was away getting provisions, in these same frail canoes they defeated three armed Spanish ships, capturing two of them. Their success continued and within a week of reaching the Pacific they had a small fleet of captured vessels including one, the *Trinidad*, of 400 tons. They speedily altered and fitted them out for their purposes. After some successful raids, one party sailed around Tierra del Fuego and up to the West Indies in the *Trinidad*. She has been described as a good sailer; she must have been sturdy too.

Later, another expedition of buccaneers, including Dampier, rounded the Horn the other way—around South America into the Pacific—after a stop in Africa. In Africa, they seized a large Danish ship and renamed her the *Batchelor's Delight*.[5] (According to another account, they traded their original small ship for sixty black girls to relieve the tedium of the voyage. This may explain the new name given to the Danish ship.) The Danes were voyaging to the East Indies at this time and their ships were armed. East Indiamen, whether of English, French, or Dutch registry, tended to be like big, undergunned frigates and, naturally, a Danish one would be similar. The *Batchelor's Delight* is described variously as being of thirty-six or forty guns.

This Danish ship was a stout one, fit for the Horn, and she made the passage fairly easily. After a successful cruise in the Pacific, she returned to the Atlantic and reached the West Indies in 1688 at the convenient time when James II was offering a King's Pardon to all buccaneers who would renounce their way of life. Dampier had left the *Batchelor's Delight* while she was in the Pacific to go into the *Cygnet*, which was commanded, fittingly enough, by a Captain Swan. Much of his new ship's cruising was recorded by Dampier. So was her fate. She wore herself out, was finally abandoned by her last crew, and sank at her anchors at Madagascar, an undramatic end, symbolic of the buccaneering profession that had ended, not with hangings, but with pardons.

Indeed, not only was one buccaneer not hanged, but he eventually became the Archbishop of York. Lancelot Blackburn's needs in tobacco, wine, and women changed much less than his occupation, and, according to Horace Walpole, "the jolly old Archbishop of York gained more hearts than souls."[6] From this time on, however, the increasing development and sophistication of government in the Americas and the wars in Europe meant the end of peacetime buccaneering. Not only would there be no scarcity of letters of marque for privateers during long years of war, but there would be no excuse for not having one. Later, in peacetime, there was to be little tolerance of pirates, whatever their qualifications and experience, or of piracy, whatever the rationalization.

While the wars were still being fought, however, Woodes Rogers, himself no buccaneer, with Dampier as one of his officers, came to the Pacific on a privateering expedition with ships named the *Duke* and the *Duchess*. Whether these names were meant to imply either that the ships were a pair and would not separate, or that they were ships of the same class (and a high one at that) can only be a guess. They were frigates, the *Duke* of 320 tons and 30 guns, and the *Duchess* a little smaller at 260 tons. Between them they carried 56 guns and constituted a potentially formidable force. However, the crew, about one third of which was foreign, was a rough lot, although Rogers said the foreigners caused less trouble than the British did. Mutiny threatened the voyage almost from the beginning over the disposition of a prize—in privateering voyages, profit was most important, and acceptable sharing absolutely vital. It was always hard to control men who considered themselves shareholders of a voyage.

Having made the Horn passage, the ships called, as ships commonly did, at the island of Juan Fernández for a rest and for wood, water, and such provisions as they could find. On this occasion, the ships found the most famous of marooned sailors, Alexander Selkirk, not famous for himself—he had a creditable but undistinguished naval career—but as the model for Robinson Crusoe. When the *Duke* and *Duchess* called, Selkirk received them in goatskins, looking, according to Rogers, "wilder than the first Owners of them."[7] Rogers took him on board as a mate, because of Dampier's opinion that Selkirk, formerly master of the *Cinque Ports*, had been "the best Man in her."[8]

Other men had lived alone on Juan Fernández. William, a Mosquito Indian from Darien, survived there alone for three years, having been abandoned accidentally, whereas Selkirk had been put ashore deliberately, like the Dutch

"Vice-Admirall." William, like Selkirk, had been happy enough to leave; he had joined the *Batchelor's Delight* with Dampier. He had succeeded as a Crusoe at least as well as Selkirk had, forging harpoons and fish hooks from a gun barrel, building a hut, and sleeping on a "barbecu" (grating) of sticks covered with goatskins.[9]

On Juan Fernández, Selkirk had learned to run down goats and kill them with his knife; later, "Quarter Master" found that the Pitcairn Islanders did exactly the same thing.[10] Persistence is the key, not speed; Canadian Indians also had a technique of pursuing deer and moose on foot and thereby simply wearing them down.

Rogers captured some ships, although, since the raids of Drake and Cavendish, and of the buccaneers a century later, the Spanish defences and warning systems had greatly improved. Where possible, privateers, like the buccaneers before them, captured towns as well as ships. Sometimes they ransomed, sometimes they simply pillaged—the chosen procedure usually being a matter of reaction to Spanish defense or surrender. Naturally, in any raid, private citizens often tried to smuggle out precious items of wealth. In his book, Drake's nephew says that one of his uncle's men from the *Golden Hind* once found "a chaine of gold, and some other jewells, which we intreated a gentleman Spaniard to leave behinde him, as he was flying out of towne."[11] This dry humour seemed in context near South America; Colnett observed that a Spaniard, when reassured that he was not in danger, "recovered his spirits but lost his liberality." Often, it was a kind of gallows humour. When everyone on board the *Speedwell* was facing imminent starvation, Bulkeley recorded the death of the purser in this manner: "Departed this Life Mr. *Thomas Harvey*, the Purser; he died a Skeleton for want of Food: This Gentleman probably was the first Purser belonging to his Majesty's Service, that ever perish'd with Hunger."[12] Spaniards in the Pacific quite sensibly developed tricks of concealment. Silver bars were found in jars of marmalade, in sun-dried bricks, or cast as pigs of tin ballast. Obviously, the more successful the trick, the less likely it is to be known. Given the standard of cooking at the time, silver and gold might have passed unnoticed in ships' bread or puddings, unless somebody actually tried to eat them. Their addition could hardly have made the food heavier.

Because of the great distances sailed, boredom was a particular problem in ships in the Pacific, even on the buccaneering voyages which are somewhat more associated with gold, girls, and orgies. Drunkenness was one vice of sailors, whether or not they were lawfully at sea, that journals of every century emphasize. Given the hardships they faced, it is little wonder that sailors drank, or that when the rum or beer ran out they would drink unusual drinks more readily than they would eat unusual foods. Sailors of different nationalities favoured their own drinks to begin with, but apparently, in the last resort, they accepted the necessity of drinking whatever was alcoholic and not completely undrinkable. Some of the recipes sound as if they had arisen from the dregs of desperation; but the Pacific provided certain new nectareous drinks as well as a few more doubtful ones. In most places, the Europeans found that potent drinks, some not alcoholic but narcotic, were part of the culture. When the men went ashore, another dimension was added to the captains' discipline problems. For example, it was hard to forbid the drinking of *kava*, when its preparation was a matter of hospitality.

Every attempt was made to keep liquor from the sailors, in spite of the resentment of the crews. Very often, these precautions failed. Hawkins described his crew as they were leaving land: "some drinke themselves so drunke, that except they were carried aboord, they of themselves were not able to goe one steppe."[13] Dana pointed out that "sailors will never be convinced that rum is a dangerous thing by taking it away from them and giving it to the officers"; "a Seaman in general would as soon part with his life, as his Grog," one of Cook's officers concluded.[14] "Quarter Master" claimed that seamen will go to any lengths to get rum, and he described some amusing ways in which spirits were stolen on board. Banks mentioned the draining of some cases of Madeira and its replacement with seawater, but even this story does not match that of the sailors who reputedly drained and drank the rum preserving Nelson's body on its way home for burial. Thus, on board Indiamen of the nineteenth century, stealing liquor by sucking it out of barrels was called "tapping the Admiral," and, even today, rum is sometimes called "Nelson's blood."

On certain important occasions, such as Christmas, in the *Resolution*, it seemed necessary, even for an able disciplinarian such as Cook, to let the men have their head—and their heads the hangovers. On the previous voyage four years earlier, Banks had noted at Christmas that "all good Christians, that is to say, all good hands, got abominably drunk. . . . Weather, thank God, very moderate, or the Lord knows what would have become of us."[15] This may be contrasted with the behaviour of sailors in the American ship *Columbia* at Christmas only a few years later, who had been given "of grog and every other thing a double allowance and to their credit be it spoken they spent the day with the greatest propriety not in noisy mirth making a drunken frolic."[16] A convivial crew was not Captain Cook's only problem with alcohol. He complained in Savu, Dutch East Indies, that the Raja and the Dutch factor in charge of the *Endeavour*'s re-supplying were not at work, and that it "might be owing to their having drank too freely of our liquor when on board."[17]

Banks was not above the appreciation of liquor; he praised the excellence of "palm wine or toddy" and took the lemon juice required to cure his scurvy symptoms in a "very weak punch" made of "lemon-juice with one-fifth of brandy."[18] Liquor was often used this way. Rogers would have agreed with Banks's methods; he described his own punch as very effective against scurvy. Francis Chichester, on one of his voyages, drank lemon juice to keep away scurvy and claimed it would also prevent, "if enough of the right kind of whisky is added to it, mental scurvy as well."[19] According to John Drake, his cousin Francis of the *Golden Hind* squeezed the juice of herbs into wine to give to those who had scurvy. The French in at least one ship added quinine to the sailors' drink issue without telling them, and Samwell, the *Discovery*'s surgeon, says that instead of water they mixed birch sap with the rum to make the grog, because it was "an excellent antiscorbutic."[20] In order to cure his gout, Shelvocke drank a drink called "hipsy," "a liquor compounded of wine, water, brandy, and sugar, which by the admirers of it is also called meat, drink, and clothing."[21] These sailors must have been operating on the gin and tonic philosophy—why not make medicine fun? And why not breakfast too? A Maine whaling captain's breakfast shared with an English visitor was "a black bottle of terrible spirit" and some biscuits "lubricated with blubber."[22]

Incidentally, Banks had picked up—as it is still possible to do—many interesting North American drink recipes with equally interesting names. One drink, called *Callebogus*, was spruce beer with rum or brandy or gin; another, "Egg Calli," was spruce beer with egg and sugar. Smollett tells of a Royal Navy recipe for a drink called "bumbo" ("rum, sugar, water, and nutmeg") which sounds just as appetizing. Many sounded less so. A drink famous among the crews of nineteenth-century Pacific wheat ships seems revolting: "in port they drank vast quantities of alcohol, especially the famous 'tarantula juice,' made up of two quarts of spirit, cooked peaches and tobacco juice diluted with water."[23]

The amounts consumed seem stupendous, even granting that the voyages were long and that in trading ships the allowance for captains was a form of entertainment expenses. A commander of an East India Company ship was allowed approximately 5,000 quart bottles of "wine, beer and other liquors"—eleven tons of liquor. A chief mate was allowed 288 bottles of wine and a puncheon of rum, and so on down the line of command. Either the captains did a great deal of entertaining, or the company made a high and sympathetic assessment of the loneliness of command. Until its recent discontinuance, rum was the standard drink for issue to the sailors in British ships. Seamen in the Royal Navy were entitled to one-half pint per day, but after 1740 when one half of the daily entitlement was issued at noon and the other half at six o'clock in the evening, it was diluted each time by a quarter pint of water. This half-and-half mixture was "grog," and even this dilution left the drink strong enough to make some men "groggy in the afternoon."[24] American merchant ships in the nineteenth century did not use grog, and Melville argued strongly for stopping it in the American Navy ships too. There is a temptation to believe that grog was issued partly so that stopping its issue could be used as a punishment.

Some argued, as did Sir Gilbert Blane, that the substitution of wine for spirits would improve the health of seamen, but this did not become a regular practice in spite of the argument that the use of wine gave the French an advantage.[25] Nevertheless, although often reserved for the men who were ill, wine was used instead of spirits in many ships and on many occasions. Dampier complained, however, that it was difficult to find a wine which would keep in the tropics. Because of cheapness and convenience, on southern voyages wine or brandy was substituted for beer even though beer was considered a preventative for scurvy. It was so easy to get full-bodied wine at Madeira or Captetown that much was used by both the officers and men in the ships that called at these places. Sometimes, either Cape brandy or arrack was used as a substitute or for a change from rum, but, with drink as with food, seamen could be very conservative when they wished.

Dutch sailors in the East had an entitlement of arrack (one and one-half mutchkins per day), and brandy was often used in the ships sailing from Holland, at one-half mutchkin per day. A mutchkin is equivalent to three quarters of an imperial pint. The Russians seem to have used gin in their North Pacific expeditions, and when gin was not available they took the very powerful brandy distilled from a sweet grass that grows in Kamchatka. Waxell claimed that gin had kept men with scurvy "in fairly good fettle," and that after it ran out the death rate increased.[26] He also said, when describing the distillation by the natives of the sweet grass brandy, that it had a pleasant taste in spite of its strength, but warned that a glass of water the morning after would make a man "become as greatly intoxicated as he was the previous evening."[27] This "two-drinks-for-the-price-of-one" quality has been deliberately avoided by commercial distillers. The Russians used brandy, presumably this kind, very successfully in their early voyages. The Ainu "took much delight in drinking of brandy" which the Russians offered as a gesture of friendship, and "the *Japannese* did not find the taste of the *Russian* brandy amiss."[28]

However, this was not the only interesting indigenous drink encountered in the Pacific. Swan's men in the *Cygnet*, according to Dampier, named an island "Bashee" after the "excellent liquor, strong, and I believe wholesome, and much like our English beer both in colour and taste,"[29] which the natives brewed from sugarcane juice and "small blackberries." A person could, he claimed, get drunk, but never sick. This seems better than the effect one early surgeon reported of fresh coconut milk when drunk "in excessive quantity"; it brought on a paralysis ("they could neither go nor stand") that lasted four or five days.[30] Less strange in effect, and certainly easier to procure than coconut milk (or almost anything else, for that matter), was the rich and strong Peruvian wine that the buccaneers found at La Nasca in Peru simply standing on the shore in eight-gallon jars. The buccaneers did not show the restraint that the Peruvians obviously were showing.

Across the Pacific, at Achin in 1602, Lancaster more than met his match in wine in spite of his training at the Guildhall banquets in London and his years at sea. One of his officers told the story this way: "This wine is made of rice, and is as strong as any of our aquavita: a little will serve to bring one asleepe. The generall, after the first draught, dranke either water mingled therewithall, or pure water; the king gave him leave so to do, for the generall craved his pardon, as not able to drinke so strong drinke.[31]

Officers and men alike were unenthusiastic about *kava*, a Polynesian drink prepared in front of the recipients by chewing the *cavah* root, spitting the emulsion into a wooden bowl, adding water, straining it, and serving. Schouten, the Dutch captain of the ship *Unitie*, said "they also presented that notable Drinke (as a speciall and a goodly Present) to our men, but they had enough, and more then enough of the sight thereof."[32] Today's version of *kava*, according to Beaglehole, is quite acceptable. Some modern voyagers would disagree: "We drank the Kava from polished half-coconut shells. It tasted like oily mud but we all survived."[33] *Kava* is not supposed to be intoxicating, although Cook said it was, but it is believed to have the same effect on the legs, if enough is drunk, that the surgeon claimed for coconut milk.

Another chewed and salivated drink, encountered by Wafer in Darien, was "chicha," made by women chewing maize. It became a very intoxicating and sour beer. The Dutch described *cici* in Chile, hundreds of miles south, as "somewhat sowerish, made of Mays, which the toothlesse old women chew (supposing that the elder the Women are, the better shall their drinke be) and steepe it in water."[34] They referred to "drunken feasts" and "drinking in a misordered order."

Bellingshausen deprecated the usual practice of offering a drink to show friendliness, believing that the longer indigenous peoples could remain unused to alcohol the better, but, as has been seen, certain places in the Pacific had forms of intoxicants before the Europeans came. In any case, local reaction to

European liquor was sometimes as negative as was the sailors' reaction to theirs. Some sailors may have objected to *kava*, but one Indian on Magon Island "roared like a Bull" at the burning that brandy produced in his throat, and an American (as the Russians called Alaskan Indians), the most eminent of them all, "screeched most horribly" on trying a beaker of gin.[35] Such a comment may well have been unfair to the gin. So much have times changed that American sailors leave their now dry ships to visit ships of other nations specifically hoping to be given a "beaker of gin."

All local reaction was not so unfavourable. In the same year that Waxell met his "most eminent" American, Captain Walton, while entertaining some Japanese in the *Archangel Michael*, found that "Russian corn-gin in particular had appealed to their taste."[36] Quirós's officers found that Solomon Islanders liked the wine they were given—no doubt Peruvian wine—and "made signs that it was good."[37]

Drink was a serious problem for Pacific ships in terms of discipline as well as of health. People argue that flogging as a punishment lasted so long in the Navy—in spite of so many attempts to mitigate or to stop it entirely—because of the seamen's addiction to drink. On the other hand, the importance of liquor—two centuries ago, there was immense hardship and little pleasure at sea—meant that the deprivation of or increase in the allowance could be used either as a punishment or as an encouragement and reward. A double allowance might be served in cold weather, after extra exertion, or for some special occasion, such as the celebration of a king's birthday or a coronation. Some captains issued a double allowance immediately before a battle began, but as early as the beginning of the seventeenth century Hawkins argued against this practice. He roundly condemned those who too freely "mingle powder with wine"; he disapproved of "the raynes of reason being put into the hands of passion and disorder."[38] The Spaniards, he pointed out, were not so foolish.

CHAPTER 24

Women

*For who could think of tumbling these artless creatures over-
board, when they had swam miles to welcome us? Their
appearance perfectly amazed me; their extreme youth, the
light clear brown of their complexions, their delicate features,
and inexpressibly graceful figures, their softly moulded limbs,
and free unstudied action, seemed as strange as beautiful.*

HERMAN MELVILLE
TYPEE, 1846

*It amused me very much to see how perfectly women are
women all the world over. There was the same incessant flow
of small talk among themselves, the same caressing and putting
their arms round one another, as would have been seen in
any other group of women in any other place from London to
Sydney. And to complete the resemblance they all persisted
in kissing and hugging an impudent young varlet of a ship's boy
who went down on the catamaran as they were going away.*

THOMAS HUXLEY
OF THE *RATTLESNAKE*

As one looked outward from Pacific ships, there were often women to be
seen—women who acted in a variety of ways. Some women waved their men
away from the dockside at Liverpool or Callao or Amsterdam; other women
swam to meet the ships, bringing love and seeking iron, and in the process
changing men's attitudes towards life—and especially to the life on board
ship. To many sailors, the choice was not a difficult one—between what a
Bounty discipline was certain to be at sea and the bounty of love that seemed
certain to be on shore. Some women braved the sea themselves. Love was
not the only factor involved, but almost every woman who was at the dock
or at sea was there because she loved a sailor—whether friend, husband, or
father; this did not lessen the contribution many of them made as officers
or crewmen. On the whole, however, it seems that the mixture of sexes was
an explosive one; murders and suicides are often mentioned. Confinement on

board small ships, intensified by Pacific distances, magnified all human emotions, and sexual emotions are strong enough to begin with. But the evidence of the journals, with the possible exception of the journals of the buccaneers, would indicate that the absence of women was less serious sexually than myth would make it seem.

French ships, and French sailors, some as buccaneers, had appeared many times in the Pacific before the *Boudeuse* came with Bougainville in 1765, a leader remembered for a number of things—one of them a flower—but most of all because he was not really a sailor, but a soldier, in a sense a throwback to the system of command of two centuries earlier. With the French flair for "la différence," the *Boudeuse* expedition carried both a prince and a woman. The prince went to find adventure, the woman to keep her lover; she found both adventure and the fame of being the first woman to circumnavigate the earth. She had disguised herself as the valet of her lover Commerson, the expedition's scientist, and escaped detection until the men of Tahiti—who knew either more about women or less about valets—spotted her. They could not understand why she then refused to grant them the same favours that their women were granting the French sailors. Perhaps she was overwhelmed by the odds against her. Unfortunately, Jeanne Baret, the *Boudeuse*'s lady-in-hiding, did not leave a diary or journal.[1]

Commerson was a good scientist, and his idea of essential equipment for a long voyage appealed to the amateur scientist in Banks; so Sir Joseph made similar arrangements for his second Pacific voyage. For various reasons he did not go, and Cook's reaction to a stowaway woman, therefore, is not known. From that same ship on his third voyage, Cook wrote to Banks saying that "nothing is wanting but a few females of our own species to make the Resolution a compleate ark." It could be that he was merely metaphorically emphasizing the number of species he had aboard and was not expressing any personal wish or allowing himself a sly dig at Banks.[2] Actually, at times, there were more women on board early naval ships than is imagined. A ship-of-the-line, the *Royal George*, had 300 women on board when she sank, although most of them were harbour visitors.[3] This event was the equivalent of a whaleship or warship capsizing at Tahiti or Hawaii when crowded with frolicking Polynesian girls.

Many women sailed the Pacific voluntarily, quite apart from the emigrant canoes and the later immigrant ships. Mary Anne Parker went in the *Gorgon* with her husband and left an excellent description of eighteenth-century voyages from quite an unusual point of view. Not all women were as hardy; one missionary's wife left the *Duff* at Spithead because of seasickness, forcing her husband to hear a call to stay in England. The women who did emigrate tried to remain feminine, whatever hardships they had to endure. There is an amusing story, but with the sadness of exile in it too, of the women in the *Charlotte Jane* who burst into tears at the rough and tiny port of Lyttelton: "they had all dressed themselves in their Sunday best, and there was nowhere to go."[4]

Some women had no "Sunday best" when they arrived in Australasia. Convict women, many of them petty offenders by modern standards, were sent out to Australia throughout the first half of the nineteenth century. In spite of the myth that the British government did not care what happened to them—easily enough disproved by correspondence on file in the Public Records Office in London—these women suffered no more hardships than most immigrants. Sickness and disease were prevalent in immigrant ships (and plenty of convict ships suffered greatly too in spite of the above mentioned evidence of efforts). Indeed, they were often the same ships, chartered for individual voyages by the government to use in these different methods of settling Australia. In the ship *Layton*, sailing in 1837, 70 out of 178 children died of measles, a disease often epidemic and fatal at that time.[5] The suffering of the mothers, already lonely and homesick and already undergoing physical and emotional hardship, may be imagined. Part of the trouble was overcrowding; in one ship, over 400 immigrants of both sexes were crowded into the space which had been considered sufficient for 300 male convicts. As a result, it became a fever ship and scores of them died. There had been no harshness, it was claimed, "except that the chief mate occasionally used a small rattan to the women who hesitated to go down."[6]

Women might well hesitate to go down to the crowded 'tween decks: "washing, indeed, was generally neglected, except on Sunday morning."[7] In another ship, there was only one bath for 400 people. In 1844, a Parliamentary committee reported of one immigrant ship that "when the hatchways were opened, under which the people were stowed, the steam rose and the stench was like that from a pen of pigs."[8] There were praiseworthy ships too, and for individual trips many surgeons could claim they did not lose one person. One captain said he had lost not one convict or immigrant, although he had commanded on many voyages.[9] In some slight mitigation of the captains' and the surgeons' burden of responsibility in the bad ships, the distances and time involved, the crowding, the tension and stress, and the sheer ignorance of sanitation have to be considered. In that age, this lack of sanitation was almost as dangerous ashore as it was afloat. Oddly enough, babies born aboard ship were more likely to survive than were those infants who came on board as passengers, probably because weaning was a particularly dangerous time.[10]

One of the problems in any ship was to keep the single men and women separated; another was the seduction—if it can be called that, given the relative positions of power and choice—of young women by ships' officers. One Australian governor protested against "the evils that appear naturally to flow from the separation of females at an early age from their natural guardians and protectors."[11] As is usual in human affairs, especially those involving sex, not all the seduction was on one side. Whymper, in his ship "bound for Vancouver Island, via the Horn," was accompanied by an

... "invoice" of sixty young ladies destined for the colonial and matrimonial market. They had been sent out by a home Society, under the watchful care of a clergyman and matron; and they must have passed the dreariest three months of their existence on board, for they were isolated from the rest of the passengers. ... I cannot honestly recommend such a mode of supplying the demands of a colony. Half of them married soon after arrival, or went into service; but a large proportion quickly went to the bad, and, from appearances, had been there before.[12]

Seduction, sickness, sadness, the loneliness of exile, even a voluntary one, make the stories of many immigrant and convict ships pathetic ones. It was not always a sad story. Many immigrant women knew happiness, both on board and in the new lands; there was also the excitement of nation building, for it was no less than that.

Some incidents on board amused the passengers. One wife who, according to Ensign Best (but perhaps with an ensign's exaggeration), was somewhat bigger than her husband of eighteen stone, obviously could not share a bunk with him in the *James Pattison*. After gentlemanly consideration, the husband was concerned that his wife might be thrown out of the berth, and "to prevent so dreadful an occurrence he got in himself" and left his wife the floor. As "Mrs. McDonald was not the right shape to repose quietly on the deck," her maid had to hold her while she slept.[13] The order of precedence is clear enough.

Other seagoing women suffered even more than Mrs. McDonald or her maid. There are some extreme examples in other parts of the world. Babies were born aboard British ships-of-the-line during the battle on the Glorious First of June, and some during the Battle of the Nile. A boy so born on the First of June in the *Tremendous* was christened Daniel Tremendous Mackenzie.

A French captain's wife who accompanied her husband to sea wrote of her journey. She described meeting an English frigate captain's wife who also sailed with her husband and had her pregnancy at sea. Since there was no battle to interrupt her plans—or perhaps to hasten those of the baby—she had gone ashore in Mauritius just in time to give birth to a boy.

There is also a most interesting description of a native child being born in the *San Pedrico*, the mother being constantly doused with buckets of seawater all through the process.[14] As stated earlier, in emigrant ships, babies often stood life well enough. The *Cap Pilar* had a baby on board for much of the cruise, and she enjoyed the life: "Jessica never showed any symptoms of seasickness."[15]

Nearly always the only women aboard were the wives of the captains. In spite of the practice being forbidden, Rose de Freycinet went with her captain-husband at the risk of his career; the career was saved by their king, Louis XVIII, remarking in a very French way that "it hardly called for punishment, since devotion was a quality that was unlikely to infect many wives."[16] Rose's accompanying her husband may have been justified by the "loneliness of command," but it was envied by the other men as a privilege. In the *Uranie*, "by her mere existence young Mme de Freycinet furnished a topic of conversation likely to disturb the good harmony, even the discipline, essential in a naval ship."[17] The men's frustration and the cast of their thoughts were demonstrated by their ensuring she could hear their ribald songs and earthy jokes. This would have confirmed some commanders' views. One of Anson's biographers reported that commander's fears about taking beautiful women on board: "Lust and envy, jealousy and suspicion would be stirred up."[18] Women were long considered unlucky on board ships, but this was not due to the disabilities of women, but to the drives of men and the troubles these caused. Certainly the presence of female convicts on board the transportation ships led to disciplinary difficulties with both crew and guards, and the troubles occurred whether or not the women were virtuous. Knox-Johnston, in the *Suhaili*, was frank about it all: "Not that I am feeling romantic at present, but if I had female company I expect I would!"[19]

Some American whaling ships had their captains' wives aboard permanently. Whalers' quarters were as comfortable as those of modern cabin cruisers, "often with a double, spring-mattress bed slung on gimbals for the captain and his wife."[20] Crewmen believed a captain with his wife on board was harder to please: "but whether to show off his authority before an admiring female . . . or simply from irritation at her presence" was a matter of much speculation.[21] To get good captains, the shipowners encouraged the captains to take their wives, one company going so far as to pay one captain's way across the United States to marry his bride and then sending them both away in the ship for their honeymoon.

Windjammers also often carried captains' wives and, as in the whalers, some women became capable officers. The *Novara* met a whaling ship in which the wife kept watch as an officer, took the helm and used "sea-phrases" as a sailor would—perhaps "sea-phrases" is an euphemism.[22] One wife, who inspected a ship before allowing her husband to accept it, agreed to the appointment because it had been the dream of her life "to have a ship with a chart house on the poop . . . so convenient to do my sewing in." Nonetheless, this wife "knew quite a lot about navigation and ship's business. . . . She signed on the ship's Articles as purser at a shilling a month."[23]

Other Pacific cultures vary in their attitudes to women in ships, and some also give women power. In the Hong Kong sampans, in which whole families live, the adult females are firmly in charge. Some cultures, however, gave women very much more power than that. In the Queen Charlotte Islands, "the women, in trade, as well as in every thing else, which came within our knowledge, appeared to govern the men." The women often beat the men mercilessly.[24] Indian tribes in British Columbia varied a great deal in this aspect as they did in other cultural matters. Perhaps reaction had set in in one way or the other, for there are reports of the great oppression of women in other parts of northwest America during the same period.

This one Canadian precedent of bark-petticoat government was not widely adopted, so some women became more directly useful at sea. In the *Garthwray*, the captain's daughter, Eva Frampton, was "allowed to take a trick at the wheel and steer the ship."[25] This was a compliment to her ability. One seagoing author compared an excellent helmswoman to a good horsewoman. There is certainly an art to both horsemanship and helmsmanship, and helmsmen varied in their skill: "whilst he was at the helm the ship was much drier, as he is a beautiful helmsman."[26] Mrs. Reed, wife of the captain of an American ship, the *T. F. Oakes*, "proved herself a far better helmsman than the majority of the men aboard the *Oakes*."[27]

Mrs. Reed successfully commanded and navigated the ship in 1897, after her husband's illness and the chief mate's death left her the responsibility; even at this late date, scurvy had decimated the crew. Lloyd's of London gave Mrs. Reed their famous Silver Medal. Spirit and competence could lead to most unusual accomplishments. Mary Patten, "a beautiful woman of refined and gentle manner," took over as captain when her husband was very ill and "navigated and sailed the heavily sparred clipper," the 1,600-ton *Neptune's Car*, around the Horn from the Atlantic to the Pacific (that is, the hard way), a feat even more impressive that that of Mrs. Reed.[28] The women's rights movements of that day "used her as the star example of woman's ability to compete successfully in the pursuits and avocations of man."[29] Interestingly, Mrs. Patten herself objected to being so used; she probably looked on her own capable efforts as survival rather than competition.

Twentieth-century women are doing equally as well. In the *Tzu Hang*, Beryl Smeeton worked to repair the ship and did "the job as properly as a professional carpenter could have done it on dry land." She could also "take a sextant sight ... work out the position line, ... and plot it on the chart," and her stints at the helm were done "sitting patiently and alert at the wheel."[30] Perhaps Beryl Smeeton's greatest contribution to the yacht was her "bright unquenchable spirit."[31] Even so, her skills and spirit were not unique. Lewis sailed the *Rehu Moana* across the Pacific with two women as crew, his only complaint being that they tended to gang up on him. The *Albatros* had two females in her crew; "Both could hand, reef, and steer," the phrase used to describe an able seaman.[32] In Australia, Coles's trimaran encountered a yacht, fittingly called the *Valhalla*, skippered by an American girl commanding a mixed crew.[33]

This girl, Mrs. Patten, and Mrs. Reed, however, did not reach the seagoing heights—or depths—of Mary Lovell, who became a pirate captain.[34] None of them was of the importance to seamen as was Ho Hsien-ku of China, who was one of the eight Taoist fairies and the only female member of that roistering band of fantastic Pacific "immortals", she invented boats—according to legend.[35] There were European legends, also. The sailors of eastern Finland, so many of whom sailed the Pacific, believed that "on board every ship there is a being, a female, watching over and guarding the ship, sometimes attending to things neglected by the crew, and at other times, if the ship is in grave danger, showing herself and pointing, perhaps at something that needs strengthening, or drawing attention in some more subtle manner to some weakness in the ship or its gear that has been overlooked."[36]

Pacific ships, often so long at sea, were fertile breeding grounds for such legends; most of the real women were encountered on shore. When buccaneers or privateers raided Spanish settlements they often captured women. The *Duke*, one of Rogers's privateering ships, captured some. Her captain commended the modesty of his sailors when searching the female Spaniards, for they merely pressed their hands firmly against the clothes of the women (no doubt with *sotto voce* comments in English to amuse their friends, yet spare the women) and, in some cases, were rewarded by finding "Gold Chains" worn modestly out of sight, perhaps to avoid flaunting wealth before the poor sailors.[37]

This same privateer leader, if most respectful toward women, was less so toward his seniors in age, for he tells that later in the same voyage he placed his female prisoners in the charge of a specially selected man: "For Being above 50 Years of Age, he appear'd to be the most secure Guardian to Females that had the least Charm."[38] The captain did not say whether he meant that the women were safe from the man or that a man of his age was safe from seduction.

In spite of the reputation of sailors as womanizers, the record of the privateers and even of a few of the buccaneers was without blemish as far as female prisoners were concerned. The *Duke* retained some black women on board as cooks, and the nature of English naval cooking probably made this a successful experiment. Although the captain said that one woman had to be whipped to make her modest and well behaved, he did not comment on her cooking—if it were as good as that of the black cooks in many American clippers, it would be good indeed.[39] The relationship of some women to the kitchen was less direct. Indian women were kept as prostitutes in the *Discovery* at Nootka Sound; whether or not they did any cooking, they received kitchen furniture in payment for their other services.[40]

Whether cooking, commanding, or kissing, the roles of women in ships in the Pacific were fascinating ones, and by no means confined to the one normally thought of—willowy girls eager to serve sex-starved sailors. This was important, of course, but with some qualifications. Rickman, who sailed with Cook, claimed that "Fresh provisions and kind females are the sailors sole delight"[41]— the order of priority is interesting.

Sex has always been a matter for fantasy, speculation, and comment. As a result, exaggeration of the eagerness and the charms of Pacific women, particularly in the South Pacific, has created a myth far beyond anything that early records justify. A myth which emphasizes the eagerness of the women of any culture to accept strangers as lovers raises a question about the potency of the men of that culture, as was made very clear in many of the journals.[42]

It is only to be expected that ships sailing an ocean covering one third of the world's entire surface encountered a great variety of reactions from women to the crews—from eagerness to complete rejection. Women of many of the northwest American Indian tribes were reported as modest and chaste, although not completely invulnerable; "still they where not all 'Dianas'."[43] Robertson said that some Polynesian girls were both afraid and reluctant. In the journals of Pacific ships, there is no scarcity of references to chaste women as well as to ones who pursued. This varied with the rank of the women in their own society. Of New Zealand women, Samwell (who was of the type who would find out) said that "none of the fine Girls were suffered to come near us but were kept with great Care at their Habitations."[44] The French thought women extremely direct in New Zealand: "The men [the French sailors] watched impassively . . . their indifference exciting the women and driving them to unequivocal gestures."[45] The *St. Jean Baptiste*'s sailors were racked with scurvy, which no doubt explains their passivity in the face of Maori charm. Count Fleurieu commented in his realistic way about a later French voyage in another part of the Pacific that when healthy sailors after a long voyage find the women unattractive, then they must be. The sailors also had to adjust their ideas and standards of beauty to fit the location. This was quite possible for young men on long cruises, as Fleurieu, the historian of Marchand's voyage, pointed out when discussing the women of the Queen Charlotte Islands. "The French began to find them passable; and we imagine that they ended by finding them pretty."[46]

One extreme of the Pacific sex myth is portrayed in a nineteenth-century story—perhaps apocryphal, and at least overdrawn—of a murder in a peculiar set of circumstances. Twenty-five Manihiki women, so the story goes, had been engaged to dive for pearls and were put down on an uninhabited island, Suvorov, to get to work. Knowing the women had not seen their husbands for a long time, a crewman from a cutter swam to shore expecting an eager welcome, but "they either squeezed him to death or dragged him to pieces; at any rate they knocked the breath of life out of him in their hurry to get him." Such bar-room talk was both a result of and an addition to the myth. The other extreme may be exemplified at Easter Island where very few women ever appeared at any time, although it could be argued that this excess of modesty might not have been the idea of the women themselves.[47]

Apart from the aspect of sex, there is also a variety of observation of the role of women in the different cultures. It makes fascinating reading, but, except in instances where women led attacks—genuinely warlike raids—on ships, these comments have little to do with the ships themselves. Sex did affect the ships, because its temptations led to desertion, theft, indiscipline, and disease among the crews; healthy and disciplined seamen were, and still are, as vital to sailing ships as fuel oil is to diesel-engined launches.

Some women made more positive contributions than mere sexual relief to the health and discipline of seamen. During a return voyage from the Pacific, Dampier found that St. Helena herbs and girls quickly and completely cured his men of scurvy, although cynics might credit the cure to the herbs alone. Others might well point out that a cheerful atmosphere in itself is therapeutic. Men with the *Dolphin*, who had been on the doctor's list with scurvy for weeks, "said a Young Girl would make an Excelent Nurse" and they would recover "faster under a Young Girls care nor all the Doctor would do for them."[48] Robertson, master of the ship and author of the journal of the voyage, quite reasonably implied that these men might not be as ill as they claimed to be. The same reasoning led one ship's surgeon to assume conversely that if the men did not react positively to Tahitian beauty they were much more ill than he had thought.

Reaction to local women by the men in various ships depended to some extent upon the nationality and profession of the voyagers. Dr. Scherzer, of the Austrian frigate *Novara*, in 1858 the largest warship ever to have visited Auckland, said that Tahitian female dancing created "mingled shame and indignation with which it fills any but a French by-stander."[49] Perhaps because of their own inhibitions, the missionaries in the ship *Duff*, which brought the churchmen to Tahiti in 1795, did not consider the women who met the ship beautiful. Inhibition apparently alters perception.

At another South Pacific island, when young women came aboard the *Duff* dressed only in skirts made of leaves, the ship's goats, apparently not appreciating the missionaries' desire for no further revelation, ate the skirts quickly and completely. Later in the day, the delighted sailors were helped at their work of tarring the rigging by these same skirtless, shirtless, and uninhibited girls, although the sailors were inhibited by the presence of the missionaries into exemplary care with their brushes.[50] Inhibitions were quickly acquired. There is the story of the two Hawaiian girls being returned home by Vancouver's *Discovery* who had become so schooled in European attitudes that they worried about the crew seeing their ankles as they embarked.[51]

In spite of the legends of beauty and love, it all may be at least partly *faut de mieux*: "and the sight of an English Lady made my heart feel all in an *uproar*, and alas! the poor Sandwich Isle Girls where entirely forgot. So it is, and we cannot help itt."[52] Polynesian female beauty is a theme of nearly every other journal. Samwell tells of men openly prepared to take a chance on eighteenth-century punishment in order to stay in those fascinating islands.

Women, forgotten or remembered, are but one part of sailing legend—and not even included in Churchill's summation of the Royal Navy tradition as "Rum, Sodomy, and the Lash." It is true that much rum sailed the Pacific in ships, and it was the chief cause of the use of the lash, but there is little mention of homosexuality. Occasionally, buccaneer journals mentioned it, and the case of Ian Pietersz and the skipper's boy named Gerret at Buton in the Indies is noted in both a sailor's journal of the *Heemskerck*'s voyage, and in Tasman's journal.[53] Barlow did say of the sea that "it was a place where many ill vices were in practice," but this is most unspecific and could as easily have meant blasphemy as perversion.[54] The absence of any discussion of a problem, especially this particular one, does not mean that it did not exist. There is evidence that the buccaneers practised sodomy fairly extensively, but it was certainly not completely accepted; at least one buccaneer captain was removed from command when charged with perversion. Nevertheless, if at all impressed with Churchill's view, many more references to it might be expected than are found. Nor could it have been prudish editorial suppression, particularly in the light of the frank discussion by observers of diverse sexual practices of the many nationalities they encountered during their voyages.[55] There did not seem to be any reluctance to discuss suspected sodomy among the Polynesians, both in New Zealand and in Tahiti. Ledyard discussed it in detail and at great length as practised in Hawaii, saying it was "very prevalent if not universal among the chiefs," but not "among the commonalty."[56] As Ledyard goes on to tell of the sailors' and officers' strong "prejudice against it," there seems to be no unwillingness to discuss the subject.

In long and close confinement, sexual practice inevitably becomes a matter of discipline, owing to the intense feelings involved and aroused, whether discussing Mme. de Freycinet or the Dutch boy in Tasman's ship. If discipline had been subverted, however, the punishment would be in the records. It so seldom is that it is questionable whether sodomy was really the problem that it is claimed to have been. If acceptance had been taken for granted, seamen would not have taken it either so humorously as at Hawaii or so seriously as the Dutch did at Buton. The Spaniards took it seriously. Sodomy in Magellan's fleet was "a crime usually punished by flogging, but technically carrying the penalty of public hanging."[57]

A chapter about women should end on a more positive note than is reached by a discussion of perversion. Yet most deep-sea sailors were denied, and to an extent still are, the real joys of heterosexual love, which are not so much the varied and unguaranteed delights of sex itself as the enduring and creative joys of family life. To read of Cook's marriage, for example, is to understand the greatest sacrifice that explorers made. It is as untrue to say all sailors were promiscuous as it is to say that all Tahitian women were unchaste, but it would be as true for the men in ships as for the women ashore to say that the pressures of long periods of separation bore more heavily on those who scorned to find relief in infidelity. Contrary to the girl-in-every-port myth of the sea, there are journals in which the stresses of being apart from someone loved are openly described. Today's life ashore would not lead to the conclusion that homosexuality and the attitudes of men toward women as "sex objects" are problems caused only by confinement in Pacific ships, nor would reading the journals lead to the conclusion that such problems are solved by freedom on Pacific islands. Emotions may be intensified or weakened by momentary circumstances, but they still exist, and still depress or delight. A ship, said Melville, "is but this old-fashioned world of ours afloat."[58]

CHAPTER 25

Music

. . . four people performed upon flutes, which they sounded
with one nostril, while they stopped the other with their
thumbs; to these four others sang, keeping very good time, but
during half an hour they played only one tune, consisting of
not more than five or six notes; more I am inclined to think
they have not upon their instruments, which have only two
stops.

SIR JOSEPH BANKS
OF THE *ENDEAVOUR*

The Malay paddlers sit twelve a-side, singing in time with
their rapid paddling, digging powerfully and deep every stroke,
between each raising their paddles perpendicularly in the air,
then "down" all together again with a splendid swing, their
naked bodies swaying, and the canoe springing forwards like a
racehorse.

LORD GEORGE CAMPBELL
OF THE *CHALLENGER*

Life in Pacific sailing ships was hard. Work and responsibility wore the seamen away, and there were few compensations. For some, and almost certainly
this was the majority, there was no real relief from the pressures except
drink, for homosexual sex on board meant a dangerous conflict with cultural
and instinctive values, and sex on shore was both intermittent and uncertain.
A few, the aged or the enthusiastic, found refuge in religion; others, very
few, in poetry. This book is dedicated to those seamen who, in greater or
lesser degree, found in literature—either in its appreciation or its creation—
some emotional balance when the small world in which they sailed seemed
more confined than usual. To them a debt is owed for the sea literature
which, while as distinctive as its nurturing, takes its place by right as a
treasured part of a national heritage.

In the ships of the Pacific there were all types of men—with as diverse interests. There were men whose minds were always on the next bottle, men whose minds seldom wandered far from women, even men who, in reaction to these, mumbled to God in their hammocks or cried aloud to Him from the foretop. Whatever else they did—they all sang. So did the men whose shy sonnets were a secret treasure, or whose journals were to make them famous. Music was far more important in ships than it ever was on land; it was needed more, and so it meant more. Sailors worked to music—at least while at the most slogging, wearisome jobs; it was not the assistance to work that mattered most, but—as with Negro spirituals—the emotional relief of raising their voices where their role almost always demanded silence. Even loud and lyrical criticism of the sacred authorities on board was allowed—provided it was sung and provided the work went on.

Sea songs, like cowboy songs, filled the role of the ancient ballads, which indeed some of them were, and preserved the name and fame of men ("Old Stormalong," for example), for later seamen to sing about. Songs immortalized ships or Spanish ladies or nut-brown maidens or cities. Songs gave vent to the sadness of exile or the joys of being homeward bound. They were often the voices of repressed spirits breaking forth, and just as often the unburdening of the high spirits of youth and health. There was drollery in the ballads too, sometimes satire crucifying the pretensions of another class, sometimes merely the expression in rough verse of the buffoonery and earthiness dear to the lower deck. There are all kinds of sea songs, just as there are all kinds of sailors.

Naturally then, the men who valued song as an aid to effort and a relief to the spirit, would be interested in the music they heard wherever they landed. Gradually, as the Pacific was explored, more and more local references to the girls or to the ports became embedded in the shanties, as the sea songs came to be called. Not all sea music was vocal; many of the journals speak of violins, drums, trumpets, and bagpipes. The instruments helped to use rhythm as an aid to ship work, from keeping in stroke with the hand pumps to hauling up anchors. Polynesians, Indonesians, and Chinese also toiled in time to a variety of instruments—gongs, drums, trumpets—and to voice chants. The Europeans who heard them compared the music to their own.

The most haunting music of the Pacific was found in British Columbia; all journals concur in this. The *Discovery* was met by Indians singing in concert as they paddled, beating time on the canoe with their paddles— always perfect time, for in Indian as in Maori canoes the paddlers sat so close together that every motion had to be perfect harmony. Indian singing was both ceremonial and therapeutic, as well as entertaining and delightful. Elements of mimicry and pantomime were sometimes involved. One Indian, telling some Americans of a Spanish attempt to convert them, sang to them and "though it was in broken Spanish and indian yet he imitated the sounds of their voices their motions and religious cants of their faces to a miracle."[1] European crews found Indian singing to be very moving in its rhythm and harmony, and one captain also wrote of Indians "Singing, with Great Melody."[2] Their war songs were impressive too: "the most warlike and awfull thing they ever heard."[3]

It was obvious that the Indians thought singing important: "Their Song was composed of a variety of strange placed Notes, all in Unison and well in tune, the words were first given out by one Man, as a parish Clerk gives out the first line of a Psalm."[4] It was one of Cook's officers who made this nostalgic comparison. His commander thought that the ending of each strain of Indian singing," "a loud and deep sigh," had "a very pleasing effect."[5] Indian women sang too, shaking rattles shaped like birds and filled with pebbles in rhythm with their voices—"a very harmonious Sound."[6] One observer said that the women did the singing: "the music was rude but agreeable it being both vocal and instrumental the vocal part being performed by the women and the instrumental by the men."[7]

Although they had only whistles and rattles (figures 54, 55, 56, 57), some made of copper, the Indians in British Columbia liked European music, being  "very attentive" when the *Resolution* gave them "a few tunes on two french Horns."[8] The ship's second lieutenant, noting the favourable reception of the fife and drums as well as the French horns, flatly stated that "these were the only people we had seen that ever paid the smallest attention to those or any of our musical Instruments, if we except the drum."[9]

Rattles and drums were not the only percussive instruments recorded in the journals. Across the diagonal of the Pacific half a century

Fig. 54. Indian Whistle (British Columbia)

later, Arago, the famed French naturalist, kept rhythm just as impressively with his castanets, inspiring "a solo dance by an elderly man" in a crowd of approving Australian aborigines.[10] Aborigines, in some parts of Australia at least, had musical instruments. Macgillivray in the *Rattlesnake* described "a piece of bamboo, three feet in length, which, by blowing into it, is made to produce an interrupted, drumming, monotonous noise."[11] The instrument is now famous in modern popular musical circles as the didjeridoo (figure 58).

In the South Pacific islands, the Polynesians preferred their own music to that of the Europeans. Their singing was "musical and harmonious," and the accompanying movements done "as one man," but "Not one of our musical instruments, except the drum did they hold in the least esteem ... as to the French horns they very seldom would attend to them attall either here [Tonga] or at any of the other islands."[12]

Polynesians liked drums; they were part of their own culture. Tongan drumming was famous; in the early nineteenth century a Tongan was bass drummer in a British army band.[13] When the *Research* called at Tonga in its search for the wrecked La Pérouse expedition, she gave a concert with her fife and drums.[14] Then a fiddler played while European, New Zealand, and what were described as "Lascar"

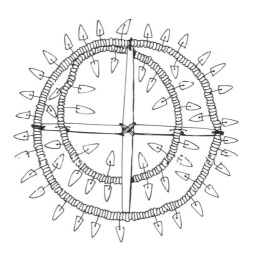

Fig. 55. Indian Rattle

dances were performed for the Tongans. Music was also used to ingratiate; it often worked, even with Polynesians who are usually reported as unresponsive to eighteenth-century European music. In a concert similar to the *Research*'s, an English midshipman "plaid on the Fiddle & some of our people danced to entertain" Indians near Cape Horn.[15] The Polynesians and Indians nearly always preferred the dancing to the music. Yet Cook entertained a king and his chiefs at Hawaii with his whole band, and one of his officers said they "were highly delighted with the music."[16] In at least one *kava* ceremony in which the Dutch with Schouten's circumnavigation in 1615-16 took part, "the Trumpets blue, and the Drumme played before

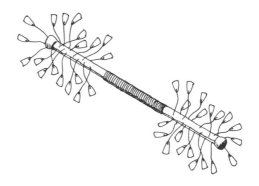

Fig. 56. Indian Deer Hoof Rattle

them wherein they [the Polynesians] tooke great pleasure."[17]

These were not the first brass instruments the Polynesians had heard, approvingly or otherwise. From the *Heemskerck*, Tasman had answered the sweet notes from Maori conch shells with a trumpet played by a sailor "who could play somewhat on the Trumpet"—a rather half-hearted commendation. The *Zeehaen*'s captain had his under-mate "do likewise."[18] A little later, Tasman gave Tongans their first taste of "complex" music, with a concert by two trumpeters, a violinist, "and one of our sailors who could play on the german flute."[19] Tasman seems to have been unappreciative of music— or perhaps he was a perceptive critic. Certainly not all Europeans appreciated Polynesian singing where "every time the oars went into the water, they made a great clamour."[20]

Fig. 57. Indian Rattle
(British Columbia)

Cook's men were not impressed by the playing of the Tahitian nose flute (figure 59) because "during half an hour they played only one tune, consisting of not more than five or six notes."[21] In discussing this particular flute music, a knowledgeable officer reasoned that "their being accustom'd to a music which consists of such few notes is perhaps the reason why they do not seem to relish any of ours, which is so complex."[22] Speaking of Tonga, Lieutenant Burney reports somewhat more technically: "Their music is mostly (but not always) in the minor key or flat 3.^{d} they want not for Variety, and the whole has a very pleasing effect, but in so uncommon a stile that I could never get hold of more than half a dozen following notes."[23] Yet it was precisely the variety in British Columbian music which set it above Polynesian music, at least to European ears.

Music was important in Pacific ships. It was not only the Polynesians and Indians who used it as entertainment and as an aid in keeping time in paddling. In the *Tartar Galley*, Captain Forrest's Malayan crew sang to help the rowers: "In rowing . . . they have always a song as a kind of tactic, and beat on two brass timbrels to keep time. I have known one man . . . with sometimes a Molucca, sometimes a Mindano Mangaio song, revive the rest, who from fatigue, were drousing at their oars; and operate with pleasing power what no proffered reward could effect."[24] Dampier described a similar galley where "Gong and the Rowers alternately answer each other, making a sound that seems very pleasant and warlike."[25]

Music, then, was an aid to effort and morale, and not merely entertainment. "The old man [the captain] knew that if chantying was curtailed in any way, the quality and quantity of work suffered, and that was all that mattered. 'Pulley-hauley' without a song would have been like marching without a band!"[26] Clark said that in the American clippers he captained "a good chanty man was worth four men in a watch."[27] So it was in English ships as well: "We took the halliards to the small capstan forward, and mastheaded the yard to the chanty of 'Away for Rio!' Jamieson singing the solo." And, "The thing to hear is a nigger crew chantying. They sing most beautifully, with splendid minor and half notes; they cannot do the least little bit of work without chantying."[28]

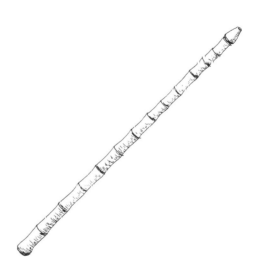

American and British ships had many black sailors, and the origin of sea shanties is sometimes attributed to those from the West Indies. The name has been ascribed to the West Indian "shantie," a movable house, but it seems to be much more logically connected with the French

Fig. 58. Australian Didjeridoo

word "*chanter*," "to sing," or even with the English "chant," as responses were almost invariably used.

There were shanties for each task: setting sail shanties, such as "Haul on the Bowlin" or "Shenandoah"; pumping shanties, such as "Storm Along, Stormie"; and purposely-long capstan shanties, such as "The Black Ball Line" or "Home, Dearie, Home."[29]

Singing was not the only music sailors knew: in one ship, ". . . the ship's fiddler couldn't fiddle fast enough for us, racing those hooks up . . . he played all the lively reels and strathspeys . . . the anchors were up in no time, the fiddler on one of the guns sawing away like a wild fellow."[30] In the *Bramble*, the ship's fiddler played while they hoisted horses overboard—but neither the type of tune nor the reaction of the horses is recorded. "The fiddler vanished when patent windlasses and steam donkeys came in; before that date his was one of the most important duties when heaving up the anchor."[31]

It was not always work that occasioned the music. There were concerts, and musical evenings when "they preferred to provide their own music" in the windjammer *Garthpool.* A violin, an accordion, a banjo ukelele, a mandolin, a Hawaiian guitar, a mouth organ: "and the carpenter performed on one of his big saws . . . one person on board suggested that the crew were better musicians than sailors."[32] In the *Illawarra,* "the hymns, *Rock of Ages* and *Star of Hope,* were accompanied by the harmonium, a viola and a muted bugle."[33] Such strange assortments of instruments seemed to match the strange assortment of men that usually manned British merchantmen.

Singing was important; in Dana's ship "were two English man-of-war's-men, so that, of course, we soon had music. They sang in the true sailor's style . . . many of the latest sailor songs."[34] Perhaps the rhythm of the work or the variety of cultures intermingling at the ports of call begot the rhythm, for although the shanties do not have the lullaby sadness of cowboy laments, they nevertheless avoid the intrusive cadence of marching songs. The internal rhyming and assonance in them are frequently used as aids to memory: "I've courted Maori beauties beneath the kauri trees," or "They dug his grave with a silver spade." It was these cheery songs—ignoring for the moment silver spades and graves—which, quite as much as the lures of scented distance and hinted mystery, are so essential a part of the glamour of the sea. Like all glamour, it is fundamentally false. With the sea, as with the cattle range or the Canadian North, much is made of the intermittent pleasures in order—perhaps unconsciously—to cloak the grim and constant reality. Songs, then, were consolatory at the best of times, if not always recognized as such. Some were frankly so. Those of the convicts in their transports were, and those of the missionaries in the *Duff,* who, impelled to leave England by conscience, seemed no less sad than the convicts compelled to leave England by conviction.[35] Rose de Freycinet's guitar in the French corvette had

Fig. 59. Tahitian Nose Flute

sadness in its notes, too, evident sometimes when she spoke of it; so had the "small upright piano" a whaling captain let his wife take to sea.[36] It is not difficult to imagine that these women were often sad, being both alone in their sex and sharing the loneliness of command as well. Sadness may be seen, however, where there is really only nostalgia. Other emotions, such as reverence, could also be mistaken for sadness. There is a description of shipboard melancholy in a report to the Inquisition, which probably owes more to the religious prejudice of the Spanish observer than to any actual emotion of the musicians in the *Golden Hind*: "they brought four viols, and made lamentations and sang together, with the accompaniment of the stringed instruments."[37]

Drake, Cavendish, Cook, and many other captains of European naval ships that explored or raided in the Pacific brought musicians—sometimes whole bands—with them. As to be expected, the musicians had non-musical duties on board, but their most important functions were to entertain guests when it seemed wise to conciliate, or to arouse the crew to battle readiness when it seemed necessary to fight. To impress one guest, Cavendish "banquetted him most royally . . . and caused his Musitians to make him musicke," but, in his fight with the Manila Galleon, he encouraged his crew "with the whole noyse of trumpets."[38] On one occasion in Tahiti, "the whole band of music" of the *Resolution* "struck up a grand military march, and the procession began."[39] On an earlier occasion, "when the King thought proper to depart . . . [we] entertained him with the Bag-pipes of which musick he was very fond."[40]

The Tahitian "King" was not alone in his appreciation of bagpipes. The pipes were not just for entertainment. The Waipu skippers, the New Zealanders who had brought their Nova Scotia sea skills with them, were no more famous than the Waipu pipers, who had preserved their art in Cape Breton Island and carried it to New Zealand when so many of them sailed there to settle. One of these piper-skippers, "commanding a brigantine, had a potent charm to dispel a calm; he walked up and down the poop playing the bagpipes, skirling for wind, giving his crew a blaw, a blaw, until he blew the ship into a breeze."[41] The pipes have not gone the way of the nose flutes. The modern trimaran *Gallinule* heard the pipes in Cairns, Australia, when a ship came in from Greenock which "appeared to have a piper aboard playing fit to bust his lungs."[42]

Less glamorous, but perhaps more adaptable to mood, were Knox-Johnston's twentieth-century tape recorder and the crews' gramophones in so many nineteenth-century American ships. Today, in most Pacific vessels, the wireless brings in music from all over the world, most of which would make the clipper-ship shanties and the Waipu bagpipes sound as soothing as nostalgic.

CHAPTER 26

The Clash of Cultures

*They were artists in reducing life to its essentials, and, though
they did not succeed in making for themselves a simple life
of the beauty of the Eskimos', theirs had quite a lot to recommend it. Their system of ethics and ideas of morality were
as simple as they were convenient; everything was permissible
that procured them satisfaction of their desires. Murder,
suicide, adultery, etc., if not actual virtues, were far from being
considered sins or even wrong.*

SVEN WAXELL
OF THE *ST. PETER*

*The skipper and some of the crew went ashore and fell in with
many natives who appeared to be very friendly. They brought
off two and showed them the vessel . . . they noticed only two
things—an accordion and some axes which latter they were
very desirous to possess. There can be little doubt that the iron
articles were in fact the cause of the subsequent attack.*

THOMAS HUXLEY
OF THE *RATTLESNAKE*

European ships reached the Pacific during the early years of the sixteenth
century in the latitudes falling between the two tropics. The Portuguese,
travelling east, came to the west side of the Pacific at the East Indies, reaped
a rich harvest of spices, and began an imperial venture which has not yet
ended. The Spaniards, travelling west, reached the east side of the Pacific by
crossing the Isthmus of Panama, reaped a harvest of gold and silver, and
continued a centuries-old tradition of conquering and Christianizing the in-
fidels. Conquest has long since ended, yet Spanish culture remains pre-
eminent in vast areas of the world. Although both the Portuguese and Spaniards
spread north and south of their initial areas of Pacific influence, the commerce
and wealth they sought had northern and southern limits which were soon
reached. These limits were set by the climate, because wealth accumulated
in civilizations, and civilizations flourished only in warmer climes before the

development of European technology during the sixteenth, seventeenth, and eighteenth centuries. This technology was both encouraged and funded by the new wealth from the ancient East, new not because what had been unknown was becoming known, but because what had been inaccessible was becoming accessible. Sailing ships were the part of European technology which made the spices of Java and the gold of Peru exploitable by Europeans, and guns, particularly the shipborne cannon, made their demands irresistible. For the variety of reasons discussed in an earlier chapter, the development of the large Chinese junks had not had the same effects.

Ships, like their guns, developed slowly by modern standards. Europeans could sail past the southern extremes of Africa and South America by the early sixteenth century—for example, as Magellan had done—but not easily or safely. The great winds and waves, and the legendary gales at the Cape of Storms (Good Hope) kept early ships from pressing south there to run eastward to Australia. Those that did so accidentally, Portuguese and Dutch, reported that there was nothing there worth the risk. The dangers of oceanic voyaging in the sixteenth century were so great—fevers, scurvy, starvation, shipwreck—that only commerce or looting which promised commensurate rewards justified the risks.

At the southern extreme of South America, the hardships and difficulties of threading the Straits of Magellan or of rounding the Horn were even greater, for in travelling westward ships were challenging the winds precisely where they had a clear run round the globe. Drake did it (and only just succeeded) half a century of ship development later than Magellan, but he, and Cavendish and Hawkins later, wished to raid Peru. They turned north and did not have to force their way westward against the Westerlies. Mendaña in 1567 and 1595 had led Spanish expeditions into Polynesia and Melanesia north of the great westerly wind belt, and so did Quirós in 1605. There was no lasting result, however. Once more the risks and losses seemed to outbalance the possible gains. Rich commerce depended on great civilization; goods had to be valuable, because the ships could carry so few of them. The ships were small, but as the rigging was still relatively inefficient the crews were large and required much space for themselves and their provisions, and the dangers of piracy or native contumacy meant that precious space had to be set aside for guns, powder, and shot. Apart from this, Spain was straining herself to protect her position in Europe and America. In the Pacific beyond America, she contented herself with the rich Philippines. This trade crossed the Pacific to Mexico, using a wind route of the same kind as that by which it crossed the Atlantic to Spain, that is, north to the Westerlies and then east, south to the trades, and then west.

These strong and persistent westerly winds protected the extreme southwest Pacific from great incursion from the east until Cook came. Byron, Wallis, Bougainville and Carteret in late eighteenth-century ships had been forced by the Westerlies to edge northwards almost as much as they had forced Magellan in 1520 and Schouten in 1615. The apparent barrenness of Australia protected the southwest Pacific from the west. It was known that there was a land mass there, but the rumours about it were not of wealth—of gold and silks and glamour—but of sand and flies and poverty. It aroused little interest.

In the far north of the great ocean there was intermittent hope of, and more intermittent effort to find, a passage from Europe to Asia around northern North America. By the seventeenth century, the northern extreme of that continent was written off, except for furs and codfish, and rather tenuous legends of gold. It was an obstacle, and far greater than realized, between Europe and Japan and China. Its westward side was still largely unknown. Drake sailed north past New Albion, named for "white bankes and cliffes which lie towards the sea" that would remind any Englishman of home. It was California. How far north of it he sailed is not certain, except that it was beyond 43°N and far enough north that in June the English—a hardy breed surely—complained of "ayre so colde, that our men being grievously pinched with the same, complained of the extremitie thereof, and the further we went, the more the colde increased upon us."[1]

The cold protected the North Pacific until in the mid-eighteenth century the steady overland expansion of the Russian Empire reached the Pacific coast and changed to an expansion across the seas. Alaska was discovered and claimed. This great Russian Empire, and that of the Chinese, are the only great eighteenth- and nineteenth-century empires to survive so far the vicissitudes of the twentieth century. The Russian Empire has even increased in size, for as a great and pragmatic nation (although she did not spare herself the exertions and sacrifices of empire building) she managed to spare her conscience the burden of guilt and vicarious responsibility which afflicts the West. Civilizations, like David and Solomon, seem to soothe their decline by producing psalms and proverbs: not the Russian. Even if the last to reach the Pacific, she is still there and seems likely to stay.

By the 1760's and 1770's, the Portuguese, Spanish, Chinese, Japanese, and Russian Empires were Pacific powers, and Britain and France, their ships improved and developed by a century of war, their appetites whetted by their experiences in India and the West Indies, were ready to explore and, where it seemed profitable, to exploit. The greatest power of all was still to come. Not yet emerged from the womb of revolution, but already conceived in a fertile independence, destined to develop the most powerful Pacific empire of them all, the British Colonials beginning to call themselves Americans were already spoken of as a world power by men as perceptive as Chatham and Burke.

The stage was set. The wealth and power existed; they sought as ever to reproduce and increase themselves by commerce or by conquest. The technical equipment existed; ships, navigation instruments, water purifiers, preserved foods, had benefited by constant development since Magellan's day, lured on by trade, spurred on by war. The attitudes existed; men were willing to be trained, men were eager to experiment, men were eager (and some were able) to explore for reasons other than the classic ones of Glory, Gold, and Gospel. Science had grown beyond witchcraft to become mature enough to face religion openly and to begin to win some of the arguments. It was the Age of Enlightenment in Europe; how far would that light be carried by her ships?

Exploration lasted for centuries. The Pacific is vast and some islands are low in fact and in visibility; whale ships and commercial vessels were discovering new land until after the middle of the nineteenth century. By the end of exploration, nearly all the islands were under, or about to come under, the protection of some European power. In the four corners of the Pacific, the Europeans governed firmly by that time. Kamchatka was part of the Russian Empire; Alaska was American, and British Columbia was Canadian; Australia and New Zealand, like Canada, were maturing settlement colonies of the British Empire; and Chile was one of the most European of the successor states of the Spanish American Empire. Already these offshoots of Europe were claiming new Pacific territories of their own. Chile governed Juan Fernández and Easter Island; America controlled Hawaii; and New Zealand, home of the most vigorous branch of the Polynesian peoples, spoke up vigorously. In the words of the eminent historian of New Zealand expansionism, ". . . the Maori people had convincingly demonstrated that New Zealand was a part of Polynesia. This thesis was virtually turned upside down by propagandists of the late nineteenth century who argued that all Polynesia should belong to New Zealand or should share the same British rule as New Zealand."[2] In New Zealand, white settlement came about because Europeans had developed skills and technology since the years when Magellan had crossed the Pacific. There was little sign that their attitudes had changed.

Throughout this book, the relationship of technique, skill, and equipment to human attitudes has been discussed. Good equipment means good morale; skilled officers lead contented crews; competence in commanders evokes responsibility in the commanded. Technique shapes attitudes as much as it results from them; therefore, the spread throughout the Pacific area of new techniques, skills, and materials brought by Europeans would cause important changes in human perceptions, and, in consequence, societies. Islanders who had laboriously built canoes from small breadfruit tree trunks could now trade tortoiseshell for sawn planks; Indians at Cape Flattery could change their copper harpoons with elk horn barbs for harpoons of forged iron by selling furs or whale oil. From such small beginnings, new values and new attitudes to commerce would develop. Europeans did not introduce trade into the Pacific, for tribes in all but the most primitive of cultures already exchanged various products, but they expanded and altered it immensely as new arrivals brought with them both new demands and new products. This meant great adjustment for the various Pacific peoples, directly in their economies, and indirectly in their societies. Nor should the changes which occurred in Europe be forgotten. There, the most important change was the shift in power from the Mediterranean to the Atlantic, which took place when the sea highways of the world enabled western Europe to cheaply and efficiently bring the products of the East to avid consumers.

The whole world altered, not just the Pacific, because sailing ships which were able to carry massive cargoes and to defend themselves with broadside cannon were developed in Europe. Paralleling this evolution, and just as important, was the maturing of techniques of navigation which enabled men to guide ships to any destination. All these technical developments, many of which had long been known in China, led to that "expansion of Europe" which discovered America, explored the Pacific, and created today's world. The attitudes of Europeans towards Asia and to the Pacific islands (including the theory of the Noble Savage), the violent clashes between newcomers and natives, and the causes of them, the influence of convicts and deserters, the thoughtlessness of land-hungry settlers and the well-meant interference—a kind of erosive goodness—of the missionaries, the use of Pacific men in European ships, and blackbirding as a labour policy, altered both the lands visited and the lands left behind. All these things spread European ideas and attitudes, fundamentally altering Pacific life.

The relationship of technique and attitude is complex enough in a study of European economics or history, and doubly so when the secondary effects of its impact on other cultures are examined. As an eminent economist put it,

. . . at first sight the problem might appear to be merely one of introducing new methods of production and the instruments, tools or machines appropriate thereto. But what is really involved is a vast change in social beliefs and practices. . . . It is because all these new activities are not independent of the existing institutions into which they have to be fitted, and which have in turn to be adjusted to them, that

Plate 61. H.M.S. *Rattlesnake*. This small 28-gun frigate became famous not solely because of the part she played in the exploration of eastern and northern Australia and New Guinea, but also for her association with the explorer Captain Owen Stanley, with the naturalist John Macgillivray, and with the great philosopher T. H. Huxley, all of whom she carried.

Plate 62. The *Golden Hind*. This galleon was the first ship to circumnavigate the world under a single captain, the great Sir Francis Drake. She returned to England so heavily laden with gold and silver from Drake's raids on the Spanish Pacific empire that it was feared she might founder at sea. Although

Plate 63. The *Dolphin* attacked by natives at Tahiti. Men from the *Dolphin*, commanded by Captain Wallis, were attacked by the Tahitians on the day of their arrival. Although willing to trade, the Tahitians seemed prepared to resist any landing. The *Dolphin*'s guns proved warrant enough to allow seamen to go ashore and begin the contact with Tahiti which altered Europe's view of the world and of mankind. The Tahitian's world would itself change beyond restoring.

Plate 64. Dumont d'Urville's *Astrolabe* in danger on a reef at Tonga in 1827. The *Astrolabe* survived this incident to round the world again ten years later.

the process of change is so complex and, if it is to proceed harmoniously, necessarily so slow.[3]

This is particularly true when those cultures differ so much from the impinging European culture as did the ancient, sophisticated and wealthy empire of sixteenth-century China at one extreme, and, at the other, the primitive and poor tribes of Fuegian Indians. Yet both of these societies, the sophisticated as well as the primitive, were altered by the arrival of Europeans in sailing ships.

There is extensive literature in many languages dealing with the clash of cultures in the Pacific. Sometimes, when reading it, as in reading that on Polynesian navigation, there is a temptation to repeat what the captain said of the officers' council—"their opinions were as divers as their names." This literature contains absorbing speculation, interesting evidence, and clever debate. I commend it to you. The conclusions reached are of no concern in a book about the problems of the ships themselves. The discussion contained in this chapter is very brief and merely illustrative, and meant to point up the value of the original journals. There is value as well as interest in seeing seventeenth- or eighteenth-century Maoris through the eyes of contemporary Dutchmen or Englishmen. It is unfortunate that there is no comparable opportunity to see things the other way round.

The authors of these journals describe the meetings with strange men and women in the new lands most ingenuously. They tell what the literate sailors saw, or thought they saw, how they reacted and, from their point of view, how the people they met reacted. So far as is possible, allowances must be made for the cultural attitudes which shaped those early European and American writers, but it is even more important that the readers be aware of the attitudes which have shaped themselves. Having tried to do this, my two main conclusions are that men under pressure seldom acted or reacted in predictable ways, and that the pressures were nearly as varied as the men.

In working out the tiny dramas on the beaches and on the decks or between deck and canoe, the positive human quality which most affected the results was curiosity—the negative ones were greed and fear. Without curiosity, ranging from a desire to study the transit of Venus to a wish to see if a sailor were really white all over, the encounters would not have occurred or taken the form they did; without greed or fear, the results would not so often have been violent or distressing. Curiosity, greed, and fear were common to both newcomers and natives, and, under the circumstances, with new products before their eyes, with profits or benefits quite apparent, although with the reactions of the other side still unclear, the cupidity and timidity alike are understandable. To understand, readers need only to ask themselves how they would react to a genuine visit of men from outer space, particularly if there had been no reason to think about the possibility beforehand. The first Europeans in parts of the Pacific were seen as men from another world, as the various traditions embedded in indigenous tradition show. Sailors on an American brig were told of a gigantic devil gliding along on the water, spreading its wings to move, able to breathe fire, spit death, and shout like thunder.

Often the reactions on each side were more realistic. There was so much that was recognizable and eminently desirable to Europeans in the wealth of China. In the wealth of the European ships there was much that was completely new but immediately desirable to the Polynesians. The reactions of these particular groups to new situations in which one of the other groups was involved were interesting, as far as can be ascertained from the reports available. The Chinese, with their stable and sophisticated society, seemed to want little from the Europeans and, far from envying them, felt contempt. The various Polynesian peoples, with materially limited, but relatively stable societies, seemed avidly eager for iron and willing to adopt new techniques to further their ambitions—for example, they used the guns to conquer neighbouring tribes in Tahiti, Hawaii, and New Zealand. The Europeans, from an expanding culture with the resulting tensions and distortions, admired and envied both the sophistication of China and the simplicity of Polynesia. They admired and envied the ancient civilizations of the Far East as civilizations; they admired and envied the Polynesians as people.

The East certainly had plenty of wealth to envy, especially when one remembers the relative standard of living of sixteenth- and seventeenth-century Europe. The cargo of the *Madre de Dios*, the Portuguese carrack carrying some of this wealth home, consisted of jewels as well as

> . . . spices, drugges, silks, calicos, quilts, carpets, and colours etc. The spices were peppers, cloves, maces, nutmegs, cinnamon, greene ginger: the drugs were benjamin, frankincense, galingale, mirabolans, aloes, Zocotrina, camphire: the silks, damasks, taffatas, sarcenets, altobarsos, that is counterfeit cloth of gold, unwrought China silke, sheared silke, white twisted silke, curled cypresse.[4]

These were the precious goods which could be bought or stolen—the outward signs of a great civilization. The Europeans acknowledged the greatness. Pigafetta, with Magellan, spoke of "Great China, the king of which is the greatest sovereign of the world. . . . He has seventy crowned kings under his dependence; and some of these kings have ten or fifteen lesser kings dependent on them."[5] But the Chinese were admired for a great deal other than their wealth and power. Marco Polo found that they "surpass other nations in the excellence of their manners and their knowledge of many subjects, since they devote much time to their study and to the acquisition of knowledge."[6]

That knowledge was productive. In Kinsai, "without doubt the finest and most splendid city in the world," Polo saw "shops in which every sort of craft is practised, and every sort of luxury is on sale, including spices, gems, and pearls. In some shops nothing is sold but spiced rice wine."[7] Polo noted that Chinese life was not all study, at least in Kinsai, "for their minds and thoughts are intent upon nothing but bodily pleasure and the delights of society."[8] With some awe he reported that the city had "the finest baths and the best and biggest in the world."[9] (Cleanliness always invoked praise from Europeans, even though in those days in Europe washing seemed to be more theory than practice. It was a characteristic of Hawaiian and Tahitian culture often praised. "They [the Hawaiians] attend to a circumstance which particularly distinguishes polished from savage life, and that is cleanliness:—they are not only clean to an extreme in their food, but also in their persons and houses."[10])

Japan was admired almost as much as China: "The people of this Iland of Japan are good of nature, curteous above measure, and valiant in warre.... They are governed in great civilitie, I think, no Land better governed in the world by Civill Policie."[11] At least so thought William Adams, the English pilot who built ships for the Japanese Shogun in the early seventeenth century. Marco Polo called Japan "a very rich island, so that no one could count its riches," and spoke specifically of a palace with its rooms "paved with fine gold to a depth of two fingers breadth."[12] As he had not seen Japan, doubtless there crept in the exaggeration which always seems to expand tales of gold. Undeniably, Japan was rich. Carletti, who did visit it, gave the standard European reaction when he said that "Japan is one of the most beautiful and best and most suitable regions in the world *for making profit* by voyaging from one place to another."[13] (Author's italics.) Profit was usually uppermost in the minds of Europeans in the East—otherwise they would not have made the effort and faced the risks to get there; however, the journals show that for commercial acumen the Chinese and Japanese were a match for anyone. Shelvocke, outswindled once again in a life well within reproach, criticized the Chinese for "their immoderate love of money."[14]

There is little doubt that early voyagers exaggerated both the complexities of Asiatic civilization and the simplicities of other cultures. Carletti argued that the Chinese were responsible for "every invention for good or for evil, of beauty or of ugliness ... or at least it can be affirmed that they have in themselves the knowledge of everything."[15] On the other hand, Pigafetta said of Palaoan (Palawan) that he and his companions "found this island to be a promised land," and Cook said of the Aborigines of Australia that "in reality they are far more happier than we Europeans."[16]

Few of "we Europeans" agreed with Cook enough to envy the Aborigines. No one at all envied the Indians of the Straits of Magellan area, "the Most Miserable Wretched Creatures of all the Human Race." Robertson put forward a theory about the Fuegians and happiness which agreed with Cook's own conclusions about the reason for the happiness of the Aborigines. Robertson thought "their greatest happyness Concists in their Ignorance of the rest of Mankind, they seem Contented with their state not knowing any better."[17] Perhaps, people would have envied the immense size of the Patagonians if, in the welter of argument, they could have decided what their size was. Byron claimed that "the Stoutest of our Grenadiers would appear nothing to these,"[18] and that a six-foot-two ship's officer seemed "a mere shrimp" beside them.[19] Somehow, the Patagonian giants were never authenticated. Few sailors envied the people in the extreme north anything, except perhaps their great physical strength.[20] Ledyard, who knew Kamchatka well, because he was the kind of man who explored a society as well as its location, did not like or envy anything there. Perhaps the North Pacific climate made people content with Europe.

In the journals, it was the Polynesians, of all the Pacific dwellers, who were most admired as people. Lord Campbell, after the *Challenger* had visited the Friendly Islands, thought that "as far as physique and appearance goes they [the Polynesians] gave one certainly an immediate impression of being a superior race to ours."[21] Another English officer, Clerke, maintained that the Tongans "in their persons surpass in beauty every Nation I ever yet met with, excepting the Natives of the Marquesas."[22] It would hardly be possible to go further in admiration than Fleurieu did when writing of the Indians of the far northwest coast of North America: ". . . we admire the efforts of genius struggling with little means, and yet with success . . . [and we see that which] inclines us to presume the existence of a sort of social compact, dictated by Nature, sanctioned by Reason, and observed among them more religiously, perhaps, than if penal laws commanded its observance."[23] Here is the Noble Savage in full perfection, decked out with all the correct words: social compact, nature, reason. Nevertheless, it was the Polynesian and not the Indian life that was envied; here was the life of the Pacific of dreams. Schouten said, after being in Polynesia, that ships should go to the Pacific "so that there men may plainly behold and see the golden World, whereof the Poets write."[24]

A recent voyager declares that "there is an unwritten law against speaking ill of the South Sea Islands or even thinking of their people in worldly terms."[25] There is at least a measure of truth in this, for the recent reaction against the values of Western civilization, as represented by Europe and America, has revived the theory of the "Noble Savage," with only the decorative words being different. The theory now applies to anyone outside Europe or America; all the people to whom it is applied accept the word "noble," but, understandably, spurn the word "savage." Whereas in Crozet's time the Noble Savage theory was almost the monopoly of the "philosophers" of whom he spoke so bitterly, today the idea is much more widespread. Many people now suspect an innocent, moderate, and trite remark, such as "there is good and bad everywhere," because it indicates that possibly there might be some good in Washington or some bad in Nairobi. Even if most of the early captains were somewhat more realistic about humanity than that, there were still as many differences of opinion as there were temperaments.

As is usually the case, the theory is not completely invalid. Vancouver, neither fool nor sentimentalist, lavishly praised some native Alaskans: "... they had behaved with a degree of modesty and decorum rarely found amongst men in a far more civilized state ... if the conduct they exhibited during the time they passed with us, is to be received as their general national character, it indicates them to be a people unactuated by ambition, jealousy, or avarice."[26]

In Tahiti, Commerson, the scientist as famous for his valet as for his observations, found something very commendable—as one might suspect he would in "the gentle impulse of an instinct that is always sure because it has not yet degenerated into reason."[27] Modern touches abound in the observations made by the sailors. New Zealanders, said Crozet in 1772, dance heavily and sing only of war or of love. Two centuries have not altered this.

Like Commerson, de Surville of the *St. Jean Baptiste* rather favoured the Noble Savage philosophy, apparently reasoning that if civilization were bad, then lack of it must be good. But the down-to-earth Norman, Labé, who was with him, pointed out that while it was good to be free of the vices of European culture, it was not good to "suffer greater discomforts through lack of the material benefits of civilization."[28] By the "material benefits" Labé probably meant medical care, for this was fervently sought by the Pacific peoples. Drake, among others, spent much time in treating the ill in California. Anderson, one of Cook's surgeons, described disease of many kinds that he found everywhere in the Pacific; Europeans were almost always asked for medical help, whenever and wherever they landed. The more open-minded of the surgeons and captains picked up in return some new ideas in medicine and some new remedies. Colnett studied Polynesian and Indian medical methods. By today's standards, European medicine then was not advanced, but, in Labé's time, the foundation of its spectacular advance had already been laid in the scientific outlook which develops only in civilization. The very reasons for sending the *Endeavour* to Tahiti, in spite of the unfortunate aspects of cultural clash, were based on the scientific outlook which later would lead to great and beneficial advances in all fields. Men who would finance a voyage around the world to best observe the transit of Venus would not be content to remain ignorant in any science.

Cook realized the tragic effect that contact with Europeans would bring to the Pacific islands, and based his misgivings on the fate of the Indians in America, but he was too accurate an observer to miss the darker sides of life in New Zealand, the Pacific islands, northeastern Asia and western America also. La Pérouse did not miss them, either: "Each canoe has one man with whom the others do not associate. . . . He may be a slave, but in any case his rank is very inferior to that of the others."[29] However, La Pérouse did not criticize the Indians as strongly as Waxell criticized the Kamchatkans: "In fact the only recognized sins that have been recorded are those of bathing in, or drinking, hot water, and of saving anyone from drowning."[30]

Broughton of the *Chatham* commented on the jealousy of the South Sea islanders of the power others held—surely a most human trait. Most observers did not miss seeing the obvious powers of the chiefs and aristocracy in many places, although they also noted that this varied widely. Ledyard described Tahitian society as "feudal," no doubt an oversimplified analogy, but indicative that the critical faculty was not completely inhibited in Tahiti. If materialism were learned only from European contact, then Hawaiians, for example, were extremely quick to learn: "The years from 1811 to 1828 saw the sandalwood boom in Hawaii when the Hawaiian aristocracy lived high for a while on the profits of sandalwood cut by the common people." Captain Clerke of the *Discovery* said that in Hawaii "the immediate pleasure of the principal People is the Law of the inferior subjects in general, and that they drive them about as they please, even to destruction."[31]

Whether or not the observers were being realistically critical, it was Polynesia which meant the Pacific to the philosophers of Europe. It still does to most people. Who means Attu or Kiska when they speak of the "islands of the Pacific?" Who sees them as places to bury treasure or to marry pleasure? It is the changes in Polynesia which have been deplored, and it is the Polynesians who have entered an adjectival mythology—even living, breathing ones: "my old friend . . . narrated the *prodigious* history of her race and clan with her own *peculiar* eloquence and the *extreme* dignity of her bearing."[32] (Author's italics.)

All romance cannot be based completely on fiction. "Had a glimpse of the gardens of Paradise been revealed to me I could scarcely have been more ravished with the sight," said Melville of the valley of Typee on Nukuhiva.[33] "Gardens of Paradise" seem mythical enough, and romantic enough, but the beauty was real. London, however, nearly a century later, "saw a wilderness" in the same valley.[34] Wildernesses can be virgin or abandoned; in Typee, depopulation resulting from disease and war had made a wilderness from a garden. It is easy to see why Villiers quotes an old Samoan prayer:

> O keep from us the Sailing Gods
> that they bring not death and disease among us![35]

Nevertheless, many islands had more inhabitants who prayed that the "Sailing Gods" would come than inhabitants who prayed that they would not.

Disease came inadvertently; violent death, to Europeans and others, could come for causes almost as mysterious. The real reason for most of the early clashes between newcomers and natives is not known. Marion's French expedition could serve as an example of a fatal clash with its causes completely obscured by misunderstanding, and one which left the Europeans aware that they had transgressed, although unaware of how they had transgressed. The French ships came to New Zealand in 1772 needing repairs. By misfortune or mismanagement, or both, the *De Castries* and the *Mascarin* had collided while preparing to anchor at the Marion Islands on their way to the Pacific. The *De Castries* lost her bowsprit and her foresails, while the *Mascarin* lost her mizzen mast and damaged her upper works at the stern. This extensive damage would take some time to repair and would require stout wood, available, as they knew from Cook's journals, in New Zealand. It was the length of time spent in New Zealand which led directly to tragedy. The *De Castries* was one of the first ships to try to use "the beautiful cedar (Kauri pine) masts which we had found on the mainland."[36] (By "mainland," the French author meant the North Island of New Zealand, an application of the word quite the opposite of the present facetious New Zealand usage.) Lying ready to be hauled to the ships, the masts were abandoned because of clashes between the Maoris and French, in which Marion was killed.

No one knows the direct cause of the clashes; stories about the incidents differ widely. Perhaps the Maoris planned the killings, thinking that the French ships had already been there too long and by all appearances were going to stay even longer. It might have been a flare-up over something specific, perhaps something comparatively trivial when judged by European standards. Some suggest an infringement of *tapu*. "I can affirm," said Crozet, Marion's lieutenant, "that not even on the slightest occasion had these savages any reason to complain of us."[37] No doubt he was sincere, but, from the Maoris' point of view, there might have been many reasons for complaining. Usually, however, there are signs of dissatisfaction and unrest before the actual attack is made.

There were two quite opposite reasons for clashes between Europeans and the inhabitants of islands or coastal areas they visited. The first was the fault of the natives, but only in the sense that they showed themselves to be very human. French "philosophers" might laud the "New Cythera," but its inhabitants were determined to have it "newer" still. The first reason then was the natives' "desire for European goods . . . the temptations of the white men's wealth . . . the temptations to plunder."[38] After discussing all the ways in which his ship's officers and crew had tried to conciliate and to deal fairly with the Indians at Nootka, on Vancouver Island, one participant decided, although some modern historians do not agree with him, that the cause of an Indian conspiracy to take the ship was a desire to plunder: "it was alone to possess themselves of our property which to them appeared immense and which in a similar situation in a more civilized country would have been a temptation to many."[39] Jacobs, of the American brig *Margaret Oakley*, gave an excellent description of the appearance of a European ship and her clothed crew as they must have looked to the inhabitants of the southwest Pacific. Obviously, the temptations were strong. Petty thieving was a major problem, and attacks on ships quite common—particularly in Melanesia and northwest America.

The second reason for conflict was the Europeans' fault, for they collected such quantities of food that the local inhabitants feared for their own supply. "The Old men fairly told him that he must go away or he would leave them without provisions," was a reaction to the purchases of the *Endeavour*.[40] Coupled with this pragmatic fear was a less tangible one, but perhaps one more important: "Coconut trees are often treated as sacred. . . . In these circumstances the destruction of a tree is of concern to the whole tribe."[41] Yet Europeans—sometimes desperate with scurvy—would cut down a tree just for the nuts or the cabbage; the resentment of the owners is understandable.

There is also the likelihood of a simple accident triggering clashes. In the *Charlotte*, a convict ship on her way to China for a cargo home after delivering her unhappy passengers, the sudden flapping of a loose sail threw several Micronesian visitors overboard and very nearly brought about an attack.[42] Captain Gray of the *Columbia* accidentally discharged his gun while in a ship's boat, and wounded an Indian: "our situation would then have been the most critical for though it was an accident yet in all probability it would have been construed otherways." Fortunately, the Indian was only slightly wounded and they "gave him a knife and he appeared to be satisfied."[43] Accidents such as this were bound to happen.

The conflicts had one result which met with the approval of the ships' commanders—many men became afraid to desert. Some men who conquered their fear and fled the ships spread European culture of a kind around the Pacific, although it was seldom of the kind that an impartial observer would recommend. Desertion usually occurred where the welcome was apparent and safety assured, and, naturally, most often where the life was apparently much more attractive than it would be on board. A few seamen were lured away to a hard life. One marine deserted in Kamchatka to stay with a woman to whom "he had been much attached," although desertion was usually not a problem in this particular area.[44] Desertion is surely one measurement of envy, of seeking another man's lot, so there was not much desertion north of Hawaii.

Ships were more likely to lose men than gain them, however, almost anywhere else in the Pacific. Some men fled discipline; the *Charlotte* found on board two deserters from H.M.S. *Sirius*, the frigate which had escorted the first convict convoy to New South Wales. Many men fled hardships; sailors were tempted by what seemed an easier life ashore. "The promise was A Large Estate and A Handsome wife," to crewmen on Cook's *Discovery*: "it seems Exactly the paradise of Mahomet in Every thing but Immortality."[45] Many men, not unnaturally, preferred this paradise to ships' life off Antarctica or Alaska; it was not simply the climate or the women which appealed to them, but a way of life. The *Duff* lost men to the islands. Even one missionary gave up the cloth for *tapa*: "He has gone to the daughters of Belial; and he says he is Happie."[46]

The Europeans who lived in close contact with the people giving them refuge accelerated cultural change; their skills were often used in boat construction or in warfare, for example. When better watercraft or better armaments were created, the society was permanently altered. Life with schooners and guns is not the same as life with canoes and lances. There was one specific group which came to the Pacific by sailing ship—the convicts—the members of which had even more reason to change their situation than the sailors had. The convicts had good reason to flee from their own kind and seek refuge wherever they could find it. They carried their skills and habits with them. It is tempting to speculate about the frustration of a Hyde Park pickpocket who ended up on a coral island where people wore no clothes.

One of the difficulties ships faced in leaving early New South Wales was to get away without carrying convict stowaways. The ships were so small that successful hiding was most difficult, but in many cases fugitives had the co-operation of the crew. Captains, chronically short of men, sometimes aided the convicts, and "by appealing to the pity of the ships' captains they often escape the punishment to which they have been condemned."[47] The *Uranie* found several convicts in her hold: "unwelcome guests," said de Freycinet realistically, "not being sailors, most of them would be no use to us."[48]

The convicts certainly had not learned much about sailing while on board the convict ships. Conditions on board were hard, but much to be preferred to life in prison hulks in English harbours, according to one literate convict. The Public Records Office in London contains many letters and documents showing that the British government tried very hard to make the voyages to Australia bearable, although not pleasant. A strong military guard aboard (Ensign Taylor was an officer in such a detachment in the *James Pattison*) backed up the strict discipline. Strictness was not resented; there was resentment only against injustice and brutality. One convict said: "A prudent, just, disciplinarian is always preferred by the well-inclined; who, under his control, do not feel themselves at the mercy of ruffians."[49] This is a point of importance often ignored today, but it was as important to the sailors as it was to the convicts. One seaman argued that on a ship "strict discipline among such a large body of men, where the very extremes of good and evil may be found, is very necessary; and though it is at times carried to undue lengths, still for my part, I never in any one instance had cause of complaint."[50]

Sanitary measures aboard ships were better developed by the 1840's, answering some earlier problems, and it is probably true to say that by then the convict ships were better run and provisioned than the majority of immigrant ships. Much depended on the quality of the ship's surgeon, for he had great power: "that personage being invested ... with paramount importance, from his absolute power, the exertion of which could alone prevent the ship from becoming a floating Tartarus."[51] One enlightened policy gave the surgeon "for each man delivered alive ... a bonus of ten shillings ... a direct interest in doing all he could to keep sickness away."[52]

The convicts, having reached Australia, were still subject to onerous restrictions. Naturally enough, they escaped to ships such as the *Uranie* or American whalers whenever possible. Like other sailors, they became scattered around the Pacific, in the islands, in New Zealand, in California or Hawaii, and their influence normally was not uplifting. Early travellers in New Zealand who admired the Maoris saw little benefit from any contact the natives had with outsiders—except possibly the missionaries. Nicholas said a Maori became "from his intercourse with our seamen, an expert proficient in turpitude." Nicholas spoke of the loss of dignity of the Maoris, and of the "coarse familiarity," and "sneering impudence" picked up from the sailors and runaways. He preferred, he said, the Maoris' "unsophisticated rudeness."[53]

Most of this is to be expected from a proportion of the men from ships of those times; it is only today that complete crews of scientists are sent on missions to explore. Many whaling journals condemn the runaways' presence in New Zealand prior to the annexation by the British; their attitudes to life and to authority, for example, and the behaviour of men of similar views who had deserted ships and joined them at whaling ports-of-call, such as the Bay of Islands in northern New Zealand, made drunken pest holes of these places. "Debauched drones" Villiers called them in his *Cruise of the Conrad,* when describing the deleterious effect on Pacific life of "a great spreading of white bums, beachcombers, and ne'er-do-wells (which has not yet ceased), runaway sailors from the whale ships, and convicts from Botany Bay and Norfolk Island." However, sometimes evil can bring forth unforeseen good. A visitor to New Zealand in the 1820's reported just such a paradox: "The natives, seeing with what admiration strangers beheld their fine young women, and what handsome presents were made to them, by which their families were benefited . . . have been latterly as anxious to cherish and protect their infant girls as they were formerly cruelly bent on destroying them."[54] There is also an interesting remark about an early deterrent effect of weapons in Ponape in the Carolines. "They are now well aware of the deadly effect of firearms, and live more harmoniously in consequence."[55]

Lawlessness was a factor in bringing about the British annexation of New Zealand. The thoughts of the sailors and outcasts about the good life were in direct opposition to those of the missionaries. An Englishman who resented missionary inhospitality at the Bay of Islands nonetheless spoke of their good influence, and condemned the example and behaviour of the whalers. "The natives of this part of the island, though very much improved in some respects, are wretches of depravity, which is owing I believe to the number of whaling ships that come to this port. The conduct of the crews of these ships is shameful and entirely counteracts the good effects which might result from the labours of the missionaries."[56] The missionaries had strong support in Britain while the sailors, much less the outlaws (for in a real sense that is what they were), had none; annexation by Britain was finally seen as essential for orderly commerce and for the safety of Maori society. Reason and emotion for once had been a team.

Reason is more important than emotion in the long run. As ships are vehicles of men, so are men vehicles of ideas and passions; Pacific sailing ships, at only one step removed, carried new ideas and age-old passions across and around an ocean as big as all the land masses on earth added together. The ideas dramatically changed the lives of Pacific peoples; the emotions they had lived with always. It is nonsense to argue that Europeans brought greed or pride or envy to a hitherto unsullied Pacific. The ideas they brought could be more damaging than the human failings ever could. The idea of private ownership of land, for example, was more important in Maori-European relations in New Zealand than was any squabble about drink or lust. The settlers in New Zealand and Australia, and Canada, the United States, Ecuador, Peru, and Chile, for that matter, wanted land and worked for personal advancement. The abstract rights of the indigenous people came a long second in their thinking, if they really thought about them at all. As much injustice came about through thoughtlessness and ignorance as came through ill intent. There were more newcomers who did not think than ones who would have admitted that they did not care.

In the case of the missionaries, much destruction of indigenous culture was a direct result of a sincere desire to improve the ethics of the natives, a desire which could be considered misguided, but which certainly was not ill intentioned. Inadvertently, the settlers and missionaries may have done more harm than the deserters or convicts did. Land hunger and the desire to convert the heathen are passions, not ideas, and are not amenable to reason. In the nineteenth century, land hunger and conversion had influence and power behind them. The Pacific world would change.

The Pacific had some slight revenge. Emotions and passions can operate on a grand scale at times. Europe was also affected by the meeting of cultures in the Pacific, for example, by the sentiment (it can hardly be called a thought) which proclaimed that to be primitive is to be pure in heart. Marie Antoinette as a milkmaid was an indirect result of the legends of the simple and generous maids of Tahiti, and this myth was a small but definite part of the decline from the Age of Enlightenment into the Age of Romance. Because this age began with wars on the largest scale—the French elevated national and revolutionary sentiment into dogma and tried to enforce the new orthodoxy on the entire continent—unhappy Europe ever since has been linked in people's minds with nationalism and war. Europeans did not introduce war to the Pacific—or national jealousies, either. From the very beginning, the journals tell of warriors and weapons. Meares, in his journal, for instance, said that "the Nootka nations are not only in frequent hostilities with the more distant tribes, but even among themselves" and argued from his wide experience that "a state of savage life is universally found to be in a state of warfare."[57] Early reports from New Zealand say much the same thing. Cook said that the Maoris "were very much divided into parties which make war one with another . . . they are a brave open warlike people."[58] The Japanese were described by Carletti as "given over wholly to war" and he thought that in weapons "the Japanese are perhaps richer than any other nation whatever in the world—and of all sorts, the offensive as well as the defensive."[59] The great armies of China were well described by Marco Polo. All these peoples adopted new weapons from Europe to pursue their old ambitions. They accepted new ways to kill as readily as they accepted new means to cure.

Ideas and the techniques which sprang from them were interchanged. Today, Europeans use watercraft developed elsewhere: kayak, canoe, and catamaran. Whaleboats became the chosen craft of the Maoris. Deserters, escaping convicts, and genuine traders took skills with them when they embraced wives and citizenship on Pacific islands. The new white settlements in the Americas and Australasia used Pacific labourers and possibly taught them more than they paid them. Islanders, Indians, and Asians sailed the world in European ships, and learned as they did so; from the beginning, Pacific sailors were pressed into service and what they learned altered their society at home as much as did direct European action.

Many of the sailors in the Spanish American ships were Indians, just as there were Chilean and other South American Indians on whalers three centuries later. The Mosquito Indians who served with the buccaneers were especially able sailors, famed for their eyesight and their skill in harpooning. Further north, the Aleuts became excellent sailors in Russian ships and in the whaling vessels of all nations, and were said to "gladly enter upon that occupation, and learn all the methods and develop the necessary skill in seafaring faster than the Russians do."[60] There was the occasional reservation about merit. In the *Tartar Galley*, Forrest commented that although Malays were excellent with fore-and-aft rig they were not good sailors in square-rigged vessels.

Chinese sailors sailed with Quirós in the *San Pedro y Pablo*, with Wilson in the *Antelope*, and with Meares in the *Nootka*. It has been pointed out in an earlier chapter that Chinese junks were developed early and were of such basically sound design that the Chinese shipwrights were reluctant to alter them in any way. Clifford still had some difficulties with this conservatism in getting the *Golden Lotus* built after World War II. "Chinese junk must have watertight bulkhead," his builders insisted, in spite of the fact that the installation of the engine required more room.[61] Chinese sailors were conservative too. Meares had trouble with them, not in matters of discipline, but in getting them to do as he wanted them to do rather than what they had always done. However, most people prefer to deal with the familiar. In spite of his frustration, Meares praised Chinese energy and skill.

The particular cultural attributes and attitudes of the southwest Pacific islanders made them especially valuable;

"I have never heard any captain of a vessel," says Wyllie, "who did not speak highly of the native seamen whom he had employed. They are eminently subordinate, docile, good-natured, and trustworthy, and, with proper training, they become good, efficient seamen. Their extraordinary expertness in swimming renders them of great use where boats are employed in surfs."[62]

Tasmanian and Australian aborigines made skilled whalemen, and Australian whalers employed them in great numbers. (The southwest Pacific bred good sailors both before and after extensive European settlement. Tasmanians, Australians, and New Zealanders of the British sea culture made fine sailors too.) During his cruise, Long became convinced that "the Polynesians are natural born sailors."[63] Certainly, these deep-sea men had sailed with Europeans from the arrival of the very first ships. Maoris shipped with whalers, and "many a tattooed Maori sailed the Pacific and found his way to the gold rushes"; they were known to learn the rigging particularly quickly and to climb well.[64] Both skills are essential in sailing ships, and there are heart-rending stories in many journals of the first frightening climbs up to the mastheads and of the constant fear of letting loose the wrong line.

Polynesians from the islands made up by far the majority of seamen in crews of the island trading brigs and schooners, which usually—but not always—had European captains and officers. Labour ships in the islands, particularly of Melanesia, often used "islanders to row the whaleboats, whilst a European steered them."[65] The labour trade supplying Melanesians and Polynesians for seasonal work on the plantations of Queensland was called "blackbirding," a word defined by a noted dictionary as "slave traffic," which it was not. Such accusations were made against the traffic by people with the most to lose—the unemployed whites and the missionaries. There is no doubt that there were abuses and frauds, aided by imperfect understanding of contracts, but that the trade was more fair than its critics admit is shown by the missionaries who bewailed the islanders' continued desire to go.[66] It was an important factor in altering island culture, creating both the demand for European goods and the means of paying for them.

The trade grew up because the Queensland plantations needed labour in the 1860's for cotton planting; it flourished because sandalwood traders had both the island experience essential for recruiting and the ships to carry the recruits. Sandalwooding taught the islanders that Europeans had goods to exchange for the scented wood which the islanders could obtain merely by the expenditure of labour to cut it. A natural enough progression was to leave the islands to labour more directly for the Europeans in order to buy their goods. Recruiting and transporting islanders could be dangerous. Not all Melanesians or Polynesians wanted to go and work, but they all wanted trade goods. Pillage might be easier than labour.

The natives kept and exercised enough control of their end of the labour traffic to ensure—by refusal either to sign on themselves or to let others sign on—that conditions remained bearable. The reputations of different plantations and different ships spread swiftly through the islands. Plantation life certainly was not slavery, and, although alcohol created some problems, there were fewer troubles than might have been expected. At the end of the contracts, which were usually for three years, almost all the islanders (called as a group, "Kanakas") went home with the goods they had come to get. Their communal culture ensured an immediate and widespread distribution of these goods throughout the tribe. But the taking home of guns and the subsequent massacres in the islands meant the end of the trade. This end was also foreshadowed by the increase in Kanaka violence in Australia. From 1880 on the trade declined; by 1900, the trade, by law, was finished.

Even at its peak it had required only twenty to twenty-five ships, mostly ex-whalers and sandalwooders of less than two hundred tons, rigged as schooners and brigantines. They operated in the hurricane-free season from March to November, cruising the islands and sending small boats ashore to barter for recruits. In spite of the unsavoury reputation of the trade, the names of many of the ships are singularly attractive: the *Dancing Wave*, the *Wild Duck*, the *Sea Flower*, the *Lapwing*, the *Mukulau*, the *Lady Darnley,* the *Native Lass*, and, more prosaic, the *Bobtail Nag*.

The men of the whale ship crews were even more varied than the men in the labour ships, for

... every West European racial and national type mixed with native-born Americans ... Japanese, Chinese, Filipinos, sundry Malayans, a few Hindus, and Singhalese; Kanakas from the West Pacific Islands; Australian Black-fellows; Amerindians; Eskimos; and even some South American Amerindians. One British vessel had a Russian Captain, Dutch purser, Arab first mate, Nigerian boatswain, and ten other nationalities among its crew.[67]

Some Pacific islands were so famous for their sailing men that they became almost denuded of males; Rapa, in the Tubuai Islands, at one time had a reputation "as a kind of dusky harem with every male of the species treated as a kind of queen bee."[68]

When the indigenous Pacific sailormen went home, the real importance of their return would not be in their reception, however eager, but in the new ways and new outlooks they brought with them. What was learned of the new world by Island or Indian or Maori sailors would alter their society permanently; Europeans did not have to settle in a new land in order to change it. When Pacific men sailed to strange places with the European "Sailing Gods," they would never be the same again. Neither would their homelands.

The Sailing Gods had not meant this to be—or, at any rate, few of their captains had. Drake excelled in his dealings with Pacific inhabitants. Magellan, Quirós, Cook, Bougainville, La Pérouse, Bering, Bellingshausen, de Freycinet, and Flinders all tried to be fair and friendly—with greater or lesser success— depending very often on the coolness or nervousness of their subordinates. Bligh's instructions to his crew for dealing with Tahitians were enlightened and thorough; Vancouver seemed, according to his biographer, "to have had a peculiar insight into the primitive mentality of the islanders [Hawaiians] and he wrote of them later with affection."[69] The crew of the *Providence* noted that the Hawaiians liked Vancouver in return. Many of the French or English who visited the Pacific in the late eighteenth century disclaimed racialism as vigorously as the sixteenth-century Spaniards had proclaimed Christianity. "I flatter myself," said Mary Ann Parker of the Aboriginals of New South Wales, "that the time is hastening when they will no longer be considered as mere savages;—and wherefore should they?"[70] It was an outlook widely shared. Sometimes, its expression, however well intentioned, sounds patronizing. When Lord Morton, President of the Royal Society, sent some advice to Cook before his first voyage he spoke of the indigenous people Cook was likely to encounter as "human creatures, the work of the same omnipotent Author, equally under his care with the most polished European; perhaps being less offensive, more entitled to his favour."[71] The advice was sound, but, circumstances varying as they do, it was fortunate for humanity that Cook did not really need it. However individuals acted, or were reacted to, the clash of cultures could have only one end; that which had been seen as ideal, however unrealistically, was to be corrupted. Innocence, even on an island surrounded by leagues of sea and the resulting protection of time, could resist neither temptation nor ravishment.

There have always been interactions between the Pacific and its inhabitants, between the Pacific and its explorers, and the Pacific and its exploiters, just as there have been, in any age and location, interactions between natives and newcomers. Always it has been the Pacific which acts and the men who react. The Pacific has not changed. To many people the word is exciting, because it brings to mind the myth of contentment, the hope of a return to simplicity. Whatever it is in the imagination, in reality it is thousands of miles of emptiness where starvation and disease can weaken the unprepared or the unfortunate. It is an ocean bounded by ice, and reefs, and earthquake-prone coasts; it is water which can lie mirror-still until a sailor screams, or which can heave and spume and pound until the strongest of men's creations has no choice but to go where the sea pushes. There is always beauty, even in the worst of gales or in the most dangerous of icebergs, and most certainly in the mountainous islands or the still lagoons. There is no other certainty except that the Pacific itself decides whether men enjoy or endure.

Men have had to adapt. They have found new materials in which strength and lightness coincide, to rig their yachts or to build their boats. They have found new techniques with which to call for help—as is often necessary still— or to keep their food fresh and their bodies healthy, to motor through calms or to enter a confined harbour against a land breeze.

These are techniques. They help, but there is no certainty in any of them. But to deal with techniques, men have had to change themselves; they have had to learn new skills and have accepted new attitudes. The hard bodies which ran to the top-gallant yards are now acute minds which supervise turbines. When disaster strikes, the hard bodies are missed, for the acute minds not only endure less, but often refuse to accept that they should endure at all. The education to deal with the techniques, in its turn, has created the need for new skills in leadership to deal with the educated. New men must have new officers. It goes without saying that there can be no Bligh, maligned as he was; there cannot even be Ansons or Cooks who operate with fairness, but with strictness and formality too. I do not suggest that it would be impossible today to crew a nineteenth-century sailing ship; but certainly the crew could not come from the crowd—any crowd—along the wharfs, as it used to do. The crew would need to be as carefully selected as is a football team, and for much the same reason—only the unusually motivated will endure once there is some other choice.

Co-operation is still necessary. In modern freighters or tankers, the teamwork needed to operate the sophisticated machinery must be as effective and as disciplined as it was in the whaleboats. But the men are selected, and not shanghaied, and have been trained by a persuasion more subtle than a bosun's rattan cane. There always was skill involved in seamen's work, but it was skill that could be forced on a type of man that today no shipping line would hire. Sailors of modern container ships are separated from sailors of seventeenth-century frigates by the same technical and psychological gulfs that would separate the drivers of Centurion tanks from the fyrdmen following Harold to Hastings directly from their fields. In the one case, they would be technicians doing their highly competent best; in the other, they would be simple spirits with the loyalty—and the swagger—that are now denigrated by people who envy the adventure, but avoid the risks.

Only by the tiny yachts or the replica rafts is the Pacific challenged as it once was. In some ways, a Chichester becomes as much a part of his boat as an Eskimo kayaker; he alone is the spirit of a sea body which dodges and endures and presses on. In these modern voyages is seen a partial re-enactment of the daring and vitality of the original navigators, and of the improvisation and self-sufficiency of the Pacific peoples.

It was my interest in the voyages of Chichester which led me to Slocum, and thence back through the centuries of sailing the greatest of oceans. It seemed to me that the problems faced by all the voyagers were constant, and that the solutions differed partly because of the materials their cultures and circumstances provided, but primarily because of the differences in the attitudes and the spirit of the individual men and women. While reading the journals, my interest was diverted from the tools of men to the behaviour of men; the intended book began to reshape itself.

To show how frail were men, how weak were their materials, and, in compensation, how great must have been their skill and courage, is a major purpose of this book. It was not so originally. What I had intended to show was the beauty, grace, and ingenuity built into the ships and canoes; what I have learned was the extent of men's courage and their will to live. If both these qualities were required of men because the Pacific is the most awesome of all the things of nature, surely men's responses met the need. Their inventiveness led them from raft to canoe to clipper, from pole to paddle to sail. With each move forward, the beauty of the craft grew just as much as its efficiency. Of all creations meant to move men where they will, surely sailing ships are the most majestic. There is majesty apparent in the form, but also in the acceptance of the contest, in the daring to pit frail material and human skill against unlimited and impersonal power. Although the wind still commands wherever it can reach, men have learned that—within obedience—they can win a subtle victory.

NOTES

CHAPTER I

1. Ronald Latham, ed., *The Travels of Marco Polo* (London: The Folio Society, 1968), p. 263.

2. Joseph D. Hooker, ed., *Journal of the Right Hon. Sir Joseph Banks During Captain Cook's First Voyage in H.M.S. "Endeavour" 1768-71* ... (London: Macmillan, 1896), p. 93.

3. J. C. Beaglehole, ed., *The Journals of Captain James Cook on his Voyages of Discovery*, vol. 3, *The Voyage of the "Resolution" and "Discovery" 1776-1780*, Hakluyt Extra Series no. 36 (Cambridge: Camb. U. P., 1967), p. 1321.

4. Francesco Carletti, *My Voyage Around the World: A 16th Century Florentine Merchant* (New York: Pantheon, 1964), p. 41.

5. Frederic W. Howay, ed., *Journal of Captain James Colnett Aboard the "Argonaut" from April 26, 1789 to November 3, 1791* (Toronto: Publications of the Champlain Society, 1940), p. 175.

6. Francis Drake, *The World Encompassed* (reproduced from London edition, 1628; Ann Arbor, Mich.: University Microfilms, 1966), p. 50.

7. William Robert Broughton, *A Voyage of Discovery to the North Pacific Ocean ... Performed in His Majesty's Sloop "Providence" and Her Tender, in the Years 1795-1798* (London: T. Cadell & W. Davies, 1804), p. 183 (hereafter cited as *"Voyage in H.M.S. "Providence"*).

8. G. R. G. Worcester, *Sail and Sweep in China* (London: H.M.S.O., 1966), p. 99.

9. Woodes Rogers, *A Cruising Voyage round the World ... begun in 1708, and finished in 1711* ... (London: A. Bell and B. Lintot, 1712), p. 284.

10. Richard Hakluyt, *The Principal Navigations Voyages Traffiques and Discoveries of the English Nation ...* 10 vols. (London: Dent, 1927-1928), 10:242.

11. William Dampier, *Dampier's Voyages Consisting of a New Voyage Round the World ... The Voyages to Campeachy ... a Voyage to New Holland ...*, ed. John Masefield, 2 vols. (London: E. Grant Richards, 1906), 1:165-66.

12. Hakluyt, *The Principal Navigations*, 8:227. See also *ibid.*, p. 231. Morrell describes meeting large balsas fifty miles out from land, see Benjamin Morrell, *A Narrative of Four Voyages to the South Sea ... From the Year 1822 to 1831* ... (New York: J. & J. Harper, 1832), p. 120.

13. Thor Heyerdahl, *Kon-Tiki* (Chicago: Rand, 1950), p. 84.

14. L. E. Elliott Joyce, ed., *A New Voyage and Description of the Isthmus*

of America, by Lionel Wafer, Hakluyt Second Series, no. 73 (Oxford: Oxf. U. P., 1934), p. 59 (hereafter cited as *Voyage by Wafer*).

15. Clements R. Markham, ed., *Reports on the Discovery of Peru*, Hakluyt First Series, no. 47. (London: Hakluyt Society, 1872), p. 14n.

16. Heyerdahl, *Kon-Tiki*, p. 83.

17. *Ibid.*, p. 85.

18. James Hornell, *Water Transport: Origins and Early Evolution* (Cambridge: Camb. U. P., 1946), p. 77.

19. Worcester, *Sail and Sweep*, p. 113.

20. Hakluyt, *The Principal Navigations*, 8:221.

21. Drake, *World Encompassed*, p. 55.

22. *Ibid.* See also David Porter, *A Voyage in the South Seas in the years 1812, 1813, 1814, with particular details of the Gallipagos and Washington Islands* (London: Sir Richard Phillips & Co., 1823), p. 23, and Morrell, *Narrative of Four Voyages*, p. 223.

23. Elsdon Best, *The Maori Canoe* (Wellington: Govt. Printer, 1925), p. 144, quoting Shand.

CHAPTER 2

1. Edwin Tappan Adney and Howard I. Chappelle, *The Bark Canoes and Skin Boats of North America* (Washington, D.C.: Smithsonian, 1964), p. 197.

2. Frederick Whymper, *Travel and Adventure in the Territory of Alaska* (1868; reprint ed., Ann Arbor, Mich.: University Microfilms, 1966), p. 137. See also Beaglehole, *Voyage of the "Resolution" and "Discovery,"* pp. 1107, 1446; and W. L. G. Joerg, ed., *Bering's Voyages: An Account of the Efforts of the Russians to Determine the Relation of Asia and America*, vol. 1. *The Log Books and Official Reports of the First and Second Expeditions 1725-1730 and 1733-1742 . . .*, by F. A. Golder, American Geographical Society Research Series, no. 1 (New York: Octagon, 1968) p. 148 (hereafter cited as *Log Books of Bering's Voyages*).

3. Beaglehole, *Voyage of the "Resolution" and "Discovery,"* p. 1138.

4. Nils Adolf Nordenskiöld, *The Voyage of the "Vega,"* 2 vols. (London: Macmillan, 1881), 2:228.

5. W.L.G. Joerg, ed., *Bering's Voyages: An Account of the Efforts of the Russians to Determine the Relation of Asia and America*, vol. 2., *Steller's Journal of the Sea Voyage from Kamchatka to America and Return on the 2nd Expedition 1741-1742*, by F. A. Golder, American Geographical Society Research Series, no. 1 (New York: Octagon, 1968), p. 96 (hereafter cited as *Steller's Journal of Bering's Voyages*).

6. John Rickman, *Journal of Captain Cook's Last Voyage to the Pacific Ocean* (Ann Arbor, Mich.: University Microfilms, 1966), p. 373. See also Golder, *Steller's Journal of Bering's Voyages*, p. 95.

7. Beaglehole, *Voyage of the "Resolution" and "Discovery,"* pp. 463, 1113.

8. Whymper, *Travel in Alaska*, p. 137.

9. *Ibid.*, pp. 195, 197.

10. Nordenskiöld, *Voyage of the "Vega,"* 2:94.

11. John Bechervaise, *Thirty-six Years of a Seafaring Life by an Old Quarter Master* (Portsea: W. Woodward, 1839), p. 199. See also Whymper, *Travel in Alaska*, p. 195.

12. John Meares, *Voyages made in the Years 1788 and 1789, from China to the Northwest Coast of America* (1790; reprint ed., Amsterdam: N. Israel, 1967), p. xv.

13. Whymper, *Travel in Alaska*, p. 249.

14. *Ibid.*, p. 89.

CHAPTER 3

1. Rickman, *Cook's Last Voyage*, p. 245.

2. Beaglehole, *Voyage of the "Resolution" and "Discovery,"* p. 1102; and Frederic W. Howay, ed., *Voyages of the "Columbia" to the North-west Coast 1787-90 and 1790-93* (Boston: Massachusetts Historical Society, 1941), p. 369. See also Beaglehole, *Voyage of the "Resolution" and "Discovery,"* pp. 316, 1394.

3. Reuben Gold Thwaites, ed., *Original Journals of the Lewis and Clark Expedition 1804-06*, 8 vols. (New York: Arno Pr., 1969) 4:31.

4. Beaglehole, *Voyage of the "Resolution" and "Discovery,"* p. 1410.

5. Michael Roe, ed., *The Journal and Letters of Captain Charles Bishop on the N.W. Coast of America, in the Pacific, and in New South Wales 1794-1799*, Hakluyt Second Series no. 131 (Cambridge: Camb. U. P., 1967), p. 81.

6. Whymper, *Travel in Alaska*, p. 30.

7. Douglas Phillips Birt, in A. Rose, *My Lively Lady* (London: Pan, 1968), appendix 1, p. 193.

8. Howay, *Voyages of the "Columbia,"* p. 197.

9. John Claus Voss, *The Voyage of the Indian War Canoe "Tilikum": across the Pacific from Canada to Australia* (Invercargill: Printed at the Caxton Office, 1903), p. 20.

10. Thwaites, *Lewis and Clark Expedition*, 4:30; and George Vancouver, *A Voyage of Discovery to the North Pacific Ocean and Round the World Performed in the Years 1790-95 . . . ,* 6 vols., (London: J. Stockdale, 1801), 2:25 (hereafter cited as *Voyage in the "Discovery" and "Chatham"*).

11. Thwaites, *Lewis and Clark Expedition*, 4:30, 3:217.

12. Vancouver, *Voyage in the "Discovery" and "Chatham,"* 3:139, 212; and T. J. Jacobs, *Scenes, Incidents and Adventures in the Pacific Ocean . . . During the Cruise of the Clipper "Margaret Oakley" . . .* (New York: Harper & Bros., 1844), p. 73.

13. Howay, *Colnett Aboard the "Argonaut,"* p. 175.

14. Hakluyt, *The Principal Navigations*, 10:239.

15. Joyce, *Voyage by Wafer*, p. 52.

16. *Ibid.*

17. Bolton Glanvill Corney, *The Quest and Occupation of Tahiti by Emissaries of Spain during the Years 1772-76*, Hakluyt Second Series no. 32, 3 vols., (1913; reprint ed., Nendeln, Liechtenstein: Kraus Repr., 1967), 1:115n.

18. George Shelvocke, *A Voyage Round the World ... Performed in the Years 1719-1722.* (London: Cassell, 1928), p. 64.

19. Corney, *Occupation of Tahiti,* 1 : 115n.

20. *Ibid.*

21. Drake, *World Encompassed,* p. 37.

22. Hugh Carrington, ed., *The Discovery of Tahiti,* by George Robertson (1948; reprint ed., Nendeln, Liechtenstein: Kraus Repr. 1967), p. 88.

23. Clements R. Markham, *The Hawkins' Voyages.* Hakluyt First Series no. 57 (London: Hakluyt Society, 1878), p. 204.

24. Robert E. Gallagher, ed., *Byron's Journal of His Circumnavigation 1764-1766.* Hakluyt Second Series no. 122 (Cambridge: Camb. U. P., 1964), p. 80. See also Morrell, *Narrative of Four Voyages,* pp. 95-96.

25. J. C. Beaglehole, ed., *The Journals of Captain James Cook on his Voyages of Discovery,* vol. 2, *The Voyage of the "Resolution" and "Adventure," 1772-1775,* Hakluyt Extra Series no. 35 (Cambridge: Camb. U. P., 1961), p. 597. See also Carrington, *Discovery of Tahiti,* p. 88.

26. Whymper, *Travel in Alaska,* p. 211.

27. John White, *Journal of a Voyage to New South Wales ...* (London: J. Debrett, 1790), p. 160.

28. John Macgillivray, *Narrative of the Voyage of H.M.S. "Rattlesnake" ... during the years 1846-50 ...* 2 vols. (London: T. & W. Boone, 1852), 2 : 140.

29. J. C. Beaglehole, ed., *The Journals of Captain James Cook on his Voyages of Discovery,* vol. 1, *The Voyage of the "Endeavour" 1768-1771,* Hakluyt Extra Series no. 34 (Cambridge: Camb. U. P., 1955), pp. 304-05.

30. Macgillivray, *Voyage of H.M.S. "Rattlesnake,"* 1 : 64. See also Frank Debenham, ed., *The Voyage of Captain Bellingshausen to the Antarctic Seas, 1819-21.* Hakluyt Second Series 91/92, 2 vols. (London: Hakluyt Society, 1945), 1 : 189; and Hornell, *Water Transport,* p. 185.

31. Ida Lee, ed., *The Logbooks of the "Lady Nelson"* (London: Grafton & Co., 1915), p. 55. See also Debenham, *Voyage of Captain Bellingshausen,* 1 : 189.

32. Julian Huxley, ed., *T. H. Huxley's Diary of the Voyage of H.M.S. "Rattlesnake," 1846-47* (London: Chatto & Windus, 1935), p. 127.

33. Lee, *Logbooks of the "Lady Nelson,"* p. 35.

34. White, *Voyage to New South Wales,* p. 160. See also James Holman, *A Voyage Round the World, including travels in Africa, Asia, Australia, America, from 1827 to 1832,* 4 vols. (London: Smith, Elder & Co., 1834-1835), 4 : 459.

35. Carl von Scherzer, *Narrative of the Circumnavigation of the Globe by the Austrian Frigate "Novara" ... in the years 1857, 1858 and 1859, etc.,* 3 vols. (London: Saunders, Otley Co., 1861), 3 : 36.

36. White, *Voyage to New South Wales,* pp. 133, 146, 148.

37. Hooker, *Journal of Sir Joseph Banks,* p. 321.

38. Macgillivray, *Voyage of H.M.S. "Rattlesnake,"* 1 : 119, 146-47.

39. Rupert Furneaux, *Tobias Furneaux, Circumnavigator* (London: Cassell, 1960), p. 107.

40. Markham, *Hawkins' Voyages,* p. 142.

CHAPTER 4

1. Peter Dillon, *Narrative and Successful Result of a Voyage in the South Seas . . . to Ascertain the Actual Fate of La Pérouse's Expedition,* 2 vols. (London: Hurst, Chance & Co., 1829), 1:272.

2. James Cowan, *Suwarrow Gold* (London: Cape, 1936), p. 76.

3. Whymper, *Travel in Alaska,* p. 251. See also Charles Wilkes, *Narratives of the United States Exploring Expedition During the Years 1838, 1839, 1840, 1841, 1842,* 5 vols. (Philadelphia: Lee & Blanchard, 1845), 4:296.

4. Edward Robarts, "Narrative of a Voyage to the South Seas" (Adv. Ms. 17.1.18., National Library of Scotland, Edinburgh), p. 19. This journal has been edited and published since this book was written; Greg Dening, ed. *The Marquesan Journal of Edward Robarts 1797-1824,* Pacific History Series no. 6 (Canberra: Australian National University Press, 1974).

5. Peter H. Buck, *The Coming of the Maori* (Wellington: Maori Purposes Fund Board, 1949), pp. 25-27. For an excellent discussion of deliberate voyages, see Porter, *Voyage in the South Seas,* p. 93.

6. Peter H. Buck, *Vikings of the Sunrise* (New York: Lippincott, 1938), p. 95.

7. Buck, *Coming of the Maori,* p. 209.

8. Scherzer, *Narrative of the "Novara,"* 3:157. See also Hooker, *Journal of Sir Joseph Banks,* p. 205

9. Hooker, *Journal of Sir Joseph Banks,* p. 186. Because of the resemblance to their canoe, it would seem natural enough for the Maoris to adopt the European whaleboat, as Wilkes said they had done by 1840, although presumably not exclusively. See Wilkes, *United States Exploring Expedition,* 2:389.

10. Brenda Guthrie, *New Zealand Memories* (London: The Bodley Head, 1930), p. 109.

11. Hooker, *Journal of Sir Joseph Banks,* p. 186.

12. Best, *Maori Canoe,* p. 57.

13. I. T. Sanderson, *Follow the Whale* (London: Cassell, 1958), p. 117.

14. Best, *Maori Canoe,* p. 62.

15. Julien Crozet, *Crozet's Voyage to Tasmania, New Zealand, the Ladrone Islands and the Philippines in the Years 1771-72,* trans. H. L. Roth (London: Truslove & Shirley, 1891), p. 41.

16. Best, *Maori Canoe,* pp. 112, 114. See also Buck, *Coming of the Maori,* p. 487.

17. Best, *Maori Canoe,* p. 171, quoting J. L. Nicholas. See also *ibid.,* p. 305.

18. W. P. Morrell, *Sir Joseph Banks in New Zealand* (Wellington: A. H. & A. W. Reed, 1958), p. 128.

19. N. M. Taylor, *The Journal of Ensign Best, 1837-43* (Wellington: R. E. Owen, Govt. Printer, 1966), p. 367.

20. Hooker, *Journal of Sir Joseph Banks,* p. 241.

21. Dillon, *Fate of La Pérouse's Expedition,* 2:353. See also Wilkes, *United States Exploring Expedition,* 2:413.

22. Taylor, *Journal of Ensign Best,* p. 245.

23. Buck, *Coming of the Maori,* pp. 203-04. See also Best, *Maori Canoe,* p. 80.

24. Best, *Maori Canoe,* p. 191.

25. Celsus Kelly, ed. and trans., *La Austrialia Del Espíritu Santo. The Journal ... Relating to the Voyage of Pedro Fernández de Quirós to the South Seas (1605-1606) ...*, 2 vols., Hakluyt Second Series nos. 126, 127 (Cambridge: Camb. U.P., 1966), 1:69.

26. Morrell, *Sir Joseph Banks in New Zealand*, p. 139. See also Hooker, *Journal of Sir Joseph Banks*, pp. 194, 241.

27. Taylor, *Journal of Ensign Best*, p. 259.

28. William Bligh, *A Narrative of the Mutiny on Board His Majesty's Ship "Bounty"; and the Subsequent Voyage of Part of the Crew in the Ship's Boat ...* (London: George Nicol, 1790), p. 56 (hereafter cited as *Mutiny in H.M.S. "Bounty"*).

29. T. M. Hocken, *Abel Tasman and His Journal, 1642-43*, a paper read before the Otago Institute, September 10, 1895, p. 9.

30. Best, *Maori Canoe*, p. 14. See also Buck, *Coming of the Maori*, p. 201, and Robert McNab, *Murihiku and the Southern Islands ... from 1770-1829* (1907; reprint ed., Auckland: Wilson & Horton, 1970), p. 113.

31. Stanley, Lord of Alderley, ed., *The First Voyage Round the World by Magellan ...*, Hakluyt First Series, no. 52 (London: Hakluyt Society, 1874), p. 70. See also Isaak Commelin, *A Collection of Voyages Undertaken by the Dutch East-India Company ...* (London: W. Freeman etc., 1703), p. 202; C. Andrew Sharp, ed., *The Voyages of Abel Janszoon Tasman* (Oxford: Clarendon Press, 1968), pp. 40, 201; Beaglehole, *Voyage of the "Resolution" and "Adventure,"* p. 515; and Dampier, *Dampier's Voyages,* pp. 311, 467, 478, 480.

32. Commelin, *Dutch East-India Company*, p. 202; and Dampier, *Dampier's Voyages*, 1:310.

33. Best, *Maori Canoe*, p. 17.

34. Sharp, *Voyages of Abel Tasman*, pp. 49, 201.

35. Buck, *Vikings of the Sunrise*, p. 254.

36. Dampier, *Dampier's Voyages*, 1:480.

37. Hornell, *Water Transport*, p. 258.

38. Crozet, *Voyage to Tasmania*, p. 94.

39. Thomas Gilbert, *Voyage from New South Wales to Canton in the Year 1788 ...* (London: J. Debrett, 1789), p. 28.

40. Jack London, *The Cruise of the "Snark"* (New York: The Regent Press, 1911), p. 174.

41. Dwight Long, *Sailing all Seas in the "Idle Hour"* (London: Hodder, 1940), p. 86.

42. Buck, *Vikings of the Sunrise*, p. 101; and William Ellis, *Polynesian Researches, during a residence of nearly six years in the South Sea Islands etc.*, 4 vols. (Rutland, Vermont: Charles E. Tuttle Co., 1969), vol. 1, *Polynesia*, p. 162.

43. Furneaux, *Tobias Furneaux, Circumnavigator*, p. 52. See also Ellis, *Polynesia*, p. 382.

44. Joshua Slocum, *Sailing Alone Around the World* (New York: Century Co., 1900), p. 29.

45. Buck, *Vikings of the Sunrise*, pp. 222ff.

46. David Lewis, *Daughters of the Wind* (Wellington: A. H. & A. W. Reed, 1967), p. 221.

47. Thomas Forrest, *A Voyage to New Guinea and the Moluccas . . . During the years 1774, 1775, 1776 . . .*, 2nd ed. (London: J. Robson, 1780), p. 9n.

48. Beaglehole, *Voyage of the "Resolution" and "Adventure,"* pp. 802, 848. See also Carrington, *Discovery of Tahiti*, p. 123, and George Colvocoresses, *Four Years in a Government Exploring Expedition . . .* (New York: Cornish, Lamport & Co., 1852), p. 134.

49. Beaglehole, *Voyage of the "Resolution" and "Adventure,"* p. 780. See also Hooker, *Journal of Sir Joseph Banks*, p. 115; and Best, *Maori Canoe*, p. 202. When describing double canoes at the Isle of Pines, one early trader (Cheyne) said, "The small Canoe serves as an outrigger for the Large one," and Wilkes thought the same of Fijian canoes. See Dorothy Shineberg, ed., *The Trading Voyages of Andrew Cheyne, 1841-1844*, Pacific History Series no. 3 (Canberra: Australian National University Press, 1971), p. 40; Wilkes, *United States Exploring Expedition*, 3:345; and David Henry Lewis, *We, the Navigators: The Ancient Art of Landfinding in the Pacific* (Wellington: A. H. and A. W. Reed, 1972), p. 262.

50. J. Cumming Dewar, *Voyage of the "Nyanza," R.N.Y.C., being the record of a three years' cruise in a schooner yacht in the Atlantic and Pacific and her subsequent Shipwreck* (Edinburgh: Blackwood & Sons, 1892), p. 3. See also Sharp, *Voyages of Abel Tasman*, p. 43.

51. Broughton, *Voyage in H.M.S. "Providence,"* p. 33.

52. C. Andrew Sharp, ed., *The Journal of Jacob Roggeveen* (Oxford: Clarendon Press, 1970), p. 101. See also Roe, *Journal of Captain Charles Bishop*, p. 36; and Beaglehole, *Voyage of the "Resolution" and "Adventure,"* pp. 352, 353.

53. Hooker, *Journal of Sir Joseph Banks*, p. 161.

54. *Ibid.*, p. 158.

55. Beaglehole, *Voyage of the "Resolution" and "Adventure,"* p. 408. For a comprehensive collection of contemporary illustrations of Polynesian watercraft, see E. Dodd, *The Ring of Fire*, vol. 2, *Polynesian Seafaring* (New York: Dodd, 1972).

56. Hooker, *Journal of Sir Joseph Banks*, p. 159.

57. *Ibid.*, p. 161.

58. Carrington, *Discovery of Tahiti*, p. 140.

59. Beaglehole, *Voyage of the "Endeavour,"* p. 130.

60. Corney, *Occupation of Tahiti*, 1:13.

61. London, *Cruise of the "Snark,"* p. 172.

62. Long, *Sailing in the "Idle Hour,"* p. 87.

63. Buck, *Vikings of the Sunrise*, p. 116.

64. Kelly, *Voyage of Quirós*, 1:174.

65. James Wilson, *A Missionary Voyage to the Southern Pacific Ocean . . .* (London: J. Chapman, 1799), p. 400.

66. Buck, *Vikings of the Sunrise*, p. 119.

67. Sharp, *Journal of Jacob Roggeveen*, p. 153.

68. Fanny Stevenson, *The Cruise of the "Janet Nichol" Among the South Sea Islands* (London: Chatto & Windus, 1915), p. 33.

69. Rickman, *Cook's Last Voyage*, p. 303.

70. Vancouver, *Voyage in "Discovery" and "Chatham,"* 3:367.

71. *Ibid.*

72. Thwaites, *Lewis and Clark Expedition*, 3:213.

73. Dillon, *Fate of La Pérouse's Expedition*, 2:78. Wilkes saw Fijians building huge canoes for a Tongan chief, see Wilkes, *United States Exploring Expedition*, 3:167.

74. Beaglehole, *Voyage of the "Resolution" and "Adventure,"* p. 762. See also Rickman, *Cook's Last Voyage*, p. 97.

75. Beaglehole, *Voyage of the "Resolution" and "Adventure,"* p. 848.

76. Colvocoresses, *Exploring Expedition*, p. 128.

CHAPTER 5

1. Best, *Maori Canoe*, pp. 246-47.

2. Bligh, *Mutiny in H.M.S. "Bounty,"* p. 29.

3. Beaglehole, *Voyage of the "Resolution" and "Adventure,"* p. 865. Cheyne gives an excellent description of this "peculiar method of sculling them [New Caledonian canoes] to windward," see Shineberg, *Voyages of Andrew Cheyne*, p. 129. See also Wilkes, *United States Exploring Expedition*, 3:19, for a description of sculling canoes at Tonga and Fiji.

4. Beaglehole, *Voyage of the "Resolution" and "Adventure,"* p. 545.

5. *Ibid.*, p. 863.

6. *Ibid.*, p. 515.

7. Kelly, *Voyage of Quirós*, 1:77.

8. Scherzer, *Narrative of the "Novara,"* 2:597.

9. Hornell, *Water Transport*, p. 208. See also James Hornell, "Boat Construction in Scandinavia and Oceania; another parallel in Botel Tobago," *Man*, 36 (Sept. 1936): 145.

10. Helen Wallis, ed., *Carteret's Voyage Round the World 1766-69*, 2 vols., Hakluyt Second Series nos. 124 and 125 (Cambridge: Camb. U. P., 1965), 1:175n., quoting G. S. Parsonson.

11. William Dampier, *A Voyage to New Holland*, ed. James A. Williamson (London: Argonaut Press, 1939), p. 200. See also W.J.J. Spry, *The Cruise of Her Majesty's Ship "Challenger"* (London: Sampson Low, Marston, Searle & Rivington, 1877), p. 266.

12. Macgillivray, *Voyage of H.M.S. "Rattlesnake,"* 2:40.

13. Huxley, *Diary of H.M.S. "Rattlesnake,"* p. 215.

14. Macgillivray, *Voyage of H.M.S. "Rattlesnake,"* 2:58.

15. Alain Gerbault, *In Quest of the Sun* (London: Hart-Davis, 1955), p. 146.

16. Huxley, *Diary of H.M.S. "Rattlesnake,"* p. 215.

17. Macgillivray, *Voyage of H.M.S. "Rattlesnake,"* 1:255; and Huxley, *Diary of H.M.S. "Rattlesnake,"* p. 217.

18. Macgillivray, *Voyage of H.M.S. "Rattlesnake,"* 2:65.

19. *Ibid.*

20. *Ibid.*, 1:204, 207.

21. Jacobs, *Cruise of the "Margaret Oakley,"* pp. 184, 201. See also Matthew Flinders, *A Voyage to Terra Australis*, 2 vols. (London: G. & W. Nicol, 1814), 1:xxxvii.

22. Wallis, *Carteret's Voyage*, 1:175n, quoting G. S. Parsonson.

23. Jacobs, *Cruise of the "Margaret Oakley,"* p. 183.

24. Sharp, *Voyages of Abel Tasman*, p. 49.

25. Long, *Sailing in the "Idle Hour,"* p. 207.

26. James Burney, *History of the Buccaneers of America* (1816; reprint ed., London: Allen & U., 1912), p. 281.

27. Richard Walter and George Anson, *A Voyage Round the World . . . 1740-44* (London: Society for Promoting Christian Knowledge, n.d.), p. 303.

28. Hakluyt, *The Principal Navigations*, 8:239.

29. Walter and Anson, *Voyage Round the World*, pp. 302-03. See also Crozet, *Voyage to Tasmania*, p. 123.

30. Burney, *Buccaneers of America*, p. 281.

31. Crozet, *Voyage to Tasmania*, p. 94.

32. Macgillivray, *Voyage of H.M.S. "Rattlesnake,"* 1:204. Wilkes, an experienced sailor, said that when Tongans and Fijians sailed, the outrigger was kept on the weather side; see Wilkes, *United States Exploring Expedition*, 3:346.

33. Burney, *Buccaneers of America*, p. 280.

34. George Keate, *An Account of the Pelew Islands, composed from the Journals and Communications of Captain Henry Wilson . . .* (London: G. Nicol, 1788), p. 46.

35. Crozet, *Voyage to Tasmania*, p. 94.

36. Jacques Arago, *Narrative of a Voyage Round the World in the "Uranie" and "Physicienne" . . . by Captain Freycinet, 1817-20 . . .*, 2 pts. (London: Treuttel and Wurtz, 1823), 1:266-67.

37. *Ibid.*, 1:270.

38. Keate, *Account of the Pelew Islands*, p. 316.

39. *Ibid.*, p. 119.

40. *Ibid.*, p. 116.

41. Drake, *World Encompassed*, p. 82.

42. Forrest, *Voyage to New Guinea*, p. 23n.

43. Commelin, *Dutch East-India Company*, p. 202.

44. Dampier, *Dampier's Voyages*, 1:478, 478n.

45. Henry Keppel, *The Expedition to Borneo of H.M.S. "Dido,"* 2 vols. (London: Chap. & H., 1846), 1:65.

46. Samuel Purchas, *Hakluytus Posthumus, or Purchas His Pilgrimes*, 3 vols., Hakluyt Society Extra Series (1625; reprint ed; Glasgow: James MacLehose and Sons, 1905), 2:321.

47. *Ibid.*, 3:442.

48. Keppel, *Expedition of H.M.S. "Dido,"* 2:20.

49. Charles-Pierre Fleurieu, *Discoveries of the French in 1768 and 1769, to the South-East of New Guinea*... (London: John Stockdale, 1791), p. 139.

50. Romola Anderson and R. C. Anderson, *The Sailing Ship* (London: Harrap, 1926), pp. 40-42. See also C. Nooteboom, "Eastern Biremes," *Mariner's Mirror* 35, no. 4 (Oct., 1949): 272-75; and Forrest, *Voyage to New Guinea*, p. 228.

51. Dampier, *Dampier's Voyages*, 1:343.

52. Hakluyt, *The Principal Navigations*, 8:244.

53. Forrest, *Voyage to New Guinea*, p. 313. See also *ibid.*, p. 228.

54. Dampier, *Dampier's Voyages*, 2:58.

CHAPTER 6

1. Brian Miles Clifford and Neil Illingworth, *The Voyage of the "Golden Lotus,"* (Wellington: A. H. & A. W. Reed, 1962), p. 39.

2. Latham, *Travels of Marco Polo*, p. 204.

3. Commelin, *Dutch East-India Company*, p. 145.

4. Clifford and Illingworth, *Voyage of the "Golden Lotus,"* p. 29.

5. Latham, *Travels of Marco Polo*, p. 204.

6. *Ibid.*

7. *Ibid.*, p. 205.

8. Carletti, *My Voyage*, p. 96. See also Lionel Casson, *Illustrated History of Ships and Boats* (New York: Doubleday, 1964), p. 177.

9. Robin Knox-Johnston, *A World of My Own* (London: Cassell, 1969), p. 122.

10. A. Basil Lubbock, *The Colonial Clippers* (Glasgow: James Brown & Son, 1924), pp. 308, 337. See also Hornell, *Water Transport*, p. 87.

11. Broughton, *Voyage in H.M.S. "Providence,"* p. 362.

12. Carletti, *My Voyage*, p. 96. See also *ibid.*, pp. 96-98.

13. Latham, *Travels of Marco Polo*, p. 213.

14. *Ibid.*, pp. 204-05.

15. Clifford and Illingworth, *Voyage of the "Golden Lotus,"* p. 61.

16. Holman, *Voyage Round the World*, 4:77.

17. T'ien-Tsê Chang, *Sino-Portuguese Trade: from 1514 to 1644* (Leyden: E. J. Brill, 1934), pp. 22-23.

18. Forrest, *Voyage to New Guinea*, p. 365.

19. Latham, *Travels of Marco Polo*, p. 176.

20. Worcester, *Sail and Sweep*, p. 37.

21. G.R.G. Worcester, "The Chinese Warjunk," *Mariner's Mirror* 34, no. 1 (Jan., 1948): 22.

22. *Ibid.*

23. Worcester, *Sail and Sweep*, p. 10.

24. Stevenson, *Cruise of the "Janet Nichol,"* p. 33.

25. Broughton, *Voyage in H.M.S. "Providence,"* p. 363.

26. Walter and Anson, *Voyage Round the World*, p. 308. See also Shineberg, *Voyages of Andrew Cheyne*, p. 80.

27. Charles E. Nowell, ed., *Magellan's Voyage Around the World: Three Contemporary Accounts* ... (Evanston, Ill.: Northwestern U. Pr., 1962), p. 131.

28. Clifford and Illingworth, *Voyage of the "Golden Lotus,"* p. 28.

29. Ernest K. Gann, *Song of the Sirens* (London: Hodder, 1969), p. 38.

30. Adam J. Krusenstern, *Voyage Round the World in the Years 1803-06 ... on board the ships "Nadeshda" and "Neva"* ..., trans. R. B. Hoppner, 2 vols. (1813, reprint ed., New York: Da Capo, 1968), 1:267.

31. Holman, *Voyage Round the World*, 4:253. See also *ibid.*, p. 41.

32. Krusenstern, *Voyage Round the World*, 1:267.

33. Holman, *Voyage Round the World*, 4:69.

34. Howay, *Colnett Aboard the "Argonaut,"* p. 247.

35. Jean Francois de Galaup, Compte de La Pérouse, *Voyages and Adventures of La Pérouse*, trans. Julius S. Gassner (Honolulu: U. Pr. of Hawaii, 1969), p. 71.

36. Sven Waxell, *The American Expedition* (London: Hodge, 1952), p. 83. See also Gerhard F. Muller, *Voyages from Asia to America for Completing the Discoveries of the North West Coast of America* (1761; reprint ed., New York: Da Capo, 1967), p. 26. For a comment on their clumsiness, see R. D. Paine, *The Ships and Sailors of Old Salem* (New York: Outing Publishing Co., 1909), p. 362; and Björn Landström, *The Ship* (New York: Doubleday, 1961), p. 223.

37. Purchas, *His Pilgrimes*, 3:454

38. *Ibid.*, 2:328, 335.

39. *Ibid.*, p. 337.

40. Waxell, *American Expedition*, p. 82. See also Muller, *Voyages from Asia*, p. 27.

CHAPTER 7

1. Herbert Warington Smyth, *Mast and Sail in Europe and Asia* (London: Blackwood & Sons, 1929), p. 290.

2. Gann, *Song of the Sirens*, p. 119.

3. Anderson and Anderson, *Sailing Ship*, p. 156. See also Björn Landström, *Sailing Ships* (London: Allen & U., 1969), p. 109.

4. Herman Melville, *White Jacket* (New York: Grove, 1956), p. 27.

5. Ian Cameron, *Lodestone and Evening Star* (London: Hodder, 1965), p. 128.

6. *Ibid.*, p. 130.

7. Landström, *Sailing Ships*, pp. 90-93. See also Charles Ralph Boxer, *Fidalgos in the Far East*, 1550-1770 (The Hague: M. Nijhoff, 1948), pp. 12-15.

8. Carletti, *My Voyage*, p. 190.

9. Charles Ralph Boxer, "Admiral João Pereira Corte-Real and the Construction of Portuguese East-Indiamen in the Early Seventeenth Century," *Mariner's Mirror* 26, no. 4 (Oct., 1940): 406.

10. *Ibid.*

11. William Lytle Schurz, *The Manila Galleon* (New York: Dutton, 1959), p. 184.

12. Boxer, *Fidalgos in the Far East*, p. 15. See also Knox-Johnston, *World of My Own*, p. 6.

13. Zelia Nuttall, ed., *New Light on Drake*, Hakluyt Second Series no. 34 (1914; reprint ed., Nendeln, Liechtenstein: Kraus Repr., 1967), p. 252.

14. F. C. Prideaux Naish, "The Mystery of Tonnage and Dimensions of the *Pelican—Golden Hind*," *Mariner's Mirror* 34, no. 1 (Jan., 1948): 42-45.

15. Nuttall, *New Light on Drake*, p. 108.

16. *Ibid.*, p. 302. See also Arthur H. Clark, *The Clipper Ship Era* (London: G. P. Putnam's Sons, 1910), p. 6; and Shelvocke, *A Voyage Round the World*, p. 111.

17. Smyth, *Mast and Sail*, p. 246.

18. Nuttall, *New Light on Drake*, p. 239.

19. *Ibid.*, p. 303.

20. *Ibid.*, p. 184.

21. Clements R. Markham, ed., *The Voyages of Sir James Lancaster, Kt. to the East Indies*...Hakluyt First Series no. 56 (London: Hakluyt Society, 1877), p. ii.

22. Michael Lewis, *The Navy of Britain* (London: Allen & U., 1948), p. 451.

23. J. R. Stevens, *An Account of the Construction and Embellishment of Old Time Ships* (Toronto: 1949), *passim*. One nineteenth-century ship-of-the-line, the *Duke of Wellington*, was reputed to have contained the oak timber from 76 acres of 100 year-old oak trees, given 40 trees to the acre. See *Sea Breezes* 31:415.

24. E.H.H. Archibald, *The Wooden Fighting Ship* (London: Blandford Press, 1968), p. 65.

25. *Ibid.*, p. 86.

26. Landström, *Sailing Ships*, p. 152.

27. Corney, *Occupation of Tahiti*, 1:147n.

28. William Foster, ed., *The Voyage of Sir Henry Middleton to the Moluccas, 1604-6*, Hakluyt Second series no. 88 (London: Hakluyt Society, 1943), p. 104.

29. Landström, *Sailing Ships*, p. 145.

30. Sharp, *Voyages of Abel Tasman*, p. 10.

31. Ellsworth Luce West, *Captain's Papers* (Barre, Mass.: Barre Publishers, 1965), p. 73.

32. Krusenstern, *Voyage Round the World*, 2:229.

33. Sharp, *Voyages of Abel Tasman*, p. 20.

34. Markham, *Hawkins' Voyages*, p. 307.

35. Landström, *Sailing Ships*, p. 163. See also Anderson and Anderson, *Sailing Ship*, pp. 200-04.

36. John Dunmore, *French Explorers in the Pacific*, 2 vols. (Oxford: Clarendon Press, 1965, 1969), 1:124.

37. *Ibid.*, p. 264.

38. Landström, *Sailing Ships*, p. 162.

CHAPTER 8

1. Hakluyt, *The Principal Navigations,* 8:204.

2. Kelly, *Voyage of Quirós,* 1:27.

3. *Ibid.,* p. 26.

4. Beaglehole, *Voyage of the "Resolution" and "Discovery,"* p. 1486.

5. Vancouver, *Voyage in the "Discovery" and "Chatham,"* 4:191-92.

6. Muller, *Voyages from Asia,* p. 26.

7. Waxell, *American Expedition,* p. 77. Muller calls this craft the *Bolschaia-reka.*

8. Flinders, *Voyage to Australia,* 1:cxix.

9. Marnie Bassett, *Behind the Picture* (Melbourne: Oxf. U. P., 1966), p. 27.

10. Drake, *World Encompassed,* p. 4.

11. Markham, *Hawkins' Voyages,* pp. 184, 256.

12. Anderson and Anderson, *Sailing Ship,* p. 165. See also Landström, *Sailing Ships,* p. 161; and M. S. Robinson, comp., *Van De Velde Drawings* (Cambridge: Camb. U. P., 1958), p. 232.

13. Hakluyt, *The Principal Navigations,* 8:155.

14. Markham, *Hawkins' Voyages,* p. 323.

15. *Ibid.,* p. 325.

16. *Ibid.,* p. 122.

17. Roger Charles Anderson, *Oared Fighting Ships* (London: Percival Marshall, 1962), p. 86.

18. William Funnell, *A Voyage Round the World Containing an Account of Captain Dampier's Expedition into the South Seas in the years 1703 and 1704* ... (London: James Knapton, 1707), p. 2.

19. A. Basil Lubbock, ed., *Barlow's Journal,* 2 vols. (London: Hurst & Blackett, 1934), 2:484, 549. See also Purchas, *His Pilgrimes,* 2:332.

20. Lubbock, *Barlow's Journal,* 1:72.

21. Alfred George Course, *Windjammers of the Horn* (London: Adlard, 1969), p. 50. See also Burney, *Buccaneers of America,* p. 186.

22. Joyce, *Voyage by Wafer,* p. 121.

23. Funnell, *Voyage Round the World,* p. 27.

24. Lee, *Logbooks of the "Lady Nelson,"* p. 220.

25. Jacobs, *Cruise of the "Margaret Oakley,"* p. 51.

26. Sanderson, *Follow the Whale,* p. 203.

27. Bechervaise, *Old Quarter Master,* p. 144.

28. John Easty, *Memorandum of the Transactions of a Voyage from England to Botany Bay 1787-93,* ed. G. A. Wilkes and A. G. Mitchell (Sydney: The Trustees of the Public Library of New South Wales, in association with Angus and Robertson, 1965), pp. 126-27.

29. John Frederick Mortlock, *Experiences of a Convict* (1864-65; reprint ed., Sydney: Sydney University Press, 1966), p. 60.

30. Waxell, *American Expedition,* p. 147.

31. *Ibid.*, p. 153.

32. Shelvocke, *Voyage Round the World,* p. 132.

33. John Bulkeley and John Cummins, *A Voyage to the South Seas in His Majesty's Ship the "Wager" in the Years 1740-1741,* 3rd ed. (London: Harrap, 1927), p. 120. See also *Ibid.*, p. 24.

34. Howay, *Voyages of the "Columbia,"* p. 343.

CHAPTER 9

1. Richard Henry Dana, Jr., *Two Years Before the Mast* (New York: Dodd, 1946), p. 249. See also Adrian Seligman, *The Voyage of the "Cap Pilar"* (London: Hodder, 1941), p. 102.

2. Dana, *Two Years Before the Mast,* p. 247.

3. Felix Riesenberg, *Cape Horn* (London: Robert Hale, 1941), p. 357; and Shelvocke, *Voyage Round the World,* p. 145.

4. Carletti, *My Voyage,* p. 35.

5. Meares, *Voyages from China,* p. 56.

6. Markham, *Hawkins' Voyages,* p. 313.

7. Cameron, *Lodestone and Evening Star,* p. 170.

8. Edward Keble Chatterton, *Seamen All,* 2nd ed. (London: Philip Allan, 1928), p. 149.

9. Vancouver, *Voyage in the "Discovery" and "Chatham,"* 5:29.

10. Dampier, *Dampier's Voyages,* 2:41.

11. Meares, *Voyages from China,* p. 348.

12. John Ruskin, *The Harbours of England* (London: George Allen, 1905), pp. 1-4.

13. John Smith, *The Sea Grammar* (1627; reprint ed., New York: Da Capo, 1968), p. 11.

14. Cowan, *Suwarrow Gold,* pp. 12-13.

15. Joseph Conrad, *Mirror of the Sea* (London: Dent, 1950), p. 121. See also Leonard John Ewens, *The Little Ships of the Pioneer Years 1836-45,* Parts 1 and 2 (Adelaide Pioneers' Association, 1952-53), 2, *passim*; and J. E. Philp, *Whaling Ways of Hobart Town* (Hobart: J. Walch, 1936), p. 12.

16. The vessel in question was named the *North West America.* Of "40 or 50 tons," it was built, with the assistance of the inhabitants of Nootka village, by Captain John Meares and the crew of the *Felice* in Nootka Sound between May 13 and September 20, 1788. See Meares, *Voyages from China,* p. 220.

17. Howay, *Voyages of the "Columbia,"* p. 390.

18. Johann Georg Forster, *A Voyage Round the World, in His Britannic Majesty's Sloop "Resolution," Commanded by Capt. James Cook, during the Years 1772-5,* 2 vols. (London: B. White, 1777), 1:228. See also Buck, *Coming of the Maori,* p. 316; Beaglehole, *Voyage of "Resolution" and "Adventure,"* p. 777; and Best, Maori Canoe, pp. 95-97.

19. Taylor, *Journal of Ensign Best,* p. 345.

20. Beaglehole, *Voyage of "Endeavour,"* p. 131.

21. Alan John Villiers, *Cruise of the "Conrad"; a Journal of a Voyage round the world*... (London: Hodder, 1940), p. 49.

22. Cowan, *Suwarrow Gold*, p. 131.

23. Elis Karlsson, *Mother Sea* (London: Oxf. U. P., 1964), p. 168.

24. *Ibid.*

25. D. W. Waters, *The Art of Navigation in England in Elizabethan and Early Stuart Times* (London: Hollis and Carter, 1958), p. 315.

26. Howay, *Colnett Aboard the "Argonaut,"* p. 279.

27. Conrad, *Mirror of the Sea*, p. 130.

CHAPTER 10

1. Carrington, *Discovery of Tahiti*, p. 17. See also Shelvocke, *Voyage Round the World*, p. 36.

2. La Pérouse, *Voyages of La Pérouse*, p. 8.

3. Morrell, *Sir Joseph Banks*, p. 40; and Krusenstern, *Voyage Round the World*, 1:89.

4. Gallagher, *Byron's Journal*, p. 62. For a ship hitting a whale by accident, see J. C. Ross, *A Voyage of Discovery and Research in the Southern and Antarctic Regions*..., 2 vols. (London: John Murray, 1847), 2.146.

5. Alan Burgess, *No Risks—No Romance*, (London: Cape, 1941), p. 70; and Howay, *Colnett Aboard the "Argonaut,"* p. 52. See also Frank Thomas Bullen, *The Cruise of the "Cachalot" Round the World after Sperm Whales*, rev. ed. (London: John Murray, 1928), p. 61.

6. For a thorough discussion of the apparent gentleness of whales, see Jacques-Yves Cousteau and Philippe Diolé, *The Whale*, trans. J. F. Bernard (London: Cassell, 1972), pp. 13, 15, 57.

7. Sanderson, *Follow the Whale*, p. 206. See also Victor Blanchard Scheffer, *The Year of the Whale* (New York: Scribner, 1969), p. 74. He suggests a maximum of "an hour and a quarter."

8. Meares, *Voyages from China*, p. 340. For a very interesting discussion of this, see Alexander Dalrymple, *An Historical Collection of the Several Voyages and Discoveries in the South Pacific Ocean*..., 2 vols. (London: The Author, 1770-71), 1:12.

9. Foster, *Voyage of Sir Henry Middleton*, p. 12. However, some writers report whales attacking boats deliberately. See Paul Budker, *Whales and Whaling* (London: Harrap, 1958), p. 98; Scheffer, *Year of the Whale*, p. 96; Philp, *Whaling Ways*, pp. 26, 65-66; and W. Lawson, *Bluegum Clippers and Whale Ships of Tasmania* ... (Melbourne: Georgian House, 1949), pp. 56, 63, 67.

10. Long, *Sailing in the "Idle Hour,"* p. 194.

11. *Ibid.*

12. Howay, *Voyages of the "Columbia,"* p. 206n; and James Colnett, *A Voyage to the South Atlantic and Round Cape Horn* ... (London: The Author, 1798), p. 89.

13. Seligman, *Voyage of the "Cap Pilar,"* p. 268.

14. Owen Chase, Thomas Chappel, and George Pollard, *Narrative of the Wreck of the Whale-Ship "Essex"* ... (London: Golden Cockerel Press, 1935), pp.

26, 41. See also Sanderson, *Follow the Whale*, p. 209; and A.B.C. Whipple, *Yankee Whalers in the South Seas* (London: Gollancz, 1954), p. 60.

15. Knox-Johnston, *World of My Own*, p. 84.

16. Francis Chichester, *Along the Clipper Way* (London: Pan, 1966), p. 92.

17. Latham, *Travels of Marco Polo*, p. 204. See also Lawson, *Bluegum Clippers*, pp. 182-83; Budker, *Whales and Whaling*, p. 112; Whipple, *Yankee Whalers*, pp. 49-61; Edward Keble Chatterton, *Whalers and Whaling*, 2nd ed. (London: T. F. Unwin, 1925), pp. 68, 122.

18. Sanderson, *Follow the Whale*, p. 335.

19. *Ibid.*, p. 41. See also Budker, *Whales & Whaling*, pp. 152-54.

20. Whymper, *Travel in Alaska*, p. 45.

21. Sanderson, *Follow the Whale*, p. 336. See also Budker, *Whales & Whaling*, p. 104.

22. Sanderson, *Follow the Whale*, p. 311. See also Budker, *Whales & Whaling*, p. 63.

23. Sanderson, *Follow the Whale*, p. 39.

24. Howay, *Voyages of the "Columbia,"* p. 66.

25. *Ibid.*, pp. 77, 78. See also Wilkes, *United States Exploring Expedition*, 4:486.

26. Beaglehole, *Voyage of the "Resolution" and "Discovery,"* p. 1325.

27. G. S. Parsonson, "Introduction" to Kelly, *Voyage of Quirós*, 1:80. See also W. Mariner, *An Account of the Natives of the Tonga Islands in the South Pacific Ocean . . .*, ed. John Martin (London: John Murray, 1817), 1:313.

28. Markham, *Hawkins' Voyages*, p. 157. A reported Japanese method was scarcely less incredible. A swimmer fastened a rope to the wounded whale's snout through a hole he cut for the purpose; see Budker, *Whales and Whaling*, p. 88.

29. Sanderson, *Follow the Whale*, p. 25. See also Philp, *Whaling Ways*, p. 48; and Lawson, *Bluegum Clippers*, p. 15.

30. Sanderson, *Follow the Whale*, p. 262.

31. *Ibid.*, p. 250. See also J. Ross Browne, *Etchings of a Whaling Cruise*, ed. John Seelye (1846; reprint ed. Cambridge, Mass: Harvard U. Pr., 1968), pp. 543, 550.

32. Marnie Bassett, *Realms and Islands* (London: Oxf. U. P., 1962), p. 102.

33. Sanderson, *Follow the Whale*, p. 256.

34. *Ibid.*, p. 236. See also Easty, *Voyage to Botany Bay*, p. 134; and Philp, *Whaling Ways*, pp. 7-8.

35. West and Mayhew, *Captain's Papers*, p. 7. See also Sanderson, *Follow the Whale*, p. 235. For a description of the very good Tasmanian whaleboats, see Philp, *Whaling Ways*, pp. 71-72; and Lawson, *Bluegum Clippers*, p. 59. These boats and their crews often showed their superiority even to American boats and crews.

36. Sanderson, *Follow the Whale*, p. 252.

37. Browne, *Etchings of a Whaling Cruise*, p. 559. See also Bullen, *The Cruise of the "Cachalot,"* p. 115.

38. Dana, *Two Years Before the Mast*, p. 176.

39. *Ibid.*, p. 177n. See also Bullen, *Etchings of a Whaling Cruise*, p. 106.

40. Clark, *Clipper Ship Era*, p. 79. For a completely contrary view, see Whipple, *Yankee Whalers*, pp. 8-9.

41. C. Bede Maxwell, *Wooden Hookers* (London: Angus & Robertson, 1940), p. 73.

42. R. D. Robertson, *Of Whales and Men* (London: The Reprint Society, 1956), p. 13.

43. Browne, *Etchings of a Whaling Cruise*, p. 504. See also Bullen, *Cruise of the "Cachalot,"* p. 95.

44. Villiers, *Cruise of the "Conrad,"* p. 246.

45. Browne, *Etchings of a Whaling Cruise*, p. 574. For a discussion of the whaling gun, see Budker, *Whales and Whaling*, pp. 103ff.

46. H. Williams, ed., *One Whaling Family* (Boston: Houghton Mifflin, 1964), pp. 44, 46.

47. Markham, *Hawkins' Voyages*, p. 322.

48. Sanderson, *Follow the Whale*, p. 238.

49. *Ibid.*, p. 250.

50. West and Mayhew, *Captain's Papers*, p. 26.

51. *Ibid.*, p. 53.

52. Sanderson, *Follow the Whale*, p. 187. See also Whipple, *Yankee Whalers*, p. 108

53. Sanderson, *Follow the Whale*, p. 187. See also Philp, *Whaling Ways*, p. 59; and Lawson, *Bluegum Clippers*, p. 21.

54. Bassett, *Realms and Islands*, p. 216.

CHAPTER 11

1. A. Basil Lubbock, *The China Clippers*, 3rd ed. (Glasgow: James Brown & Son, 1916), p. 274.

2. Conrad, *Mirror of the Sea*, p. 42.

3. Bullen, *Cruise of the "Cachalot,"* p. 371. See also Chatterton, *Seamen All*, pp. 167-68.

4. Gann, *Song of the Sirens*, p. 19.

5. Lubbock, *China Clippers*, p. 288. See also *ibid.*, p. 283; and Chatterton, *Seamen All*, p. 123.

6. Long, *Sailing in the "Idle Hour,"* p. 251.

7. Clark, *Clipper Ship Era*, p. 338; and H. T. Chappelle, "The First Clipper," *Mariner's Mirror* 34, no. 1 (Jan., 1948): 30.

8. Kenneth E. Slack, *In the Wake of the "Spray"* (New Brunswick: Rutgers U. Pr., 1966), p. 198.

9. Chichester, *Along the Clipper Way*, pp. 71-72.

10. Carl E. McDowell and Helen M. Gibbs, *Ocean Transportation* (New York: McGraw-Hill, 1954), p. 21, and *ibid.*, p. 21, quoting S. E. Morison.

11. Anderson and Anderson, *Sailing Ship*, p. 188.

12. McDowell and Gibbs, *Ocean Transportation*, p. 22.

13. Clark, *Clipper Ship Era*, p. 60.

14. *Ibid.*, p. 8.

15. Chappelle, *"The First Clipper,"* p. 31.
16. Lubbock, *Colonial Clippers*, p. 64, quoting Daily Atlas, Boston, Mass.
17. A. Basil Lubbock, *The Blackwall Frigates* (Glasgow: James Brown & Son, 1922), p. 125.
18. Course, *Windjammers of the Horn*, p. 161.
19. Clark, *Clipper Ship Era*, p. 237.
20. Riesenberg, *Cape Horn*, p. 357.
21. Alan J. Villiers, *Set of the Sails* (London: Hodder, 1949), p. 212.
22. Clark, *Clipper Ship Era*, p. 127.
23. *Ibid.*, p. 124.
24. Lubbock, *Colonial Clippers*, p. 27.
25. *Ibid.*, quoting *Illustrated London News*.
26. *Ibid.*, p. 28, quoting *Illustrated London News*. See also *ibid.*, p. 40; and Chatterton, *Seamen All*, p. 127.
27. Lewis, *Daughters of the Wind*, p. 230. See also Alfred Fell, *A Colonist's Voyage to New Zealand under Sail in the "Early Forties"* ... (Exeter: J. Townsend, 1926), pp. 8, 12, 27, 32, 49.
28. Riesenberg, *Cape Horn*, p. 335.
29. Clark, *Clipper Ship Era*, p. 105.
30. A. Basil Lubbock, *Round the Horn Before the Mast* (London: John Murray, 1915), p. 130.
31. Karlsson, *Mother Sea*, p. 79.
33. Villiers, *Set of the Sails*, p. 221.
33. Landström, *Sailing Ships*, p. 177.
34. *Otago Daily Times* (Dunedin), 8 July 1974, p. 4.
35. Karlsson, *Mother Sea*, p. 83.
36. Leslie Morton, *The Long Wake* (London: Routledge, 1968), p. 65.

CHAPTER 12

1. Waters, *Art of Navigation*, p. 98.
2. *Ibid.*, p. 405.
3. *Ibid.*, p. 419, quoting William Oughtred.
4. *Ibid.*, p. 3.
5. London, *Cruise of the "Snark,"* p. 45.
6. *Ibid.*, p. 49.
7. Nowell, *Magellan's Voyage*, p. 256.
8. Albert G. Osbun, *To California and the South Seas* (San Marino, Calif.: Huntington Lib., 1966), p. 131.
9. Alan Moorehead, *Darwin and The Beagle* (London: H. Hamilton, 1969), p. 218.
10. Carrington, *Discovery of Tahiti*, p. 29.
11. Waters, *Art of Navigation*, p. 289.
12. Dampier, *Voyage to New Holland*, p. 69.

13. Albert Hastings Markham, *The Voyages and Works of John Davis, The Navigator,* Hakluyt First Series no. 59 (London: Hakluyt Society, 1880), p. 283.

14. Waters, *Art of Navigation,* p. 76. See also Bligh, *Mutiny in H.M.S. "Bounty,"* p. 11.

15. William Bourne, *A Regiment for the Sea and other Writings on Navigation* ... (Cambridge: Hakluyt Society, 1963), p. 237.

16. A. J. Villiers, *Captain Cook, The Seamen's Seaman* (London: Hodder, 1967), p. 39.

17. Waters, *Art of Navigation,* p. 433.

18. Slocum, *Sailing Alone,* p. 112.

19. Kelly, *Voyage of Quirós,* 1:52.

20. Hocken, *Abel Tasman and His Journal,* p. 5.

21. Wallis, *Carteret's Voyage,* 1:57.

22. Dunmore, *French Explorers,* 1:73.

23. Geoffrey Rawson, *"Pandora's" Last Voyage* (London: Longmans, 1963), p. 22.

24. Walter and Anson, *Voyage Round the World,* p. 87. See also *ibid.,* pp. 85-86.

25. Dorothy Burwash, *English Merchant Shipping, 1460-1540* (Toronto: U. of Toronto Pr., 1947), p. 16.

26. Markham, *Hawkins' Voyages,* p. 135.

27. Purchas, *His Pilgrimes,* 2:503; Carrington, *Discovery of Tahiti,* p. 5; Markham, *Hawkins' Voyages,* p. 135ff; and Debenham, *Voyage of Captain Bellingshausen,* 1:111. See also Ross, *Voyage in Antarctic Regions,* 2:136.

28. Beaglehole, *Voyage of the "Endeavour,"* p. xxxv. See also Eric C. Hiscock, *Beyond the West Horizon* (London: Oxf. U. P., 1963), p. 79; and Vancouver, *Voyage in the "Discovery" and "Chatham,"* 2:48.

29. Debenham, *Voyage of Captain Bellingshausen,* 1:176.

30. Beaglehole, *Voyage of the "Endeavour,"* p. 392.

31. Beaglehole, *Voyage of the "Resolution" and "Discovery"* p. 1501. Others were taught or had learned, too. Paine quotes an Italian astronomer who met, on an American ship, a Negro cook who used to make lunar observations. He had been Captain Cook's cabin boy; see Paine, *Ships and Sailors,* pp. 237-38.

32. Debenham, *Voyage of Captain Bellingshausen,* 1:47n.

33. Gerbault, *In Quest of the Sun,* p. 52.

34. Lubbock, *Blackwall Frigates,* p. 111.

35. J. Randier, *Men and Ships Around Cape Horn,* 1616-1939 (London: Arthur Barker, 1968), p. 90, quoting Gemma Frisius.

36. Beaglehole, *Voyage of the "Resolution" and "Adventure,"* p. 17.

37. Seligman, *Voyage of the "Cap Pilar,"* p. 91.

38. Beaglehole, *Voyage of the "Resolution" and "Discovery,"* p. 1541.

39. Macgillivray, *Voyage of H.M.S. "Rattlesnake,"* 1:16. Flinders had chronometers stop for the simple reason that they had not been wound up; see Flinders, *Voyage to Australia,* 2:161-62.

40. Chichester, *Along the Clipper Way,* p. 192.

41. Debenham, *Voyage of Captain Bellingshausen*, 1:xv.

42. Waters, *Art of Navigation*, p. 104. See also *ibid.*, p. 328; and E.G.R. Taylor, *The Haven-Finding Art, A History of Navigation from Odysseus to Captain Cook* (London: Hollis and Carter, 1956), pp. 174ff.

43. Nuttall, *New Light on Drake*, pp. 75, 208. See also Charles H. Cotter, *A History of Nautical Astronomy* (London: Hollis and Carter, 1968), pp. 309-11.

44. Course, *Windjammers of the Horn*, p. 47.

45. G. S. Parsonson, *"The Settlement of Oceania,"* in Jack Golson, ed., *Polynesian Navigation,* 3rd ed. (Wellington: A. H. and A. W. Reed, 1972), pp. 31-32.

46. Harold Gatty, *Nature is Your Guide* (London: Collins, 1958), *passim*; and Lewis, *We, the Navigators, passim*. During the Second World War, corvettes of the Royal Canadian Navy were provided with a complete kit for Polynesian celestial navigation from Harold Gatty, *The Raft Book:Lore of the Sea and Sky* (New York: George Grady Press, 1943).

47. Debenham, *Voyage of Captain Bellingshausen*, 2:310.

48. Arago, *Voyage of "Uranie" and "Physicienne,"* 2:14.

49. Voss, *Voyage of the "Tilikum,"* p. 27.

50. John Claus Voss, *The Venturesome Voyages of Captain Voss* (London: Martin Hopkinson, 1934), p. 108; and Voss, *Voyage of the "Tilikum,"* p. 27. See also Lewis, *We, the Navigators*, p. 87.

51. Clifford and Illingworth, *Voyage of the "Golden Lotus,"* p. 207.

52. Slocum, *Sailing Alone*, p. 110.

53. Bligh, *Mutiny in H.M.S. "Bounty,"* p. 35.

54. Villiers, *Captain Cook*, p. 189.

55. Lewis, *Daughters of the Wind*, p. 220.

56. Gann, *Song of the Sirens*, p. 160.

CHAPTER 13

1. Drake, *World Encompassed*, p. 42.

2. Commelin, *Dutch East-India Company*, p. 328.

3. Chatterton, *Seamen All*, p. 39.

4. Walter and Anson, *Voyage Round the World*, p. 72.

5. Lubbock, *Round the Horn*, p. 201.

6. Chichester, *Along the Clipper Way*, p. 152, quoting L. Draper of the Institute of Oceanography; and F. S. Russell and C. M. Yonge, *The Seas*, 2nd ed. (London: Warne, 1947), p. 239. See also Wallis, *Carteret's Voyage*, 1:126.

7. Course, *Windjammers of the Horn*, p. 79.

8. Long, *Sailing in the "Idle Hour,"* p. 74.

9. Course, *Windjammers of the Horn*, p. 79. See also A. B. Becher, *Navigation of the Pacific Ocean ... including extensive extracts from the Nautical Magazine* (London: J. D. Potter, 1860), p. 15. One of the ships in this book, the *Garthwray*, flying the Canadian flag in 1922, gave up trying to

defeat the Horn and turned east to reach Iquique past Australia and New Zealand. Her voyage from Britain to Chile on that occasion took 559 days, by far the longest on record.

10. Broughton, *Voyage in H.M.S. "Providence,"* p. 12. See also Becher, *Navigation of the Pacific Ocean*, p. 128, quoting Lieutenant Bowers.

11. Walter and Anson, *Voyage Round the World*, p. 12; and Gallagher, *Byron's Journal*, pp. 78, 83.

12. Julian S. Corbett, *Papers Relating to the Navy during the Spanish War 1585-1587* (London: Navy Records, 1898), p. 104, quoting Despatch from Drake to Walsingham, 2 April, 1587 (S. P. Dom. C.C. 2) (hereafter cited as Navy Papers).

13. Slocum, *Sailing Alone*, p. 77; and Lewis, *Daughters of the Wind*, p. 115.

14. Stanley, Lord of Alderley, ed., *The First Voyage Round the World by Magellan . . .*, Hakluyt First Series, no. 52 (London: Hakluyt Society, 1874), p. 53; and Purchas, *His Pilgrimes*, 2:90.

15. Gallagher, *Byron's Journal*, p. 83. See also Becher, *Navigation of the Pacific Ocean*, p. 120.

16. Villiers, *Captain Cook*, p. 48.

17. Whymper, *Travel in Alaska*, p. 8. See also Morrell, *Narrative of Four Voyages*, p. 77; and Porter, *Voyage in the South Seas*, p. 17, for interesting discussions of the dangers.

18. Course, *Windjammers of the Horn*, p. 148.

19. Lubbock, *Round the Horn*, p. 235.

20. Wallis, *Carteret's Voyage*, 1:53.

21. A. J. Pazolt, in C. W. Domville-Fife, ed., *Epics of the Square-Rigged Ships: Autobiographies of Sail* (London: Seeley Service, 1958), p. 199; and Chichester, *Along the Clipper Way*, p. 78.

22. Villiers, *Cruise of the "Conrad,"* p. 51.

23. *Evening Star* (Dunedin, New Zealand), June 20, 1972, p. 14.

24. Morton, *Long Wake*, p. 17. See also Karlsson, *Mother Sea*, p. 97; and Becher, *Navigation of the Pacific Ocean*, p. 15.

25. Hakluyt, *The Principal Navigations*, 8:180.

26. Lewis, *Daughters of the Wind*, p. 210. For a thorough discussion of this point, see Dodd, *Ring of Fire*, pp. 24-25.

27. Gerbault, *In Quest of the Sun*, p. 38.

28. Markham, *Hawkins' Voyages*, p. 114.

29. Ernle Bradford, *Drake* (London: Hodder, 1965), p. 32.

30. Wallis, *Carteret's Voyages*, 1:20.

31. Carrington, *Discovery of Tahiti*, p. 114.

32. Wallis, *Carteret's Voyages*, 2:440.

33. *Ibid.*, 1:106. See also 1:112.

34. *Ibid.*, 1:143.

35. *Ibid.*, 1:126.

36. Clements R. Markham, *Early Spanish Voyages to the Strait of Magellan*, Hakluyt Second Series no. 28 (1911; reprint ed., Nendeln, Liechtenstein: Kraus Repr. 1967), p. 203.

37. Debenham, *Voyages of Captain Bellingshausen*, 2:366.

38. Drake, *World Encompassed*, p. 61.

39. Moorehead, *Darwin and the "Beagle,"* p. 169.

40. Kelly, *Voyage of Quirós*, 1:253n.

41. Joyce, *Voyage by Wafer*, p. 124.

42. Course, *Windjammers of the Horn*, p. 95; and Henry Brett, *White Wings*: *Fifty Years of Sail in the New Zealand Trade, 1850-1900*, 2 vols. (Auckland: Brett Printing Co., 1924-28), 2:165.

43. Captain C. P. Boughton, in Domville-Fife, *Square-Rigged Ships*, pp. 147, 148. For another description of proximity to an unexpected volcanic eruption, see Morrell, *Narrative of Four Voyages*, pp. 191ff.

44. A. J. Pazolt in Domville-Fife, *Square-Rigged Ships*, p. 235.

45. Chichester, *Along the Clipper Way*, p. 75. See also Dana, *Two Years Before the Mast*, p. 255.

46. Elis Karlsson, *Pully-Haul: The Story of a Voyage* (London: Oxf. U. P., 1966), p. 73. For a similar procedure used by a Maori captain of a New Zealand coastal vessel, see Allan Alexander Kirk, *Ships and Sailormen: A Collection of Pen Portraits of Some Australian Shipmasters and Others whose Lives have been dedicated to the Sea* (Wellington: A. H. & A. W. Reed, 1964), p. 146.

47. Conrad, *Mirror of the Sea*, pp. 60-61. See also Becher, *Navigation of the Pacific Ocean*, p. 120.

48. Chatterton, *Seamen All*, p. 119.

49. Markham, *Voyages of Sir James Lancaster*, p. 93.

50. Dampier, *Dampier's Voyages*, 1:441.

51. Beaglehole, *Voyage of the "Resolution" and "Adventure,"* p. 141; and William Bligh, *A Voyage to the South Sea...in His Majesty's Ship The "Bounty"* ... (London: George Nicol, 1792), p. 145.

52. Karlsson, *Mother Sea*, pp. 142-43.

53. Dampier, *Dampier's Voyages*, 1:443.

54. Beaglehole, *Voyage of the "Endeavour,"* p. 433.

55. Mary Ann Parker, *A Voyage Round the World in the "Gorgon" Man-of-War* ... (London: J. Nichols, 1795), p. 66. See also Keppel, *Expedition of H.M.S. "Dido,"* p. 248; and Colnett, *Voyage to the South Atlantic*, p. 15.

56. Lubbock, *Blackwall Frigates*, p. 128.

57. Marilyn J. Copland, "Refrigeration: Its Impact upon New Zealand 1882-86" (B.A. Honors Thesis, The University of Otago, 1972) pp. 12-13.

58. Maxwell, *Wooden Hookers*, p. 61; and John Dunmore, *The Fateful Voyage of the "St. Jean Baptiste"* (Christchurch: Pegasus Press, 1969), p. 41.

59. Markham, *Hawkins' Voyages*, pp. 144-45.

60. Lubbock, *Barlow's Journal*, 2:526.

61. Nuttall, *New Light on Drake*, p. 311.

62. Lubbock, *Round the Horn*, p. 284. See also James Bisset, *Sail Ho! My Early Years at Sea* (London: Hart-Davis, 1961), p. 72.

63. Brett, *White Wings*, 2:71; and *ibid.*, 2:72.

64. Morton, *Long Wake*, p. 14.

65. Lubbock, *Round the Horn*, p. 286.

66. Dana, *Two Years Before the Mast*, p. 31.

67. Villiers, *Set of the Sails*, p. 173.

68. Melville, *White Jacket*, p. 320.

69. Golder, *Steller's Journal of Bering's Voyages*, pp. 115-16.

70. Hakluyt, *The Principal Navigations*, 8:185.

71. Hooker, *Journal of Sir Joseph Banks*, p. 111. According to Bisset, a twentieth-century captain had a shark caught so that nailing its tail to the jib-boom would bring a wind. It did; see Bisset, *Sail Ho!*, p. 156.

72. Joyce, *Voyage by Wafer*, p. 123. See also Burney, *Buccaneers of America*, p. 227.

73. Colnett, *Voyage to the South Atlantic*, p. 166.

74. Markham, *Hawkins' Voyages*, p. 105.

75. Hakluyt, *The Principal Navigations*, 8:98. See also Landström, *Sailing Ships*, pp. 102-06.

76. Waters, *Art of Navigation*, p. 233. See also Markham, *Hawkins' Voyages*, p. 93; and M. Lewis, *The Hawkins Dynasty: Three Generations of a Tudor Family* (London: Allen & U., 1969), p. 163.

77. Markham, *Hawkins' Voyages*, p. xxiii.

78. Conrad, *Mirror of the Sea*, p. 134.

79. Lubbock, *Colonial Clippers*, p. 115. See also A. J. Pazolt in Domville-Fife, *Square-Rigged Ships*, p. 257; and Fell, *Colonist's Voyage*, p. 45.

80. Domville-Fife, *Square-Rigged Ships*, p. 257; and Rogers, *Cruising Voyage*, p. 23. See also Beaglehole, *Voyage of the "Resolution" and "Discovery,"* p. 743; and Paine, *Ships and Sailors*, p. 421.

CHAPTER 14

1. Markham, *Hawkins' Voyages*, p. 306. See also Boxer, *Fidalgos in the Far East*, p. 15; and Knox-Johnston, *World of My Own*, p. 6.

2. Markham, *Hawkins' Voyages*, p. 203.

3. Lewis, *Hawkins Dynasty*, pp. 140ff.

4. Russell and Yonge, *The Seas*, pp. 135-42.

5. Peter Pye, *Red Mains'l* (London: Hart-Davis, 1961), p. 17.

6. Markham, *Hawkins' Voyages*, p. 202.

7. *Ibid.*, p. 201.

8. Markham, *Discovery of Peru*, p. 4.

9. Russell and Yonge, *The Seas*, p. 152. See also Dampier, *Dampier's Voyages*, 1:366; and Burney, *Buccaneers of America*, p. 289.

10. Dampier, *Dampier's Voyages*, 1:366.

11. Wilson, *Missionary Voyage*, p. 398. See also Dodd, *Ring of Fire*, p. 100.

12. S. E. Bradfield, *Road to the Sea* (London: Temple P. Bks., 1964), p. 3.

13. Wallis, *Carteret's Voyage*, 1:19. See also Riesenberg, *Cape Horn*, p. 365; and Conrad, *Mirror of the Sea*, p. 48.

14. Carrington, *Discovery of Tahiti*, p. xxxi.

15. For the reaction of penguins, see Ross, *Voyage in Antarctic Regions,* 1:195.

16. Broughton, *Voyage in H.M.S. "Providence,"* p. 53.

17. Herman Melville, *Redburn* (Chicago: Northwestern U. Pr., 1969), p. 4; and Jacobs, *Cruise of the "Margaret Oakley,"* p. 37. See also Broughton, *Voyage in H.M.S. "Providence,"* p. 2.

18. Carrington, *Discovery of Tahiti,* p. xxxii.

19. Nuttall, *New Light on Drake,* p. 302. I wish to thank Señor J. Ignacio Rubio Mañe of the *Archivo General De La Nacion* of Mexico City for his courtesy and assistance. He wrote: "Please find enclosed herewith the transcription of the original document which is in Volume 85, Exp. 12, f. 3 of *Inquisicion* in these National Archives of Mexico. The copy is only of the paragraph you are interested [*sic*], underlining the words you desire to check (*No es Nuevo ni emplomado*).

   My opinion is that *emplomado* in Spanish is not *coppered* nor *ballasted* in English. The word *emplomado* comes from *plomo* which means *lead* in English."

20. Lewis, *Daughters of the Wind,* p. 119.

21. Hooker, *Journal of Sir Joseph Banks,* p. 93. See also Beaglehole, *Voyage of the "Endeavour,"* p. 95.

22. Carletti, *My Voyage,* p. 97.

23. Lewis, *Daughters of the Wind,* p. 253.

24. Commelin, *Dutch East-India Company,* p. 275.

25. Adrian Hayter, *"Sheila" in the Wind: A Story of a Lone Voyage* (London: Hodder, 1959), p. 221.

26. Commander Capstickdale, "a Master Mariner of the days of sail," in Domville-Fife, *Square-Rigged Ships,* p. 268.

27. Purchas, *His Pilgrimes,* 2:241.

28. Rogers, *Cruising Voyage,* p. 227.

29. Hakluyt, *The Principal Navigations,* 8:229.

30. *Ibid.,* p. 230.

31. Bradford, *Drake,* p. 143. See also Riesenberg, *Cape Horn,* pp. 247, 249.

32. Villiers, *Cruise of the "Conrad,"* p. 232.

33. Beaglehole, *Voyage of the "Endeavour,"* p. 344.

34. *Ibid.*

35. Markham, *Hawkins' Voyages,* p. 238.

36. Markham, *Voyages of Sir James Lancaster,* p. 215.

37. Stanley, *First Voyage by Magellan,* p. 145.

38. Roe, *Journal of Captain Charles Bishop,* p. 69.

39. Bassett, *Realms and Islands,* p. 201.

40. Long, *Sailing in the "Idle Hour,"* p. 107. See also Voss, *Venturesome Voyages,* p. 80.

41. Captain R. Barry O'Brien in Domville-Fife, *Square-Rigged Ships,* p. 108.

42. Conrad, *Mirror of the Sea,* p. 67.

43. Long, *Sailing in the "Idle Hour,"* p. 304.

44. Beaglehole, *Voyage of the "Resolution" and "Discovery,"* p. 575.

45. *Ibid.*, p. 749.

46. *Ibid.*, p. 8n.

47. Markham, *Hawkins' Voyages*, pp. 114-15. See also James Grant, *The Narrative of a Voyage of Discovery Performed in His Majesty's Vessel "The Lady Nelson" . . . in the years 1800, 1801, and 1802 . . .* (London: T. Egerton, Military Library, Whitehall, 1803), p. 27.

48. Markham, *Voyage of Sir James Lancaster*, p. 222.

49. Debenham, *Voyage of Captain Bellingshausen*, 1:143, 218.

50. Dunmore, *French Explorers*, 1:123. Nor was this only a Russian, French or British problem. For American navy yard shortcomings, see Robert Erwin Johnson, *Thence Round Cape Horn: The story of United States Naval Forces on Pacific Station, 1818-1923* (Annapolis, Md.: Naval Inst. Pr., 1963), p. 27.

51. Keate, *Account of the Pelew Islands*, p. 124.

52. Hornell, *Water Transport*, pp. 207-13.

53. Lee, *Logbooks of the "Lady Nelson,"* p. 1. See also Grant, *Voyage of the "Lady Nelson,"* pp. 185-95, for reports praising the design of the *Lady Nelson*.

54. Bullen, *Cruise of the "Cachalot,"* p. 13. See also Budker, *Whales and Whaling*, p. 96.

55. London, *Cruise of the "Snark,"* p. 18.

CHAPTER 15

1. Howay, *Voyages of the "Columbia,"* p. 238n. See also Charles Bateson, *Gold Fleet for California: Forty-Niners from Australia and New Zealand* (Auckland: Minerva, 1963), pp. 89, 126; and Shineberg, *Voyages of Andrew Cheyne*, pp. 86-87.

2. Conrad, *Mirror of the Sea*, p. 26.

3. Harold A. Underhill, *Deep-Water Sail* (Glasgow: Brown, Son & F., 1963), p. 90.

4. Roe, *Journal of Captain Charles Bishop*, p. 258.

5. Casson, *Ships and Boats*, p. 138.

6. Landström, *Sailing Ships*, p. 181. See also Donald George Macintyre, *The Adventure of Sail* (London: Elek, 1970), pp. 32, 192.

7. Underhill, *Deep-Water Sail*, p. 53.

8. Anderson and Anderson, *Sailing Ship*, p. 206.

9. Clark, *Clipper Ship Era*, p. 273.

10. Lubbock, *Colonial Clippers*, p. 62. See also Clark, *Clipper Ship Era*, p. 107.

11. Landström, *Sailing Ships*, p. 171. See also Fell, *Colonist's Voyage*, pp. 19, 65.

12. Miles Smeeton, *Once is Enough* (London: Hart-Davis, 1959), p. 70.

13. Long, *Sailing in the "Idle Hour,"* p. 171. For the beauty of square-rig as opposed to other rigging, see Bisset, *Sail Ho!*, p. 170.

14. Villiers, *Cruise of the "Conrad,"* p. 9.

15. *Ibid.*, p. 14.

16. Underhill, *Deep-Water Sail*, p. 96. See also Landström, *Sailing Ships*, p. 177.

17. Lubbock, *Barlow's Journal*, 2:570. See also John H. Parry, *The Age of Reconnaissance* (London: Weid. & N., 1963), p. 63; and Rogers, *Cruising Voyage*, p. 153.

18. Villiers, *Captain Cook*, p. 133. See also Anderson and Anderson, *Sailing Ship*, pp. 140, 166; and Landström, *Sailing Ships*, pp. 127, 151 and 165.

19. Lewis, *Daughters of the Wind*, p. 94.

20. Knox-Johnston, *World of My Own*, p. 53.

21. A. J. Pazolt in Domville-Fife, *Square-Rigged Ships*, p. 189.

22. Lewis, *Daughters of the Wind*, pp. 44, 48.

23. Beaglehole, *Voyage of the "Resolution" and "Discovery,"* p. 481.

24. Eric Newby, *Grain Race: Pictures of Life before the Mast in a Windjammer* (London: Allen & U., 1968), p. 11.

25. Lubbock, *Round the Horn*, p. 147. See also Dana, *Two Years Before the Mast*, p. x; and Fell, *Colonist's Voyage*, *passim*.

26. Long, *Sailing in the "Idle Hour,"* p. 188. For a good discussion of this particular danger, see Whipple, *Yankee Whalers*, p. 138.

27. Karlsson, *Mother Sea*, p. 67. For an excellent discussion about the skills of a seaman, see Bullen, *Cruise of the "Cachalot,"* p. 204.

28. Robert Cunningham Bruce, *Reminiscences of a Wanderer* (Wellington: Whitcombe & Tombs, 1914), p. 9. See also Taylor, *Journal of Ensign Best*, p. 120.

29. W.R.S. Harris in Domville-Fife, *Square-Rigged Ships*, p. 208.

30. Beaglehole, *Voyage of the "Resolution" and "Adventure,"* p. 126; and Dana, *Two Years Before the Mast*, p. 246.

31. Wilson, *Missionary Voyage*, p. 130.

32. Karlsson, *Mother Sea*, p. xii.

33. Dana, *Two Years Before the Mast*, p. 298.

34. *Ibid.*, p. 12.

35. Lubbock, *Round the Horn*, p. 220.

36. Markham, *Hawkins' Voyages*, p. 96.

37. Beaglehole, *Voyage of the "Endeavour,"* p. 257; and *ibid.*, p. 34.

38. A. J. Pazolt in Domville-Fife, *Square-Rigged Ships*, p. 189.

39. Hooker, *Journal of Sir Joseph Banks*, p. 254.

40. Markham, *Hawkins' Voyages*, p. 310.

41. Stanley Walter Croucher Pack, *Admiral Lord Anson* (London: Cassell, 1960), p. 90.

42. Landström, *Sailing Ships*, p. 132.

43. Gallagher, *Byron's Journal*, p. 67n.

44. Hocken, *Abel Tasman and His Journal*, p. 4.

45. Shelvocke, *Voyage Round the World*, p. 3.

46. Lee, *Logbooks of the "Lady Nelson,"* p. 5.

47. Slack, *Wake of the Spray*, p. 209.

48. Conrad, *Mirror of the Sea*, p. 46.

49. William Falconer, *Marine Dictionary—1780* (reprint ed., Newton Abbott, England: David & Charles, 1970), p. 299.

50. Beaglehole, *Voyage of the "Resolution" and "Adventure,"* p. 587.

51. Lubbock, *Barlow's Journal,* 2:331.

52. Beaglehole, *Voyage of the "Resolution" and "Adventure"* p. 5.

53. *Ibid.*

54. Richard Henry Dana, *Dana's Seamen's Friend,* ed. James Lees (London: George Philip and Son, n.d.), p. 73.

CHAPTER 16

1. Slocum, *Sailing Alone,* p. 2.

2. *Ibid.,* p. 6.

3. *Ibid.*

4. *Ibid.,* p. 7.

5. *Ibid,* pp. 63, 233.

6. Slack, *Wake of the "Spray,"* p. 213.

7. Slack, *Wake of the "Spray,"* p. 247; and *ibid.,* p. 192.

8. Slocum, *Sailing Alone,* p. 40.

9. Hakluyt, *The Principal Navigations,* 8:296.

10. Smeeton, *Once is Enough,* p. 198.

11. Lewis, *Daughters of the Wind,* p. 38.

12. *Ibid.,* p. 76, quoting Charles Darwin.

13. Worcester, *Sail and Sweep,* p. 97.

14. Slack, *Wake of the "Spray,"* p. 203.

15. Dana, *Seamen's Friend,* p. 83.

16. Edward J. Wakefield, *Adventure in New Zealand,* 2 vols. (London: John Murray, 1845), 1:166.

17. Nuttall, *New Light on Drake,* p. 48.

18. Worcester, *Sail and Sweep,* p. 25.

19. Forrest, *Voyage to New Guinea,* p. 302.

20. Voss, *Tilikum, passim.*

21. Charlie and Ruth Gould, "Astrocyte," *British Columbia Medical Journal,* 10(1968): 171.

22. Knox-Johnston, *World of My Own,* pp. 88, 220; and *ibid.,* p. 124.

23. London, *Cruise of the "Snark,"* p. 30.

24. Course, *Windjammers of the Horn,* p. 86. For emergency sea-anchors, see Bateson, *Gold Fleet,* p. 118; Johnson, *Round Cape Horn,* p. 18; and Morrell, *Narrative of Four Voyages,* p. xxv.

25. Lee, *Logbooks of the "Lady Nelson,"* p. 15.

26. Course, *Windjammers of the Horn,* p. 34. See also Voss, *Venturesome Voyages,* p. 316.

27. Villiers, *Cruise of the "Conrad,"* p. 291. In his book *Old Whaling Days* (Cardiff: Conway Maritime Press, 1970), p. 124, William Barron points out that British whaling vessels sometimes used to "hang a whale's tail across the stern that the constant dropping of the oil from it would break the heavy seas when running before a westerly gale."

28. Broughton, *Voyage in H.M.S. "Providence,"* p. 26.

29. Conrad, *Mirror of the Sea*, p. 14.

30. Slocum, *Sailing Alone*, p. 165.

31. London, *Cruise of the "Snark,"* p. 31.

32. Smeeton, *Once is Enough*, p. 36.

33. Lubbock, *Colonial Clippers*, p. 305.

34. Waters, *Art of Navigation*, p. 314.

35. Anderson and Anderson, *Sailing Ship*, p. 169.

CHAPTER 17

1. Stanley, *First Voyage by Magellan*, p. 64.

2. Broughton, *Voyage in H.M.S. "Providence,"* p. 176.

3. Lubbock, *Round the Horn*, p. 152. See also Beaglehole, *Voyage of the "Resolution" and "Discovery,"* p. 749.

4. Nordenskiöld, *Voyage of the "Vega,"* 2:252.

5. Beaglehole, *Voyage of the "Endeavour,"* p. 39n.

6. Carrington, *Discovery of Tahiti*, p. 82.

7. Sharp, *Journal of Jacob Roggeveen*, p. 64.

8. Debenham, *Voyage of Captain Bellingshausen*, 1:159.

9. Waxell, *American Expedition*, p. 129.

10. Christopher Lloyd, *The Health of Seamen* (London: Navy Records, 1965), p. 284, quoting Dr. Thomas Trotter.

11. Rickman, *Cook's Last Voyage*, p. 20.

12. *Ibid.*, p. 21.

13. Sharp, *Journal of Jacob Roggeveen*, p. 150.

14. Christopher Lloyd, *The British Seaman, 1200-1860* (London: Collins, 1968), p. 229.

15. *Ibid.*, p. 294.

16. Melville, *White Jacket*, p. 82.

17. Rickman, *Cook's Last Voyage*, p. 9.

18. Lloyd, *Health of Seamen*, p. 267, quoting Dr. Thomas Trotter. See also James Lind, *Lind's Treatise on Scurvy*, ed. C. P. Stewart and Douglas Guthrie (1753; reprint ed., Edinburgh: Edin. U. P., 1953), pp. 86-87.

19. Beaglehole, *The Voyage of the "Endeavour,"* p. 441.

20. Dana, *Two Years Before the Mast*, p. 237.

21. Burney, *Buccaneers of America*, p. 217.

22. Walter and Anson, *Voyage Round the World*, p. 72.

23. Taylor, *Journal of Ensign Best*, p. 114.

24. James Kenneth Munford, ed., *Journal of Captain Cook's Last Voyage*, by John Ledyard (Corvalis, Oregon: Oreg. St. U. Pr., 1963), p. 235 (hereafter cited as *Ledyard's Journal*).

25. Gann, *Song of the Sirens*, p. 188. For a series of four men overboard without rescue on a Pacific Voyage of U.S.S. *Macedonian*, see Johnson, *Round*

Cape Horn, p. 21. For a more cheerful tale of a man rescued because his boots floated him, even if upside down, see Wilkes, *United States Exploring Expedition*, 1:150.

26. Markham, *Voyages of Sir James Lancaster*, p. 26.

27. Lubbock, *Round the Horn*, p. 252.

28. Howay, *Voyages of the "Columbia,"* p. 365.

29. Dana, *Two Years Before the Mast*, p. 13. See also Burgess, *No Risks—No Romance*, p. 69.

30. Markham, *Hawkins' Voyage*, p. 126.

31. Markham, *Early Spanish Voyages*, p. 212.

32. Spry, *Cruise of H.M.S. "Challenger,"* p. 41.

33. Lloyd, *Health of Seamen*, p. 152.

34. Beaglehole, *The Voyage of the "Endeavour,"* p. 370; and Villiers, *Captain Cook*, p. 243.

35. Jerry Allen, *The Sea Years of Joseph Conrad* (New York: Doubleday, 1965), p. 150.

36. C. S. Forester, *Commodore Hornblower* (Boston: Little, Brown and Co., 1945), p. 80.

37. Edward Ward, *The Journal of Edward Ward 1850-51* (Christchurch: Pegasus Press, 1951), pp. 27, 30. See also Fell, *Colonist's Voyage*, pp. 34-35.

38. A. J. Pazolt in Domville-Fife, *Square-Rigged Ships*, p. 229.

39. La Pérouse, *Voyages of La Pérouse*, p. 101.

40. Whymper, *Travel in Alaska*, p. 129.

41. Alexander Ross, *Adventures of the First Settlers on the Columbia River*, March of America, Facsimile Service, no. 58 (Ann Arbor, Mich.: University Microfilms, 1966), p. 312.

42. Bassett, *Behind the Picture*, p. 74.

43. Morton, *Long Wake*, p. 161.

44. Tobias Smollett, *The Adventures of Roderick Random*, (Oxford: Oxf. U.P., World's Classics, 1930), p. 190.

45. Foster, *Voyage of Sir Henry Middleton*, p. 9; and Hakluyt, *The Principal Navigations*, 8:304.

46. Pack, *Admiral Lord Anson*, p. 37.

47. Howay, *Voyages of the "Columbia,"* p. 224. See also Flinders, *Voyage to Australia*, 2:173, 226.

48. Burney, *Buccaneers of America*, p. 193; and Macgillivray, *Voyage of H.M.S. "Rattlesnake,"* 1:198.

49. Burney, *Buccaneers of America*, p. 142; Hooker, *Journal of Sir Joseph Banks*, p. 299; and Colnett, *Voyage to the South Atlantic*, p. 88.

50. Long, *Sailing in the "Idle Hour,"* p. 77. See also Crozet, *Voyage to Tasmania*, p. 91.

51. Beaglehole, *Voyage of the "Resolution" and "Adventure,"* pp. 469-70.

52. *Ibid.*, p. 470n.

53. Waxell, *American Expedition*, p. 174.

54. Hayter, *"Sheila" in the Wind*, p. 236.

55. Roe, *Journal of Captain Charles Bishop*, p. 108; and Vancouver, *Voyage in the "Discovery" and "Chatham,"* 4:45.

56. Carrington, *Discovery of Tahiti*, p. 120; and Markham, *Hawkins' Voyages*, p. 168.

57. White, *Voyage to New South Wales*, p. 145; and *ibid.*, p. 178.

58. White, *Voyage to New South Wales*, p. 58.

59. Lubbock, *Round the Horn*, p. 198.

60. *Ibid.*, p. 195. See also Bullen, *Cruise of the "Cachalot,"* pp. 191; 210, 279.

61. Morton, *Long Wake*, p. 74. See also Colnett, *Voyage to the South Atlantic*, p. 140.

62. Colnett, *Voyage to the South Atlantic*, p. 82n.

63. Dillon, *Fate of La Pérouse's Expedition*, 1:301; and Scherzer, *Narrative of the "Novara,"* 3:148.

64. Roe, *Journal of Captain Charles Bishop*, p. 45.

65. Lind, *Treatise on Scurvy*, p. 333n, discussing a book by Sinopeus.

66. Rogers, *Cruising Voyage*, p. 253.

67. Lind, *Treatise on Scurvy*, pp. 304-05.

68. Hakluyt, *The Principal Navigations*, 8:286.

69. Smollett, *Adventures of Roderick Random*, p. 250; and *ibid.*, p. 185.

70. Hakluyt, *The Principal Navigations*, 8:286.

71. Dunmore, *Voyage of the "St. Jean Baptiste,"* p. 57.

72. Dana, *Two Years Before the Mast*, p. 236.

73. Foster, *Voyage of Sir Henry Middleton*, p. 9.

74. Markham, *Hawkins' Voyages*, p. 316.

75. Maxwell, *Wooden Hookers*, p. 94.

76. Melville, *White Jacket*, pp. 240, 247.

77. Smollett, *Adventures of Roderick Random*, p. 189.

CHAPTER 18

1. Wallis, *Carteret's Voyage*, 2:452.

2. Markham, *Hawkins' Voyages*, p. 138; and Lind, *Treatise on Scurvy*, p. 301. See also *ibid.*, p. 70.

3. Walter and Anson, *Voyage Round the World*, p. 80.

4. *Ibid.*

5. *Ibid.*, p. 81.

6. White, *Voyage to New South Wales*, p. 107.

7. Waxell, *American Expedition*, p. 200; and Walter and Anson, *Voyage Round the World*, p. 82. See also Lind, *Treatise on Scurvy*, pp. 123-24.

8. Beaglehole, *Voyage of the "Endeavour,"* p. 349; Wallis, *Carteret's Voyage*, 2:377; Corney, *Occupation of Tahiti*, 1:116; Dunmore, *Voyage of the "St. Jean Baptiste,"* p. 114; Colnett, *Voyage to the South Atlantic*, p. 176; Dana, *Two Years Before the Mast*, p. 295; and Chichester, *Along the Clipper Way*, p. 91, quoting Vito Dumas.

9. Lind, *Treatise on Scurvy*, p. 306. See also Carrington, *Discovery of Tahiti*, p. 104.

10. Muller, *Voyages from Asia*, p. 53; and White, *Voyage to New South Wales*, p. 103.

11. Lind, *Treatise on Scurvy*, pp. 93, 105. See also Debenham, *Voyage of Captain Bellingshausen*, 1:46.

12. Browne, *Etchings of a Whaling Cruise*, p. 563.

13. Waxell, *American Expedition*, p. 122.

14. Gallagher, *Byron's Journal*, p. lxii.

15. Beaglehole, *Voyage of the "Resolution" and "Discovery,"* p. 659n.

16. Scherzer, *Narrative of the "Novara,"* 2:574.

17. Debenham, *Voyage of Captain Bellingshausen*, 1:46. See also Colnett, *Voyage to the South Atlantic*, p. 83; Meares, *Voyages from China*, p. xviii; and Ivan Goncharov, *The Voyage of the Frigate "Pallada"* (London: Folio Society, 1965), pp. 26, 52.

18. George Godwin, *Vancouver, A Life* (London: Philip Allan, 1930), p. 37; and Debenham, *Voyage of Captain Bellingshausen*, 1:140. See also Flinders, *Voyage to Australia*, 1:227; and Ross, *Voyage in Antarctic Regions*, 1:242.

19. Meares, *Voyages from China*, p. 76.

20. Lind, *Treatise on Scurvy*, p. 342.

21. Lloyd, *Health of Seamen*, p. 149, quoting Dr. Gilbert Blane.

22. Muller, *Voyages from Asia*, p. 24. See also Debenham, *Voyage of Captain Bellingshausen*, 1:46; and Meares, *Voyages from China*, p. xx.

23. Chichester, *Along the Clipper Way*, p. 58. See also Wilson, *Missionary Voyage*, p. 309; and Lloyd, *Health of Seamen*, p. 140.

24. Lind, *Treatise on Scurvy*, p. 215. See also Markham, *Hawkins' Voyages*, p. 140.

25. La Pérouse, *Voyages of La Pérouse*, p. 117.

26. Lind, *Treatise on Scurvy*, p. 315.

27. Lloyd, *British Seamen*, p. 43.

28. Markham, *Voyages of Sir James Lancaster*, p. 66.

29. *Ibid.*, p. 62. See also Foster, *Voyage of Sir Henry Middleton*, p. xviiin.

30. Beaglehole, *Voyage of the "Resolution" and "Adventure,"* p. 51.

31. Markham, *Hawkins' Voyages*, pp. 141, 163.

32. *Ibid.*, p. 163.

33. *Ibid.*, p. 161.

34. Lind, *Treatise on Scurvy*, p. 5.

35. Waters, *Art of Navigation*, p. 293.

36. Smith, *Sea Grammar*, p. 96.

37. Lind, *Treatise on Scurvy*, Appendix p. 434, quoting Meiklejohn, Passmore and Stewart.

38. Beaglehole, *Voyage of the "Resolution" and "Adventure,"* p. 600.

39. Howay, *Voyages of the "Columbia,"* p. 60.

40. Nordenskiöld, *Voyage of the "Vega,"* 1:480. See also La Pérouse, *Voyages of La Pérouse*, p. 34; and Golder, *Steller's Journal of Bering's Voyages*, p. 58n.

41. Hakluyt, *The Principal Navigations*, 8:51.

42. Wallis, *Carteret's Voyages*, 2:451, quoting Dr. Thomas Trotter. See also Bullen, *Cruise of the "Cachalot,"* p. 298.

43. Lloyd, *Health of Seamen*, p. 305, quoting Dr. Thomas Trotter.

44. Lind, *Treatise on Scurvy*, p. 366.

45. *Ibid.*, p. 156.

46. Morrell, *Sir Joseph Banks in New Zealand*, p. 35; and Hooker, *Journal of Sir Joseph Banks*, p. 72.

47. Lloyd, *Health of Seamen*, pp. 280, 305, quoting Dr. Thomas Trotter.

48. Lubbock, *Round the Horn*, p. 107. See also Knox-Johnston, *World of My Own*, p. 171; Browne, *Etchings of a Whaling Cruise*, p. 563; and Morton, *Long Wake*, p. 8.

49. Karlsson, *Mother Sea*, p. 91.

50. Lind, *Treatise on Scurvy*, p. 166.

51. Lee, *Logbooks of the "Lady Nelson,"* p. 10.

52. Lloyd, *Health of Seamen*, p. 302, quoting Dr. Thomas Trotter.

53. Sidney J. Baker, *My Own Destroyer* (Sydney: Currawong Publishing Co., 1962), p. 51. See also *ibid.*, pp. 49-51; and Flinders, *Voyage to Australia*, 1:230.

54. Carrington, *Discovery of Tahiti*, p. 111n.

55. Lind, *Treatise on Scurvy*, p. 179. See also Beaglehole, *Voyage of the "Resolution" and "Adventure,"* p. 191n.

56. Villiers, *Captain Cook*, p. 99.

57. Drake, *World Encompassed*, p. 41; Colnett, *Voyage to the South Atlantic*, pp. 74, 118; and Lind, *Treatise on Scurvy*, p. 274.

58. Wallis, *Carteret's Voyage*, 1:184.

59. Charles McKew Parr, *So Noble A Captain: The Life and Times of Ferdinand Magellan* (New York: Thomas Y. Crowell Co., 1953), p. 253.

60. Markham, *Voyages of Sir James Lancaster*, p. 4.

61. Lind, *Treatise on Scurvy*, p. 91.

62. W.R.S. Harris in Domville-Fife, *Square-Rigged Ships*, p. 207.

63. Carrington, *Discovery of Tahiti*, p. 73.

64. Randier, *Men and Ships*, p. 333.

65. Dunmore, *Voyage of the "St. Jean Baptiste,"* p. 84.

66. Golder, *Log Books of Bering's Voyages*, p. 238. See also Waxell, *American Expedition*, p. 142.

67. Burney, *Buccaneers of America*, p. 194. See also Wallis, *Carteret's Voyages*, 2:445-46.

68. Bassett, *Realms and Islands*, p. 118. See also Wallis, *Carteret's Voyages*, 1:162.

69. "Family Doctor," New Zealand Broadcasting Corporation Broadcast, July 8, 1972.

70. Dana, *Two Years Before the Mast*, p. 297. See also Grant, *Voyage of the "Lady Nelson,"* p. 180.

71. Roe, *Journal of Captain Charles Bishop*, p. 124.

72. Lee, *Logbooks of the "Lady Nelson,"* p. 48.

73. Furneaux, *Tobias Furneaux, Navigator*, p. 78.

74. Lind, *Treatise on Scurvy*, p. 160; and Beaglehole, *Voyage of the "Endeavour,"* pp. 612, 633.

75. Gallagher, *Byron's Journal*, p. 156.

76. Carrington, *Discovery of Tahiti*, p. 99.

77. Beaglehole, *Voyage of the "Endeavour,"* p. 74. See also *ibid.*, pp. 187, 633.

78. Debenham, *Voyage of Captain Bellingshausen*, 1:11.

79. Lind, *Treatise on Scurvy*, p. 282.

80. Brett, *White Wings*, 2:107. See also Lind, *Treatise on Scurvy*, p. 302.

81. Beaglehole, *Voyage of the "Resolution" and "Adventure,"* p. 955.

82. Markham, *Hawkins' Voyages*, p. 215.

83. Gallagher, *Byron's Journal*, p. 52n; and Wallis, *Carteret's Voyage*, 2:521.

84. Wallis, *Carteret's Voyage*, 2:445.

85. Beaglehole, *Voyage of the "Endeavour,"* p. 103n.

86. Stanley, *First Voyage by Magellan*, p. 68.

87. *Ibid.*, p. 122.

88. William Bligh, *The Log of the "Bounty...,"* 2 vols. (London: Golden Cockerel, 1936-37), 2:205.

89. Cowan, *Suwarrow Gold*, p. 139.

90. Dillon, *Fate of La Pérouse's Expedition*, 1:6, 256. See also Chatterton, *Seamen All*, p. 46; and *Dampier's Voyages*, 1:296.

91. Whymper, *Travel in Alaska*, p. 241; and Meares, *Voyages from China*, p. xix.

92. Meares, *Voyages from China*, p. xxx.

93. Markham, *Hawkins' Voyages*, p. 167; Beaglehole, *Voyage of the "Endeavour,"* p. 349n; and Lloyd, *Health of Seamen*, p. 248.

94. Howay, *Voyages of the "Columbia,"* p. 369.

CHAPTER 19

1. Rickman, *Cook's Last Voyage*, p. 266. See also Krusenstern, *Voyage Round the World*, 1:23.

2. Sharp, *Journal of Jacob Roggeveen*, p. 130.

3. Broughton, *Voyage in H.M.S. "Providence,"* p. 82.

4. Waxell, *American Expedition*, p. 154.

5. Beaglehole, *Voyage of the "Resolution" and "Adventure,"* p. 287.

6. Seligman, *Voyage of the "Cap Pilar,"* p. 79.

7. Dana, *Two Years Before the Mast*, p. 248.

8. Christopher Lloyd, *William Dampier* (London: Faber, 1966), p. 96.

9. Dana, *Two Years Before the Mast*, p. 242n. See also Villiers, *Captain Cook*, p. 98.

10. Karlsson, *Mother Sea,* p. 93.

11. Lloyd, *Health of Seamen,* p. 58, quoting James Cook.

12. Lubbock, *Round the Horn,* p. 14.

13. Villiers, *Captain Cook,* p. 98.

14. Lubbock, *Round the Horn,* p. 96.

15. Morton, *Long Wake,* p. 7.

16. Markham, *Hawkins' Voyages,* p. 244. Sir James Bisset tells us of the penury of ships' owners at the beginning of the twentieth century: "The pork and beef came out of the harness casks green and yellow and stinking, but we had to stomach it or go hungry"; see Bisset, *Sail Ho!,* p. 144.

17. Sharp, *Journal of Jacob Roggeveen,* p. 75.

18. Roe, *Journal of Captain Charles Bishop,* p. 275.

19. Lubbock, *Barlow's Journal,* 1:54.

20. London, *Cruise of the "Snark,"* p. 25.

21. Stanley Walter Croucher Pack, ed., *Lord Anson's Voyage Round the World,* by Richard Walter, abridged ed. (New York: Penguin Books, 1947), p. 210.

22. Smeeton, *Once is Enough,* p. 63.

23. Lubbock, *Barlow's Journal,* 1:68.

24. Beaglehole, *Voyage of the "Resolution" and "Discovery,"* p. 482. See also Lloyd, *Health of Seamen,* p. 271.

25. Lewis, *Navy of Britain,* p. 178. See also Lloyd, *British Seamen,* p. 98.

26. Seligman, *Voyage of the "Cap Pilar,"* p. 170.

27. W. E. Giles, *A Cruize in a Queensland Labour Vessel to the South Seas,* ed. Deryck Scarr (Canberra: Australian National University Press, 1968), p. 28.

28. Beaglehole, *Voyage of the "Resolution" and "Adventure,"* p. 185n.

29. Markham, *Voyages of Sir James Lancaster,* p. 232.

30. Bassett, *Realms and Islands,* p. 188.

31. Waxell, *American Expedition,* p. 137.

32. *Ibid.,* pp. 141, 192.

33. Golder, *Steller's Journal of Bering's Voyages,* p. 234.

34. Macgillivray, *Voyage of H.M.S. "Rattlesnake,"* 2:24, 25. See also John Moresby, *Two Admirals* (London: John Murray, 1909), p. 292.

35. Clifford and Illingworth, *Voyage of the "Golden Lotus,"* p. 146.

36. Roe, *Journal of Captain Charles Bishop,* p. 88; and Munford, *Ledyard's Journal,* p. 187.

37. Whymper, *Travel in Alaska,* p. 215.

38. Henry N. Stevens, ed., *New Light on the Discovery of Australia* . . . Hakluyt Second Series no. 64 (London: Hakluyt Society, 1930), p. 139; and Burney, *Buccaneers of America,* p. 212.

39. Osbun, *To California,* p. 155.

40. George Campbell, *Log-letters from "The Challenger,"* 5th ed. (London: Macmillan, 1877), p. 417.

41. Beaglehole, *Voyage of the "Resolution" and "Discovery,"* p. 33n.

42. Whymper, *Travel to Alaska,* p. 242.

43. Hakluyt, *The Principal Navigations*, 8:71.

44. Seligman, *Voyage of the "Cap Pilar,"* p. 218.

45. *Ibid.*, p. 254.

46. Hakluyt, *The Principal Navigations,* 8:71; and Macgillivray, *Voyage of H.M.S. "Rattlesnake,"* 1:97.

47. Stevens, *Discovery of Australia*, p. 167.

48. Knox-Johnston, *World of My Own*, p. 226.

49. Waxell, *American Expedition*, p. 154.

50. *Ibid.*, p. 148.

51. Howay, *Voyages of the "Columbia,"* p. 220.

52. Beaglehole, *Voyage of the "Resolution" and "Discovery,"* p. 1354.

53. *Ibid.*, p. 458.

54. Munford, *Ledyard's Journal*, p. 96.

55. Karlsson, *Mother Sea*, p. 93.

56. Slocum, *Sailing Alone*, p. 32.

57. Seligman, *Voyage of the "Cap Pilar,"* p. 169.

58. Smeeton, *Once is Enough*, p. 44.

59. Long, *Sailing in the "Idle Hour,"* p. 192.

60. Dana, *Two Years Before the Mast*, p. 25.

61. Seligman, *Voyage of the "Cap Pilar,"* p. 80.

62. Karlsson, *Pully-Haul*, p. 23. See also Dana, *Two Years Before the Mast*, p. 25.

63. Beaglehole, *Voyage of the "Resolution" and "Adventure,"* p. 564.

64. Sanderson, *Follow the Whale*, p. 19.

65. Dampier, *Dampier's Voyages*, 1:100.

66. Drake, *World Encompassed*, p. 19.

67. Cowan, *Suwarrow Gold*, p. 240.

68. Hooker, *Journal of Sir Joseph Banks*, p. 138.

69. *Ibid.*, p. 65. See also Funnell, *Voyage Round the World*, p. 121; Shelvocke, *Voyage Round the World*, p. 31; Vancouver, *Voyage in the "Discovery" and "Chatham,"* 2:213; and Dampier, *Voyage to New Holland*, p. 169.

70. Hooker, *Journal of Sir Joseph Banks*, p. 270. So did Flinders, see Flinders, *Voyage to Australia*, 1:170.

71. Jean Cole, *Trimaran Against the Trades* (Wellington: A. H. & A. W. Reed, 1968), p. 121.

72. Hayter, *"Sheila" in the Wind*, p. 232.

73. Gallagher, *Byron's Journal*, p. 22; and Slocum, *Sailing Alone*, p. 44.

74. La Pérouse, *Voyages of La Pérouse*, p. 19.

75. *Ibid.*, p. 83.

76. Hooker, *Journal of Sir Joseph Banks*, p. 138.

77. Chase, Chappel and Pollard, *Wreck of the "Essex,"* p. 48.

78. Slocum, *Sailing Alone*, p. 117; and Heyerdahl, *Kon-Tiki*, p. 114.

79. Gerbault, *In Quest of the Sun*, p. 51. See also William H. Wakefield, *"Tory* Diary 1839" (M, I, 119, Hocken Library, Dunedin, New Zealand), p. 8.

80. Wallis, *Carteret's Voyages*, 1:159.

81. Rickman, *Cook's Last Voyage*, p. 15.

82. Ward, *Journal of Edward Ward*, p. 23. For enthusiasm about shark meat, see Wakefield, *"Tory* Diary 1839," p. 14.

83. Dillon, *Fate of La Pérouse's Expedition*, 1:180.

84. Roe, *Journal of Captain Charles Bishop*, p. 28; and Beaglehole, *Voyage of the "Endeavour,"* p. 206n. See also Colnett, *Voyage to the South Atlantic*, p. 171.

85. Lubbock, *Round the Horn*, p. 115.

86. Hooker, *Journal of Sir Joseph Banks*, p. 312.

87. Beaglehole, *Voyage of the "Endeavour,"* p. 276, and Burney, *Buccaneers of America*, p. 128.

88. Hakluyt, *The Principal Navigations*, 8:97. See also Carrington, *Discovery of Tahiti*, p. 62.

89. Kelly, *Voyage of Quirós*, 1:213.

90. Dampier, *Dampier's Voyages*, 1:289; and Beaglehole, *Voyage of the "Endeavour,"* pp. 183, 585.

91. Howay, *Voyages of the "Columbia,"* p. 261.

92. Beaglehole, *Voyage of the "Endeavour,"* p. 358n.

93. Morton, *Long Wake*, p. 8.

94. Seligman, *Voyage of the "Cap Pilar,"* p. 296.

95. Lubbock, *Round the Horn*, p. 93. See also Lind, *Treatise on Scurvy*, p. 167.

96. Beaglehole, *Voyage of the "Resolution" and "Adventure,"* p. 16n.

97. Lubbock, *Barlow's Journal*, 1:84.

98. Crozet, *Voyage to Tasmania*, p. 88.

99. Kelly, *Voyage of Quirós*, 1:201.

100. Gallagher, *Byron's Journal*, p. 16.

101. Funnell, *Voyage Round the World*, p. 220.

102. Lloyd, *Health of Seamen*, p. 271, quoting Dr. Thomas Trotter.

103. Beaglehole, *Voyage of the "Resolution" and "Discovery,"* p. 96. See also Kelly, *Voyage of Quirós*, 2:348; Wallis, *Carteret's Voyages*, 1:152; Lewis, *Daughters of the Wind*, p. 64; Thomas Burns' Diary, 27 November, 1847 to 15 April, 1848, M.,1 440/18, G. C. Thomson Papers, Hocken Library, University of Otago, Dunedin, New Zealand, pp. 13, 34; and Fell, *Colonist's Voyage*, pp. 34, 39. For a twentieth-century emergency collection of rainwater on a large sailing vessel, see Bisset, *Sail Ho!*, p. 203.

104. Dampier, *Journey to New Holland*, pp. 104, 126. Porter tells of the drinking water to be obtained, when thirsty enough, from inside a land tortoise, see Porter, *Voyage in the South Seas*, pp. 47, 67.

105. Course, *Windjammers of the Horn*, p. 2.

106. Markham, *Hawkins' Voyages*, p. 164. For an emergency still, see Flinders, *Voyage to Australia*, 1:xliii.

107. Markham, *Hawkins' Voyages*, p. 164.

108. Scherzer, *Narrative of the "Novara,"* 1:5.

109. Brett, *White Wings*, 2:128.

110. Debenham, *Voyage of Captain Bellingshausen*, 2:386.

111. Browne, *Etchings of a Whaling Cruise*, p. 28.

112. *Ibid.*, p. 187.

113. For "hare soup" made from penguins, see Ross, *Voyage in Antarctic Regions*, 1:90.

CHAPTER 20

1. Howay, *Voyages of the "Columbia,"* p. 368. See also *ibid.*, p. 180.

2. Campbell, *Log-Letters from the "Challenger,"* p. 104; Funnell, *Voyage Round the World*, p. 49; Clifford and Illingworth, *Voyage of the "Golden Lotus,"* p. 106; Keate, Account of the *Pelew Islands*, p. 30; Dampier, *Dampier's Voyages, passim;* and Burns' Diary, p. 16.

3. Beaglehole, *Voyage of the "Endeavour,"* p. 122.

4. Hooker, *Journal of Sir Joseph Banks*, p. 101.

5. Huxley, *Diary of H.M.S. "Rattlesnake,"* p. 182.

6. *Ibid.*

7. Beaglehole, *Voyage of the "Resolution" and "Endeavour,"* p. cxi.

8. Ward, *Journal of Edward Ward*, p. 67. See also Dunmore, *Voyage of the "St Jean Baptiste,"* p. 44; Bassett, *Realms and Islands*, p. 192; and Vancouver, *Voyage in the "Discovery" and "Chatham,"* 4:305.

9. Lubbock, *Barlow's Journal*, 1:400. See also Osbun, *To California*, p. 161. Porter claims live Galapagos tortoises could be stored aboard, stacked in the hold like barrels, for up to eighteen months; see Porter, *Voyage in the South Seas*, pp. 47, 66.

10. Macgillivray, *Voyage of H.M.S. "Rattlesnake,"* 2:21.

11. Hakluyt, *The Principal Navigations*, 7:38.

12. Burney, *Buccaneers of America*, p. 172.

13. Bassett, *Realms and Islands*, p. 105.

14. Debenham, *Voyage of Captain Bellingshausen*, 1:161; and Lind, *Treatise on Scurvy*, p. 425, quoting Meiklejohn, Passmore and Stewart.

15. Baker, *My Own Destroyer*, p. 50.

16. Rickman, *Cook's Last Voyage*, p. 232.

17. Dunmore, *French Explorers*, 1:94.

18. Beaglehole, *Voyage of the "Resolution" and "Discovery,"* pp. 226, 226n.

19. Markham, *Hawkins' Voyages*, p. 217.

20. Bruce, *Reminiscences of a Wanderer*, p. 21.

21. Beaglehole, *Voyage of the "Resolution" and "Adventure,"* p. 135n.

22. Burgess, *No Risks—No Romance*, p. 65. See also Villiers, *Cruise of the "Conrad,"* p. 252.

23. Seligman, *Voyage of the "Cap Pilar,"* p. 38.

24. Course, *Windjammers of the Horn*, p. 75.

25. Beaglehole, *Voyage of the "Resolution" and "Discovery,"* pp. 137n, 579. See also Charles-Pierre Fleurieu, *A Voyage Round the World Performed during the Years 1790-91-92*, 2 vols. (1801; reprint ed., New York: Da Capo, 1969), 2:10.

26. Karlsson, *Pully-Haul*, p. 71.

27. Course, *Windjammers of the Horn*, p. 75.

28. Williams, *One Whaling Family*, p. 38.

29. Campbell, *Log-Letters from the "Challenger,"* p. 182.

30. Lubbock, *Round the Horn*, p. 260.

31. Bulkeley, *Voyage in H.M.S. "Wager,"* p. 105.

CHAPTER 21

 1. Michael Lewis, *Navy of Britain*, p. 195. Admiral Moresby speaks of "mathe-matical study" under "dear old Star, our Scottish instructor." In his auto-biography he refers many times, with respect and affection, to his various teachers within the Royal Navy of the nineteenth century; see Moresby, *Two Admirals, passim*.

 2. Lubbock, *Blackwall Frigates*, p. 116.

 3. Melville, *White Jacket*, p. 326.

 4. Kelly, *Voyage of Quirós*, 1:29. See also Waters, *Art of Navigation*, p. 313.

 5. Markham, *Hawkins' Voyages*, p. 275.

 6. Dewar, *Voyage of the "Nyanza,"* p. 279.

 7. Albert B. Armitage, *Cadet to Commodore* (London: Cassell, 1925), p. 173.

 8. Markham, *Hawkins' Voyages*, p. 100.

 9. Kelly, *Voyage of Quirós*, 1:141. See also Flinders, *Voyage to Australia*, 1:42.

10. Waters, *Art of Navigation*, p. 463.

11. Sharp, *Journal of Jacob Roggeveen*, p. 85.

12. Karlsson, *Pully-Haul*, p. 44.

13. Dana, *Two Years Before the Mast*, pp. 284-85. See also Browne, *Etchings of a Whaling Cruise*, p. 250.

14. Dana, *Seamen's Friend*, p. 102.

15. Markham, *Hawkins' Voyages*, p. 275.

16. Nuttall, *New Light on Drake*, p. 105. See also Joyce, *Voyage by Wafer*, p. 83.

17. Markham, *Hawkins' Voyages*, p. 292.

18. Bradford, *Drake*, p. 116.

19. Nuttall, *New Light on Drake*, pp. 206-07.

20. Dorothy Shineberg, *They Came for Sandalwood* (Carlton: Melbourne University Press, 1967), p. 82; and Chatterton, *Seamen All*, p. 160. See also Drake, *World Encompassed*, p. 54.

21. Allen, *Sea Years of Joseph Conrad*, p. 259.

22. Waxell, *American Expedition*, p. 31.

23. *Ibid.*, p. 120. See also Golder, *Steller's Journal of Bering's Voyages*, pp. 156-57.

24. Conrad, *Mirror of the Sea*, p. 6.

25. Dana, *Two Years Before the Mast*, p. 8.

26. Waxell, *American Expedition*, p. 120.

27. Debenham, *Voyage of Captain Bellingshausen*, 1:xxii. See also Beaglehole, *Voyage of the "Endeavour,"* p. 380.
28. Smollett, *Adventures of Roderick Random*, p. 204.
29. Lubbock, *Round the Horn*, p. 3. See also *ibid.*, pp. 140-41.
30. Cowan, *Suwarrow Gold*, p. 238; and Lubbock, *Round the Horn,* p. 33.
31. Wallis, *Carteret's Voyages*, 1:109-10. See also *ibid.*, pp. 111, 135.
32. Allen, *Sea Years of Joseph Conrad*, p. 167.
33. Karlsson, *Mother Sea*, p. 161.
34. Wallis, *Carteret's Voyages*, 1:111.
35. Beaglehole, *Voyage of the "Endeavour,"* p. 173; and Nuttall, *New Light on Drake*, p. 18. See also La Pérouse, *Voyages of La Pérouse*, p. 104.
36. Bechervaise, *Old Quarter Master*, p. 275.

CHAPTER 22

1. West, *Captain's Papers*, p. 20.
2. Randier, *Men and Ships*, p. 244.
3. Nuttall, *New Light on Drake*, p. 252; and Markham, *Hawkins' Voyages*, p. 273.
4. Browne, *Etchings of a Whaling Cruise*, p. 495.
5. Slocum, *Sailing Alone*, p. 104.
6. Browne, *Etchings of a Whaling Cruise*, p. 495. See also Clark, *Clipper Ship Era*, p. 120; Melville, *White Jacket*, p. 357; Cowan, *Suwarrow Gold*, p. 229; Bullen, *Cruise of the "Cachalot,"* p. 4, *passim*; and Randier, *Men and Ships*, p. 245.
7. Lubbock, *Barlow's Journal*, 1:213.
8. Lubbock, *Round the Horn*, p. 11.
9. Smollett, *Adventures of Roderick Random*, p. 182.
10. Browne, *Etchings of a Whaling Cruise*, p. 43.
11. Huxley, *Diary of H.M.S. "Rattlesnake,"* pp. 149, 177n.
12. Bassett, *Behind the Picture*, p. 39. See also Fell, *Colonist's Voyage*, p. 82; and Burns' Diary, *passim*.
13. Huxley, *Diary of H.M.S. "Rattlesnake,"* p. 320.
14. Cowan, *Suwarrow Gold*, p. 195. See also Long, *Sailing in the "Idle Hour,"* p. 250.
15. Karlsson, *Pully-Haul*, p. 26.
16. Karlsson, *Mother Sea*, p. 106.
17. Conrad, *Mirror of the Sea*, p. 38.
18. *Ibid.*
19. Villiers, *Captain Cook*, p. 112.
20. Villiers, *Cruise of the "Conrad,"* p. 28.
21. Kelly, *Voyage of Quirós*, 1:142; and Bechervaise, *Old Quarter Master,* p. 163.
22. Browne, *Etchings of a Whaling Cruise*, p. 561.

23. Dana, *Two Years Before the Mast*, p. 41.

24. Villiers, *Cruise of the "Conrad,"* p. 274. See also *ibid.*, p. 277.

25. Vancouver, *Voyage in the "Discovery" and "Chatham,"* 1 : 338.

26. Taylor, *Journal of Ensign Best*, p. 219. See also Melville, *White Jacket*, pp. 352, 353; and Dana, *Two Years Before the Mast*, p. 103n.

27. Waxell, *American Expedition*, p. 135.

28. Golder, *Steller's Journal of Bering's Voyages*, pp. 148-49.

29. *Ibid.*, p. 149.

30. *Ibid.*, pp. 5-6.

31. Waxell, *American Expedition*, p. 25.

32. Golder, *Steller's Journal of Bering's Voyages*, p. 5; and Villiers, *Captain Cook*, p. 194.

33. Debenham, *Voyage of Captain Bellingshausen*, 1 : 247.

34. Moorehead, *Darwin and "The Beagle,"* p. 86. See also Bassett, *Behind the Picture*, p. 5; and Flinders, *Voyage to Australia*, 1 : 193.

35. Flinders, *Voyage to Australia*, 1 : 193.

36. Baker, *My Own Destroyer*, p. 44.

37. Long, *Sailing in the "Idle Hour,"* p. 316.

38. *Evening Star*, Dunedin, New Zealand, June 2, 1972, p. 9.

39. Villiers, *Cruise of the "Conrad,"* p. 305.

40. Bassett, *Realms and Islands*, p. 126; and Flinders, *Voyage to Australia*, 1 : 42.

41. Whymper, *Travel in Alaska*, p. 82.

42. Browne, *Etchings of a Whaling Cruise*, p. 494; and Lubbock, *Barlow's Journal*, 2 : 341, and 1 : 90.

43. Bruce, *Reminiscences of a Wanderer*, p. 346.

44. Nuttall, *New Light on Drake*, p. 207.

45. Hakluyt, *The Principal Navigations*, 8 : 120.

46. Purchas, *His Pilgrimes*, 2 : 193; and Bulkeley, *Voyage in H.M.S. "Wager,"* pp. 40, 61.

47. Golder, *Log-Books of Bering's Voyages*, p. 209.

48. Pack, *Admiral Lord Anson*, p. 107. See also Lewis, *Ships and Seamen of Britain*, p. 23.

49. Seligman, *Voyage of the "Cap Pilar,"* p. 164.

50. Villiers, *Cruise of the "Conrad,"* pp. 30-31.

51. Villiers, *Set of the Sails*, p. 222.

52. Newby, *Grain Race*, p. 7.

53. Smith, *Sea Grammar*, p. 96. See also Waters, *Art of Navigation*, p. 40.

54. Markham, *Hawkins' Voyages*, p. 223.

55. Pack, *Admiral Lord Anson*, p. 54.

56. Kelly, *Voyage of Quirós*, 1 : 45.

57. Bulkeley, *Voyage in H.M.S. "Wager,"* p. 107.

58. Peter Heywood, *The Court-Martial of the "Bounty" Mutineers*, ed. Owen Rutter (London: Hodge, 1931), p. 38 (hereafter cited as *"Bounty" Court Martial*).

59. Brett, *White Wings,* 2:87.

60. Meares, *Voyages from China,* pp. 25, 128. See also Holman, *Voyage Round the World,* 4:78.

61. Markham, *Hawkins' Voyages,* p. 99.

62. Lloyd, *British Seamen,* p. 220; and Bassett, *Realms and Islands,* p. 176. See also Fell, *Colonist's Voyage,* pp. 24, 83.

63. Villiers, *Cruise of the "Conrad,"* p. 236.

64. Heywood, *"Bounty" Court Martial,* pp. 7, 8, 11. See also Villiers, *Cruise of the "Conrad,"* p. 277.

65. Bligh, *Log of the "Bounty,"* 1:110.

66. Villiers, *Cruise of the "Conrad,"* p. 274.

67. *Ibid.,* p. 277.

68. Heywood, *"Bounty" Court Martial,* p. 32.

69. Melville, *Redburn,* p. 272; and Bligh, *Mutiny in H.M.S. "Bounty,"* p. 41.

70. Lloyd, *British Seamen,* p. 239. Moresby, the explorer of New Guinea's coast and a sailor of decades of experience, claimed that a "strict, flogging captain . . . secured his men without difficulty, so long as it was felt he was just and impartial." He also claimed that "many men preferred a short and sharp five minutes at the gangway [i.e., being flogged] to a long-drawn-out black list. . . ," See Moresby, *Two Admirals,* p. 68.

71. Lloyd, *British Seamen,* p. 25.

72. Melville, *White Jacket,* p. 265.

73. Bruce, *Reminiscences of a Wanderer,* p. 56. Bisset also thought American discipline much tougher, and the methods of enforcing it much rougher than in British ships. See Bisset, *Sail Ho!,* pp. 143, 183.

74. Nuttall, *New Light on Drake,* p. li.

CHAPTER 23

1. Joyce, *New Voyage by Wafer,* pp. 77, 92.

2. *Ibid.,* p. 159.

3. Maxwell, *Wooden Hookers,* p. 164.

4. Worcester, *Sail and Sweep,* p. 47.

5. Dampier, *Dampier's Voyages,* 1:533.

6. P. K. Kemp and Christopher Lloyd, *The Brethren of the Coast* (London: Heinemann, 1960), p. 74.

7. Rogers, *Cruising Voyage,* p. 125.

8. *Ibid.*

9. Dampier, *Dampier's Voyages,* 1:112.

10. Bechervaise, *Old Quarter Master,* p. 173.

11. Drake, *World Encompassed,* p. 62. See also Hakluyt, *The Principal Navigations,* 8:61.

12. Colnett, *Voyage to the South Atlantic,* p. 128; and Bulkeley, *Voyage in H.M.S. "Wager,"* p. 108.

13. Markham, *Hawkins' Voyages,* p. 108.

14. Dana, *Two Years Before the Mast*, p. 258; and Beaglehole, *Voyage of the "Resolution" and "Discovery,"* p. 189n.

15. Hooker, *Journal of Sir Joseph Banks*, p. 44.

16. Howay, *Voyages of the "Columbia,"* p. 256.

17. Beaglehole, *Voyage of the "Endeavour,"* p. 419n.

18. Hooker, *Journal of Sir Joseph Banks*, pp. 69, 345. See also Flinders, *Voyage to Australia*, 1:25.

19. Francis Chichester, *The Lonely Sea and the Sky* (London: Pan Bks, 1967), p. 331.

20. Beaglehole, *Voyage of the "Resolution" and "Discovery,"* p. 1244; Nuttall, *New Light on Drake*, p. 42; and Dunmore, *French Explorers*, 1:266.

21. Kemp and Lloyd, *Brethren of the Coast*, p. 202.

22. Lubbock, *Blackwall Frigates*, p. 126.

23. Randier, *Men and Ships*, p. 169.

24. Lloyd, *British Seamen*, p. 256.

25. Lloyd, *Health of Seamen*, pp. 148, 163.

26. Waxell, *American Expedition*, p. 121.

27. *Ibid.*, p. 182.

28. Muller, *Voyages from Asia*, p. 70, and *ibid.*, p. 32.

29. Burney, *Buccaneers of America*, p. 296.

30. Joyce, *New Voyage by Wafer*, p. 114.

31. Markham, *Voyages of Sir James Lancaster*, p. 77.

32. Purchas, *His Pilgrimes*, 2:267.

33. Gould and Gould, "*Astrocyte.*"

34. Purchas, *His Pilgrimes*, 2:194; and Joyce, *New Voyage by Wafer*, p. 91.
    Wine prepared in the same way is still proffered strangers in the Japanese Ryuku Archipelago. A young girl chews about one-tenth of an amount of cooked rice and spits it into the remainder as leaven. Kava made from rice the hostess has chewed is still drunk among some aborigines of Formosa, while a wine made from millet chewed by men is favoured by other groups. See Ling Shun-sheng, "Kava Drinking in China and East Asia," *Bulletin of the Institute of Ethnology, Academia Sinica* (1957), no. 4:25-30, *passim*.

35. Funnell, *Voyage Round the World*, p. 227; and Waxell, *American Expedition*, p. 115.

36. Waxell, *American Expedition*, p. 78.

37. Stevens, *Discovery of Australia*, p. 111.

38. Markham, *Hawkins' Voyages*, p. 302.

CHAPTER 24

1. Dunmore, *French Explorers*, 1:94. For a woman who for months successfully disguised her sex while living in the forecastle of a whaling ship, and who was known as the best man in the crew, see Whipple, *Yankee Whalers*, pp. 152-54. Another of the French captains of Pacific exploration played a part in bringing a much more famous lady out of hiding. Dumont d'Ur-

ville recognized the importance of the beauty of the newly found **Venus de Milo**, and his report helped to have her placed in the Louvre.

2. Beaglehole, *Voyage of the "Resolution" and "Discovery,"* p. 1521.

3. Melville, *White Jacket*, p. 220.

4. Brett, *White Wings*, 2:74.

5. Maxwell, *Wooden Hookers*, p. 26.

6. *Ibid.*, p. 47.

7. *Ibid.*

8. Lubbock, *Colonial Clippers*, p. 4. See also Burns' Diary, pp. 14-15.

9. Maxwell, *Wooden Hookers*, p. 29.

10. *Ibid.*, Chap. 2, *passim*. See also Fell, *Colonist's Voyage*, pp. 22, 29, 52; and Burns' Diary, pp. 13, 35.

11. Maxwell, *Wooden Hookers*, p. 38.

12. Whymper, *Travel in Alaska*, p. 3.

13. Taylor, *Journal of Ensign Best*, pp. 180-81.

14. Stevens, *Discovery of Australia*, p. 171.

15. Seligman, *Voyage of the "Cap Pilar,"* p. 174.

16. Bassett, *Realms and Islands*, p. 14.

17. *Ibid.*, p. 148.

18. Pack, *Admiral Lord Anson*, p. 56. See also Burns' Diary, p. 17.

19. Knox-Johnston, *World of My Own*, p. 50. See also Lawson, *Bluegum Clippers*, p. 68.

20. Sanderson, *Follow the Whale*, p. 251.

21. Course, *Windjammers of the Horn*, p. 64, quoting Joseph Conrad.

22. Scherzer, *Narrative of the "Novara,"* 3:256.

23. Course, *Windjammers of the Horn*, p. 56.

24. Howay, *Voyages of the "Columbia,"* p. 208. See also *ibid.*, pp. 96n, 235, 325.

25. Course, *Windjammers of the Horn*, p. 74.

26. Lubbock, *Round the Horn*, p. 191.

27. Captain R. Barry O'Brien in Domville-Fife, *Square-Rigged Ships*, p. 60.

28. Riesenberg, *Cape Horn*, p. 331.

29. *Ibid.*, p. 332, quoting Captain Clark.

30. Smeeton, *Once is Enough*, pp. 13, 41.

31. *Ibid.*, p. 82.

32. Gann, *Song of the Sirens*, p. 179.

33. Cole, *Trimaran Against the Trades*, p. 137.

34. Pye, *Red Mains'l*, p. 14.

35. Worcester, *Sail and Sweep*, p. 1.

36. Karlsson, *Pully-Haul*, p. 33.

37. Rogers, *Cruising Voyage*, p. 179.

38. *Ibid.*, p. 243.

39. Clark, *Clipper Ship Era*, p. 108.

40. Beaglehole, *Voyage of the "Resolution" and "Discovery,"* p. 1095.

41. Rickman, *Cook's Last Voyage*, p. 294.

42. Nowell, *Magellan's Voyage*, pp. 167, 185, 214; Beaglehole, *Voyage of the "Resolution" and "Discovery,"* p. 1373; and Crozet, *Voyage to Tasmania*, pp. 28, 65, 68.

43. Howay, *Voyages of the "Columbia,"* p. 371. See also Krusenstern, *Voyage Round the World*, 1:153ff; Shineberg, *They Came for Sandalwood*, p. 12; Joyce, *New Voyage by Wafer*, p. 78n; and Wallis, *Carteret's Voyages*, 2:510.

44. Beaglehole, *Voyage of the "Resolution" and "Discovery,"* p. 996. See also Shineberg, *They Came for Sandalwood*, p. 12; Krusenstern, *Voyage Round the World*, 1:153ff; and Carrington, *Discovery of Tahiti*, p. 166.

45. Dunmore, *Voyage of the "St. Jean Baptiste,"* p. 89.

46. Fleurieu, *A Voyage Round the World*, 1:297. See also *ibid.*, 1:220.

47. Cowan, *Suwarrow Gold*, p. 82. See also Colvocoresses, *Exploring Expedition*, p. 35, and Krusenstern, *Voyage Round the World*, 2:155.

48. Carrington, *Discovery of Tahiti*, p. 167; and Dampier, *Dampier's Voyages*, 1:527.

49. Scherzer, *Narrative of the "Novara,"* 3:219.

50. Wilson, *Missionary Voyage*, pp. 130, 137.

51. Vancouver, *Voyage in the "Discovery" and "Chatham,"* 3:385.

52. Howay, *Voyages of the "Columbia,"* p. 428.

53. Sharp, *Voyages of Abel Tasman*, pp. 259, 309. See also Rogers, *Cruising Voyage*, p. 166.

54. Lubbock, *Barlow's Journals*, 1:28. Cheyne reports that, while at Bornabi, his "chinese Blacksmith and Carpenter" committed "unnatural crimes with native boys" and the natives had never "heard of such a thing before." This would be most unlikely if it were as common on European ships as has been claimed. See Shineberg, *Voyages of Andrew Cheyne*, pp. 292-93.

55. Carletti, *My Voyage*, pp. 182, 211ff. See also Crozet, *Voyages to Tasmania*, p. 28; Nowell, *Magellan's Voyage*, p. 167; and Bligh, *Log of the "Bounty,"* 2:35.

56. Munford, *Ledyard's Journal*, p. 132. See also Beaglehole, *Voyage of the "Resolution" and "Discovery,"* 3:1373, quoting King; and Fleurieu, *A Voyage Round the World*, 1:248.

57. Cameron, *Lodestone and Evening Star*, p. 132.

58. Melville, *White Jacket*, p. 368.

CHAPTER 25

1. Howay, *Voyages of the "Columbia,"* p. 245.

2. Roe, *Journal of Captain Charles Bishop*, p. 70.

3. Beaglehole, *Voyage of the "Resolution" and "Discovery,"* p. 315n.

4. *Ibid.*

5. *Ibid.*, p. 315.

6. *Ibid.*, p. 316n.

7. Howay, *Voyages of the "Columbia,"* p. 257.

8. Beaglehole, *Voyage of the "Resolution" and "Discovery,"* p. 1088. Admiral Moresby said that the Indians of British Columbia "had a remarkable appreciation of music, and our band was a mingled amazement and delight to them." See Moresby, *Two Admirals,* p. 124.

9. Beaglehole, *Voyage of the "Resolution" and "Discovery,"* p. 1395.

10. Bassett, *Realms and Islands,* p. 88.

11. Macgillivray, *Voyage of H.M.S "Rattlesnake,"* 1:151.

12. Beaglehole, *Voyage of the "Resolution" and "Discovery,"* p. 109.

13. Dillon, *Fate of La Pérouse's Expedition,* 1:293.

14. *Ibid.*, p. 279.

15. Gallagher, *Byron's Journal,* p. 81.

16. Rickman, *Cook's Last Voyage,* p. 308.

17. Purchas, *His Pilgrimes,* 2:267.

18. Sharp, *Voyages of Abel Tasman,* p. 121.

19. *Ibid.*, p. 155.

20. *Ibid.*, p. 44.

21. Hooker, *Journal of Sir Joseph Banks,* p. 82. For the earliest description of the Melanesian "pipes of Pan," see William Amherst and Basil Thomson, *The Discovery of the Solomon Islands by Alvaro de Mendaña in 1568,* 2 vols. (London: Hakluyt Society, 1901), 1:114, 2:233.

22. Beaglehole, *Voyage of the "Resolution" and "Discovery,"* p. 940.

23. *Ibid.*, p. 1341.

24. Forrest, *Voyage to New Guinea,* p. 303.

25. Dampier, *Dampier's Voyages,* 2:10.

26. W.R.S. Harris in Domville-Fife, *Square-Rigged Ships,* p. 219.

27. Clark, *Clipper Ship Era,* p. 110.

28. Lubbock, *Round the Horn,* pp. 205-06, 244.

29. *Ibid.*, pp. 170, 246. See also Fell, *Colonist's Voyage,* p. 4.

30. Cowan, *Suwarrow Gold,* p. 127.

31. Lubbock, *Blackwall Frigates,* p. 120.

32. Course, *Windjammers of the Horn,* pp. 160, 165.

33. A. J. Pazolt in Domville-Fife, *Square-Rigged Ships,* p. 192.

34. Dana, *Two Years Before the Mast,* p. 224.

35. Wilson, *Missionary Voyage,* p. 8.

36. West, *Captain's Papers,* p. 68; and Bassett, *Realms and Islands,* p. 16.

37. Nuttall, *New Light on Drake,* p. 355.

38. Hakluyt, *The Principal Navigations,* 8:247; and Purchas, *His Pilgrimes,* 2:170.

39. Rickman, *Cook's Last Voyage,* p. 137.

40. Beaglehole, *Voyage of the "Resolution" and "Adventure,"* p. 208.

41. Cowan, *Suwarrow Gold,* p. 19.

42. Cole, *Trimaran Against the Trades,* p. 129.

CHAPTER 26

1. Hakluyt, *The Principal Navigations*, 8:62, 66.

2. Angus Ross, *New Zealand's Aspirations in the Pacific in the Nineteenth Century* (Oxford: Oxf. U. P., 1964) p. 1.

3. C. M. Cipolla, *Guns, Sails and Empires: Technological Innovation and the Early Phases of European Expansion*, 1400-1700, (New York: Pantheon, 1965), p. 130, quoting Frankel.

4. Waters, *Art of Navigation*, p. 233.

5. Stanley, *First Voyage of Magellan*, p. 156.

6. Latham, *Travels of Marco Polo*, p. 134.

7. *Ibid.*, pp. 179, 181.

8. *Ibid.*, p. 185.

9. *Ibid.*, p. 187.

10. Meares, *Voyages from China*, p. 210.

11. Purchas, *His Pilgrimes*, 2:339.

12. Latham, *Travels of Marco Polo*, pp. 206-07.

13. Carletti, *My Voyage*, p. 132.

14. Shelvocke, *Voyage Round the World*, p. 250.

15. Carletti, *My Voyage*, p. 164.

16. Stanley, *First Voyage by Magellan*, p. 109; and Beaglehole, *Voyage in the "Endeavour,"* p. 399.

17. Carrington, *Discovery of Tahiti*, pp. 61, 92. See also Morrell, *Narrative of Four Voyages*, pp. 97, 156; and Wilkes, *United States Exploring Expedition*, 1:122.

18. Gallagher, *Byron's Journal*, p. lxxvii.

19. *Ibid.*, p. 48.

20. Waxell, *American Expedition*, p. 209. See also Bechervaise, *Old Quarter Master*, p. 244; and Munford, *Ledyard's Journal*, p. 168. Morrell spoke of the remarkable strength of some natives of the Carolines; see Morrell, *Narrative of Four Voyages*, p. 425.

21. Campbell, *Log-Letters from the "Challenger,"* p. 138. See also Wilkes, *United States Exploring Expedition*, 3:25; and Moresby, *Two Admirals*, p. 282.

22. Beaglehole, *Voyage of the "Resolution" and "Discovery,"* p. 1308.

23. Fleurieu, *A Voyage Round the World*, 1:339.

24. Purchas, *His Pilgrimes*, 2:269. See also Bullen, *Cruise of the "Cachalot,"* p. 206; and Ellis, *Polynesia*, p. 20ff.

25. Gann, *Song of the Sirens*, p. 209.

26. Vancouver, *Voyage in the "Discovery" and "Chatham,"* 5:173.

27. Dunmore, *French Explorers*, 1:110.

28. Dunmore, *Voyage of the "St. Jean Baptiste,"* p. 50. See also Drake, *World Encompassed*, p. 78; Beaglehole, *Voyage of the "Resolution" and "Discovery"* p. 1026; and Osbun, *To California*, p. 120.

29. La Pérouse, *Voyages of La Pérouse*, p. 92.

30. Waxell, *American Expedition*, p. 219.

31. Shineberg, *They Came for Sandalwood*, p. 7; Beaglehole, *Voyage of the*

"*Resolution*" and "*Discovery*," p. 1323; Broughton, *Voyage in H.M.S. "Providence,"* p. 70; Roe, *Journal of Captain Charles Bishop*, p. 63; and Munford, *Ledyard's Journal*, p. 57.

32. Gerbault, *In Quest of the Sun*, p. 94.

33. Herman Melville, *Typee* (London: Cassell, 1967), p. 52.

34. London, *Cruise of the "Snark,"* p. 147.

35. Villiers, *Cruise of the "Conrad,"* p. 265. Yet Wilkes reported that many natives prayed for the arrival of the European ships; see Wilkes, *United States Exploring Expedition*, 3:157.

36. Crozet, *Voyage to Tasmania*, p. 57.

37. *Ibid.*, p. 62.

38. Shineberg, *They Came for Sandalwood*, p. 200. See also Macgillivray, *Voyage of H.M.S "Rattlesnake,"* 1:98; Huxley, *Diary of H.M.S. "Rattlesnake,"* p. 139; and Flinders, *Voyage to Australia*, 2:207, 213.

39. Howay, *Voyages of the "Columbia,"* p. 272. See also Jacobs, *Cruise of the "Margaret Oakley,"* p. 96ff.

40. Beaglehole, *Voyage of the "Endeavour,"* p. 244n.

41. Wallis, *Carteret's Voyages*, 1:162n, quoting G. S. Parsonson.

42. Gilbert, *Voyage to Canton*, p. 37.

43. Howay, *Voyages of the "Columbia,"* p. 258.

44. Beaglehole, *Voyage of the "Resolution" and "Discovery,"* p. 709n.

45. *Ibid.*, p. cxiii.

46. Cowan, *Suwarrow Gold*, p. 161.

47. Bassett, *Realms and Islands*, p. 193.

48. *Ibid.*, p. 195.

49. Mortlock, *Experiences of a Convict*, p. 58. Wilkes, a non-British observer, and of the officer class, discusses the power of the surgeon on British convict ships, and the treatment of convicts generally. See Wilkes, *United States Exploring Expedition*, 2:209.

50. Bechervaise, *Old Quarter Master*, p. 121.

51. Mortlock, *Experiences of a Convict*, p. 58.

52. *Ibid.*, p. 60. See also Fell, *Colonist's Voyage*, p. 97.

53. John Liddiard Nicholas, *Narrative of a Voyage to New Zealand Performed in the Years 1814 and 1815 . . .*, 2 vols. (London: J. Black and Son, 1817), 1:136, 183.

54. Augustus Earle, *A Narrative of a Nine Months' Residence in New Zealand in 1827* (Christchurch: Whitcombe & Tombs, 1909) p. 195.

55. Shineberg, *They Came for Sandalwood*, p. 153.

56. George Eaton Stanger, "Journal of a Voyage from Hobart-Town to England in the Barque 'Seppings,' 1838," D543 (Acc 226), Gloucestershire Record Office, Glos., England, p. 149.

57. Meares, *Voyages from China*, p. 267.

58. Beaglehole, *Voyage of the "Endeavour,"* p. 281.

59. Carletti, *My Voyage*, pp. 113, 131.

60. Aleksandr. I. Andreev, ed., *Russian Discoveries in the Pacific, and in North America in the Eighteenth and Nineteenth Centuries*, trans. Carl

Ginsburg (Ann Arbor, Mich: J. W. Edwards, Publisher for the American Council of Learned Societies, 1952), p. 88.

61. Clifford and Illingworth, *Voyage of the "Golden Lotus,"* p. 40.

62. Browne, *Etchings of a Whaling Cruise,* p. 546. See also Bullen, *Cruise of the "Cachalot,"* p. 207, and *passim.*

63. Long, *Sailing in the "Idle Hour,"* p. 316.

64. Cowan, *Suwarrow Gold,* p. 24.

65. Giles, *Cruise in a Queensland Labour Vessel,* p. 38n.

66. G. S. Parsonson, Paper delivered to the Canterbury Historical Society, Christchurch, N.Z., 1967.

67. Sanderson, *Follow the Whale,* p. 261. Nor was this true only on whaling ships. Johnson tells of an American warship crewed by sailors of nineteen different nationalities, see Johnson, *Round Cape Horn,* p. 130.

68. Burgess, *No Risks—No Romance,* p. 278.

69. Godwin, *Vancouver, A Life,* p. 88. See also Beaglehole, *Voyage in the "Endeavour,"* p. 553; Debenham, *Voyage of Captain Bellingshausen,* 1:202; Waxell, *American Expedition,* p. 78; Stevens, *Discovery of Australia,* p. 111; and Broughton, *Voyage in H.M.S. "Providence,"* p. 34.

70. Parker, *Voyage in the "Gorgon,"* p. 102.

71. Beaglehole, *Voyage in the "Endeavour,"* p. 514.

GLOSSARY

ADZE – a large wood-cutting tool, with the blade at right angles to the handle. It is used for shaping and smoothing planks in boatbuilding. In European shipyards adzes were first made of iron and then steel, but in pre-iron cultures they were made of stone or shell.

AHULL – drifting with all sails furled and the helm lashed.

ALMANACS – books which contained a calendar and tables giving the major astronomical events in the year, along with the terrestrial events which the former affected. For example, many almanacs had tables giving both the phases of the moon and the tides.

ALOFT – above the deck.

AMIDSHIPS – the middle of the ship in either length or breadth.

ANTI-SCORBUTICS – any agent, such as a food or a drink, which contains Vitamin C and hence prevents scurvy.

ASTROLABE – an early navigational instrument used for measuring the angle of stars or the sun from the horizon in order to find latitude. Normally it was a heavy brass ring suspended from a small ring, marked in one quadrant with degrees from o to 90 and equipped with a movable sighting bar with two vanes containing small holes through which the sight is taken. The degree of altitude is read off the marked quadrant at the position of the bar.

AZIMUTH COMPASS – an instrument like the mariner's compass but having sights for taking the angle between N and the position of a celestial body when near the horizon.

BAIDAR – a large open East Asian skin boat, like an Eskimo umiak.

BAIDARKA – a small enclosed East Asian skin boat, like an Eskimo kayak.

BALANCE-LUG – a type of lug sail used on Chinese junks.

BALSA – a raft—of various kinds but, in particular, the large rafts built of logs from the balsa tree for use on the coasts of Peru and Ecuador. *See* figure 2.

BALTIMORE CLIPPER – a late eighteenth-century American schooner from which the later clippers were developed.

BARGE – a large boat, used by the commander of a naval vessel.

BARNACLE – a shellfish which is often found on ships' bottoms.

BARQUE – a vessel with three masts, the forward two rigged like a ship's, with square sails and the after or mizzen mast fore-and-aft-rigged with a spanker and a gaff-topsail. *See* figure 48.

BARQUENTINE – a vessel square-rigged on the foremast, with two or more other masts rigged with fore-and-aft sails. *See* figure 48.

BATTEN – a long thin strip of wood.

BEAKHEAD – a triangular continuation of the deck and bulwarks which extended beyond an early ship's bow under the bowsprit. It was perhaps a survival of the ram of the galleys.

BEAM – the greatest breadth of a vessel, or, in context, one of the strong pieces of timber running across the ship to support the decks.

BEARING – the direction of an object from the observer.

BEATING OR TO BEAT – to sail a ship towards the direction of the wind by sailing on alternate tacks.

BECHE-DE-MER – a sea slug picked from reefs and, after drying, sold to the Chinese for food—an early and important article of trade.

BILGE – the most nearly horizontal parts of the floor of a ship, on either side of the keel, and upon which a ship would sit when aground.

BINNACLE – a box enclosing a ship's compass, on a stand located near the helm.

BITTS – strong pieces of timber placed vertically in the fore part of the ship and bolted to the beams. They are used to secure things such as cables or the end of the bowsprit.

BLACKBIRDING – a form of labour contracting in which the plantations of Queensland recruited labour from Melanesia in the late nineteenth century.

BOATSWAIN – the warrant officer in the naval service who is in charge of the rigging and hence, like an army sergeant major, also in charge of the men who do the work.

BOLTROPE – the rope edging a sail (as a kind of frame) around which the canvas is sewn.

BONAVENTURE-MIZZEN – a fourth mast, aft of the mizzen mast, in some big ships of the late sixteenth and early seventeenth century. It carried a lateen sail.

BONNET – additional pieces of canvas laced to the bottom of sails to enlarge them.

BOOM – a spar used to extend the foot of a studding sail or a fore-and-aft sail.

BOWLINE – a rope attached to the leach, or outer edge, of a square sail, used to keep the weather-edge of the sail tight when the vessel is sailing close hauled. In very early European ships, the weather edge of the large square sail was pulled taut by a rope fastened to the bowsprit which had been invented for that purpose.

BOWSPRIT – a large spar pointing forwards and, usually, upwards from the bow of a vessel.

BRACE – to turn a yard horizontally; also the lines by which this is done.

BRIG – a square-rigged vessel with two masts, in contrast with the three of a ship.

BRIGANTINE – a two-masted vessel, originally square-rigged, but in the eighteenth century using a fore-and-aft sail instead of a mainsail on the mainmast. In the nineteenth century, the usual meaning of the word was a two masted vessel, square-rigged on the foremast, fore-and-aft-rigged on the mainmast, but having upper masts with ship proportions.

BROADSIDE – all the guns a ship could mount on one side or the other, that is, the port broadside or starboard broadside. The firing of the guns all at the same time was also called a broadside.

BUCCANEER – a type of semi-pirate originating among the West Indian islands but at times operating in the Pacific.

BULKHEAD – a vertical partition between decks to separate cabins, etc.

CANNON – the largest type of muzzle-loading gun.

CAPSTAN – a machine placed vertically in the deck by which great weights can be lifted. Bars are fitted into square holes in its circular head so members of the crew can turn it to wind in cables or lines. *See* figure 51.

CARAVEL – a small handy Portuguese ship which developed from fishing boats. It carried lateen sails on two or three masts but, by the end of the fifteenth century, Spanish caravels often had square foresails and mainsails. Caravels were important vessels in early Iberian exploration. *See* Plates 16, 17; figure 30.

CAREEN – to heave a vessel over for cleaning her bottom, usually by pulling on her masts. *See* figure 42.

CARRACK – a large ship developed in Portugal from the old "round-ship." It had a high aftercastle and an even higher forecastle. *See* figure 30.

CARVEL-BUILT – a vessel was said to be "carvel-built" when the planks of her side were laid edge on edge, with the seams caulked. *See* figure 43.

CASTLE – the construction on the bows and sterns of early ships on which men were stationed in battle. These later became the forecastle and aftercastle, permanent structures which housed the crew and officers, respectively.

CAT – a type of northern English merchant ship with a very round bow and almost flat bottom. Some of them won fame as exploration ships, especially Cook's *Endeavour*.

CATAMARAN – either a vessel with two hulls joined together with beams and a platform, or a raft made of yoked logs.

CAULK – to fill a vessel's seams with oakum or other material.

CENTREBOARD – a type of retractable keel. *See* figure 44.

CLEW – the lower corners of a square-sail or the after corner of a fore-and-aft sail.

CLINKER-BUILT – a vessel was said to be "clinker-built" when each plank of her side overlapped the one below it. *See* figure 43.

CLIPPER – a type of beautiful and speedy cargo ship developed in the United States in the second quarter of the nineteenth century. *See* Plates 25, 26, 27.

CLOSE-HAULED – a vessel is sailing "close-hauled" when her yards are braced so as to allow the ship to sail as close to the wind as possible, that is, with the yards in a vessel with square sails hauled as close as possible to the shrouds on the lee side.

CLOSE-TO-THE-WIND – sailing as closely as possible into the wind, that is, in the direction from which the wind is blowing.

COMPASS – the instrument that tells direction by means of a magnetized needle which points to Magnetic North.

CONNING – to direct the steering of a ship.

COOPER – the skilled man in a ship who made, repaired, or set up barrels and casks.

COPRA – dried coconut kernels.

CORACLE – a wicker and skin boat, found in Wales or Ireland, like the Indian skin boat on the North American plains.

COURSE – the lower sail on the masts, *e.g.*, the mainsail is sometimes called the maincourse. Also the direction in which the ship is meant to go.

CRANK – a vessel is said to be "crank" when she leans so easily that she is in danger of oversetting.

CROJACK YARD – the lower yard on the mizzen mast of a square-rigged ship.

CUTTER – a small vessel with one mast, gaff-rigged, and with more than one head sail. *See* figure 48.

DEAD-RECKONING – estimating a ship's position by observing her courses and distances run. The word is said to derive from deduced reckoning.

DORY – a small rowing boat.

DRAUGHT – the depth of water required to float a ship.

DUBBING DOWN – cutting away extra wood in order to shape a boat.

FATHOM – a unit for measuring the length of ropes, cables, etc., and the depth of water. It is six feet, a length based on the distance from fingertip to fingertip of a man's outstretched arms.

FIGUREHEAD – a carved head or figure at the bow of a ship.

FILLING – protecting a ship from shipworms by putting square-headed nails into her planking so closely that they form an iron sheathing.

FLOOR – the inside of the bottom of a vessel on either side of the keel for as far as it remains reasonably flat.

FLUTE – a European merchant vessel of the seventeenth century, round bodied but very narrow at the top. It was called a flyboat in England.

FLYING-PROA – a very fast Micronesian single outrigger canoe. *See* Plate 14.

FOOT-ROPE – a rope running underneath a yard and upon which the men stand when reefing or furling a sail.

FORE-AND-AFT RIG – consists of sails, usually triangular, spread more or less along the line of the keel on stays, sprits, gaffs, and booms rather than on yards across the ship.

FORECASTLE – the deck forward of the foremast and the space underneath it between decks in which the crew lived in most vessels.

FOREMAST – the forward mast of vessels with more than one mast.

FOTHER – to draw a sail filled with loose material under a ship's bottom to temporarily stop a leak.

FREE-BOARD – in a boat, the distance from the gunwale to the waterline; in a ship, from the lowest port to the waterline.

FRIGATE – speedy and easily handled warship with one gundeck. It was rigged as a ship, that is, with three square-rigged masts. *See* Plate 21.

GAFF – a spar along which the head of a type of fore-and-aft sail is spread.

GAFF-TOPSAIL – a small fore-and-aft sail set over rather than under a gaff, so that the foot of the sail is spread by it.

GALIOT – a small trading vessel, usually rigged as a ketch with particularly large foresails on a long jib-boom, used by the Russians in the North Pacific. *See* figure 48.

GALLEON – a type of fast, weatherly ship developed mainly in England from Venetian prototypes. It was lower and narrower than other ships of its day, and had the distinctive galleon beakhead. *See* Plate 19; figure 30.

GALLEY – a type of ship which could be rowed, associated mainly with the relatively smooth seas of the Mediterranean; or, in a quite different meaning, the place in a ship where the food is cooked.

GROMET – a type of oar-lock.

GUNWALE – the upper rail of any vessel or boat.

HALYARDS – the lines used to raise or lower the yards and gaffs.

HAMMOCK – a length of canvas, suspended at each end, for a sailor to sleep in. Adopted from the American Indians.

HARPOON – a spear with a line attached to its iron head which is used for capturing whales or large fish.

HAUMI – a portion of a Polynesian dugout canoe which has been joined on to either lengthen or repair it.

HEADSAILS – all sails set forward of the foremast.

HEAVE-TO – to adjust a ship's sails so that they counteract one another and the ship lies-to or stays motionless.

HEEL – to lean over to one side.

HELM – the machinery used to steer a ship including the rudder, the tiller, and the wheel.

HERMAPHRODITE BRIG – a two-masted vessel square-rigged on the fore-mast and fore-and-aft-rigged on the mainmast, now called a brigantine. *See* figure 48.

HOGGED – a vessel is said to be "hogged" if she has been strained so that she droops at each end.

HOLD – the stowage space for cargo in the interior of the ship.

HOOKER – a small trading vessel developed in the Baltic, rigged like a yawl but with the large Baltic foresails. Hookers were built by the Russians in the North Pacific, probably because they were familiar with them in the Baltic. *See* figure 48.

HULL – the body of a vessel.

JIB – a fore-and-aft sail set forward on a stay to the jib-boom.

JIB-BOOM – a removable spar extending the bowsprit to which the tack of the jib is fastened. In modern yachts the term can mean an inboard boom used to spread the foot of the jib.

JOLLY BOAT – a small ship's boat, usually hoisted at the vessel's stern.

JURY – as a prefix to the name of any nautical equipment it means that it is a temporary repair or replacement, *e.g.*, jury foremast.

KAYAK – the small enclosed Eskimo skin boat which was usually built to carry one man for hunting but which occasionally was designed for trans-porting two or three. *See* Plate 7; figure 9.

KAURI – a type of very large New Zealand pine tree.

KEDGE – a small anchor used to warp the ship, that is, the anchor is carried by boat to be dropped some distance from the ship and the ship is pulled up to it by winding in the anchor's cable with the capstan.

KEEL – the main timber of the ship, in a sense its spine, which runs the whole length of the bottom and supports the whole frame.

KETCH – a small vessel with two masts, the after mast smaller, usually completely fore-and-aft-rigged.

KNEE – a heavy right-angled piece of timber which joins the ship's ribs or timbers to her beams. To be strong a knee had to be made from the natural growth of the wood at branch or root. *See* figure 33.

LARBOARD – the left side of the ship when one looks forward. The name has been changed to "port" to save confusion with "starboard," the right side as one looks forward.

LATEEN – a triangular sail spread usually along the length of the ship on a long yard hung at an angle of 45° from the mast.

LAUNCH – a large ship's boat, usually called the longboat.

LEAD AND LINE – the weight on the line and the line used to sound, or to make soundings, that is, to measure the depth of the water.

LEAGUE – a measurement of distance, about three miles.

LEE – the side of a ship or an island opposite that from which the wind blows, that is, the sheltered side.

LEEBOARD – a wide board put down deeply into the water on the lee side of a flat bottomed boat to prevent the wind drifting the boat to leeward.

LEE SHORE – the dangerous shore on the leeward side of the ship, that is, toward which the wind is blowing at a given time, and hence towards which the ship tends to drift.

LEEWAY – is the rate at which a vessel drifts to leeward, measured in points.

LETTER OF MARQUE – a letter from a governmental authority authorizing a captain of a ship other than a warship to carry out acts of war against his country's enemies.

LIE-TO – a vessel is said to be "lying-to" when by the counteraction of the sails, or by taking off all sails, she makes no progress through the water. Vessels would lie-to in order to pick up pilots for harbour or to exchange visits.

LIGHTER – a flat bottomed boat used to tranship goods from ship to shore.

LOG – a book in which anything important about the vessel, crew, winds, weather, distances and courses is set down systematically.

LOG AND LINE – a piece of board attached to a long light line which, when thrown into the sea, enabled an officer to measure the speed of the ship by gauging the rate at which the line ran out.

LONGBOAT – the largest boat in a merchant vessel. It was usually stowed between the fore and mainmasts and was often used as a handy enclosure in which to keep small livestock such as pigs.

LONGSHIP – the clinker-built rowed ships of the Vikings.

LORCHA – a type of hybrid boat in East Asia with a European hull and junk rigging.

LUG SAIL – a fore-and-aft sail used in boats and small vessels which is spread on a yard hanging obliquely on a mast with about a third of the yard's length before the mast. East Asian junks use a type of lug sail.

MAIN – the prefix used for the largest mast on a ship and for the yards and sails on it.

MAST – a vertical spar upon which the yards are suspended to spread the sails.

MATE – an officer under the master or captain of a merchant vessel. It can also mean an assistant, *e.g.*, a surgeon's mate or a carpenter's mate.

MESSENGER – a rope used on the capstan to haul in the cable.

MIZZEN MAST – the aftermost mast of a ship, that is, the mast nearest the stern.

MON – a Solomon Island plank-built boat, beautifully finished and decorated.

MOON SAIL – a light square sail sometimes used in light winds above the sky-sail on a clipper.

NAO – a general word, something like ship, for large Portuguese merchant vessels.

NIPPER – a short piece of small soft rope used to tie the anchor cable temporarily to the messenger as the cable was heaved in by the capstan. Though constant tying and untying were necessary as the cable came in it was light work, suitable for boys, and done by any in the ship. Hence the word "nipper" for boy.

NOCTURNALS – an early navigational instrument by which one could find the time at night by observing the position of "the guards" relative to the North Star.

OAKUM – rope-yarn which has been picked to pieces so that it is a loose fibrous material, good for caulking and similar uses.

OARPORTS – the small square holes in the sides of galleys, sloops, or early frigates for the oars or sweeps.

OUTRIGGER – a device for balancing narrow canoes, usually a light log set out on a frame on the right side of the canoe. *See* figures 18, 19.

PEAK – the outer upper corner of a gaffsail or a lateen.

PINK – an eighteenth-century English merchant vessel very like a flute—commodious and slow.

PINK-STERNED – having a high narrow stern.

PINNACE – in the sixteenth century a pinnace was a small vessel which could be rowed but which was big enough to sail in company with a fleet. By the middle of the eighteenth century it was a ship's boat, carried aboard, and smaller than the longboat.

PINTLES – the hooks bolted to the rudder by which it hangs and pivots in the braces bolted to the stern.

PIRAGUE – a type of wood canoe on the west coast of South and Central America.

PORTS – holes in the side of a vessel out of which the guns fired; *see also* oarports.

PRIVATEER – a civilian ship or captain legally commissioned by the government to make war.

PROA – an Indonesian or Micronesian canoe.

QUARTERDECK – the upper deck aft of the mainmast. As it was reserved for the officers the word "quarterdeck" is sometimes used as a collective synonym for officers.

RAKE – the inclination of a mast from the vertical, usually but not always rearwards.

RATLINES – lines put across the shrouds to use in climbing aloft.

RATTAN – a palm with long thin multi-joined flexible stems which were used to make ropes or whipping canes.

RAUPO – a New Zealand bullrush used for caulking.

REEF – to reduce a sail's area by taking in part of its head, if a square sail, or its foot if a fore-and-aft sail.

RIBS – a term used to describe a ship's timbers.

RING DIAL – a form of portable sun dial ring intended to help find astronomical time at other times than noon. It was of little practical use in normal conditions at sea because it had to be set accurately for latitude, aligned accurately north and south, and held stationary.

ROYAL – a light sail just above the topgallant sail, used only in light winds. The name is said to be used because the *Sovereign of the Seas* of Charles I was the first ship with them.

RUNNING RIGGING – the lines in a ship which are used to move yards and sails, *e.g.,* the halyards or the braces. *See* figure 46.

SCARF – to fasten pieces of wood together, fitting them by tapering or shaping them in such a way that the joint is no thicker than the pieces at either side.

SCHOONER – usually a small two-masted vessel with the mainmast larger than the foremast, and no tops on its masts. There are different types of schooner named according to the way the two masts are rigged. There have also been large schooners with up to seven masts, *e.g.,* the *Thomas W. Lawson. See* figure 48.

SCULL – to scull is to impel a boat by imparting either a sideways or rotary motion to an oar or oars which do not leave the water.

SCURVY – a disease of malnutrition caused specifically by a shortage of ascorbic acid in the diet.

SCUTTLE-BUTT – the butt of water open on deck from which the crew can normally drink freely, and because of this a slang term for ship's gossip.

SET – the direction in which a current or tide flows.

SHAKES – the unassembled staves of casks.

SHALLOP – a later name for a pinnace, and an earlier name for a sloop.

SHEATHING – an extra wooden or metallic covering on the bottom of a ship to protect her, for example, from ice or shipworm.

SHEER – the longitudinal curve of a vessel's side, and sometimes decks.

SHIP – a general term for a large vessel, but if used specifically, a vessel with three masts, each of which has tops and yards.

SHIP-OF-THE-LINE – a ship built strongly enough and carrying enough heavy guns (over 50) to take its place in the line of battle. The great ships sailed into battle one following the other because nearly all of their heavy guns fired only to the side. *See* Plate 20.

SHIPWRIGHT – someone who actually builds and repairs ships, as opposed to designing them.

SHROUDS – ropes from the mastheads to the sides of the vessel which support the masts. In more recent times these ropes are made of metal.

SKY SAIL – a light sail above the royal. Used only by such ships as clippers where a cargo such as tea made speed profitable enough to justify the extra effort and risk.

SLOOP – a small vessel with one mast, but also a naval classification for the smallest ships of war, whatever their rig. *See* figure 30.

SNOW – a kind of brig, with an extra mast just behind the full-rigged main-mast to carry the gaff "brigsail" or trysail.

SOUND – to measure the depth of water with a lead and line.

SPANKER – the fore-and-aft sail, set with a boom and gaff, on the mizzenmast of a ship or barque.

SPAR – a general term for all gaffs, booms, yards, and masts.

SPRIT – a small boom used in some small boats, such as whaleboats, to spread the sail. The lower end of the boom rests at the foot of the mast allowing it to cross the sail diagonally so that the upper end raises the upper outer corner of the sail.

SPRITSAIL TOPSAIL – a small sail originally set far forward on a tiny mast standing upright on the outer end of the bowsprit, later set under the jib boom ahead of the spritsail, the small sail spread under the bowsprit to aid manoe-vring.

SQUARE SAILS – sails which hang from yards and are spread across the line of the keel.

STANDING RIGGING – the part of the rigging which supports the masts and is not moved, *e.g.,* shrouds and stays. *See* figure 46.

STAY – large rope or wire used to support a mast in a fore-and-aft direction.

STAY SAIL – a sail set on a stay.

STERN – the after end of a vessel.

STERNPOST – the piece of timber or metal running upward from the after end of the keel to which the two sides of the vessel are joined.

STIFF – a quality of a vessel which enables her to carry sail without heeling too much. It is the opposite of crank.

SWEEP – a large oar used in galleys or pinnaces.

TACK – to tack is to alter the direction of the ship by swinging her head across the wind in order to place the ship on the other tack when beating into the wind. If the wind is from the west you alter direction by turning from south-west through west to north-west or vice versa. A vessel is said to be on the starboard tack if the wind is blowing from the starboard and on the port tack if the wind is blowing from the port side. *See* figure 38.

TAPA – a Polynesian coarse cloth made by pounding the bark of the paper mulberry, the breadfruit or various other plants.

TAPU – declaring by ceremony that a thing or person is sacred or accursed, or a prohibition of certain actions by general consent.

TENDER – a ship is said to be tender or tender sided when it heels over too easily and too far in a wind.

THWART – cross support in a boat or canoe.

TILLER – the large bar, usually of wood, fastened to or into the head of the rudder to turn it.

TIMBERS – the large pieces of wood in a vessel, particularly the long curved pieces which form its ribs.

TOP – a platform on the head of a lower mast which spreads the rigging and is useful as a resting place for men aloft. In war riflemen were stationed here, and it was a rifleman in one of the tops of the *Redoutable* who killed Nelson.

TOP-GALLANT MAST – the third mast above the deck.

TOP-GALLANT SAIL – the sail set on the top-gallant mast; like the topsail it was divided in later years.

TOPMAST – the second mast above the deck.

TOPSAIL – the sail set on the topmast, in the later nineteenth century and twentieth century often divided into two sails for easier handling in the biggest ships.

TOPSTRAKE – the top plank in a longship or built-up canoe.

TRAVERSE BOARD – was a navigational device which consisted of a small board with eight holes, representing the half-hours in a four hour watch, bored at each of the four points of the compass. In these the navigator pegged the courses made by a ship in each half-hour.

TREENAILS – long wooden pins for nailing planks to timbers.

TRIREME – a Greek or Roman galley with three banks of oars.

TRYSAIL – today a triangular fore-and-aft sail set on the spanker boom in bad weather but originally the sail set with gaff and boom at the mainmast of a full-rigged brig.

TUMBLE-HOME – the sloping in of a ship's sides above the gundeck or lower hold. The idea was to put the main stowage room for heavy materials low down and to reduce the weight above. Some sailors claimed it kept the ship slightly drier when the waves were from the beam.

UMIAK – the large open skin boat of the Eskimos. *See* Plate 8; figure 12.

WALES – planks of extra thickness set in a ship's side to add strength. They run the full length of the vessel.

WALL-SIDED – a ship is said to be wall-sided when her sides are perpendicular as opposed to tumbling home or flaring out.

WARP – to move a ship from one place to another by pulling it up to a fixed object, such as an anchor.

WATCH – a division of time in a ship. There are seven watches, five of four hours and two of two hours. In most merchant ships the crew was divided into two watches, the port and starboard watches, one of which was on duty and one off at any given time.

WEATHER – in the direction from which the wind (that is, weather) blows, the opposite to lee. If a ship is sailing north and the wind is from the west then the port, or left, side of the ship is the weather side.

WHEEL – the device by which the ship is steered. In older ships the wheel operated on the tiller, and hence the rudder, by rolling ropes on a shaft or barrel to shorten or lengthen them. In later ships screw devices were used.

WHERRY – a small rowing boat pointed at each end.

WHIPSTAFF – a lever device used to steer the ship by moving the tiller by means of a pole running through to the deck above. It was superseded by the wheel in the early eighteenth century. *See* figure 50.

YACHT – usually a vessel of pleasure or state, but the Dutch used war-yachts for exploration, presumably because they would handle easily if conditions became difficult. *See* figure 30.

YARD – a spar hung to a mast to spread a sail upon.

YARD-ARM – the extremities of a yard. (This was a convenient place for hanging mutineers or pirates.)

YAWL – a small vessel with a mainmast and a very small aftermast.

YULOH – a sculling oar of ancient Chinese invention worked in a rotary motion. Some were huge and, when worked by several men, could propel large heavy ships of up to several hundred tons.

SELECTED BIBLIOGRAPHY

UNPUBLISHED SOURCES

Although I consulted and found to be of great assistance in the preparation of this book more than two hundred ships' logs and journals and several hundred late eighteenth- and early nineteenth-century documents held in various French, British, American and New Zealand libraries and museums, I have not listed them individually here.

Aldred, Rev. J. "Journal of Rev. J. Aldred, Passenger on the *Triton*, 1839-1840." Typescript. Dunedin, N.Z: Hocken Library, University of Otago, M.,1,115.

Burns, Thomas. "Diary, Nov. 27, 1847-April 15, 1848: An Account of his Passage to New Zealand on the *Philip Laing*." Typescript. Dunedin, N.Z: G. C. Thomson Papers, Hocken Library, University of Otago, M.,1,440/18.

Copland, Marilyn J. "Refrigeration: its Impact upon New Zealand, 1882-86." B.A. Honours Thesis, University of Otago, N.Z., 1972

Edinburgh. National Library of Scotland. Adv. Ms. 17.1.18. "Narrative of a Voyage to the South Seas" [by Edward Robarts].

Ferens, Thomas. "*John Wickliffe*, Diary, Nov., 1847-July 24, 1848." Typescript. Dunedin, N.Z: Hocken Library, University of Otago, M.,1,440/16.

Gloucester, England. Gloucestershire Record Office. D543(Acc 226). "Journal of a Voyage from Hobart-town to England in the barque *Seppings* 1838" [by George Eaton Stanger].

Wakefield, William H. "*Tory* Diary 1839." Typescript, copied from the original in the Turnbull Library, Wellington, N.Z. Dunedin, N.Z: Hocken Library, University of Otago, M.,1,119.

PUBLISHED SOURCES

A

Adney, Edwin Tappan, and Chapelle, Howard I. *The Bark Canoes and Skin Boats of North America*. Washington, D.C.: Smithsonian Institution, 1964.

Akerblom, Kjell. *Astronomy and Navigation in Polynesia and Micronesia: a Survey*. The Ethnological Museum, Stockholm Monograph Series, no. 14. Stockholm: The Ethnological Museum, 1968.

Allen, Jerry. *The Sea Years of Joseph Conrad*. New York: Doubleday & Co., 1965.

Amherst of Hackney, Lord, and Thomson, B., eds. *The Discovery of the Solomon Islands*. 2 vols. Hakluyt Second Series, nos. 7 and 8. London: Hakluyt Society, 1901.

Anderson, Roger Charles. *Oared Fighting Ships from Classical Times to the Coming of Steam.* London: Percival Marshall, 1962.

Anderson, Romola, and Anderson, R. C. *The Sailing Ship.* London: George G. Harrap & Co., 1926.

Andreev, Aleksandr I., ed. *Russian Discoveries in the Pacific and in North America in the Eighteenth and Nineteenth Centuries.* Translated by Carl Ginsburg. Ann Arbor, Mich.: American Council of Learned Societies, 1952.

Anson, W. Vernon. *Life of Lord Anson, 1697-1762.* London: Murray, 1912.

Appleton, Marjorie. *They Came to New Zealand.* London: Methuen & Co., 1958.

Arago, Jacques. *Narrative of a Voyage Round the World in the "Uranie" and "Physicienne" . . . during the years 1817, 18, 19, 20. . . .* London: Treuttel and Wurtz, 1823.

Archibald, E. H. H. *The Wooden Fighting Ship in the Royal Navy, A.D. 897-1860.* London: Blandford Press, 1968.

Armitage, Albert B. *Cadet to Commodore.* London: Cassell & Co., 1925.

Arrow, Neill. *Painted Ocean.* Christchurch: Caxton Press, 1961.

B

Baker, Sidney J. *My Own Destroyer.* Sydney: Currawong Publishing Co., 1962.

Bassett, Marnie. *Behind the Pictures*: *H.M.S. "Rattlesnake's" Australia, New Guinea Cruise, 1846-1850.* Melbourne: Oxford U. Pr., 1966.

—————. *Realms and Islands*: *Journal of Rose de Freycinet.* London, Oxford U. Pr., 1962.

Bateson, Charles. *Gold Fleet for California*: *Forty-Niners from Australia and New Zealand.* Auckland: Minerva, 1963.

Beaglehole, John C., ed. *The Journals of Captain James Cook on his Voyages of Discovery,* 3 vols. Hakluyt Extra Series, nos. 34, 35, 36. Cambridge: Hakluyt Society, 1955-1967.

—————. *The Discovery of New Zealand.* 2d. ed. London: Oxford U. Pr., 1961.

Becher, A. B. *Navigation of the Pacific Ocean, Illustrated by Charts.* . . . London: J. D. Potter, 1860.

Bechervaise, John. *Thirty-Six Years of a Seafaring Life, by an Old Quarter Master.* Portsea: W. Woodward, 1839.

Best, Elsdon. *The Maori Canoe.* Dominion Museum Bulletin, no. 7. Wellington: Government Printer, 1925.

—————. *Polynesian Voyagers*: *The Maori as a Deep-Sea Navigator, Explorer, and Colonizer.* Dominion Museum Monograph, no. 5. Reprint. Wellington: Government Printer, 1954.

Bisset, Sir James. *Sail Ho! My Early Years at Sea.* London: Rupert Hart-Davis, 1961.

Bligh, William. *A Narrative of the Mutiny on board His Majesty's Ship, "Bounty," and the Subsequent Voyage of part of the Crew in the Ship's Boat.* . . . London: George Nicol, 1790.

—————. *A Voyage to the South Sea . . . in His Majesty's Ship The "Bounty" . . .* London: George Nicol, 1792.

—————. *The Log of the "Bounty"*: *being Lieutenant William Bligh's Log of* the Proceedings of His Majesty's Armed Vessel "Bounty," in a Voyage to the South Seas. . . . 2 vols. London: Golden Cockerel Press, 1936-37.

Bourne, William. *A Regiment for the Sea and Other Writings on Navigation.* . . . Edited by E. G. R. Taylor. Hakluyt Second Series, no. 121. Cambridge: Hakluyt Society, 1963.

Boxer, Charles Ralph, ed. and trans. *A Portuguese Embassy to Japan (1644-1647)*. . . . London: Kegan Paul, Trench, Trübner and Co., 1928.

————————, ed. *A True Description of the Mighty Kingdoms of Japan and Siam.* 1663. Reprint. London: Argonaut Press, 1935.

————————, ed. *Fidalgos in the Far East, 1550-1770.* The Hague: M. Nijhoff, 1948.

————————, ed. *Francisco Vieira de Figueiredo: A Portuguese Merchant-Adventurer in South East Asia, 1624-1667.* The Hague: M. Nijhoff, 1967.

————————. "Admiral João Pereira Corte-Real and the Construction of Portuguese East Indiamen in the Early Seventeenth Century." *Mariner's Mirror* 26, no. 4: 388-406.

Bradfield, S. E. *Road to the Sea.* London: Temple Press Books, 1964.

Bradford, Ernle. *Drake,* London: Hodder and Stoughton, 1965.

Brett, Sir Henry. *White Wings.* 2 vols. Auckland: The Brett Printing Co., 1924-1928.

Brockett, William Edward. *Narrative of a Voyage from Sydney to Torres Straits in Search of the Survivors of the "Charles Eaton".* . . . Sydney: Henry Bull, 1836.

Broughton, William Robert. *A Voyage of Discovery to the North Pacific Ocean . . . in the Years 1795, 1796, 1797, 1798.* 1804. Reprint. Amsterdam: N. Israel, 1967.

Brown, John Macmillan. *Maori and Polynesian, their Origin, History and Culture.* London: Hutchinson and Co., 1907.

Browne, J. Ross. *Etchings of a Whaling Cruise.* rev. ed. Edited by John Seelye. Cambridge, Mass.: The Belknap Press of Harvard University Pr., 1968.

Bruce, Robert Cunningham. *Reminiscences of a Wanderer.* Wellington: Whitcombe and Tombs, 1914.

Buck, Sir Peter H. *Explorers of the Pacific.* Bernice P. Bishop Museum Special Publication 43. Honolulu, Hawaii: Bishop Museum, 1953.

————————. *The Coming of the Maori.* 2d. ed. Wellington: Maori Purposes Fund Board, 1966.

————————. *Vikings of the Sunrise.* Philadelphia: Lippincott, 1938.

Budker, Paul. *Whales and Whaling.* London: George G. Harrap and Co., 1958.

Bulkeley, John, and Cummins, John. *A Voyage to the South Seas in His Majesty's Ship the "Wager" in the Years 1740-1741.* . . . 3d. ed. London: George G. Harrap and Co., 1927.

Bullen, Frank T. *The Cruise of the "Cachalot."* 1910. Reprint. London: John Murray, 1928.

Burgess, Alan. *No Risks—No Romance.* London: Jonathan Cape, 1941.

Burney, James. *A Chronological History . . . of the Discoveries in the South Sea or Pacific Ocean Illustrated with Charts.* London: G. and W. Nicol, 1803-1817.

—————. *History of the Buccaneers of America.* 1816. Reprint. London: George Allen and Unwin, 1912.

Burwash, Dorothy. *English Merchant Shipping, 1460-1540.* Toronto: University of Toronto Pr., 1947.

C

Cameron, Ian. *Lodestone and Evening Star: the Saga of Exploration by Sea.* London: Hodder and Stoughton, 1965.

Campbell, Lord George. *Log-Letters from "The Challenger."* 5th. ed. London: Macmillan and Co., 1877.

Carletti, Francesco. *My Voyage around the World.* Translated by Herbert Weinstock. New York: Pantheon, 1964.

Casson, Lionel. *Illustrated History of Ships and Boats.* New York: Doubleday and Co., 1964.

Chambers, B. M. "Infinite Inexactitude of Longitude in 1622. . . ." *Mariner's Mirror* 20, no. 3: 376-378.

Chang, T'ien-Tsê. *Sino-Portuguese Trade: from 1514 to 1644.* Leyden: E. J. Brill, 1934.

Chapelle, Howard Irving. *The National Watercraft Collection.* United States National Museum Bulletin 219. Washington D.C.: United States National Museum, 1960.

—————. "The First Clipper." *Mariner's Mirror* 34, no. 1: 26-33.

Chase, Owen; Chappel, Thomas; and Pollard, George. *Narrative of the Wreck of the Whale-Ship "Essex". . . .* London: Golden Cockerel Press, 1935.

Chatterton, Edward Keble. *Whalers and Whaling: the Story of Whaling Ships up to the Present Day.* London: T. F. Unwin, 1925.

—————. *Seamen All.* 2d. ed. London: Philip Allan and Co., 1928.

Chichester, Sir Francis. *The Lonely Sea and the Sky.* London: Pan Books, 1964.

—————. *Along the Clipper Way.* London: Pan Books, 1966.

—————. *Gypsy Moth Circles the World.* London: Hodder and Stoughton, 1967.

Cipolla, Carlo Maria. *Guns, Sails and Empires: Technological Innovation and the Early Phases of European Expansion, 1400-1700.* New York: Pantheon, 1965.

Clark, Arthur H. *The Clipper Ship Era: an Epitome of Famous American and British Clipper Ships, their Owners, Builders, Commanders, and Crews, 1843-1869.* New York: G. P. Putnam's Sons, 1910.

Clifford, Brian Miles, and Illingworth, Neil. *The Voyage of the Golden Lotus.* Wellington: A. H. and A. W. Reed, 1962.

Cole, Allan B. ed. *With Perry in Japan: the Diary of Edward Yorke McCauley.* Princeton: Princeton University Pr., 1942.

Cole, Jean. *Trimaran against the Trades.* Wellington: A. H. and A. W. Reed, 1968.

Colnett, James. *A Voyage to the South Atlantic and Round Cape Horn into the Pacific Ocean . . . in the Ship "Rattler."* Compiled by William Combe. London: the Author, 1798.

Colvocoresses, George Musalas. *Four Years in a Government Exploring Expedition [to] *Australia—Antarctic continent—New Zealand....* New York: Cornish, Lamport and Co., 1852.

Commelin, Isaak. *A Collection of Voyages Undertaken by the Dutch East-India Company ... Containing an Account of Several Attempts to find Out the North-East Passage ...* London: W. Freeman, 1703.

Conrad, Joseph. "The Nigger of the 'Narcissus,'" "Typhoon Falk," and Other Stories. London: J. M. Dent, 1957.

——————. *Mirror of the Sea.* London: J. M. Dent, 1950.

Cooke, Edward William. *Sixty-Five Plates of Shipping and Craft.* London, 1829.

Corbett, Julian Stafford, ed. *Papers Relating to the Navy During the Spanish War, 1585-1587.* London: Navy Records Society, 1898.

Corney, Bolton Glanvill, ed. and trans. *The Voyage of Captain Don Felipe Gonzalez in the Ship of the Line "San Lorenzo" with the Frigate "Santa Rosalia" in Company to Easter Island in 1770-1....* Hakluyt Second Series no. 13. Cambridge: Hakluyt Society, 1908.

——————, trans. and comp. *The Quest and Occupation of Tahiti by Emissaries of Spain during the Years 1772-1776.* 3 vols. Hakluyt Second Series nos. 32, 36, 43. London: Hakluyt Society, 1913, 15, 19.

Cotter, Charles H. *A History of Nautical Astronomy.* London: Hollis and Carter, 1968.

Course, Alfred George. *A Seventeenth-Century Mariner, 1642-1703.* London: Frederick Muller, 1965.

——————. *Windjammers of the Horn: the Story of the Last British Fleet of Square-Rigged Sailing Ships.* London: Adlard Coles, 1969.

Cousteau, Jacques-Yves, and Diolé, Philippe. *The Whale: Mighty Monarch of the Sea.* London: Cassell and Co., 1972.

Cowan, James. *Suwarrow Gold.* London: Jonathan Cape, 1936.

Coxe, William. *The Russian Discoveries between Asia and America.* 1780. Reprint. Ann Arbor, Mich.: University Microfilms, 1966.

Coxere, Edward. *Adventures by Sea of Edward Coxere....* Edited by E. H. W. Meyerstein. Oxford: Clarendon Press, 1945.

Crozet, Julien, *Crozet's Voyage to Tasmania, New Zealand, the Ladrone Islands and the Philippines in the Years 1771-1772.* Edited by H. Ling Roth. London: Truslove and Shirley, 1891.

D

Dall, William H. "A Critical Review of Bering's First Expedition, 1725-30, Together with a Translation of his Original Report upon it. With a Map." *The National Geographic Magazine*, vol. 2. Washington D.C.: National Geographic Society, 1891.

Dalrymple, Alexander. *An Historical Collection of the Several Voyages and Discoveries in the South Pacific Ocean....* London: the Author, 1770-71.

Dampier, William. *Dampier's Voyages....* Edited by John Masefield. 2 vols. London: E. Grant Richards, 1906.

——————. *A Voyage to New Holland.* Edited by James A. Williamson. London: Argonaut Presss, 1939.

Dana, Richard Henry. *Dana's Seamen's Friend*. New rev. ed. Edited by James Lees. London: George Philip and Son, n.d.

—————. *Two Years Before the Mast*. 1847. New York: Dodd, Mead and Co., 1946.

Danielsson, Bengt. *The Happy Island*. Translated by F. H. Lyon. London: George Allen and Unwin, 1952.

—————. *From Raft to Raft*. Translated by F. H. Lyon. London: George Allen and Unwin, 1960.

—————. *What Happened on the "Bounty."* London: George Allen and Unwin, 1962.

Darwin, Charles. *Journal of Researches into the Natural History and Geology of the Countries Visited during the Voyage of H.M.S. "Beagle" Round the World.... *2d. ed. London: John Murray, 1876.

Davis, Ralph. *The Rise of the English Shipping Industry in the Seventeenth and Eighteenth Centuries*. London: Macmillan and Co., 1962.

Debenham, Frank, ed. *The Voyage of Captain Bellingshausen to the Antarctic Seas, 1819-1821*. 2 vols. Hakluyt Second Series nos. 91, 92. London: Hakluyt Society, 1945.

Dewar, J. Cumming. *Voyage of the "Nyanza," R.N.Y.C., being the Record of a Three Years' Cruise in a Schooner Yacht in the Atlantic and Pacific and her Subsequent Shipwreck*. Edinburgh: W. Blackwood and Sons, 1892.

Dillon, Peter. *Narrative and Successful Result of a Voyage in the South Seas ... Performed by Order of the Government of British India to Ascertain the Actual Fate of la Pérouse's Expedition*. 2 vols. London: Hurst, Chance and Co., 1829.

Discombe, Reece, and Anthonioz, Pierre. "Voyage to Vanikoro." *Pacific Discovery* 13, no. 1.

Dodd, Edward Howard. *Polynesian Seafaring: a Disquisition on Prehistoric Celestial Navigation and the Nature of Seagoing Double Canoes....* New York: Dodd, Mead and Co., 1972.

Domville-Fife, Charles William, ed. *Epics of the Square-Rigged Ships: Autobiographies of Sail*. London: Seeley Service and Co., 1958.

Drake, Sir Francis. *The World Encompassed*. 1628. Reprint. Ann Arbor, Mich.: University Microfilms, 1966.

Dunmore, John. *French Explorers in the Pacific*. 2 vols. Oxford: Clarendon Press, 1965 and 1969.

—————. *The Fateful Voyage of the "St. Jean Baptiste."* Christchurch: Pegasus Press, 1969.

E

Eaddy, P. A. *'Neath Swaying Spars: The Story of the Trading Scows of New Zealand*. Auckland: Whitcombe and Tombs, 1939.

Earle, Augustus. *A Narrative of a Nine Months' Residence in New Zealand in 1827*. Christchurch: Whitcombe and Tombs, 1909.

Easty, John. *Memorandum of the Transactions of a Voyage from England to Botany Bay 1787-1793*. Sydney: Trustees of the Public Library of New South Wales, with Angus and Robertson, 1965.

Ellis, William. *Polynesian Researches*. Rev. ed. 4 vols. Rutland, Vt.: Charles E. Tuttle Co., 1969.

Ewens, Leonard John. *The Little Ships of the Pioneer Years 1836-1845*. 2 pts. Adelaide: Pioneer's Association, 1952-53.

F

Falconer, William. *Marine Dictionary*. 1780. Reprint. Newton Abbot: David and Charles, 1970.

Fell, Alfred. *A Colonist's Voyage to New Zealand Under Sail in the "Early Forties"*. Exeter: J. Townsend, 1926.

Firth, Sir Charles Harding. *Naval Songs and Ballads*. London: Navy Records Society, 1908.

Fleurieu, Charles-Pierre, Compte de Claret. *Discoveries of the French in 1768 and 1769, to the South-East of New Guinea, with the Subsequent Visits to the Same Lands by English Navigators. . . .* London: J. Stockdale, 1791.

——————. *A Voyage Round the World Performed During the Years 1790-91-92 by Etienne Marchand. . . .* 1801. Reprint. 2 vols. New York: Da Capo Press, 1969.

Flinders, Matthew. *A Voyage to Terra Australis; Undertaken for the Purpose of Completing the Discovery of that Vast Country and Prosecuted in the Years 1801, 1802, 1803*. 2 vols. London: G. and W. Nicol, 1814.

Forester, C. S. *Commodore Hornblower*. Boston: Little, Brown and Co., 1945.

Forrest, Thomas. *A Voyage to New Guinea and the Moluccas, from Balambangan. . . .* 2d. ed. London: J. Robson, 1780.

Forster, Johann Georg. *A Voyage Round the World, in His Britannic Majesty's Sloop, "Resolution," Commanded by Capt. James Cook, during the Years 1772-3-4 and 5*. 2 vols. London: B. White, 1777.

Foster, Sir William, ed. *The Voyage of Sir Henry Middleton to the Moluccas, 1604-1606*. Hakluyt Second Series no. 88. London: Hakluyt Society, 1943.

Funnell, William. *A Voyage Round the World Containing an Account of Captain Dampier's Expedition into the South Seas in the Ship "St. George" in the Years 1703 and 1704. . . .* London: James Knapton, 1707.

Furneaux, Rupert. *Tobias Furneaux, Circumnavigator*. London: Cassell and Co., 1960.

G

Gage, Thomas. *Thomas Gage's Travels in the New World*. Edited by J. Eric Thompson. Norman: University of Oklahoma Pr., 1958.

Gallagher, Robert E., ed. *Byron's Journal of his Circumnavigation 1764-1766*. Hakluyt Second Series no. 122. Cambridge: Hakluyt Society, 1964.

Gann, Ernest K. *Song of the Sirens*. London: Hodder and Stoughton, 1968.

Gatty, Harold. *The Raft Book: Lore of the Sea and Sky*. New York: George Grady Press, 1943.

——————. *Nature is Your Guide: How to Find Your Way on Land and Sea*. London: Collins, 1958.

Gerbault, Alain. *In Quest of the Sun: The Journal of the "Firecrest."* London: Rupert Hart-Davis, 1955.

Gibbings, Robert. *Over the Reefs*. London: J. M. Dent, 1948.

Gilbert, Thomas. *Voyage from New South Wales to Canton in the Year 1788.* London: J. Debrett, 1789.

Giles, W. E. *A Cruize in a Queensland Labour Vessel to the South Seas.* Edited by Deryck Scarr. Pacific History Series no. 1. Canberra: Australian National University Pr., 1968.

Godwin, George. *Vancouver: A Life.* London: Philip Allan, 1930.

Golder, F. A. *Bering's Voyages: An Account of the Efforts of the Russians to Determine the Relation of Asia and America.* Edited by W. L. G. Joerg. 2 vols. American Geographical Society Research Series no. 1. New York: Octagon Books, 1968.

—————. *Russian Expansion on the Pacific 1641-1850.* 1914. Reprint 2 vols. Gloucester, Mass.: Peter Smith, 1960.

Golson, Jack, ed. *Polynesian Navigation: A Symposium on Andrew Sharp's Theory of Accidental Voyages.* 3d. ed. Wellington: A. H. and A. W. Reed, 1972.

Goncharov, Ivan. *The Voyage of the Frigate "Pallada."* Edited and Translated by N. W. Wilson. London: The Folio Society, 1965.

Gough, Barry M. *The Royal Navy and the Northwest Coast of North America 1810-1914: a Study of British Maritime Ascendency.* Vancouver: University of British Columbia Pr., 1971.

Gould, Charlie and Ruth. *"Astrocyte." British Columbia Medical Journal* 9: 137-40, 177-81; 10: 137-41, 169-72; 11: 176-78; 12: 12-14.

Grant, James. *The Narrative of a Voyage of Discovery, Performed in His Majesty's Vessel The "Lady Nelson" ... in the Years 1800, 1801, and 1802, to New South Wales.* London: T. Egerton, Military Library, Whitehall, 1803.

Grimble, Arthur. *A Pattern of Islands.* London: John Murray, 1952.

Guthrie, Brenda. *New Zealand Memories.* London: Bodley Head, 1930.

H

Hakluyt, Richard. *The Principal Navigations Voyages Traffiques and Discoveries of the English Nation....* 10 vols. London: J. M. Dent, 1927-1928.

Harker, Jack. *Well Done "Leander."* Auckland: Collins, 1971.

Hayter, Adrian. *"Sheila" in the Wind: a Story of a Lone Voyage.* London: Hodder and Stoughton, 1959.

Henderson, G. C. *The Discoverers of the Fiji Islands: Tasman, Cook, Bligh, Wilson, Bellingshausen.* London: John Murray, 1933.

Heyerdahl, Thor. *American Indians in the Pacific: the Theory behind the "Kon-Tiki" Expedition.* London: George Allen and Unwin, 1952.

—————. *"Kon-Tiki": across the Pacific by Raft.* Translated by F. H. Lyon. Chicago: Rand McNally and Co., 1950.

—————. *Aku-Aku: the Secret of Easter Island.* London: George Allen and Unwin, 1958.

Heywood, Peter. *The Court-Martial of the "Bounty" Mutineers.* Edited by Owen Rutter. London: William Hodge and Co., 1931.

Hickling, Harold, *One Minute of Time: the "Melbourne"—"Voyager" Collision.* Sydney: A. H. and A. W. Reed, 1965.

Hilder, Brett, *Navigator in the South Seas*. London: Percival Marshall and Co., 1961.

Hiscock, Eric C. *Beyond the West Horizon*. London: Oxford University Pr., 1963.

Hocken, Thomas Morland. "Abel Tasman and his Journal." Reprinted from *Transactions of the Royal Society of New Zealand*, vol. 28, by the *Otago Daily Times* in 1895.

Hockin, J. P. *A Supplement to the Account of the Pelew Islands Compiled from the Journals of the "Panther" and "Endeavour"* . . . *Two Vessels Sent by the Honourable East India Company to those Islands in the Year 1790*. . . . London: Capt. Henry Wilson, 1803.

Holman, James. *A Voyage Round the World, Including Travels in Africa, Asia, Australasia, America, etc., etc., from 1827 to 1832*. 4 vols. London: Smith, Elder and Co., 1834-1835.

Holmes, R. C. "Sea Fare." *Mariner's Mirror* 35, no. 2: 139-145.

Hooker, J. D., ed. *Journal of the Right Hon. Sir Joseph Banks During Captain Cook's First Voyage in H.M.S. "Endeavour" 1768-71 to Terra del Fuego, Otahite, New Zealand, Australia, the Dutch East Indies etc*. London: Macmillan and Co., 1896.

Hornell, James. *Water Transport: Origins and Early Evolution*. Cambridge: Cambridge University Pr., 1946.

——————. "The Origin of the Junk and Sampan." *Mariner's Mirror* 20, no. 3: 331-337.

——————. "The Making and Spreading of Dugout Canoes." *Mariner's Mirror* 34, no. 1: 46-52.

——————. "The Sources of the Clinker and Carvel Systems in British Boat Construction." *Mariner's Mirror* 34, no. 4: 238-254.

Houghton, Philip. *Land from the Masthead: the Circumnavigation of New Zealand in the Wake of Captain Cook*. London: Hodder and Stoughton, 1968.

Howay, F. W., ed. *Journal of Capt. James Colnett aboard the "Argonaut" from April 26, 1789 to Nov. 3, 1791*. Toronto: Champlain Society, 1940.

——————, ed. *Voyages of the "Columbia" to the North-West Coast 1787-90 and 1790-93*. Boston: Massachusetts Historical Society, 1941.

Hudson, G. F. *Europe and China*. London: Edward Arnold and Co., 1931.

Hugill, Stan. *Shanties from the Seven Seas*. London: Routledge and Kegan Paul, 1961.

Huxley, T. H. *T. H. Huxley's Diary of the Voyage of H.M.S. "Rattlesnake."* Edited by Julian Huxley. London: Chatto and Windus, 1935.

J

Jacobs, Thomas Jefferson. *Scenes, Incidents and Adventures in the Pacific Ocean, or, the Islands of the Australasian Sea, During the Cruise of the Clipper "Margaret Oakley" under Capt. Benj. Morrell*. New York: Harper and Bros., 1844.

Jayne, K. G. *Vasco da Gama and his Successors, 1460-1580*. London: Methuen and Co., 1910.

Johnson, Robert Erwin. *Thence Round Cape Horn: the Story of United States*

Naval Forces on Pacific Station, 1818-1923. Annapolis: United States Naval Institute, 1963.

K

Karlsson, Elis. *Mother Sea.* London: Oxford University Pr., 1964.

——————. *Pully-Haul: the Story of a Voyage.* London: Oxford University Pr., 1966.

Keate, George. *An Account of the Pelew Islands, Situated in the Western Pacific Ocean, composed from the Journals and Communications of Captain Henry Wilson and Some of his Officers, Who, in August 1783 Were There Shipwrecked in the "Antelope". . . .* London: G. Nicol, 1788.

Keene, Donald. *The Japanese Discovery of Europe: Honda Toshiaki and Other Discoverers, 1720-1798.* London: Routledge and Kegan Paul, 1952.

Kelly, Celsus, trans. and ed. *La Austrialia del Espíritu Santo.* 2 vols. Hakluyt Second Series, nos. 126 and 127. Cambridge: Cambridge University Pr., 1966.

Kemp, P. K., and Lloyd, Christopher. *The Brethren of the Coast.* London: Heinemann, 1960.

Keppel, Sir Henry. *The Expedition to Borneo of H.M.S. "Dido" for the Suppression of Piracy, With Extracts from the Journal of James Brook, esq. of Sarawak.* 2 vols. London: Chapman and Hall, 1846.

Kirk, Allan Alexander. *Ships and Sailormen: a Collection of pen portraits of some Australasian Shipmasters and Others Whose Lives Have Been Dedicated to the Sea.* Wellington: A. H. and A. W. Reed, 1964.

Knox-Johnston, Robin. *A World of My Own: the Single Handed, Non-Stop Circumnavigation of the World in "Suhaili."* London: Cassell and Co., 1969.

Koester, August. *Ship Models of the Seventeenth to Nineteenth Centuries.* New York: E. Weyhe, 1926.

Krusenstern, Adam John. *Voyage Round the World in the Years 1803, 1804, 1805 and 1806 by Order of His Imperial Majesty Alexander the First, on Board the Ships "Nadeshda" and "Neva". . . .* Translated by R. B. Hoppner. 2 vols. 1813. Reprint. New York: Da Capo Press, 1968.

L

Lach, Donald F. *Asia in the Making of Europe.* 2 vols. Chicago: University of Chicago Pr., 1965, 1970.

Laird Clowes, G. S. *Sailing Ships.* 2 pts. London: H. M. Stationery Office, 1932.

Landström, Björn. *The Ship.* New York: Doubleday and Co., 1961.

——————. *Sailing Ships.* London: George Allen and Unwin, 1969.

Lane-Poole, Vice Admiral, R. H. "Primitive Craft and Mediaeval Rigs in South America." *Mariner's Mirror* 26, no. 4: 333-338.

La Pérouse, Jean Francois de Galaup. *Voyages and Adventures of La Pérouse.* Translated by Julius S. Gassner from the 14th. edition of the F. Valentin abridgement, 1875. Honolulu: University of Hawaii Pr., 1969.

Latham, Ronald, ed. and trans. *The Travels of Marco Polo.* London: The Folio Society, 1968.

Lawson, W. *Bluegum Clippers and Whale Ships of Tasmania. . . .* Melbourne: Georgian House, 1949.

Ledyard, John. *Journal of Captain Cook's Last Voyage.* Edited by James Kenneth Munford. Studies in History no. 3. Oregon: Oregon State University Pr., 1963.

Lee, Ida, ed. *The Logbooks of the "Lady Nelson," With the Journal of Her First Commander, Lieutenant James Grant, R.N.* London: Grafton and Co., 1915.

Lever, Darcy. *Lever's Young Sea Officer's Sheet Anchor.* 1819. Reprint. New York. Edward W. Sweetman, 1955.

Lewis, David. *Daughters of the Wind.* Wellington: A. H. and A. W. Reed, 1967.

——————. *We, the Navigators: the Ancient Art of Landfinding in the Pacific.* Wellington: A. H. and A. W. Reed, 1972.

Lewis, Michael. *The Ships and Seamen of Britain.* London: The British Council, 1946.

——————. *The Navy of Britain.* London: George Allen and Unwin, 1948.

——————. *The Hawkins Dynasty: Three Generations of a Tudor Family.* London: George Allen and Unwin, 1969.

Lind, James. *Lind's Treatise on Scurvy.* Edited by C. P. Stewart and Douglas Guthrie. 1753. Reprint. Edinburgh: Edinburgh University Pr., 1953.

Ling Shun-sheng. "Formosan Sea-Going Raft and its Origin in Ancient China." *Bulletin of the Institute of Ethnology, Academia Sinica* (1956), no. 1:25-54.

——————. "Kava Drinking in China and East Asia." *Bulletin of the Institute of Ethnology, Academia Sinica* (1957), no. 4:25-30.

Lloyd, Christopher. *Pacific Horizons: the Exploration of the Pacific before Captain Cook.* London: George Allen and Unwin, 1946.

——————. *The Health of Seamen.* London: Navy Records Society, 1965.

——————. *William Dampier.* London: Faber and Faber, 1966.

——————. *The British Seaman, 1200-1860.* London: Collins, 1968.

——————. *Mr. Barrow of the Admiralty: a Life of Sir John Barrow.* London: Collins, 1970.

London, Jack. *The Cruise of the "Snark."* New York: The Regent Press, 1911.

Long, Dwight. *Sailing all Seas in the "Idle Hour."* London: Hodder and Stoughton, 1940.

Lubbock, A. Basil. *Round the Horn Before the Mast.* 4th. ed. London: John Murray, 1915.

——————. *The China Clippers.* 3d. ed. Glasgow: James Brown and Son, 1916.

——————. *The Blackwall Frigates.* Glasgow: James Brown and Son, 1922.

——————. *The Colonial Clippers.* 3d. ed. Glasgow: James Brown and Son, 1924.

——————. *The Nitrate Clippers.* Glasgow: Brown, Son and Ferguson, 1932.

——————. *The Opium Clippers.* Glasgow: Brown, Son and Ferguson, 1933.

——————. *The Arctic Whalers.* Glasgow: Brown, Son and Ferguson, 1937.

——————, ed. *Barlow's Journal.* 2 vols. London: Hurst and Blackett, 1934.

M

Macgillivray, John. *Narrative of the Voyage of H.M.S. "Rattlesnake".* . . . 2 vols. London: T. and W. Boone, 1852.

MacGregor, D. R. "Some Early British Tea Clippers." *Mariner's Mirror 34,* nos. 2, 3, 4: 67-82, 184-195, 280-293.

Macintyre, Donald George. *The Adventure of Sail.* London: Elek, 1970.

Mack, James D. *Matthew Flinders, 1774-1814.* Melbourne: Thomas Nelson, 1966.

Mackaness, George. *A Book of the "Bounty."* New York: Dutton and Co., 1938.

Malinowski, Bronislaw. *Argonauts of the Western Pacific.* 5th. Impression. London: Routledge and Kegan Paul, 1960.

Mariner, William. *An Account of the Natives of the Tonga Islands in the South Pacific Ocean. . . .* Edited by John Martin. 2 vols. London: John Murray, 1817.

Mariner, William. *The Sea, The Ship, and The Sailor.* Salem, Mass.: Marine Research Society, 1925.

Markham, Albert Hastings, ed. *The Voyages and Works of John Davis the Navigator.* London: Hakluyt Society, 1880.

Markham, Sir Clements R., ed. and trans. *Early Spanish Voyages to the Strait of Magellan.* Hakluyt Second Series, no. 28, 1911. Reprint. Nendeln, Liechtenstein: Kraus Reprint, 1967.

——————, ed. and trans. *Reports on the Discovery of Peru.* London: Hakluyt Society, 1872.

——————, ed. *The Voyages of Sir James Lancaster, Kt. to the East Indies, With Abstracts of Journals of Voyages to the East Indies during the Seventeenth Century, Preserved in the India Office.* London: Hakluyt Society, 1877.

——————, ed. *The Hawkins' Voyages during the Reigns of Henry VIII, Queen Elizabeth and James I.* London: Hakluyt Society, 1878.

Martyr, Weston. *The Southseaman: Life Story of a Schooner.* Edinburgh: Blackwood and Sons, 1926.

Maude, Henry Evans. *Of Islands and Men: Studies in Pacific History.* London: Oxford University Pr., 1968.

Maxwell, C. Bede. *Wooden Hookers: Epics of the Sea History of Australia.* London: Angus and Robertson, 1940.

McDowell, Carl E., and Gibbs, Helen M. *Ocean Transportation.* New York: McGraw-Hill, 1954.

McNab, Robert. *Murihiku and the Southern Islands: a History of the West Coast Sounds, Foveaux Strait, Stewart Island, the Snares, Bounty, Antipodes, Auckland, Campbell and Macquarie Islands from 1770-1829.* 1907. Reprint. Auckland: Wilson and Horton, 1970.

——————. *The Old Whaling Days: a History of Southern New Zealand from 1830 to 1840.* Christchurch: Whitcombe and Tombs, 1913.

Meares, John. *Voyages Made in the Years 1788 and 1789, from China to the Northwest Coast of America.* 1790. Reprint. Amsterdam: N. Israel, 1967.

Melville, Herman. *Typee.* London: Cassell and Co., 1967.

——————. *White Jacket: the World in a Man-of-War.* New York: Grove Press, 1956.

——————. *Moby Dick.* New York: Harper and Row, 1966.

——————. *Redburn: His First Voyage.* Edited by Harrison Hayford; Hershel Parker; and G. Thomas Tanselle. Evanston and Chicago: Northwestern University Pr. and the Newberry Library, 1969.

de Mierre, H. C. *Long Voyage.* London: Harold Starke, 1963.

Moorehead, Alan. *Darwin and the Beagle*. London: Hamish Hamilton, 1969.

Moresby, John. *Two Admirals*. London: John Murray, 1909.

Morison, Samuel Eliot. *The European Discovery of America: the Northern Voyages, A.D. 500-1600*. New York: Oxford University Pr., 1971.

Morrell, B. *A Narrative of Four Voyages to the South Sea . . . from the Year 1822 to 1831. . . .* New York: J. and J. Harper, 1832.

Morrell, W. P., ed. *Sir Joseph Banks in New Zealand*. Wellington: A. H. and A. W. Reed, 1958.

Mortlock, John Frederick. *Experiences of a Convict: Transported for Twenty-One Years*. 1864-5. Edited by G. A. Wilkes and A. G. Mitchell. Sydney: Sydney University Pr., 1966.

Morton, Leslie. *The Long Wake: from Tall Ships to Narrow Boats*. London: Routledge and Kegan Paul, 1968.

Mosely, H. N. *Notes by a Naturalist: an Account of Observations made during the Voyage of H.M.S. "Challenger" Round the World in the Years 1872-1876. . . .* London: John Murray, 1892.

Muller, Gerhard Friedrich. *Voyages from Asia to America for Completing the Discoveries of the North West Coast of America. To which is Prefixed, a Summary of the Voyages Made by the Russians on the Frozen Sea, in Search of a North East Passage. . . .* 1761. Reprint. New York: Da Capo, 1967.

N

Naish, F. C. Prideaux. "The Mystery of Tonnage and Dimensions of the *Pelican-Golden Hind*." *Mariner's Mirror* 34, no. 1: 42-45.

Newby, Eric. *Grain Race: Pictures of Life Before the Mast in a Windjammer*. London: George Allen and Unwin, 1968.

Newman, C. E. T. *The Spirit of Wharf House: Campbell Enterprise from Calcutta to Canberra, 1788-1930*. London: Angus and Robertson, 1961.

Newton, Arthur Percival, ed. *The Great Age of Discovery*. 1932. Reprint. New York: Lennox Hill Pub. and Dist. Co., 1970.

Nicholas, John Liddiard. *Narrative of a Voyage to New Zealand Performed in the Years 1814 and 1815, in Company with the Rev. Samuel Marsden, Principal Chaplain of New South Wales*. 2 vols. London: James Black and Son, 1817.

Nordenskiöld, A. E. *The Voyage of the "Vega" Round Asia and Europe*. 2 vols. London: Macmillan and Co., 1881.

Nooteboom, C. "Eastern Biremes." *Mariner's Mirror* 35, no. 4: 272-275.

Nowell, Charles E., ed. *Magellan's Voyage Around the World: Three Contemporary Accounts: Antonio Pigafetta, Maximilian of Transylvania, Gaspar Correa*. Evanston: Northwestern University Pr., 1962.

Nuttall, Zelia, ed. and trans. *New Light on Drake: a Collection of Documents Relating to His Voyage of Circumnavigation, 1577-1580*. Hakluyt Second Series, no. 34. London: Hakluyt Society, 1914. Reprint. Nendeln, Liechtenstein: Kraus Reprint, 1967.

O

Osborn, Fairfield, ed. *The Pacific World*. New York: W. W. Norton and Co., 1944.

Osbun, Albert Gallatin. *To California and the South Seas: the Diary of Albert G. Osbun, 1849-1851.* Edited by John Haskell Kemble. San Marino, California: The Huntington Library, 1966.

P

Pack, Stanley Walter Croucher. *Admiral Lord Anson.* London: Cassell and Co., 1960.

——————, ed. *Lord Anson's Voyage Round the World, 1740-1744.* By Richard Walter. London: Penguin Books, 1947.

Paine, R. D. *The Ships and Sailors of Old Salem....* New York: The Outing Pub. Co., 1909.

Parker, Mary Ann. *A Voyage Round the World in the "Gorgon" Man-of-War....* London: J. Nichols, 1795.

Parr, Charles McKew. *So Noble a Captain: the Life and Times of Ferdinand Magellan.* New York: Thomas Y. Crowell Co., 1953.

Parry, J. H. *The Age of Reconnaissance.* London: Weidenfeld and Nicolson, 1963.

Philp, J. E. *Whaling Ways of Hobart Town.* Hobart: J. Walch, 1936.

Porter, Captain David. *A Voyage in the South Seas in the Years 1812, 1813, and 1814 with Particular Details of the Gallipagos and Washington Islands.* London: Sir Richard Phillips and Co., 1823.

Price, A. Grenfell, ed. *The Explorations of Captain James Cook, 1768-1779.* Melbourne: Georgian House, 1958.

Purchas, Samuel. *Hakluytus Posthumus, or Purchas his Pilgrimes.* 1625. Reprint. 3 vols. Glasgow: James MacLehose and Sons, 1905.

Putnam, G. G. *Salem Vessels and Their Voyages.* Salem, Massachusetts: Essex Institute, 1924-1930.

Pye, Peter. *Red Mains'l.* London: Rupert Hart-Davis, 1961.

R

Randier, Jean. *Men and Ships Around Cape Horn, 1616-1939.* London: Arthur Barker, 1968.

Rawson, Geoffrey. *Ships and Seamen.* London: Thornton Butterworth, 1934.

——————. *"Pandora's" Last Voyage.* London: Longmans, Green and Co., 1963.

Rickman, John. *Journal of Captain Cook's Last Voyage to the Pacific Ocean.* Ann Arbor: University Microfilms, 1966.

Riesenberg, Felix. *Cape Horn.* London: Robert Hale, 1941.

Riley, Carroll L.; Kelley, J. Charles; Pennington, Campbell W.; and Rands, Robert L., eds. *Man across the Sea: Problems of Pre-Columbian Contacts.* Austin, Texas: University of Texas Pr., 1971.

Robertson, George. *The Discovery of Tahiti.* Edited by Hugh Carrington. 1948. Reprint. Nendeln, Liechtenstein: Kraus Reprint, 1967.

Robertson, R. B. *Of Whales and Men.* London: The Reprint Society, 1958.

Robinson, Gregory. "The Evidence About the *Golden Hind." Mariner's Mirror* 35, no. 1: 56-65.

Robinson, M. S., comp. *Van de Velde Drawings: a Catalogue of Drawings in the National Maritime Museum: Made by the Elder and the Younger.* Cambridge: The National Maritime Museum, 1958.

Roe, Michael, ed. *The Journal and Letters of Captain Charles Bishop on the N.W. Coast of America, in the Pacific, and in New South Wales, 1794-1799.* Hakluyt Second Series, no. 131. Cambridge: Cambridge University Pr., 1967.

Rogers, Stanley. *The Pacific.* London: George G. Harrap and Co., 1931.

Rogers, Stanley Reginald Harry. *Freak Ships.* London: John Lane, 1936.

Rogers, Woodes. *A Cruising Voyage round the World . . . Finished in 1711.* London: A. Bell and B. Lintot, 1712.

Rose, Sir Alec. *My Lively Lady.* London: Pan Books, 1968.

Rose, J. Holland. *Man and the Sea: Steps in Maritime and Human Progress.* Cambridge: W. Heffer and Sons, 1935.

Ross, Alexander. *Adventures of the First Settlers on the Columbia River.* March of America Facsimile Series 58. Ann Arbor: University Microfilms, 1966.

Ross, Angus. *New Zealand Aspirations in the Pacific in the Nineteenth Century.* Oxford: Clarendon Press, 1964.

Ross, Sir James Clark. *A Voyage of Discovery and Research in the Southern and Antarctic Regions, during the Years 1838-43.* 2 vols. London: John Murray, 1847.

Ross, J. O'C. *This Stern Coast: the Story of the Charting of the New Zealand Coast.* Wellington: A. H. and A. W. Reed, 1969.

Roth, Walter Edmund. *Ethnological Studies among the North-West Central Queensland Aborigines.* Brisbane: Edmund Gregory, Government printer, 1897.

Ruskin, John. *The Harbours of England.* London: George Allen, 1905.

Russell, F. S., and Yonge, C. M. *The Seas: Our Knowledge of Life in the Sea and How it is Gained.* 2d. ed., rev. London: Frederick Warne and Co., 1936.

S

Sanderson, I. T. *Follow the Whale,* London: Cassell and Co., 1958.

Scheffer, Victor Blanchard. *The Year of the Whale.* New York: Scribner, 1969.

Scherzer, Karl. *Narrative of the Circumnavigation of the Globe by the Austrian Frigate, "Novara". . . .* 3 vols. London: Saunders, Otley, and Co., 1861.

Schurz, William Lytle. *The Manila Galleon.* New York: Dutton, 1959.

Seligman, Adrian. *The Voyage of the "Cap Pilar."* 2d. ed. London: Hodder and Stoughton, 1941.

Sharp, Charles Andrew. *Ancient Voyagers in the Pacific.* Wellington: Polynesian Society, 1956.

——————. *The Discovery of the Pacific Islands.* Oxford: Clarendon Press, 1960.

——————. *Ancient Voyagers in Polynesia.* Auckland: Paul's Book Arcade, 1963.

——————. *The Discovery of Australia.* Oxford: Clarendon Press, 1963.

——————, ed. *The Voyages of Abel Janszoon Tasman.* Oxford: Clarendon Press, 1968.

——————, ed. *The Journal of Jacob Roggeveen, 1722.* Oxford: Clarendon Press, 1970.

Shelvocke, George. *A Voyage round the World. . . .* London: Cassell and Co., 1928.

Shineberg, Dorothy, ed. *The Trading Voyages of Andrew Cheyne, 1841-1844.* Pacific History Series, edited by H. E. Maude, no. 3. Canberra: Australian National University Pr., 1971.

——————. *They Came for Sandalwood: A Study of the Sandalwood Trade in the South-West Pacific, 1830-1865.* London: Cambridge University Pr., 1967.

Slack, Kenneth E. *In the Wake of the "Spray."* New Brunswick, N.J.: Rutgers University Pr., 1966.

Slocum, Joshua. *Sailing Alone around the World.* London: Sampson, Low, Marston & Co., n.d.

Smeeton, Miles. *Once is Enough.* London: Rupert Hart-Davis, 1959.

Smith, John. *The Sea Grammar.* 1627. Reprint. New York: Da Capo Press, 1968.

Smollett, Tobias. *The Adventures of Roderick Random.* Oxford: Oxford U. Pr., World's Classics, 1959.

Smyth, Sir Herbert Warington. *Mast and Sail in Europe and Asia.* London: Blackwood and Sons, 1929.

Spry, W. J. J. *The Cruise of Her Majesty's Ship "Challenger."* London: Sampson Low, Marston, Searle and Rivington, 1877.

Stanley, Lord of Alderley, ed. *The First Voyage round the World by Magellan.* London: Hakluyt Society, 1874.

Stephens, H. Morse, and Bolton, Herbert E., eds. *The Pacific Ocean in History.* Papers and Addresses Presented at the Panama-Pacific Historical Congress, 1915. New York: Macmillan Co., 1917.

Stevens, Henry N., ed. *New Light on the Discovery of Australia: Journal of Captain Don Diego de Prado y Tovar.* Hakluyt Second Series, no. 64. London: Hakluyt Society, 1930.

Stevens, J. R. *An Account of the Construction and Embellishment of Old Time Ships.* Toronto, 1949.

Stevenson, Fanny. *The Cruise of the "Janet Nichol" Among the South Sea Islands.* London: Chatto and Windus, 1915.

Stevenson, Fanny and Robert Louis. *Our Samoan Adventure.* Edited by Charles Neider. London: Weidenfeld and Nicolson, 1956.

Suggs, Robert C. *The Island Civilizations of Polynesia.* New York: New American Library, 1960.

T

Taylor, E. G. R. *The Haven-Finding Art: a History of Navigation from Odysseus to Captain Cook.* London: Hollis and Carter, 1956.

Taylor, Nancy M., ed. *The Journal of Ensign Best, 1837-1843.* Wellington: R. E. Owen, Government Printer, 1966.

Temple, Sir Richard Carnac, Bt., ed. *The Papers of Thomas Bowrey. 1669-1713, Discovered in 1913 by John Humphreys, M.A., F.S.A., and now in the Possession of Lieut-Colonel Henry Howard, F.S.A.* 2 pts. Hakluyt Second Series, no. 58. London: Hakluyt Society, 1927.

Thomas, Pascoe. *A True and Impartial Journal of a Voyage to the South-Seas, and round the Globe in His Majesty's Ship the "Centurion". . . .* London: Printed by S. Birt etc., 1745.

Thompson, Laurence G. "The Junk Passage across the Taiwan Strait: Two Early Chinese Accounts." *Harvard Journal of Asiatic Studies* 28: 170-194.

Thwaites, Reuben Gold, ed. *Original Journals of the Lewis and Clark Expedition, 1804-1806.* 8 vols. New York: Arno Press, 1969.

U

Underhill, Harold A. *Deep-Water Sail.* Glasgow: Brown, Son and Ferguson, 1963.

V

Vancouver, George. *A Voyage of Discovery to the North Pacific Ocean and round the World, Performed in the Years 1790, 1791, 1792, 1793, 1794, and 1795, in the "Discovery" Sloop of War and the Armed Tender "Chatham". . . .* 6 vols. London: J. Stockdale, 1801.

Verne, Jules. *A Voyage round the World.* London: George Routledge, 1877.

Villiers, Alan John. *Vanished Fleets: Ships and Men of Old Van Diemen's Land.* New York: Garden City Pub. Co., 1931.

——————. *Cruise of the "Conrad": a Journal of a Voyage round the World. . . .* London: Hodder and Stoughton, 1940.

——————. *Set of the Sails: the Story of a Cape Horn Seaman.* London: Hodder and Stoughton, 1949.

—————— *Captain Cook, the Seamen's Seaman.* London: Hodder and Stoughton, 1967.

Voss, John Claus. *The Voyage of the Indian War Canoe, "Tilikum," across the Pacific from Canada to Australia. . . .* Invercargill: Printed at the Caxton Office, 1903.

——————. *The Venturesome Voyages of Captain Voss.* 2d. ed. London: Martin Hopkinson, 1930.

W

Wafer, Lionel, *A New Voyage and Description of the Isthmus of America.* Edited by Elliott Joyce. Hakluyt Second Series, no. 73. Oxford: Hakluyt Society, 1934.

Wakefield, Edward Jerningham. *Adventure in New Zealand.* 2 vols. London: John Murray, 1845.

Wallis, Helen, ed. *Carteret's Voyage round the World 1766-1769.* 2 vols. Hakluyt Second Series, nos. 124, 125. Cambridge: Hakluyt Society, 1965.

Walter, Richard, and Anson, George. *A Voyage round the World in the Years 1740, 1741, 1742, 1743, 1744.* London: Society for Promoting Christian Knowledge, 1748.

Ward, Edward. *The Journal of Edward Ward: the Voyage of the "Charlotte Jane" from Plymouth, England to Lyttelton, New Zealand, 1850-1851.* Christchurch: Pegasus Press, 1951.

Warner, Oliver. *English Maritime Writing: Hakluyt to Cook.* London: Longmans, Green and Co., 1958.

Waters, D. W. "Chinese Junks. An Exception: the *Tongkung.*" *Mariner's Mirror* 26, no. 1: 79-95.

——————. Review of *The Junks and Sampans of the Yangtze*, by G. R. G. Worcester. In *Mariner's Mirror* 34, no. 2: 134-137, and 35, no. 3: 253-254.

—————. *The Art of Navigation in England in Elizabethan and Early Stuart Times.* London: Hollis and Carter, 1958.

Waxell, Sven. *The American Expedition.* London: William Hodge and Co., 1952.

Weckler, J. E. Jnr. *Polynesians, Explorers of the Pacific.* War Background Studies No. 6. Washington: Smithsonian Institution, 1943.

West, Ellsworth Luce, and Mayhew, Eleanor Ransom. *Captain's Papers: a Log of Whaling and Other Sea Experiences.* Barre, Massachusetts: Barre Publishers, 1965.

Whipple, Addison Beecher Calvin. *Yankee Whalers in the South Seas.* London: Gollancz, 1954.

White, John. *Journal of a Voyage to New South Wales....* London: J. Debrett, 1790.

Whymper, Frederick. *Travel and Adventure in the Territory of Alaska.* 1868. Reprint. Ann Arbor: University Microfilms, 1966.

Wilkes, Charles. *Narrative of the United States Exploring Expedition during the Years 1838, 1839, 1840, 1841, 1842.* 5 vols. Philadelphia: Lee and Blanchard, 1845.

Williams, Glyndwr. *Anson's Voyage 1740-1744.* London: Navy Records, 1967.

Williams, Harold, ed. *One Whaling Family.* Boston: Houghton Mifflin Co., 1964.

Williamson, James A. *Cook and the Opening of the Pacific.* London: Hodder and Stoughton, 1946.

Willis, William. *The Epic Voyage of the Seven Little Sisters.* London: Hutchinson and Co., 1956.

Wilson, James. *A Missionary Voyage to the Southern Pacific Ocean....* London: T. Chapman, 1799.

Wilson, T. B. *Narrative of a Voyage round the World ... the Wreck of the Ship "Governor Ready" in Torres Straits....* London: Sherwood, Gilbert and Piper, 1835.

Wood, C. F. *A Yachting Cruise in the South Seas.* London: Henry S. King and Co., 1875.

Wood, G. Arnold. *The Voyage of the "Endeavour."* London: Macmillan and Co., 1926.

Worcester, G. R. G. "The Chinese War-Junk." *Mariner's Mirror* 34, no. 1: 16-25.

—————. *Sail and Sweep in China.* London: H.M.S.O., 1966.

Wray, J. W. *South Sea Vagabonds.* London: Herbert Jenkins, 1939.

Wycherly, George. *Buccaneers of the Pacific.* London: Rich and Cowan, 1935.

INDEX

The numbers in italics are principal references

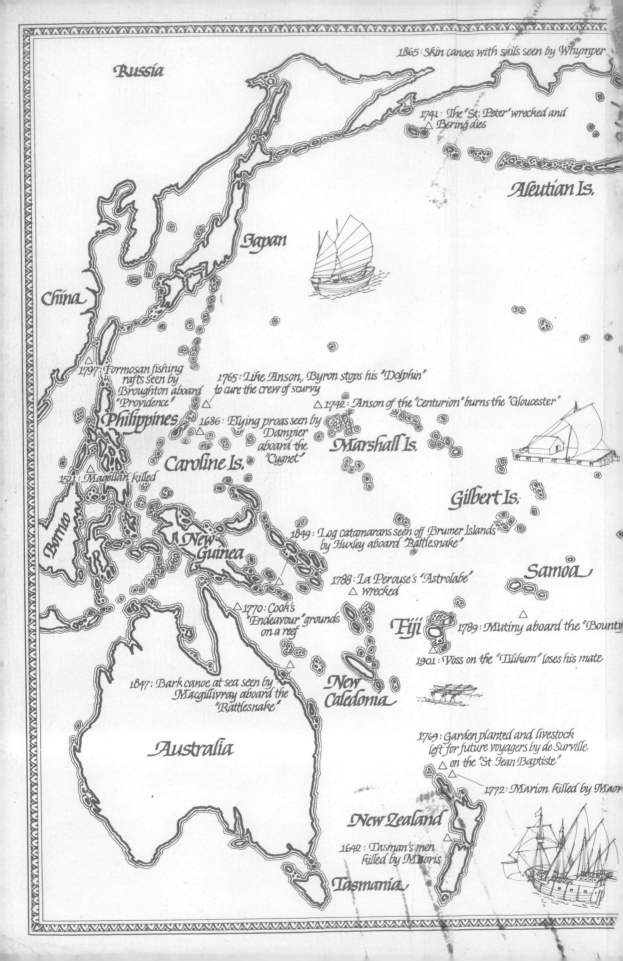

Russia

1865: Skin canoes with sails seen by Whymper

1741: The "St. Peter" wrecked and
△ Bering dies

Aleutian Is.

Japan

China

1797: Formosan fishing
rafts seen by
Broughton aboard
"Providence"

1765: Like Anson, Byron stops his "Dolphin"
to cure the crew of scurvy

△ 1742: Anson of the "Centurion" burns the "Gloucester"

Philippines △ 1686: Flying proas seen by
Dampier
aboard the
"Cygnet"

Marshall Is.

Caroline Is.

1521: △ Magellan killed

Gilbert Is.

Borneo

New
Guinea

1849: Log catamarans seen off Brumer Islands
by Huxley aboard "Rattlesnake"

Samoa

1788: La Pérouse's "Astrolabe"
△ wrecked

△ 1770: Cook's
"Endeavour" grounds
on a reef

Fiji 1789: Mutiny aboard the "Bounty

1901: Voss on the "Tilikum" loses his mate

1847: Bark canoe at sea seen by
Macgillivray aboard the
"Rattlesnake"

New
Caledonia

1769: Garden planted and livestock
left for future voyagers by de Surville
△ on the "St. Jean Baptiste"

Australia

1772: Marion killed by Maor

New Zealand

1642: Tasman's men
killed by Maoris

Tasmania